THE DIARY OF OTHERS

Anaïs Nin in her New York apartment, 1959. Photo: Stanley Haggart

THE DIARY OF OTHERS

The Unexpurgated Diary of Anaïs Nin

1955-1966

COPYRIGHT INFORMATION

ALL RIGHTS RESERVED. This book contains material protected under International and Federal Copyright Laws and Treaties. Any unauthorized reprint or use of this material is prohibited. No part of this book may be reproduced or transmitted in any form or by any means, electronic or mechanical, including photocopying, scanning, PDF download, recording, blogging, internet posting, content syndication, e-mail or by any information sharing, storage and retrieval system without express permission from the publisher, except by a reviewer or scholar who may quote brief passages in a review or article.

All content unless otherwise noted copyright © 2021 by The Anaïs Nin Trust
Introduction copyright © 2021 by Benjamin Franklin V
Preface copyright © 2021 by Paul Herron

Excerpts from THE DIARY OF ANAIS NIN, Volume Five: 1947-1955. Copyright © 1974 by Anais Nin. Used by permission of Houghton Mifflin Harcourt Publishing Company. All rights reserved.

Excerpts from THE DIARY OF ANAIS NIN: Volume Six: 1955-1966. Copyright © 1976 by Anais Nin. Used by permission of Houghton Mifflin Harcourt Publishing Company. All rights reserved.

Unless otherwise noted, photographs are courtesy of The Anaïs Nin Trust.

Library of Congress Cataloging-in-Publication Data
Names: Nin, Anaïs, 1903-1977, author. | Herron, Paul (Paul S.), editor. | Franklin, Benjamin, 1939- writer of introduction.
Title: The diary of others : the unexpurgated diary of Anaïs Nin, 1955-1966 / Anaïs Nin ; [edited by Paul Herron ; introduction by Benjamin Franklin V.]
Description: State College : Sky Blue Press, 2021. | Includes bibliographical references and index.
Identifiers: LCCN 2021028164 (print) | LCCN 2021028165 (ebook)
ISBN 9781735745930 (paperback) | ISBN 9781735745947 (ebook)
Subjects: LCSH: Nin, Anaïs, 1903-1977--Diaries. | Authors, American--20th century--Diaries. | LCGFT: Diaries.
Classification: LCC PS3527.I865 Z46 2021 (print) | LCC PS3527.I865 (ebook) | DDC 818/.5209 [B]--dc23
LC record available at https://lccn.loc.gov/2021028164
LC ebook record available at https://lccn.loc.gov/2021028165

Sky Blue Press

State College, Pennsylvania

ACKNOWLEDGMENTS

The editor would like to thank the following for their contributions to the realization of this volume: the Anaïs Nin Trust, Angela Enos, Joel Enos, Lana Fox, Benjamin Franklin V, Jennavieve McClelland, Jooyeon Rhee, Chrissi Sepe, Cari Lynn Vaughn, Deanne Wells.

This book is dedicated to Alan Swallow and Gunther Stuhlmann.

PREFACE

The *Diary of Others* is so named because after 1958 Anaïs Nin's diary consisted mainly of correspondence with "*des autres*"—family members, friends, and colleagues—as a way of documenting her life. In all, some 1,600 pages of original text were used to edit the book into its present form.

Editing this volume was challenging for a number of reasons. One is that the source material was written on loose pages that were sometimes out of order or misfiled, which involved detective work to locate and place them in proper sequence. And, sometimes, materials such as notes, calendar entries, and letters were kept separately from the original diary and had to be sequentially (and contextually) integrated with the rest of the manuscript.

This book is divided into two sections: "The Trapeze Life" (1955-1958) and "Others" (1958-1966). The "Trapeze" section, beginning in April 1955, details Nin's double life, which she compared to a trapeze upon which she oscillated between New York, where she lived with her legal husband Hugh (Hugo) Guiler, and California, where she lived with Rupert Pole, the lover she bigamously married in early 1955.

The "Others" section, beginning in 1958 after Nin ceased writing frequent and detailed diary entries, consists of correspondence describing her increased efforts to promote her fiction and to edit her diary in such a way that it could be published in her lifetime without doing harm to those she held dear. Her frequent communications with her literary agent and various publishers, along with trips abroad to get her titles published in foreign markets and to film one of her novels, precluded her lifelong habit of diary writing, which all but ceased for years. Also, in 1962 Nin reveals that she "stopped writing in the Diary because everywhere I turned lay pain," which possibly includes Nin's crumbling marriage with Guiler, her frustrations with the bourgeois attitudes of Pole, and her failure to find a dedicated publisher who would keep her work in print. The editorial decisions as to what would be included in the "Others" section were made in order to provide a seamless documentation of Nin's determined and patient planning for what would soon be recognized as her most important publication: the diary itself.[1]

Paul Herron
State College, Pennsylvania
August 2021

Note

[1] The divorce of Renate Druks and Ronnie Knox, which occurs in 1964, is described in what could be perceived as confusing passages written between 1963 and 1964. The time gaps between the passages seem to indicate that they have been misplaced, but given the fact that Druks and Knox had a bohemian, on-and-off relationship, it is feasible that they agreed to a divorce in 1963 but then either reconciled briefly or ran into unforeseen legal or logistical problems before it was finalized in 1964. Because Anaïs Nin does not offer any explanations, the order of the entries has been preserved.

INTRODUCTION

I feel in my bones that you are soon, and suddenly, going to become a figure of great prominence in the literary world.
—Henry Miller, letter to Anaïs Nin, March 2, 1965

In *Trapeze: The Unexpurgated Diary of Anaïs Nin, 1947-1955* (2017), Anaïs Nin (1903-1977) mainly details her relationships with husband Hugh Guiler in New York and lover Rupert Pole in California. They fulfilled different needs, though both men frustrated her: the dull banker Guiler provided financial security; the dilettante forest ranger Pole, sex. She divided her time between them. Her romance with Pole became so intense that he, incorrectly believing she had divorced her husband, insisted that they wed, which they did in 1955, thereby making her a bigamist. With this event *Trapeze* ends.

The Diary of Others: The Unexpurgated Diary of Anaïs Nin, 1955-1966 records numerous aspects of Nin's life in the decade following her second marriage. Among other specifics, it documents the unease Nin feels in public, the help she receives from psychoanalysis, the nature of her experience taking LSD, the lesbian sensations she feels but on which she does not act, her enjoyment of jazz, her need for love, her illnesses, and her inability to tolerate criticism, including from friends whose actions benefited her, most prominently Gore Vidal. The book exposes her vanity and occasional nastiness.[1] In time Nin overcame some of what she considered deficiencies (she became a gifted public speaker, for example); others she never surmounted (such as rejecting friends and critics who displeased her).

Interesting though these and additional characteristics and occurrences are, two subjects are of greatest importance. One concerns Nin's need for secrecy about both her bigamy and at least one—and probably all—of her affairs. Mainly she fears that her husbands will realize that they share her. Keeping them ignorant of this reality complicates her life to the degree that she likens it to being on a trapeze. She flies back and forth from coast to coast, spending time with one husband here and the other there. (She could afford to do this because of Guiler's generosity.) She lies to them. She pleads with people who know about her domestic situation to keep it confidential, as they seem to do. Yet her commitment to Pole is only the most recent of her betrayals of Guiler.[2] Continuing to conceal her first infidelity—with Henry Miller in Paris in the 1930s—remains a priority. In a diary entry dated June 1955 she writes, "I am suffering from guilt. The exposure of my relationship with Miller frightens me." The desire to keep it secret causes her to demand that Alfred Perlès remove from his ready-for-publication *My Friend Henry Miller* (1956) the details about Miller and her that she thinks are too revealing. Perlès alters the text, grudgingly.

While Nin strove to keep people unaware of her unconventional personal life, she craved recognition as an author. Her fiction had been largely ignored or often derided. During the time covered in this volume she struggled with it, both creating it and placing it with publishers, who judged it commercially unviable. She was relieved when British Book Centre released the novel *A Spy in the House of Love* (1954), though it did so only because Guiler paid for its publication. She believed that the text has cinematic possibilities, but people in the movie industry, including director Robert Wise, disagreed. She wrote her next book, the novella *Solar Barque*, in fits and starts. Since the manuscript generated no interest, in 1958 she published it with the Anais Nin Press, which she established in 1955 to make available some of her previously published books.[3] Though in the late 1950s her career as a fiction writer was in jeopardy, she did not stop trying to locate a publisher that would keep her novels, novellas, and stories in print.

Her perseverance paid off. In possibly the most significant letter she ever composed within the context of her writing, in February 1961 she wrote to Denver publisher Alan Swallow, explaining her plight and asking if he would like to publish her new manuscript (an expansion of *Solar Barque* titled *Seduction of the Minotaur*) and reprint *Winter of Artifice* (novellas) and *Cities of the Interior* (collected novels). She asks, "I wonder if there is anything we can work out together." To entice him she states that to the firm that publishes her novels she "will give an option on the Diaries (for the future)." After they discussed possibilities in subsequent letters, on March 6 he responded to her proposal with words she had long yearned to read, no matter from whom: "I think it makes just about perfect sense that I become your U.S. publisher…I am indicating my willingness, even my eagerness to do this."

Their arrangement, which validated Nin as a fiction writer, laid the foundation for her rise to literary prominence. Despite the modest size of Swallow's business —a one-man operation—it was noted for publishing serious literature by the likes of Janet Lewis, Allen Tate, and Yvor Winters, as well as books about the American West by Vardis Fisher and Frank Waters. That is, there was some cachet attached to being known as a Swallow author. For over half a century since affiliating with him, her fiction has remained in print as Swallow books.[4]

Nin had told Swallow that the publisher of her fiction would have what amounts to first refusal on publishing her diary. He did not refuse. However, the magnitude of the project caused him to require assistance. Nin attempted to help him by contacting such established New York companies as Putnam's and Random House, but they declined to become involved. By early November 1964, Nin believed that such a venture might appeal to Hiram Haydn, an editor at Harcourt, Brace & World; Gunther Stuhlmann, her agent, agreed. They were right. The diary impressed Haydn, who thought that publishing an edited version of it was practicable. In 1965 his organization decided to publish, under his editorship, a volume dealing with the years 1931-1934 and to credit Swallow as co-publisher.[5]

When published in 1966, the book became a sensation. Many if not most reviewers applauded it, though there were naysayers such as Nora Sayre, who mocks Nin and criticizes her prose. Paramount among those commending it were Jean Garrigue on the front page of the *New York Times Book Review* ("a rich, various and fascinating work"), Robert R. Kirsch in the *Los Angeles Times* ("a chronicle of a life lived with extraordinary intensity and sensitivity, recorded with great empathy and luminous understanding"), and Deena Metzger in the *Los Angeles Free Press* ("a warrior against the cult of callousness and insensitivity").[6] Some less notable commentators were similarly enthusiastic.

At least partly because the publication of this book and several later volumes of the *Diary* coincided with the rise of second-wave feminism, many women were attracted to them. Believing, wrongly, that Nin had succeeded in life without financial backing from a man, some readers, including critics, considered her a liberated woman and idealized her. Erika Duncan, for example, deems her "a role model for working relationships," while Diane Wakoski thinks her "the closest thing we have to Venus living among us." Kate Millett goes so far as to characterize her as "mother to us all, as well as goddess and elder sister." Nin encouraged and reveled in such adulation. As Helen Tookey observes, Nin "did her best to enable, or maximize, her symbolic standing as the ultimate liberated woman."[7]

The Diary of Others concludes a month after the diary's publication with Nin's response to its favorable reception:

> A month of good reviews, love letters, appearances on television. Has the sniping really stopped?
> *Diary* selling well. Hiram Haydn thought its sale would be limited. He only printed 3,000. They were sold in a week.
> A month which made up for every disappointment, every poison pen, for all the past obstacles. The sound of opening doors is deafening! Suddenly love, praise, flowers, invitations to lecture.

Nin was correct. Accolades came to her in abundance. The book sold so well that Harcourt committed to publishing more volumes of the *Diary* and, later, additional works by her.[8] She became popular on the lecture circuit. At last she received the acclaim—and fame—she had long sought while keeping secret certain aspects of her life. The publication of the *Diary* elevated her from essentially an underground writer to a celebrity author. With her fiction in print and her *Diary* being published and admired, her belief in her artistry was vindicated.

Benjamin Franklin V
University of South Carolina
June 2021

Notes

[1] Nin states in May 1963 that she has retired "as the major character of this journal"; subsequently, she will consider it the *journal des autres* (of others). Indeed, correspondence drives much of the narrative in *The Diary of Others*, in which Anaïs Nin seems less a persona than does the character so named in earlier volumes of the *Diary*. An instance of her powerlessness to accept criticism occurred when Nin ended her association with Oliver Evans after the publication of his *Anaïs Nin* (1968), which, as the initial scholarly book about her, served her well. See Deirdre Bair, *Anaïs Nin: A Biography* (New York: Putnam's, 1995), 480. Commenting on Vidal on May 2, 1957, Nin acknowledges that she terminates friendships: "He maintains that my pattern is to break relationships, but he does not recognize that this happens only when I am hurt." She betrays her vanity in June 1957: "I am today probably one of the handsomest women of fifty-four walking the streets…" Her mean-spiritedness is evident in her April 1955 disapproval of Mrs. Lindsley's looks and her unflattering description of Hazel McKinley in February 1956.

² Guiler knew of some of his wife's adulteries by the early 1940s. When Nin stopped making payments (with money Guiler earned) for the poet Robert Duncan's subsistence in 1942, out of spite Duncan told Guiler about several of her lovers, information he received with equanimity. See Bair, *Anaïs Nin*, 260, 272. Guiler understood the nature of Nin's life with Pole by the mid-1960s.

³ For information about the publication of *A Spy in the House of Love*, see Bair, *Anaïs Nin*, 369, 372, 591 n. 9. No movie of this novel has yet been made. Nin especially struggled writing *Solar Barque* during the first half of 1956. That May she despaired: "The [compositional] 'flow' was not only inhibited, but I felt total *doubt* about what I was doing. I felt I no longer could write well." To a degree, she blames this problem on her inability to accept the death of her mother, who died in August 1954. For a discussion of Nin's publishing enterprise, see Benjamin Franklin V, "Advertisements for Herself: The Anais Nin Press," *Papers of the Bibliographical Society of America* 91, no. 2 (June 1997): 159-90.

⁴ For Nin's reflections on Swallow, see Anaïs Nin, "Alan Swallow," *University of Denver Quarterly: A Journal of Modern Culture* 2, no. 1 (Spring 1967): 11-14, as well as her "Alan Swallow" in *Publishing in the West: Alan Swallow, Some Letters and Commentaries*, ed. William F. Claire (Santa Fe: Lightning Tree, 1974), 12-15. The Swallow Press is now an imprint of the Ohio University Press.

⁵ The publication of Nin's diary was announced as forthcoming as early as 1937. See Henry Miller, untitled statement, *The Booster* 2, no. 8 (October 1937): facing 1. Putnam's published Henry Miller's *Letters to Anaïs Nin* in 1965. Placing the correspondence there caused a rift between Nin and Swallow, who believed that his commitment to her fiction entitled him to publish the letters. See Bair, *Anaïs Nin*, 469-71. Swallow died in November 1966, seven months after the publication of the first *Diary* volume.

⁶ For a summary of critical commentary about Nin's work published into 1977, see Rose Marie Cutting, *Anaïs Nin: A Reference Guide* (Boston: G. K. Hall, n.d.). Nora Sayre, "Miss Nin," *New Statesman* 72 (September 16, 1966): 402; Jean Garrigue, "The Self behind the Selves," *New York Times Book Review*, April 24, 1966, sec. 7, p. 1; Robert R. Kirsch, "Journal of a Troubled Journey," *Los Angeles Times*, April 17, 1966, sec. B, p. 2; Deena Metzger, "The Diary of Anaïs Nin, 1931-1934," *Los Angeles Free Press*, April 29, 1966, p. 7. Positive though the Garrigue review is, Nin complained to her about it. See Bair, *Anaïs Nin*, 609-10 n. 2.

⁷ The critics Philip K. Jason, Duane Schneider, and Daniel Stern are among the men who admired the diary and Nin's work in general. Susan Manso and Erika Duncan, "Anaïs Nin—Two Views," *New Boston Review* 2 (Fall 1976): 27-28 (the quotation is from 28); Diane Wakoski, "The Craft of Plumbers, Carpenters, & Mechanics: A Tribute to Anaïs Nin," *American Poetry Review* 2 (January-February 1973): 46-47 (the quotation is from 47); Kate Millett, "Anaïs—A Mother to Us All," *ANAIS: An International Journal* 9 (1991): 3-8 (the quotation is from 4); Helen Tookey, *Anaïs Nin, Fictionality and Femininity: Playing a Thousand Roles* (Oxford: Clarendon Press, 2003), 190. Too often Gunther Stuhlmann's introduction to the first *Diary* volume was unread or forgotten. There, he indicates that Nin's unnamed husband is among the

people requesting that Nin omit them from the published *Diary*. See Gunther Stuhlmann, introduction to *The Diary of Anaïs Nin, 1931-1934* (New York: Swallow Press and Harcourt Brace & World, 1966), xi.

[8] During the time it published the first editions of Nin's books, Harcourt was named variously: Harcourt, Brace & World; Harcourt Brace Jovanovich; and Harcourt Brace. The firm published seven heavily edited volumes of the *Diary* that cover the years 1931-1974. They were so successful that Harcourt offered three different boxed sets of the paperback versions, as well as a book of photographs of Nin and selected friends. Next, it published four volumes of Nin's *Early Diary* that document her life from 1914 to 1931. Then, it released four supposedly unexpurgated *Diaries* that alter the nature of Nin's activities from 1931 to 1939 as depicted in earlier books. Additionally, it published a collection of Nin's essays, correspondence between Nin and Henry Miller, and two volumes of erotica that became best sellers and were later packaged as a boxed set.

BOOK ONE
THE TRAPEZE LIFE
1955-1958

New York, March 1955

Hugo and I have undergone a rebellion against each other similar to the rebellion of children against parents. The peace treaty we made in the kitchen—a true, detached sympathy for each other's problems—ended the rebellion. The last time we got violently angry, we clarified the misunderstanding that caused the anger; we realized that our way of fighting, the power we had over each other, was by anger...but this is the second phase (the first being the power we had to make each other feel guilty).

Hugo received me eagerly, with desire. We had one quarrel (because he wants me to get elated at the potential of his new business, when the reality is that we are living on borrowed money). But I am not angry. I can listen to his interminable talk about business.

When we went to dinner, a cocktail and a movie, he did not relax but chose that moment to explain the most intricate workings of the stock exchange. I grew sad because he seemed incurable; he thought I was sad because I did not believe in his capabilities to make money.

We have separate rooms now, because he snores, because he awakens at 2:00 or 3:00 or 4:00 AM and reads, or gets up.

We live like friends. Millicent and I have to remind him to shave!

But his honesty is disarming, as are his efforts. He talks about his weaknesses, his troubles.

The other night Brooks Clift, a little high, got into a taxi with us, and we discovered the driver was not in his seat. The motor was running. Jokingly at first, Brooks took the driver's seat and drove the taxi a few yards. Nothing happened. Thus emboldened, he drove several blocks. Hugo was entirely concerned with the taxi driver's plight. I was divided: feeling for the taxi driver, yet laughing at Brooks' prank, elated by the danger and guilt. But neither Hugo nor I could stop Brooks, because he represented the rebel.

Brooks Clift's amusing dream: "Anaïs is there. Hugo comes in and says: you must leave. I say: 'I just paid $500 for this apartment, but if Anaïs wants to come in and do her writing in it, I will gladly leave.' There is an iron shutter that rolls down, as in my brother's apartment (Montgomery Clift). I pull it down. Anaïs is now taking notes. I ask Hugo: 'Which woman did I marry?' Hugo answers, 'Anne Miller.'"

Brooks has just married for the third time. We met him because he read my books at his analyst's home... We pressed him for the name of the analyst: Dr. Bogner!

So Dr. Bogner has to hear the story of the stolen taxi (which is left in front of the movie house we were going to!), about Brooks, whom she analyzed for two years and has not seen for a year.

"I won't tell her about your dream!" I said. But he was still worried about whom he had married; and because I know and like his new wife, I was concerned about his confession. Like so many immature people, he is full of charm.

What makes Hugo's immaturities so lacking in charm?

Then last night, I had a dream of a godmother. She invites me to stay with her at the beach. But the weather is dark and we have to stay in the house. I was unable to swim and felt disappointed. The clothes she loaned me did not fit. We took a plane to leave the place, but a helicopter flew near us, so close that it frightened me. I felt they would collide. I even felt it must be attached to us, the way it followed us about.

This led me to a talk with Dr. Bogner about my real godmother who gave me disappointing presents—a dark-haired doll when I wanted a blonde one, real jewelry that she worried about me losing. She and Mother quarreled. I do not remember why I turned against her. I showed no feeling at her death, which hurt my mother. I have been meditating on my sudden and irrevocable breaks—(once there is a break, I cannot *feel* anymore, as with Gore Vidal). I talked about my uncontrollable anger at Rupert in Acapulco—or at Hugo, of my fear of *explosions*.

I saw an automobile accident, one car hitting another, causing the gas tank to explode. The fire's violence awakened my fear of more explosions, the fear of explosions in stories of coal miners—all sudden. I have awakened during atom bomb tests although I could not hear them, and in one instance did not even *know* it was to take place.

New York, March 1955

Yesterday I asked myself whether I had lost my power to create because of the many humiliations America has inflicted on me, and the disastrous failure of *A Spy in the House of Love*. Am I beaten by the coldness and stupidity of the critics, the low level of life here in general? Has America's treatment of me triumphed?

The answer came this morning. The inner music started again. I reread what I had done on *Solar Barque* and liked it. Tonight I *hear* the music, and all my feelings are awake.

My greatest problem is one inherent in the experiment itself. Because I follow the pattern of free association, the design is sometimes chaotic even for me. The attempt to construct a novel in this way *is* difficult. I wanted to show how the adventurer does not forget his past or escape it when he enters paradise... The doctor gave Lillian the drug of remembrance and refused her the drug of forgetfulness. He is killed for that, because people want to forget. Lillian does not escape... so she returns to remember and liquidate the past.

New York, April 1955

Dream: Heavy atmosphere. I am leaving Rupert and trying to carry away some things he must not see. I am leaving Hugo and also trying to take away pennies and semi-precious stones. But they meet. Rupert comes to me, very upset, and says: "Hugo just told me in French that you are going to marry him." I answer: "You misunderstood him. Of course not."

Now I have to face the truth: the smokescreen of my accusations against Hugo were intended to conceal the unbearable truth: *I do not love him.* This I have been unwilling to face. I thought it was all the neurotic walls we had created, neurotic quarrels, neurotic estrangements, but after seven years of analysis, his character, although altered, retains basic themes I do not love. I did not want to part in anger, to part because of this neurosis: *I felt a responsibility.* Also, I have always suspected my emotions. My head said: stay with Hugo. My feelings were with Rupert.

But I'm frightened.

Yesterday I helped Hugo all day with his tax papers. We talked quietly and without anger about many things, mostly practical. It so happened that because his new job has not yet brought in anything, I am the one who is bringing in money.

Royalties for *A Spy in the House of Love*: $178.00
Lecture & film showing at Brown University: $100.00
Lecture & film showing at Chapel Hill: $100.00
Reimbursement from British Book Centre on an unfair charge: $144.00

But the *pleasure* I might have in helping him is marred by his "error" at the bank, which made him think he had lost $150 by his foolish expenditures: for example, he made an expensive telephone call to Caresse Crosby in Washington to see if she is coming on Wednesday when it is Caresse who should let us know if she is staying with us! So I persuaded him to let me write an airmail letter. Then he made another call to Hollywood to discuss terms with Warner Brothers over a few feet of film they *might* buy!

We each have our madness, I know. That is why I confide my true feelings to the Diary, but not to him. I try to protect him from me and from himself. He is like a thorn in me. I can't free myself. And I can't love him.

Everything is wrong. He is either overly passive and weak, or overly aggressive and stubborn... He either demands too much (to be waited on hand and foot), or gives too much (like the Chrysler I did not want in California).

Another session with Bogner after this. She disregards my statement about Hugo (which is always accompanied by tears) but focuses on my need of independence. It is true there is a superimposition of my economic status as a child—my mother was very optimistic about all the money she thought she had earned, but it was in the form of commissions on purchases charged by clients, and many of these clients never paid, so we accumulated debts and had a house we could not pay for. My secretarial work for Mother was overwhelming; the bills from the shops had to be examined and each item charged to a separate person.

My reaction, finally, was to go out and get a job. But today I cannot solve the problem as easily—I have two homes and too much work to do in each. But when I work *for* Hugo, I feel it is wasted, because he makes errors and is wasteful. I can't help feeling if I worked for myself I could organize my life so that I could achieve my wish: that finances are not in the foreground.

Anyway, Bogner is harsh. She is probably trying to say independence is a *feeling*, not a thing to be taken literally (a job). Whatever Hugo does (and he is not my mother—he struggles against his irrationality in money matters) should not make me feel helpless and overwhelmed by destructive forces. Hugo destroys, just as Gonzalo and Henry did. But at least he is struggling against all his negativities.

But I have no *faith*. Even if he made a fortune I would not enjoy it. I would have paid too dearly for it.

I'm baffled because when analysis seems to arouse self-suffering, it also suggests aggression or the desire for power.

Am I angry (not loving Hugo) because leadership was Hugo's only gift to me? He did not give me life or pleasure; he gave me protection—and this protection was false.

Of all the ironies: even though this month I am the one who *earns*, I have no vote, no say, no power, no control, nothing in the way money is spent! Hugo tells me what will be.

Of course, he has no faith in me, having looked upon me as a dependent. When I wanted to handle the problems with British Book Centre, he said: "I'll go. You get emotional." Then he bungled it. But I did not have to obey—I could have said, "No, I want to go. I understand the situation."

The persistence in my relationship with Hugo was due to my hope that our dissonances were neurotic—but today I do not believe this.

The "money" subject was so painful that I wept. An unsolved mystery, for I have worked very hard. I am still working. I filed hundreds of film-showing papers. I entered Hugo's films in festivals (and *Jazz of Lights* won a prize). I see Kossoff, Hugo's distributor. I run errands for Hugo.

Hugo was to be my indirect fulfillment, but, by his perversity, I failed to accomplish even this. I did not fail *him*, not in his desire to be helped as an artist, but I did fail to be the wife he needed. He needed a nurse, servant, slave, housekeeper, cook, listener.

Last night he was so kind—analytic—because I was in a weak mood and distressed. He is at his best then.

New York, April 1955
To each his madness.

I asked Dick Duane (who is changing prodigiously under analysis) why some people's *masks* (we were looking at hideous masks from Peru) are so monstrous... are they defenses? I was thinking of Hugo's face. It is a mask of torment, a distortion of his former face. His mouth has become thin—at first, it was sensuous. His nose seems more aquiline, the furrows between his eyebrows are a quarter inch deep.

Rupert makes me feel tender. Hugo antagonizes me.

In the life of the soul and emotions, there are undertones, treacherous downward forces.

Yet, when I go out, I feel the sun, the air of spring. I enjoy the Easter window dressings. I enjoy the massage at Arden's—I'm happy because I have my own bedroom.

I follow all the developments of Jim Herlihy's life. He is the only American who has learned the *value* of life from me, who prizes it like a work of art, and who broke through surface writing into a subterranean level—because he *feels*. Yet when we first met years ago, his feelings were not in his writing... The gift I offered America, which they did not want, Jim accepted. It proves that the boy from Detroit, denuded, from a sterile background, uneducated, could take me and my work and be nourished...and he has grown quickly. I read his diary with interest, quote from it. He does his best writing there. Why does one's best writing require secrecy, silence and darkness? A locked-up diary. What we give the world is grey and diluted.

Dick and Jim "divorced," but then Dick rushed into analysis. I felt so clearly that neurosis is a possession by the devils of destruction. You become compulsive. You destroy. It is not your voice, your true self. But your body is inhabited. It is the spirit of the past, past selves superimposing themselves over the present, blurring it, choking it. An Anaïs of fourteen seeing her mother working so hard and in debt, an Anaïs baffled by bookkeeping, feeling helpless—and later, feeling clairvoyant and judging my mother's errors, then working for immediate needs with a small salary for my family of four—and then I returned from modeling all day at Jaeckels and posing all evening for artists only to discover my mother has signed a contract for a "sidewalk" ($600) when we did not even have a properly working furnace!

The irrationality of the mother—that was the terror. The inability to reason. The illusion that my father could reason, and then the illusion about *logic—man's logic*—when I met my father I was shocked by his falseness, his irrationality—he died insane.

Hugo's "hearing problem" is similar to my father's ignoring his family. When Millicent and I stand at the door to *prevent* his returning and we say in unison: "Do you have a handkerchief? Do you have your keys? Wallet? Newspaper? Fountain pen?" he invents a new complication: he says *yes*—but he does not *hear* us. And after he is downstairs, he returns for the pen.

Hugo's disintegrated personality frightens me—that is why I am obsessed with it. I repeat: he is very ill, very ill. I must take care of him.

But it's strange. For the first time I understand why, long ago, they treated the insane like criminals: because the destructive demons are apparent, even in the neurosis, and destruction is *criminal.*

New York, April 1955

Caresse Crosby, author of *The Passionate Years* in a passionless era, appears. Her dress is airy, winged. It is of a black but transparent material, inflated and crisp by new methods as organdie once was by starching and ironing. It gives her the silhouette of a young woman. Her hair, though grey, is glossy, brushed, starched and the opposite of limp, because the spirit of Caresse is airy and alive. Age can wrinkle her face, freckle her hands, ruthlessly drop the lids over her eyes, tire her, but it cannot kill her laughter, her enthusiasm, her mobility.

Her second husband, Harry Crosby, committed suicide at the side of another woman. Her beloved son Bill died asphyxiated by a faulty gas heater in Paris. But Caresse wears a huge bow at her neck because her dress and body and hair reflect the alertness and the discipline of her spirit. She told me, "I went to a cocktail in Washington, at Huntington Cairns', and I was appalled how little interest people had in each other."

Hugo and I took her to dinner. Some say she is a silly woman. Perhaps she has not lived at the deepest levels, but at the level of a chic Pollen, a smiling international serpentine, a *chargé d'affaires* of the heart, a public relations director among lovers, a personal representative of the artists, a publisher who "played" writers as others played horses, the purest example of *mouvement perpetuel* of fervors... Certainly a woman like this is worth more than Paul Bowles and John Goodwin, who are blind, deaf and dumb to all human beings, writing about their infantile tantrums, sadisms and distortions.

I finally saw clearly today the true flaw in American writing. It poses as realism. John Goodwin writes a novel about Haiti. He mentions politics, economics, prices, costs, etc. and establishes the "realism" so dear to Americans. To all appearances this is an objective novel (in contrast to mine), but soon the characters appear and they are thoroughly distorted by a psychotic homosexual insight. And this is what the American public swallows. It is a documentary. It deals with a black and white problem, with voodoo and retired alcoholics. No one dares to say the book belongs at the galleries where they hang paintings by the insane.

At the same party there was a lady, Mrs. Lindsley. Unlike Caresse, Mrs. Lindsley aged without illusory fiesta dresses, without the blessings of cosmetics, without skillful reconstructions. It may have been that she decided from the beginning that no art or charms could reduce the prominence of her nose. At this moment, with her memory almost gone, with her hair like an accidental pile of hay, her skin dry and coarse, she seemed partly animal and partly mummy.

But she told a story: "When I went to Nairobi and went out lion hunting in a jeep, one negro was driving and the other carried my gun. The rule in this kind of hunting is to remain in the jeep and to keep driving. Well, when we reached a particularly deep gully, the jeep got stuck, and while they were working to get it going, I left them and went for a walk along the gully. I was walking back peacefully when I saw, on my right, that an enormous lion had been walking alongside me. I was calm. I continued to walk towards the jeep. So did the lion. Then where the gully turned towards the left, the lion continued towards the right, but before parting of the ways, he looked back at me as if to say goodbye."

One felt that the lion had determined that Mrs. Lindsley did not belong to the human race. That furthermore, there was an affinity between her hair, skin, bones, and some aged animal. Or that perhaps there was nothing there to stimulate his appetite. The friendship, in any case, the peaceful walk, was understandable. If I had been walking along the gully, and I had seen Mrs. Lindsley, I would have not cried out or run away—I would have continued my walk too.

Meanwhile, Mrs. Keating of *Cue* magazine and I were discussing the review of Tennessee Williams' new play. *Cue* is the magazine I am (mythically) working for, to explain to Rupert my trips and various activities, my involvement in film showings, museums, exhibits, etc. I have also dreamed of starting *Cue* in California.

At my right sat Caresse, whom I had "met" twenty years earlier in fantasy and with whom, I told Hugh, I had shared the country life at the *Moulin de Soleil* (to explain my absences) and with whom I actually shared the country life at Hampton Manor, her southern mansion in Virginia, with Dalí and Miller (escaping from both Hugo and Gonzalo).

Hugo, at the French restaurant, is acting like a man of distinction, talking brightly; his skin is rose-toned; he is smiling. No trace of weaknesses, hesitations, insomnias, torments. (The loss of money, constant, is now discovered in analysis to be due to his father's love and obsession with money, so that Hugo, while sharing the obsession, when he gets money, feels that it burns his fingers and he must throw it away...) We are throwing it away now on a pseudo-French dinner, and I am aware that almost all of our evenings are directed and regulated by business. The difference is that I am aware I owe Hugo all the care that has kept me from insanity (Dr. Bogner) and given me health (Dr. Jacobson) and part of the pleasures of my life with Rupert. In turn I am aware that I have given Hugo an ocean of friends...so it balances, everything balances except my desperate longings for Rupert. I can only calm the desperation by reminding myself:

"Tonight, if you were in Sierra Madre, you would be setting out for another dinner with his family and another evening of quartet music." But at midnight we would be going to bed together.

Whereas here at midnight Hugo and I go into our separate rooms.

Another evening of Men of Business. But the French men of business are socially charming, witty, flirtatious, gallant, and never talk business. One, a refined, cultured Jew, well traveled, well read, quoting Valéry, is an amateur photographer. There was talk of Yucatan culture, of China, of Saint Phalles' *History of the World*, hand-kissing, teasing, admiration of Hugo's films, etc. He even blew into my coat as skiers do to warm each other!

Irina Aleksander is off to live in France—her husband is now in a high position in the U.N. Departures by ship are still more emotional than departures by air. The cabin was filled with flowers, and there was champagne. India, Japan, Scotland, Yugoslavia and Russia were represented. It seems more portentous, a more definitive voyage.

The fascinating contradiction in Irina is that she utters "*mondaine*" clichés with gestures, facial expressions, fervor and exaggerations of Dostoevskian characters. She is only saying: "Oh what beautiful flowers you sent!" But she seems to be saying: "Do you or do you not believe in God?" Her grey tailored suit is rigorously conventional, her small grey hat and small veil standardized chic, but she thanks the minister and the members of the U.N. for their collective present in the tone of voice of a Russian actress who has received a diamond tiara—and embarrasses everyone with a display of humility and negation worthy of a Chinese: "It is too much. We don't deserve all that!"

The same with her lavish praise of others and detrimental self-portraits. She calls attention to the pockets under her eyes, signs of age, fatigue, strain… Observes my renaissance, and Hugo's, knows the secret of it, lived on the same street as Dr. Bogner for years…yet repudiated salvation…

"Goodbye, goodbye," in the style of a Russian Sarah Bernhardt. It is the language of politeness in which Irina has sought to breathe emotion. The illusion of politics is dead. But unlike other illusions (those about love), that of politics is usually fatal to all other illusions. Politicians are as narrow-minded as priests. You can have no other love—so the rest of the personality is atrophied. At least in the drama of personal illusions, one recognizes the disillusionment with a lover, but meanwhile one has possessed life and pleasure. In politics one has possessed nothing.

I see around me that those who believed in communism are more bitter than those who believed in a lover who betrayed them.

New York, April 1955

Bogner led the talk to the three things I failed to do: to make money, to drive a car with pleasure, and to operate a camera—the three were symbols of Hugo's prerogatives, leadership, excellence. I was afraid to take over his masculine expressions. He was in the driver's seat. All the more reason, if he did not do it well, for me not to take over and humiliate him. As soon as this was clear (which actually means to separate the impure from the pure), Bogner said, "When you took a job to help your mother; it was seemingly a pure motivation, but you felt guilty not because you stepped in to help in a crisis, but because originally you had wanted to take your mother's place in your father's affection, because originally (original sin!) you were angry with her for driving away your father, angry with her for bringing you to America when you were happy in Spain. So these are hidden angers, covered by *good* reasons for taking a job, because in one of your dreams you're taking your mother's place when she drove badly."

This may even explain why I repudiated music (my father's prerogative) and why I never entered politics (Gonzalo's prerogative). But writing? I did not fear to write when Henry did... Anyhow—the impure and the pure mix. The conscience is aware of the evil thought—and is uneasy.

Parties

Dick looks like Pinocchio at the piano, but sings like Caruso in *Plus Léger*. Pepe, just back from Cuba, has rediscovered his mother: "So beautiful, Anaïs, with a skin like yours and eyes like mine. And I had her all to myself, my brother and sister being married. And I loved her. I realized how much I loved her, in the way Freud said..."

The smokescreen of the homosexuals' true feelings about women is over-praise and gushing, which I once enjoyed innocently as a sign of my power to transcend taboos.

Letter from Anaïs Nin to Rupert Pole:
New York, April 8, 1955

Darling:

Your letter written on the beach made me homesick and restless.

My writing looks like yours, not only because I am thinking of you, but also because I am in the subway! Very busy with a film festival during the day and evenings, and also a photo exhibit. No time for anything but my job.

Plans for *House of Incest*: I can get 1,000 copies offset, an exact reproduction of the orange [Gemor Press] book, bound for $200 or $300 when the time comes, so that we can make $2,700 ourselves by slow, continuous sales as I have done the last few years. I can do that with all my titles as they get sold.

The subway now has red leather seats and shaded lights!

Caresse Crosby is off to Greece to work at her Citizens of the World scheme. She has a house in Delhi where we can stay anytime! And she bought a mountain so that Citizens of the World could be legal. The airline did *not* charge her $15 for excess baggage because she told the man she was traveling for peace.

Never too busy to think and feel your presence vividly just before sleep.

Your wife

New York, April 12, 1955

A dream last night in which Hugo and I were being drafted to fight a war. My job is dangerous. I have to push some earth into a pit and I'm in danger of sliding down into the pit with the moving earth.

And before that: *the lake that cures everything*. Hugo and I are swimming in it. Other people take boats. Boats are like carnival floats. They ride over us and endanger our lives. Hugo never notices them. I feel I have to watch out for both of us. I get angry at the boats and bang on them.

The most painful operation this month is related to money. I have a feeling of inadequacy in that realm, of helplessness. But following Bogner's clarifications about my father's disdain for money, I have handled all my affairs well.

Talked clearly and firmly to my agent James Brown: "I want to find a collector who will buy the original of the Diary, and a publisher who will buy the copy for *future* publication."

"When?"

"When certain people have died—10 or 15 years."

The only woman the homosexual loves is the one who can, outwardly, bear a few signs of semblance to the mother, but seems younger than the mother, an idealized version. Now, for Jim, I at once conceal the mother (I don't *look* maternal), yet I have enough resemblance with his mother (in this case temperamentally—she is Irish, very emotional). My best relationship is with Jim—the most truthful. Because we are not lovers? I suppose it is easier to be sincere when you are not lovers. But what I like is attainable in the lover relationship too. An agreement upon basic attitudes and wishes: to live richly, to make a work of art of life, and to create a work of art that is alive.

Dream: Rupert is driving my car (the big Chrysler Hugo gave me). He is attempting to scale a steep and rugged hill. I protest. But Rupert (full of determination as he is on such occasions) tries anyway. Of course we fall off. I hear by the sound that the car is utterly smashed. I am aware that Rupert smashed it because it was Hugo's car.

Thursday, April 14, 1955
Received check from university $40
Took films to Providence, Rhode Island
Taxi $1.30
Train to Providence $12.85
Tip $0.50
Lunch $1.30
Taxi $0.75
Taxi $0.75
Hotel $5.00
Tip $0.50
Breakfast $0.40
4:00 film showing
8:00 film showing and talk

Letter from Anaïs Nin to Rupert Pole:
New York, Thursday April 14, 1955

Darling:

This morning packing for the film showing in Providence was very sorrowful, as it reminded me of packing for Los Angeles. Sometimes it hurts so much I wonder if I will have the courage to do it again, even if we are building a house. I recognize the human pain of separation...no matter how busy I am, when it hits me, it hurts. However, I also realize its practical necessity. The practical results are obvious.

With James Brown, I settled the British Book Centre problem. The owner, in England, went bankrupt, and that is why they got tight at this end and got rid of Felix Morrow, my old publisher. Brown said I could sue them for my royalties, but it would cost $500 in lawyers' fees to get $200 or $300—and the suit would bring attention to other publishers how little I sold. So I went myself and arranged a friendly settlement.

The other good news is that *Spy* was sold to England, 50 pounds advance and 10% royalties.

The third is that the French translation of *Ladders* has gone to Plon in France—a big house who wants to read the Diary. I said the Diary would be later, after they do the novels to establish my reputation first. I also made it clear to Brown what I wanted to do with the Diary (which is our capital). He said it was perfectly possible that I could sell the original manuscripts to a collector, and an abridged, revised copy to a publisher to be published after death of certain persons... So you see our Five Year Plan is practical.

I continue to push the California *Cue* idea.

You should have gone to see the Spanish dancers, darling. My weeping was only because I would have liked to be a dancer, if I had not been stage shy—but this, like your occasional regrets for a life as an actor or a musician, is only occasional and not deep. I also have, occasionally, a twinge of homesickness for Spain and France, but that is not deep or basic, only a mood. The only *basic*, fundamental essential country and profession I have is *you*.

Love,
Mrs. Pole

Letter from Rupert Pole to Anaïs Nin:
Sierra Madre, April 1955

Darling:
Intended to write such a good letter this eve—but just can't now—so desperately tired. Such an exertion. Was going to a movie but then decided if I'm ever to be a violist I must practice, so started to play at seven and now it's midnight and suddenly I realize I've been playing intensely (all the hard parts) for five hours—backache, eye-ache, so silly...

Of course I was inspired by a quintet I heard last night—a Hungarian group—so wonderful I was determined to become a good violist *overnight*, and now I just ache, but it numbs and dampens the ache of missing you, which is so much more intense.

My love, I realize you must keep your books in circulation—that is a must even with *H. of I.* I only felt you should charge more for it now that it has become a valuable edition. If there's enough demand for it we might have it offset now, sell those inexpensively and raise the price on the first edition. I feel *you* should gain something back from all work and money you put into that special printing.

Warm and clear here—just waiting for you to return so we can ride and swim and love under the sun—and continue *our life.*

R

P. S. Don't like "Mrs. Pole." Looks terrible. Like "A" much better.

New York, April 23, 1955

In analysis there is a constant study of *displacement.* Thus I discover that the bad habits of Hugo's I cannot bear and fight in him are the same habits I had conquered in myself. I made superhuman efforts to discipline my dreamy, chaotic childhood. I succeeded. I *was* as Hugo is now. And so I hate his self-indulgence. Just as the ex-alcoholic hates the alcoholic but often marries him, I felt betrayed by Hugo's errors. They are my *potentialities of error.* Then I discovered his economic life is as complex as my love life ("I want to go to Paris, and I want to get business here too," says Hugo, just as I want both Rupert and Hugo). He manipulates the "facts" to suit his fantasy. No wonder he confused me (or wanted to) as I confuse him to conceal my life with Rupert. He had to confuse finances to cover his love of gambling (his association with adventurers).

Always two wishes pulling at each other.

I had asked Bogner: "Please deliver me from anger and irritation with Hugo." The night before I had gone to bed early, weary, and he had gone to the film-makers' evening. He returned *two* times, once for the projector, and once for the reel, which is *always* an integral part of projecting. The *error.* The error and forgetfulness control and dominate him.

Now I see the disappointment. Bogner forces the insight back *into* the self that persists on fighting by projection (such as Lila Rosenblum's occupation with fighting off alcoholism in others after suppressing her own).

By coincidence or by the effects of analysis, I have handled my life so well that this month I have earned money, sold books.

"Get a load of this," says Jim over the telephone when he has a story to tell. "Get a load of this," I said to Jim. "I met Samuel Roth, who has a publishing house downtown. He is a poet. The whole family works there. He gave me $100 right off for the right to reprint six short stories. The money is made on nude magazines and an anthology for subscribers only, where classics and trash mix under the sign of 'Planet Sex.' He may be the one to publish my diaries." Jim was excited. "Because, Anaïs, I have just read volume 46 and I almost called you up at midnight— only the thought of Hugo asleep kept me from calling. That volume 46! It contains the most beautiful writing that was ever done in the English language! I had to read passages to Dick! I was ready to explode!" Thus he returns to me the fervor I poured into the volume.

To balance the total indifference of the Big Critics, I have a personal, intimate fervor…in Chapel Hill…the first person who brought my books there and made others read them. A girl said: "But why, why, why didn't I know, why wasn't I told about you? I read everything good, yet I never *knew* about you until Paul Chase made me read you." Why? Because I have received no honors, no Serious

Critical Study, because I am omitted from all anthologies and studies of American literature.

26 years ago in Paris, a boy was born to whom I paid little attention. Paul is the son of Gilbert Chase, my American cousin. 26 years later I received a neat, precise letter from Paul about my books. He wrote from Chapel Hill College. I sent him the books he did not have and we corresponded. He announced his marriage. He planned my visit to the college, and a showing of Hugo's films. He was enthusiastically helped by Kenneth Ness of the art department.

So yesterday, I arrived on a small plane, and found waiting a neat, slender young man, with a delicate, narrow face, and enormous, beautiful eyes. Neither Uncle Gilbert nor Gilbert were handsome, but Paul is, and alert and quick, with finesse. We recognized each other. He drove me to his little house, where I met his wife Deirdre. We left my bag at the inn. He rapidly informed me of my schedule. At 4:00, after talking with them (Deirdre is pretty and intelligent), I had barely time for a bath when Kenneth Ness appeared. A teacher of painting, dressed negligently, blue eyes distressed, gestures febrile, jittery. I thought he was nervous at meeting me...but this nervousness is constant, and I wish I had followed my impulse to ask him: "Are you in trouble?" We talked about the plans for the evening, details only. Later I went to his house for dinner. I met a teacher of creative writing from Duke University and an art historian. I saw a few of Kenneth Ness's paintings, which are bold, alive, and full of charm. We talked about films. We went to the auditorium. About 200 people. A good attendance. Ness introduced me. I presented the films—showed them, talked again. Then a party at Mrs. Chapman's, who owns two of my books.

After the party I talked with Paul and Deirdre until 1:00 AM. Went to bed exhausted. Awakened aching from fatigue. Breakfast in bed, stood on my head... At 10:30 I saw Ness's other paintings, *all* of them. The paintings are joyous, and rich... I hope what I said helps him, as he does not feel ready for an exhibit. Lunch with Jessie. Jessie is masculine, big, homely, but very pleasing, direct, lusty and humorous in spite of distress, recovering from a breakdown, writing a novel. The lives of these people touched me, the great distress in such peaceful, relaxed, Southern surroundings. She understands my work. Her class I met later, about 20 students. We had a lively discussion, reading. I told them the story one told me: her mother asked her one day: "Tell me about this subconscious I've been hearing about."

"But Mother, I've been talking to you about it for 20 years!"

"Oh, that, but the way *you* talked I thought it was something you had that I didn't have!"

Letter from Alfred Perlès to Anaïs Nin:
c/o Henry Miller, Big Sur, California, Monday, April 1955

Dear Anaïs,

Neville Armstrong, of Neville Spearman, Ltd., London, who, I understand, is publishing your book *A Spy in the House of Love*, asked me in a recent letter to sound you out on the possibilities of bringing out your fabulous diary. I gave him a rough idea of the size of the journal, telling him it must by now have grown to a work of at least 20 large volumes, possibly more. Was that too exaggerated an estimate? Neville, who seems very keen on your diary, now suggests an edition of a one-volume selection from the journal. Would that be of any interest to you? You apparently have a small but enthusiastic public in England, and the appetizer of a one-volume selection, if judiciously selected, may well lead to increased demand for your work.

As you know, I've been staying with Henry at Big Sur for the last five months; now my visit is coming to an end: another couple of weeks and I'll be on my way back to England (where I've been living since 1938), via Chicago and N.Y. I'd been hoping I would have a chance of seeing you again after all these years. If I had a car and if I were sufficiently mechanically-minded to drive it, I'd drop in on you. Seems there are as many ifs as in the good old days.

Do drop me a line, though, if you can spare the time. Let me know if it's all right for me to give Neville your address so he can get in touch with you directly. My own book on Henry Miller is coming out this autumn (same publishers) and you are affectionately evoked in it.

Affectionately yours,
Fred

New York, April 1955

Made my peace with Max Geismar over his review of *Spy*.

Max: "I hurt easy."

I explained: "At that time I did an unrealistic thing: I set you up as a symbol. You were going to make an absolute statement, the voice of America, to say what no American critic said, total allegiance—but I see now that I was wrong. You couldn't do that, because you have your own integrity…"

"I could not say that for the Diary."

"I believe that."

"But I do admit I let you down, failed. I did not write what *I* felt about *Spy*, but what I thought would sell the book."

"Yes, that was wrong. I didn't want that. I wanted you to write what you said over the telephone: 'The book is alive!' But I am sorry I hurt you. I felt you were my last link with America. After that, I broke away. I accepted America's rejection. Then, when I resign myself, I do the lectures and discover the 'small and fervent following.'"

Last talk with Bogner: I said, "I understand the *displacement*—when I had a talk with Hugo in which I asked his forgiveness for seven years of irritability, as soon as I realized his absent-mindedness *was* mine, which I disciplined, I went out and took two wrong subway trains! To prove that as soon as I relinquish the discipline I act like Hugo? *Also*—I reminded Hugo that for 25 years I idealized him. He was the man without *flaws*. Then analysis opened up the rebellions, etc.

(Incidentally, I asked Hugo: "What about what you projected onto me? Did I let you down? Did you want me to be the artist and rebel?" "Yes. And you sure were!" said Hugo. "You sure did it for me!")

Bogner pointed up the extremes: projecting onto Hugo an ideal figure (which I needed) or its reverse: a figure full of flaws. This is what made adjustment difficult. With Henry, there was no idealization at the base...none with Gonzalo either.

Bogner made the subjective metamorphosis very clear. I could see it. I could also see it all originates with and returns to the self. But when she *seems* to imply that I use this subjective vision in my work, too, I get very disturbed. I'm willing to admit errors in living—but not in my work. I take her implication as a threat to the integrity of my work. She did not mean that. She *meant* that all truth lies in the *relationship* between subjectivity and objectivity, not in one *or* the other. "But subjectivity has been used as a judgment *against* my work..." She stopped me. Because I had misunderstood. Although I defend the validity and value of subjective art, when she says something that sounds like doubt, I feel she is implying psychological blindness (pathology, madness?). But she didn't. All she said was *truth* was an interplay between them. Hemingway was not an objective writer or he would have written a case history. It was Hemingway's vision of war, bullfights, etc.

The only other time I misunderstood Bogner was again in reference to writing. *To remain objective she has not read my books.* She asks me about them. She seemed to disagree when I said I used a psychoanalytic way of approaching the truth about character... She didn't mean *all* of character, just the focus on neurosis or the secret or irrational self... I felt *she* of all people should understand what I am doing. But she questions all extremes, all separations. Nothing is separate. (*I* have separated them.) Everything is interrelated. Outside. Inside. Body. Psyche. In my art I meant to *begin* in the subconscious and arrive at objectivity...to unite them.

She has declined to accept guardianship of the original Diary volumes: I wanted that because she is the only objective person I know, and also the only one who would not be hurt by it.

And now she is gone on vacation all summer...but I feel stronger and more whole. I think Hugo and I served as guinea pigs for analysis and added a contribution to science. It took patience, courage, intelligence. Bogner was the only one who accomplished the job properly.

Sylvia and Ted Ruggles: At first they were the neighbors in our apartment building. We greeted them in the elevator. We greeted him when he promenaded his dog. They were both rotund and pleasant in different ways. She rosy-faced, fresh, open, with a tinkling southern accent. He more reserved, dark-eyed like a Latin, silently alive. Once or twice we invited them to our parties. But the friendship began when we showed Hugo's films at the Young Men's Hebrew Association. Then they were devoted, helpful, rich in suggestions and advice. Both of them are as busy as we are, so it was an intermittent friendship. But last night we had our best evening together.

"Fresh out of Harvard," said Ted, "I got a job with a famous and wealthy psychoanalyst who was writing books—a study of Bonaparte was one. He was given to plagiarism and I was employed to de-plagiarize his books. We lived in a sumptuous apartment overlooking the Park, near the zoo. He liked to get up early, but I didn't. Not wanting to be too direct about it—too gauche—he never made an issue of this. But when he took his early morning walk around the reservoir, on his way home he would stop at the zoo and awaken the lions who roared angrily and so loudly they awakened me!"

Meanwhile Sylvia works for the U.N. children. Ted and Hugo compared their Scotch clans. Ted brought out the separate mouth flute on which they practice for the bagpipes. Sylvia showed us an anthology called *Garden Poems* she gathered together.

They did not feel that the sale of the Diary to a collector was a fantasy but a very concrete plan that could bring me money. So now I will pursue this "fantasy" until it is fulfilled.

It is astonishing how hostilities cease as you clarify your projections. If I gave Hugo full material power over our life (and rebelled against having no capital of my own), he gave me not only the role of artist but that of critic and evaluator of our spiritual values (and consequently he rebelled against my dictatorship in that realm). No sense of equality is possible under such a regime. I had to acquire my own status in financial matters, and he acquired his spiritual direction in analysis. Furthermore, we had to find our individuality and our own insight into ourselves and no longer live at the mercy of others' images. Others' images are doomed to be destructive, whether they are "ideal" or critical. They are subjective.

My image of Hugo has undergone a thousand transformations—from idealization to total rejection. The theme of images. Val Telberg does a photo-montage for *Fortune* magazine ("Crack-up of Executives") and chooses Hugo for a model, who makes what I see as a tormented, strained face. Bogner sees it merely as a man "concentrating."

My last photographs are healthy and joyous! None of them are sad and tragic as they once were.

On parting from Hugo—as the neurosis disappears, the human relationship reasserts itself—mellowness, tenderness...

Now if only Rupert would make a faux pas (an exhibition of flirtation) I would get "cured" of him and achieve a mature life with Hugo. As much as I desire Rupert, I dread the shrunken life, the absence of mutual creativity and Rupert's goal of a home and a domestic woman.

Hugo admitted his perverse balkiness, his sabotages, etc. And I my criticalness, perfectionism, etc.

New York, Wednesday, April 27, 1955
Leave for California
Flight 5 at 12:00 Idlewild

For the first time I made Hugo the beneficiary of my travel insurance—an expression of protectiveness. I usually reserved this for Rupert and Joaquín. I always felt Hugo was rich enough—I never would take his economic problem seriously, but now I realize it was a neurotic problem, and he suffered by it and I wanted to relieve it.

Letter from Anaïs Nin to Anne Metzger, Nin's French translator:
Sierra Madre, April 1955

Dear Mrs. Metzger:

A French literary agent wrote me recently that the publisher Plon had been inquiring about my Diary. I answered that the publication of my Diary would be for the future, and that I felt any publisher who was interested should begin by publishing my novels and thus establish my reputation in France. The Diary would later be of greater interest. So I told the agent about your translation, and if Gallimard is not interested I suggest you show it to Plon as the agent Georges Borchardt is writing to Plon giving them my answer.

Incidentally, it may interest you to know that the Diary from the age of eleven (a very humorous account of my arrival in America) to the age of sixteen is in French, which might interest Plon or any other publisher you are in contact with. It could be put out as one volume, to be followed later by the others, much later. This is actually my life's major work, said by the critics to be better than the novels.

I would like so much to be able to read your translation, but I understand you cannot mail your only carbon copy. Let us hope I may be able to get to France this year. Do let me know what Gallimard says.

Sincerely yours,
Anaïs Nin

Letter from Alfred Perlès to Anaïs Nin:
Big Sur, Thursday, April 28, 1955

Dear Anaïs,

To put your mind at rest, I am dispatching to you, by separate post, a carbon of my book on Henry.

I gather from my publisher's last letter that the book is already with the printers, so it would be a hell of a job to make any alterations. However, I do not anticipate that you will want me to change a word. You are the only person in the book I did not want to hurt, and I don't think I did, and I'm sure you will sense the intention. There isn't a single reference to you in the book that could be taken for anything but a glowing tribute to your personality. Moreover, I've tried to be as discreet and tactful as possible, and there's no mention of Hugo or even the fact that you were married. Naturally, there must be quite a number of people who knew about your relationship with Henry; I'm not telling them anything they did not already know: no shocking revelations, nothing sensational or scandalous. If you do insist on certain alterations, suggest them in a way that doesn't necessitate resetting the whole damned book.

Very much love,
Fred

Letter from James Brown to Anaïs Nin:
New York, May 1955

Dear Anaïs:

Of course it is all right for Mr. Borchardt, as the agent for Plon, to consider your work. If Plon is interested, then of course arrangements would be made by this office through our agents. You should make it very clear to Mr. Borchardt that he cannot act as your agent.

Yes, this office and our representatives abroad are interested in you and your work. You must realize that agents do not sell things. The only thing that sells writing is the writing itself. It is a fallacy to assume that anyone would do more than show something and let the chips fall where they may. If, through your connection with Mr. Borchardt, Plon decides they want to publish something, then we agents step in to represent you and to protect you in every way.

Yours,
Jim

Letter from Henry Miller to Anaïs Nin:
Big Sur, May 7, 1955

Dear Anaïs,

I hasten to reply to your letter, which just came, to say first that I will endeavor to use what influence I have with Neville and with Fred, and second to say that I think you do them wrong when you say that it was all planned and premeditated. No one was aware—not even I—of the circumstances you are in. None of us, now that we know, can see how a mere change of name would truly protect anyone. However, I am writing both Neville and Fred immediately—carbon is enclosed—in the hope that some compromise can be arranged. Fred is entirely innocent, whatever you may think. I know that he is distressed about the whole situation and in a dilemma. He did his utmost to give a good picture of you—and it is a "good" picture—never dreaming that the past had not been liquidated, so to speak. I had told him you were not married to Hugo any longer, that being the impression we received when we had a visit from [Rupert's] father. When we got your first letter recently I thought that possibly I had heard wrong, but Eve, who was present during that visit, assured me I had heard correctly. If I have been discreet all these years, why would I have urged Fred not to be? I've written a preface to the book, making it plain that I was a witness to the event. I hope you don't think I anticipated pleasure in dealing you injury indirectly. I couldn't possibly think that way.

It's true that Neville Armstrong planned to tie everything up, but why wouldn't he think that way, being your publisher, Fred's and mine? It's only natural, and how could he have foreseen your reaction, knowing nothing about these complications? As the publisher of what purports to be a "biography," it's only logical that he should want the real names of all the persons mentioned. Sooner or later someone is going to do another biography, or a study of my work, and without asking permission, perhaps without any of us knowing a thing about the book, use your name openly—in a way that you won't like, I mean. I understand your position and even the necessity you feel for concealing certain facts. But to ask others to join you in a conspiracy of silence is another matter, and that is where the real problem lies, for you more than for anyone. I hope this doesn't sound harsh or critical. It isn't meant to be. As you will see from my letter to Neville (the same goes to Fred), whatever motivates your deepest behavior is not for anyone to question.

Finally, you may have a better suggestion to make, regarding a change in text, than what I am suggesting to Fred and Neville. If so, please do so. I can hardly urge them to eliminate your personality from the book altogether. I doubt if I would have the courage to do it, were it my own book.

And one other thing...I did as little as I possibly, humanly, could to alter Fred's views about persons and events. Each of us would tell the story differently. There are things I could object to, things I could improve on, and so on, but I am not the author. I tried only to help him say what he himself felt impelled to say. Being the "subject," it was not an easy position to be in. I am trying to tell you, and do believe it, or you work an injustice upon yourself, that no one tried to be unfair to you or take advantage of you. And, if it comes to the worst—I don't think it will!—remember that you are one of the protected ones. What you and I, and others like us, need to learn, however, is this—what do we seek to be protected from? And how can we protect those who do not need our protection?
Rest easy!
Henry

Letter from Henry Miller to Alfred Perlès and Neville Armstrong:
Big Sur, May 7, 1955

Dear Neville and Fred:
I've just had another letter from Anaïs, one I can't ignore. So long as the book is not out, and I know it isn't yet, I too implore you to stop and think about the situation, find some expedient that will overcome Anaïs's fear and anguish without destroying your project. In her letter Anaïs tells me that she is still married to Hugo and altogether dependent upon him for support. Further, that she would do anything to prevent him from being hurt, as she is certain he will be should the book be printed as it stands.

In spite of all the objections that can be advanced, and I have given much thought to the matter since the situation has arisen, I would say that human considerations should take place over any other. If *you* feel, as I suspect you do, that Anaïs exaggerates the harm that may result in permitting her name to be used, I must also say that *you* exaggerate in thinking that a change would kill the book. I have racked my brains to think of a good solution, knowing both sides in the controversy. The only suggestion I can come up with at the moment is to put an asterisk after her assumed name (Zenobia, let's say) the first time it appears, and in a footnote say something like this: "To the regret of author and publisher alike, the real name has been changed in this instance. It is the only one in the book that has been altered."

I venture this without having consulted Anaïs about it. But you will probably hear from her shortly after the receipt of this, as I am sending a copy of this letter to her. She is the one to listen to, not me. I am simply joining my voice to hers in a plea for understanding. Being the "subject" of the book, I now find myself attempting to act as arbiter. What a situation! The worst is that Anaïs now believes me to have aided and abetted you villains!

But seriously, since nobody wishes to hurt anybody, and since it is to everyone's benefit that the situation be rectified, what is so difficult that four intelligent, sensitive people cannot solve? I want to say to you two, as I say to myself, that "we" are not to judge whether Anaïs is right or wrong in her assumption of the harm that can be wrought to Hugo. Mind you, she is not trying to protect herself, but another. And even if that argument seems specious, it should be heeded. As one who has lived a "complicated" life, I should certainly never want my motives examined with a cold, worldly eye. I know (now) that there is no border between self and non-self, between selfish and unselfish intentions, and so on. I know that when we judge another, it is always for our own convenience and to conceal from ourselves a blemish we are only all too aware of possessing.

And so I say: Do something! You don't have to turn the world upside down to grant the favor that is asked of you. You can only suffer aesthetically or financially, and what is that compared to a mental torture, which is what Anaïs is now suffering and will obviously suffer much more unless you listen to her.

I can't say any more to you. It's your responsibility more than mine. There's only one thing I will say, yes... Don't give "excuses." You know me, you know I am everyone's friend. Forgive me if I speak plainly to you.

Sincerely,
Henry

Letter from Anaïs Nin to Neville Armstrong:
Sierra Madre, May 1955

Dear Mr. Armstrong:

I am writing to you as one human being to another. Your use of my name will damage a *life-long marriage*. It may be Fred has not explained this to you.

Until I am sure that you are incapable of such an unethical action, I naturally could never trust you with the Diary. It is strange that until now I have believed only in America did people do ruthless and inhuman things to make money. Also, if you read the Diary you would blush for the inaccuracy of Fred's book, which will someday be exposed and embarrass you (in a few years when the Diary comes out).

My name in that book is totally unnecessary. I am not publicity material on that level. My agent will make it impossible for you to publish *A Spy in the House of Love* under the conditions you described to me. And naturally, I would never think of entrusting you with the Diary. I believe the entire scheme suggested by Alfred Perlès will not be as successful economically as you may imagine. I am not a person who appeals to scandal lovers. Do think all this over, and if none of these arguments mean anything to you, I have offered to pay the expenses of the change of name, and I know the book is not yet at the printer for its final printing.

As one example of Fred's inaccuracies: the passage that he assumes to be Miller's comment on the Diary was written about *House of Incest*, a prose poem. Also, when the Diary does come out it will make your life of Miller an absurdity.

Anaïs Nin

Letter from Georges Borchardt to Anaïs Nin:
New York, May 12, 1955

Dear Miss Nin:

Thank you for your letter, about French rights in your books, which reached me at the same time as a letter from James Brown Associates; I am enclosing a copy of their letter to you.

I have of course no intention to interfere with your regular agent's work (from what you had told me I had understood that you were free to make arrangements for translation rights), and therefore suggest that he instruct his representative in Paris to submit both *The Four-Chambered Heart* and *A Spy In the House of Love* to Librairie Plon, unless, of course, he has those books out with another French firm at this time.

I am sending a copy of this letter to Mr. Brown who, I think, is much too modest when he says that "agents do not sell things." Some do! Particularly (and this is true both here and in France) where books written in a foreign language are concerned.

Sincerely yours,
Georges Borchardt

New York, May 1955

Reading the diary of Virginia Woolf was such a confined, narrow and dry experience that it drove me not to suicide, but to write in my own.

The last entry was of the kind known as the stagnant cycle. But I emerged light and strong. Not only am I able to dissolve (once more) my rebellion against Hugo (which should be a rebellion against what I failed to achieve), but to help Hugo dissolve his dangerous and destructive rebellion against *his* boss, Claude de Saint Phalles, for his impatience, lack of organization and lack of coordination in *his* papers! Hugo was going to write him a letter (defending himself, his slowness) accusing *him* of inefficiency! So I helped him and decided to give his film to a distributor, leaving me free to face my own economic problem. The rebellions exist because I look upon Hugo as the master of my destiny. Poor Hugo.

Jim's fascination with the Diary 41-42-43-44—his constant excitement warms me. Why should it be *more* vitally important to a young man of 27 than even to Geismar? Jim is my only link with the future. He reads me, makes me feel that even if America succeeds in destroying literature—which is what it is doing actively, and people like Geismar are helping—they cannot afford to destroy life, and it is the *life* in the Diary that Jim is drinking up in contrast to the writing of his contemporaries, which he can't read because it is dead.

Yesterday he called me up, exaltingly: "I don't kid myself, Anaïs, there is no relation between the best of my writing or the best of writing being published today, and yours. They simply do not meet on any conscious level. I know that. But I feel that I got your secret in my diary—there, at least, I feel I can reach something deep, sincere."

I'm always a little amazed—for Jim is refractory to Proust, to Genet, to the ones I consider great. But the Diary never bores him, never bogs him down, never ceases to make him feel alive.

I went to see him at his lunch hour. He talks compulsively. I read his diary—the incredible madness of Dick—the quarrels—the classic bit about Dick's constant talking… I said, "The drama is not a homosexual drama. You could write this about a man and woman and it would be the same…"

He encourages me to take out all the fragments concerned with the personality of the Diary itself—its character—he sees it as a personage…

People are asking for fragments, but I know, and Jim agrees, that a fragment will be damaging to the Diary—an injustice.

It is frightening how Rupert loses his power over me when he is not present.

Letter from Anaïs Nin to Rupert Pole:
New York, May 30, 1955

Darling Chiquito:
Was very upset after talking to you. I understand your disappointment [for my delay in returning], darling. Mine was submerged in the determination to have *no more* separations. They are too painful. I was driven into this when I saw the interest from the library in the Diary, got filled with hope, and this sustained me. Darling, bear with me and my effort for us. It may mean not only the house, but no more trips. I could take a small job near Sierra Madre—I know it's hard for you to accept the change. I know I was impulsive—but I feel it's the right moment. Here I am with a weekend's worth of makeup, a small toothbrush, two dresses—thank god I can wash my nylon blouse. What set me off were the letters of introduction from the librarian to the Guggenheim Foundation, to two collectors in N.Y. and four in Washington. I am seeing the Columbia Fund Raisers today—the three Tuesday and Wednesday—will try to get to Washington Thursday or Friday and try to stay with Caresse Crosby. Darling—we are only sacrificing a week, for you will be away. You won't have time to write me... I will call you up again *Sunday* from Washington—I may have news then... I may be dreaming, but I was amazed at the interest. The second Chicago collector suggested giving me $100 a month— too slow—only totally $10,000—and the library feels that's too little. But when I return we will talk it all over, and we'll make a decision together.
   Te quiero, y no quiero viajar sin ti mas [I love you, and I don't want to travel without you anymore],
   A

Letter from Rupert Pole to Anaïs Nin:
Sierra Madre, May 1955

Darling:
Another loused-up call. It's so hard when we have only three minutes and both of us are keyed up and somewhat on the defensive. I did so want to hear from you and to learn how things were going, where you planned to go next to sell your diary and whether you were encouraged or discouraged, how you were getting along with only two dresses. And you wanted me to talk, and I had nothing to say but the same old stuff you know so well: 283 lightning fires in northern California and feared I would have to go and miss your phone call, but luck was with us when they left me here.
   The meeting went very well with everyone saying the hit of the week was the film I obtained and showed, and a skit I worked into one of the lectures (using your blow-up breasts) portraying Miss Edith Titwell, a bird watcher, which was so

successful I had to do it again next day so they could film it. One big forester laughed so hard, he choked and had to be given first aid.

Very upset to get your letters saying our phone calls had made you ill. I blame only myself and know now how you must have felt trying to push this diary thing through though you wanted to come back, and I only hope my letters explained a little. But try to put yourself in my place too, love—Friday, Nichols told me you'd called and only said you'd call again—so I waited in anticipation all evening—no call. Then I thought you'd call Sunday as agreed so I worked in the field Saturday to get back and find you'd called just five minutes before. Nichols said you sounded terribly anxious to get me, so I imagined all sorts of things from a jubilant victory announcement to the fear you might be ill and need me—again, all Saturday and no call. Then finally Sunday you called, and for all my anticipation your first words were "Darling, I can't come out Friday." I was disappointed and I know it showed and that made you sad and by the time I was adjusting myself to this and trying to go on from there, the call was over. I wanted to call you in Washington to tell you to take all the time you needed and to push it while you were there and above all not to worry about me—but I had no idea where to call. Love, you may have thought you explained everything on the phone—but you didn't—or at least I didn't get it—only later when your letters came did I realize how complicated this was and the time and effort that went into seeing each collector and the fact that you had to wait for Joaquín so he could bring the other originals so you could show them to collectors.

If you have to go away again, love, we'd better give up the calls and I'll try to write every day to keep you posted without misunderstanding.

I keep thinking of you pushing yourself so hard, forcing yourself to meet and put up a good front to all these people in your two little dresses and feel more power than the serpent's belly by so stupidly adding to your troubles instead of really strengthening and helping you when you need me—but know always that I love you and that I know you are forcing yourself into this for the sake of the relationship, that it's our best immediate chance to be free together—just don't push yourself too hard, love. Both you and I do things too intensely, but nothing is worth your health. We'll make our decision when you come back to rest and warmth *y tu estupido hombre*,

R

Letter from Anaïs Nin to Rupert Pole:
New York, June 6, 1955

Darling:

Your letter was nice and I know you meant to show me you were with me on this, but over the telephone you sounded hesitant, and not in agreement, and I am conscious of the fact that I have only a few minutes to explain what I am doing... The result is such a conflict that I got ill the last time we talked, and again today. I'm so depressed I don't know whether I should give up. But, love, this is one time I do not understand you. You put up with the trips to N.Y., yet when I make an effort by selling the Diary to *stop* the trips, to build a house, to get out of what you called a "rut," you pull back, you do not give me courage. Would you prefer I come back this week and then have to return in September and stay longer?—the collectors will be away for the summer, probably. I wouldn't be able to do anything or have an income—and each one I see is a long, drawn-out affair—a talk, a visit to their collections, they have to read the books, see a volume and the clippings.

I will call you up next Sunday as you said. Even about Joaquín—you know I gave up seeing him for months so as to stay one day longer with you on my way and back from N.Y. *twice.* Then we didn't go to S.F. in May. Now I would like to see him before he leaves for the summer. And your remark that you didn't know I had original diaries in S.F.—you forgot I asked you several times to drive there so I could pick up those in the vault. We never had time.

This phone call, which I had so looked forward to, upset me. What is it, darling? Are you telling me everything? I'm desperately anxious to see this through, but I can't do it without your consent.

I hope you read this before I call you up Sunday.

Darling, *te quiero,*

A

Letter from Anaïs Nin to Rupert Pole:
New York, Thursday, June 9, 1955

Sweet love:

I'm writing you hoping our phone call Sunday will be happier. I want to tell you I understand your ambivalence, for I suffer from the same one: my heart says go home, and my head says I must go on. Your letter said: I understand. But by phone your heart rebels and you seemed to question all I do...especially when you said: "You're going to sit around waiting for Joaquín!" Darling...this is like a chain. The Library gave me seven letters of introduction, then Harvard gave me three, then Ruggles from Columbia two and the Spewacks one to Walter Chrysler, a homosexual who owns the biggest collection of diaries... But our talk Sunday made me ill. I felt you were not *with* me; I needed encouragement. I lost all my energy, and if you were not going to be at the fire camp I would have come home. This is worse than a job...it's a 24-hour job—telephone, interviews. All these people are wealthy, spoiled, busy and wary. I have to make a good impression. Today I came back from Washington to see Jacobson because I couldn't go on. I kept hearing your voice, impatient, demanding, making me feel your disappointment. Not being there to talk it over, I felt you questioned the necessity of all I did ("A *week* in Washington?"), all your negativity. Jacobson gave me energy for my interview with Chrysler. When Joaquín arrives with two more originals (the first one is under glass at Northwestern so that collectors can look at it) I can show them to the Harvard manuscript purchasers (handwriting makes it more valuable). In Washington I got one higher bid...$12,000, but that you know is not enough to free us for the future...

Letter from Anaïs Nin to Rupert Pole:
New York, June 1955

My emotional state has been jittery and nervous... Fears for our relationship—the inability to go ahead if I feel I'm making you unhappy. I hope my call Sunday will put an end to that...or else I can't continue. I've lost four pounds, don't sleep well... Yet you know I want to be home as much or more than you want me home. Why were you cross, hesitant, questioning everything I did...putting the obstacles forward...not *with* me? Why did you question my saying half of the originals were in San Francisco? Why can't you *trust* me? Your letter said you understood, but when I call I get into a mess... I wanted to talk until I felt you with me, but I was also conscious of the expense.

Anaïs

Letter from Rupert Pole to Anaïs Nin:
Sierra Madre, June 1955

Love:

So worried that I sounded negative when you phoned—didn't mean to at all but had been working so hard on staining the walls, which had taken so much time and had been going badly (terribly difficult to get it even—each board reacted differently and I had to rub it in, erase, rub it in again ad infinitum) and was so sure you would be back this week that the news you would stay in New York hit me hard in beginning.

Querida, I do realize how much this means to us, perhaps even our freedom, and you must do everything you can now while the thing is hot. I had thought of you seeing all the people when you went back for your job, but I see now that N.Y. was necessary to get the rest of the diary so we can base our decision on the overall picture when you get back. Even a monthly payment is OK if you're sure of their sincerity. I trust you completely and know you're doing all this to be free of the N.Y. separations and perhaps even free of the routine side of our life.

Don't know what's happened to me. Never slept well when you were away, but now I hardly sleep at all—so tired and yet lie awake—can't even sleep in morning. Beer and wine by gallon seem to have no effect. Your drug is too potent—I am becoming immune to all others.

I leave for fire school Monday evening. Back about 5:30 PM Friday. But I can go directly to the airport. Try to arrive Friday evening. If you don't know the plane time soon enough to reach me before Monday evening then wire Mother. I'll call her on way back from fire school.

We'll have Saturday together—and soon every day together, to live every moment completely.

Siempre
R

Letter from James Brown to Anaïs Nin:
New York, June 13, 1955

Dear Anaïs:

I have been giving a great deal of thought to your representation by this office. You know that we have always considered your name on our list as a real honor. Few lists have the distinction of so good a writer.

When René de Chochor left we went over our list very carefully and at that time cut it rather drastically. In spite of this cutting, I have very definite feelings of regret at my inability to give the time I should be giving to you and others on the list.

The appearance of Mr. Georges Borchardt in the picture set me thinking. That process has led me to the conclusion that you would be better represented by someone like Mr. Borchardt, whom I now remember I have met, and with whom I have been impressed. His European background, it seems to me, would be particularly helpful to you.

This most recent experience in England, which has caused you such distress, has only added to my decision to write this letter to you. It is not an easy letter to write, but I do think that my decision is completely in your interest.

I note that Mr. Borchardt is sailing for England and France on June 20, which gives you only a few days to speak to him. It might be well for you to make the decision before he leaves so that he would take your problems and interests along with him.

I shall look forward to hearing from you.

Yours,
Jim

New York, June 13, 1955

The *Saison en Enfer* began with the necessity of appearing at Northwestern University May 25 after barely a month with Rupert, and my not daring to tell Rupert I would go on from there for a month of separation. I felt his resistance to the separation. So I packed two or three dresses for four days' absence, a small weekend makeup kit, and built a myth to explain the continuation of the trip. A myth born of a fantasy, and of a wish: I would look for a collector who would buy the original Diary and free us economically from trips to N.Y. and enable us to build a house.

To this tension about the trip was added a letter from Henry, another from Fred, announcing a *My Friend Henry Miller* to be published in England…and telling me what a pretty portrait Fred had painted of me! I asked to see the manuscript. Everything that I had feared and avoided all these years had finally happened: the relationship with Henry exposed, and Hugo in danger of pain… The fact that the book was journalistic, petty and inaccurate was only part of my irritation. I wrote to Henry, to Fred, asking that my name be changed. Fred pretended to sympathize, said he would speak to his publisher, etc. But the trap was well set and I was already caught… I had signed a contract with Neville Armstrong for publication of *Spy*—and all along they had intended to exploit the publicity created by *My Friend Henry Miller*. My letters to Neville Armstrong were ineffectual. They all pretended it was too late. I appealed to James Brown to at least try to cancel the publication of *Spy* to minimize publicity. He wrote a letter, but it was answered by Armstrong cynically. And today Brown dropped me off his list of writers. I tried for a month…in vain.

During that same week, I used too heavy a broom, wrenched a muscle in my back and was in too much pain to drive the car, do housework…yet I had to get well for Northwestern, and I did.

Felix Pollak, the librarian who encouraged the trip, was at the station after driving through rain-flooded roads in a taxi; poor Felix, an extravagance for his modest life. He looked like his handwriting...small, delicate, with big, sad, Spanish eyes, a gentle smile, the hands of a violinist. He kissed my hand like the Viennese he is. In the taxi, a long drive to his home, a long talk. He had been nervous, but he was not nervous any longer. As I found out later, he was being metamorphosed from a man of forty to an adolescent of eighteen.

A metamorphosis not without inconvenience, for with it were reawakened his adolescent romantic longings and desires. All of Chicago's sky rained angrily upon such lyrical states. They tried to drown Felix, the Curator of Special Collections, as he rushed to meet a famous writer who confirmed his inner world. It made him dissatisfied with the present...with Evanston, the library, his director Mr. Nyholm, and his wife Sara's cooking. Warm, maternal Sara—seeking to please him by cooking a Viennese dish. "It is too sour," said Felix.

His violin was there, his beautiful chess pieces, the piano, Sara's cello, the books, and once more Europe and America tried to live together. Felix was dazzled. I had to expend energy to protect and include Sara.

He had quietly manipulated the entire situation: the library's purchase of 43 manuscripts, the exhibit in the glass cases, originals of my books, engravings, records, publicity on the campus, but so quietly, so subtly that nobody noticed it. So he is overlooked, not invited to lunch and dinner, invisible. He was, however, asked to introduce me, which he did at the film showing, too lavishly for everybody's liking, overlooking Hugo's film...

The film showing was a success, but any pleasure was destroyed by jealousy and intrigues. Too many people joined us for coffee afterwards. Each table expected my presence. Each person wasted time with foolish questions: "How much footage of film did Mr. Hugo take for *Jazz of Lights?*" "Were the effects achieved in the laboratory or with the camera itself?"

The Film Group made it clear that since they paid for my trip they felt I should sit at their table, so I did. Exhaustion—sleep. A busy day the next day, a lunch with university people.

Felix. What can I give him? When you give someone flavors of other worlds, you also give the poison of discontent. Life is dull at Evanston, as it is all over America. I took a walk, to see the surroundings. The lake was bilious. A cold wind. The houses are big chambers. No drinking allowed. The atmosphere of a hospital, school, factory. I know what Felix feels. People live here as if disconnected. There are no relationships because they have denied the self. The students stand about, glued to each other like still-blind puppies in a warm nest, not seeing or knowing each other.

The hall for the reading was a cold, windswept place. Always present is the massive lecture desk I avoid to face the public with all of myself. Those pulpits are not for me or my words. I read badly because there was too much noise from other rooms, the light was as violent as in a cafeteria, and I was physically and emotionally frozen. Afterwards Dr. Douglas had a gathering at his apartment. Felix said: "I have fallen hopelessly in love with you!" And as if divining the danger, Sara came to sit beside me. The one in need of protection touches me more, the wife... People talk, but it is all in a void. It could be that I, fallen from other planets, am falling away from earth even more.

No one said anything I can remember, though I listened with all my attention. *Ils parlent de leurs petites affaires*—the rain, exams, the effect of spring upon the students.

When I arrived in New York, Hugo was studying for his Stock Exchange exams. His pattern was designed this way: After dinner, at 8:00 PM, to sleep until 4:00 AM. From 4:00 AM to 7:00 AM to study. Then to work. He spent the weekends studying. We settled into the routine. I emptied, gradually, a rotten flower box of its earth. I found the very last engraving block from 215 W. 13, forgotten in a closet. I reframed soiled engraving frames on the wall. I answered a big correspondence. Each telephone call to Rupert was an ordeal. He was openly rebellious: "I can't sleep at all! Why another week? Can't you do all that when you go to New York for your job?"

Hugo passed his exam after three weeks of imprisonment. We took a few moments off to have a *café express* at McDougall's place, to see a movie. In the middle of it all, symptoms that had manifested themselves before reappeared: my heart began either to race or pump heavily. One night I felt very close to death. Hugo was asleep at nine o'clock. I felt so strangely—usually I know how I feel, quickly diagnose myself and proceed to remedy. But that night I felt *drôle*—queer—nonspecific. The pain in the chest was clear, the shortness of breath. But the tremors, the missing beats... I walked around. I finally slept sitting up, with the light on. Is it guilt, anxiety over Hugo, or organic damage? Jacobson treated me. I can't read a letter, carry a diary, climb stairs without agitation. Was I breaking down?

Letter from Maxwell Geismar to Anaïs Nin:
New York, June 1955

Dear Anaïs,

What bothers me most in this whole thing is your conviction that you are "through" as a writer, at least in this country, and that it is useless to go on writing, if that is what you really feel... This is death for a writer, and you must not accept this statement except as a momentary revulsion... If you are really convinced of this, why not get the diaries published in Paris or Italy, go over there yourself, try to get the right arrangements, or print them yourself, as D. H. Lawrence did with *Lady Chatterley* and *Pansies*, and you can possibly even make money from them; this may be a desperate recourse, but valid if you feel it is the only thing left. (And then, of course, they will print a censored American version!) Otherwise, why *not* try to write that novel based on a cycle of diaries, which would still not impair the final worth of the diaries, but might be halfway between what you have published and what you haven't. I think this is the way you should move; but do *anything* rather than give up!

Best love as always,
Max

New York, June 1955

Blow after blow after blow after blow. Strongly tempted to burn the Diary. Unless I go to Paris and openly live the life of Genet, the criminal and monster, I will die. The atmosphere of America...puritan, middle class, hypocritical, afraid of reality...is a lack of oxygen.

I have paid the price for not breaking with the bourgeois world and living with the artist. Why, why, why didn't I have the ultimate courage to be what I am as Genet is what he is—*le poète maudit*—to not be in the wrong world, like my father? For protection you pay with your life.

Jim and I talked about this—dared each other. "How your diary has helped me to grow—helped me to deepen. But I still can't write everything in my own diary. I think I might die and Dick may read it."

He is running everywhere for his new play, which is being produced...rewriting, at the castings, at conferences, over-incorporating, etc. He has anemia. He is indeed my son! But the interesting fact is that he proved once more (I proved it once) that he is doing his best writing in his diary.

Bella and Sam Spewack, the critics, say over the telephone about *Under a Glass Bell*: "Beautiful writing—as beautiful as it can be—but a word painting. No story. It has to move. You could have written *Bonjour Tristesse*. For example, the 'Mouse' story. You write a sketch. You do not tell enough. We should have known more from the point of view of the maid. You should be out of it. Your being there is egotistical writing. But if you had not been in it..."

And the two of them are in misery, suffering blindly, desperately in their marriage, she saying: "Only death will free me!" They understand each other less than Hugo and I, hurt each other because they write and live "objectively" and think that you can blot out the self!

Finally, a good letter from Rupert calmed my anxiety over his protest. Jacobson healed me. I picked up my work again.

En route to Los Angeles, June 16, 1955

On the plane, less desire, less pleasure in flying towards Rupert. I don't know if it is because my last nightmare was so violent and I am still under its effect, or if it is pain, sickness, aloneness, or that in my fantasy of selling the Diary to be free, I realized how deeply I hate the mediocrity of the life I lead with Rupert. I feel nausea at the idea of the house, the driving, the evenings with his family, the evenings of music with uninteresting musicians, housework, the paltriness of it all, the narrowness, and worse than that, Rupert will not help me create a different life. I remember the day he took me to see the property Lloyd wants to buy, and we drove into the mountains over Malibu, climbing, climbing, and no matter how much sea or mountains, it is all barren, sterile and empty.

I know this now. And if I succeeded in creating the life I love, it would not make Rupert happy. He would be ill at ease.

The conflict will kill me, but I cannot surrender. I cannot surrender to the moronic life of California or to the business-obsessed life of Hugo. I wonder whether my hatred of America is not at the bottom a rebellion against a side of Rupert and Hugo that destroys me, that I cannot live with.

We punish others for being enslaved to them. I punish Hugo because I can't separate from him. I can't separate ultimately and permanently. Yet I'm happy to be leaving New York and I do not want to return.

I am beginning to consider the destruction of the Diary—because I feel unwanted as an artist, cast off.

The Diary is me, and nothing the world has done will convince me it can be trusted with the truth. To me, the world has been a jungle, full of fierceness, meanness, malice.

The Diary will hurt the only three people I consider good, human, almost saintly: Hugo, Rupert and Joaquín.

America hates the artist. My Diary would prove that the artist is wrong because he goes mad or dies with grief. The world won't say: the artist is my soul and I want to kill my own soul.

Anne Geismar has successfully cut all my contact with Max. She sensed the danger. She always answers the phone: "Max is working," and Max never calls. It is Anne who arranged the evenings together. And she is right, for the last time we went out together and danced, Max said: "Oh Anaïs, it is not dancing I want." But the relationship is a failure because they too have the Shame of the Self while this Self is clearly visible to me, and no amount of alcohol or physical illness will drown it. They think they have liquidated it, but they have only disguised it under the cloak of politics and historical writers, the ones blessed by the Popes of the Past.

I look down from the plane upon the Colorado River. No matter what you look upon, America looks empty—a décor—but no Persons, no Individuals, only masses and no identities. The canyons, the rivers—I have traveled through them and not one Person stands out in my memory. I looked at them in cafés, restaurants, in other cars, all along the 3,000 miles, and no one stands out. I spent hours studying them and they seem like "extras" in a film from which the main characters are absent. Nothing distinguishes them.

Enough.

I, who thought I would always love and never hate…

It will make dying so easy—and I must remember this— to think that the future is America and Russia, countries subconsciously similar, who will one day fall into each other's arms. They have both destroyed the same values. The workman will inherit the world, but not before all that was worth inheriting has been destroyed. To give him three meals a day we did not have to destroy everything else. And we have.

I remember Richard Wright saying he could not expand as a writer in America because the race problem festered in him. I am in danger of the same festering from America's ruthless treatment of me… I must rise above this constant irritant or it will poison my work. That was why I wanted to write about Mexico. I want to write only about what I love.

Sierra Madre, June 1955

A nightmare made it clear what is making me ill:

I was condemned to die by means of an injection in the head administered by a negro. I had sympathy for my executioner and kept promising I would not make it difficult for him. I was making arrangements for the Diary. Then came time for the injection. As its effect began, I began to suffocate slowly. My mother was there. I suddenly realized that once I died she would read my Diary. My dying words were: "Promise me you won't read it." Then, as the suffocation increased, I awakened. I found Rupert's arm across my chest. I had palpitations. So I sat up and analyzed the dream. I am suffering from guilt. The exposure of my relationship with Miller frightens me. Selling the Diary frightens me. I must burn it. Nothing is worth harming other human beings. The truth cannot be told. The truth is destructive. I must burn the Diary.

I must act to protect Hugo, Rupert and Joaquín from harm. I had one more bad night—pains in the chest, the heart acting erratically as if it were tired of pumping.

I faced my fear. Then last night, after Rupert had expressed his love and passion after a day at the beach and sun, I slept well for the first time in four or five weeks without sleeping pills. I know the heart is damaged. But I will have time to make arrangements about the Diary. Because I know also that I will die suddenly. I reminded Rupert of his promise to divorce me if my health should break and his answer was, "But you know if you ever left me you would destroy me!"

I realize the idea of death is the answer to the idea of guilt. Guilt is punishable by death. And I know what my crime is: what human beings only dream, I acted out. I obeyed the dream.

But I was unable to free myself of guilt. And Dr. Bogner was unable to give me absolution.

This is the truth which human beings cannot bear, the truth revealed in their dreams. You can fall in love with your father and brother. You can revolt against your mother. You can kill your rivals. You can steal others' loves. You can betray your husband and lovers...in dreams. You can be amorous, and orgiastic, you can be a thousand women, in your dreams. But enact one of your dreams, and you are a criminal, in your own eyes, in the world's, and *you are condemned to death.*

Yet, I gave so much to others! I know that there is no one else who has given to as many people in one lifetime the feeling *of not being alone.* I know that is why Hugo clings to me, to a half-wife, because even when I am not there he feels less alone. The strain of the lectures was due to that same concept, to give as many human beings as possible an instant of relationship—to see, hear, feel what they want seen, heard, felt.

For this I have been hated too by the Americans who hate intimacy and the personal, the frigid ones like James Brown who chose to give me up at the most inhuman moment of all.

This life is healing, thanks to Rupert's depth of feeling, his own enjoyment of music, the beach, his games with Tavi. He had stained the dreadful brown walls so that they look now like silver bark or wood bleached by the sea. Now the paintings stand out, as does the yellow couch. Nature around us is serene, the neighbors and their little lives.

I marvel at Lloyd's ferocious selfishness, but I know how to dissolve his attacks now. When he begins to erupt with anger (always on the theme of his work versus the world's ignorance and stupidity or its actual plagiarism), I give him sympathy. And this is sincere, for even if one's character is one's destiny, he was frustrated in great part by the stature of his father (Frank Lloyd Wright, impossible to surpass) and in great part by America's hatred of imaginative architecture. He has to suffer Huntington Hartford, a millionaire, an uncouth, uncultured grocer's son who persecutes modern art and buys a whole page in the *Times* to give vent to his ignorance, who after ordering a building from Lloyd, cancels the whole project and sends Lloyd as a Christmas present a basket of the cheapest A&P peaches and other "delicacies" from his father's store.

Then I seek to distract Lloyd's attention by, for example, discussing the wonderful restoration of Mexican sculpture in a book Rupert bought for him.

When someone is wounded, first give sympathy, then first aid, then combat negativity with creativity.

Letter from Neville Armstrong to Anaïs Nin:
London, June 1955

Dear Miss Nin,

This is to acknowledge with thanks your letter of this month regarding Alfred Perlès's Henry Miller biography. Following a spate of letters between Henry, Fred and myself, and a number of round table conferences, we have finally agreed to your petition to remove the offending passages relating to yourself from the book since it seems to mean so much to you. Fred had brought me a new draft, and I know you will be satisfied with the changes, although from our point of view it is unsatisfactory and most unartistic.

As you know, the book was already set and ready for printing, and these changes are going to cost us money, which, frankly, I feel you should absorb. The sum is around £33 ($100), and since you said earlier you would be prepared to meet all corrections I should be happy to have your cheque for this amount. I must make it clear, however, that we are making these changes against our better judgment; there is no question of possible libel arising with such changes, but we have all bowed to your wishes in the matter without being compelled to do so. I hope this will bring you some peace of mind.

It was never anybody's intention to play havoc with your emotions or private life, and for the life of me I am surprised that events of twenty years ago should have any bearing on the contemporary scene. Apparently, they do.

Yours sincerely,
Neville Armstrong

Excerpt from Perlès's letter to Miller:
"What I actually did was to split up Anaïs into two women, which enabled me to make reference to the diary, Louveciennes, etc., while blaming her 'misconduct' on a fictitious character, called Liane de Champsaur. Anaïs is safe."

Sierra Madre, August 1955
Double exposure month, with all the images blurred and truncated. I started to work on the Diary, which meant several trips to the Pasadena bank vault, a hurried, one-day trip to San Francisco to bring back half of the originals I had there, trips to Bekins' Storage in Arcadia, where I keep the copies. It meant renumbering them, rechecking dates (there was an error). It meant copying volume 50, which contains

sexual adventures in New York and Paris, the disintegration of my relationship with Henry, the meeting of Gonzalo. It also contains the trip to Morocco and Spain.

First of all, these images, as they appeared upon the images of my life with Rupert, created strange superimpositions. For example, the description of Morocco, with its pure images without political undercurrents—the poetry and the music and the realism of it—this floating, beautiful, mysterious image is now superimposed upon the harsh, nasal voice of the radio commentator: "Riots in Morocco. 30 persons killed. Arabs kill Jews and French," and in the newspaper, images only of the dead and wounded lying in the streets.

Henry, in volume 50, is concerned with aging and is pale and faded in comparison with the fiery, volcanic Gonzalo. But now, twenty years later, he has married Eve, a 30-year-old actress, and must be a satisfying lover still! He was fading only in my own heart and body.

But twenty years later he writes me: "I am writing about Moricand. Do you remember the name of the restaurant on the way to the Porte d'Orléans, on the right, where I first met him? And who was the friend he talked so much about—not Cendrars—the other? Do you know his birth hour?" It reminded me of Proust's visits to ascertain the kind of flowers Madame X wore on her hat many years before at a party.

So while we correspond about Moricand, I type out the feverish pages about Gonzalo. Gonzalo was like an eruption. I was completely absorbed by the fire, the intensity, the communion of senses and feelings. This dark, fervent Gonzalo casts no shadow on the present. That experience consumed *all* experiences with fire, but was it a phoenix—am I not living with another Scorpio—a fire sign, in the same terms of senses and feelings—but someone less violent, less overwhelming? In the dark, you could superimpose the heavier, earthier body of Gonzalo over Rupert's slenderer, lighter one; the density, the substance, is different, but chemically both are fire. Rupert has more electricity, more air, less earth. But there are similarities: like Gonzalo, he procrastinates. Like Gonzalo, he sees the obstacles.

When Rupert came home, I said: "Curtis Harrington just called up. He has a new job with Columbia. He wants me to recommend books and plays. I suggested Jim's play—and Georges Simenon, whose adventure books would make marvelous films. I could translate them."

"You won't get very much money for that. It would be better if you got an option from Simenon."

"But I tried in New York. I could not get through to him. His wife is his business manager. Only a studio or an agent can get an option."

"They will cheat you. After they get your synopsis you will be out of the picture."

After a while, I relinquished both the idea and the work. I haven't the energy to push it. The only thing about which I have become avaricious is my energy. I try not to waste it.

But this superimposition taught me a truth I have never faced. In every relationship there are two aspects, and I have always combatted one of them. It is true Rupert is poised here, can listen to the ugliest voices in the world, discuss the price of the new Hilton hotel, read *Time* magazine, and accept mediocre people.

But there are those few moments of heightened life—last night, with the curtains drawn, the garden glistening, one moment... And so, Anaïs, you have always been enslaved by that high moment and spend the rest of the time rebelling against *human life*. What frightens me is that my energy is lessening, so I will soon accept mediocrity, resign myself. The energy I have left I had hoped to use in getting out of America and finishing my major work. But America is *in* Rupert—it is always my own inability to accept the *total* human being; I'm in love with an *aspect*, but not *all* of Rupert, not the Rupert who cannot read any of the books I love, whose mind is literal. Poor Rupert. He may feel the same way about me. For the heightened moments he has sacrificed all that he could have had: a sturdy young woman, a home-lover, a domesticated wife, someone who would listen to the radio and read *Time* with him. He is mentally alone with his American mind filled with the problems of incinerators, smog, maintenance, petty talk, economics and politics—the last because it is inseparable from economics, not for any high, philosophic or humanitarian reasons.

Is rebellion an irreducible part of me?

In the double exposure, what I saw was what Bogner had tried to show me: not the drama of my life being enacted by conflict with Hugo, Henry, Gonzalo or Rupert, but me fighting my own self... It is I who love divided men and cannot give myself to any one life, always rebelling against some element I cannot digest: in Hugo it was the bank (because it wanted to swallow me too); in Henry it was the begging and borrowing and an irresponsible life, dependency on others, parasitism (and he wanted me to live the same way); in Gonzalo it was the slavery to Helba's madness (and he wanted me to share this slavery); in Rupert it is the American lifestyle (the lowest form of life).

Other superimpositions: the Tahitian party I gave in Paris, with real Tahitians playing and dancing, overlaying the evenings with Rupert's family, or with Reginald, or with movies...

Renate Druks and Paul Mathieson, however, could walk into volume 50, into 1936, and install themselves. They would have understood Moricand, and the others would have loved them.

Renate's story: when she was five or six years old her father took her to a doctor for a precursor to the Rorschach test. The doctor put on a record and asked Renate where the music came from. She meditated for a moment, then pointed to her heart and said, "From here." Another story: At sixteen she wanted to be an actress. Her father took her to a famous teacher, who was also a Don Juan and taught his pupils far more than the art of acting. Renate knew this, and knew specific instances of his seduction. When he first saw her, he said brutally: "You can't be an actress. Your mouth is too small." At this Renate became very angry, and she began to violently accuse him of all his evil acts. He grew red and was about to burst out in self-defense when Renate stopped herself short, bowed, smiled, and said: "Now, wasn't that good acting?"

Paul. Angelic blue eyes, and small boy's mouth. A little animal whose wish is to go around kissing everybody. But his nestling is homosexual and Renate suffers from his promiscuity. He does not do this cleverly or protectively. Instead he says, "A man must be cruel."

When Paul and Renate talk to me, I am torn between them; I feel for Renate, yet I behave as Paul does. I tell Paul that cruelty is unnecessary, and to Renate I say, "Paul loves you, and this sexual wandering is adolescent and superficial."

Lloyd, Helen, Rupert and I were invited to hear a quartet at the home of Bob Balzer of the American Aristocracy of Grocers, Butchers, Bakers, Cleaners, etc. Like the A&P grocer Huntington Hartford, Bob inherited a fortune. He travels. He is a friend of Gloria Swanson. He built himself a Japanese house. It was situated on top of a hill overlooking Hollywood. We drove up to it. Three young Japanese men in white kimonos met us at the door. We took off our shoes and were given slippers. The house was beautiful; it could not be ugly, being an imitation of the most beautiful of all styles. There was a sense of space, serenity and stylization—sliding panels, concealed closets, screens and statues, the simplicity of the isolated *unique* object—the separate and unique beauty, the antithesis of American life, which believes in multiplicity. Even a representation of a Japanese house was still an aesthetic experience. On the terrace, after the music, we drank champagne. But just as the beauty of the canyon, the sea, the southern marshes are so obviously external and contain no flavor of legends, no mythological essences, this evening offered but a shell that did not move one deeply. Every experience in America gives me the feeling of a stage set, because not one person there is capable of creation. This reproduction, like a reproduction of a painting, was purchased, not created. Imitation is not a proof of love, but of the satisfaction with a semblance of the original. Lloyd was there, and he is capable of creating, but because Japan is now in fashion, because Lloyd has not received the approbation of fashion, the blessing of popularity, Bob could never let him create an original home. What we enjoyed was a copy, not too faithful, but containing a few genuine objects.

During the music, because the music was not good, I felt nevertheless reconciled to the idea of my personal death. It would be a pity if I died before completing my work, because I am an exceptionally fine instrument for human consciousness. But if I should, at least music will always continue.

In this beautiful Japanese reproduction I alone can produce an inner music that harmonizes with the house. The people will disappear without a trace.

Rupert was sitting on the floor near the musicians so that he could watch their hands. I wondered whether he felt alone in this group, unable to identify with them. I looked at his hands, which are not beautiful, and felt tenderness. Whenever a young man talked to me, sooner or later, Rupert appeared. I wondered whether, if I died, Rupert would be able to flow more easily into the common stream of life. At the same time I realized with greater clarity, that it is the highest levels that are perpetuated… Then I drank the champagne, and this, combined with the illusion of beauty (an illusion strongly aided by the three young Japanese men), the summer night and my ability not to hear the trivial conversations, I went into a spatial flight and reached enjoyment.

In the car driving home, I consoled Lloyd. "Yes, we knew the difference between original creation and imitation. We have the original with us." I tapped his shoulder. Helen was in her vague, abstract moon character, dissolved like all Pisceans who then take on the round globular fish eye and cannot *see* other human beings in a focused way, but look bewildered as if they would collide with them, just as fish do when the deep sea divers appear.

Still under the euphoria created by a synthetic beauty, I sat in Eric's little boyhood bed and talked. "I want to explain why I hate the mountains: they isolate you from other human beings, and I was born isolated and am always struggling to come closer to others. You see, even Pam Campion thinks of me as 'strange.' It took a long time for her to trust me. I feel strange and lonely at times, like tonight."

"But don't you see? I do too—I feel just the same way. You know I feel like that, but I am resigned to not fitting in anywhere—I don't struggle," said Rupert.

I said much more, but it has vanished from my memory like a dream. I was inspired. I was like a woman who had spent an evening walking on the highest and loneliest mountains of the world, higher than Annapurna, where I had discovered and conquered a realm that does not die and where I am at home, glad to be buried in the pyramids of art. And there, at least, I will be able to rest.

Rupert felt this strangeness and sense of isolation, just when I had been meditating on his relation to the most common forms of life; he did not give his whole self to anything except to us, to me, to our relationship, which was why he wanted a home for it.

We looked at another house, and Rupert said: "That is good. I want you to see many houses" (so I will share his obsession). A modern house, built around a pool. As simple as the Japanese house, uncluttered, clear, spacious. Again an empty house.

We returned home suntanned, sleepy and tired. Rupert had asthma from too much swimming. And I returned to my double exposures. They proved, over lapses of 20 years, that we were wrong when we blamed my mother for Joaquín's restricted life. Mother died and Joaquín is still self-restricted, cautious, not free. I blamed Henry, Helba and Gonzalo for the destructive demons in my life, but when the three disappeared, I accomplished their role alone and acted out my own destructiveness. The image of myself struggling against Helba's and Gonzalo's destructiveness (an image I admired) was not entirely accurate. When they left, Hugo and I enacted our own, even down to the scenes of ferocious quarrels similar to Helba's and Gonzalo's. And then I handed over to Rupert the Don Juanism I felt less able to live out directly because of my loss of youth. Yet in each case we all fight the other's living out his assigned role. Hugo and I quarreled violently as June and Henry did. Yet when Hugo first saw one of their quarrels, he tried to suppress it. He could not bear it. Thus we make the others scapegoats; they assume the role we do not dare to live ourselves.

How beautiful it would be if we recognized the hidden wish, and when handing to the other the keys to the city we were not able to conquer, we also consented to the perversion; but on the contrary, Hugo fought my fantasy life (the houseboat, Acapulco, etc.) and only regretted it when we planned to "separate."

I fought Henry's promiscuity (which I wanted). I fought Gonzalo's surrender to dark drugs and alcohol, to irresponsibility (years later, I regret this and yearn to live as Genet has, risking jail). But this time I have safely entrusted to Rupert the "safety measures" I appear to disregard. It is Rupert who opened a savings account, Rupert who wants me to free him and yet fights liberation at every level.

I watch him now as he plays—a very serious musician, tense—his slim body erect, his right foot keeping tempo, and begin to understand why he plays so often, several evenings a week. He wants to shut himself away from a world that causes him trouble. He has the love he needs, vigilant, attentive, untiring, and he wants a nest. Away from there, he is strained. At parties he plays a role. He is not free, not at ease. He finds Renate's and Paul's flighty conversations hard to follow.

We fight the part of ourselves that is unhappy, and we instinctively fear it. Because we fear it, we stifle it. Because it is stifled, it must breathe through another. But with the revelation of this aspect (Henry's promiscuity, Gonzalo's drugs of forgetfulness), we cannot come to terms. The proof of this is the reversals that take place. Remove Henry, and I have to do my own living and writing. Remove Gonzalo, and I have to achieve my own violence. Remove Hugo, and I become practical and organized in finances. Remove me, and Hugo no longer fears to be overwhelmed by tropical languor, Mexican inertia—he recognizes his need of it. (When he was in Acapulco he feared to abandon himself because I had...and I represented the spectacle of a drugged tropical native.)

The untransformed lives, all around me. Most of my rebellions are against mediocrity. What I want comes from the depths and it does not exist here.

Now and then Rupert and I get the same nervous irritability, and then there are clashes. I seek to rid the house of non-essentials; I seek the Japanese house with only the beautiful, the essential. He returns from his patrol with an old belt he found on the road, an old rug someone threw away, or else he pulls out of the garbage can a broken object I threw away. Rupert is a rag-picker, showing the symptoms that created a Reginald Pole—unkempt, unclean, with frayed clothes, carrying his belongings in cartons, with cartons of empty medicine bottles, every object shabby, sordid, wrinkled, *dead*—none of them alive or beautiful. So strange a trait in a man of such radiant beauty as Rupert.

Now and then he also feels the need of acting like Lloyd. He shouts at me because the beer was not delivered cold as it should have been, just as Lloyd shouts at Helen. Also, since I have returned, one month now, we have only spent our evenings as he wanted us to, music, family, movies, and I was not able to see Renate and Paul.

For a week I was rebellious, and I tried to escape by writing, but I lacked the energy. I had a checkup to prove I had a bout of rheumatic fever in New York after the cold lecture halls of Evanston (which explains the heart condition). My energy has been low. At Rupert's family's home we slept in his old room—and I in an alcove built for Eric, because the beds are small.

One night after the music, when I was glad to sleep alone because I was angry deep down, he stood by my bed, leaning down to kiss me goodnight, his body so firm, like the statue of Donatello, brown with suntan, all but his firm milk-white behind, and his roseate, delicately tinted sex. I saw his body more acutely in that instant than in all our years of life together. The strong legs and arms. The few, well-placed black hairs on his chest, just between the nipples, a triangle, not too bushy, just a few black curled hairs. The strong, powerful legs and arms give him earthiness. The poetry is in the long neck, the carriage of the head, the cheek line of such sharpness, the flesh glued to the bone structure, economy, streamlined, with the aerodynamics of a jet liner, and the earthy way of standing squarely, his hands and feet not beautiful, but primitive, coarse, and again the poetry in the stance, in the turns of the head, in the flow of the hair on the back of the neck. And tonight, bending over, the triangle of black curly hair above the tender shell rose of the sex, some curly, and three or four so black, more curled than others, glistening.

The skin on the hands rough, wrinkled; the skin on his face that of a woman, flushed. The ears polished, brown, sensitive. One feels the tension of the muscles —I feel his firmness against my body. He is so tall; I put my arms around his waist, indented like that of a woman.

He sleeps naked. When his strong arms and legs emphasize his strength in bed, his spare shoulders, narrow chest and slender neck make him seem vulnerable and adolescent. He has the proportions of an adolescent. But he weighs more. He now looks, at times, more like a man and less like an adolescent.

Last night we were next door at the Campions', eating a barbecue dinner on the patio. The three little girls were in their nightgowns and kimonos, fresh out of the bath, with their hair parted and tied on each side of the ear like two wings—and sitting like photographs so they would be allowed to eat with us. In the middle of the evening when we were left alone, Rupert walked over to me and said, "I love you," which is unusual for him to say in public.

I wore a yellow Mexican handwoven skirt, a black top, wicker straw sandals, a straw bag, and living seemed simple and sweet. And when we came home Rupert made love to me fiercely.

Today he has gone to fight a fire. Renate and Paul also think that his great fear of being like his father, alone, nomadic, poor, dissipating time and energy, guides many of his efforts at roots, permanency, his lack of adventurousness. He fears to lose me by flirtations as Reginald lost two wives, to accomplish nothing, to become negative.

So we put money in a savings account. We plan a house. And like the wandering Jews I have to create an inner world because I reject this one. It is not mine.

At 6:00 AM yesterday the telephone rang and a sleep-webbed Rupert answered. While he dressed I prepared his breakfast and his lunch box. Rupert's dressing consists of questions: Where is the shirt I wore yesterday? Where are my keys? Where is my wallet? This is the need of an immense love mentioned in his horoscope. It means: be there, keep me, notice me, do not leave me alone. It means a man's task is a difficult one. It means he lives in a chaotic world. It means he is not prepared. Living is chaos. It means anxiety. It explains why he does not seek quality, high moments, fascinating characters, an audacious life—they are all intimidating. If I rebelled at this constant demandingness from Hugo because he was twenty years older than Rupert and cast in the role of the father, I am now resigned. I take the tray and I arrange the coffee, toast, eggs, vitamins. At this hour of the morning Rupert does not taste his food. In the morning he is not alive. He looks somnambulistic. His eyes do not see. He is silent. He is slow to combustion. The fire is low. His hands are cold. He drives off without the lunch box so I will spend an hour trying to find out where he is until I am told they set up a camp where food would be available.

I was glad to be alone. Because aside from the time he spends reading *Time* magazine, Rupert is never quiet. If he works at a repair job on his viola it is wild curses, and I must, even if I am lying down, come and see how the string has failed him because it is too old.

So I was glad to have a day of meditation. I organized and reconstructed myself. The Mexican novel is difficult—the theme I like is once again too subtle and symbolic and difficult to dramatize. It is disheartening to find everybody extolling

Bonjour Tristesse with an enthusiasm they never had for me…the trite, superficial story, shallow and melodramatic, one to be forgotten soon. There is no doubt people want to remain on the surface, and the adolescent world, above all others, appeals to Americans.

Letter from Anaïs Nin to Jim Herlihy:
Sierra Madre, August 1955

Dear Jim:

The fascinating problem of the irresponsible life…that has been the theme of the month. Just as we discussed it more clearly and openly, I realized that I had lived an irresponsible life—in secret—and that the occasional dangers of exposure proved that I feared exposure and reacted with a violent attack of guilt, which means obstacles: the human obstacle. The unwillingness to cause pain as well as the unwillingness to accept judgment of others. You notice one of the most inspiring elements in our relationship is that we pass no judgment. I should not even state it as negatively as that: we accept each other's most unconscious self, the hidden one. Completely. And this gives us an elating state of freedom. Now, I solved the problem of not hurting (or hurting with amnesia and chloroform) by lying. But I have never solved the problem of guilt, which is proved by me to be masochism…I can only get rid of the guilt by atonement. Atonement to Hugo (working on his films, etc.), atonement to Rupert (nursing his impossible, diseased and repulsive father).

And so a petty Hamlet haunts our house, to telephone or not to telephone, to eat or not to eat, to talk or not to talk…and by this time Anaïs is ready to be healthy, having atoned for over a month.

Anaïs

Letter from Jim Herlihy to Anaïs Nin:
New York, August 1955

Dear Anaïs:

Sitting at a cocktail table in my newly air-conditioned salon! Which explains the strange handwriting. Summer is severely hot here, but we're enjoying machine-made coolness.

Had dinner and evening with Hugo on Sunday.

Your letter was a very special treat. One doesn't expect the average letter to be so well written. The line about the Hamlet in Anaïs's house was lovely.

Your paragraph on guilt, ironically enough, arrived the very morning after I had dreamed that I had been guillotined.

No further comment necessary!

Our fear of *not* being punished seems to plague us even more than the fear of suffering, which is a shame, because we seem to have built-in crucifixes anyway, so what the hell!

I would love to talk to you tonight! Rehearsals are okay. Leading lady out with a fever for a few days, and we can't afford the time; but I think it will come out well anyway. Opening date draws closer!

It's so strange, so funny, that you and I suffer so at our own hands when our greatest flaw is probably that we are *too* careful of others, *too* considerate.
Love,
Jim

En route to New York, August 1955
I always like to write by the cold, clear light of the airplane cloudscape. It is a special light, not gold as I imagine the light of Greece, not blue like the light of snowy mountains. It is intensely white—sharp. But I see everything clearly in this light—it is not due to the light itself but the altitude and separateness.

No amount of analysis has made me drain-proof. My men drain me. And I allow this. My love never seems to wane, to lie fallow, to hibernate, to be listless, indifferent, lazy, inert, passive, negative, in repose. It is attentive. I can only reach indifference by weariness. The last month frightened me, because I felt I was without energy. And I was indifferent.

I did not care so much about my discipline. At four o'clock I usually bathe, exercise, dress afresh. Also, I could not write, not because I didn't feel like it but because I feel that nobody cares. I think Jim is the only one actually in love with what I write. Nobody else. Hugo, certainly not, partly because it hurts him since he reads it only as fantasies that are voyages without him...and partly because he does not understand it. Now he reads Giraudoux carefully—who is more difficult than I am...

Loneliness. It is difficult to write for an empty hall, to know I will have to struggle to get the book published, struggle to sell it and struggle against hostility. When I extended friendship to Bella Spewack I never imagined such a sudden turn against me and such a destructive letter: "Take yourself out of it. *Tell a story.* Dylan Thomas tells a story, as does Françoise Sagan in *Bonjour Tristesse. They tell a story.*"

Paul and Pam Campion. They have chosen their level. They exclude the depths. I catch glimpses of this through the cheerful, joking surface. They dispose quickly of the depths. The death of Pam's father, scarcely noticed, scarcely acknowledged, the trauma of a big fire. Pam's mother's guilt about surviving the father. Their unfulfilled wishes. How Pam's father, after being a workhorse for forty years, wanted to go around the world and his wife refused because it was too late and she was now old—and soon after he died.

They cement their lives in their twenties. At 36 and 38 they like the Dixieland music they danced to at twenty. They read the books of the month and magazines. Their orbit is small. I like them as human beings, but to me they are like the untouchables—untouched by life's great mysteries or storms or high moments. I can't write about them. I see little difference between the three playful little girls and Pam—they are sweet, kind and industrious, but how can one write about them?

Character is as much revealed by what we fear as by what we manifest. I feared my father's Don Juanism because I possessed the same propensities, and all I accomplished was to avoid a superficial Don Juanism; I deepened mine, but it was still Don Juanism. I feared my mother's temper and jealousy, yet I possess it within myself, and recently (since my mother's death) I have had to face her bad temper and jealousies in myself. The flowing of both my mother's qualities (unselfishness, devotion) and her defects (temper, jealousy) increased not only with her death, because of her death, but also because my Don Juanism was almost completely erased by Rupert. My faithfulness to Rupert, contentment with Rupert as a lover have almost annihilated my desire for other men—in seven years only a few lapses, when Bill Pinckard returned from Korea, when Carter Harman sought to retrieve a lost opportunity, once with Chinchilito (Edward Graeffe). With the lessening of the male role—seduction—came the increase of the maternal elements, and with them the negative aspect: possessiveness, irritability...

Strange that again I superimpose myself twenty years ago selecting an *angry* Henry when I seemed incapable of hatred and anger, over today when I am much more consumed with anger and hatred of America and the traits of my mother. The relativity, the shifting quality of character becomes more and more apparent.

I wonder if my mother felt the humiliation, the enslavement, the submissive serving role of woman and was constantly in rebellion against it, as I am. Femininity is accomplished by such a loss of prestige and power, such a servitude, that assertion could only assume a negative form: anger.

New York, August 1955

Leaving Rupert was so painful that I felt I never could do this again. But a greater pain awaited me: that of seeing, inexorably, the death of my love for Hugo.

He had been working hard at his new job and was also taking a Dale Carnegie course in public speaking. He had suffered the death of his mother. He was expecting consolation and pleasure. He wept over his mother when he recalled the terms of her last request that her ashes should be scattered. Hugo broke down. "Why scattered? My father's ashes are buried in Scotland. Why didn't she realize what this would mean to me? I have nothing to go back to—I think of her blue eyes and her crooked smile, all gone. All the hardness has gone out of me. I have had so much hardness. And now she is dead, and I will never fight anything again."

"But darling, you had to fight, for your own survival... And isn't it better that her ashes are scattered than to think of her rotting in a tomb?"

Consolation. Then pleasure. He had bought champagne for my arrival. He wanted to see plays. He wanted to go to the beach. But he did not make love with me, and we kiss like brother and sister.

At night I suffer anxiety. Rupert is not beside me. Deprived of his physical closeness, his physical passion, I feel myself dying. But I cannot desert Hugo, not until Bogner comes back. I once believed it would harm Hugo, but now I feel I am as bad for him as he is for me. He needs more love, more identification with all his interests.

Hugo and I are in the kitchen.

Anaïs: "I want you to forgive me my impatience with your errors. I have become aware that my greatest weakness was in my inadequacy in life, in facing economic and practical problems, and that my greatest need was of someone adequate. The most difficult thing I ever had to do was to accept your *inadequacy*. It was as if your not doing things well *doubled* my weakness, and I felt anxious and overburdened. That is why I have been rebellious. Please forgive me. I am sure I have disappointed you equally. I am sure I failed to fulfill your greatest need. What was your greatest need?"

Hugo: "I wanted someone who would be there all the time."

And I...in order not to desert him altogether...deserted him intermittently. After this admission it seemed like the end. Ironically, his particular neurosis (vagueness, absence, obsession with business, fatigue) gives me the feeling that he is not there either. So we are living with ghosts...the way families live together, out of loyalty, but not truly there, the way I lived when I visited my mother: filling up the hours, finding the time dragging and wishing to leave.

I always promised I would be patient—but I cannot be. In the middle of the night (Joaquín is visiting, sleeping in my room, so I sleep with Hugo) he gets up—he tries to be quiet. When he returns to bed, he lies down half on the bed and half on the bedside table, which gives way to his weight; the glass top breaks, the heavy lamp falls and nearly hurts him. In my sleep I say: "Did you get hurt?" And I feel a terrible pain of compassion and, at the same time, a desire to escape, and the feeling of his heaviness and clumsiness stays with me. In the morning I tell myself Hugo is ill. I need to be compassionate. He opens a can of tomato sauce and splashes my new dress. He leaves the gas lit under an empty pan.

We go to the beach. He swims well. But as he stands on the edge smiling at me, the pose of his body is dolorous, like that of a cripple. He looks at me with the expression of a cripple. He has an abnormally low voltage. Although the doctor said there was nothing wrong with his hearing, he always makes you repeat what you say, leans over as if he were a little deaf, and often misses the beginning of a story and asks a question that shows he did not get the point. The slightest act—how to arrange our things on the beach—is accomplished hesitantly. Now, all this should make me compassionate, and the truth is that it makes me angry. Why?

I make errors—but I have made such superhuman efforts to avoid them.

The women Hugo likes (Peggy Glanville-Hicks and Bogner) are precisely the same as I am—quick-witted, dynamic, impatient, accelerated. If I left him I believe he would choose the same elements that are antithetical to his temperament. He *should* like easy-going, slow, patient, passive women.

What has hardened me against Hugo? To say I do not love him is not enough, for I love him as I love Joaquín—I don't want him hurt or lonely. Is this hardness like the hardness of the partner who feels he must compensate for the weakness of the other?

Combined with the disintegration is a continuous kindness. It is demoralizing.

What alarms me is that he arouses the same hardness in his business partners. St. Phalles treats him like a son, scolds him, although he is only five years older than Hugo.

"I promise you," said Hugo, "that this summer I did not sabotage my work. The errors I made that Claude accused me of are normal. I am learning a new profession."

"I believe you, darling."

He spends a sleepless night because St. Phalles offended him. He spends a sleepless night because his sister Edith is here to contest their mother's will.

For all this I should show sympathy, as I show sympathy for Reginald, and recently I could not.

41

I am baffled and hate myself for this. I try first of all to understand and then am unable to, so I turn away and escape...movies, the beach, Joaquín's visit, Jim, a new dress, gin. I am going through, for the first time in my whole life, a phase of irresponsibility. I am not answering letters, not writing, am reading Simenon, and above all learning to live in the present, casually, letting life flow.

Letter from Rupert Pole to Anaïs Nin:
Sierra Madre, August 1955

Darling:
Sitting here on a tall, tall mountaintop watching the puny efforts of man to combat nature with 41 Mexicans. The Mexicans, of course, are very amused by the whole thing—the whole idea of fighting fire seems silly to them. But they're here and they like the mountains and like me, so they're doing good work widening and digging trenches. Of course, the good money they're making will make them the enemy of all the other Mexicans when they return home.

Strange fire. I was home Saturday after patrolling another fire. I was called Sunday for this one. Some more fires are just down the river. Then, Monday morning, just as we were getting ahead of this one, the old one broke out again and spread all over the mountains. Now as we sit here on top of a second mountain looking back at the first mountain, they're beginning the fight all over again. The fires are like two planets drawing towards each other—one just cooling and the other still flaming, each in a different time period. Mountains here give a tremendous feeling of energy in repose—as you look down those incredible gorges and chasms (remember how it looked from the top of Josephine Lookout?) you feel the gigantic surges of energy the earth must have made to heave them up so high so suddenly. I'm sure now these mountains of mine are the result of a great earth orgasm of the past.

Don't know when I'll get back, love, but glad all this is happening when you're in N.Y. I have a special arrangement with the mountain gods to have no more fires after you return to me (but had to sell them myself in return—only for now, though, not forever).

Tavi should be fine. Left his food with Phyllis with instructions to call Mother if I'm not back in a day or two.

Love, you'd better make a person-to-person call next Sunday—cheaper than station-to-station, plus you may get a telegram from me. That way if I'm not back you'll get news of me without paying.

Hope you're not trying to work too fast and hard—remember to save some of yourself for our next swim!!

Fire on next mountain looks better now—will probably lose my days off again, but should be home about Saturday.

R

Letter from Anaïs Nin to Rupert Pole:
New York, August 22, 1955

Darling Chiquito:

When we get a bad phone connection I become more aware of the 3,000 miles between us! So you went on a fire that very Sunday? I never imagined that (did not want to). It must have been a bad one if it lasted through your days off. I get *no* news about California—not one line in the *N.Y. Times*. I read just to see if you have had as much rain as the East and hoped the fire season was over.

Sunday—you may not have heard me—I was at Reis Beach with Ruth Witt-Diamant, her sister, Jim and Dick. One inch between each person, and all except the negroes, who are beautiful, look as if they eat nothing but hot dogs, millions of them... But the sea was warmer than in L.A. and so I spent more time swimming... I wanted to know if you were tired from the fire, but the three minutes were up and I could not tell from your voice as I usually can. Was it a signal for you again?

Why don't you ask Nichols never to answer while I am away, evenings—no, I guess you can't do that. I feel so frustrated not to be able to call you spontaneously—but I can see he has to answer, in case of fire.

I'm glad Lloyd got the land he wanted. I suppose you've had no time to see about a possible job nearer your future home. Everybody sends you love...

Jim says I always arrive radiant and begin to look less radiant each day away from you.

Te quiero—and I wish I were there to rescue you in my arms when you come back looking smokier than Smokey the Bear in the ad—a smoked bear.

Anaïs

Letter from Anaïs Nin to Rupert Pole:
New York, September 7, 1955

Darling Chiquito:

Ruth, Joaquín and I went to the Paramount in Brooklyn because they told us it was the best negro singing in town. It's a huge movie house, big as an opera. You have to sit through a bad movie first, then come all the singers we've ever heard on records (late at night, remember) and all the popular songs—a fast, wonderful show. But the most interesting thing was that it was a crowd such as we only saw at bullfights—excited, tumultuous teenagers, "gangs" of boys with special shirts, in fact delinquents, all clapping, answering the songs, delirious, standing on the seats, and behaving like voodoo dancers! It was supercharged and high voltage atmosphere. It was very exciting. All evening I wished you were beside me, for one of the many reasons I love you so much is that at times like this you are always *high voltage*.

So glad to have your letter, darling. You are having the weather the East had before I came. Too bad because of bronchitis you won't be able to cool off in the pool.

Darling...I'm thinking of you, and very happy you are not risking your life right now because it is *our* life—that is the greatest proof of love.

Te quiero,
A

New York, September 1955
Everybody is concerned with the fact that great and powerful America has not produced a great and powerful American novel—only puny, effeminate works—or uncouth war novels.

Hugo says the theme of America should be that of its scientific and industrial energy. I say that it should be that of human beings not collapsing inwardly under the forces of science and industry, but controlling them with an equivalent inner force. The tragedy has been the inner collapse.

The negro alone has not collapsed. Possibly the *only* expression of American energy will be scientific, industrial, and jazz, which matches up to it, holds its own, has an equal vitality. Possibly the American novel will never be written. Certainly not by writers twenty years old. Certainly not by Tennessee Williams, who instead of maturity now gives *Cat on a Hot Tin Roof* hysteria in place of feeling, brutality in place of strength, clichés in place of revelation, obscenity in place of vitality. The proof of his immaturity is that he appeals to Jim, who is 27, and to American audiences in general, who are seven years old.

But when William Goyen writes a beautiful, poetic novel, he is assassinated and derided as much as I was. There is nothing in between crudeness, puritanism, and poetry. Poetry is rejected.

New York, September 8, 1955
Joaquín left yesterday. It is strange to see him *today*, with today's eyes. He is disciplined and organized. He conforms to all his duties. On Sunday he went to mass early—at 6:00 AM. He visited all his old friends from his childhood days on up. He went to see a music publisher. He enjoyed his cocktail like anyone else, slept well. During the summer, while teaching in Aspen, he swam, got brown. He accepts bad movies or dull people quietly. He plans wisely and with practicality for his sabbatical in Europe. He manages his life smoothly and wisely. He nearly married a girl, but when the obstacle vanished (my mother), he got frightened.

I had a dream that I was walking up the façade of a house, looking into an apartment. A mother and a boy of seven or eight years scream. Everybody is alarmed. I go down and explain: "I am a trapezist practicing." Two handsome women are listening to me. I explain: "I must first get my handbag, which I left hanging between floors." I climb up; it is difficult. I climb on to a porch (similar to ours on 215 W 13th) and finally reach for my handbag, which is resting on a rotten box full of earth (the flower boxes on our porch have rotted away). On the porch there are half-emptied bottles of champagne. I think it is a party such as only Hollywood can give—extravagant and wasteful. Now I am in bed with a boy—seven years old—he has an erection. I am amazed. He holds me and we lie quietly with his sex between my legs.

New York, September 15, 1955
The first time I saw Bogner after her summer vacation she listened to all I said and then commented: "Of course, you realize that you are still related to Hugo even if in a negative way, which seems to be the obverse of love."
Anaïs: "I am happier with Rupert, closer to Rupert."
Bogner: "But that happiness may be achieved only because Hugo is there."

Bogner suspected my extremes of violent compassion for Hugo when I am far away, and violent irritation with him as soon as I am near him.

Today we focused on irrationality and my fear of it (Lloyd Wright, Reginald Pole, Gonzalo, Helba, all unreasonable), my effort to dominate and control it (by creation, psychoanalysis).

She always operates and releases immediately the intolerable pain of the break. The decision is postponed. I begin to enjoy the present.

I spend an evening at the Palladium watching mambo competitions—the women dressed in the new skin-tight fashion with a ruffle only below the knee, revealing every ripple of the body. And Teddy Brown (remember New Year's Eve when we spent the evening desiring each other?) was there winning prizes, surrounded by beautiful girls. When he saw me, he said: "I'm very sorry I saw you, Anaïs. I will have bad dreams again." I had discouraged his desire. "Can I call you tomorrow?" he asked, attracted as so many of us are by defeat and the need to conquer. And he called at nine in the morning while Hugo and I were having breakfast.

And when the desperate moment comes, when I feel I can no longer bear the separation from Rupert, I either drink or write or go out again.

I am bringing back to Rupert an improved Anaïs, teeth fixed so I am no longer afraid to smile. And to Hugo I gave hours of sympathy to his task of business, which is continuous.

I write on the bus, while waiting at the dentist, etc.

And last night the inevitable dream: Rupert and I are in his car driving to Mexico. He is taking me to see my family. On the way he notices a girl. He tells me: "While you're visiting your family I will go and find the girl." And I cry out: "But why do you tell me this?"

Dream: There is a married couple, but he always has another woman living with them as part of the household. I realize the wife is tortured, so I force her to listen to me. She is hostile, suspicious. I say: "You must be objective and understand this and then it won't hurt you. It isn't that he doesn't love you; he is circuitous (like Paul Mathieson) and you are too direct. So he gets shocks from you, and the other woman is there merely as a shock absorber, as a kind of deviation to deflect your storm." I am very eloquent and very forceful, and finally pacify her.

Sierra Madre, September 1955

To sum up an extraordinary change caused by analysis: five weeks without depressions, anxieties or nervousness—only occasional and less severe forms of it. I feel installed in the present. I give myself to it. I no longer feel anger, walls, hostilities with the world. My criticalness has lessened. I enjoy what comes. I am not nervous beforehand. I drink, I am gay, I am free. The *fears* have decreased: not afraid of being unable to earn a living, not afraid of losing Rupert. There is less jealousy, less rebellion—much more smoothness and lightness in living, an ability to throw off anxiety. My feeling has changed about America. The hatred has gone. I do not get disturbed by Lloyd. I went to a party at the Campions', and whereas before a part of me would hold back because the people were not individually interesting, this time I entered uncritically into it on its proper level. Contentment. It took me a lifetime to know that happiness is a quiet thing, not a peak of ecstasy.

Having fewer conflicts, I get less tired and accomplish more. I can do housework half a day, type half a day and still go out at night. No hangover from drinking at the party, where for the sake of comedy I made fun of my "falsies," which I have to wear with off-the-shoulder dresses only!

Lightness and a feeling of strength. It all consolidated this month. It is true I may die without seeing Bali, but then I have other things. I can make one human being happy. I am close to one human being and closer than before to others. My genuine gentleness is returning. I do not expect others to love or understand my work. I feel like a minor Einstein, a mathematician of the emotions whom only a few can read. I am not bitter or hurt—so much has been accomplished.

Letter from Anaïs Nin to Maxwell Geismar:
Sierra Madre, September 1955

Dear Max:
I know you are genuinely concerned about the Diary and wanted me not to feel blocked. And I am grateful for your advice. But I will try and explain something now that will make you happy and improve our relationship on the ideological side (nothing needs improving on the human side). This year I finally achieved objectivity. Very difficult for a romantic. The divorce from America, as I call it, was painful, but has proved very creative and liberating. It was like breaking with a crabby, puritanical, restrictive, punitive, sour parent. Immediately after I overcame the hurt, I began to write better than ever. America, for me, personally, has been oppressive and destructive. I am completely free of it. I don't need to go to France or anywhere else. I don't need to be published. I only need to continue my personal life in full bloom, as it is, and to do my major work. I merely forgot, for a few years, what I had set out to do. To prove that problems are primarily psychological, and that no Marxism, no economic security, and no social obsession will solve them. American history has proved the fallacy of this. You have to begin with the self, the personal and the human being and then proceed to your community. Psychoanalysis was right. And in that sense it is altruistic. Having settled this in my own mind, I have settled down to complete, fill out, round out the Diary. I feel now that all American accusations and attempts to batter this self have failed to destroy me, as they nearly did. So I am doing my life's work quietly. I am in a cool, serene laboratory. The self in the real sense, as you know in all creation, in all experiment, in all research or exploration or invention, is not important. I have proved something, I believe, of value to humanity when they get weary of trying to solve everything from the outside. This has to wait, because the world is in its material phase and has to see that dialectical materialism will destroy it more totally than the romantics or neurotics ever could. It's an interesting stage. And now I understand also why I hurt you, but will never do so again because this is no longer a hurtful, emotional thing, but history, psychology, philosophy... I also can explain to you why I felt so compelled to take the Diary away from you...it happened after I read your review of Hemingway in which you took him to task for living outside the United States and for not keeping his nose to the political grindstone. At that moment you were no longer my well-loved friend, but a

symbol of what I do not believe. Then, when I became free and objective, you were yourself again, and the ideas you have, or the beliefs, no longer threaten me. I don't live here anymore. I live in the future. And it is all lighter and freer, and more humorous... Quite different from escape.

In escape you abandon your life's work. This is more like the scientist going into his laboratory and keeping the uninitiated out merely so they won't break the bottles, or ruin the formulas, spill the precious liquids. It's altitude. Good for work.

I don't know if I have made myself clear, that the ideas you have no longer interfere or blur the friendship, because I feel sure within myself.

You see, I feel that if the whole world sought reality and truth, it would mean the end of war. To *remove* what makes you angry, or unjust, or aggressive, or unable to allow others to think and be different...that can't be done from the outside. It is then you are ready to live for bigger aims and better friendships.

Sierra Madre, September 1955

The title of this story is: If you suddenly look upon human beings' behavior as insane, then it all makes beautiful sense.

Lloyd wants to build a home on a mountaintop. It is a symbolic act dramatizing his alienation from the world. He lives entirely on the negative pole of his being. He detaches himself and fumes with hatred of human beings' behavior. He has not received his due from the world. He seeks isolation. So he chooses the top of a mountain when he could go to the architectural centers he loves—Japan, Mexico, South America. He could have escaped the American culture he hates. He could even have been loved and admired in more romantic, more imaginative countries.

Rupert is not eager to live next to Lloyd, but this is a more practical plan: Lloyd has found a good buy, 20 acres, and the dream can only be fulfilled by a concerted effort on the part of Lloyd, Rupert and Eric. I understand and accept this. We could not buy our own lot of such beauty or size by ourselves.

Lloyd and Helen are both tired and old without having lived or traveled. Helen has a lame leg that slows down her activity. She has difficulty driving. They have money difficulties, tenants who do not pay for their other houses. Yet to get away from the smog, she is willing to go up to this mountain where earning a living and doing errands will be more complicated. Lloyd has his office at home and should be accessible, but on the mountain he won't be.

Though Rupert would like not to live close to the family, he wants his own home at any price. I don't want this way of life at all.

But Friday we all dressed in our oldest clothes. I helped Helen into her slacks. Helen often looks as one imagines the people from the moon. She worked all morning at making sandwiches while Rupert slept in an effort to recover from the strain of the day before: in a few hours he blazed 2,000 feet of a mountain trail, arriving at the top in near collapse, his heart beating wildly, his delicate chest completely overwrought.

That first day I had resolved not to rebel. We climbed for six miles, up steep, sharp, curved mountain roads. I hate mountains. They look stolid, irrevocable, oppressive. When we reached the top we were above the smog. The sun was shining—but on what? A stark mountain and boulders. Not the red sepia earth of Spain and silver olive trees. Not the velvet and silk foliage of Mexico with giant flowers. Instead, a green from the paint pot of natural greens. Below a coarse meadow. The only touch of beauty, a surprise, were imprints of seashells in the sandstone. To this I gave all my attention. If I could not have the sea, here I had, symbolically, a distant evocation of it, a proof of its existence. But why should I live where the sea *has* been? I collected them in a pile. I said: "We will use them in the building of the house." Rupert was glad that I loved the fossils, for he could see the mountain was, to me, a mere pile of earth weighing like an obstacle on my body—a Wall of China between me and the world. I did not try to deceive Rupert. I told him what I felt. It is like death. I had rebellions—but how well he knows how to subdue them. He does not fight. He becomes gentle and reasonable. "You are very clear about what you don't want, but so vague when I ask you what you do want. California is a compromise. I can earn a living here. If I have a home I feel I can travel. It will be a good investment. I will be able to rent it as Mother rents her houses, and we can travel on that."

What can I say? That we should go to New York and both of us work and live in an apartment, when Rupert will spend all his time driving away from it, seeking nature? Traveling adventurously, gambling, working our way through life, Rupert cannot do. It is not his temperament to have no home, to live as I do, not thinking of the future...

On Friday the fog covered even the mountain top. Lloyd was so disappointed. Sasha Heifetz and his wife had come as they will share the land. In the fog we climbed down the mountain. We examined the fossils, the deer droppings, the coyote droppings, the rabbit holes. No snakes: it is too dry. In the fog we sat in the meadow and ate our sandwiches. Because of the fog, the place looked more as I saw it than as Lloyd saw it.

Rupert climbed the highest boulder. He was silhouetted against the pearly fog, surrounded by it. He seemed like a ghost. The voices echoed. They carried an empty wine bottle to break on the rock. Everybody was laughing. Before they broke the bottle I walked away unnoticed. What I felt was I could not participate in this ritual. I could see Rupert's slim figure alone on the rock. I could not be there. I would not be there. I would be dead and he would be married to someone else. When they broke the bottle, the sun came out for a few minutes. Lloyd could survey his kingdom. He talked about building projects. Helen came down towards me. She wanted to be in the meadow and rest a moment. One can tell Helen what one feels: she understands, and when she does not, she still conveys sympathy. I said: "This is like being dead. I love life and human beings. All the fog, and the solitude. It is the way I imagine death."

Then we made the arduous climb up. Helen was out of breath, panting fearfully, as Rupert had done the day before.

Once home, we had a drink. Lloyd was discussing a map with Rupert. I kept hearing: "And nobody will be able to build near us." From where I sat he looked so big...and I thought of Ibsen's architect building, the tallest spiral. It was at this moment that I saw them all pursuing their own madness. And then it all made sense. It was at this moment also that I recognized the responsibility for loneliness. It was I who was cutting myself off from the family's dream, because temperamentally I didn't belong in it.

Over breakfast Rupert and I had one more talk—I raised a few more objections—having so little money, the house would take years to build, and all our time and energy. (I never can tell Rupert how little time I have left—I do not like to sadden him—but I am fully aware of it. It is the only possession that I have now begun to economize and save for my work's completion.)

I have not said what I wanted to say. Each one has a fantasy, a personal, irrational fantasy he seeks to live out. He will live it out at any cost, in human life, one's own or that of the loved one... The house is Lloyd's moment, his Egyptian tomb. For Rupert it will be a source of joy, but only if the woman is *right*—and if my life is shortened by the enormity of the task, then Rupert will have paid dearly for his fantasy.

Bogner would question how I failed to avoid becoming entangled in the family's fantasy. Truthfully, I do not know how to avoid it. It is true it has been spun around me, but it is Rupert's fulfilment that, in the end, wins over my rebellion. I see he is happy. He has the feeling he is doing a wise thing. I see that he is working for solidity, for the most essential of all things: to own one's own house.

And I should be living on Varda's barge, in Varda's way.

But Paul and Renate, a week later, are not alarmed. "Of all the people we know, Anaïs, you have the greatest share of the fairytale—you *are* a symbol of the spirit. You will not be overwhelmed by rocks. And it is highly comical to see you, between the giant Lloyd, and even the giant Rupert, builders in rock and earth…"

Everyone smiles because they bet on me, on the one Ruth described to Auden as "everybody's fairy princess." They are sure I will remain as I wish—fluid and mobile.

Rupert is so touching, so sincere, that he wins me. He wants to build me an Acapulco—tropical plants and water…

He is happy, and yet sweetly concerned… His sweetness disarms me. I surrendered. He reminds me that in all his horoscopes the basic theme is the home, the nest.

Renate understood what I felt. Paul is Nordic and sees beauty in the neutral colors and plain stones…

I find that the origin of misery is rebellion against reality in favor of a romantic fantasy. This month I have lived more harmoniously with what I have. I have Rupert. And from there on I have accepted what makes my life with Rupert happen: sharing his fantasy. Not rebelling against his profession, his family. I have lived well with his family two days and nights a week. I have taken up first aid because at the station I was called upon three times to give first aid and felt helpless. Monday I went from 8:00 AM to noon for Red Cross instruction. I faced one of my greatest fears: the fear of looking upon physical wounds. I never feared psychological horrors—but I dreaded to witness an automobile accident. I was always impressed with Thurema Sokol's rescue of a man cut by glass and closing the wound with her hand and stopping the blood. I learned to make bandages. After 18 hours of instruction I will get my first aid certificate.

Then—I found it easy and enjoyable to take care of Christy, Kitty and Mollie Campion because they are fairytale children, sensitive, delicate and poetic. I genuinely love them. But next door on the other side, Nichols and his wife moved in. Phyllis is a Swedish farmer's daughter from Wisconsin, but unhealthy and negative and neurotic, with skin allergies, asthma, and a lifeless quality. Nick is religious, fanatically dutiful, severe with his two boys. The boys are made of oatmeal, not well cooked. Lumps. Big, heavy, and without charm. Yet—when she went to the hospital to bear a third boy, I took care of the other two, and I cooked dinner for the whole family on the first chaotic day. The night before she went to the hospital, as Rupert was on a fire, I offered to babysit so they could enjoy a movie. Awaiting news of the third oatmeal boy, I felt excited—even without personal love. I was finally reinstated to the fraternity of an anonymous community life—*la vie de famille*. Of course, I am a fake, for I am impersonating a good human being doing her human duty while knowing I am not entirely submerged in it. They are not my children. But there was a deep change, and the change was in my absence of rebellion—my accepting the human in place of the marvelous... Rupert left Sunday at noon. When he returned Tuesday afternoon, I felt closer to him, less guilty, because I had been useful. I had sold Paul's and Renate's Xmas cards to help them economically. It was in this way that I reintegrated the warmth of family life when I was a child.

I have Rupert. And Rupert has a large share of earthy qualities under his romantic exterior, so I have to make my peace with the Earth. I, who have struggled to fly from its chores, its monotonies, its animal weight... What new loveliness there is in Mollie carrying a bottle of milk that is half of her own size and knocking gently for me to make a chocolate drink. And how she sits under my arm, or shows me a bruise on her incredibly small elbow. Pam I truly love, too. She is sensitive, and although undeveloped in experience or knowledge, she is without hostility towards what she does not know. She is thoughtful, humorous and touching—limpingly doing all her work, and potentially an artist.

This has been a month when I have felt whole and made my break with Hugo completely.

Loneliness increases as you ascend to more rarefied atmospheres. What Rupert gives me is human life, uncomplicated.

Letter from Anaïs Nin to Anne Metzger:
Sierra Madre, September 1955

Dear Anne:
I give you the fullest right to do anything with *Ladders to Fire* that you think wise. You can cut, eliminate, subtract and dilute, whatever Plon wants. I have for twenty years endured so much from American puritanism, American inability to evaluate literature, American commercialism, that I am absolutely unable to feel anything but indifference to the irrationalities of the publishers or the public. When I received your letter—after having spent all these years constructing an impossible image of the intelligence, the tolerance, the complete liberation of the French mind, the largeness of its life and concepts—Plon's feeling made me laugh at myself. They sound like American publishers. Are they Catholic? Anyway, it is of no importance what they do. I do want to be published in France. I am particularly amused, having just finished reading Genet and some of Colette's early and unequivocal books... The stupidity of Plon amazed me, for it is so much like American stupidity. *Tant pis.* My wishes in all matters concerning my writing have never been fulfilled, and I can see they won't be in France either. The next thing will be the French critics writing like the uncultured American reviewers,

saying I should be writing about women who live in the suburbs with children, and not about artists...

I do hope, dear Anne, that after all the work and faith you expended on me, that the contract, if it comes through, will be the way I want it, that you, the translator, should be paid first out of whatever advance they give me...the writer later. It was the understanding we had.

I am rushing this off to you. Do whatever you please. I trust you and I like you.
Anaïs

November 1955
Return to New York.

Letter from Rupert Pole to Anaïs Nin:
Sierra Madre, November 1955

Love:

Your voice sounded good—strong and cheerful—hope you weren't trying to fool me. Be careful of too much work the first days back—and remember—the more you give them the more they'll expect each time.

Lots of fires for a while but blessed by rain today—hope this will end the season and we'll be free as the wind when you get back. One bad fire burned right down to the ocean but didn't bother the property. The property, by the way, is hopelessly bogged down with not one, but four separate owners.

Was a little tired when you called—big rescue Saturday night—two boys stopped by and told me about a bad accident on Chantry Road—of course I was the first one there and had to climb down 500 feet to a car with a man and woman trapped in it—I had already called the sheriff and ambulance and sent for Forest Service help. I had to pry the door open, comfort the man (in severe shock) and apply first aid to the woman (fractured clavicle and a possible broken pelvis). After ages, the F.S. crew arrived with a stretcher and we first pulled the woman, and then the man, for what seemed like miles straight up. An ambulance and dozens of policemen were there by then, but do you think any of them would come down to help? Ha!! Both will be OK—they were so drunk they rolled with the punches. The car is still down there, so I went to see the man at home today. He was in bed with no phone and had botched up things with his insurance company. So tomorrow I have to call the company and arrange to get the damned car out of the canyon. So goes the life of a forest ranger.

But I do make good martinis, don't I, love? I'm getting 'em so dry now so you have to dust off the glasses before you can drink 'em. I place the vermouth bottle so that just its shadow falls on the gin! The martini craze has even hit the F.S., who is using 'em in its newest survival kits. You're lost in the frozen wasteland, and night falls, and then you fall. What to do? You get out your little F.S. survival kit, open it, and inside, neatly packed, you find one vial of gin, one vial of vermouth, an olive and a cup. And without fail, the minute you begin drinking, some jerk rushes out of the forest to tell you you're doing it wrong!

Why don't you come back soon, and I'll mix you one. Next to us, it's the most potent little mixture ever devised. Maybe if we fill the bathtub with martinis we can lure your fish back into the aquarium—right after you left they all curled up and escaped—that is, all but me, and I just curl up and wait, right here.

R

New York, November 1955

Last night Hugo and I went dancing at the Palladium. The absence of physical contact was frightening. He must suffer from it, but he would not realize it. My knowledge of the truth always makes me seem crueler.

I bought a veil from France, which has "the fingers of a rainbow" designed to touch the edge of the eyes. I bought Hugo's Xmas present: a miniature planetarium to give space to his room at night. His room is so shut in. He is the man who could live with covers on the furniture and the shades down.

For Jim I bought a Japanese notebook—and a "perpetual movement machine"—four small metal squares turning by the effect of the sun or electric lamp, so that he can look at it when he is stopped in his writing.

The moon is thin and metallic. It is not Rupert's full moon (which always affects me sensually).

When can I tell Hugo; when will he be ready, strong, independent and capable of other relationships? His relationships all fail, with his partners, with the Barrons, with Millicent. He has no close friends and no woman in love with him.

Dream: Hugo looks *grey*. I cannot tell him the truth because I identify with the deserted.

I say to Dr. Bogner: "I still feel the same way. Hugo and I have reached tenderness and understanding, but no physical contact. I cannot live this way. It makes me destructive. I do not give Hugo my best self. I feel we have a dead relationship. I know I can't ask you: is Hugo ready? Lately I have interpreted his not sleeping well and his destructiveness as being caused by not having a basically alive, lusty, physical relationship."

"This is *your* interpretation."

She has spent all these last hours trying to find a flow, a break, a pretense, a weakness in my decision. But I have felt no ambivalence. *I only hesitate to damage Hugo.* I want to time it right. I am losing patience because Hugo, with twice as much analysis as I, is so far from lucidity. He lives in a fog.

I gave him the planetarium. "When you awaken at night you will think you are out of doors, watching the stars." He was very touched. I spent three weeks fixing up the house. It is clean, refreshed, repaired. Finished reframing a whole wall of block engravings...

But I bought my ticket for the 30th and I will be glad to escape.

Bogner worries me. I realize what she is doing. But I remain certain, quiet. Not happy. Of course not. I am tempted to tell Hugo the truth. I wish Bogner would help me, but her task is to question, to examine. She says my "interpretation" of Hugo's symptoms (his need of a woman, a physical relation) is my *wish* that Hugo should feel this as it would free me of responsibility.

Our talk is inconclusive. It makes me irritated.

If I am running away from the endless complications of Hugo's sickness—why should I not want to escape from a Hamletism much deeper and more terrible than mine? Why should I not want to escape his lifelessness? Another woman might *give* him life—make love to him—warm him.

"It is all too…smooth," says Bogner.

"Not smooth. But clear. I see everything clearly. I want to act. I feel I can't act without first talking to you."

"You say you have considered every alternative. You say you know what you want—but you don't want to damage Hugo. You say you feel Hugo feels as you do—but suppose he does not—suppose he has never considered separation—then what will you do?

"I feel that he would if he were capable of either clarity or decisions. But he isn't. And I cannot wait any longer. I want a life of wholeness…"

Bogner's attitude—of seeming not to believe I am well and ready to live out what I want—is naturally a setback.

She said, "You are always talking about Hugo."

"Because he is my only concern. I have settled my own indecisions."

En route to Sierra Madre, November 30, 1955

I could be happy in Sierra Madre except for the excessive domestic duties that swamp me and suck all my energy. Rupert coming home for lunch makes me responsible for three meals a day. We never go out to eat. On our free days we dine at Helen's, which frees me from cooking, but there are many more dishes to do. Then at eleven I have to serve beer and snacks to the musicians. Breakfast there on our day off also means many more dishes. Helen is tired, and I have to help her.

Rupert is careless and creates more work for me—he comes through the house like a cyclone. When he is around I can't write or concentrate. He is cursing because he can't find this or that. He expects me to help him look. After a month of no writing I get sick and rebellious. The doctor says I must rest every day. If I carry laundry, vacuum, carry food, I feel tired and my chest constricts. I have to carry garbage cans and incinerate all the papers. How will I escape from this? We save money, but I not only waste my energy, I am also unhappy.

I don't know if Dr. Bogner undermined my contentment this last month, made me doubt it, but I have to keep balancing the beauty of my passion for Rupert against a slavery to all I hate: housework and family and a rigid, bourgeois life.

Rupert enjoys Paul and Renate, their spark of creation and fantasy, but not enough to stay long—he wants to leave for a movie! Movies and music encircle me until I feel angry and rebellious.

I was glad to see him go away on a fire for two days and nights. I slept ten hours, cleaned the house, wrote letters, and felt whole again.

I've lived my life upside down. I look more beautiful now than I did at thirty—I also enjoy holding a child and watching him stop crying and fall asleep!

For three weeks I told Bogner I feel sure and strong and determined. Our last talk:

Anaïs: "I know you can't *say* openly: the analysis is not finished. Or, Hugo is ready to accept your departures and feels as you do."

Bogner: "I cannot make your decisions."

Anaïs: "But when I say I have decided, you question. Of course I realize you have to be sure. Your questions have not aroused the old depressions and confusions. Does this mean I'm well?"

Bogner (to Hugo at his session): "I have been impatient with you. I am sorry about that."

Hugo: "And I have not been benevolent" (referring to an expression in Bible we always used playfully: a husband must be benevolent to his wife—at least once a week). "But when I was, it was with a cry: I love you!"

Hugo got up after three days in bed with a cold to go and see Bogner. Returning, he said in a moment of rare humor: "I was foggier today than I usually am."

The Barrons said: "Hugo is better when you are not there. You are too glamorous, too exciting. It makes him passive. When you are not there then he is the handsome, active one, radiant. Sometimes he needs to be the glamorous one."

Even if I have returned obsessively to this relationship, it is to observe an extraordinary growth of personality and liberation; if analysis could free Hugo, bound like a mummy, it is a greater value to human beings than religion. He was indeed a man *dead* from neurosis, killed by it.

My study of Georges Simenon revealed an interesting truth. Because I consider him the best of the realists, I made the following discovery: realism is given by the observation of the physical detail, but mostly by the *ugly* detail. Simenon is fertile in the homely, plain, small, everyday details, the animal details—also the deformity, the mannerisms, the neckties, the clothes. He stands at the opposite pole from me. But this is not the surprise—the surprise is that I *see* all this, but I choose to ignore it, by turning away, by escaping from it, which has caused me to leave it out of my work. I did not want to include it. I did not want life made heavy, ugly. It was a choice, a deliberate choice.

In my life the human has been exceedingly present. In the airplane, flying towards Rupert, I see vividly not only what is beautiful in him—his eyes, features, body—but even more often his hands, which are not beautiful. They touch me, even from afar. He handles them in a particular way, roughly and firmly. They are strong. He does strong and deft work with them. Yet at rest, they have a tender expression. No one would imagine them to be a musician's hands. He adds to their ruggedness by treating them badly—cuts and burns.

This year, after meteoric expeditions, I have come closer to the earth. I want to concentrate on the physical detail.

Ne touchant à la terre que par le sexe! [Not touching the earth except by sex!] I wrote this during my surrealist period.

I was proud of my handiwork in Hugo's home. I left the house beautiful, orderly. For two days I struggled with wall washers and rug cleaners, emptying each room and refilling it. Hugo's room is always, as Millicent said, like that of the Collyer Brothers. Two days after we fixed it up, it returned to the same look. Why do objects take the expression of our character? Why do Hugo's shoes lie each one pointing in a different direction? Why is he surrounded by used, empty envelopes, used pipe cleaners, old newspapers and yellowed clippings?

Sierra Madre, December, 1955

Christmas in Hollywood...Anne Baxter was a successful movie star with all that a movie star is privileged to enjoy. But like all of us, she was cursed with a family. This family left her in Hollywood at seventeen to fend for herself. She did. The family spent the rest of the time stunting her and passing judgment on her. Finally, when the husband she divorced died (John Hodiak), the accumulated guilt the family created came to a crisis. On Christmas Day she decided to atone. She would give a big family dinner. She would get her grandmother of eighty, who has been senile in a hospital for five years (the mother of Lloyd Wright and many other Wrights), and who was brought on a stretcher and sat on a wheelchair. The house, luxurious, full of outsized presents for her little girl, giant glass candy containers as in the fairytales, a butler, a cook, millions of candles, superb food, and all the family around, all disliking each other deep down, one quarrel almost erupting because of the martinis, and then Anne, not content with this, opened a bottle of champagne and popped the cork into her eye. Great pain. A bandage. A doctor. But on with the show. The family show. "Grandmother, do eat some turkey." "Rupert, sing us a song on your guitar." "Here comes the minced ice cream mixture to be burnt à la Cossack"...served flaming blue. "Anaïs, take those obis" (two long beautiful Japanese brocade bands the Japanese women wear around their waist). "Oh, the beautiful Japanese writing paper. I must have a lot of it. Can you order more for me? I want to put my crest on it." She is thirty or so, slender and delicate, but she has a lusty Tallulah Bankhead voice, with fair hair, and a flexible waist, and humorous rather than sentimental eyes... The family, like all families, proud of her fame, but moralizing... "Hodiak was such a fine man"...and her man of the moment is impossible (he was not allowed at the party). The daughter was spoiled and interrupted Rupert's singing, which caused the grandmother to awaken from her stupor and menace the little girl with lightning-like angry gestures.

(George Bernard Shaw was right. The family is an artificial bondage. It is false and meaningless. Why do people continue to pay tribute to it...to feed its jaws, submit to its verdicts... In friendship, at least, there is sincerity and selection.)

So Anne got what she needed, absolution from Helen and Lloyd, a blessing for her charity, she paid the ambulance, she made her contribution to the petty and non-understanding gods of the family, she injured her eye (probably at that moment she was inwardly cursing them all), and the two most beautiful young men in the world, Eric and Rupert, were there in bondage and consequently less strong, less integrated, more childish because of it.

"Goodbye...goodbye. It was a beautiful party, a beautiful party. You are generous and kind to do this. Grandmother was very happy." (Not at all, she was humiliated, and probably more aware of how far she was from living, how close to death...)

Sierra Madre, January 1956

The other day I went alone to see Paul and Renate. There is always inside Renate this high-voltage motor that propels her exterior. Her face grimaces with intensity. She moves her entire body as she talks, and there are no breaks.

Paul always looks like a man who has seen the midnight sun, the look of a blond angel who has just come from a black mass. The Black Suns do not tan him. He smiles innocently, although one is certain he has undressed the angels and the choirboys, and made love to them. He never leaves out the sexual baton from his drawings or paintings, nor does he leave out the extreme pleasure he has in looking at his own body in the mirror, on the canvas, on the drawing paper. He has the small smile of Pan, and the predilection for pale blues and pinks and gold of the Christmas tree decorations, and the decoration of homes meant for blue-iced adolescents not yet determined, but not for savage primitives, lusty or fierce women such as Anna Magnani. All embellishment with paper and print is a coat of innocence. *Le joli. Le bonbon.* Butterflies and birds. Sugar and no marrow. I have only seen him angry and fierce when Renate, who cannot bear souls like secret Japanese boxes one fumbles to open and can only open with patience and gradually with a feeling there is always one part of the box that remains inaccessible, violates this box, tears it open and destroys it. Paul, who knows what she finds each time is a pagan animal with the face of an angel, says: "You know, what I give to others is nothing that is taken away from you, nothing that belongs to our relationship." But Renate feels that this sexual angel is the monster who will destroy her. It is the monster who leaves her alone in her house at Malibu, who leaves in their only car so that she has no time, no warning and no transportation to retaliate against his pagan unfaithfulness with a Christian attempt at unfaithfulness, one without pleasure. Only the pagan can enjoy his sensual life as one enjoys fruit.

Renate looks anguished, her sea-petal eyes afloat on a dubious pond, unable to float to the sea, to the turmoil of waves, feeding on a static water with a surface of fears...and when will Paul emerge from his airy houses and bend over her to console her? How can he console her for not being pagan? Consolation is a Christian act, and Paul's only Christian act is that he likes Pan dressed in choirboys' suits with wings, incense, flowers to eat, and angels.

Paul exploits his unconscious, producing an artificial product. But that is no reason for feeling that all adornment, all improvisations are artifice. Paul prefers to call on magic, to use costumes and ritual, to study mythology. While I visit, we have to delve within for our mythology and archaeology and rituals. For example, why crown Rupert's newfound dreaming self with the same laurels used for Caesar?

Renate's painting is the largest in the room. It faces us as we sit around the table. At the end of the afternoon, it is a luminous naked woman reclining beside a giant cat sitting on his haunches. The face of the cat and the face of the woman are the same size. The eyes of the cat are larger than the woman's. The cat holds all the dark power of the night, also of vision into the night. The woman holds all the light of the flesh. They are the Beauty and the Beast, after a long marriage from which they both emerged equally beautiful. But later, when it grows dark, it was the body of the woman that began to shine with all the phosphorescence of the animal, and the cat disappeared into the darkness, and one could only see his eyes. She has absorbed the beast and turned it into lighted flesh, but the beast still had the vision of the alchemy.

Now Rupert has had a shock. The Forest Service wants us to move out of Sierra Madre and go and live one hour up the mountain, 4,000 feet up in cold and solitude—two hours away from music, friends and movies. The Forest Service believes in moving the men around. And the man who wants our place, Nichols, has three children who must be near a school. Rupert is immediately disturbed, distressed. He uses my health as a defense: I cannot live in the altitude. Fortunately, the Sierra Madre doctor is the one who believes I have rheumatic fever and a handicapped heart.

This forced me out of a month-long unconquerable and incurable depression in which I float at the bottom of the unconscious ocean where there is no light, and no luminous fish either!

So I floated up to Rupert.

Letter from Anaïs Nin to Jim Herlihy:
Sierra Madre, January 1956

Dear Jim:

Here is a report on Christmas...confidential. Movie stars live in terror of adverse publicity... New Year's Eve was better. Renate was hostessing at Holiday House, which is run by Dudley Murphy, once a filmmaker (*Ballet Mécanique* with Léger and *Emperor Jones*). A modern place overlooking the sea. I was given a royal welcome because of the books, and we were treated with large bottles of champagne. I danced a great deal, kissed strangers for New Year's by proxy, intending to kiss you and Dick.

A clear day... Usually they shatter into a thousand pieces. Have you noticed that some people (particularly the kind I am twice married to, who fuss, fret and fume) can make shredded wheat out of the days? They lack some catalyst that makes the day whole, abstract and free of small irritants... But I have peace this afternoon. Hugo is still in Cuba and will be there until January 8, but as he talks of going to Cuba again I may not return till the end of January, which will give me a month to finish *Solar Barque* for the English publisher who has asked for something new...

Hugo did give me a big present of money, which I put in a savings bank, but which I feel is not my own somehow...you know why. Because in myself I have made the break. So I am not touching it. *Bells of Atlantis* was shown in Cuba, with success. And in Brazil. I did not finish the 1955 Diary properly. I love to wind it up, as in a work of art. To point out the climax and to make prophecies... But voilà.

Do you have the feeling that the Diary is a finished work and does not need reediting or filling in? When I feel my time growing short, I wonder...

We will try to see Dick's show at a neighbor's who has TV. But TV reception here is bad because of Mount Wilson. We are right *under* the station. Just miss it.

For our underground experience: please remember that a new carbon paper will take a very clear imprint of all you write and can be easily read by being held against the light!

Love,
Anaïs

Sierra Madre, January 1956

A long distance call for Rupert. It is a friend calling: "Reginald is very ill. Can you come to see him?"

So we drove out, on Thursday, one of our two free days. We drove to Riverside. We drove to a hotel so typical of the hotels Reginald chooses—we could easily single them out in any city. They are the hotels for hobos, derelicts, the homeless, the old. They are hotels one step away from rest homes. He never stays long at people's homes. He gets restless when he is comfortable. His home is in such hotels. They are not chosen to harmonize with his old age pension, because we give him whatever he needs above this. It is his setting as well as that of his illnesses. He refuses to wear the good suits Rupert gives him. He has a theatrical integrity. The drama of *look at my wounds* requires such a setting, and such costumes. The hotel looks like a tall wall in a lightless, sunless city. A skylight sheds a diminishing light four floors through a shaft stairway. Frosted glass windows are all you see as you ascend in a caged elevator. Rugs are mended, patched with unmatched rug fragments. In the rooms, the beds are copper, the lights are bulbs on a wire, there is a washstand, a cracked mirror, a torn black window shade. When we arrive at one o'clock the black shade is down. Reginald is scarcely breathing. He is holding on to the copper bedrail as if he were a paralytic and this were the only way to pull himself into a sitting position. Every space in the room—window sill, dressing table, washbowl, shelf, chairs—is covered with medicines, milk bottles, cans of food, as well as empty medicine bottles, empty milk cartons, empty cans. He has energy to visit people, and to talk, but none to throw away an empty can. When his energy is low he takes a shot of insulin. When he can't sleep he takes sleeping pills. He wears cracked eyeglasses, which need to be cleaned. He urinates in cans and milk bottles when the bathroom is a few steps away. His cartons of dirty clothes, soiled letters, torn books are on the floor.

He wants Rupert to repair his truss for a hernia because it hurts him. We are not sure that he has a hernia. Friends, older and weaker than he, fetch his food.

I raise the black window shade and let the sun in. I begin to throw away empty cans and bottles. I feel if I throw away some of the dead objects he is surrounded with I will be throwing away a little of the death and decay that has already disintegrated so much of Reginald.

The presence of Rupert there is difficult to believe. But there is a relationship, and Reginald looks like a very sick, decayed, grey shadow of the radiant Rupert, who brings home old blankets and old rugs people throw away in the canyons.

Reginald is the reason why Rupert hates doctors and medicines. He is also the reason why Rupert chose a rugged profession, to overcome a weak chest.

Rupert is fixing the truss. I have emptied the room of three scrap baskets.

We will not be civilized until such lives are not maintained and sustained by sentimental doctors. The desire and fear of death that incites a human being to kill himself slowly and involve other human beings in a progressive, gradual decay should be recognized, and his death should be accelerated rather than protracted. He should be put out of his misery and the misery he causes. He is reaching the age of 70 and has no moments of happiness.

I do not feel pity for Reginald. I do for Rupert, who is always depressed by this spectacle and frustrated in his desire to change his father's life. When we leave him alone to live out his restlessness, to exhaust the friendships offered him, then people call us as if we were neglectful—for every new person repeats the feeling of compassion for Reginald, seeking to help him, failing, and then being horrified by what he demands. Look at my wounds. Stay with me at the bedside of this suicide by shabbiness. Share these repulsive foods. Wash my clothes.

How little people know—as little as I knew when I met Helba—that his gradual suicide is impossible to reverse.

The empty cans and bottles I threw away were only my own small personal victory against dead objects, but none over Reginald's Tomb of Tutankhamen. If the outer signs all depict our interior landscape, then Reginald is already decomposed inwardly and we are visiting the dead.

These years in Sierra Madre, with relationships based entirely on human values, proved to me that the simple human life as laid out by uncreative human beings is impossible for creative people, because it is narrow, monstrous, not deep. My relationship to the Campion family is purely human, affectionate, interdependent, devoted. We are able to laugh together for an evening, to share troubles, to be kind to one another. (Pam's mother said I was the kindest women she had ever known.)

But it is not enough. I get desperately restless.

Unfortunately, Rupert is such a human being. He can be content with mediocre people. He belongs in a purely human world. His qualities as a human being touch me, but I am bored with the people he likes, bored with the music that does not get better and does not vary or seek change or renewal. He has the proper static quality necessary to "human" life. The only poetry in our life is his beauty.

Have I time yet to meet the artist I want to marry? Am I imprisoned forever in human life because I myself am basically human?

Renate and Paul discuss this before me. It is their drama. Renate is a human being, primarily, with artistic gifts and intelligence. But Paul is both a human being and a dreamer.

The dreamer is going to dream his mythological life whether they betray human values or not (as I did). The mythological personage commits non-human acts (as I did). We sit at the Café de Paris while Rupert plays music with Lloyd. And Paul and Renate lacerate each other. His blond, angelic face with blue eyes can look absolutely inhuman. Hers is warm, unstable, distressed and in pain. He says to Renate severely: "You insisted on entering a world that was locked to you. You crashed through. And now what you found hurts you. And it's only your insecurity that hurts you. *I have never given anyone else what belongs to you.*"

Renate does not see this. She only feels, blindly, and wholly, what she calls the *agonía* of Paul's body given to another. (In her faulty Viennese English she uses *agonía* instead of agony, and I don't know why it sounds more terrible. It brings images of torture, of Christ's crucifixion. In English, agony does not exist, truly, except as a prelude to death. Emotion does not reach such proportions. In Spanish, it implies all the slow torture of jealousy.)

I feel for both. I am both. If the Diary is still a secret, it is because I have to protect human beings from the terrors of mythology, or what happens when you live with *all* of yourself, *all* your dreams, *all* you contain.

This door Renate forced open revealed Paul's multiple lives. She could not close her eyes.

With Bogner's help now, I have fully accepted the multiple Ruperts, among which there is a seventeen-year-old boy who feels related to younger girls, a very commonplace Rupert who could sleep with Hazel McKinley or Paulette Goddard.

It all lies outside me. I have been so much less jealous. It proves that non-jealousy can be achieved. Unfortunately, to achieve it, I have also had to draw upon the help of hatred. When Rupert flirts with mediocrity or banality or superficiality, I look upon his nakedness and hate it, like something that exposes its mediocrity or banality. He ceases to be desirable or beautiful. Now, it may be that what a lover most hates in the other's promiscuities is the very revelation of a minor self, a self that is less than one's dream, one's passionately designed great love. Rupert diminishes himself in my eyes. In jealousy there may be this struggle to maintain a fervent integrity between the idealized lover and one's idolatry—to exclude the *proof* that there exists another Rupert, unrelated to me, who is mediocre and can desire or admire mediocrity. It is similar to when I hated Alfred Perlès—I should have known that he was revealing to me, against my will, a minor, clownish Henry who was blind to the fact that I did not want to see this distortion because it threatened the scale, stature and dimension of my relationship with Henry.

This jealousy is not only an effort to keep a love all for one's self, but to keep the unity of the lover's image that is caught in the dream, and to prevent reality from corroding this image. It is the minor Rupert who threatens my relationship with the ideal Rupert, as it was the destructive Gonzalo mirrored in Helba whom I hated in her. Jealousy can be annihilated only by the recognition of the Ruperts who are foreign to me, by allowing those Ruperts to exist, by not fighting their manifestations, because they only destroy the relationship when there is war between them. It was the war between Gonzalo's destructive self and me that separated us—not its existence personified in Helba.

It is not a one-dimensional young girl who will deprive me of Rupert, but a one-dimensional Rupert who will lapse from the deeper relationship—naturally. The beauty of a relationship based on a disparity of age is that youth abolishes the twilight and conceals and retards the reign of death. The tragedy is that I, who have discovered my identity by painstaking efforts, live with someone who has not, who is still in a state of flux, shadow imitations and negative rebellion. Rupert's maturity lies somewhere between his imitations of Lloyd's tantrums and door-slamming autocracies, and Reginald's passivity. I see his face glistening, wet from tears shed at the Spanish dancing of Antonis. And then I hear him harshly shouting in the flattest and most nasal of Western voices: "Goddamn it, why did you put all the newspapers in the garage? I need one to light the fire for the meat!"

Maturity is first the shedding of what you are not, and then the balancing of what you are in relation to the human beings you love.

New York, February 1956

Came back to find Hugo in great spirits. He has been given a drug for anxiety. He enjoys his business, his evenings with clients, his occasional evenings of pleasure. His depression has lifted. This makes me very happy. He treats me with tenderness and the homosexual's way of expressing physical closeness. He tells me I'm beautiful, he embraces me, he bites my shoulder, but he does not take me. It is what I wanted. Did it happen because he felt I did not want him? Did analysis free him of desiring a woman who does not desire him? Here, my depression takes place at bedtime. A day that does not unite me with Rupert. In Sierra Madre the depression (or rebellion, which is worse) comes when I feel trapped in a net of mediocre living. But the most frightening experience has been that of disorganization in my thinking and writing.

I reread *Solar Barque* as if someone else wrote it. I forget what I have written. Jim commented on this. Is it the strain? Such a dual life is an enormous strain. From the smallest detail to the largest emotional crisis. To remember to remove the drugstore label on my vitamins, which is marked Mrs. Guiler, and to remember to remove the labels on my medicine labeled Mrs. Pole—to the large conflict I feel each time I leave Rupert.

Hugo is his own sweet, tender self again—as he was before the eight years of anger and rebellion—but naturally so, not forced. And above all, he has a life of his own, separate and not dependent on me. He can enjoy his life when I am not there.

In this I achieved my wish: to leave Hugo only when he is happy and self-sufficient.

We don't quarrel. We enjoy the movies, plays, talking together.

Yesterday Bogner telephoned me that I could come at 12:15. Was it because I was going to see her that I am able to pull myself together and write three good pages? Yesterday I pulled myself together by force. I wrote letters, wrote pages on the hitchhiker Fred, whom I called "Christmas."

After Bogner: The primitives were so wise when they enacted rituals of possession by the dead. It proves they *knew* it happened, and they knew *when* it happened. And they also could prepare rituals of dispossession. The same thing takes place in us, in the so-called civilized man—but as it is not externalized (we have a ritual for burying the dead and then we believe that the relationship is over); we are not aware of the time and place when they re-enter our being and occupy our souls. I did not experience my mother's death completely when it happened. I suffered a natural, human, physical pain, a natural sorrow. But it was only a year later that I developed a heart illness (she died of heart failure) and prepared to die as she had, to die with her, and also took on her negative traits of irritability and rebellion. I took on the traits I hated and suffered from, and her illness. (I could have taken on her cheerfulness and courage, but if I had it would have added to my sorrow at her loss.)

It is a natural, common mechanism, said Bogner. And I understood also how the feeling of disorganization, of inner breakdown, was also born of that "possession." It may have had its inception in my Florence Nightingale period—the nursing of Rupert in Acapulco, then the intermittent care of Reginald gave nascence to the identification with my mother and her other traits, her nursing, care, rebellion, anger, disorganization. Thus we do live by a sequence of associative moods and feelings. And it is necessary to separate them from our "unpossessed" self—a self free of intrusions of others, of amalgamations with others.

That is why I have been so ashamed these two months, not of myself, but of the aspects of my mother I did not like, together with the aspects I once did like and felt deprived of: her nursing.

Proust had a great deal to say about possession by the dead, but nothing about the act of dispossession, which is the role of the analyst.

I wonder how the primitives were able to time these crises so mathematically (this is the age of puberty, this of marriage, this is the time for the ceremony to chase away the haunting of the dead) because all these are individual rhythms and have no relation to calendric time. The spirit of my mother imbedded in her sewing machine and her gold thimble did not make me love housework. It may have been that my mother's irritation was due to her rebellion against the supremacy of her mother role, and what I identified with was a deeper truth. I had never consciously seen a mother who did not want to be a mother all the time, who at one time had wanted to be a singer.

Because of one of the new drugs, Hugo sleeps through the night, has more energy, and is in good spirits. We go out every evening, either with clients or by ourselves. The expression of pleasure on his face, of elation, is not due to bringing home more than $800 a month, but to the fact that all day at the office they have been telephoning Budapest and London as go-betweens for the sale of the Bank of Monaco so that Grace Kelly's father will not gain control of it! The fantasy of Big Business and the possibility of making a great deal of money excites him. I now understand that these delusions, illusions and mirages are similar to those of the world of love if you are a lover of wealth. I respect Hugo's pleasure because now it is acknowledged as pleasure, whereas before it was seemingly the cause of his anxiety.

I ask, "Can I buy new towels? Can I buy handkerchiefs for you, and new table mats?"

"Wait a little while. Any day now…if this thing goes through. Last month we made $10,000 in commissions."

"Where is it?" I ask playfully.

"We had expenses. We have $3,000 left, to be split between Claude and myself, but we decided to leave it in the account as a guarantee for when the firm no longer gives us a salary."

And then he talks about a trip to Europe and adds: "People say now that for two people to go to Europe you really need $5,000."

Of course, I may say that in the world of love I also showed more anxiety than pleasure, but it was a world of deep enrichment and the profit of a treasure house of memories. If wealth takes your whole life like *one* difficult mistress and grants you wishes only when you are old, she is certainly more often a cheat than the lover who always leaves her wealth within you. And anyway, the sale of the Bank of Monaco is certainly not as beautiful as Rupert.

We have decided to enjoy what we have.

I wrote to Frances Field about what I found in volume 68. It may be that the world is like a parent who cannot believe his little son could possibly be one day a great statesman, a general, a president or a famous playwright. When I think of Frances as I once knew her—familiar, self-disparaging, sustained by me and analysis, bewildered or submerged in housework—the possibility that she could be as good a painter as my great love Paul Klee never occurred to me. It may occur to someone who does not know her.

When I met Marguerite Young, who looked like the most unwashed and disheveled of Village lesbians, I turned away from her diarrhea of talk and never imagined she was writing a remarkable book of which fragments have appeared in *New Writing*. Marguerite settled all problems with the public by establishing that her mother was mad, and then she was able to install herself and expose all the vagaries and fantasies… Labeled as madness, the wild animals born of fantasy are like the animals in the zoo. There is a cage between these rare specimens and the spectator. My mistake, in public relations, was to disregard the cage.

I write on the bus, on my way to Jacobson, on my way to Bogner, on my way to see Frances's new batch of paintings.

The expression Hugo has when contemplating the sale of the Bank of Monaco is the same one Max Jacobson has when he has cured someone, when I say I feel better. The greatest pride and delight appear in his eyes and he is illumined by it; he has once again triumphed over death.

Eyes have a definite landscape. Renate's evoke the sea. They are marine eyes. One is aware of their motion—of the flickering dots of light, of their seascape animation. Paul's eyes are born of icicles upon which a blue sun is reflected. The icicles formed as stalactites. The drops of tears were cold. They do not melt. They are mineral. In Rupert's eyes the green and gold are warm. They sparkle. They melt. They are Venetian eyes, canals of reflections, and the gold moves in them. They do not move so much from left to right, but remain lighted like nightscapes on the water. Then there are the earth eyes. They are without horizons or depth. They have all the browns of the earth the sepias of animals, of the forest. The brown of fox eyes, doe eyes. Black eyes are coals from the mines. They catch fire. They smolder. They burn. Then there are the neon-lit eyes—toneless. A bulb, a wire, a current, that is all. Mazda eyes.

I read Huxley's *Heaven and Hell*. What we called the mystic or the artist was actually the one who, through art or some departure from the conscious mind, achieved what he calls the antipodes by genius, by hunger, by madness, or by ritual. He left out psychoanalysis.

From Jim's diary:
> Anaïs's diary is having a powerful effect; her power to breathe life, through writing, into even the most difficult periods of her neurosis. I cannot help but be inspired by this, and strengthened: the spectacle of beauty from ashes, the phoenix rising from the flames; something surreally fundamental, the great indefatigable phallus, which is life, life, life, drawing one through the thickness and the mud, giving one survival power against the death rays everywhere. Anaïs, who, at this very moment, is in bed with bronchitis, suffering from low energy, is the strongest woman alive. If at times there are manifestations of weakness, it is only because her sensibilities are greater. She needs desperately all of the staying power and resilience, which she definitely possesses, because she enjoys the curse and the privilege of a kind of sainthood—sainthood being the name for high sensitivity and awareness and an inhuman or rather superhuman sort of vision. Laugh loud, weep deeply… I

want to protect Anaïs from pain. Impossible. It was my first feeling, my first response to Anaïs in 1947: I want her not to be hurt…

Copying this from Jim's diary, and reading about his moods, struggles with writing, dreams, refurnished the loneliness and bareness of my writing world.

Working blindly on *Solar Barque*, and without the impetuous fire that once fed me, I pushed the words out like volcanic eruptions. I felt I had been doing listless, lifeless writing. And perhaps it is true.

This is the longest period I have had of low energy and depression. Two months, almost continuously grey.

The first few days with Hugo only confirm the abstract friendship our marriage has reached.

He came to my bed early in the morning, took off his pajamas, and fell asleep against me. But nowhere, nowhere will he face the truth, grasp it, discuss it. His whole nature is evasive, non-committal…and I can see why analysis is taking so long. All his statements are vague. And when I present a feeling I have, he acts as if he has not heard me. He makes no comment. It is what I call his absence.

I was writing this in Bogner's waiting room. Then I took up with her the "certainty and definiteness of my decision to act…" and the fact that her statement before I left in December had again arrested me: "You are arranging reality again in terms of what you wish. You wish to think Hugo feels as you do. It would be more convenient for you. The truth is that *you* have doubts."

"No, I do not. I only have doubts about Hugo's state. None about how I feel. In fact, when I first came to you years ago, it was not doubt about how I felt, but guilt and the inability to cope with this guilt. This guilt has diminished considerably, as I gradually discovered Hugo's own perversities and his share of responsibility in what happened to our relationship. When will I ever know how Hugo feels, if you keep saying I distort reality, that my mechanism is to 'arrange' facts to suit what I want?"

I know she can't make a direct statement, but I want her to admit I am closer to reality, able to make a choice and abide by it.

She seemed severe and difficult. Questioned every word I said. If I said "analysis," she said it was not analysis because it had been interrupted and haphazard. If I said I didn't want a direct statement but certainly an assurance that I was seeing facts clearly, she said: "You are not." But then she shocked me by saying: "The only direct statement I can make is that if it is Hugo you are worried about, Hugo will *never* be ready to cope with your leaving."

"Never?"

"Never."

This was a deep shock, because it was like a condemnation to live in this duality forever.

"Why are you disturbed when I say you are still distorting reality?"

"Because that is like being told you are still sick and have to stay in a sanitarium another year. *And I don't have much time!*"

Has my destructiveness towards Hugo been an effort to lessen his stranglehold on me, to kill his clinging to me?

When I tell him what the doctor in Sierra Madre said, that the damaged heart will only get more troublesome as I get older, he weeps. My reaction all day is how can I leave such a tender, loving man?

We talk like friends over dinner. I try to tell Hugo the curious experience I have about dimensions—like an abstract painting—of one Hugo I can see, and a rarely visible one who exists, but which I only infer, mostly through others' eyes. I hear about the parties he goes to, the nightlife in Cuba, etc. I heard about his affair with Faith, in which he showed such intensity that it frightened the white-blooded American girl. Obliquely, this portrait is slowly accrued, filled in. But it is like the other side of the moon. Neither one of us can bring this into the marriage.

New York, February 7, 1956

Sunday, after the type of trivial quarrel that always becomes bitter, I finally had to take the initiative and make Hugo admit he is not happy. A part of the truth was unveiled. We did not give each other what we both wanted—closeness—and with this lacking, we became destructive towards each other. Hugo cannot and never has accepted my trips. They have made him sullen and withdrawn. He admitted the first break took place far back when, because of a raise in salary, he decided to go and live in London when I wanted to stay in Paris where life had fully opened up for me. He said, "I was always too practical, and this, as far as you are concerned, was a mistake." I tried to tell him: "Our marriage is dead. I went to analysis hoping to restore it. It hasn't happened."

"Above all," I begged, "let us not blame each other or ourselves. What happened was, for the greater part, neurotic on both sides. Your depression and lack of vital contact destroyed me."

What has not died is the pain it causes us to definitely part. I wept. Hugo wept too. We felt shattered and shocked.

"Go away for a year. And let us see what happens," said Hugo.

"But you must try to find someone you can be close to."

I admitted being the first one to cause hurt, with John Erskine, but who is to say what caused my desire? After six years of marriage, Hugo seemed grey and lifeless, at thirty-two! Erskine seemed vital.

I refused to turn back and delved again into the causes. We had genuine pain—a fraternal pain.

"I don't want a separation that will leave bitterness and anger," I said.

We were both quiet and very unhappy. I told him the quarrels were a way of having a relationship, and also an indirect way of expressing resentment at our frustration.

After nine years of analysis, he is no nearer the truth. I had to bring it out. A terrible role to have to play alone. But once I took the first step, he did admit he was not happy.

A terrible Sunday. When our marriage died it is as if we both died for each other. It hurts.

He wanted to destroy his engravings on the wall because, he said, "I became an artist to get close to you and it didn't work!" Like his destruction of his beloved kite as a child.

He knows now that he gave me *things* (dresses, cologne, etc.) as a substitute for real, whole *feelings*. His love was mixed with so much destructiveness.

A part of the truth, without Bogner's help this time…I had to decide alone that I could no longer bear to see Hugo's life empty, or bear his retaliation for my "desertions." I can never be faithful to Hugo. I can to Rupert. Bogner implies I am going towards an uncertain future. But what do I care, at 52…where is my *future?* Rupert's love will end in a few years. But I have had it for nine years. If only Hugo could have this for a few years… What appalling loneliness.

Hugo always receives the truth as a series of traumatic shocks, never as a direct, frontal encounter with life itself. He has built a fortress *not* to confront truth. His smoke screen was *impenetrable. It also shut out life.* The rigidity is so great that it makes him cling to the past, to stagnant unfulfillment, to debris, to anything rather than the flow and changes of life and feeling. He can exist in this neutrality, in this twilight, as he can exist in his curtained, darkened bedroom. There is in his soul the same stagnation and murkiness that he creates outwardly.

He was saying: "I suffer more because it comes as a shock to me. I can see you have been more aware of the deficiencies of the marriage."

"Well, I took my suffering over a longer period of time, as anyone who is aware and cannot delude himself. Awareness is a long-term suffering, Yours is that of continuous blindness and sudden lucidities."

"There hasn't been enough love…"

"Or too much neurosis. I prefer to think the destructive element was the neurosis."

His pain hurt me so much. I was ready to yield again. But he has cornered me into this, by rejecting the trip that was my only solution against total separation. I felt as if instead of helping him to make another life, to have other relationships during my absence, I merely left him lonely and hurt him each time. I can't bear this anymore. I can't bear the guilt over my life with Rupert.

It is so strange that our relationship began with Hugo saying: "I do not love you enough."

I thought the kindest thing was not to mention Rupert. When Hugo said: "You are too much of an individual to be married," I wanted to say: "But I *can* be married, I *can* be close to someone." But I wonder if I did mention Rupert whether it would help him to throw the blame on a rival instead of on ourselves and the unhappy chemistry of our temperaments. I wanted this separation to be *human.* I kept repeating: "We are two human beings in trouble. We must help each other. We must not crush each other with guilt."

Image-making…fantasy-making. We both contributed to this abstract relationship.

I can't work or forget or rest. I don't know why—I keep thinking of something that happened in the public library at 42st St., the painful experience I had walking down to the manuscript room. It was locked. And not only was it locked, it was a heavy iron-grilled door, like that of a prison. It was more terrible to me, this burying of manuscripts, than the burial of a body, which is necessary. Perhaps because I had been tormented by the ethical problem of the Diary—destroying it for the sake of human beings, or keeping it because it has a value for human beings.

I got my life from books, so I would be killing a life-giving thing to save Hugo from the truth. But who saved *me* from the truth? Henry Miller never spared me, and opened his whole self and life. So did Gonzalo.

The world needs truth, no matter how painful, because when people bury the truth it festers.

Bogner's implication was that I don't see reality. And she quibbled over the word "analysis" or the length of time I was in it, *to prove to me* that I "arranged" the facts. I was saying that I went to analysis to repair my relationship with Hugo or to free myself of it, and to free him of it.

The grilled, locked room of the manuscripts in the public library is also the tomb in which we lock the truth.

"Now," said Hugo, "you can go and live out all these fantasies you wrote about. You can go and live as you write," proving how wrong he is about what I want, which is closeness. And how he misunderstood what I wrote about, that passion was an illusion of closeness.

New York, February 10, 1956

I finally unraveled what I called Hugo's jiu-jitsu—the negativism or passivity that made me hurl myself against a void. *He was not there.* He was playing ostrich. That is how we progressively arrived at a non-relationship. He only came out of his cave to quarrel. And quarrels were the only moments of life.

We had a totally opposite attitude towards reality. I went forward to meet its blows and prepared myself for them by awareness, such as thinking every day Rupert will love a younger woman. Hugo's defense was to lock the door and live in a fortress. He took only the blows, and every time I hurt him he withdrew. He was sullen, sulking. He died. But he did not take the good, the good I have to give—the aliveness. He had no existence of his own, no soul of his own. He fed on me. I even had to unbury the artist in him, which he quickly buried again.

I got hurt a million times more than he...but I went on living. My cure was awareness, more living to cure myself, more loves. I healed myself like a homeopath, by the same passion that killed me. More love, more passion.

The agony of the weekend was our act born of intolerable conflict. When I realized my trips and Hugo's life in between did bring us closer but at the same time increased the distance—because Hugo's withdrawals increased to the point of no longer being able to make love and because of my guilt for inflicting loneliness on him—I had to expose this. For Hugo it was a "shock." And nothing else. For me it was one step closer to the truth. He has denied suffering from the trips. All his life he has denied what he feels. That was why I was always confused between the tolerant Hugo who conceded, understood, and the sullen, angry Hugo bent on subtle "reprisals."

New York, February 1956

Jim and I were talking about the people who used to see us alone, intimately, but who make us feel they are taking us into their wombs. "Some wombs are more alive than others." Lila Rosenblum: first were the dramatics of neurosis, alcoholism and bohemianism, but from this she passed into neutrality. No neurosis, no alcoholism, no bohemianism, but no life. When she saw us recently (before, it was phone calls after taking too many sleeping pills, S.O.S. and rescue), it was to present a case history. "I am better, but I have ulcers, and I still fall in love with women who do not want me." The cave is grey. The death bed. I hope I have the courage to die alone, not to drag others into the caves to hold my hand. Particularly if you decide to die continuously, or to be dead in life, you should not expect company. If you are going to bury yourself alive—and plenty of people do—you should not demand the companionship of the living.

Hugo, who always lives in a climate evenly low and evenly depressed, when faced with a sorrow, drowns. I weep—die—and am reborn. Even through our earthquake this weekend I persisted in keeping the house alive and warm, persisted in staying alive.

When Hugo says "I died in London," there does not seem so much difference between his death in London and his low, flat spirits with which he lived in Paris.

He says, "I enjoy business," but I have never heard him talk about business with delight, humor, or nonchalance.

C'est toujours la messe basse sans musique. [It is always the low Mass without music.]

Couldn't some woman's passion warm him into life? Hugo laughs bitterly because I don't know the "law"—the law won't allow this.

Jim laments absence of enchantment, but American life itself is without enchantment. The Practical is Supreme. He states it only exists in art. He finds people empty.

We discuss Stanley Haggart, who opened a nightclub for Norma, a friend, and gave her dresses, who gave Jim furniture and much help in decorating. Was he doing all this to enhance his life, out of love? But in each case (Jim, Norma, and me) he has been subtly destructive...as when he told me the details of Hugo's affair with Faith, the dancer.

We excused Stanley when he was unhappy with Woody Parrish. Now he has Tom, who is gifted, young, handsome. But he still chips away at those he loves.

When I first met Stanley, he was utterly commonplace. He analyzed handwriting as a way to connect with people. It was intuition on a level of a machine that tells you your weight and fate for a penny.

Woody would grimace at every banality. Stanley was not creative but ingenious, clever at effects. Motherly. When he and Woody separated, Stanley became "original," adopted Dadaist and surrealist games with décor, became lighter, and the strangeness and obscurity of Woody became the style of Stanley. But no single element was original. He was a clever borrower, a deft imitator, a skillful assembler of others' ideas. I used to amuse myself finding the "origin" of his ideas. He would point to the flat plywood couches on four iron legs. They were Sasha Hammid's idea. Several matches in a bowl were his "signature," he said once. And people talk about the ego of the creative artist!

When they were poor I admired their ingenuities—but they were Woody's camouflages. Today he is not poor.

One day he confessed he had been born in Sierra Madre, and then the image was clear. A handsome young man, well-fed, such as they raise there, good physical specimen, six feet tall—then a model in New York, a man's body and female domesticity, but made a nest for delinquents, for children so he could feel mature. Strange how this negative aspect (sharp, sour, petty, little denigrations) only appeared when Woody left, who once did all the satirical demolition work.

Woody talked such esoteric Dadaism then, to counteract Stanley's prosaicism. I wonder now if, without Stanley, he talks plain, unadorned English.

Peggy Glanville-Hicks is in trouble, facing a painful operation, so a human relationship is established, whereas previously the sparks and fusing of intelligence and the mythological roles short-circuited this. By an effort to eliminate the trite, the earthy, the homely, you eliminate all traces of the sick animals we are. So now Peggy is a sick animal. Afraid. Alone.

"Thanks for extending a lifeline," she said, in her brusque, short manner of speech.

I comforted, consoled. "If you prefer to stay in your corner, as you say, I can come over and attend to your needs." (She lives four doors away.)

She once said: "Everything I reach for seems to move away." She loved the unattainable Paul Bowles.

Yet she gives the impression of a hummingbird—violently vibrating and never touching the branch. One does not dare reach towards a hummingbird. You feel its insistence on the little bit of space. But now Peggy is ill. We cease to be mythological personages. Once she said of me: "You are so devilishly vital and yet so devilishly elusive!"

The mythological personage protects a frightened human being. It is the tournament armor.

Peggy was frightened of the hospital, but she continued to predicate and assert art values. There have always been folk art and classical art. They cross-fertilize, but they should not be confused. America thinks all art can be folk art—and it cannot. They are succeeding in destroying art. And leadership. They will soon have masses of uneducated people.

And I hated America with a hatred so great, so magnificent, that it is the equivalent of a great love. It is such an absolute, unmitigated hatred. I curse it. I wish it were destroyed. It has released upon the world the greatest flood of vulgarity. And the hostility contained within it—power—will someday explode and seek to destroy the rest of the world. America is destructive. Because it is not creative. It can't create, and so it will destroy. Because if Europe exploited the people and kept them poor, America has committed a greater crime: it enriches them but exploits their ignorance, denies them education and refinement and erases growth. It exploits them as buyers to their salesmanship. So this well-fed monster will someday eat the monster who fed it only monster food. And the minority who possessed the knowledge will not be there to guide this blind monster—the masses.

Hazel McKinley arrives at the Museum of Modern Art like an enormous bonbon from Shraft, a patisserie, a *gateau à la Reine*. Puffed in body, topped by a hat of white furry mushrooms, Hollywood blond hair, a hard candy necklace, a pale blue dress, balloons of flesh. Once, long ago, her nose was too prominent—and she had it diminished, but now on the swollen face it looks too small. It is losing ground. To achieve a Hazel you take a young girl and use a bicycle pump, and then you let a little air out, and you obtain this figure both faded and young, infantile and without effect. It is still baby fat. The smile is very bright, the eyes a good quality of sea green. But the fairy godmother was not kind when it decided that she will grow old without maturing. Yet she paints delicately in watercolor. And her love for poetic young men—homosexual—remains a mystery until one observes her hands. They are delicate and sensitive, even beautiful hands. The coarse, slovenly self-indulgent body grew thus in spite of the artist hands, the green eyes and the bright smile. One feels like picking up the scattered glance, the broken phrases, the asides (she screws her mouth on one side to murmur: "He was impotent during the first week of our relationship"), the chaos, and pouring glue over them. After all these years she sustains a constant flux without change or climax. The last man, Alex Kirkland, the actor, is not young, but like Hazel, is immature. He is handsome and charming. Effeminate. He must like pillows, large feather quilts. He resembles her father. She resembles her mother. They quarrel. "Do you think he hates women and likes little boys? As soon as he is out of my sight, I get anxious. Yet I don't dare marry him. He's a Christian Scientist and he takes me to church. I want to take him to Dr. Jacobson so he will improve his virility."

They both glue shells on baskets in the purest Woolworth taste. *Très homme du monde.* He kisses her hand and keeps his dignity. He is slender, well-groomed.

Her confessions remain the same: "He is jealous, and he treats me badly when he drinks." She is a Baronne de Charles...and the scenes that took place in New Orleans when she fell in love with two young men who had been in jail may resemble some of Charles' most underworldly scenes. Do the men flay her because she is the whore-mother Mollie Bloom, or because this maternal flesh has to be sexually worshipped and all of them would like her castrated?

Letter from Anaïs Nin to Rupert Pole:
New York, February 1956

Darling Chiquito:
Thinking hard about Annette's house in Acapulco last night and wondered if you will agree with me. At fifty pesos plus the cost of breakfast, I know it is less than the other place. But...we have no access to the kitchen to make ourselves lunch, or drinks (since the servants are there), which we save money on, and we have no privacy because Annette will send other people to occupy the top house and we may or may not like them. As I remember the last time, they were all more or less parasites who fasten on to us as we do not know how to say no to people without feeling badly...if we don't like them... What do you think? The kitchen, you know, was part of the upper house and always occupied by the maid and her man...anyway, it was a coal kitchen, which means that the maid would want to do the lunch (and charge us) instead of our scrambled eggs we made so casually—it would be a fuss. What do you think? Another problem is that in Annette's house everything was being stolen...and we never lost anything at La Roca. I have not heard from La Roca yet... have you? I forgot if I gave your name or mine... anyway, "Pole"...

Last night I read a book about the life of Erik Satie (one of my favorites) in French, which I borrowed from Joaquín, and it was fascinating. He was the one who liberated Debussy and influenced all the music of that period, but he was not taken seriously because he was witty and full of jokes…and because he had "no form"…isn't that delicious?

After finding out how little people understand each other, I can sleep better and more philosophically. Otherwise I brood on the evil of the world, like the blind negro woman friend of Millicent who can only get $37.50 a month from Welfare. I am trying to do something about this with Community Center. Filling out forms she can't fill out, etc.

Love love love
A

New York, February 1956
"Pseudo Heart Trouble"
Symptoms:
At dawn I am sometimes awakened by this feeling: a faint trembling, a feeling that in the region around the heart a liquid is trying to pass through a rough channel, or canal. It lasts for a few moments.

At other times I feel a kind of suspense: then I distinctly feel what seems like a heavy fall in rhythm.

At other times, if I carry heavy things or do housework, I will feel a compression of the chest as you do at 7,000 feet altitude. A tightness. At other times, after a heavy meal or drinking (I do not drink excessively, in fact, moderately) the heart accelerates and I have palpitations.

Now and then my feet are slightly swollen.

On damp days I feel worst of all. My breath is short. None of this is continuous. I used to do fifteen minutes a day of exercises, now I do only five because the chest tightens.

On the emotional level, I have been disturbed, but I have been under analysis for six years.

Other illnesses: typhoid, chronic anemia until the last few years. Jaundice at thirty. Stopped menstruating at forty-two. Have had hot flashes ever since with very little relief. Basically depressed, with temporary elations.

New York, February 16, 1956
After Bogner. It was very simple. I let Dr. Grath in Sierra Madre diagnose me with rheumatic fever, without laboratory tests, and tell me that my heart would get worse with time and to accept limitations in my activity. I allowed the physical symptoms to overwhelm me. I *wanted* to have a bad heart, and to die. But last week I wanted certitude. I wrote down the symptoms and saw a heart specialist who gave me tests for an hour and a half. I have no disease of the heart. He could not say what did cause the symptoms. But Bogner reminds me that anxiety can create *all* the symptoms. I used this certitude to get well, climbed back to health and a severe confrontation with my attempt at "suicide." Images of my "fatal" heart disease were followed by the image of my mother running to the door impulsively to talk to the milkman (while Joaquín and I sat at lunch on our last day together before she died) and how Joaquín and I looked at each other with the same fear of the fatal consequences of her rapid, impulsive, violent exertion (she had already had a stroke a year or so before). There was the image of myself at

seventeen inventing a big strike drama on the tram to excuse my being late for Tia Anaïs. The power of the spirit is frightening—for miracles, for creation, for destruction...

Peggy is so small and thin that she looks like a girl of fifteen with breasts. Small head. She wears her hair brushed up severely and bunched into high pompadours of curls. She has utterly delicate hands. This slightness, this delicacy is violently jarred by the callousness, noise, vulgarity, the sordid atmosphere of an American hospital. Nowhere is American lack of humanity more revealed than in their hospitals.

We drove her home on Saturday. She had been operated on for a growth in the colon. And so each evacuation was torture. She was hysterical with pain. So small and fragile, in pain. I tended to her with great compassion and helped to quieten her nerves, and therefore the contractions that increased the pain.

At 6:00 AM she summoned me by "wishing," and I arrived in the dark to help her. I was giving back to her all the care I had received from others, passing on all I had been given. Aside from the critical moments, she was quiet and cheerful. She ate with pleasure. And slowly, from this small body, the energy, which is all in her mind, began to sparkle again. All her strength is in her mind, to sustain a timid, frightened, hypersensitive body. Doctors are blind to treat such a person as they would others. She is a finer specimen, more complex, and in need of careful handling. She is convalescing now. I lived only for her for four days.

Now I find it hard to describe her. She studied, first of all, anthropology. She lives by astrology and mysticism. She won a music scholarship when she was very young, in Australia, and went to England. Very young, she married Sydney Bates, the composer. There was a musical affinity, but he was emotionally unbalanced. He was frustrated as a composer, so the imbalance grew and he became an alcoholic. He behaved so erratically that Peggy feared he would be locked up in an asylum. In preference to that, she locked him up with paints, and he painted well and was exhibited. But he hated his jailer. He beat Peggy and took her money. She worked. And still she felt "responsible" for him. She finally guided him into another marriage. He also had homosexual tendencies, a problem that he tried to solve with hormones, which added to the imbalance.

Then, just before the end of the marriage, she met Paul Bowles. They were in love. Jane Bowles was like Helba—a cripple—and Paul felt responsible for her and was dedicated to her as Gonzalo was to Helba. Jane interfered violently with the relationship (although it was she who had rejected Paul sexually), threatened and separated them (which took Helba ten years to achieve with me).

Now Peggy lives, at 43, with a feeling of renunciation. She cannot separate sensuality and her loves. She has a small, perfect, childlike smile—a pixie quality that makes her appear young. She is intensely active in the music world. Has a quality of leadership. She feels it is man who has been unable to cope with liberated women, to deal with equal relationships. The imbalance is in the man. It is truly a curse for a woman to be intelligent just as it seems to be a curse for a man to be sensitive. The whole sexual balance is disturbed. Sensitive men can't make love to women, and intelligent women can't accept the brute. This is her interpretation. She reviles psychoanalysis.

We talked quietly while I sewed, touching lightly on our lives, not too fully. I teased her about the Barrons, and I nominated her as a candidate for Hugo's next wife, or Joaquín's... But I can see that when Peggy contradicts Hugo, he is furious. She hates Proust. She hates analysis.

This morning I conquered both my boredom and irritation at Hugo's need to discuss, for exactly two hours, whether I should put money in a savings and loan association or a savings bank. I realize he enjoys this as other men enjoy chess or crossword puzzles—so I entered the game.

His life is 90% business. So I am grateful that this obsession enables us to help Peggy with a maid for a few days, or pays for my dentist, heart specialist and massages. In other words, I have *to pay*—by a more intimate and continuous association with practicalities than I had wanted.

Until now I believed it was a sickness—but I was wrong.

The wall is there. The break. The death.

The mere detail: a man who never directly answers a direct question—what havoc this causes! He is always eluding, ducking...it is like shadow boxing.

Why is it that in man, sexuality is related to power in the world or in art? Why is it that when woman is free, he turns away from her? Why does development in a woman not affect her sensual life?

Dream: Bella Spewack is there. I insult her violently for the cruel, destructive letter she wrote me. And when I am all through, I come up to her, weeping, and I say: "And the worst of it is that I love you."

Dream: Hugo leaves the door of the car unlocked so that I will fall out and die. When I realize he wants me to die, I am very undone.

Hugo and I laid down plastic tiles in the entrance to our apartment—a two-day, arduous job. He worked solemnly. I was the one being playful and gay. I wonder if his gay self is as impossible for him to relate to me as it is impossible for him to relate to other human beings. How can he live without sex? How can he live doing business all day and going to the movies at night? He believes we should not psychoanalyze each other or share analyses, so now we have nothing to talk about. I know nothing of what he feels or thinks. We discuss objective themes.

I suffer being away from Rupert...I miss his physical warmth—his aliveness.

Letter from Rupert Pole to Anaïs Nin:
Sierra Madre, February 1956

Love:
Real tired trying to get everything done and get off, but still have time for a line. All is well and going according to schedule—am sure I'll get off next Monday—a good time to be going—we both need Acapulco now, to say nothing of each other. Do hope you got your plane reservation. No word from La Roca—have written them again—but no worry, there are lots of places to stay there now. The main thing is to get there together.

I saw Dane Rudyar at a slide show, and he kept asking me about you—and the Solomons asked about you—everyone asks about you—but they can only ask—*I know*. That's why I'm working harder and harder to hurry the time till we're

together again. The moon is full tonight, and now is when our eternal honeymoon should begin again. But the moon in Mexico is always full—with love…
R

New York, February 1956
After seeing Bogner, all the fragments of my life (even babysitting) group themselves under the theme of belonging or not belonging. To belong or not belong with the writers of *The Nation*. To belong or not belong to a community on a human level only. To be admitted into Bogner's "busy" world even at the cost of washing dishes (which Bogner knows I hate). Problem of loneliness and efforts to belong—as a child I tried to belong to the family by "service" when I gave up reading and writing and dreaming to wash dishes and take care of my brothers.

A relief from solitude in my passion for Rupert at the cost of creative solitude activates my hunger for France.

Erik Satie's life is moving. His innovations. His humor. His complexity and imagination. His influence and contribution to music are unacknowledged.

It is so sad to read Romain Gary's novel, in which the war orphans, too young and surrounded by disaster, begin to see the American gangster and roughneck as an ideal hero who alone can win in a mad world! Humphrey Bogart. Or *Wages of Fear* and the fantasy about American life where food and shelter are attainable.

Hugo is much farther from the truth of his feelings than I am, and that is why he is much farther from relationships. He is also without courage and without strength in living. That was why he has needed twice as much analysis.

Bogner was wrong when I "interpreted" Hugo's feelings. She said I was projecting onto him that *he* was unhappy to make it easier for myself.

But I was right.

I tried to make him admit the vital contact was absent from our marriage, and to that he would not concede.

I think of how Gonzalo came *forward* to meet me in our emotional encounter, how Rupert holds his ground (not Henry—he was another evasive one).

The weeping we did (caused by affection and a long life together) and the admissions we made, will they bring on a separation without bitterness?

After seeing Bogner:

Mise au point.

Hugo is not happy, but he does not want separation.

I want a separation, but without destructive consequences.

I wanted Hugo to find closeness with somebody else while I was away.

Letter from Rupert Pole to Anaïs Nin:
Sierra Madre, February 1956

To: My Love
From: Your would-be Mexican husband
Subject: Separation or "How Long"

Can't give you an earlier date yet, love. This forestry film is lousing everything up, but it's very important and I must see it through—if I leave before it's completed they'll try to complete it alone, and even if they have it done well by professionals, I'll miss the experience of working with them. Hope to know more soon.

The plans for life in our Sea House, and now your absence, have made me realize much too intensely that only one relationship gives my life meaning—that everything we do must in some way contribute to the growth of the relationship or to its beauty. That which doesn't contribute is wasted time and without meaning. All that is beautiful and meaningful for me is only found in you.

R

February-March 1956
Trip to Acapulco with Rupert.

Letter from Jim Herlihy to Anaïs Nin:
New York, March 1956

I have been more active than ever since my retirement from Keyes Fibre Co. Did you know that last Friday they moved away? With the bonus they gave me, plus the option money for the play, I now have $400 in the bank and will not have to work for most of the summer.

The really important thing I wanted you to know is that since my "retirement" I have had much more time for reading, and am having a beautiful and incomparable experience with the black children of Anaïs Nin. I am nearly through volume 55 now; the person and the writing grow steadily in clarity and wisdom and beauty. It is a great saga of an individual, very possibly the greatest that exists. No important step is missing; the floundering, the searching, the backsliding, the bold and magnificent steps forward in consciousness and freedom. I feel the full weight of this tremendous trust you've shown by leaving them in my hands. Every now and then I think I have hit upon sections that can be used separately to help you in your own relationship with the world, in the present, but quickly find that their content and wholeness are dependent on their existence in a framework. Even so, I do think I have some ideas that, with editing, and a certain effort in collage, might be used for publishable fragments. I really don't know. We never really sat down with the books in front of us and fully investigated this possibility. I only know that you are the greatest woman I have ever known or heard of. Don't let this embarrass you, or make you uncomfortable. I would love you as deeply as I do if you had never written a word. This paragraph, however, is addressed to the artist. You must make that distinction when you read it; I don't want you to feel alienated personally by such pronouncements!

The play's new producers, James Hammerstein and Barbara Wolferman, seem to be aggressive and good at their jobs.

There's more to say, but I must flee. I'll write soon again.
Love,
Jim

Letter from Anaïs Nin to Jim Herlihy:
Sierra Madre, March 1956

Dear Jim:

Your letter moved me deeply. It contained such a perfect response and understanding. You have indeed given back to me whatever it is you feel the Diary gives you. You have taken the place of the entire world, and what more can a writer ask than to build a pyramid of writing that someone can enter, feel at home with, enjoy and inhabit. It is as wonderful an experience as reciprocated love. In fact, it is the same.

Your letter was wonderful to receive. In a sense, this is a desert. Rupert the dreamer was only born a few weeks ago. In Acapulco he began to have and remember dreams. The friends I like are in Malibu. I see them rarely.

You must imagine your letter arriving in a dull little village, in the little tin box among others, and how I take it to the coffee shop and sit there to escape from the paper plates awaiting me. I feel like the grounded aviator who receives his command to fly again. And immediately I obey. I'm glad you wrote me, also because you have often talked, talked, but it eluded me. I wanted to keep it. I never could seize it and write it down, what you said, because, as you say, it evaporated. I see now that like the thousand and one nights, I have to continue the Diary to entertain you. *But we will have the marvelous again.* You must believe that. When it is within one, inevitably it will take shape.

Love and gratitude,
A

Sierra Madre, March 1956

Dream: I was talking over the telephone with my mother. I could hear myself saying "Mommy." But after a while her voice grew faint and she was silent. I kept calling her in vain. Then I tried to find her. She had shrunk. She was so small. She was small and looked like a long, thin cat (as Mitou does when we hold her straight by her two legs—she looks as long as a rabbit...). I felt terrible sorrow.

Dream of a few nights ago: My wallet (like my real wallet, which is a large one called the "international traveler," big enough for airplane tickets, traveler's checks, etc.) lay on the sidewalk, between Hugo and an artist. I felt I had to do an errand, concerned about the wallet, but feeling the two people would take care of it. When I returned it was gone. In the dream I was very angry with Hugo. But as I awakened, gradually it occurred to me that it was my fault and I should be angry with myself because I *knew* Hugo was absent-minded and therefore not capable of taking care of the wallet, and I *knew* that certainly the artist was completely irresponsible.

This month is a *Mea Culpa* month, for I blame myself entirely for my estrangement from Hugo. I exonerate him. I have examined all my relationships and exonerated all of them and condemned myself. I wage a constant war against reality in favor of the dream, and that is how I have destroyed my relationships.

Mea Culpa is heavy to bear.

At Bekins' Storage there are three huge files with all the diaries. As soon as I copy one I return the original to the file and send one carbon copy to Jim.

Copying volume 68 brought into vivid focus Frances Field (then Brown), Lanny Baldwin, Harry Herskovitz, Thurema Sokol, Gonzalo, the Press, etc. Jim's letter mentioning organization was accurate, and it is my problem... I must organize. I must complete. I must fill and round out the portraits. Each character I live with for a few days, I see in both lights, the human light of the Diary and the essence and abstraction of the novels. In the Diary I follow the life-line. In the novel, the fantasy. Where to begin?

Tavi lies at the foot of the bed. He is fourteen years old, the equivalent of eighty years in a man. At the beginning of my life with Rupert, on the days when I felt old, I imagined growing old with Tavi and going off with him to hide somewhere. But Tavi in eight years has grown old. He is deaf. He does not see very well. He is not too eager to go out with Rupert and climb up and down the canyon. He prefers to stay with me and sleep. He sleeps most of the day. And in eight years I have not changed. I get up at seven or eight, make breakfast, clean the house, do errands, go to the post office, carry laundry and objects to be cleaned, cook lunch and rest a few minutes; in the afternoon I type and write letters, mail books, read other people's novels. Almost every evening we go out. I don't feel a lack of energy except during cycles of depression. Working on the Diaries seems to cure me of depression. Why?

The development of Frances's life is remarkable—from tuberculosis, a bad marriage and poverty, to health, a good marriage, a child, a more glamorous, better life and the creation of good paintings. But the subtle element I would like to capture is that the secret inner world she concealed, protected, expressed only in dreams and in talks with me is the one she is now painting. Before, she pictured the outer world as brutal and cruel, but when she exposed her delicate inner world in painting she was loved, praised, bought... She managed all this with mediocre analysts: Martha Jaeger and Clement Staff. She knows there were errors. But in spite of this defective assistance, she flowered.

The *visibility* of this secret world before it developed into painting is what I would like to describe even though what Frances manifested was an intellectual toughness, an analytical sharpness by which she defended her sensibilities and fantasies. Yet, she did not recognize this in my writing at the time—at the time she questioned me. It is only now that she understands the imagery and that the similitudes that we shared took the form of similar symbols in her work and mine.

I am ashamed of my withdrawals from Frances when she became over-analytical, almost exclusively so because she was physically handicapped for living; she offended my strong aesthetic sense, once by exposing her legs up to the thighs at a party, another by using a roll of toilet paper to blow her nose when she had a cold. This was Frances's background—contradicting the delicacies of her mind and dreams.

Sierra Madre, Spring 1956

Bob Leach brings me a novelist—Sydney Omarr. They are both prosaic, ugly and hopeless in a way that does not arouse pity. Bob adds up the times he has taken out the garbage. Omarr is vulgar and thinks he is writing like Miller.

When Rupert left for training camp, I bought paper, let the house go, and settled into the diary world. I continued copying volume 68. I was happy. I was in a full, rich world. The Press. Gonzalo. Chinchilito. Friends. Analysis with Martha Jaeger.

Is it distance that makes these people more interesting? I once made a decision that I would never describe anything I was not in love with. Never to write about what I hate. I have broken this promise.

Jim's ardor incited me to copy more diaries. I couldn't finish *Solar Barque*. He is my one faithful reader. I owe him so much. He has never failed me. The only difficult moment we had once was when he lost his week's pay twice, when he misplaced a journal, and when he said: "I am going to bed, and I am going to stay in bed so that no more catastrophes happen." I was leaving for California. I was alarmed, and I began to stress his need of analysis. I almost lost him then.

It was Dick who went to analysis, when they separated once. But Dick's improvements do not affect Jim or make him want analysis. Not even his knowledge that Bogner saved me from self-destruction, possibly madness.

This was the only crisis in our friendship. Otherwise, I like everything he does and the way he does it. I like that he combines humanity with amorality. He is free and yet never betrays, or cheats. He could commit a crime and it would be justified. He is proud and independent. It is difficult to give to him materially. But otherwise he is responsive, devoted, faithful, and miraculously articulate. He is spiritually and psychically a trapezist. He is agile and knows how to leap. Depression is his only enemy, as it is mine.

New York, May 1956

Waiting for Godot, one of the few "antipodes of the mind," is mysteriously accepted by the people. Why? Because its human aspect and comic spirit are common—smelly feet, passivity, hobos' fantasy of someone who will save them. The language is not authentic (in the antipodes people speak the language of the dreamer), but people have the illusion they have seen a profound spectacle. As when Tennessee Williams presented his private nightmare blown up in *Camino Real*.

But it had quality, inventiveness, the courage of *depaysement*. Some lines are moving, others stir laughter. It was superior to most plays. The aftertaste was good, as aftertastes of quality. I don't know why it is not completely moving—no more than Joyce. Is it because it is not born of the antipodes, but an intellectual simulation again, a reproduction, not a direct expression? It's carefully charted.

Jim and I tried to analyze why we did not fall in love with the play. Was it because the theme was personally distasteful: waiting, empty days, seeking to pass the time, passively waiting for a rescuer? Was it that blending of rough humanity, sore feet, with complexities about time born of Einstein? Whatever it is, we must be loyal to all the explorers of man's dreams and nightmares.

New York, May 1956

Story of a Possession, continued...

Unknowingly, I had continued to mourn my mother and, failing to die with her of heart disease, I took on her trait of irritability. I'm told that it is a common form of mourning. I suddenly could not work on *Solar Barque*. I was not only arrested, the "flow" was not only inhibited, but I felt total *doubt* about what I was doing. I felt I no longer could write well. With this came anxiety and the need to see Bogner.

I went early to my appointment and wandered about in her neighborhood. At the same time, Hugo left for Cuba after spending his last evening with another woman. And while this is what I had wanted, I did not experience it as the fulfillment of my wish (total separation from Hugo) but as a child losing its father. I realized with the sexual wall that had been erected between us early in the marriage, that he was my father and not my lover, and now he became the father who deserted me for a mistress. I relived the loss of my mother simultaneously with the loss of my father. I had to call Rupert twice, and, as Bogner said, relived the separation not with the mature knowledge that separation is not an absolute break in the relationship, but as a child whose parents leave the house for an evening and never come back.

Only yesterday with Bogner did I remember that my mother had condemned my writing. I wept. Bogner was unusually gentle and tactful.

I wept in the taxi.

I became calmer. I came home and ate dinner alone. I was able to write letters, attend to my book orders. Before sleeping I took a bath, read Pierre Molaine, another multi-dimensional writer. Before sleeping, another attack of anxiety. The heart beats. The body is now cold, almost blue, now hot, and I have to open the windows. Took a sleeping pill. This morning I went on with the writing of *Solar Barque*—the costume party on the Mexican general's yacht.

Dream: The Wright family was composed of eight or ten tall men (as it is in reality). I was staying with them. But because there was no room I was sent to sleep with one of the wives, who had a little girl. She disapproved of my presence. There was something immoral about me. I was rereading my diaries, the early ones. I found a photograph that surprised me because in it I looked very beautiful. The woman went on attending to her child...hardly concealing her disapproval.

Before he left, Hugo kissed me tenderly, fraternally, and said: "I was very happy with you this time."

New York, Thursday, May 17, 1956

Dream last night: We are at an orgy with soldiers, another woman and myself. When we see a woman who has been raped, we try to run away. She is running far ahead of me down the stairs when a young man, by a trapeze act, swings on a rope and catches me and lifts me up in midair. I experience pleasure at being caught. He says he has a role for me in a play. The play is put on. I notice the audience is very small, and in fact there is no audience. There is a handful of people connected with the play, and the props are made of the discarded blue felt curtains I cut up in strips for my rugs in Sierra Madre. Then the young man and I go off together. He takes me to the house of the woman who was in the play, to show me why she cannot be in it any longer: she has grown fat and wrinkled. She exposes her belly—I feel badly that she let herself go. I feel young by comparison.

Reliving the death of my mother, and the father *going away* (sexually, and on a trip), after the talk with Bogner I was able to write. *Solar Barque* is, for the greater part, invention. Very little reality. And now I realize it has been so difficult to write because it is on the periphery of the Diary—all that I cannot touch in the Diary and have to circumvent.

Sitting at the White Horse with Eduardo, discussing his life, etc. The tragedy of his ninety-year-old father dying but leaving all his children at the mercy of the oldest brother. And the brother becomes like the father, a tyrant, so Eduardo is not free financially. Talking about the Diary, he expressed real anxiety for himself and others at the consequences of publication. I came home feeling I must transpose it. It is too dangerous to human beings. I realized how much I suffered from Perlès's distorted portrait. Even if my portraits are truer, they are truer to the part of themselves that people wish concealed.

Telegram from Hugh Guiler to Anaïs Nin:
New York, June 7, 1956

Letter received. No question of separation. Also please disregard my reference to guilt in today's letter.
Love, Hugo

Sierra Madre, July 1, 1956
Until today I felt unequal to the task of writing about what happened in May. It was too painful. When I arrived Hugo was a changed man. He was taking a new drug that made him sleep all night and therefore he was less tired, less depressed, less dead. But very soon I became aware of the other change. I cannot be lied to. When I went out Sunday to telephone Rupert, Hugo made a call that he abruptly cut off when I returned. When we were out one Saturday afternoon he telephoned several times (as I did). When he went to Havana for a few days, he did not give up his last evening's business appointment to spend it with me as he usually would have. I went out with Jim, about one evening a week, and was surprised to find Hugo in bed and asleep by midnight. Now it had happened, and I was going to behave as I should. If Hugo was happy…

What baffled me was that his attitude towards me was better. He was more loving, mellower, seemed even amazed at how I looked at breakfast, seemed to enjoy going to the theatre with me, seemed to appreciate me more. Returning from Cuba, he brought back perfume for both women (as I used to get the same shirt for both Hugo and Rupert). For three weeks we went out, lived pleasantly. At night I felt the same emptiness without Rupert, the same sleeplessness. I felt at last I was free. Hugo was happy. He would understand and forgive me. At last we could stop feeling guilty towards each other.

One morning I awakened early and felt: now that we are no longer lovers, he will understand. I can talk to him. We can have a different kind of relationship. I got up and found he was awake. I slipped into his bed and talked very quietly and tenderly, trying to say it was right that he should have a mistress, since I had left him alone, and, barely hinting at our freedom, I told him I have had a casual lover lately, only the smallest fraction of the truth, to test him, pleading for his understanding and acceptance.

Well, I was wrong. I did not get it. He said, "But what did you expect me to do, to live without your desire?" Hugo, who has never faced any reality directly, went into his usual "shock." He suffered. Suffered like a heavy, gloomy animal, made me feel like a criminal. Once more the very thing that made our life together so unreal, so unvital, his lack of courage, appeared. "I have to talk to Bogner. I can't bear it." He didn't sleep. We spent a miserable Sunday. I kept consoling him, reassuring him. He had failed me in the same way he had all his life. He didn't behave like a man, but like a child.

Then I saw Bogner. She did not agree that I had done right. She reminded me that she had told me Hugo would never be able to face a separation. But I said there is no question of a separation. If he has a mistress, surely he can face that I should have a lover.

I spent the rest of my time there just helping Hugo. He did not help me. I said: "This is one time when you are not going to withdraw or sulk, because that is how you drive me away. We are going to face this together. Why do I accept the situation and not you?"

The one thing I had never been able to face is Hugo's selfishness. All our life together he prevented me from living. He was a weight on me, and now, in spite of all, he still refers to the "shock." He still laments for himself. The one love I had believed selfless… We spent a month healing up. I not so much from the fact of the mistress, but of Hugo's wails and agonies over my having a lover!

Then my feelings were mixed: pity for his neurotic vulnerability and anger at his weakness…great anger.

I concealed the disappointment and the anger. It made me physically ill. I behaved humanly towards Hugo—but I also knew in my heart what he is: a coward. He could only live with help from every side.

So once more, lies. I wanted him to be what he is—and to let me be what I am. But what he demanded was a sickening softness and pampering for his great suffering.

Then last night I had a clear dream: I returned to New York. Hugo was making love to me. A woman interrupted us (a maid?). Then Hugo, I noticed, was absentminded and thinking of business. He did not complete the lovemaking. I found later many bottles of perfume on the dresser. I said: "You gave this woman more perfume in one month than you ever gave me in my whole life!"

To get well (I had a burning, painful stomach and nausea) I had to face my anger. Hugo's attitude angered me. It was egocentric. All his reactions to life are to go into shock. His most recurrent phrase is "I died." He died when he broke with his family. He died when he chose to go to London and I would not go. He died when I said we had not given each other what we most wanted.

Now, I did not particularly enjoy what happened. It might mean the end of the marriage. But I took it better. I realize it is difficult to face the ending of such a long marriage. What I took my strength from was my love for Hugo, for all he had given me, and this made me want to help him. So there we are. All our life it was I who acted—and it was Hugo who reacted. We are so different in this. I plunge into reality even if it hurts. He avoids it.

He said: "I have speculated on your trips for years."

"Why didn't you merely ask me? I would have told you."

I am so tired of his evasions—fogs.

I took the "pain" of knowing about the mistress as something that had to be, that I had caused, wanted, and which was inevitable. Why not he? I didn't wail and howl about it. Now I see that Hugo's attitude made all sincerity impossible. I said, "I thought we could have another closeness, based on truth, giving each other freedom, understanding. You indirectly want me there, something to count on."

Another cause for anger was that Hugo should be *now* what he should have been when we first married: gay, assured, fond of going out, fond of pleasure, which may have changed our whole life and marriage.

Returning to Rupert's passion was healing. He had built a fireplace. He cooked steaks in it. We made love wildly. I felt now perhaps I will be free of guilt, and be no longer haunted by Hugo. But of course I wasn't. I spent my time writing him comforting letters.

To rid himself of the pain, Hugo said: "Stay away all summer and then we'll see what happens." If I leave it to him nothing will happen. He will outwait me, out-patience me, and again out of anguish I will take action.

Then I tried to get Rupert to move to New York, because the mediocrity of our life is sapping the relationship. He is changing professions, and I felt now is the time. But he would not agree, because of Reginald; because getting teaching experience in N.Y. would not help him here later; because he wants to build his house in Malibu and get his degree as a teacher.

Today I had to look at my angers in the face so they would no longer poison me.

It is strange that the simple truth of inner responsibility and self-created unevenness should be so difficult to grasp. That my own self-created guilt was what I projected onto Hugo. That Hugo's obsession with security was projected onto the need of protecting a helpless woman (which is why he never let me take a job). That Hugo blamed his rebelliousness on me. That I blamed him for caution, control and duty. That my obsession with pleasure was threatened by Hugo's dedication to work.

Many events that could have been pleasurable were transposed into pain by my own alchemy. For example, when I had won the lover of my fantasies (Rupert, who was both passionate and warm-hearted, both passionate and tender), I proceeded to destroy the joy with anxiety over its potential loss. Going to parties became an ordeal. The extent to which Hugo and I did this to each other was incredible. Most of our analysis was spent blaming each other for this or that. Our dualities were expressed through the other. This morning I awakened understanding how this related to pleasure. Because I have expected pleasure from a person, or a country, or a way of life I had imagined to be pleasurable, when I was confronted with reality—a Hugo who was a neurotic, depressive type, or a Rupert who seeks a small, inartistic life in which he feels comfortable, or a country and a way of life I do not like—I feel pleasure is unreachable. But this is suicide. When Rupert was called on a fire yesterday at 3:00 AM and would be gone for days, instead of reacting as I sometimes have—merely to give Rupert the pleasure of finding me at home when he returns weary and grimy, dreading to stay in this hateful place—I proceeded instantly to find what I could enjoy: uninterrupted hours of work, visits by Chris, Kitty and Mollie (yesterday I gave them all my old Spanish dance costumes, and they have had a joyous time trailing them along the lawn), languorous sleep, meditating on the novels. Pleasure was not an attitude, not a person or a place. Guilt was my greatest tormentor, the cause of my masochism, and I made Hugo the incarnation of this guilt…

The battle I still have to win is the battle with my anger.

A series of dreams made my feeling about Hugo clear. They opened with a tidal wave so enormous that people swimming in it seemed the size of a fly. I was engulfed but did not drown. Then came one in which Hugo explained how he had met the other woman and his admission that she was 69 years old. Then I said to him, "It is the mother you were always looking for!"

Today I awakened more whole. I have been trying to face my anger.

1—I am angry at the English publisher who was to pay me $100 on the date of publication in March—and it is now July.

2—I am angry at Henry for allowing Fred to paint such a shabby picture of our relationship.

3—I am angry at British Book Centre for offsetting my own edition of *Spy* and selling it without paying me a cent, instead of selling mine as per agreement and taking a distributor's fee.

4—I am angry with Hugo for sulking for thirty years and only smiling and expanding now, because if he had been more expansive thirty years ago our marriage might have been happy.

I could go on.

One is ashamed of anger.

If I had not had to live dually and divert my passion from the marriage I might have had children. I love Pam's children, and they love me.

Well, enough for today.

Letter from Anaïs Nin to Hugh Guiler:
Sierra Madre, July 1956

Darling:

By a devious way, I have arrived at a serious step forward. I had started to tell you about the Campion children, but I did not finish telling you how it affected me. It was while watching *Moby Dick*—the inhumanity of obsession—and while watching the children feeling the loss of me (I am moving soon), but only for what *they* were losing and unable, of course, to feel anything within me (how *I* would miss *them*, etc.), and I followed this thread of the inhumanity of the neurotic until I arrived at the same thing you described: that every time something unexpectedly bad happens to the child (or the neurotic or the romantic), he either sulked, withdrew, or closed the door. The neurotic, like the elephant, neither forgets nor forgives... The neurotic (another image which came to my mind) is like the monkey who scratches the insect bite that hurts him until he destroys himself. Anyway, all this suddenly caused a gradual transformation. Something fell away, which is what you describe as maturity ...the fixation on past reactions, primitive emotional reactions...and I felt I was stepping out of the shell of old pains, scars and sensibilities. A new motivation appeared—the *human*. Because of the idea of you as a human being, quite separate from me, not feeling well, working away, waiting for Bogner (that's a good one, Waiting for Bogner!), seeking wholeness, I felt that all my anxieties had shifted... No complicated reactions anymore. The point was to jump out of one's personal sensibilities and accept the other's behavior as it is, accept life as it comes...when we did not exhibit or receive ideal behavior, we were unforgiving to each other, you know. I used to say I wish you were more easy-going, but I wasn't either, could not be teased, etc. Well, I have made the jump. If I return before Bogner does from her vacation, it will be because you need me as a human being, because you are not as deliriously happy as I pictured you (my fantasy of how much better the Other Woman is for you than I am). We both behaved in such a way as to bring about what happened, and life itself creates this every day for everybody, but we couldn't imagine it happening to us.

Darling, in intelligence we have been above average, but we have nurtured each other's childlike sensibilities to excess so that even the slightest offense, the slightest interest in another was a drama... Well, I am ready to take things as they come, as I cause them, as you cause them, as nature causes them, as time causes them. My mind is now on our marriage; we are each other's whole family. We have (alas, to the detriment of other kinds of man-woman relationships) tried to be brother and sister, mother and father, grandfather and grandmother, children, cousins, aunts to each other! I don't look upon my return home as such a solemn crisis anymore. In a few days, it seems to me, I have grown up, no longer having a dependency on you, an identification with you. It was even humorous, how I proceeded to create you within me, to replace you by having stomach trouble, by losing my address book, by forgetting things, by awakening at four in the morning. All this has disappeared. I am beginning to feel well, and I am concerned about you. As I said, you only have to say the word. I will come when you say. And from me, at least, you will not have any trouble.

Enjoy your life, darling, you have lost nothing and gained everything. Have your cake and eat it too!

Your cake

A

Sierra Madre, July 1956

Rupert describes our relationship very simply. "Everything else is unreal. Even my life in the Forest Service. I feel I am playing a role. I do not feel at home. I do not belong. When the men go on fires and find themselves in interesting places (such as the canyons in Arizona last week) they want to stay longer and visit. I want to come home."

"But at school—when you were young..."

"In school I was not at ease. I couldn't feel close or get close to the other students. At Harvard it was the same. Everybody had a group, a clique they belonged to—I didn't—I tried. When I studied music and I realized they thought I was an artist, I took up track and boxing—sports."

"Your mother always says you were such a happy boy."

"No—my life began to open up when I met you. It has improved ever since. I feel, at least, my life with you is real. When you are away I get the same feeling of unreality."

Last night we went to see *Moby Dick*. Huston understood and integrated its deeper meaning. The captain's obsession, not with a profession (whaling), earning money, or the well-being of his crew, his duty, but with his neurotic account to settle with Moby Dick who defeated and crippled him. Every neurotic sacrifices human beings and himself, his human life, to such an account. Hugo and I did. We sacrificed the marriage. And now? Now we have regrets. I don't know why, but I cannot get rid of the image of Hugo haunting me. Why? Why can't Rupert displace and replace Hugo? Because they are one and the same man, father and son?

Finished volume 68, which was 215 pages long. Cannot complete *Solar Barque*. Enjoying the heat, the pool and the children.

Letter from James Brown to Anaïs Nin:
New York, July 6, 1956

Dear Anaïs:
I have from Mrs. Lena I. Gedin of Stockholm, Sweden, who represents us there, the following:
Anaïs Nin, *The Four-Chambered Heart*
Wahlström & Widstrand Forlag have finally made up their mind to publish a Swedish edition.
Terms: $150 advance. 7½ % for 3,000 copies, 10% thereafter.
If you agree, please mail contracts with one copy for my files.
Many congratulations to you on this sale. Mrs. Gedin doesn't know that you are no longer represented by us. Would you be good enough to turn this over to whomever is representing you? Or, take this up directly with Mrs. Gedin. I am sending Mrs. Gedin a copy of this letter to you so that she will know. I do hope you are both well.
Yours,
Jim

Letter from Anaïs Nin to Jim Herlihy:
Sierra Madre, July 21, 1956

Dear Jim:
It has been a long time away, but this time I am obliged to consider Hugo's wishes in the matter, and he wishes me to postpone my return until September. He needs time to accept the new situation that threw him into a tailspin...but he absolutely refuses to consider a separation.

A great deal has been happening here. Rupert's disillusion with forestry is based mainly on three new men on the force who do not appreciate him as the others did, the necessity of being moved as in the army, never having a home, and his weariness with being always on duty even when we are at the beach. (Last Thursday they called us back to put out fires set by the crew themselves because they were bored and wanted excitement!) He will have a job beginning September 15 in a school in the Silver Lake district. We are looking for a place to live, and there are plenty. He will work fewer hours, from 9 to 3, earn a little more, be free three months in the summer, and no slavery or army discipline... I am glad I had the patience to wait until he was sick of it, for I hated the place, the profession, and the amount of time it took from me (answering the phone, people at the door, etc.).

Did I tell you *Spy* sold out in England? And *Four-Chambered Heart* was sold to Sweden?

Anaïs

Letter from Thomas Payne of Avon Books to Anaïs Nin:
New York, July 30, 1956

Dear Miss Nin:
I am writing in connection with your work *A Spy in the House of Love*, which we are most interested in publishing as a reprint. I am informed that you handle the rights to the work yourself; accordingly, I should be most anxious to hear from you as to whether the reprint rights are available to us. As soon as the question of availability is cleared up, I am sure we shall have no trouble working out mutually satisfactory terms.

Sincerely yours,
Thomas Payne, Editor-in-Chief

Letter from Joaquín Nin-Culmell to Anaïs Nin:
Paris, August 19, 1956

Dear Anaïs:
Your letter did greet me upon my arrival in Paris and I was delighted to receive it.

Paris is simply wonderful. Everything and everybody is alive and kicking. I was met at Le Havre by Jean Viqué, my old schoolmate from the Schola Cantorum, and at the Gare St. Lazare by Marie-André Peiquot, the French pianist who first played my very early compositions. Jean made me cancel my hotel reservation and took me to his apartment. Every morning I walk out on the balcony and salute l'Arc de Triomphe. From the station we went to Marie-André's and had a light supper. We talked and talked and talked. I was dead tired from the trip but so very happy. The next morning I went to the American Express and picked up my mail and found your letter. That same evening I went to see *En Attendant Godot*, a tremendous production of a terribly moving play. Thanks again for letting me read it beforehand. Today, Sunday, I have just returned from Mass. Will have lunch soon and then will spend the evening at Marie-André's. Tomorrow I will have lunch with Graciella [Sánchez-Archibald]. I will also buy my tickets for St. Jean de Luz, Madrid, Barcelona and back to Paris. Will be leaving Friday but plan to be back by October 1. Mail to the American Express in Paris will always reach me.

Paris is *not* expensive providing you are willing to live like a Frenchman. Is there any better way to live? Will find a room for my return in October. Meanwhile, Jean Viqué insists that I stay with him.

I think I am going to like it here...

Joaquín

Sierra Madre, August 1956
Dream: I am taking care of Tia Antolina. I want her to return to New York where my mother is. As soon as I say this I realize I have forgotten that my mother is dead. Hugo goes off with Tia Antolina's nurse.

Dream of Saturday night: I am traveling on a submarine. I am holding on to it by a long strap like the strap of the airplane seats. I glide along the surface as water skiers do. Other people are traveling the same way, in the opposite direction. Some are on horseback. The sea is dotted with travelers, and all the ships are under the surface. But I feel my submarine is traveling too deep, and if it goes down any deeper it will pull me below where I can't breathe. I contemplate letting go of the strap, but someone tells me that if I do, the submarine will sink to the bottom. I have a feeling of responsibility towards the submarine, so I hold on. It is strenuous, but I hold on.

Letter from Thomas Payne to Anaïs Nin:
New York, August 1956

Dear Miss Nin:

I am writing in answer to your recent letter regarding our interest in reprinting your work *A Spy in The House of Love*. I am delighted to hear that the book is available and eager to get underway so that our edition may appear the first part of next year.

We propose selling the book at 25¢; the standard royalty against that price is 1¢ for the first 150,000 copies and 1½¢ thereafter. Our proposed initial printing is somewhat more than 200,000 copies (this would include a Canadian distribution, which I trust is available to us). As an advance against royalty, we offer $1,250, half on signing of our contract and half on publication of your work.

I am extremely hopeful that the foregoing terms are agreeable to you—it would give me a good deal of personal pleasure to reprint *A Spy in the House of Love*.

Sincerely yours,
Thomas Payne

Letter from Jim Herlihy to Anaïs Nin:
New York, August 31, 1956

Dear Anaïs,

Now I know what we will do with the bottle of Mumm's '49 champagne that has been cooling for some worthwhile event for several weeks: celebrate the Avon sale. This has made me very happy. I am not dissatisfied with the price either, since you are, of course, out of their "category." It will give you a good prestige among the bookkeepers who do the publishing of books when *Solar Barque* is ready. It is good news for all possible reasons, I think; I can only say "high time."

I am saddened to discover that Dick has taken to reading my journal again, even though I keep it locked. For this reason, I cannot write freely about Boshkar, the greatest dancer of India, with whom I shared an adventure in the mountains last weekend. Oh, well. But I do think that this lack of control over curiosity is vulgar and despicable. I am afraid that I have begun to wish that the world had better manners, even though I realize that manners are often a terrible mask for decay. Now I have a wonderful and shabby little room in which to work; it suits me better than the elegant study on 48th St. I paint in it, and when I can, I will write in it.

Poor Dick is passing through one of his most neurotic periods, ruled by his anxieties; terrible to watch. But he is trying to help himself out of it. I am afraid that his analysis last year and early this year was a fraud, not one perpetrated by the analyst, but by himself. He was merely buying an illusion of wholeness, just as one buys a new silk suit or a tube of grease paint. It was as if he had been coached in a performance rather than helped deeply. I think he is using the excuse of finances to avoid further analysis. He hasn't returned to the doctor since his return from his tour. But I learn to accept, and I learn ways of liberating myself from the restrictions his neurosis would impose. I begin to believe he will never be well, but that at best, he will learn ways of hiding his anxieties from me, so that they won't repel me.

I find, Anaïs, that his needs, emotionally, are exclusively "female" ones, so that I can only fulfill them when they seem to be male; that is, when he is deluding me! All very curious!

Jimmy Spicer was here for a few hours on Tuesday. His mood is soured by the prospect of going to work this fall at a job he will dislike. He is becoming more and more concerned with finding "direction." I have great sympathy for him, and wish there were a way to help.

Am now reading vol. 68, the one you recently typed for me. It is still the only totally readable writing I can find anywhere, except for slivers and bits and pieces of other writers.

I hope you will not harm yourself with work. Please don't take unnecessary chances, over-guessing your strength, etc.

Love,
Jim

Letter from Eve Miller to Anaïs Nin:
Big Sur, September 4, 1956

Dear Anaïs,
Forgive my delay in answering your letter, which seemed to call for a prompt reply. Henry has taken the children into town (Monterey) for the day, and I find myself with the first "free" hours I've managed all summer. In retrospect—our summers are *all* happiness and joy...living through them is often another story! Due to ennui and isolation, our two seem to need more than should be humanly expected from *any* parent. However, we do it. How Henry finds the energy or time for his work—I can't imagine! The household is a three-ringed circus from the time summer starts—anywhere from five to seven children living with us, visitors, fans, etc. on into exhaustion. Now it's about over, and I'm already less tired!

But—about your letter. Since I typed the MS of Henry's entire book [*A Devil in Paradise*]—unless my memory is failing me entirely—I don't think he makes further mention of you. I won't discuss the questions regarding Moricand—I wasn't there. That you are upset over Henry's words comes as a surprise to me, as well as to him.

As far as trying to urge Henry to treat you with "silence" in future works, I can't do that. I wouldn't presume to urge Henry to do one thing or another, where his work is concerned. Everything he stands for is tied up in his own "personal" integrity, vision...I couldn't possibly tamper with it. I shouldn't worry about it, however, if I were you—I'm absolutely certain he would never be tempted to harm you with either truth or distortion, or in any way. That you are hurt in this instance, as I said before, is a great surprise. It is such a small issue, if you'll forgive me... isn't it? In fact, I think Henry is more affected by your response than merely "surprised." I'm sure you're the last person he'd ever expect would read into his words an "attempt to hurt." Nothing in your relationship would have prompted such an aberration. He has a tender, deep understanding of you, as a woman, let alone an artist.

Do rest easily, will you? We're sorry that this past year has caused you any distress.

Our warm best to you, *always...*

Eve

Letter from Rupert Pole to Anaïs Nin:
Los Angeles, September, 1956

All goes well. I'm one of the few new teachers being kept at King Jr. High—not because I'm any good but because I'm in math!

Don't see what can stop our house—even Lloyd—but I do hope he'll design it—he's such a poetic architect, doing stunning houses and churches here. Eric is sympathetic to the house idea. Have been hoping to soften Lloyd.

So very tired and it's only Monday. I need the strength you give me always.

Soon,
R

Letter from Anaïs Nin to Hugh Guiler:
Los Angeles, October 1956

Darling:
Got your special delivery letter Saturday and was glad because it was a nice one. Believe me, knowing how your week goes, I do not expect you to write me until the weekend when I know you have a little leisure time.

Solar Barque is finished, as I told you, and I am still sitting for hours trying to see why I feel it is not finished. This period of transition by analysis is deadly to the work. Change is easy to express in action, in being, but certainly hell to express in a novel that began two years ago. Evidently change is preventing me from crystallizing the novel as I should...mutations are too quick, and the medium of a theme does not lend itself to all the changes of attitude.

I have been concerned about the world news, humanly, and also wondering how it affects your work. I remember your being concerned about the Suez Canal situation, but now it is so much worse. Do you think it will bring on another world war?

Ruth Witt Diamant sent me an invitation to hear two young, wild poets from the slums of Brooklyn. I went to hear them. It was pathetic, and rather moving. One of the poems was called "Howl." It was a pathologic cry, or struggle to make poetry of all they had been born in, and at times they reached a kind of American surrealism, bitter irony, which was interesting and not without power. At other times they did indeed howl like animals...just like dogs baying at the moon... It reminded me of Artaud's mad conference at the Sorbonne... Then someone in the audience challenged the poets in a dull and stupid way: "Why don't you write about something beautiful...why do you choose the slums?" One of them, Allen Ginsberg, got in a frenzy of anger, all the while remaining symbolic, and he challenged the man: "You come and speak a poem as beautiful as ours. You come and stand here, stand naked before people, I dare you. Take your clothes off. Stand naked before the world, as I have. Will you dare?" The man began to hem and haw. Then the poet took all his clothes off and stood naked. "Now let someone dare to insult a man who offers what he feels, who stands naked before everyone..."

Strangely enough (though he was no beauty), the way he did it was not shocking, but it was so violent and direct and had so much meaning (in terms of all our fears to unveil ourselves). After a while everyone threw his clothes back at him. It was really like the old surrealist-dadaist fights. The man in the audience was booed and hissed after being told he looked like Nixon, and what could you expect... The poets went on reading and shouting for hours, and I left. It was really like hearing surrealism born in the Brooklyn gutters... Jewish, of course...

Off to walk to the post office to mail this.

Anaïs

New York, October 1956

Hugo was grinning like a young man at the airport, but actually he has not been well. Definitely, he shows me his crippled side—and is perhaps quite capable of a joyous, earthy one with someone else. I know already, from his letters, that his affair is over. We live like friends, concerned with each other's well-being. We went to the beach. We went on a shopping spree. He bought a suit. He bought me a cape. He expresses his love with gifts. He buys champagne and caviar. We kiss tenderly. After a week I was ready to do anything to see him alive again. Even to give him a mistress. So I called Karon Kehoe.

I had met Karon during a stay in New York, at Sylvia Ruggles'. I expected the editor of *Charm Magazine*, but not the soft, sensuous camellia-skinned woman with white hair—a young, smooth face, cat-grey eyes, small and sensitive hands.

Hugo was ill. I took him some of Sylvia's curried rice upstairs.

Karon smiled, talked a little (her mouth is full with teeth slightly curved outward, giving one the impressions of a mouth that seems to offer itself as if set permanently in the fullness of a kiss). She drank two martinis and fell asleep after murmuring that she had not slept for two nights. She looked very beautiful asleep, and it was difficult to follow the conversation with the Ruggles and a boring lawyer.

After this evening, Karon, Sylvia and I had a lunch together in such a noisy restaurant that we could not hear each other.

Karon was preparing to leave for a vacation and said casually, "Why don't you come with me?" At the time I thought of this as a light and free pleasure I wished I had the freedom to accept. I gave her all my books and we corresponded.

The next time we met I wanted her to go to the beach with us after a lunch we had together with Hugo. Hugo, of course, would not manifest any reaction. In his usual, non-committal way, he said quietly: "She is very pretty. Why doesn't she dye her hair?"

Monday evening she came beautifully dressed in black, heavily bracleted, and necklaced with silver. Karon took Mitou in her arms and enacted with her such a sensuous mock battle that I could tell (even if I had not divined it with my own senses) the extent and vitality of her physical duels. She tamed an unwilling cat—but not with gentleness. In the dissolved, warm light of the room, luxuriant, pale, alive, I felt like Mitou, truly hypnotized by her vividness and the startling incarnation of all my women—Djuna, Sabina, Lillian. On the couch, while Hugo was in another room, she touched my arm lightly at first—all the musicians and artists of love know the power of that first light touch. But in the bedroom she uttered passionately: "You are someone I want in my life for always. We have a great deal of time—I don't want to rush anything. I love you." All the faces of women I loved flowered in hers, with one continuity of intensity and fever—June's, Thurema's, Tana's...

Hugo had dinner with us, but he did not give up his drumming lesson. He left us, and then Jim and Dick, who had come in for a little while, left us too.

After they left, Karon sat on the floor. Her words were so incoherent I cannot retrace them. "I am so happy. I know I was beginning a new cycle. I love your gentleness."

I took her hand and said very tenderly, "I never had a complete relationship with woman."

This startled her. "I had heard...I had been warned...but your books..."

I knew all the time that I was entranced by a passion I could not share, but it was difficult to subdue the incandescence of her face and voice, and I felt responsible because I was aware of my attraction and had obeyed the impulse without being fully aware of its direction.

I did not refuse her kiss; it was too beautiful an offer. But I felt as Gore once said: "When I kissed a woman I did not like the softness." I missed the hardness, the firmness of a man. She continued to live out her dream. She questioned me. I was truthful about Hugo and Rupert. Soon I would be leaving. I was already torn between two loves.

Then another kiss—the strong, grey hair, the beautiful, softly rounded shoulders.

The telephone rang: It was Jim.

"Rupert telephoned" (I am supposedly living with Jim and Dick). "I told him I did not know when you would be back. But I heard him tell the operator to try again in a few minutes."

I tried telephoning Rupert, but the long distance operator was keeping the line for *his* call. Karon came to the bathroom while I telephoned, kissed my hands, bit my fingers—but the telephone call had made Rupert a reality. She saw me tense and concerned. I said: "I have to go to Jim's and be there when he calls again." We walked to Jim's, only ten minutes away. Jim and Dick received me gaily, like two conspirators in one of my novels. I went to Jim's bedroom, and Jim and Dick kept Karon away. Rupert's phone call came through: "I have so much work, swamped in papers to correct. I feel so tired. Hated to miss your call Sunday, but Reginald and Hilda came, and so I went to the family's to stay. When are you coming back?"

We talked. I was concerned about his disappointment—about his future in teaching. When we went out again, Karon and I, she was feeling the shock. I reminded her that I had told her the truth. We sat at a bar.

"But I love you, and I had imagined you free, and we could be so happy together." In the street she had tears in her eyes. This disturbed me. I called a taxi for her. I was exhausted and numbed.

I would not see her until Wednesday—when we were both quieter. I did not want her hurt. I felt such love of her passion, and her abandon—and perhaps I was wrong, because she continued to court me, to use all her seductions on me. But I was never confused. I knew it was not desire. And my dream last night made it clear: Karon took me, but she had a penis. And as I awakened, Karon became Rupert.

Karon is fascinating. A new passion is always fascinating. I did feel I could have been happy with her, and with Hugo. But my body did not respond to her vehemence, her caresses.

Monday night we went out, the three of us. She charmed Hugo. And I felt: what a delightful mistress she would make for him. She is intelligent, enthusiastic, sensuous, pleasure-loving. But Karon was preoccupied with stealing caresses, holding my hand.

Telephone calls. She has a light voice. A strange mixture, her body so voluptuous, her light voice and chiseled hands.

I was tempted.

I felt the passion has lessened in my life with Rupert. He has made a marriage of it—a domestic life—and I have two homes, two husbands.

But at no moment did I have the feelings towards Karon that I had for Rupert.

Tonight Karon is in Dallas on a business trip. Hugo is with a negro drumming class. I telephoned Rupert, who was at his desk correcting papers. I told him I, too, was at work in my room.

Karon called me from the airport. Her emotionalism forces me to answer. I feel ungenerous. It is not real. But I could not have her with that feeling of shock she had after her passion the other night. I remembered the times I behaved as she did...and how no one came to my rescue (the first time Albert Mangones kissed me, roused me, and then I did not hear from him for days and days).

Letter from Anaïs Nin to Rupert Pole:
New York, October 1956

My darling:

I felt so deeply for you last night after our talk—darling, I never imagined this teaching job as it turned out to be—I'm very concerned. I want so much for you to be freer—and it seems to me it was *misrepresented* to you. I wish I were there to talk it over with you—my darling Chiquito—you are so trusting in spite of your intelligence and your knowledge of facts. How could such an intuitive and clever young man get in such a trap? Well, enough said about the trap. What will you do? Sincerely, I don't feel you burned any bridges behind you if you went back to the job the Forest Service offered you. It is not easy to admit to a mistake but I think it can be done without loss of dignity or prestige. I keep turning all this in my head and wish we could talk.

Darling—above all—don't feel trapped—nothing is ever final and we are both too clever to get enslaved. Remember we are the best jail-breakers of all.

A

New York, October 1956

Waiting for Bogner. For the first time in my life I have had to deal with fog. *Le brouillard.* As if the clear, sunny climate of my thoughts was related to the climate of my Latin countries. This fog was characteristic of Hugo (Scotland), the same one he still wraps himself up in. Last night he said Bogner accused him of concealment. When I teased him and playfully said, "You tell *me* what you're concealing," he answered as in the old days: "I don't know." And today I know it is true.

I felt the same way. Fatigue? A need to sit down. After arriving by great efforts at the peak of Annapurna, taking responsibility for everything, the self as director, producer, actor, spectator, I wanted to sit down. Yes, it is I, not Hugo, France, America, Rupert, health, and now I do feel the hard core of reality. But having touched it (put a flag on it), I fell into vagueness and diffusions. I, who placed so much pride in my clarity, focus, sharpness.

Fog. The analysis that once seemed the most real of all moments (beside my passion for Rupert) now also appeared vague.

But what was *I* concealing?

I was clear about Karon. It was her own charm and vehemence that extracted from me the words she wanted to hear, which I must retract tomorrow. Once over the telephone she said, "I am tired and I'm getting a cold, I'm going to bed early."

"No more nightmares," I said, referring to three she had described to me.

"If I can imagine you beside me, I won't have nightmares. Will you let me imagine you beside me?"

Could anyone say "no"? And then, while watching Hugo's films in the semi-darkness, when I believed she was immersed in the images, she said swiftly: "Is it absolutely impossible?" Surprise attacks. I answered "No," but as one answering to pacify a feverish child. She is Rupert's age, nearing forty—but fresh and adolescent. No fog there.

Telephoning Rupert the one night Hugo went drumming—establishing a line between two desks full of papers (only Rupert hates papers and I don't). A long, relaxed talk this time, not from a phone booth. But the violent, powerful pull is gone, because what awaits me is a small cage of domesticity and family. Once, when I had given up trying to understand why Rupert did not want to see Paul and Renate as often as I did even though he likes them, it was revealed in a light conversation during which I suddenly remembered he had once talked a great deal about skiing. We went once together, near San Francisco. My sense of balance being good from dancing, I managed to stay on my skis in the lowlands. But as soon as I tried to climb, even sideways, I went downhill more than uphill and wore myself out. It was like a nightmare in which you lose ground. The rest of the group made it to the hilltop. I quietly disappeared and watched him descend several times. After that day, Rupert stopped skiing, so I asked him: "You used to love skiing—why did you never go again? Because I couldn't keep up with you? But you could go with other people…you mustn't give up things just because I can't do them."

"Oh, no," said Rupert. "I wouldn't enjoy it without you. We both prefer swimming, anyway. I wasn't any good at skiing."

"You didn't give it up because of me?"

"No, any more than you would give up seeing Paul and Renate because I can't keep up with their flights of fancy."

But that's just it, I thought; he does avoid spending time with them, and this is the reason. He is uncomfortable in the only world in which I am happy. I remember the expression of his eyes while Paul and Renate talked surrealistically about events at Holiday House. Rupert would tend the fire in the fireplace, or make coffee, all the while looking at me as if I were going up in a balloon.

Waiting for Bogner. Last night Hugo came home very depressed. "I was completely blocked at Bogner's. She let me flounder. She just sat and repeated I was avoiding something. A blank wall."

"Yes, I know. We're both settling down. We are comparatively at peace and we're afraid to be stirred up again. But don't be hurt when she lets you flounder. Evasion was one of your main defenses. She must let you see that evasion leads nowhere."

His mood was heavy—but I helped him get out of it by my own methods, which are not indulgent.

"Come on, it's sulking, you know. This summer I treated my depressions roughly, and it helped. I realize they were not in proportion to reality—not justified by reality. Treat it roughly. I am in sympathy with you. I know how you feel. But let's pretend you're taking out one of those young things who think you're so marvelous, so you can't be depressed, you just have to be charming and gay."

He laughed. At first we had walked through the Village mournfully, looking for an external cure. But after my talk we went to a bad movie—came home—and I gave him pleasure by expressing pleasure at an extravagance he had committed for me: to cure me of gin, he bought me a split of champagne to drink that night.

And then to sleep.

Actually, what we are making such a romantic to-do about is what the French accepted long ago, the division between marriage and sensuality. After nearly separating this summer, we got frightened, are together again, faced with the same impasse: no sensual life.

I long for Rupert again…and Hugo?—what does he feel?

When I told Bogner how simply and clearly I saw the two relationships, I asked her: "Am I over-simplifying…eluding some deeper truth?"

"I don't know yet."

I feel clear and comfortable.

I'm proud of not having dissolved into depression. I was sad last night to have written Rupert about delaying my trip a week. Four weeks was too quick. I was not ready.

Bogner: "You seem to reach peace, comfort or serenity only when the sensual life is excluded."

"Yes. At the same time I feel myself dying (or aging, which is the same), and I identified with Anne in *The Mandarins* living out her last love affair and then retiring (wanting to die). What has happened to my sharp, keen, wild passion for Rupert?"

When I describe the life I dreaded being condemned to, it sounded bourgeois, dull, the music every Thursday night, the same pieces, the same words, the same people, nothing new, no modern composers. At the same hour, at ten or eleven, they ask for beer, and then Helen either goes to sleep, or we talk about Anne Baxter's life as parents would...

When Rupert doesn't know what to say, he doesn't draw anything from within himself, but rather delivers Lloyd's tirades on architecture, on how other architects copy Frank and Lloyd, how misjudged, unappreciated Lloyd is. He is like a robot with Lloyd speaking through him. He has inherited both from his mother and Reginald an actor's mimetics. Only I know exactly at what moment he is Rupert. This struck me the first day we talked together, at a stop at a gas station, while he attended the car, pipe in mouth, and a Tyrolian hat on his dark hair—and he talked to the man who was filling the tank. My god, he is *acting* a bigger, heavier, older, more important man. Rupert was then twenty-eight—but his frame, the delicacy of his face, the shape of his hands were adolescent. When Rupert cannot talk as Rupert, he acts or talks like Lloyd. Sometimes I feel he does this because to a boy's eyes (he was ten when Lloyd became his stepfather) it must have seemed to him that Lloyd was a *man*, as Reginald was not. Lloyd was taller, stouter, had a bigger voice, a violence Reginald did not have. It must have seemed to Rupert that Reginald lost out to a stronger man (Lloyd is healthier, with a peasant's strength. At sixty he can work on his mountain as well as a younger man). Rupert also set out *not* to be Reginald.

New York, October 1956

In a dim bar, Karon arrived with several silver bracelets clinking, and we exchanged gifts. "I want you in my life forever, Anaïs." Then I quietly told her the truth again, that I am in love with Rupert, that I love Hugo and I am trying to make him happy, that I have never loved a woman except with friendship.

She constantly contradicts herself. One moment she accepts everything, the fact I have so little free time, yet at another moment she says intensely: "Will you call me at eight?"

"I have people for dinner."

"Call me."

At eight I called, left the Geismars and Hugo talking. She wanted me to come to her place Monday night (while Hugo drums). She would make dinner. How early could I come?

Worse, she spoke the language of lovers, and I could not answer. I could tell by her voice what she expected Monday night. Then she repeated: "I love you. I miss you."

"I have to go now," I said.

"But you have only talked with me five minutes. Will you call me at midnight?"

"No, Karon."

Then she said the fatal words: "You know, all that you said at the bar—it was all nonsense. We'll talk about that."

I don't know which element awakened me, her possessiveness, her aggressiveness, but I knew the charm was gone, and I knew I could no longer pretend—I did not feel like going Monday and was struggling against her invasion.

For the first time I was able to free myself. I called her Saturday and told her I could not come, and why. She cried. But I was gentle and firm.

After this I understood that freedom is within you too. *I was always compelled by the needs of others.*

Katarina Castle telephones (I met her twice at Peggy's). She lost her husband. "And I have to talk to you. You are the only one I can talk to. I know you look so fragile but you have so much strength, spiritual strength."

Then last night, as Hugo sat beside me on my bed and we drank our last drink, I saw his hand, and I felt *reverence* for it. And the thought of it shocked me, for it is not what a wife should feel. Speaking of it to Bogner, I wept.

And now?

"What has affected my passion for Rupert? Was it the shock of separating from Hugo this summer, the real loss of Hugo? Was it because he has immersed me in a marriage when all I wanted was a lover?"

I can see in Bogner's eyes that I handled the mirage of Karon clearly and well.

Now I feel humble too, because I acted somewhat as Karon did when I had my infatuation for Gore, and once or twice I acted like this towards Bill Pinckard out of anxiety. He used to rebel against my calling when he was slow in starting his day, and I could not bear the silence, the not knowing if I would see him.

I tried to be more human with Karon than Bill or Gore were with me—but when someone is at a peak of desire there is no cure but a break. And to be with someone who desires you and whom you don't desire is very painful.

Just before Bogner's today I had a moment of sharp aliveness—as I have rarely these days. Was it because I was decompressing, reaching freedom? If only people would realize it is all inner. I projected my guilt, or exaltingness onto others.

Karon was not only Karon to me, but also myself intoxicated by a passion that the other did not answer (Gore), and this made me understand her and seek to cure her without damage.

But Karon was also aggressive—I did not fling myself upon Gore. Of course I tried to charm him and expressed all the tyrannies of anxiety: "Call me—call me."

How Karon talked! How strange to create characters like her and then have them spring out of your book and into your life. The first night I blamed the martinis, but she was always the same. "Rutteridge—I love him deeply. We have known each other for seven years. At first he was married, then two years ago he left his wife. He has the gentleness you have—only less. I don't know what he wants. It is always good."

But over the telephone: "When I came back from Dallas I wanted to be with you. But it seems to me I was with you, Rupert and Hugo. Why can't you go away with me? Next week I have some holidays."

"I'm leaving for California soon."

"But you'll come with me sometime? I feel like swooping down and carrying you away from both men."

It is strange how possessiveness can suddenly distort the image of a beautiful woman into a faceless force that is ugly. Yet the possessiveness of Gonzalo, Rupert, Hugo never bore such a face...it is different when you love.

I lost my first image of Karon—the soft contours, flawless skin, electric grey hair, grey eyes, the childish voice and small, very supple hands.

I felt at peace to be delivered of her intensity.

Above all, I could not say "I love you."

Letter from Anaïs Nin to Rupert Pole:
New York, October 1956

Darling:

Felt better after our telephone talk, although I can tell your cold was *bad*...and I wondered how you *really* felt. I must confess, I hate your new job already! We'll find a solution together, I know...in peace, clarity and closeness.

Please don't wear yourself out fixing up the house Saturday...please, darling— for my sake—I had a chance to replenish my energy, and you haven't.

Last night, after working until ten, Jim and Dick returned and asked me to go for a stroll through the Village. We saw a Hindu poet in his soiled white costume and dirty blue jacket—negroes in red shirts and berets and *beards* looking like ancient biblical Africans—women in new fashions (cloche hats, pale makeup and heavily made-up eyes) looking like flappers of the '20s.

I need Friday because that's the last visit to Jacobson—what he gives me is too strong to take more than once a week—something new (probably from the fins of Moby Dick!). "Now all we need to do is find the secret for your bronchitis that *you* share with Yul Brynner"—Jacobson is experimenting on him: Brynner gets it every time he has a play opening! He looks so strong on film, but he had bronchitis while filming the death scene in *The King and I*.

As you see, I'm trying to win on every front: The freedom problem we'll lick too.

A story on segregation. Two successful, wealthy negroes came to N.Y. for a fling—went to plays, nightclubs, etc. and had a fine time, but they wanted a little feminine companionship and they were told just to telephone the hotel desk. So they did and immediately two blondes appeared at the door. The two negroes hesitated a little... One said: "Do you think we should?" The other decided: "Why not? We only want to sleep with them, we don't want to go to school with them."

All my love, darling—a double dose for the cold to combat microbes!

A

New York, October 1956

Instead of an evening of struggling to dissolve Karon's unanswered desire, I chose a carefree evening with Jim and Dick. I like to slip into black tights and a beige car coat, hair down my back, a black velvet circle to keep the front in place. We started the evening with a parody of Karon's exigencies because they knew if I did not laugh at this I would feel badly at depriving her of this evening. I used the large clock for timing eggs and received them with it placed against my heart.

"You are one minute late! When it rings exactly at zero you must say you love me!"

They did. I said: "Such a lovely, spontaneous expression of love!"

But we gave up the game because it reminded us of the times we had taken the clock too seriously. We went off walking springily and lightly to the Rienzi, a café atmosphere. In the bohemian crowd there I feel at ease. I do not know what they read, but I share their love of jazz. I know they believe Beckett to be profound because they don't understand him, but I know, in spite of *Godot*, that he is not. Whoever has made an effort to deviate from the trite is not necessarily meaningful. However, we must be grateful to them. I do not attack them in public, because the antipodes of the mind must be explored, and Beckett's ramblings are more alive than the frozen foods and taxidermist products we get from American publishers.

Perhaps they do read Beckett. Jim and Dick do not. They talk about their happiness. It took years for the relationship to become harmonious; they had to recognize their need for each other and accept happiness. Jim shed his masochism and rejection of happiness. They both shed their defenses. Jim is less critical of Dick's talk and recognizes in its moments of frivolity a true feeling he cannot put into words. Drunk, Dick expatiates on "rag pickers," Jim on his flow of writing, and I on my regret that I have missed several important metamorphoses. Dick truly climbed into Jim's world by feeling.

Dream: I am flying to Los Angeles in a plane that has no wings. It is a new kind of jet plane, they tell me. But I am a little anxious. It is all nose—all body—and two small wings at the end. But I land at Chicago. It is not a non-stop flight. There I am stranded, and Rupert is expecting me at six o'clock. I try to charm the airport officials into taking me into another plane so I will get there in time. Otherwise I will be three hours late. I am beginning to persuade them. One of the officials has something to do in Los Angeles. I am standing around anxiously while they are telephoning, filling out papers, etc.

I have difficulty returning to Rupert. But he is so depressed, discouraged, and after talking with him (overwhelmed by work, seeing no one but his family, working for Lloyd, Helen, Reginald), I felt such compassion for his distress. I bought my ticket for the 20th. "I have a sense of failure," he says about teaching.

Meanwhile, my life with Hugo is harmonious. My energy is so much lower that I no longer rebel against the price I pay for comfort, for doctors' care, for dentistry, for rugs, for trips: my life. You give your life, your whole life, to bourgeois demands and in return you have a bed and good food, but no leisure, no time to live as you wish.

But I get the same at the other end—work, housework, family, boredom, a mediocre world—I have ceased to struggle.

Hugo talked last night about his need of a home.

If I were twenty I would break with all of it. Today I am beaten by my health and diminishing strength—I am afraid the artist is dying.

I spent these five weeks working on the home and repairing the damage of three and a half months with Rupert (low blood count, pre-ulcer conditions). I have produced in two years only 84 pages of writing.

Next day

I wrote that last page so pessimistically, after what seemed like a peaceful Sunday (Sunday was always my most hated day). Hugo and I finished a screen made of Japanese rice paper and his large engraving with a light behind it, which has astonished and enchanted everyone (it was originally conceived to conceal a monstrous air conditioner). Then we drove to Riis Park Beach, passing near Karon's apartment in Brooklyn Heights. Hugo asked me about Karon.

I explained that Karon was possessive like Thurema and that I was shying away from her (to explain not inviting her so often).

We walked along the boardwalk. He took a quick swim. Watching him walk into the water, I remembered weeping at Bogner's because the weight of Hugo's depression and lifelessness had always made me feel guilty, as Rupert's irritability does, or Gonzalo's rages, or Henry's remoteness—until I found out the cause of them. With Henry I quickly realized it was due to his writing. When he was *in* life he was wholly in it, but when he was writing he was dehumanized, cold and remote. Knowing this calmed me. About Gonzalo: I found out most of his rages were born of jealousy or guilt. And this helped me to cope with his storms. But with Hugo, I never knew.

I imagine that Bogner wants me to not repeat myself...wants me to continuously move forward. I say that we have already talked about this (the concept that my father was not happy at home, that he was very happy *away* from home).

"The facts and observations are exact," said Bogner. "It is your interpretation that is erroneous. Your father did have preoccupations outside his life at home, but from this you deduced you were not pretty or intelligent enough to keep him there."

Interpretation of Hugo's depressions... Because I did not love him with passion? But he was depressed when we were first married, when I did desire him. He was sick before I met him, with nervous indigestion, etc.

I felt lighter. And whoever thinks this exploration is self-centered and futile, from what I learned today I helped Hugo, Jim and Dick, Millicent, Karon, Rupert (letters), and affected shopkeepers, bus drivers, policemen, cleaners, etc., more people than those who *set out* to be selfless or without self-exploration!

I *could* stay here with Hugo, with just the tenderness, devotion and friendship. I could forget Rupert because I can't play roles anymore. I can't be what Rupert needs. What he needs I am not—the relationship is false—only the desire and feeling are real. We only touch as lovers. Everything else is wrong.

A summerlike day in October. I went to Dunhill's to get Hugo's favorite cigars. The room where the boxes are kept is like a sacristy of sandalwood. A man officiates among the pale and odorous boxes. Two Italian priests are indulging the sin of orgy of the sense of smell. The door keeps dust and dryness away, ideal temperatures for the leaves.

Out on Fifth Avenue again. I drop in at the French bookshop for two new Simenon books and one more Simone de Beauvoir. The salesgirl asks me: "Pardon me, but aren't you on a television program?"

Out on Fifth Avenue again. Only one new dress this month, because I concentrated on redecorating the apartment and making Hugo comfortable.

Hugo came home early to practice his drums. We talk quietly in the kitchen and I tell him I would like to leave on the 20th to work on the possibility of a scenario for *A Spy in the House of Love*. "But I want to be sure we can do what we like without hurting the other."

He assured me he no longer reacts to my trips, that we had had a happy time together. Peace, even. But underneath do we suffer from the death of physical connection, from pain at *knowing* there is a lover somewhere? I am not happy to imagine Hugo and Karon together, and I understand Hugo's animal suffering at imagining me with a lover.

This we would not think of this month. But it was there. Hugo concealed it from himself by creating a profusion of dreams and at the same time a smokescreen. I faced it with Bogner, but most of the time we tried to forget it.

Annette Nancarrow came from Mexico on her way to a tour around the world for the Mexican Tourism Bureau. But Annette is not well physically, and it hurts me to see the disintegration of a woman's beauty. A man's aging is different. He ages like a bronze statue, acquires a patina, but it has a character and a quality.

Peggy was there, in a red dress, too brittle, too sharp-witted, telling of her visit to Paul Bowles, his house in Tangiers.

"The light is clear, as it is said to be in Greece—incredibly luminous. His apartment is at the top of the tallest building and he sees all of the city, and the sea, and the ships. As soon as I saw it, I realized again he was the only man for me, and why no other man could get to first base. He is so wise, and so subtle, and we always think the same way. I had hoped my wound was healed (they had had an affair many years ago) but when I sailed away I felt the same way, as if an unbreakable cord were being pulled out of me, stretching between us but never breaking. He was very truthful. Jane Bowles, though, not a true wife, is a fixture, and the Arab boy who has become a very good painter is his son. He had a tooth missing and hair uncombed and sloppy clothes, but after a few days of my presence all this improved... He also had a small tower house in the Carlsbads, a native house."

But her eyes do not see the Paul Bowles I sensed though his novels, which he conceals. And it is Jim who tells me why Paul had to leave Mexico.

"In Mexico he lived in San Miguel de Allende. He employed young boys. He whipped them, or at times let them whip him. One day they went out in the woods, and cut down branches, and he was whipping the boy when one of the villagers came upon the scene and they were arrested. To save himself he explained he was whipping the boy because he had stolen his watch. The boy was put in jail for three years. He sent Paul a message: 'When I get out I will kill you.'"

Now that Jim and Dick have found a level of communication and acceptance, we go out together. Dick is caressing and gay. Jim is always tense, even when we consume a bottle of champagne together, while Dick sings impossible songs with an exquisite voice. "Love For Sale." Jim is writing a play and they are both marveling at Jim's facility. Jim feels it is a good play. High, we discuss our destructive demons and when and why they appear. Dick becomes a demon when Jim's writing is attacked. "Jim's writing is Dick's purity," I say, "because in the world where we live, a voice is a commercial commodity, and Dick has been manipulated by merchants from the beginning. In writing, one has a choice."

Jim says: "Anaïs's demon is self-destructive. When she is about to destroy, she turns on herself."

Jim is self-destructive too. He remembers that from the very beginning at Black Mountain I did not say: "This is good writing," but instead I said, "Go on, go deeper and it will become good—like the pitch in a voice. Find your level. This is not yet you."

Six o'clock. I await Hugo, who is at Bogner's. He will take a long bath and read the paper and drink a scotch while I make dinner. We can talk about *The Mandarins* or about Hugo's desire to make a film in Venice. He will mention with familiarity Proust's passage on Venice.

He is not tense and irritable like Rupert, but he is often depressed. He is resigned to waking up at four (in spite of the drugs Bogner gave him) and to read. We are at peace. He has the same heaviness, slowness of tempo, which makes me feel anchored. But now he is no longer a man I wanted different. I need peace. It still saddens me that he never opens the curtains, that he prefers the air conditioner to an open window, cigars, that he temperamentally is my opposite—but I appreciate other things. He is thoughtful of me, he is tender, he is more articulate than he was. He is intelligent, and creatively we have the same aim.

No doubt the way he bows over me and kisses me is paternal. But this paternity has masked the truth that I mothered him!

Last night with Jim and Dick, we went to the bookshop, we bought James Baldwin's second novel and one by Camus.

Why do I write like this without stopping? At Dr. Jacobson's, in the bus, and now with the cat sitting next to me.

Last night, Monday (the night Hugo goes drumming), Karon called up. She talked naturally, said it had been a misunderstanding, that what she felt was too deep, and that she wanted to see me, to be my friend. I said: "Let's wait till I return. It is too soon." Why do I think of her and Hugo together? To hurt myself, to punish myself for my life with Rupert.

Peggy was saying: "The exquisite thoughtfulness and subtlety of Paul. While I had to work with Olin Downes, collaborate with him, Paul held back the story of his experience with Downes' destructiveness, but when I was a victim of it (he used my contacts to foster the presentation of his opera while pretending to be working for mine) only then did he tell me all."

Does she know by what violent acts Paul achieves relationship to human beings? Does she read the end of his novel in which the man sadistically kills the Arab and says: "This murder, at least, was a moment of relationship to a human being"?

Some time ago I wrote about the *sympathy* of Simenon, and now I am reading a study of him in which this sympathy is stressed. "Nothing repels him. Physical sickness, crime, vices, perversions." He has sympathy for *all* of man.

This sympathy was once my main motivation. As a child I knew that the presents made to us by Mrs. Rodríguez, because of her wealth, were not sufficiently appreciated and I made her the following speech (which became a subject of laughter in the family): "You know, Altagracia, it isn't the luxuriousness of your presents for us children that I appreciate as much as your *thoughtfulness* in choosing them."

What became of this sympathy? Neurosis corroded it. Neurosis is a kind of unhealable wound. A man with an unhealable wound does not have much sympathy for others. People have always *felt* this sympathy but it did not come through in the work. This year I feel it was restored to me in its fullest scope because I am not drained by my anxieties.

Rationalization: It is natural for a couple to lose sexual interest in each other after thirty years of marriage.

Analysis: But I lost my interest in Hugo early in the marriage—as soon as I met Henry. No, before that.

So we retrace our steps—to the beginning. Why did I consider my father's leaving as a sexual defeat...because I somehow became convinced it was the *sexual* which drew him out of the house, away from us? Did I, as a little girl, compare myself with the women who came to the house? Overhearing my mother's scenes, was the sexual betrayal stressed? Is this where the concept that sensuality and love are not reconcilable originated? It was sensuality that led me to Henry, certainly not love. Sensuality also with Gonzalo. Sensuality with Rupert. The addition of a human love and devotion was a feminine expansion, an excrescence, but it did not withstand the test of time, which is the test of love.

New York, October 18, 1956

Now that Hugo and I have ceased making our marriage a battlefield, I can finally understand what this means. Hugo is capable of sustaining his destructive sulkiness for three months, as he did when he lay on his back with a slipped disk. The true reason behind his impossible behavior then was that Bogner had told him: "If you feel you urgently need analysis I will come down and see you, but don't expect me to come and hold your hand!" The last part of the phrase she uttered flippantly and later recognized as a mistake, but Hugo took it so seriously he swore he would never call her, and instead vented his anger upon Millicent, Jim and myself, straining our devotion to its maximum! Bogner had merely intended to warn him against exploiting his physical helplessness for sympathy, and to imply he had to continue an analytical relationship. He was sulking for these past five weeks because she let him flounder in silence and his typical *buté* [mulish] attitudes, in which I used to get trapped while vainly seeking the reason. In reality I did commit many acts that were hurtful, but Hugo's revenges were more than compensatory.

(So funny, when you write in the bus, while waiting for red lights to change, the stops seem too short, and the "go" too long. I have to keep my phrases suspended, waiting for the bus to stop lurching!)

The deepest aspect of this drama of Change is that Hugo is shedding his heaviness, and this month we achieved smoothness, harmony and lightness, a rhythm that was the dream I could not reach in maturity. The pieces began to fit, accords were made. While Hugo shed the anxieties that oppressed me, I shed my own. I asked him seriously and yet lightly too: "Will you please tell me one thing: was it my trips that made all the trouble between us?"

"Honestly, darling, I don't know. I'm in a morass, a chaos still. I did not feel as before that a door was shut in my face, that I was left out, felt lonely and unrelated. Nor did I feel, as I did as a child, responsible for my father's unhappiness at home, unrelated to him except when I was bad and he spanked me. No demonstration of love or tenderness—but anger, yes."

This morning I awaken at eight o'clock and see that Hugo is asleep. Through the eyes of Simenon I see his bedroom, which I once hated, differently. Hugo *is* a heavier kind of animal than I am. Like some of Simenon's characters, he likes his cave, his hole, his *autre*. He is comfortable there. It is his nest. He needs it. It is a womb. It protects him. *The Mandarins* is open on his bed. His light is on, which means he was awake for a while during the night.

Quietly I close the door and take a shower, make up my face, get ice from the kitchen (my beauty secret), pack my bags already half-packed, and just as I am finishing he awakens. We embrace with tenderness.

While he takes a shower I start breakfast. The Celestial Housekeeper has installed new charcoal grey linoleum in place of the worn and soiled one of indeterminate pattern. I look into the front room to admire the new couches, no longer the bohemian couches of poor quality made by an Irish carpenter who could sing but not make furniture—but neat, modern, pale wood ones with well-tailored foam mattresses covered by grey tweed, smart and perfect. The Celestial Housekeeper had the old phone changed, whose dial numbers were effaced, ordered a new rug, commissioned a painter. I leave a tender Hugo, as he was in my admiring eyes during the early part of our marriage before the neurosis gave him a lifeless quality I could not live with.

This morning he is alive, cheerful, tenderly regretting my leaving but not depressed, not heavy—and we drove to the beach and took a quick walk. I said, "You know, what is happening is that I am very slowly, very cautiously, very, very gradually falling in love with you again, but like Mitou I am putting only one paw down at a time as she does with everything new—and you are a new person, you know."

This process reminds me of the beautiful film *Secret of the Reef*, in which there are the births of baby turtles, pushing out from egg shells, the baby octopus pushing out from an egg that seems to be made of plastic, the lobster painfully pushing out from its old shell…

The painful explosions (from too much repression) Hugo and I suffered devastatingly are over, and we have fewer depressions and anxieties.

During our War—similar to a war between countries—many caricatures and distortions took place.

Last night's dream: Rupert asks me to go down to the cellar and bring back bottles of wine. I feel, as I often have when he has asked me to do things so difficult for me (like driving for ten or twelve hours or moving all in one day, changing the Sierra Madre house in half a day) that I can't do it. I look down the stepladder into a congested cellar. The bottles will be too heavy, too heavy. I tell him so, and he acts (as he often has in such cases) with impatience. He goes down with me, but impatiently. I am frightened and I hold back. There is a blank. The next thing I know Rupert has dived down in a diver's suit, and he is hammering away at the cellar, hoping to get in from the outside (as if the way of the ladder was impractical). I feel very uneasy and guilty. It is a dangerous job (as all sea-diving is, and his lungs are not strong). I can hear his hammer blows.

Actually, I am only returning to Rupert for *human* reasons. I cannot separate from him violently. He is a tender human being. But he is unaware of my tiredness, my inability to cope with his life. Being younger and stronger, he cannot understand how I feel. He cannot understand that when we go to his family for dinner, that cleaning up for four people and then running up and down the stairs several times an evening, I feel so tired I could weep.

But at this moment he is in trouble. He hates his job—and he is sick.

How can I break without damaging him? If I stay with him I will damage him more because I cannot live his life. His life is the way he is, and when I rebel against his life, I am rebelling against what he is, unless, like Hugo, he could *shed* his fears, negativism and neurosis. He is not as capable of deep analysis as Hugo. He rejects help. *He wants to do it from the outside*, hammer a hole. But he wanted me to go down the impossible ladder.

Los Angeles, October 1956, 1729 North Occidental Boulevard

I have learned to separate my private, personal experience from reality. The nightmare contains a truth. At the airport I see both the charm of Rupert and what dilutes my love. I find the same tenderness and desire, but something lighter and less painful. But I am caught in his needs. He shows the traces of his ordeal: the overwhelming new job, bronchitis and loneliness. He is thin and has dark shadows under his eyes. I am full of sympathy and love to see him happy, but deep down I am more detached. It is early, and we have dinner at the Café de Paris, and we go and see a Tahitian film. Then we go to bed and make love as before, but it does not have for me the unbearable keenness and sharpness. The next morning he makes breakfast for me (which he always does the first morning I am home, but only once). It is his way of saying he is happy I am home. He shows his happiness. He tells me how much he missed me, and I can see it is true.

Letter from Jim Herlihy to Anaïs Nin:
New York, November 1956

Dear Anaïs,

I am glad for all the news in your letter, and that your return helped Rupert; I hope you can help him in some way in his dealing with the youngsters. They would adore you. Why don't you teach them! Also glad your new apartment is what you wanted it to be, simple and light.

Yes, it is true, of course, that we did have less direct contact the last time you were here. I think I felt it a little bit. I'm sure there are lots of reasons, but not important ones. For instance, I was in a daze of awareness after what seemed like an interminable sleep. This is odd, and I can't quite explain it. But for the first few weeks happiness amazed me so much that I found myself musing over it, as much as the things and people around me. I love you more than ever, probably because I am freer than ever; and it may seem at first strange since I have no will to prove anything to anyone, even myself. Can you understand that something as novel as this and as wonderful would create something transitional in my relationships too?

Because of guilt (also recently abandoned, of course) I felt that even though I was loved marvelously, by you, I had to continue earning and earning and earning it. Now I don't believe that. I accept it. Anaïs loves me. I love Anaïs. It is simple. It is not something earned or even given or received, but something that exists, a constant transmission of power, what you have called "flow."

There is, Anaïs, absolutely nothing that I would not tell you, or that I would hide from you. You and I have viewed one another's demons and skeletons with sympathy, love, and without judgment, and I think this is one of the reasons we can enjoy one another so keenly. This has not changed and never will. I would feel very badly if you withheld pain from me now out of fear of affecting my new-found condition. Because I love you, you are entirely beautiful to me and I welcome all of you. After all, you are the one who taught me this!

I finished the play last night, or rather this morning. Yes, I think it was this morning as the sun had been up for an hour or two. I love the play. It is strange and funny and beautiful. The best first draft I've written, and by far the best play I've written. I had no will for letters at all during this period, which accounts for the lateness of this. I enjoyed yours keenly, but having answered it when I didn't want to would have been dangerous to me, and false to you. The play is called *Crazy October*, and it was written during the craziest October of my life.

I am going to see if I can defy your notion that one cannot stay high. I must admit it does seem ridiculous to imagine remaining up. But I have already set a record, for myself at any rate. I have never been this high this long. (Seven weeks! And no ground in sight!)

Love,
Jim

Letter from Anaïs Nin to Hugh Guiler:
Los Angeles, Tuesday, November 13, 1956

Darling:

I haven't been to the post office yet, but I want to mail this off to you and will write you anyway.

Now, my love, I know we are making a superhuman effort in every direction to rebuild our life together, and as I have told you nothing that you do will affect our relationship in any way, but as I told you before, we can only be close if we retain a certain open communication about night thoughts too... In my night thoughts I ask you not to let me return if you are in the middle of a love affair. Do not let me return at the wrong time. I had the intuition when I was there that you were attracted to Karon. She has the kind of figure you like. It was, in fact, one of the unconscious reasons for my accepting this job. Unless you ask me to delay my trip, I think that I can be all through by Monday the 26th (on Sunday the 25th I will be on the radio once more), and if I am completely wrong, just remember what the night thoughts are and do not be concerned. You have so many of them! I no longer think that all my intuitions are right. Tell me also where you are with Bogner...if you are still in difficulties, or flowing easily, etc. Probably your letter this morning will answer all my questions. Do you still plan on a vacation?

Thanksgiving day will be dinner at Anne Baxter's. I cannot get cured of this dislike of holidays. Last night my dream was quite terrible: my mother had died and I had to prepare her body for burial. I felt it was a sacred ritual. At the same time I felt it was a horrifying experience: to take care of my mother after death.

It was so strange to be lying on a hot beach (99 degrees) and thinking that in New York you were freezing.

Let me know if you need reading matter.

Anaïs

December 1956
Return to New York.

Letter From Rupert Pole to Anaïs Nin:
Los Angeles, December 1956

Love:

So unmitigatedly, miserably *tired.* Friday is always the worst day—films—films—films—math—broken projectors—math—no power—math—where's the film strip projector—QUIET—Mr. Pole, the other teacher wants to keep the projector for the next period—math—Mr. Pole—Mr. Pole—I'm surrounded, hemmed in, caught, trapped, caged, and right now I just can't take any more.

But I must write you, love, as you leave Wednesday, so I'll fatten this up by putting other things inside (as you sometimes do).

Reginald is driving me mad again—he spent two days in Riverside and is now back here at the Lombard again. He'd gotten used to cooking and having an ice box, so he comes here each day to cook. I have so little time and need a quiet dinner and rest, so I told him he'd just have to find his own place. He's getting a new pension of $105 a month now and they will pay all his medical needs in addition. He can well afford his own apartment.

Leona is bringing a second cello player tonight so I hope good music will cheer me up—but I'm so down now I fear this will be a lousy letter...

Better wait for my darling to bring my true life back to me—*muy pronto.*

R

Los Angeles, January 1957
Hugo had wanted us to go to Haiti for Christmas at the same time Rupert had two weeks for which he had been obsessively planning. I chose this time to satisfy Hugo and disappoint Rupert. I went to New York, but Hugo surrendered the trip (for business reasons), so I gave myself to Christmas shopping for him and to finishing redecorating the house. I bought incredibly beautiful gifts—I left them all wrapped, a house truly beautiful and elegant, and returned against my will to Rupert. And I returned to all that I hate: Helen was in the hospital. Lloyd was in a fury. Helen got well, but then we had the responsibility of taking Eric out too. And then there was Christmas, and Lloyd making of every occasion, including trimming the Christmas tree, a Hitler and coolie affair. It was oppressive. Then Reginald came to stay with Rupert and me, was there every day.

A few days at the beach were marred by the Malibu fire, which caused us anxiety for Cornelia Runyon and Renate. Then the fire rushed up to Lloyd's property, (at the time *no one* was allowed through) and burnt only a small part of it. Lloyd turned his fury against Rupert—Rupert should have saved the property! Why was he not there? The injustice and the irrationality of this! We watched the fire leaping across roads with all the equipment, men, water and airplanes impotent to stop it, and Rupert alone was going to accomplish this! Rupert, though upset, was not crushed by guilt as Lloyd wanted him to be. We were told by Helen to stay away for a while, believing Lloyd's fantastic accusations. She often thinks as he does but maintains balance by not getting angry.

It was a gloomy week. Rupert got ill (vomiting and dysentery), so we did not enjoy our New Year's Eve party. Renate came with a new lover, and a vengeful Paul appeared at same party with Yvonne, the woman Renate had been most jealous of...none of this helped. Nevertheless, Lloyd accuses us of only seeking pleasure and acting like the playboys of the Western world.

It took me days to re-integrate myself—and when Rupert began to work again, it was time to think of New York—memories of a gentle Hugo, so adoring, so generous, so appreciative, everything but the physical contact. But now we realize we were in deep trouble and look upon the last eight years as years of madness.

In New York Hugo was working with success, but still depressed. And I was investigating (for both of us, it seems) the theme of the *triangle*. In neurotic relationships there are never just *two*. There is always a third person. This was a mystery for me, but I can now see that in my relationships there was always another presence. It is not the simple figure of the other woman, the rival. It is far more intricate. It appears in literature, but it has been over-simplified. For Hugo, it is not the other man, the rival, the younger man in his dreams. This is a mask for the true triangle of our lives. Anaïs *and* her father and mother. Hugo *and* his father and mother. *He* is the young man, fearful of defeat, crushed by the union of the other two, jealous, seeking to divide them and possess one. The third figure is the parent who is never truly dispossessed, cast out, liquidated. In my case, it was the other woman who took my father away, my first defeat, the kind that condemns one to suffer a pattern of defeats. So in the triangle of Henry, June and me, I was the outsider imagining a great, violent union between them—I struggled to survive. How? By identifying with June, incorporating myself into her or *becoming* her: all of them were maneuvers of the weak. With Hugo, his father and mother, he was the young man who tried to get rid of his father (Hugo tried to horsewhip him when his father came from Puerto Rico) and possess his mother. So when I appeared, he had already been defeated. Another young man will arise to punish him in the same way, rise against him. We feel like usurpers of the parents' thrones. With Gonzalo, Helba and me, I was the third again. I came upon a union already sealed. I sought to disunite them, and I failed. I read *l'Invitée* by de Beauvoir. A husband and wife, not to be disunited, love the same young girl, and the girl does anything to not be shut out of the triangle.

"Dr. Bogner, all my life I have had the feeling that I was living a *ménage à trois*. With Hugo, at the very beginning, I imagined there was another woman. With Henry, June existed within our relationship, whether or not she was present. I live with both Rupert and Hugo, never alone with Rupert. And I saw a younger woman as Rupert's rightful wife."

The triangle was the parents and I. I seeking to displace one parent. Hugo's "sister" Karon came to displace Hugo and win her mother (me).

Thurema resembled my mother. Karon too.

At that time, too, I had the dream of *La Fausse Petite Fille*. I dreamt of three cold little girls. We were at the pool. The water was cold. I made them come out (as I did with the Campion children) and dried them. But the eldest died of the cold. Her bones were to be thrown over the high ledge of a mountain, to be scattered. When we reached over the ledge I peered down and found it was so high I could not see the bottom. I felt the bones would be scattered into *infinity*, irretrievable, so I said they should not be scattered there.

At that time too, my hatred of Rupert's life was made clear. "Imagine," I explained honestly to Rupert this time, "imagine your life without music, without musicians—well, that's my life here. It is constrictive."

His job only brings him $300 a month. He could do as well in New York. We could get away from the family. Could he be happy without nature? "Oh, I don't need nature *all* the time. I could be happy anywhere with you."

"But," he added later, "I cannot leave my father."

"Why couldn't your father live in New York?"

"He used to get terrible bronchitis there."

"But yet he gets that here too, just as you do."

He uses *external*, minor, petty reasons to rationalize what he doesn't want to do.

I don't want to do Rupert harm, but I have tried living his life for eight years, and neither of us is happy.

Am I reverting to my same pattern of living with Hugo *and* the lover? I am unable to separate from Rupert. When I am far from the spell of his body, or of his tenderness and emotionalism, I feel I can break with him, but when I am here it seems impossible.

Los Angeles, January 9, 1957

Dream last night: We are invited to have dinner with Marlene Dietrich. I am fixing up my face. I take such a long time making my face up that the dinner is over before I join them. I go off to some dangerous, gloomy place, full of wells, landslides, tunnels. I am in trouble.

The passion and tenderness for Rupert is so strong! I cannot fight it. I tried to dissolve it by adding up all that I hated: his family, his way of life, California, his friends—but when I build up my case he demolishes it all with an embrace. With tenderness. And his needs are so great. His family oppresses him. Reginald exploits him. He looks tired—and so the conflict goes on, and it will destroy me.

Just as when Helba tormented Gonzalo and I felt I had to give him happiness, I feel I must give Rupert happiness. And that means shining all his shoes, washing his socks, cleaning and cooking, listening to quartets, going to movies. I finally understand that for Rupert, a movie, a radio program, or a TV show is more important than being in touch with the world and life through other human beings. I find *life* is more important, being in touch with the world intimately, personally, not vicariously.

I have never gone of my own free will alone to a movie!

When Hilda arrived from Jerusalem, thousands of miles, to see Reginald, and arrived at the house, and sat down, Rupert was going to turn on his commentators at five o'clock as usual. Hilda had more to say than Edward R. Murrow ever did.

It is as if he prefers the *indirect* contact.

In New York I felt the intellectual harmony with Hugo, the graciousness and intelligence of our life together. If I lose Hugo I not only lose someone I love in a different manner, but a life that we have finally achieved by amalgamating his gifts and mine would be lost. There is strength in it. Alone with Rupert, I feel helpless and orphaned.

The great changes in Hugo are difficult to believe. *He is fighting against his own heaviness.* He is full of responsiveness and curiosities and possesses a flowing interest in life.

In a strange, ironic way, Hugo is now the young man and Rupert the older one: Rupert's fears make him static, a creature of habits and manias.

Renate and Paul have separated. Paul was childishly and insultingly faithless, not careful or delicate. As a hostess at Holiday House, Renate has met many people. When I first knew her, she was a romantic, but now she has undergone many changes. She is desecrating her own romanticism. She took a physical lover, a young man the opposite of Paul, who sells advertisements and likes deep-sea diving.

She is reinventing her life. When I saw the blonde girl whose portrait she was painting, I could not find the cold, destructive woman of Renate's description. Her language has changed.

She still says things like: "My paintings have a life of their own. The woman and the cat caused a scandal. The portrait of X got burned in the fire when nothing else did." But now she is trying to learn jive and the talk of the Malibu beach boys.

New York, January 15, 1957
    Arrived here at 6:30 AM.

Letter from Anaïs Nin to Rupert Pole:
New York, January 1957

My darling:
    This time the going away was very difficult and painful and I haven't recovered from it. I lost my enthusiasm for my work, my optimism… I could not make out whether you truly wanted me to give up my job, which has given us so much and is about to help give us a house. I hope it was just because it happened too often recently. It was the first time you made remarks like Lloyd's…about my wanting a good time! A good time indeed. That hurt me, darling, even that you could think I would separate from you for that. When you know how I work when I am in New York, so much so that I never see plays or movies, one or two in a month, and write most of my evenings. I hope you did not mean all this, and that it was merely the blues we always have when we part. Anyway, it affected me. I am dragging myself around, have no interest or pleasure in my work.

I had to be on TV twice for *Spy*, and Tom Payne is hoping for reviews. He and his wife invited the press to meet me at the Avon offices.

It is fifteen degrees with snow on the ground. I arrived in a snowstorm, and it was lucky you bought me those booties. I know you were tired when I left and I hope you caught up on your sleep. I am mailing you vitamins.

Here is my "good time" schedule: Up at seven-thirty, out at eight, drugstore breakfast, bus ride to office, get assignment, work, drugstore lunch, home, dinner on the wing and typing what I took notes about all day. Also typed two pages I wrote to add to the new novel for England, which the publisher found too short. Mailed them today, mailed book orders... I am staying at Eduardo's until he returns as I can get more work done alone. He arrives in a week or ten days, then I move back to Jim's. But, darling, don't write me, as I sincerely hate to see you tied to that desk any more than you absolutely have to. I will phone often.

When I tried to paint New York at its best, it was with a foolish notion to free you from schoolteaching and from the family pressures, but I see I was wrong. It only bothered you. You know, I am like a rain maker and I think of impossible dreams and solutions and magic to improve upon reality, and that is not your way of living. But meanwhile, we are working for the house, and it is becoming a reality.

Te quiero mucho, and don't forget that it is only because I have you, and am working for you and with you, that everything seems better. New York would be a bleak, impossible place if you were not there to return to.

A

New York, January 18, 1957

Perhaps because in an effort to lure Rupert away from a job that seems to have killed his spirit, and an oppressive, exacting family that gives us nothing but trouble, I painted an alluring picture of New York life...and this time I met with his resistance to my leaving.

I said, "But, darling, we need the money to build the house, to free ourselves of working forever!"

He clung to me, nevertheless. We made love hungrily and sadly, slept badly, and I felt that I couldn't bear this any longer, I couldn't bear to make one man happy and the other unhappy... I was shattered by the pain of seeing Rupert unhappy. Before going to sleep, I asked him: "What is it you want, darling?"

"I want you here. I will work for both of us."

"But that means no house, no trips." (I couldn't bear to say that his $300 a month would not pay for my doctors and medicines, my struggle for health on all fronts.)

I arrived in New York shattered. All month I have been unable to write, have felt tight, nervous.

Hugo was so happy to see me and said so, and seemed deeply contented. He slept the whole night through. (He too! Rupert can't sleep when I am gone!)

I felt torn and sick when I went to talk with Bogner.

"You are taking the *whole* responsibility yourself" were her first words. "Just as Helen chooses to live with such a man as Lloyd, Rupert and Hugo could choose another woman, another life. They do not have to live with you."

I said, "I feel disorganized." My throat, chest, stomach were constricted. My inability to write comes from this tightness, this not flowing.

She was in a sweet and gentle mood. I asked humorously: "What I feel now is different from a few years ago, when I felt driven to escape from one life into another, when Hugo's depression drove me towards Rupert's aliveness, or when Rupert's negativism drove me towards Hugo. Now all I feel is the human difficulty of keeping Hugo and Rupert happy...I cannot stop loving them or feeling related and bound to them."

This will destroy me. Already it is sapping all my strength, which I should use in editing the Diary, in my work. It is an illness, and to live in two pieces is a real torment.

When I arrived, Hugo had borrowed a sphere from the window display artist of Bergdorf Goodman—one piece, all mirror, like a half of a sun, and within it, rotating, a plastic planet, the concave mirror creating a thousand reflections. Shining on this was a spotlight with changing colors. The first night, after I arrived and we had dinner, we worked on photographing this, and then again the next morning. It was a beautiful spectacle.

And then the next evening Jim and Dick arrived, my two *light* children, very gay and very fulfilled. Jim sold his second play to Walter Starcke, to be directed by John Van Druten. First they admired the salon in its new aspect: the deep grey rug, so spongy and deep one could sleep on it. The curtains are of a rough hand weave, natural, with hand-blocked squares of soft colors that have the lightness of Miró. There are grey tweed divans, the large, square, well-filled pillows of different colors. What does the room express that reveals the changes in Hugo and myself? More solidity in the basic colors, more construction, a sense of design. The room stems from Hugo's engravings: black, white, grey, and the colored ones. The colored engravings are not in frames but all welded together now like a mural. The Japanese screen, with Hugo's large engravings on Japanese paper and a light behind it, is strikingly beautiful. The decorator (I) extended, embroidered and displayed Hugo's work—made a setting for it. It is truly the product of a magical collaboration.

A joyous evening. Hugo *participated* in it, gave and took his share of affection. The four of us interpreted the sphere in four different ways. Jim was concerned that it had no "core." Reflections and interplay were geometric, peripheral. Dick saw it as a giant Christmas tree ornament—a bubble of color, a ball, round and finite. Hugo saw the trickeries and elusive designs made by the lights. I saw what I always see in beauty and art: metamorphosis, mutation, an image of our souls, refracting lights.

With Bogner I dare myself to question my perfectly just, perfectly reasonable objections to Henry's shoddy friends (such as Fred), to Helba's insane domination over our lives, to Hugo's obsession with business (anxiety), and to Rupert's family...

On the surface, it is all reasonable, but I feel that in this lies a subtle form of destructiveness, which I am ready to face.

There is, concealed in this, an exaggerated discharge of anger. Is it that I cannot bear to say: Well, my love Henry has within himself, and is, in part, the white trash

I despise; my love Gonzalo was, in part, a psychotic who was related to Helba because they shared the same madness; my love Hugo was a man basically concerned with economic success; my love Rupert is a man who loves a home, a family, land, property, California, driving, bourgeois living, domesticity. There *is* something else, and I want to know what it is. Jealousy? Possessiveness? An alibi for partial relationships? I can't marry Rupert's life. Rupert is warm and emotional, but not imaginative or creative. I would not mind this, except he persists in domesticating me.

New York, January 29, 1957
Evening: watching films with Hugo, the ones we took of the plastic sphere. His new lens for photographing at night with ordinary lights was unsuccessful—but the ones I took during the day, by sunlight, were a success. Hugo is very pleased. I was delighted at my first footage of filmmaking. I saw Tiffany's windows and suggested Hugo film them.

New York, January 30, 1957
Dream: I am in a big house. The ceiling in the bathroom has been slit where it meets the wall, and the furniture has been syphoned out. I see this. I say, "We must telephone the police." There is a man there. I do not know if it is Hugo, who is slow to act. I rush out and think I can corner the criminal. I find a truck all loaded and ready to go. The one who is driving it is Rupert—a gangster Rupert, angry and full of hatred. When I call out to him he makes hideous faces at me. I think to myself it is my fault. His love has turned to hatred. Now I can't call the police.

Same dream: A Mexican is cutting my hair. I get angry because he is cutting into the back and I only wanted the front cut. There is a silence. I wonder what he is doing. Then I feel the razor blade entering the center of my head. I scream and escape him. I show the wound to two old people there, then to Rupert. But the emptying of the house is continuing. I say: "This house must be watched. Call the police and get four men here on guard." The man (Hugo?) says: "I can't do this because I am working with Latins and this will antagonize them." I have a feeling I am responsible for the change in Rupert.

In the play *Take a Giant Step* there is a dramatization of two contrasting attitudes about one's behavior as a Black person. The parents preach humility, self-effacement and apologies for rebellion, but the young negro discovers this attitude obsolete and takes a stand of pride, dignity and self-assertion. It was acted with such feeling that I forgot I was in a theatre. Caresse and I wept.

The moment Jim Herlihy describes his liberation from fears, his moment of freedom, I felt a change of atmosphere I could not define. I thought it was his emancipation from me (a good thing). But this time I realized he had entered a more surface world. He had given up intimacy with me, with his diary and with himself. He wrote a comedy—an objective one. He said he owed me this freedom, but it was not the kind my Diary teaches! It was a change of level. There is a lightness I love, but this is not the one. For the first time I saw a Jim I did not know. He was reading his play. It is a comedy based on a story about repulsive people on which I had commented lightly. A fat, slobbery mother and an infantile son. With his "success," his self-assertion has been stronger. It must be this way with real children too: at some moment they enter a world that is foreign to you.

Hugo said the other morning at breakfast (which we have in my bedroom in bed): "I like having you here. I feel complemented and expanded."
Anaïs: "I am so happy at the change in you, so happy to see you joyous and high at cocktail parties. It has relieved me of a terrible weight, for I took the blame for your depressions. I always felt like a criminal."
He also says: "Sometimes you are a vixen."
He knows me.
I asked: "What percentage?"
"35 percent," he answered gaily.
In the evening, I said: "As I never studied mathematics I can't figure out what 35 percent means in *hours*. How many hours a day am I a vixen?"
He laughed.

Rupert says over the telephone: "It is exam time and I have so much work that the days fly by, but the nights, darling, I can't sleep."
Bogner did track down today the origin of guilt, of vague anxieties, and malaise—it was what I was writing about: the anger and rebellion against each man, displaced and deflected in order not to be directly at them (Henry's friends, Gonzalo's Helba, *her* madness, not his, Hugo's "business," or Rupert's family). All of them *were* an integral part of the self I could not love, live with. With Hugo this is over because he has changed. He no longer *suffers* his business life but displays all the pleasure it gives him. He enjoys life. He is creative. He has friends and activities outside me. He is warmer, more alive. Rupert is a limited human being, contracted by fear, shrunken, and much more like Reginald than I care to admit. At times I have been struck by the resemblances: the boring expansion upon trivialities, the petty minds. A two-hour discussion of practical problems. When Reginald Hamletizes about places to live in, it is very much like Rupert's dismissal of *all* his professions. He was not a good enough actor, not a good enough violist, not a good enough forester, not a good enough teacher, but then he reassures himself in the truth that he gave *all* of himself to no profession. When he talks about them, he only enumerates their disadvantages, their negative aspects. I have been angry and disappointed with Rupert. He has no power, no will, really, no dedication, no persistence. He romanticized forestry, and the men above him knew this.
Rupert is sensitive enough to know I was angry, but we avoided facing that it was with *him*, not his family or California. Thus one can find the blind angers and render them harmless. How can I make all this knowledge useful and accessible to others?

To Tom Payne I said: "I thought of a way of presenting *Children of the Albatross*. Say on the jacket it is a name game for bastard children."
Tom has long-fingered sensitive hands, and long dark hair that he does not cut to the bone as most men in business do. He has dark, intelligent eyes, an aquiline

refined nose, full emotional mouth, a smile that is full. He wanted to be an architect—then the war came. His appearance is that of a writer.

We had a lunch appointment for next Thursday. Yesterday he called up: "I'm so sorry, I made a mistake, I was looking at the wrong week. I'm not free Thursday, but could I come down today?" Was this true, or did he want to come sooner?

I'm so pleased that I can still charm men off trees! How long, how long, oh lord, does charm endure?

Wednesday: Up at 7:30 with Hugo, so that we can have breakfast together. At 9:00 I am on the Fifth Avenue bus writing in the Diary at stop lights. At 10:00 I am discussing with Bogner the mysterious resistance to learning music, learning to type with the touch system, learning how to drive completely well, mechanics, science. Thorvald has a mechanical mind. My father did. He invented a machine for copying music when he did not know one existed in America. He admired the German mechanical progress. He would have liked American gadgets. Typewriting? My father did not type. It was my mother who typed the manuscript of his first book, *Pour l'Art*.

Driving? I fear my moments of inattention, absent-mindedness, getting into an accident, but I can drive well. What I did not learn is how to park, which is the easiest aspect of driving. Mystery.

How did I learn to print with the hand press perfectly, technically a difficult craft? Mystery.

Why was I so nervous during my lunch with Payne? Spanish taboos on woman's usurpation of man's role? No, I broke other taboos early (renunciation of Catholicism, sexual fidelity, etc.).

I felt calm and worked. But at 6:30 when I telephoned Rupert, all my strength disappeared: "I'm just about to go take an exam. I'm so tired. Send me sleeping pills. I fought off bronchitis. I can't sleep. Mother's tenants left the Black Oak Drive house without paying back rent. I will have to help her Saturday to fix up the place to rent it again. When are you coming back?"

I felt such pity, imagined him saving on food and drinking cheap vodka, nervous and irritable. This helped me to buy my ticket for February 15. *For myself I do not want to go.* The passion is there, but it is blocked and stifled just as with Gonzalo and Henry by the impossibility of a life together, of marriage, of unison, of a deeper rapport. I see him as young, and yet so stubborn in his resistance to all my influences, locked up in his static life, not recognizing neurosis, not able to see how he is taking on his father's patterns. What can I do now? I understand his fear of failure ("I can't give a woman a comfortable, easy, plentiful life," he said once). His loneliness. His lack of stability and physical endurance. Rupert the human being, alone, draws me, but everything else repels me. Have I poetized and imagined him? Why, why did he insist on being a husband? What shall I do? Break suddenly, or gradually? I have left him so much alone.

I know now from the time I rebelled against Hugo's way of life, it was not the life, it was Hugo. But Hugo has changed, and I love the way he lives, the way he has struggled with himself and his way of thinking. We understand each other. We function harmoniously.

What has happened to my love for Rupert? For years I have been immune to desire for anyone but Rupert. This time I find myself susceptible to the charm of Walter Starcke and Thomas Payne, to a physical warmth in their presence. The image I carry is of Rupert placing me in a box without oxygen, in which I not only cannot live, but cannot love, as they are interdependent. Being in love with my life in New York, I can love not only its flow, color and creativity, but the people in it, the livingness of it, Hugo's similar interests, his varied and complex mind, his expansiveness and maturity.

With Rupert everything is *etriqué* [tight]. He has too many fears. This makes him cling to habits, traditions, monotony.

New York, February 2, 1957
Party: Eduardo, Donald Maggini, Cuca and Jack, Graciella and Roy Archibald.

Telephone call:
Anaïs: Darling!
Rupert: What a surprise! I didn't expect a call today. I'm so glad.
Anaïs: I knew you were strained by the exams and I wanted you to know I'm thinking of you. Did you get my letter?
Rupert: Yes, I did. I understand it has to be four weeks. But then no more trips until May! And we have the whole summer together.

(His childish dictatorship is truly against all reality, for we cannot live on what he makes, let alone save for a house. If I had a job, he could not decide when I work or do not work. He does not consider the development in my writing, either. But these commands from a childish heart do not have power over me anymore. He is increasing his demands for care, protection and my presence while disregarding the elements I need in order to exist, and for this self he wants me to grow on *his* soil, which is barren for me. Does he ask for more *because* he feels I am moving away, to stay home, be a wife, see no one but Reginald and the Wrights?)

For the second time he uses precious long distance time to tell me his difficulties with an overdrawn bank account and how he has to go and give them hell. Then he says, "People have been calling up and asking about you: Samson de Brier, Kenneth Anger..." The comparison between them and my friends here gives me a chill...

New York, February 4, 1957
Stanley Haggart tells me, "Anaïs, do not give parties. Everyone feels cheated. They all want a private, personal relationship with you. At parties, even though you are a gracious and perfect hostess, you are not really there yourself—because you do not really appear on that level."

The unattended party, my own! But I am here with Stanley and Tom Payne. There is a fire in the fireplace—the couches are all around...but we sit on the floor, leaning against them. Tom is pale, tired, and at twenty-five or so has deep rings under his eyes. Stanley no longer speaks in a trite language. When Woody Parrish left, he found his tongue. He mixes prophecies and intuition with herbs of malice unknown to himself, because the role of father and mother allotted to his big body must irritate him as sometimes the female dog is irritated by the puppies' voracious tugging at her breasts.

Why have I lost my trust of Stanley, his goodness? Is it because I have lost the protectiveness and goodness, and I see in Hugo and myself the revolt at being idealized *and* used? Karon only calls to talk about herself. When she arrived at the party in a cocktail dress, her first remark was upon seeing the Japanese hair ornaments on my head: "But you didn't tell me it was a party! I would have worn my black dress!" Twice she repeated this. Then she asked me: "Why didn't you wear my butterflies in your hair?" "It would have been too much!" I answered. Her aggressions only drive me further away. I have lost all feeling for her. She no longer looks beautiful to me, or to Hugo.

Deep down, I am tormented by my feelings for Rupert, his nervousness, anxieties, fears, but it is not love. I can no longer love what hurts me. I have such a resistance to returning to Los Angeles, to a becalmed, petty life. Tavi howls whenever I leave so I cannot even go out without feeling guilt.

Hugo and I understand each other, give each other strength. In the evening after dinner we turn on the colored lights behind the screen and lie down to watch the magical effects! Magic, creation, art...all absent from my life with Rupert.

Sometimes if we turn on the red lights and a jazz record, the place looks like a nightclub. We read the same books. When he awakened at five this morning he came to my bed and fell asleep holding me. No passion. But a deep protectiveness, a fraternity.

I feel tired. I need peace and tenderness. I see myself arriving at Los Angeles, but the wild joy at seeing Rupert is no longer there. He is always irritable at the airport, angry at the airline for being late or for being early, for not allowing Tavi to come through without a leash. I always have to remind him not to spoil a happy moment. Just before I return, the house would look like Reginald's hotel rooms. Rupert tells me he has been eating canned fish (the cheapest) or chopped meat (the cheapest), which he covers with catsup. The thrifty vodka is harsh. The very night I arrive, or perhaps the next, the family awaits us. Lloyd will beam with pleasure, but his small, cold eyes wait in ambush to attack. I no longer talk about New York. They do not want to hear. Lloyd wants to talk about how impossible women are when you build a house for them. Eric misses the companionship at his Fellowship. No one of any value ever comes to the Wrights' house. We discuss movies. Lloyd searches for a theme for one of his tirades. He is astonishingly ignorant of contemporary literature, painting or sculpture.

Helen overfeeds them. They eat until satiation. Eric rebels against the large platefuls. He is lean and wants to remain lean. If there is an interesting event, such as Frank Lloyd Wright's exhibition of all his designs at Barnsdall Park, then the pleasure will be destroyed by Lloyd's temper. He once took us around and talked about his father. A few strangers became interested and listened, mistaking him for a guide. Lloyd exploded in childish anger.

I am again lost in detours, byways. I do not want to look at my changed feeling for Rupert. I cannot bear to look at Rupert, at how far he has driven me away. But has *he* driven me away? No. He was himself—I let him create the life he wants. Beautiful things are to be laid away in closets. The Japanese rug I bought in San Francisco is too beautiful to place on the floor. Gil Henderson's rug, too. The

Mexican poncho is in mothballs... Against this bourgeois conservatism I have no power. I cannot face the simple truth: I am tired of difficult relationships, inharmonious lives. I want to stay here in New York, quietly, help Hugo, work with Hugo, enjoy the calm and writing.

When you stifle a human being you also stifle his love.

New York, February 6, 1957
Saw Jacobson. I have a kidney infection.

New York, Saturday, February 9, 1957
The Barrons invited us to Gore's play for which they made the incidental music. A chic crowd, pretty women, furs, Tennessee Williams, Claire Bloom. The play was amusing. We went backstage. Reconciliation with Gore. I spoke to him for the second time since we quarreled—the first time I could not call him as I promised because I was afraid of being hurt. I am no longer afraid. I complimented him on his play. He kissed me on both cheeks and said: "You never change." At nine the next morning he telephoned. Made me promise to call him in L.A.

He said, "You are the only one left of my old friends. They all have died. John Latouche and Mrs. Astor, Nicolas Wreden."

"But you have new ones," I said.

"It is not the same."

The Barrons, who composed sounds for the play, were ignored. In spite of the fact that they used the same themes for the science fiction film *Forbidden Planet* and the play, we shared their nervousness, comforted them, and finally went out with them for a snack to talk over the play.

Dream of *the two pearls*. A man stole an object studded with jewels. Fearing to be caught, he extracted from it two pearls, dropped the object, threw the pearls over a wall into a bed of leaves, and escaped. My relationship with him is undefined. But I did pick the pearls out of the leaves and gave them to him when he returned.

Pearls are, for me, a symbol of bourgeois life, conventionality in luxury. Never liked them. Hugo and I made fun of the uniform of luxury: pearl necklace and fur. As a child I gave away or lost all the jewels given to me by my aunts. Why? Recently I saw the Sánchez-Archibald clan with distaste. All but Eduardo. Graciella and Cuca wear pearls; Hugo likes my lack of interest in jewelry and furs.

I have begun to distinguish between luxury and the kind of life Hugo and I have made. I do appreciate analysis, the doctor's care, massages, and the aesthetic beauty of the apartment. I do realize my need of them.

I was wrong about Jim. He has entered a lighter world, but he has not surrendered the other. When he finished *Crazy October*, and, celebrating its sale, he took up the Diary again (volume 60). He telephoned me to read me passages, responding to it wildly, and then came to talk to me alone because the Diary gives him nourishment. "Every artist should be able to read it."

What schizophrenic separation takes place between Jim's devotion to the flights, the powerful flights that always *took* him somewhere and never disappointed him (like the flights in jazz) and *Crazy October*?

"I am aware, aware and frightened to see that all those who started with me have already fallen by the wayside. People are wrong to say the teens is the critical age. Not at all! In your teens your life is still being composed, you are studying, experimenting, but at thirty you have had your big encounters with life and you have to adopt a course."

I had been afraid he would adopt a course of comedy. But last night he talked as before. It is not that I do not believe in comedy: it is that to stay on the surface without communication with the depths is dangerous. If I am still a fountain of meaning to Jim, all is well.

He, besides his personal devotion, is my only communication with young America, and the role I play is ironic, for it is I who would like to relate his writing to jazz, because jazz is the only expression of manifestation of the senses in America. American writing has gone too far in its stultifying copying, its photography of life and books as dead as postcards. Its only salvation is through jazz. In *Solo*, the novel by James Whitmore, there is life, a complexity of character, a style which I feel is good, fecund, original. Jazz, or jazz writing, is what I consider the only lyrical expression of emotion, of heightened living. It corresponds to the era of romanticism in Europe, surrealism before the war.

This flight, this "high" mood unknown to middle-class literature, this "living"— I must find it its equivalent in writing. Certainly the academicians will not look for it. Only the teenagers can hear it. I saw the jazz musicians reach and arouse these frozen, hardboiled teenagers. I wish I could write that way! But I was not born here. I do not speak the language. I have a sense of rhythm, but it is of a different order.

Dream of the Water Wheel: I am standing in front of a water wheel in full motion. There is someone else there, I do not know who it is. As I watch the wheel rotate I hear the cries for help of a little girl caught on the wheel. I feel helpless. I stand there unable to move, frozen with horror. Then later, either it was a second dream, or the second part of the first one, the same scene, same wheel and little girl crying, I move forward and with great strength stop the wheel and pull her out of danger.

Association with the wheel: water—my obsession with *flow*—the flow of life. Image of water frequent in my dreams. Thirst. I am never thirsty. I read about the function of the kidneys in a medical book. My water balance is out of order. The new novel begins with search for sea and river.

Neurosis really occurs when everything is *accroché*, stuck, not flowing. Water makes the wheel turn, but the child is caught, endangered (my childhood is stuck on the wheel—I have to rescue my childhood so the wheel can turn harmlessly).

Obviously the child is me (neurosis).

After a long, rambling talk with Bogner, I have concluded that life in California is *unreal*. It is not human to be suddenly detached from a whole life…it is neurotic to allow life to become suddenly unreal.

Jim was so excited by the Diary page about my father's final departure from Paris, he called me up. I remembered that outwardly there was no feeling. I had frozen my emotions. I believed my love for my father dead, but when I saw him after he fainted at his concert, I felt an acute and terrible pain. The page is a cry of despair. I loved this man still, and also hated all that he was! The emotion was so violent that it made Jim jump up and call me.

"Isn't it beautiful, incredible writing?" he asked.

"I can't tell," I answered honestly. "I can't tell if I am moved by the experience or the writing."

A talk with Bogner recalls this incident... I am withdrawing from Rupert's life. But the effort *not to feel* divests the life of its reality (emotion and meaning). I know only when I see Rupert will I have the feeling and reality of his presence.

Bogner: "When you do not want to experience great pain you withdraw, from your father's leaving, from Rupert's life. Then, once you are emptied of feeling, they become what you call unreal."

This unreality once frightened me. It seemed inhuman. Human beings like Millicent do not behave this way in the face of trouble. They suffer openly, they cry, they break down.

I am relieved to have discovered that this "inhumanity" is merely the freezing of feeling and pain when it becomes too intense. I have occasionally worried about how I can suddenly stop feeling for Reginald, Helen, Lloyd, Eric. Am I inhuman?

In certain areas, I do seek escape.

Jim: "What saved you from 'breaking' under really hellish experiences, Anaïs, was your faculty for passing into other levels."

New York, February 12, 1956

Yesterday I felt ill. Saw Bogner. And suddenly I discovered that there was a whole area that I controlled and filtered and censored before exposing it to Bogner. It was what I described as direct questions (What shall I do? How can I break with Rupert?) or obsessional, repetitive "blocked" thinking, what I considered "shameful," or non-analytical. The pressure of this was so strong that I could *feel* it pushing up. My attempt to filter it was equally strong. It produced silence. Bogner was aware of this. When I expressed it, it resembled the naked cry in the Diary.

It was a demand, an asking, not within analytical form—a direct request—Help me!

"Why was it so difficult for you to ask something of me?"

It was for this reason I could not write to her that summer when Hugo and I were semi-separated—and I envied Hugo that he could write to her and ask for help.

When this abscess opened, I wept copiously, and later felt relieved.

I came home and made dinner for Hugo. We were tired, and we both fell asleep early. He awakened me at dawn, came into my bed, caressed me, saying "I love you... I love you..." I responded without desire. Does he feel this, know this? I felt love and I wanted to please him. I gave him the caresses he asked for—but he also was led by love, not desire. He wanted to want me. When it didn't happen he was unhappy and I had to console him. "I don't understand this," he said. "I have never felt so close to you."

What irony that all my life should come to this—passion and love divided.

My talk with Bogner today did not add any new element. On the last day with her I am always afraid to tread new ground.

If nothing else, Hugo and I have served for an experiment which, if many people had given themselves to it, might truly change the world far more deeply than a devotion to politics.

Break. Break. Break. I can see my future with Rupert. A house, yes, but a home in which the inner illumination is missing. A home to which nobody of value or quality will come, because they will be *dérouté* by Rupert's talk. His presence promises so much, his charm, his beauty, his singing. He will like parties where there are "pretty girls" and be disappointed because the pretty girls give him the same sense of unavailability that he now gives me, when I am far from the spell of his beauty. The substance is in Hugo, not Rupert.

How can I break from Rupert? How? Will it hurt him? Ultimately it may push him into the life he belongs to, the wife who suits him.

Los Angeles, February 1957

Human life and human feelings are always different than what the imagination contrives. Rupert was not irritable, but happy. Tavi was delirious. We drove home. I was quiet. I had arrived without emotion. But Rupert's mood, his sweetness, his delight all affected me. He had stolen a bottle of champagne from his family. He bought me a steak (a great gesture, for the inevitable chopped venison loaf, rancid, was still in the icebox). Teaching had gone better; he had a better batch of brats. He was well, physically, and so passionate. There was his beauty to rediscover. He has the firmness of a warm statue. His joy was intense, but I could not respond. I had forced myself so far away. I had to make the journey back to him, not across three thousand miles of land, but a million light-years of the subtle space between our thoughts. But strangely, his knotted resistance to change seemed lessened. He showed me, with humor, a drawing of a man being pulled in three directions. "That's me," he said.

"But that's not funny," I said, "You must be uncomfortable, even unhappy."

But he was not.

I said, "And anyway, my love, it is I who am pulled. You have chosen your life and stuck to it—it is I who am divided between New York and your life."

In the morning, I responded to his passion even though it was physically painful, for the kidney infection I had in New York brought on a swelling of the clitoris. That night I satisfied his desire with my mouth. Just lying beside me, his sex is erect and leaping... I gave myself to my enjoyment of him. He brought me breakfast in bed. We even talked about New York. I told him that contrary to his idea that I am not practical, I live in the present and am concerned about the future in a different way—I was facing the reality that my energy was diminishing and, for the sake of the future, I should now seek to cull all the benefits of writing in New York. He was not as rigid. Before falling asleep he had said: "I do not want a static life. I won't let our life become static." Intuition? A delayed response to my emphasis on flow, variety, movement of life? We talked. *But his dream goes on.* Building the house. Strangely, he does not talk about building the house and staying in it, but of renting it to enable us to travel. His sincerity, his wholeness. Hugo had this too. One would believe them to be simple—but why do they love me and let me be the rebel, the restless creation, the artist? Rupert was making notes on his personal history (for his psychology course). It was lying on the desk. At the end of it, he wrote: "I married a woman who has enriched my life and stabilized it."

I was ashamed to be ill. We had planned a festive weekend. Eyvin and Alice Earle had a party. We went, and I was gay and danced while Rupert and Eyvin went swimming in the pool. Rupert came out rather quickly. He said: "I can't go and swim and let everybody else dance with you." We were magnetically close. A radiation of bodies. But Sunday I was weak and I could not go to a dinner for Caresse and a party afterwards—I tried to make Rupert go, but he wouldn't. We went quietly to the movies. I called up Doctor Otto Neurath, who is a cellist, whom Rupert knew in Vienna, a sensitive man, and now I'm at the clinic getting a checkup.

I felt the same depression at the life around me...the houses, the cars, the mediocrity, the kind of friends who telephone me... The same familiar atmosphere. I bought chopped beef but fixed it according to a French recipe, seeking to transform the plain into something else.

To transform...to change.

I have helped Rupert to see Lloyd's irrationality (as I could not help Gonzalo see Helba's) and it is pathetic to see him, Eric and Helen seeking to work, live, think clearly in the doomed, heavy, confused, bitter world of Lloyd's madness. Eric seeks to stop Lloyd's shouting, seeks to talk reasonably, but no matter what we do, he is louder, more belligerent, more brutal, and overwhelming. Yesterday at a family reunion, Helen was tired and out of breath, affectionate but drunk; Lloyd was ranting and always on the negative side. Eric tried to stop him: "You are always talking negatively—when will it end?" Helen said, "At the beginning I used to fight back, pack up my bag and leave. But I knew he would always find me, never let me go, and that he needed me."

She is unaware that she delivered to his sadism two helpless children. But Rupert is becoming aware. He finds now in his child psychology courses the same truths I once tried to convince him of. The child is first of all repressed, then thrown into the world and told to be aggressive, to fight, to conquer, to win. The child is told to obey blindly, then later asked to use initiative and insight. "I found in the course all you told me about the fear of failure. I realize I have this so *strongly* that I avoid at all costs any attempt that might bring me face to face with failure. I avoid the gamble at all costs."

I don't know why I cannot give to the Diary the unity and continuity of a Proustian work.

First, I would have to leave out incomplete portraits, sketched-in scenes.

Second, I would have to fill in more detail about the characters outside my relationship with them. For example, Albert Mangones. I do not feel Albert is all there in the Diary.

At times I feel I can't do this because *outside of feeling* there is no reality for me. That is why I can dissolve my relationship with Rupert when I am in New York and become unable to feel his presence—his falling asleep, feeling his body next to mine, seeing him play with Tavi like a boy, hearing his voice, seeing the tired face, the violet shadows under his eyes.

Sometimes I feel desperate when all these sensations form a chain around me, and then when I feel warm and tender, he suddenly repeats word for word the obsessional tirade Lloyd makes against Bauhaus architecture, followed by all of Lloyd's enumerations of betrayals and injustices committed by people against his work.

I never mention any subject that will draw out all the negative obstacles he concocts: if it is Paris, he says how cold he was there and how he had bronchitis; if it is New York, he says how much he hates the crowds.

Lunch with Gore at Romanoff's. He appears much the same after eight years. In the sunlight his hair looks drab and lifeless, his lips chapped, his skin pale. Success, travel, friendships, love affairs, money ($6,000 a week!) do not leave their mark. "When I drink I feel so badly—I still have those terrible depressions and so many thoughts about death. Did you read *Messiah*? It was my best book, my most serious book, but nobody likes it, and it only sold three or four thousand copies. I would have starved. Then I started to write for TV. People love me for *Visit to a Smaller Planet*—a comedy. I nearly got married, believe it or not. A lovely girl, an actress." (I remember how he told everyone I was his mistress. I wondered if he still needed the world to believe he could possess a woman.)

Sensing my doubt, he added: "It cost me $300 not to have a child. I got panicky. The idea of someone there all the time. I would have liked to been a monk. I could have lived in a monastery happily. I'm happiest in my house on the Hudson, alone, with my little one who acts as a secretary. He is my child. I have no desire for him. In fact, I have very little desire."

"No grander passions?"

"No."

The image of Eduardo superimposed itself over Gore. For the first time I saw a resemblance between them. This was a bond with the dead. This scene was strange, Gore sitting there in an absurdly pretentious restaurant, high-ceilinged and splashed with red, where the waiter, instead of showing the tact which a French waiter would accord to a wealthy man, showed the usual American tastelessness. When Gore asked for a bloody Mary without vodka but with clam juice, the waiter corrected him: "A bloody Mary does not have clam juice." So no matter how wealthy you are in America you cannot be waited on with politeness. The women who go to Elizabeth Arden are treated with the same lack of politeness.

James Mason sat a table away from us.

I was concerned with Gore's sadness. I realized it was this that had created our bond, one entirely based on distress.

But sorrow never killed me. The only time I nearly died was when I tried to live with Hugo, and only for Hugo, who was not alive then.

But why was I so infatuated with Gore? I have the same feeling for his detachment now, except that I see *all* of Gore—not only someone who has a fear of death because he is so close to it—but a dual personality, one that is simultaneously compassionate and cruel. Almost everything he says has malice in it. When he said, "I love *Confidential* magazine; don't you?" he had such gloating delight in the exposure of others' secret lives, the gloating of the voyeur, the delight of a savage.

It is strange that both Gore and Rupert are impervious to the *tone*, the level, the quality of what they read (*Confidential* and *Time* magazine have the same hatred and viciousness, a kind of sadism), and his malice when Rupert appeared was such a shock. Today I am not surprised when he says: "The other day I bought a large jar of caviar and ate it all myself."

He talks like a man who has been poor and now delights in the symbol of wealth. But he was never poor. It is not a gloating over wealth. It is more of a gloating over solitude and not having to share his caviar (life) with anyone.

I don't know why, but after a break with someone I believed in, loved or trusted, I can never recover the original feelings. I see Gore differently now.

It made me so grateful for the sincerity, the warmth of Rupert, his openness and his aliveness. This month I made myself adapt to his way of life. I did not seek to escape or vary or improve it. Is it because I know I can leave it any time I want? I gave myself to Rupert as he is.

Walter Starcke: I met him at Jim's. He is Jim's producer. He is small, dark-eyed, dark-haired, warm-faced—from Texas. I liked him. He was alive and intelligent. He was charmed: "Anaïs is a woman who can make you feel you are a man without the silly frou-frou kind of femininity." He wanted to take me to dinner. We spent several good, lively evenings, Jim, Dick, Walter and I. He came to our apartment, saw Hugo's films. In Jim's apartment we sat and drank champagne. I gave him my books. He came with a poem.

Jim said Starcke was completely charmed by me. He is very direct and very sensitive.

Strange, about Jim—we have less person-to-person contact, because he now includes Dick. He feels I freed him, made him flow. Is this how it should be in this kind of relationship? Like the sons leaving their parents to go into the world? He is out in the world now.

Letter from Anaïs Nin to Rupert Pole:
New York, March 1957

Darling Chiquito:
In case I don't reach you today I'll send you this letter in place of a talk.

Joaquín has met all the dancers and musicians of Spain and refuses to leave! He's having such a good time that he asked for a year's leave of absence without pay. Late dinners, café life, easy, warm friendships, colorfulness of the life have completely seduced him. You can imagine what Berkeley seems like after seeing the gypsies in their caves, and hobnobbing with the best composers, and being made a fuss over. Joaquín says Spaniards are so demonstrative in their friendships that you almost don't need a wife! He needs that warmth, poor thing.

Already visited one of the MS collectors of the Harvard collection, but his hobby is diaries of sportsmen, hunters, and Hemingway, letters about Africa, hunting, and English racing, racers, cars, etc. Wasted trip. He is listed as collector of diaries! We may have to go and kill a lion in Africa to be eligible!

Te quiero,
A

New York, April 3, 1957
    The frightening experience I am traversing now is that with Bogner I am acting out scenes that prove, in the end, the strength and vividness of my fantasies superimposed over reality. It is such a subtle, elusive happening, I cannot seize upon it. It is as if you see and hear clearly for a while, and then become drunk, confused or drugged. And all the time a part of me is aware of the distortions. It is frightening because it causes self-doubt—a doubt of what I have always believed in: my intuition.
    For example, there are direct questions I feel tempted to ask of Bogner but have controlled for years because my intelligence tells me all too clearly that the function of analysis is not to answer such questions directly but to explore what *lies behind* them, what causes me to ask them. They always lie at the back of my mind, tabooed. Then, once such a question broke through the restraint, as soon as I uttered it, I censored it myself: I knew it was wrong to ask it. When Bogner realized I had withheld my questions, she encouraged me to state them, because nothing should be withheld in analysis.
    Encouraged, I allowed all of them to be expressed. They were the human questions everybody asks me, which I seek to answer when people are not helped by analysis. (What shall I do? What shall I say? Why can't I make a choice, a decision, instead of living torn like this between two lives? Why do I turn against Hugo sexually?)
    This month I returned, after a month of physical and mental illness in Los Angeles, appalled by the full awareness of my dependence on Bogner, Jacobson and Hugo! I can't live *one month* without them. I was ill before I left (kidney infection). Jacobson's penicillin caused violent reactions. I did not know what it was, so I went for X-rays and tests in Los Angeles, thinking the kidney infection was growing worse. (I had fever, chills, swollen glands, painful breasts, swollen clitoris.) The doctor gave me sulfa, and I got more ill. My face swelled up. And just before I left I had a recurrence of my jealousy, which hurt Rupert by its injustice.
    The jealousy, as usual, was not based on reality, but a galloping fantasy. We went to a concert and we met a young pianist who immediately invited Rupert to a party and gave him her telephone number. It was the day before I left, and I wept. Rupert attributed it to emotionalism over my leaving. But he was angered by the injustice. "I have loved you faithfully for nine years."
    It was a fantasy that I called "intuition." But the *same* intuition made me *feel* that Bogner encouraged me to express all the questions that troubled me and then *reproached* me for asking them and not trying to get at their causes, and *exposing* my dependency and humiliating me. With my intelligence I could reconstruct the dialogue as it took place.
    "Why do I immediately imagine that Rupert will love this girl? She is a pianist, she lives in the Malibu hills, which he loves, she is young and strong, she has long hair..."
    "Ever since you came back you have done nothing but ask me questions, and you are not trying to find what lies behind this."

But these words were not uttered reproachfully. And it was not Bogner's intent to bring out feelings of shame and humiliation. It was I who felt I revealed something of which I am ashamed (dependency?).

I *felt* so strongly when she had encouraged me to reveal something I had not revealed and then betrayed me, that I considered destroying the Diary (because you can't reveal the truth to the world; the world will betray you, turn against you, judge you).

Talking to her, I could *see* that the feelings I had were distinct from the simple content of her words, just as my feelings about Rupert and the pianist were distinct from the casual reality. I was trying to remember Bogner's expression. I felt she had become severe—displeased.

To quietly understand our talk, leaving out the distortion, frightened me. I proved that I can completely distort reality—I distorted reality about Rupert too.

This only increased my distress.

The only gain was the knowledge that what I call my intuition is more often a *defense* against reality. I seek always to *precede*, to intuitively anticipate what I feel may happen ultimately.

Asking questions, to me, is an expression of immaturity (a very typical American trait).

It is a symptom of confusion.

I allow the other to decide, to *take over*. It is not Bogner's role. But she must know what troubles me.

Intuition and fantasy…I must distinguish between them.

Creatively, the way Hugo and I are using this overlapping is in composing a film: I suggested the use of a negative past (black lines are white, and white are black) superimposed over the colorful present. Walter Starcke is right when he says I have described states of consciousness.

Walter Starcke was there one evening when I went to see Jim and Dick. He is thirty-six years old, medium height, trim and compact, firm of bearing, natural and direct. He has very round, dark eyes, glowing, warm and intelligent—he is quick, but no dreamer. He has beautiful teeth, a beautiful smile, a slightly flattened nose, which gives him a boyish appearance. He has a glow.

His presence did not change the atmosphere of my relationship with Jim and Dick. I liked Walter. He had a warmth and a directness I like, together with the soft, burning, dark eyes.

I knew his history. He had had a long relationship with John Van Druten. Then, slowly, the relationship dissolved. I also knew he had relationships with women.

There was a contradiction between the vitality of his physical presence and his talk of religion, of six years of abstinence, etc. I did not know then how strongly his religious fervor had influenced Jim and Dick. I knew that a few months ago, *suddenly* Jim and Dick stepped into a new realm. They shed their anxieties. But Jim, who tells me everything, did not tell me this. Why? Was he afraid I would disbelieve? Was it a mystical experience he could not describe or share? I asked him: "How did this change come about?"

Jim told me his first white, loving lie: it was the Diary. But it wasn't—it was Walter's fervent, fanatical belief.

Not knowing this, I continued to see Walter as a glowing, warm man—and I was pleased and flattered when Jim and Dick reported: "Walter is terribly attracted to you. All the time you were away he devoured your books. He finds them erotic and mystical."

And later: "Walter said you are a woman who makes a man feel like a man."

At our party I felt attracted to Walter, but I was alarmed by Jim and Dick's eagerness to create a relationship between us. Jim, particularly. Before I left New York he talked to me over the telephone: "Walter is fighting his attraction. I don't think either one of you should fight it."

Of course, for me, the feeling for Walter was completely dissolved in the intensity of my feeling for Rupert. The physical passion is so strong it fuses us again. Walter was someone I liked with a little more sensuousness than Jim and Dick.

When I returned to New York, Jim, Dick and Walter had been to Key West for three weeks. Walter was suffering from the harshness of Van Druten's break, from loneliness and the effort to build a new life. It was partly out of love and concern for Walter that they sought to unite us, and partly because Jim knows my way of life with Rupert is intolerable.

I felt cornered by their wishes and fantasies, and then I felt: I must see Walter alone, make a friendship of this, not keep it in suspense.

So at Jim's cocktail party I suggested to Walter: "Let's spend an evening together."

We went out in the Village. He was dressed neatly and conventionally like a businessman. I said: "Jim and Dick have created a relationship between us and it is time we made our own." At dinner he smiled shyly: "I feel tongue-tied with you." But this opening loosened a flood of talk. The story of his relationship with Van Druten. Story of the break. Story of his religious experience. Slowly, the religious talk predominated. I listened. Such talk from anyone else would have made me laugh, but Walter's sincerity and vigor touched me. It was with such naïve charm that he would say: "Just one more sermon!" I was occupied in trying to understand why he talked so much about this. I felt that he was frightened by his attraction to me and that this was a smokescreen.

My desire for him, which had been gentle, was dissolved by talk of god and healing, of meditation and abstinence. Any atmosphere of religion destroys my sensuality. Perhaps if I hadn't loved Rupert I might have disregarded this, but I held back enough to sense danger: fear and guilt. It is his idealization of me that drew him—and the knowledge that I am not free gave him courage.

For the first time I experienced a sad *dédoublement* in the very heart of an attraction. A mature, experienced Anaïs remained aloof and even ironic, for the desperate proselytizing was transparent to me.

He said, "When I first saw you, you were radiant with an inner light, a kind of illumination." And I saw only a lover...a dark-skinned southerner.

Later, over the telephone, he retracted: "I pounded too hard. I talked too much. I've been this way ever since my religious experience at the top of the volcano in Hawaii."

Religion, twin beds, and occasional guilt-ridden lovemaking with Van Druten.

Dream: A woman has broken her bracelet. She gathers the pieces and leaves to get it repaired. I find a piece that had fallen into a pail of water or beer. I run after her. Then I take the car and drive to catch up with her.

Dream: Joaquín has married an old woman, as old as my mother. My mother is still alive—I cannot understand Joaquín marrying such an old woman.

Dream: Rupert is with another man. They are planning a trip on skis. I watch them making preparations. It is a new kind of ski with a highly-colored plastic platform. They tell me about all its advantages. Then they run off gaily and I am left standing with two women somehow related to Rupert and his friend. I feel broken, shattered at being left alone. I complain about the poverty of my life with Rupert. The two women and I return to the house. We move from one room into another. They are going on a journey. One of the women is pregnant—I offer to take them to the train in my car. I do. The train is also like a ship. They have no sleepers. I say: "That is too difficult for a pregnant woman. I will pay for the sleeper. She must have one." I caress her and find she is in a state of desire and wants more intimate caresses. She lifts her dress and I caress her lips. Then, because she gives a sigh of relief when I caress her legs, it turns into a massage and the erotic mood vanishes. I rush to get her a sleeper. The man at the desk says sleepers are free for pregnant women. Then I offer to pay for her sister's sleeper so that they will be able to travel together. The man agrees and hands me the keys to the new cabin. But I have no money. He is put out by this. I promise to return immediately with the money. Time is running short. There is a feeling in me that these two women are Hugo's sisters. Then the man with Rupert must be Hugo.

The dream was long, and included my uneasiness at driving, my fear of not finding my way back from the station. The realism of the pregnancy—advanced—was very heavy. The atmosphere was shabby and colorless, like California.

It is strange that although I have seen beautiful homes in California, my image of it is of mediocrity and shallowness, of middle-class living—and the Hollywood or Malibu life is only a more glamorous emptiness. The absence of richness paints all of Los Angeles when I dream—the shacks, cellars, motels and homes with Rupert in my dreams are all shabby.

Returning to Bogner and the discussion of intuition. After she stressed the differential between intuition and fantasy, and how I reacted to this (self-doubt), it became clear that this intuition, clairvoyance, or insight was my one talisman, my one magic power. Deprived of my faith in its *infallibility*, I felt powerless. And as it is connected intimately with my writing, its source, I felt doubly weakened.

Bogner said repeatedly that she has no doubt I am particularly gifted in insight, understanding and intuition, but that in a few instances (jealousy or fear of loss of love) I had been imagining and fantasizing, due to the fear of my loss of insight, and I had been wrong.

The idea of infallibility is unreal and inhuman, dangerous too. I began to understand that there was no reason for despair or abdication. I need only to think, observe, question, seek facts and not blindly trust my "intuition." I have been mistaken in my judgments of people (the Spewacks, etc.).

Last night, a free evening spent at Jim's and Dick's. First, we cleared the air about the secret of their religious conversion. It was not what I imagined. Out of kindness, because Starcke was in trouble, they let him talk religion, and Starcke assumed he had affected them. Their transition in September was no miracle—it came of much struggle and trouble.

At midnight Starcke came (he had been engaged and I thought I would not see him). Immediately I felt excitement. I felt the warmth. I wondered at it. We sat around the fire. I would have kissed him. When I went home and passed Hugo's closed door on the way to my bedroom, I had a moment of physical pain. I wished Starcke were there; I could not bear the physical emptiness. I longed for Rupert. I was restless, angry that my marriage has not fulfilled this need, fearful that by desire I would get entangled in a relationship I do not want. I am in love with Rupert. In passion, we possess each other deeply.

Anger at passing a closed door—a closed door. My relationship with Hugo was like the compartment of a ship. Always one closed door. "His mind is far away," said Millicent this morning. A closed door. Anger. But how can I be angry at Hugo —Hugo is so tender, devoted, unselfish, patient, faithful—I must be a monster. When I *knew* he suffered at the time of our marriage, had severe problems, had been castrated, I acted with gentleness and sympathy at his awkwardness, impotence, difficulties—the more gentleness, the deeper the anger is buried, the anger and the hunger, the unsatisfied woman whose core was not possessed in the shallow sexual games he played. He fondled me with his hands as he fondled his sisters, but once inside me, he was too quick.

Anger. The anger seems monstrous, yet it was there, and in my pursuit of the lover there was a revenge, an anger, as there was an anger the other night when I passed by his door (in reality we had agreed that the first one home would close the door so as not to be awakened by the second). *Because* of Hugo I was forced to find passion outside. And this night I had resisted passion, and when I had passed the door and entered my room I suffered a physical pain to have restrained myself from making love with Starcke, and I wished I could go out and find him and have a night of passion. I imagined him coming in through the window. My body ached. But this night, deprived of all the drugs that obscure such feelings, unable to drink, having given up sleeping pills and tranquilizers, I was rewarded with lucidity. This great, abysmal craving was only temporarily assuaged by passion, but not permanently and definitely. So it must be something else, something else that an intermittent closeness in passion to Rupert, or to Starcke, did not solve, answer, fill. I felt like an alcoholic deprived of alcohol. *I had to face my hunger.* I did not rush into an affair, rush to the children's tenderness with Jim and Dick, rush away from Hugo, who had given me everything but this union. Now I see why I was, at times, bad to him, why his giving was never enough—it was a substitute for something else. All that he gave me, protection, sympathy, security, physical gifts, clothes, care, a home, comfort, all these things did not fill the empty core of union.

But I couldn't be angry. He expressed desire. He took me. He admired me. He worshipped me. He photographed me with love.

The others, the lovers, who gave me less of what Hugo gave me, gave me the feeling of union. Union in passion. But it was a union I had difficulty maintaining outside the passion (with Henry, Gonzalo, Rupert), and I chafed and was restless in the relationship, was lonely.

When I talked to Bogner about this unknown hunger, the gnawing (like the gnawing in my stomach that a little food will quieten, but which begins anew because I'm suffering from hyperacidity), she said: "I am glad you came to this

I hope he did not regret his openness—there is a hangover due to confidences. I hated to abandon him to his distress.

We talked from one to four o'clock—and in between I was to see Bogner and Jacobson, and through an unwillingness to dig further I made an error and wasted most of my talk to Bogner. I barely had time to tell her of a dream: Rupert and I are on the high seas. I am floating on a surfboard. Rupert is swimming. The waves are very high. I wish Rupert would get on the surfboard with me. We manage to keep afloat and together. Then we enter calmer waters—and watch the skeleton of a wrecked ship that has been tossed against the rocks, pounded and shattered before it sinks again.

Before I leave, I'm unwilling to dredge deeper. I let the skeleton ship sink. But it is a dream of fear. Rupert swims, and I can't. The waves are high and threatening.

Jacobson finds my blood count good and is illuminated, obsessed with his new discovery. People mistrust his "experiments." He, naïvely, takes it for granted everyone wants to experiment, everyone is willing to gamble, everyone is willing to explore with him. I have always loved this trait in him, and I submitted and was willing to risk catastrophe. (The static doctors make errors too; all doctors make errors.) I felt a love and identification with his research work. I asked Hugo to contribute to it. It is his joy. Jacobson sits quietly beside me, and I have known him for twenty years. I have never seen him sit down for more than a minute. He is filled with excitement. He tells me, in his hazy, overly quick way that no one can follow, what it is. There is something about finding more nourishment in the kidney than in the liver. His language is unknown to us, but the delight and certainty animates the words with such a faith that I take his injection and we embrace, an embrace he always sustains like a thrust of love. It is no longer erotic, but it transmits a contact, a kind of love; at the moment I am his creation, he gives me life, and he watches me and loves me as his own handiwork. What share he has had in my youthfulness, I do not honestly know. A great deal, I believe. He alone has conquered my anemia. I ask him about his research. He says he has started enough trends to keep a big laboratory occupied—enough feelers, tests, checkups. The magic potion, which he has explained in technical language, is bottled, and I forget all my handicaps and feel well at that moment with the same power of physical illumination one might feel in nature.

I am no longer ill.

From there to Starcke's anonymous hotel room. The books on the table I could not read. They are religious. The dried fruit, the theosophist foods, are all in opposition to the warmth of his body, its vitality.

He talks: "My mother and sister are Southern women who make you feel sex is an insult, an offense, a crime from brutal men upon fragile women. My father died when he was only 35—so he had no time to leave us comfortable. My mother taught acting. My sister was very pretty, a flirt, and she kept all the men around but held on to her virginity until she had a breakdown. There was a man I liked, who was like Will Rogers, and I asked my mother why she did not marry him because he loved her so much. She turned and said with a look of disgust on her face: 'How can you say such a thing? Imagine being in bed overnight with such a man!' My sister left pubic hairs in the bathtub, and when I innocently scolded her for washing her hair in the tub, she turned on me and said: 'Shut your dirty-minded mouth.' She was older, five years older, and I was small, and she picked on me, tyrannized me."

So he ran away from the women into homosexuality. He went into the navy, and wore a tight sailor suit and led a wild life. On leave he went to orgies in Miami. And *then* he was treated like an animal, arrested, dragged through the streets with policemen on each side, brought in for questioning, thrown into a house with all the other homosexuals. Brutal questioning, brutal treatment, and finally a dishonorable discharge.

Then came John Van Druten, discretion, no more bars or promiscuity, and religion. And once a girl he liked "practically had to rape me, I was so shy, and it worked for a while, but she was too aggressive… We knew it was bad and we stopped before we destroyed each other…"

Later: "I would like to take you away to Key West for a week and make love to you…"

And still later: "If you were ten years younger I would have *forced* you out of this life you're in, but now I feel you are resigned—you have accepted it…"

Last night at Harold Feinstein's. A long room, a loft, all across one floor, the floor immense and with knotholes. Harold is tall and round-faced, Mongolian-like behind his eyeglasses, showing his work. His wife, pale and blonde, is pregnant. In the front, his photographic equipment. In the middle a bed. In the back an electric stove, a table, a closet. But the talk is rich. And he smiles.

He loved my records first of all, the *House of Incest* reading, then the books. Above all, live jazz musicians.

That night it crystallized, my vision into jazz not only as music, but a way of life, an attitude. It has passed into the bloodstream. It is the only rebellion against conformity, automatism, commerce, middle class and death of the spirit. It all accumulated, really the blues, the only poetry in America, the only passion, the only livingness of the blood. Not delinquency, not the lower depths of Nelson Algren, but poetry, a heightened state.

I was talking to a young man who is writing a thesis about Miller—"What happened to Miller when he returned to America?"

I said, "He repudiated it, perhaps because it repudiated him, because he needed so much care, devotion and faith, and got that in France, from France and from me."

Miller could have written the surrealist jazz of America. He didn't. He was the man of the street. He talked their language.

He lost his way: as critic, as philosopher, as essayist, he was a failure.

The men who are doing what Miller should be today, such as Nelson Algren, do not have his power.

Meanwhile, Geismar says: "No writer unacquainted with big business can write the great American novel."

What absurdity! There is no *one* novel of America. Big business is its inhuman, monstrous product—which will end in robots—but jazz is the living romantic expression of true potency, the potency of *feeling*, of living, the lyrical force—the antithesis of big business—and politics, Mr. Geismar, is a part of big business, its twin. Big business is the monster that will destroy everything, corrupt everything. It is a dehumanizing, corroding contemporary expression of all tyrannies, the Caesars, emperors, thugs and dictators.

Los Angeles, April 19, 1957

The split is showing even in my handwriting—I'm dividing my words.

So saddened by Hugo's letter, moved by it. I was writing him last night while Rupert was playing quartets, saying all I could to free him of regrets for the past and what we did to each other, and acknowledging my far greater and heavier burden of guilt. Then I had a dream:

I saw my father clearly. He was my height, he had a small bald spot at the top of his head. He was neat and trim, but he was old, older than when I last saw him in Paris. He had asked me to bring him special sleeping pills, terribly expensive ones. In fact, they were made of emeralds. I brought them to him. Then he confessed for the first time in what mental distress he was. I did not know this (in my dream). The sleeping pills were very essential. But I had the same ambivalent feeling about his need as I have about Reginald: I do not quite *believe it*. (Was it because both of them used dramatization to obtain their needs, and as soon as they had obtained care or devotion or sacrifice, they were "off" again to enjoy their irresponsible pleasures?)

Was this dream related to Hugo? Hugo's needs, Hugo's lack of contact?

On this last trip he said to me: "You always gave me the feeling of *responsiveness*, of *being there*, of comfort. You always gave me that. I didn't give you that."

I was amazed that all my "desertions" of him, my gift of myself to others, had been accomplished without making him feel a broken contact on my part... amazed.

We are both struggling to face the same terrible truth. I covered my loneliness with passions and many ardent friendships, but in truth it masked a difficulty in connecting.

At the same time I read about Proust: his unique insight into character was founded on the observation that a single face can wear a thousand masks, that personality is reducible to a discontinuous series of psychological states.

I must write my novels with my Diary work. I must find a way by which they can flow together.

Los Angeles, April 1957

I am copying volume 69, concerning the split love between Bill Pinckard and Gore Vidal.

The power of the Diary to recreate the emotional intensity of the relationship with Gore makes it so potently real, that while I am copying it, it is more alive than my relationship with Gore today.

What mystifies me is: did the relationship die because we hurt each other, or because it was illusory, and reality shattered it? When I had lunch with him it was without feeling. When I saw Bill unexpectedly a month ago, in a hardware store in the Village, I felt nothing. He was wearing sloppy clothes stained with paint. It was Bill less his beauty. I examined the face that had stirred me so much. The eyes seemed smaller, the skin no longer luminous, his nose seemed more aquiline, and I could not find the sensual modulation of the mouth. He introduced me to his wife, a very ordinary girl, short and squatty, not beautiful in any way—and the whole encounter was so deprived of the iridescence I had adorned the relationship with, that it made me jittery. I was very nervous when I returned home, not because of meeting Bill or any echo of the old feelings, but at the shocking disappearance of those feelings, their death. *It was the terrible experience of death in life that I have experienced more often than most human beings because I preserved them at their most heightened moment.* What hurt me—and with Gore too—was the experience of the death of feelings so powerful that I wanted to give all of myself to them.

While copying the pages in which Gore was alive and comparing them with the Gore I saw today, I felt the horror of death. For two years I only knew a Gore out in the world, from hearsay, gossip, newspaper columns.

Our quarrel I cannot remember clearly. Did it start when I could not stay with him in Antigua but preferred the animation and aliveness of Acapulco? Was it when I appeared with Rupert in New Orleans, and I saw Gore looking at him murderously? Was it later in New York when he came to see me and was sarcastic and destructive?

He would come and it was like a wake. I realized that his cruelty came from jealousy. He would come late and always leave a hurtful phrase with me. I may have done the same when he telephoned his boy and talked body language to him. He invited me to hear him speak at City College, and he praised Tennessee Williams, Carson McCullers, but not me. He wrote a review about writers of the 1940s and did not mention me. He humiliated me, and finally one evening when we went to the ballet with Hugo and Curtis and sat in a restaurant later for a drink, he telephoned for one of his young whores to join us, and Hugo and Curtis were shocked by his lack of delicacy.

Our relationship deteriorated. I was tired of his lifelessness, his boredom, his writing.

Finally it was he who wrote me a letter, a very long one, about my destructiveness in *all* my relationships, which I returned to him with this written on the envelope: "Misaddressed. Intended for your mother—not me."

Then silence. For two years.

It was the Barrons who told me he asked about me, and talked quietly about me, and that he regretted our quarrel.

But behind this irrational second phase (following upon the idealized one) was the bare truth that we could not give each other what we needed at the time. He wanted a passionless mother, and I wanted a passionate lover.

When we met, although it was now a highly successful Gore who had just had a big success on Broadway with *Visit to a Smaller Planet*, he still talked of depressions and fatigue. But now he has friends his own age, is very wealthy, and can stop working if he wants to.

Death. It is Gore's theme, not mine. Is it the death of *illusion*, or natural death?

Rupert bought his land by the sea some time ago—and now we have saved enough to begin the house with a loan. His dream.

I have told him the truth about my loneliness in California, that I consider it cut off from vital life, from my life, that I am here only for him. It was then he articulated his fear of negative propulsion of his life: "I have to have a home, roots. If I thought if I would ever be like Reginald, I would rather die."

Not to be Reginald. Reginald's life has put a curse on all freedom, wandering, improvisation, bohemianism, and has given value to all the stabilities. It is also in order to not be Reginald that Rupert chose a love he could be faithful to.

This fear has kept him from enjoying a wider life with me, *my* life—and someday he may regret it, for the more he withdraws from what I consider life, the more I struggle to separate from him and a life I cannot bear.

Los Angeles, May 2, 1957

As I worked on volume 69, the relationship with Gore came to life again. I was able to meet him at the Beachcomber with gayety and softness. He was his charming self, confiding. I like when he talks about the present. Gore was attracted to Joanne Woodward, the actress, who has been for three years the mistress of Paul Newman. He says he could not win Paul, so he took Joanne (this I doubt; it is a fantasy). After a while she had a film to make in England, and Paul was there, and Joanne and Paul resumed their relationship. "She wants us both—but I can't understand this—I cannot take a sensual interest in anyone for more than two or three times. And I don't want to give pleasure to the other, I want to *rape.*"

He grimaced with disgust and pain at the experience of publishing novels, the facing of reviewers, the sales concerns. He wanted to publish quietly, secretly almost, go underground. All of us have experienced the ferocity of the book world. It is an ordeal. We will never know how many writers have died of it.

But he has the belief that the novel is dead, a belief he says is shared by Christopher Isherwood and Tennessee Williams. I said this was only because the novelist will not write about the intimate inner experiences, complex and unconventional to live through, such as Gore's relationship *à trois* with Joanne and her young man (*à quatre* because Gore has a boy living with him non-sexually).

We were drinking. I do not remember all we said, but we talked easily. We drove back in his small, open MG.

He was enjoying making a great deal of money. His family respects his success. He repeated the same words I was typing this morning: "I am constant."

He maintains that my pattern is to break relationships, but he does not recognize that this happens only when I am hurt. Otherwise my intimate relationships are remarkable for their longevity. I said, "I was afraid we would not trust each other again." He seemed more like Eduardo at this moment, when speaking of his enjoyment of his home, books, quietness. And he is born under my father's sign, Libra, in October, desiring harmony.

He drove me home and talked to Rupert a little while (Rupert had been busy with Father's Night at school).

The next day Paul Mathieson came and told me his story of Acapulco.

When he went to Mexico in 1947, he inquired where I was and was told I was in Acapulco. This was the year I had met Rupert and then gone there alone. He drove down. He arrived during a party at the Mirador, a dinner dance, while Annette

Nancarrow and I were surrounded by young men (two of them were Gore's friends from Antigua, who had followed me there).

Paul had come in a Gauguin mood, wanting a primitive life, and a relationship with me. But he found me in this frivolous atmosphere. I saw him as a dreamer, as a remote, legendary boy, a mystic (who had slept with me in Monterey and had not been able to take me)—*all that I was running away from.* I made an effort to communicate with him. His silence and remoteness, I felt, were endangering my pagan mood. I wanted pleasure and sensuality. (He wanted pleasure and sensuality!) I still remember Paul in Acapulco, so blond, with his dreamer's remoteness, and no sensuality was manifested. His blondness set him apart, his refusal to talk lightly. The other two boys were frivolous. One was my best dancing partner. We swam, we danced. Paul hovered in the background. I did not divine that he wanted to take me away and live a primitive life with me.

He went to the most dangerous beach with the boys, and confident in his swimming, swam far out, although all the Mexicans warned him of the riptides. And he was caught in one, which prevented him from returning to shore. He called for help. At that time they had no lifesavers, no boats, no cords. The boys tried to get some Mexicans to swim out, tried to telephone, but no help came. Paul was in the water several hours. He thought of his death. What he could not bear was the idea of darkness, of not seeing the sun anymore. He could see the people on the beach, some unconcerned, drinking their drinks, others just watching, and even at one moment a mariachi band was playing! He was getting exhausted. He took off his bathing trunks because he felt that if he had to die he wanted to be naked, not wearing a foolish suit with the word "Catalina" stitched on it. Finally, two Mexicans swam out and brought him in unconscious. The water was pushed out of his lungs. He was ill for several days in his hotel room. And I never knew this. The boys did not tell me. And the truth was that I could have liked a relationship with Paul then; I was lonely. I was uncertain about Rupert then. If only he had spoken to me. His muteness and his withdrawal irritated me. I remember one night when we went dancing in the whorehouses, and Paul left us. When we came out, very late, he was eating fish soup with the Mexicans seated at a table in the street.

Later he met Renate, and I went to join Rupert.

When we talked about this it seemed like a shocking lack of communication, a sad abortion. He seemed entirely asexual at the time—and yet, later, at the party at Malibu, he seemed voluptuous and I thought: Renate has sexualized him. But it was not this. Renate was seduced by the voluptuous quality, a sensuousness she had not known with her husband.

Anaïs: "And I thought you were having affairs with boys, and I would not interest you. I never asked you to stay with me for that reason."

Paul: "And I thought you were surrounded by lovers!"

In the sunny, small room of our apartment, 1729 North Occidental, Paul and I stood talking while I prepared dinner for Rupert.

He had just finished reading *Solar Barque* and found it beautiful.

He is lonely without Renate, and his life has shrunk. He is aware of this reduction, so he wants to join Kenneth Anger in Paris, and I want to help him get there. I gave him travel books, and he said, "I feel wings growing out of my elbows. The artist is like a flautist; he wants to throw his flute in the air to see what music it will make."

His blue eyes are so close together that they give him an animal look rather than a man of thirty. Renate painted him naked, and from near his face looked innocent; from afar the nearness of the eyes gave him a satanic look.

Renate was good for him because she lived hysterically on the outside and pulled him out of his caverns. But even then, when she dragged him into tornadoes, ransacked his privacies, violated his thoughts—even then he said (like Sabina), "I always had to have, in all my love affairs, an emergency exit!" The "emergency exit" was the boys, which Renate fought ferociously, from the first time they lived together until the last day of the break, which happened when she came home early and unexpectedly from work and found Paul was having an assignation with a French boy. After she retaliated by taking a lover, Paul never touched her again.

Now Renate is having a *Confidential* magazine affair with Edward G. Robinson's adopted son, twenty-four years old, a drug addict and alcoholic under the power of a fifty-year-old "moll" with paid gunmen, who threatens Renate's life. Even when Renate gives it a romantic Viennese flavor—the older woman who keeps him drugged is the "dragon" whom he cannot kill himself but wants Renate to deliver him from; he is the "sleeping beauty" waiting to be rescued.

There was a sudden change in Renate after Paul left, a de-poetization, a certain atmosphere of whorishness instilled in her emancipation from faithfulness. I first attributed her disillusion with her "romantic" view of Paul, but now I see that her life has coarsened. She tries desperately to invent poetry or myth her life does not possess. Our last visit there left a painful impression. Renate wanted to be the femme fatale, to live sensationally. The lovers succeeded each other too quickly. One of them spent a night on the roof wrapped in wet blankets to save her house from the Malibu fire, but he was an Irish Catholic, and she had to fight Catholicism. Another night was the symbol of a mysterious underworld of sea-going men, but he broke away, frightened by her art life and her sophistication. She says, "Robinson's son is a combination of James Dean and Marlon Brando."

Renate's eyes bulge out slightly, devouring all of life. Paul had been the one investing her with a poetic aura.

When we last talked, she asked me: "Am I inventing my life?"

Los Angeles, May 10, 1957

Rupert and I go to Mssr. and Mme. Romain Gary's party to celebrate his selling *Les Racines du Ciel* to the movies.

Rupert seems so "sage," so neat and trim, slim and young—young when compared to the other men; he is half their width, exquisite, and as the evening passes, he exposes his tender, unaggressive self, only occasionally crystallizing into a stubbornness that is his way of affirming himself. He is intent on presenting me to James Mason because I had once mentioned being impressed with him—why does he do this? To test my love, his power—he seems to be giving me away, but I do this too, offering him to the *jeunes filles*. Then, after having made love before the party (to reassure ourselves?) we made love again afterwards, as after a victory, so happy to find intimacy again, after our flight, stimulated by our adventure into a difficult world because we had talked about our timidities.

Before the party I had said: "Darling, I have the same fears you have, only I have the courage to go into it because, although I know it is difficult and demanding, it has a certain beauty, whereas the little people we are comfortable with I dread so much because they make life so colorless, and if we allow ourselves to sink into the comfortable life, it loses its flavor." Rupert didn't know I had any fears. But how I have increased his confidence! And how I have triumphed over my own fears and jealousies—I had none last night.

But I do know that my life, as well as Rupert's, is constricted by fears—his is to not become Reginald, and mine is not to die alone and mad as my father did.

Romain Gary followed me to the bedroom to help me with my coat, but there is no communication between us. I don't know why. Perhaps it was his obvious, flamboyant mistress spilling out of her dress, or his Don Juanism—I actually understand her better.

My life here: Getting up at 7:00 AM to make breakfast for Rupert. He leaves at 7:30. Dishes and housework. Typing the Diaries. Rupert is home at 3:00 PM. I serve him a snack. I have errands to do. Sometimes he leaves from seven to ten at night for extra college courses. I helped him by typing his thesis. My only outing is a walk to the post office (along ugly streets), errands. The endless complication to meet people. I had to take a taxi to meet Gore, and they're expensive. Gore had to drive me home. I can't see Renate, or Paul. Paul traveled an hour and a half by bus to come and see me. Every now and then I explode with loneliness and constriction. Rupert is satisfied with movies and quartets two or three times a week. Tonight it is music (I stayed home). Tomorrow music, Sunday music. I can't even buy typewriting paper in this neighborhood. It takes a day to go to Hollywood for a typewriter ribbon! My explosions hurt Rupert, because he feels helpless. But the truth is that he has been completely selfish and has constructed a life entirely to suit himself and never gave up any of his habits, family, friends, pleasures, patterns. He lives exactly as he wishes to. And I am the one who is trapped.

Los Angeles, May 11, 1957

From volume 69 ("The Transparent Child") there is another book to be written that is not *Children of the Albatross*. It is on the theme of how to dissolve the trap of a hopeless love. *There is a way.* The closeness that establishes a contact between two persons (Gore and myself) is due to identification of the feelings, *according to the self you are at the moment.* At the moment I met Gore, having failed in my relationship with Gonzalo, I was seeking a closer union, a merging, and what merged were his wishes and mine—his to be protected, mine to hold and protect. This seemed to cause the nearness. But as I explored the bond, I changed. I became less like a part of Gore, and the tie was already dissolved. I changed. I moved. Many people are trapped in such loves for life, like Peggy with Paul Bowles, her conviction that he is the twin, the singular other half of herself. This has incapacitated her for other loves and has left her a nun. I must make this clear.

New York, May 24, 1957

Dream: I am talking with an older man, who is reproaching me for not having really loved him, and I deny it sincerely. I say: "You are quite wrong about this. I have an enormous respect for you. I would not have pretended love." He seems satisfied. I am looking at an extraordinary scrapbook in which the pictures of our lovemaking are encased in cellophane, and with the very water of the sea in which we made love.

Dream: I am waiting for a long time for someone. I am carrying a violin. Finally I decide to leave the violin in the care of the luxurious shop on the ground floor of a hotel. The woman accepts, but also tries to sell me *un kimono de luxe*, which is too expensive for me ($45). I go out again to watch for the person I am waiting for. Then I see my watch is wrong and that it is *too early*.

New York, May 29, 1957

When I arrived I found Hugo utterly dejected—so much so that I was alarmed and disappointed (after ten years of uninterrupted analysis). I gave up my own depression to help him. He, as usual, could only half-express it. "It's the awareness of reality, which I have avoided all my life. It's my image of myself and myself in our marriage."

He referred to our wedding night. I didn't know what to say. I can't let him take the responsibility for the sexual break, but I can't tell him the truth. I said: "Many couples make bad beginnings. It doesn't mean that you failed all the way, darling. I think what is far more important than regrets for what we lost is this *destruction of the present* by depression, which you are doing right now, destroying the present with regrets about the past."

After the constriction and boredom of life with Rupert, I was ready to enjoy the present and to dwell less on the past. Breakfast in bed. No radio going on all day. The beauty of the apartment. A lively talk with Jim and Dick. Being able to go around the corner to the post office, to buy summer clothes, to sit in cafés. Being able to talk with Bogner, seeing Jacobson to find out why I have been suffering so much from backaches (a diseased disk and arthritis, alas), to get the care I need. My mood lightened. I was in life again.

Even if analysis reveals the truth *gradually* with support and help, it is still so difficult to take. The neurotic romantic is the cripple who cannot bear the truth. Then, I feel, it is impossible for me to discuss with Hugo what happened to our sexual connection. If he recoiled, sank into depressions for six or seven weeks at the mere realization that all was not well with our physical life, it meant that Hugo was much sicker than I. I was able to take shocks, pains and betrayals, but Hugo withdrew from life entirely, except for a tenuous contact with me. Because of my gift for creating contact, was more possible? It was Jim who said the other night: "Why is it that with you everything becomes illuminated and exciting? That's the secret of your seduction. You create an intimacy, an atmosphere in which each one has an intimate feeling of existing."

We were talking about Renate's "spectacles." I said: "I'd like to be like Renate. She talks and behaves like my characters. She is propelled to act, say anything, almost hysterically, and turn it all into a marvelous spectacle." It is true Renate's impulses carry others along. She was marvelous for Paul, who was withdrawn and mute.

Now, the crucial point of "contact" that I gave to Hugo: was it due to my maintaining the realm in which we had contact, devotion, tenderness, care of each other, or was it due to my ability to give an *illusion* of contact by sympathy, by *always* responding (even when ill or despondent), by listening, by "tuning in" when I am called? I do the same with Rupert. Outside the moments of anger, when he says I "go away into an icy silence," I am there, and I am aware of his mood as he enters the apartment, aware of how he feels, and receptive *before* I begin to act.

Tuning in…tuning in.

Hugo, for example, often interrupts the other person, very often does not answer questions. He does play "solo." Annette told him he does this in dancing. Jim finds him "blowing hot and cold," near and far. "I never know," said Jim, "whether I will find Hugo as friendly or open as he was the last time."

The "deadpan" is highly developed in America (Gregory Peck, for example, added to inarticulateness, added to the incapacity to tune in). It all goes together. Not talking together. And all these needs manifested in such a perverse way. Rupert does not like an evening of talk, but he will listen to drivel on the radio for hours, the old maids' convention called *Invitation to Learning*, elemental psychology in parents' and students' interviews, etc.

With Bogner, we discovered that since I cannot bear criticism (it was criticism that made me break with Dutton, with Gore, with James Merrill, with the Spewacks). I also cannot bear to inflict this upon others. So I direct it at what *surrounds* them.

When offended or criticized, I break away. But that is not all. I have to break when offended because I fear my anger. I must avoid the object of my anger. The real problem is how to stifle anger. I have done it so much, so long, so often, that I have "packed" it like dynamite, and now it comes out in the "explosions" I fear, uncontrollable outbursts.

The day we discussed my anger I could only express bodily pain: a constricted throat, backache, headache, tension, tightness. I was using all my energy to repress it. And I left Bogner with the rising tide of anger controlled.

I displaced it by attaching it to peripheral objects, places, people.

After this I felt lighter. I accepted that I have a fiery temper.

The refusal to be angry is crippling.

New York, June 3, 1957

It is so amazing to return home and to find on my bedside table the book I was reading that I left open when I stopped, face down. To find in the salon Rank's *Art and Artist*, which Maxwell Geismar returned to me when we all spent an evening together.

After Hugo emerged from his depression I began to enjoy myself, in spite of the painful talk with Bogner, and having to face intermittent pains of arthritis in all of my back, especially in the third lumbar section where a disk, or cushion, is fused—I could see it in the X-ray. It concerned me that, not being able to exercise, I would lose my figure, that I might not be as skillful with my rotations in lovemaking. I felt threatened in my suppleness and bodily freedom. I have to walk less, and stand less.

But I tried to forget.

I love the Café Figaro on Bleecker Street. It has character. People play chess, and genuinely talk together. I went several times with Jim and Dick. I enjoyed seeing René de Chochor during a short visit, a very affectionate René who has missed us during his sojourn to Europe, enjoyed seeing the myth of the common man savagely attacked by Budd Schulberg in *A Face in the Crowd*. Enjoyed a negro play, at which I always weep.

Annette Nancarrow still has the same provocative walk, showing more of her luxuriant brown breasts as age blurs the purity of the lines of the throat, but she gallantly asserts: "I am a dethroned queen. But I enjoy being a dethroned queen. My friends love me more than when I was the top-billing star: they feel sorry for me! And there is much to enjoy backstage; I let the younger women worry about being at the top, quarrel and struggle…" Evidently, while young women take the center of the stage, there are still plenty of men who prefer autumnal women. *Jeunes filles* are for the daytime, but autumnal women are for the night.

Her freedom to come and go, her gayety and ability to live alone made me weep with envy. Could I have done this if I had been economically protected as she was? No, she has more courage than I. She is back from a trip around the world, alone. She lives by caprice, change, variety. She rid herself of her apartment in New York (in which she tried to live as a wife) because: "Think of all the places I have not yet seen and all that one can do with $150 a month elsewhere."

When Tom Payne writes me he is willing to give *Solar Barque* to Viking, I became paralyzed. I thought: one more insulting letter. I cannot take it (the last letter from Viking was apropos of *A Spy in the House of Love*, calling it an "erotic fantasy" and refusing to publish it). More damage. More anger. More feelings of being unwanted.

This seriously impairs my career as a writer. I must take the blows and insults, offenses and stupidities. They are a part of all work in the world. Dr. Bogner gets insulted in the name of analysis, or rather by those who hate it.

I do not miss Rupert. I do not even miss the physical presence, his body, his caresses. The "house" that gives him happiness crystallized all that I reject—solitude, living in a "colony," the Hollywood atmosphere, sports in a perpetually cold sea, drinking, the family—but all this is a displacement of my unwillingness to say: "Rupert *is* all these things. He is not the man I imagined—a dreamer, poet, adventurer—but a very practical, very prosaic, very limited and rather rigid person, very down to earth, very uncomfortable with my friends.

This is painful. Yet it is also my salvation, because spending the rest of my life with Rupert would have been catastrophic, with my increasing physical handicaps, need of constant care, my loneliness in his world, his evasion and avoidance of mine (he has made no effort to share or penetrate my world—he only takes the superficial aspects of it, parties, etc.).

Last night an evening with René de Chochor, James Herlihy and Dick Duane—and Hugo. Dinner at the Sevilla, eating a paella, and René talking as he has rarely talked, very seriously and intelligently about painting, Portugal, France. He has discovered, meanwhile, that he cannot live in the unpainted nature of Portugal, without, now and then, a Chartres Cathedral.

It was this I touched upon in *Solar Barque*.

Then on to the Vanguard and Professor Irwin Corey. Laughter. René suggested we try the Five Spot in the Bowery. A Grove Press editor had told him it was the place of the moment, that all those who wanted to avoid the "voyeurs" who haunt the Village by looking in through windows, had moved here. And it was the best café, with a free, natural jazz band. We sat there, but the drinking depressed me. I was angry…angry at my physical limitations. I fell asleep restlessly, too lightly, and had a nightmare:

In a room there was a person (man or woman). A tiger leaped into the room. I closed the door upon them. The person faced with the tiger cried out to me: "Bring me a knife!" but I continued to close doors, one after another. No matter how many doors I closed I could hear this person calling for a knife, and sobbing. I closed the last door, and, not knowing what happened, I awakened shaken and sick. I thought the person was Hugo, that I had left him to fight his own battles. That I had refused to give him a knife. I was so shaken, so filled with anguish and guilt that I talked to Hugo. I attributed the dream to his telling me: "I have had a problem with my passivity. I have been passive towards you and in many situations in which I was expected to take the lead." (He had been passive all evening, not taking the lead with the headwaiter, though he was not only the oldest, but the host, and this always irritates me.)

He wanted to put my name on his new film because it was I who suggested representing reality and the present in color, and the past and ghostly fantasies in black and white, negative printing.

I said such a mere suggestion or inspiration was not enough—I had merely "jump-started" him. (It occurred to me also that when people ask me why Miller has never written as well as he did in France I give many reasons, but I actually believe it is that Miller needed to be lit afire and fecundated, and I served him beautifully in this.)

A stormy session with Bogner. I misinterpreted the dream. It is not Hugo in the room. It is the conflict of aggression (the tiger) and murderous defenses (the knife) that I closed many doors upon. Spilling the dream to Hugo was a way of diluting the anguish, and hurrying to interpret it was also a way of combating the anguish. I should have brought it to her undiluted. When she infers resistance, or evasion, or not wanting to see, I get upset. It is a reproach. I am obviously not resisting or evading, since I am there with her going through a painful crisis. "But," she said, "you forget that resistance or evasion is necessary, it is good, it is your character; without this you would be fluid, a nonentity. It is no crime to assert or defend what you consider your truth. I am only trying to show you how, when you face your violence or aggression, you go about closing doors upon it, leaving your tiger and yourself to fight it out, refusing to use the knife."

"But why did I immediately think of Hugo, whose passivity disturbs me?"

Or did I mean Hugo, Rupert, Eduardo, who hate *aggressive* women yet do not love the passive ones either? What would Hugo have done with a hesitant, uncertain woman who changes her mind and is unable to make decisions? He did not like Karon's and Thurema's aggression, but he does not like passive or colorless women.

142

And I...am I not in the same difficulty? I hated Edmund Wilson for his aggression. Yet the men I did choose I wanted to *incite* to action. I believed Rupert was more dynamic and active than Hugo, and he is, but only at home. In the world he is a timorous, anxious man, very unsure of himself. He attacks only the minor characters who cannot hit back: the ticket seller at the movie house who is not responsible for the bad film, the red lights. It is displaced anger. He does not dare to attack me directly, but he is hostile to France, etc.

The nightmare still hurts me. I can still hear the sobs and howls.

It is five o'clock on a summer afternoon. I wear a cotton dress with a good design made by The American Painters Association, green, white and brown. I am sunburnt, beautifully so. My skin is soft because of my beauty secrets—sweet almond oil, olive oil, etc. A massage has unknotted my nerves. I'm awaiting Hugo, and then the Geismars.

New York, June 1957

Jim said: "You know, I have been thinking about your fucked-up relationship to the world. There's a remedy. You produced an aesthetic work, too beautiful; you attempted the impossible, demanded too much. You had failures...not in the stories, but in the novels. I have an inkling of what the failure is. You wouldn't at any moment be hell-bent on directness as you are with me. The diary kills me. I wept when I read your letter to Bill. Giving. It was on giving. There's nothing like it in *Children of the Albatross*. It's too distilled. The diary lifts me off my feet, devastates me."

Giving—the letter on giving to Bill, who was afraid and held on to his possessions. The secret may be in the giving. I didn't give all to the world.

Every time you grasp at a root, it is tangled with another root. This story began this summer. Life at the beach with Rupert. Packing the basket, suntan lotion, bathing suits, sandwiches, Tavi's leash, *Time* magazine, parking always at the same spot if possible, running for the same corner by the wall, and laying out the Japanese mats to conceal Rupert's clinging to the old and dirty army blanket. Tavi went off to cool his belly in the pool formed by a river coupling with the sea, where all the children bathe. The students, teenagers, arrive in groups and settle in groups. The girls are beautiful. Rupert is interested in them. This is his youthful external world, the physical surface, which *he is*. I am sitting on the beach with a beautiful teenager. I am not losing him to another world. He *is* this, in part, and from the beginning this teenager was not related to me, except in his moments of distress, or at the time when the savagery of the young had struck at him (his wife and his mistress).

In any case, I suffer. I suffer not only from the fear of loss, but also because I am angry, ugly. I not only feel estranged, but cut off from Rupert. When I left for two weeks to meet Hugo in Mexico, Rupert entered his world, timidly perhaps, not comfortably, but he sought it out. He did confess that he was, with his wife and mistress, like Romain Gary, feeling his closest contact with me, and trying to make it with others, but not truly. Yes, I know. I could see how he acted. Unnatural, striking poses, making efforts, cramped. But physical beauty lures him on, and then I am thrown back into the past. I was jealous of my father's interest in pretty women. A shallow interest. Nevertheless, even though purely sexual and mostly as conquest, it was this interest that deprived me of his love and tenderness.

The summer made me jittery and shook my unity with Rupert. The union with Rupert was always condemned by the knowledge that it was shallow, physical. But what always disoriented me was that when I wanted to push Rupert into the world I felt he belonged to—middle-class family life, mediocre musicians, the young, athletic worlds (surfers)—he would say, "No, I belong with you. I am at home with you."

When I leave, these worlds cease to exist. They do not fill his life. He awaits my return.

But my shaking and trembling, with all the anger and jealousies, I had to bring to Bogner. I *felt* old, I *felt* ugly, I *felt* I couldn't walk past these rows of teenagers.

None of these *feelings* were actual facts. What I felt, which seemed to be visible to all, was an ugliness. It was I who determined that what I felt was ugly. I never *wanted* to be jealous or angry. I wanted to be tolerant and indifferent.

So the life at the beach was not a drama between Rupert and me and the teenagers, but again between me and my father and mother. A jealousy of Rupert too. Weeping, I said, "It is so easy for *him* to get love. All you have to do to get love is look beautiful."

Again I excluded myself from this—I was not loved. There could only be *one* reason. I must have heard my father say so many times of women, "*Elle est jolie*, or "*Elle est belle*." Since this was the only requisite for his interest, I felt lost in this *beauty contest*. The apple was never given to me. All the beauty contests of the world I lost, and in one final outcome. A child's version of reality. No truth is final. For many players this first defeat is the terminus. For others it is to be transcended. I proceeded to transcend it. In action. I became beautiful. I made myself so. I not only grew inwardly, but I also acquired outer beauties. I won love and lovers, many loves and lovers. But it was not a beauty contest I wanted to win, it was love. In reality I became beautiful and I won my love. But in the psychic body there is a germ carrier intent on maintaining the eternal continuity of microbes.

The Diary is the museum, the storeroom, the attic of the mind. The past, intact, and the child are here. Whenever the love has a moment of inattention, or gives it to some other matter (business, art, other women, friendships), what I recall is not what I am, but rather this angry child who clamored for love and did not get it. I have no memory of physical closeness to my father. He was incapable of tenderness. His second wife complained of this. I was physically close to my mother and my brothers. And so later, I was in the same constellation: physical closeness to Thurema, none to Hugo the father, but desirous of his younger brothers Bill, Gore and Rupert. Old forms of union. Yes, I remember, I was very close to Joaquín, he was my child. When I was thirty, once, in the park, I remember Hugo, Joaquín and I were taking a walk. I was wearing a spring coat, and Hugo suggested we sit on a bench for a while. I said: "Oh, I can't. I'm going to be cold." Joaquín took off his spring coat and laid it on the bench. I sat on it. It was warm. I had a flash of desire. It was just a flash. It never clouded my relationship with Joaquín.

144

Dr. Bogner, today I bring you only a curtain. I dreamed of a curtain. Just a curtain. Nothing else. It is ridiculous, but I have been wishing for new curtains in my bedroom and I have looked at curtains in the shops. I do remember other curtains. I remember a table in Brussels. At that time tables were covered with long red felt all the way down to the floor. This was our playhouse. I was eight years old, Thorvald was six and Joaquín two. I do not remember any sexual games, but it must have been warm and intimate.

I begin to remember *moments* of union with parents and brothers, moments of love, proofs of love. It was not, as I had crystallized it, all pain and estrangement. I didn't believe in my father's love because he only appeared (in my memory) to spank us, or to watch us during siesta time because I refused to sleep. Did I refuse to sleep so that he would come and watch me? Did he come and watch me and was I uncovered and did I feel pleasure at being (at last!) looked at? In the mature woman it is these moments that marked erotic forms, such scenes that unleashed eroticism. Out of the source I drew fantasies to help myself when I felt no passion. One of them was my father lifting my dress, pulling down my panties, spanking me...no, not spanking me; he is caressing me, he is making love to me. (Fact or fantasy, said Bogner, the guilt is the same.)

And with the fantasy I overcame the guilt for seducing the father, which made me cold at the moment.

The Diary was not originally a depositor for sexual secrets. It was written for my father to read. To make him share our life. My mother read it. I left it in the library with the books. Anyone could read it. I read it to Hugo. I never concealed it, until my first affair, and even then only because Hugo read the episode I had with John Erskine.

Bogner and I explored the "blush," which is the effect of menopause. It is medically impossible to experience the hot-and-cold for ten years. I have. Medicine has not helped.

Dream: I arrive at a hotel where I have been staying and had made friends with a girl and two boys (one is called Miguel, a Cuban). I wanted to buy chicken for a dinner I had to cook for friends. I opened the kitchen. The cook was in the middle of the room on his knees praying, and his wife was intoning a Jewish prayer. I withdrew.

As I came to the entrance I found a small Mexican policeman writing out a ticket because there was a law against leaving a hotel without a car.

We wanted to go swimming. I could not find my swimming panties, only the top. Rupert offered to go and get it. He had to swim to it. It was aboard a ship in a big trunk. He opened the trunk and looked in. Other women surrounded the trunk. I felt that Rupert was making a spectacle of this search for the benefit of the women. At first I had been touched by his goodness in swimming for me. I could see all this from the shore. I decided to go and see. He was amazed that I had come.

Dream: I seek to enter a house where people are gathered. A strong magnetic atmosphere prevents me from entering. A woman tells me to push harder—I do not find myself inside. The men have bohemian beards. They believe in praying only in front of a painting. A painting is brought in. Then, a printing shop on a truck is driven in. The great noise of a fire engine is outside. The truck follows by crashing through the window and then goes out. We all leave. A flood begins, with stones and water rushing down. I'm standing on an island growing smaller. A man comes with a dog. We leap to safety, into a city. Helen's belongings are brought from the cellar, all mildewed. I have to wear stained and torn clothes.

It is only the sick who drag their past along, who decide that life is like a novel written once and definite, like a photograph. This is the way it is. But not for me. *Today*, when I break with those who offend me, is it not possible that the origins of such acts are rooted in the fact that at my parents' first "error," the first careless gesture, the first inadequacy, I reacted unduly and deepened and sharpened my anger, my revenges, my wounds? Yes, it is possible. Just as the criminal remembers only the wrongs, never the kindness, who retaliates more violently than the act against him justifies, as does the neurotic. So the child, wanting all, and obtaining but a fraction, harbors an exaggerated grudge.

A new relationship is unburied from the past, one never known. A new relationship with the parents born of the recognition of one's own role in the *interpretations* in turn alters our relationship with others. My bad relationship with certain publishers (because they denied me what I demanded, which was respect, faith and devotion) does not necessarily distort my relationship with Thomas Payne. What I see now are human parents, neurotic parents, and myself as a neurotic.

The "blush." No memories of incidents, only of fantasies. I was searching for incidents. All I brought to Bogner were sensations: curtains, tablecloths, veils, capes. Capes! Veiled from the world.

Ugliness was not, in reality, an ugliness of body or face, for I am today probably one of the handsomest women of fifty-four walking the streets (I get invitations from taxi drivers, offers of drinks on Madison Avenue, compliments from the handsomest negro bartender at Romero, desire and obsession from men living in our apartment), but my own disparaging and caricatured image is of a jealous, angry, sulking child. This image is what I imagine shows. On the beach, too, I felt it showed. I was no longer smooth and tanned and charming with, as my masseuse says, the body of a seventeen-year-old girl.

After examining all the embarrassing secret fevers of erotic fantasies, the shames, the blushes, the heat of excitement and fears, I came back with a dream of grafting a totally new skin over my scarred stomach. Scars of the past (my appendectomy as a child and my operation for a cyst a few years ago), as I said upon awakening, and wishing a new skin would cover them.

Bogner: "This is because you don't want to dig any deeper into these scars. You would like me to leave them as they are and cover them up."

The idea or concept of not being loved is painful, but the realization that living under the terms that were possible to my parents, *their* terms, *not mine* (mine must have been of a total, unshared, fanatical, prostrated, exclusive and flawless love), is infinitely more painful. The realization that breaks, separations, losses and loneliness are self-created is painful. *And you can aggravate them.* You can make extreme claims. You can make inflexible choices. I could say, for example, that the world of dancing was closed to me because I could no longer dance deliriously, but when I finally had the courage to face a dance club with friends at "7," I found

I could take pleasure in watching a delirious negress who danced into a frenzy as if she were in the jungles of Haiti at a voodoo ceremony, and I did not need to be in the spotlight.

Thus, too, with the vastly traumatic moment of abdication or retirement, which, being "breaks," only reflect the intransigencies, the neurotic inflexibility: if I cannot be at the center, *the* center of life, I would rather die. But at the center of what? Not of life, because life is relationship. You can be related to dancing without being the dancer. It is the center of attention, of love, of the world, where the child's prerogative is maintained. So I was not the beloved in the group of friends sitting at "7" while the negress danced.

I was seated next to Bill Barker, twenty-six, across from Zina, his ex-wife, and Diana, his present mistress. Bill is a handsome Irish young man. I met him in Los Angeles, in the quiet house of Burton Holmes, introduced to me by Caresse.

Bill had barely spoken, once in English, once in French, when I sensed his atmosphere—Paris, Italy, society and the artists, Cocteau and Prince Ruspoli, de Sicca and the movies, Jean Genet and ambisexuality. It was like oxygen. We could have talked for twenty-four hours. A disturbing light in his Irish eyes, irony, anger, passion. (Rupert, as usual, produced the alchemy that kills my life in California. Whenever fantasy and freedom appear, Rupert drags me back to earth because he cannot follow.)

We took Bill to Renate. There were no sparks. Bill was in an angry mood. He has been in other worlds. He is hostile to his present environment. I had let him stay in our apartment while Hugo and I were in Mexico. Then we met at Jim's, and he attacked California as a tranquilizer, a cheap heroin mixed with bicarbonate and toothpaste. He was with Diana, a beautiful child-woman, innocent, touching, naïve, tender. But when I met Zina, the image I had of Bill became as sharp as it had been mysterious before.

Zina is tall, has the body of Venus and the head of a young Greek man. Her blond curls are like a *casque*, a *casque d'or*, espousing the head, ears, forehead. The ice-cold, blue eyes are slanted in a faunesque slyness. The nose is slightly flattened, the mouth just full enough but not too sensuous. At times her expression is hard. She frowns. She peers into the café. She is a man. Then she laughs fully with her head thrown back, and she is a charming woman. At moments she talks so softly one cannot hear her. At another moment she springs like a tigress and shouts. She wears her scarf not languidly or floatily, but severely stretched across her wide shoulders like a Greek costume on a statue. She wears a dirty raincoat and shorts, or a heavy, dark wool dress, or a gay skirt and blouse. Her father was a Russian grand duke, her mother an American millionaire. She has acted in films, worked in nightclubs, married and divorced the Count of Harcourt, lived notoriously with a woman, tried drugs. At times she sits at the café completely abstracted, withdrawn. One never feels one is looking into the eyes of a human being. Bill said: "Zina is a myth. One feels she would not mind the sight of suffering. She plays roles. *Un abîme insondable* [An unfathomable abyss]."

I said, "Jim, we cannot go on calling 'characters' the people who either come out of novels or will soon be inside them, like Zina-Sabina-June. The word has been mutilated, corroded. We must find a new one." Later that day I added: "I have it. It will be Flora and Fauna. Flora for the sweet ones, Fauna for the fascinating ones."

This month the most fauna-like relationship was not with Hugo (discovering he had suppressed his aggressiveness, his self-assertion, his weeping over the fear of the loss of love, which dictated his surrender), or with Jim in spite of our jam sessions hell-bent on direction and freedom, or with Zina whose fascination affected me for a few days, or with Bill's charm (his saying Anaïs has a genius for life), but with Lawrence Durrell via his book *Justine*. Twenty years ago Larry appeared in Paris, and in the Diary he is a small, blond, blue-eyed, soft-gestured, tanned, endless talker-poet, with yogi suppleness of body, and the power later manifested in the mystifying *Black Book* not yet apparent.

The *Black Book* (Obelisk Press) was banned and remained known to very few people. He continued to write poetry and to be published in England. Twenty years later Gore mentions *Justine*, and then Bill loaned it to me. A banquet! An orgy of words and colors, riot of the senses. A male counterpart to my novels. Erratic, elusive, penetrating, a sensuous jungle, a trapezoid of images, a juggler, a master of all prestidigitations.

There was an epidemic of Durrell. Hugo read *Justine*, and so did Tom Payne. I talked about it.

The image of Larry as a young man was so clear. He had a softly-contoured face, he was not lean, in spite of sailing his boat in Greece. He had a rounded nose, humorous and earthy, comfortable. He passed certain judgments on Henry.

An absurd accident had cut the thread between us. It was he who had paid for the publication of *The Winter of Artifice*, *Black Spring* and the *Black Book*. During the war he found himself needing money. He wrote to Henry. It was at the time when I was drowning in debts. I could not help. Henry borrowed from friends. I felt so guilty. The guilt paralyzed me. We could have been writing to each other. I would have followed his life. Of the three of us, he was the best writer.

1729 North Occidental Boulevard, Los Angeles 28, July 20, 1957
Part of the failed relationships I now understand were the *invented* ones.

One of them was with James Merrill. When I first met him he was a very young poet, touching and childlike. He wrote a discerning letter about my work, a thesis on Proust. He was in love with Bill Burford and concerned over my friendship with him, of my admiration of his writing. He seemed human and sensitive. I was shocked when he suddenly turned against my work, but it all became clear when I read the novel he wrote about his father. The Jimmy Merrill in the novel was childish, prosaic, limp, loveless and unloving, boring. Could I have been that devoid of insight? The possibilities were there. In the novel he blames the possession of wealth for separating him from *reality*, for making the world *unreal*. Even though he wrote this after analysis, it is the novel of a blind infant, without any feeling, a sickly, crying sensibility, absolutely non-human.

Could Burford and Merrill turning against my work, which has not changed and has consistently developed on the same level, be due to an irrational anger at what they could not possess, not follow, not ever be? It was the sudden irrational quality of these attacks that made me suspect their motives.

Could the key lie in Gore's saying he could not write as I do and therefore had to stick to the objective novel?

One night I was sitting at the Bel Air Hotel bar with Gore, who was drinking Pernod and talking… "You don't realize that when I met you I was on the way to becoming another Hemingway with *Williwaw*. Your writing and your attitude towards writing blew me up. I had never encountered this before—the seriousness, the depths. I had intended an entirely different novel than what I finally wrote in *A Yellow Wood*. Meeting you caused me to dramatize the choice between convention and art. The young man made his choice. The woman symbolized art. It was my choice, but only because I couldn't write as you did. You disturbed all my organization. I no longer wanted to be a professional writer, just a good craftsman. I was impressed with the depths, by your story about Hemingway seeking another dimension and being unable to get beyond the hard surface of his writing. It was because of the confusion, the split in my writing that my novels probably failed. Now, you know that I am an excellent critic. I know the uniqueness of what you have done, the purity, the depth. I can't bear to read my early novels. I don't know what would have happened if I had not met you. The course of my writing would have been easier, more successful, and more ordinary."

I was very moved and very disturbed by his honesty, by guilt. He remembered he was twenty when I met him and that I had treated him as an equal.

He got up and left me for a moment, returning with a book of stories in which, almost ten years later, he had attempted the fusion of realism and surrealism. I read one right there. It was better than the novels. Tennessee Williams admired them. I felt the same guilt I feel towards Jim Herlihy. I am not sure that this encounter of American realism with French surrealism gave birth to anything, but who knows what will happen to Jim and Gore ten years from now? I reminded Gore that my first novel written at twenty years of age was not as good as Gore's first and second novels, nor Jim's first plays at the same age.

Then, under the influence of alcohol and music, we entered the realm of what had separated us. Gore admitted his great shock at the break and his fear that it may occur again. But I was able to explain it to him.

"You became sarcastic with me and said several things that offended me. Then, at the time when reviewers and publishers were sinking me, you chose to write about Williams and McCullers, to lecture about them and to overlook me. I understood your going towards Tennessee Williams, saying he was the King—I accepted this because he was a writer of value and masculine principle who was natural for you to follow instead of me, the woman. But when you praised Carson McCullers—then I was hurt. Today I would not break for such a reason, but at the time I felt wildly hurt, persecuted, and I wanted to break with everything that caused me pain. I have spent all these years in between seeking to understand what made me break with you, to objectify the vulnerability—so this cannot happen again. I didn't lose my feeling for you, I lost my confidence."

The air was clearing. Gore read accurately in these words the vulnerability he suffers from—and it touched him.

"I am always the same. I never change," he repeated.

As we got into his open sports car, a young man's car, I felt light and trusting and close to Gore again. It made me happy that we could overcome our distortions. I had discussed this with Bogner, and my tendency to escape. If I had died in the New York hospital after my cyst operation, Gore would have carried the burden of a failed relationship throughout his life, a break he did not understand. We both felt elated.

"We rescued the best of it," I said. In the book of stories, he wrote "*Comme toujours.*"

The next day he said over the telephone: "Alcohol is a great purge—I feel wonderful today." (Usually he feels depressed after drinking.) He did not know that the great purge was possible because of analysis—mine—the harrowing hours with Bogner.

This study of the escape from pain and difficulties was a painful revelation because its motivation was so deeply concealed in the richness and profundity of what I escaped into, from what seemed like an arid friendship with Gore to the elating one with Jim.

It is strange, the relationship I have had with static characters. Perhaps I need them.

And who could have predicted then that ten years later Gore and I would be driving in Hollywood in a sports car, both of us tanned, and both of us having, as he said, obtained what we wanted, he success and I love?

Los Angeles, Summer 1957

One evening I went to the French Consulate to have dinner alone with Leslie Blanch, Romain Gary's wife.

This time I was determined to memorize her face. The eyes are beautiful, rather large, green-blue, but golden at times and quite Mediterranean. It is the delicate English skin and the anonymous nose and mouth (like those in water colors) that I cannot fix in my memory—but it is a face easily imagined in English paintings of other centuries, pretty and diffuse as her character later developed—vague, chaotic, floating, fluid—but courageous and more colorful and alive than one at first suspects. To my great astonishment, this woman, with a maternal body and the heavy, masculine legs of English amazons, emerged as well related to her four heroines of *The Wilder Shores of Love*, quite capable of leaving England and her family to marry an Arab or live in a harem, to live in a tent or adopt a new religion. She has been buying Turkish rugs, not because they harmonize with the furnished Consulate house, but probably because they recreate for her the life she loved the best, in Turkey. She held in her hand the bright yellow beads of a Mahometan rosary. She wanted to take me to the Turkish rug merchant and have tea.

"I have married a rug peddler," cries Romain.

The visitors of the Consulate made her seem utterly out of place, and I understood now why she seemed lost and bewildered at the soirées.

My timidity and my own façade of a woman of the world force me to await a sign of unfamiliarity and *dépaysement*, by which I recognize those who belong to my native land, which is nowhere and everywhere.

By the time Rupert arrived, we had transformed the trite patio of a pseudo-Spanish house into a Turkish patio, and she had brought out an ancient Hindu elephant of painted wood for an airing.

Every day this month, since Rupert was not teaching and only attending courses in the evening, we went to the beach. At first I was frightened by my talk with the doctor and the X-ray of my back. The cushion between the third lumbar was diseased with arthritis, and looked half the size it should be (collapsed). This happened after some injury, and it meant no more carrying heavy loads, no exercise. (No dancing? Swimming? Lovemaking?) He had prepared me for pain and stiffness.

But the dry desert sun tanned me and healed the pain. I began to do more and more, to swim a little, to make love, to walk, to carry small packages, to do all except vacuuming or waxing floors. Rupert was kind. His own great inferiorities always make him capable of compassion, and my disadvantages and handicaps always bring out a kind of relief that our accounts balance. When I first confessed my age, oh so painfully, he was happy because "I have so little to offer; I am glad to have my youth to give you." And when I returned from New York still stiff and in pain and asked if he was going to feel tied down by my restricted activities, he said, "Of course not. Why, *I* was the one who felt I was heavy and lifeless when I couldn't dance in Acapulco and you danced so well. I always felt I weighed *you* down!" He likes my dependency—it makes him more loving.

Meanwhile, just as I felt I could not be permitted to be ill with Gonzalo because Helba weighed him down with so much illness, I feel I cannot be ill with Rupert because Reginald weighs him down so terribly. His attacks of anxiety are worse than the illness—he telephones us no matter where we are: "I must go to the hospital tomorrow. I cannot go on any longer. I need care." But he is so terrified of the hospital's discipline that when we offer to take him there he backs out of it and uses all his cunning to find a new victim, some compassionate woman who could be turned into a nurse until she grows weary.

The appalling truth is that Reginald is only an extreme form of a childish selfishness that is growing in Rupert. What deceived me with Rupert for so long was the charm and the tenderness with which he does certain unselfish things, like helping me wash the dishes at Helen's, or washing the windows. But if I examine our life, I find *everything* is done for his pleasure. No time to see Renate or Paul. Paul wanted to go to the beach with us. Rupert refused. I did go out with Gore on one of the music nights.

When he is home, I have to bear the radio, but he can't bear the typewriter or the vacuum cleaner. I have said, "Let's compromise. You listen to four commentators, but not to all the news reports. And in the evening when we are in bed and I want to read, let's have music, not news."

Yes, I have love, but no freedom, and incredible monotony. At the beach we go to the same corner, and if the corner is not free, Rupert is upset. We never, even on the hottest day, sit near the water as I like to.

We buy the same beer, make the same kind of sandwiches, cook the same meat loaf. If there is any change in routine, if Leona can't come to play and wants the musicians to go to her place, Lloyd has a tantrum and so does Rupert.

For Rupert closeness means being a part of him, wanting what he wants, doing what he wants to do. He knows I hate California. Only once did he acknowledge: "Yes, I realize our life is a little one-sided." But he believes it is because I want something he cannot give me: New York, as if it were an impossible luxury ("I would have to get a job and begin all over again") whereas the truth is that New York is associated with his failure as an actor and his failed marriage to his cousin Janie, who was hard, brittle and too intelligent an actress. Also, here he has created a life that suits him—security. When I once said passionately: "You don't want my kind of life," he seemed very hurt. I didn't add: "Because if you did you couldn't bear your own." But he can bear this one. He likes the monotony, the absence of challenge. When he finds better and more interesting musicians he gets so nervous and panicky, he avoids them and returns to the "comfortable" ones.

I don't find Gore or Leslie Blanch "comfortable," but the difficulties, the dangers, the risks are elating! I like hearing a description of Eartha Kitt not wanting to admit she did not know how to ride horseback when she went riding with Gore and Paul Newman, and getting carried away by her panicked horse. I like hearing about Claire Bloom's desperate ambition, and Gore's conversation with Anita Shell by the Bel Air pool (she is playing in *Brothers Karamazov*). Or the life of Joanne Woodward. Even though I know Gore's image of them all is more often a caricature, they are still in life while Rupert is in stagnant pools of mediocrity.

Letter from Jim Herlihy to Anaïs Nin:
New York, August 1957

Dearest Anaïs:

I have been sitting up all night every night for the past ten or twelve days ...*reading!*...and now, at four o'clock on a Saturday morning, I am forced to stop!

At any rate, it has been a beautiful ten or twelve days. I have read voraciously, about six volumes—and I have *never* in my life read with such involvement, pleasure, fascination. I am in this life that I'm reading as I have never been in anything else in literature. That is perhaps the most significant aspect of my response to this diary: I am gripped by it. And that is the *art of literature*. I'm amused by the references, even in the diary, to the "artlessness" of your work—because that is the most artful thing about it: your own faith in your choice. I'm certain that was the essential strength of Shakespeare and Dostoevsky and Lawrence and Tennessee Williams (his earlier work)—their fidelity to their own voices—no room for doubt, no time for it. You can't doubt a river when you are riding on it, when it is carrying you—you know that it will flow even if you drown in it, and that even then you will go on flowing with it. (I have decided that the people who don't know how to read you are the ones doomed to sit on the banks all their lives loathing their own inability to navigate.)

You know, Anaïs, that I am unable to read any more; I mean that during these past few years I have lost my faith in the power of books to enchant me, hold me. These volumes restore that faith. Now I'm hungry for more, for the rest of it, and then for *Don Quixote* and Dostoevsky and Proust in a way that I have not been for years—because they are writers and works that have held *you*.

Hurry back! I've got to talk to you, pour out all that I'm being filled with by this reading. This is the only writing I've ever read that does not even tire my eyes; it is life. And life is contagious, regenerates everything it touches

(You know I don't mean it when I say hurry back. You are here already.)

152

It is amazing that at the deepest moments of your neuroses, you were still in contact with truth and beauty and love; they saved you. Otto Rank, who wanted you to abandon the diary, was sadly in error. This could have been a tragic mistake; advising a bird to abandon its wings while it is *in flight!* And it could have been tragic for everyone in your life, because your "children," as you called them, were sustained by you, and you *were* the journal. I don't think there was anything split or schizoid or what-have-you about your contact with the journal; it was one of your organs, as vital to you as your heart. There are so many jokes about the mother-children metaphor of artists and their work; but it is not a joke, it is a fact. And it is truer of you, probably—because your work is truer; you don't make the separation of life and art, and so to an outsider (the analyst) the connection seems unwholesomely intimate. On the contrary: the further removed an artist is from his work (removed by artifice, invention, technique, etc.) the less "wholesome" his relationship is to the product.

Exciting, this growth and its record, the privilege of witnessing an act of creation, not just "reading about it." And the creation, of course, is you! That is the quality of the diary that makes it unique in literature: it is alive. I have often described it to you as an "organism." I see more and more how true that is, how accurate.

I can't talk enough about its holding power; perhaps it is shallow of me to stress that so urgently. But I don't think so. Such terribly clever people spend their powers endlessly, working for a design that will fascinate their audiences, readers, viewers, etc.; but I have begun (again!) to believe that those efforts are self-defeating. Yet I do believe in design. But I also believe that design is intrinsic, a byproduct of truth when it is simply seen and rendered by the artist. It is like a love message from a child: all he does is hug you; and no amount of art can recreate it. The "form" is the child itself.

It may seem odd to you that I can see this so clearly when my own work seems to have taken a totally different turn. But it hasn't. My own work is also becoming more and more *me.* A lot of my earlier work—my journals, for example—were a miniature you, an imitation; I mean that in this sense: I had chosen *your* method of creating *myself*—but your method was not mine. I am beginning to find that there are in me a brood of mad children, simple, crazy, inexplicable people, who are anxious to create *me* by speaking *through* me. I let them do as they please, and that is the closest to truth that I can reach—at least at the moment. In many ways I have a nostalgia for my old way of doing it, but I refuse to control it; control makes it a pseudo-me. I feel now very deeply and strongly that it is incumbent on me to love my children and let them breathe in their own odd, simple and crazy tongues. The new play is another expression of this: it is a play that I would never in a million years have written if I had planned it in advance and *decided* to. It is so simple and light that at times I don't believe I'd have given it room, if I'd known in advance how frivolous it would be. And at other moments it seems, along with its lightness and simplicity, just as dear and loving and profoundly alive as anything I've ever touched. All of which adds up to only one thing: we must not kill our progenies with judgment. We are creators, not judges. Let others do that. And I believe that if our "children" are properly loved, they'll survive even criticism.

Dear Anaïs, how I love you these days! You said once that you were afraid you might have led me somewhat astray in my work. But the truth is more like this: for years now you've been my one contact with a world that would otherwise have seemed, by now, illusory, non-existent. You are, in other words, the only artist I've known through these many years who fulfills my child's dream of an artist: one who is true, devoted to beauty and dedicated to transcending the world through it. That is the quality in you that I am most proud of having imitated. I wonder if, without you, I'd have known what to do with my own voice now that I am hearing it and using it. I could easily have become one of those who doubt it and throw it away, so that it might just as well never have existed at all. (And a couple of years ago, when I wanted to break with Dick, I wonder what would've become of me if you hadn't warned me, through interpreting my dreams, that I was not ready for that; it is certain that even my present happiness would not exist!)

This is a 4:00 AM letter, and I am certain that it must read like one—but I'm almost painfully full and happy and rich, and so much of it I associate with you and the gift of your friendship and now this gift of the journals—that I probably wouldn't have slept without expressing some of it first.

Van Druten writes that he's looking forward to meeting you at Gore's luncheon party soon. I must close this, but something in me resists; alas, it is my love for you!

Jim

August 20, 1957
Acapulco with Hugo.

Letter from Anaïs Nin to Rupert Pole:
Acapulco, August 1957

Darling Chiquito:

Your *pez vela* did fall into a family trap. My love, as soon as Joaquín was here, Kay [Thorvald Nin's wife] told the truth and the real reason why she had engineered a family reunion: Thor had a second and fortunately mild heart attack just before coming. The doctor told him to rest for two weeks. He refused, said he would die of boredom. But this is also the reason why he wanted to "make up" and be reconciled with all those his autocracy alienated from him. Kay knew she could not keep him here without help. Joaquín cancelled his concert and postponed the Catholic mass for the reburial of my mother. I sent you a night letter. I pictured you disappointed. Now, my darling, I have my ticket definitely for Sunday, Sept. 1. It is a deadline. Thor will go back to work then.

Very sad to miss your family's house conference, but you and Lloyd know best and I have complete trust in both of you.

We are saving money by my being here, but no siesta here is as good as ours in Los Angeles.

Te quiero, Chiquito,
A

Los Angeles, October 14, 1957

I left New York *very high*. I felt strong. I was able to help Rupert. He looked so tired. "I was so down, so blue, so tired, yet as I was driving towards the airport I began to feel better!" I felt I had strength to give him if only I could hold on to my mood. I held on. Rupert was in an "economizing mood," so I had to begin the struggle. I feed him well without spending money. He was distressed and worried by the neighbors whose building equipment had opened a road right through our property and pushed the rocks towards the sea and destroyed the ice plants. We went on the weekend to photograph the damage. I spent the days all alone, copying the Diary and writing letters. The serenity is due to the stability of my life with Hugo, the *inner decision* that I cannot stay with Rupert, who causes me too much fear in the very realm in which I am the weakest, the sickest.

Slowly, the narcissism of the life compressed me again. One night of wild passion, and then: "What did you do with my grey pants?"

"They had a hole in the seat, quite large. I thought of having it mended but it would not pay. I held them to the light and the whole seat was worn and they would have torn again."

"I don't believe it."

I had to go out to the garbage can to show them to him.

He is unhappy and overworked and so he has to complain.

"Did you enjoy your lunch?"

"The ham was not good." (He says nothing about the asparagus salad, the fruit.)

He is blue.

I work all day. I had the house cleaned thoroughly. When he came home I was gay, the house was clean, the dinner was good. We went to the movies, and saw the best Mexican film, *Roots*.

Tonight he is at his desk and I am writing letters. What sustains me is that I will be able to return to New York, to freedom, to richness. I would die here, and it would ultimately kill my passion. In Los Angeles I am like a passion flower in a geranium pot.

I stay high. I do not hear the radio. I know America is childishly, neurotically upset because Russia sent a satellite into the sky first!

Ten days later. Maintained serenity and cheerfulness. Helped Rupert Saturday at breakfast: "What shall we do today?" "I have a suggestion. See what you think of it. Let's go out and visit John Reid, the young architect whose place we went to for a party once, where the bathroom was made of the most beautiful tiles I have ever seen—and find out if we could have them for our house."

"But tile bathtubs leak. It may leak."

"Let's ask him anyway."

We finally did go. The bathtub did not leak. There is a new process Rupert did not know. The tiles were made by the architect's wife and we could have them. Furthermore, Reid offered to help, with his decorator's discount, a carpenter, places where to buy plumbing, etc. Rupert was delighted, loved the tile, and was enthusiastic. But the truth is that all this has to be forced-fed, and the "high effect" does not last because it does not come from within him. He lacks self-propulsion.

After this visit to a charming, humorous and whimsical house, he was elated. Anything connected with the house elates him. We went to a Balinese shop I had wanted to go to for years. (Also a job of persecution. "Textiles would be too expensive for the bedspread we need; Balinese textiles are too expensive.") Once there, it was a delight of original and interesting objects, and Rupert bought an inexpensive shirt and ordered East Indian cotton for a bedspread. We came back pleased, but for the first time the inner mechanism was apparent to me, and disillusioning. What Bill Barker describes as my "genius for life" was seriously frustrated by Rupert's negativity in life. Either I have to work at luring him, or I am myself defeated. I don't understand this altogether, because during our first trip West he took over, he assumed leadership, and I enjoyed his active role.

Anyway, the days pass sweetly and modestly. At seven I get up first and powder my face, comb my hair and make Rupert's tea and his sandwiches for school. Then he gets up. In the morning he is dead, even though his face has that English flushed, warm tone. He takes his tea, grabs his briefcase, his sandwiches and goes. Tavi always follows him, a habit from the forestry days when Rupert always took him along in the truck. At eight the dishes are washed and the bed is made. Rupert is trying to read *Justine*, but prefers *Time* or the evening papers. I alternate between typing, errands and housework. When my back gets tired, I move about or go and get a massage nearby from a Belgian woman. We talk French. Her house could be my mother's—the same taste, same neatness and care for the silver, mended clothes, austerity. *Petite vie*—all arranged, and so Belgian in flavor even here, the clock on the mantelpiece, the bric-à-brac, the little tables.

Once my back is straightened again, I recover my agility and get back to work. At four or five or six Rupert returns. Tavi and I greet him deliriously. He is tired. But the house is clean, the socks mended, the dinner good—and he feels it.

And at night, the lovemaking.

In human life we are close. He has the same need of touch, of warmth, of intimacy as I do. He likes to live in a state of twinship—he likes me to be there while he plays, even if the music is bad.

Whatever collisions take place in the outer spaces, the human life is good, and I appreciate it. If Rupert feels the need to curse the red lights all the while he is driving, or to curse the "bad luck" when he hits them wrongly, he is also full of tenderness and sweetness because he hates so much to give a child a bad report.

When a child remains in the man, it is always irresistible. I don't know why. It is the secret of charm. All charm seems to come from the child in ourselves. I can't remember "adult" charm or whether it exists.

His distress and blues at all work is childlike, his procrastination, his losing and forgetting, his living in the present only as far as immediacy is concerned (the old Rupert, who saw only the obstacles, lived in the future, and now the future is an obstacle to living in the present).

What a beautiful, ironic paradox. The man who brings me passion is the man who denies most often what I call life. For example, I have often tried to tell him that after a week of not going out evenings, when Friday comes and we begin to feel free and elated, it is a terrible anticlimax to go to the family for dinner and music. But Rupert not only does not understand that he seeks to attenuate, to suppress the elations that become high moods, he truly interferes with them.

"We *could* have the music Saturday," I said.

"No, Saturday I like to be free."

I have failed to change any of these routines, not with gentleness, subtlety, or with anger and revolt.

A quiet evening. I write in bed as Rupert is at the desk. *But no depression.* I don't know which god to thank, Bogner or Jacobson, massage or astrology, having prayed to all of them!

Letter from Anaïs Nin to Lawrence Durrell:
Los Angeles, October 1957

Dear Larry:

The advent of *Justine* was a phenomenon, after the miserly, sterile, frigid, plain, homely, prosaic, stuttering world of American writing. It was truly a fiesta, a banquet, an orgy. As soon as I began reading, the world expanded. It was not only the great tactile richness, the colors, the smells, the flavors of the surfaces, the atmosphere, but the sudden depths of insight, the senses and the intelligence both so keen. I was tempted to say this is not writing, but witchcraft. Whatever it is, dear Larry, I must tell you I have an immense respect for what you have done.

What are you doing in France? How are you living? I am mailing you my books today. You re-entered the flow of the Diary (a mighty river now) to have your portrait added to.

I live a divided life. One in New York with Hugo-the-father, a graceful apartment, chic clothes, white heat living, many friends, café life in the Village, trips to Mexico, business, and another life here with Rupert-the-son, [step-] grandson of Frank Lloyd Wright, nature man, beach man, and professor by mistake, by temperament a guitar player who hates work. We wear sloppy clothes, rush off to the beach whenever possible, dream of a catamaran, of surfboarding, have friends, but they are colorless because California is colorless, like a cheap drug that has been mixed with bicarbonate and toothpaste, a pseudo-tranquilizer. And I just finished a novelette on Mexico, on a mythical city called Golconda.

Is there anything you want from America? If you ever come we can put you up in New York. Are there any books you want? Anything, in fact?

Do write me.

Anaïs

Letter from Gunther Stuhlmann of Hinshaw & Stuhlmann, Literary Agents, to Anaïs Nin:
New York, October 28, 1957

Dear Anaïs:

I have been trying to get hold of you for a while, since, unfortunately, I lost my address book with your L.A. box number as well as the N.Y. phone number of your apartment, which is no longer listed with the phone company under your or Hugo's name. So I hope that perhaps this letter will reach you.

The news I wanted to convey is that I have recently become a partner in a young and active agency and that we have started to create some interest for your work in Europe, including the diary.

We are also trying to line up some young, talented writers for our stable and I would appreciate it if you would steer anybody our way whom you consider worthwhile.

Please let me hear from you so that we can discuss some things in detail—this is just a last trial balloon that I hope will reach you.

All my best,
Gunther

Letter from Anaïs Nin to Rupert Pole:
New York, November 1957

My love:

The situation at Avon is chaotic and critical for Payne. The owner died in Hollywood after being forced to drink with a bleeding ulcer. I tell you all this because my job depends on the uncertainty of Payne's future position.

But—he was so enthusiastic about my reprint of *Under a Glass Bell*, its appearance, my cutting through red tape, obstacles, commercial wholesale quantities, etc. that he is taking care of distribution of *any book I do*. He said: "How exciting and wonderful it is to be doing a book one loves after all day doing books one despises!" His help is free and very valuable. So I redesigned *Solar Barque* with [Renate's son] Peter Loomer's drawings—and I will do Durrell's *Black Book*, which is selling for $45 a copy—and Payne will take 2,000 and I'm in business—even after paying the writer, I can make money.

Cost of reprinting Durrell: $400

Distributor pays $0.40 a copy on 2,000: $800

Mailing list has bought 150 *Bells* to date, so suppose they buy 150 Durrells: $150.

Conservative earning estimate is $1,000—of which I can give Durrell whatever is fair.

Payne says I'm very practical. But oh, the work! Correspondence to *start*. Afterwards all I have to do is deliver the books to the distributor (all *big* paperback shops) with a mailing list.

Peter's drawings look beautiful.

In spite of work there always comes a moment when I miss you so painfully that my body and heart *ache* as if I had the *flu*. Separation *hurts*, really hurts.

Anaïs

Letter from Lawrence Lipton of "Eve" magazine to Anaïs Nin:
Playa del Rey, California, November 14, 1957

Dear Anaïs:

I discussed your participation in *Eve* with Jane Morrison, the Editor, and we decided that, for the present, a kind of "letter" would be the best editorial form for your material. A kind of diary of your comings and goings, conversations with the people you meet and reports on things you do and places you go—whatever you think would be of interest to our imagined character Eve, whom I am sure you know very well, for, after all, she is really you.

I can think of no better description of the sort of thing we would like to have from you than your own "reportage, to make women feel they had been there."

Of course, anything in the way of fiction that you may have at the present time will be more than welcome. I hope that some of it is winging its way to me right now. If any ideas occur to you for nonfiction material, essays of opinion, etc., drop me a line just to give me an idea what you have in mind and we will talk it over here and let you know.

Affectionately,
Larry

Letter from Renate Druks to Anaïs Nin:
Malibu, November 25, 1957

Dearest Anaïs,

Your letter made me very happy. An image came in, with your letter—you are riding the crest of a wave, the reins are red thread. Ariadne's thread, probably. The horses are foam and fish—the whole image is like the Persian miniatures you love so much.

Yes on *anything* you have in mind about Peter's work. $100 is very generous, and Peter was delighted. He wants to be known as Peter James. He was eleven when he did the drawings. He already did a few sketches for the *Solar Barque* cover in the same style as the others, of course. A king holds a sun in one hand and a boat in the other. The boat is in the shape of a dragon. He also designed a few boats in the shape of fish. How have you inspired him!

I missed you so much at the opening of my show and the party. I felt like crying "author, author." Sometimes, I feel like you invented me. But how the role fits. It's almost always the same thing with me. The dream, the role, the invention, seem more real to me than reality (what people call reality).

I should have a car within the next few days, I am negotiating for one, and then I will be able to see all sorts of people.

When will you be back?
Much love,
Renate

New York, November 1957

Activities:

Mailed 4,000 penny cards announcing *Solar Barque*, wrote hundreds of letters. Every day I wrap up books, go to the post office, answer letters.

I did things for *Eve* magazine: collected articles, made notes, pursued Erich Fromm, saw Henrietta Weigel (after 10 years), a friend of the editor.

I wrote notes for my "Letter from New York" for *Eve*.

Saw Georges Borchardt, literary agent. Saw Gunther Stuhlmann, literary agent.

Sent books to India on my own, since James Laughlin, my greatest enemy, is in charge of inter-cultural exchange for the Ford Foundation.

Helped Peggy and Sylvia in their efforts to present Peggy's opera.

Went to the Barrons' party, Eric Hawkins' dance recital, to Harlem with Stanley, Karon, Tom, Wifredo Lam and his young wife. Narrated Persian poems for a film on Persian Miniatures—three hours of work. Was paid $125. Gave check to Hugo.

Los Angeles, December 1957
Rebirth—November 1957
The liberation from guilt caused a rebirth, a flowing that was free of fixations upon the past. The past traumas cause crystals in the joints, spiritual arthritis. Suddenly I could relate to everyone, even those who had hurt me. I recaptured old friends, like Wallace Fowlie. The same people I knew before, but could not connect with, I can work with, like Gunther Stuhlmann. I had forgotten to take change into account, a change in Gunther, and in me! He is now a literary agent and helping me. He is an intelligent German who loves literature, does translations, worked with films.

I connected with Tom Payne—too well. From the very first we talked truthfully. But each time there was more intimacy. He was in trouble, between his wife, children, and his mistress Gloria, a negro dancer. He had a housing problem, where to get a home for Gloria; he was undergoing analysis, and the analyst had betrayed his confidence to his wife's analyst. I helped him. I even spoke *for* Gloria (interpreting his vacillations as she would!). We talked so easily, and he was charmed by my own publication of *Under a Glass Bell*. He liked its appearance and the act of independence. I said playfully: "Be my partner in publishing for pleasure only!" He gave me advice. He talked about his analysis, his wife and Gloria: "My wife did not come to New York for four years" and "I sent Gloria away. I couldn't stand the tension anymore. Once, after a few cocktails, she threatened to commit suicide."

The last time I left New York, he came down to bring me a borrowed *The Black Book* so that I could read it on the plane. He stood there and said, "I'm sorry you are leaving." When I returned this time he came down for dinner. Hugo was going to work on his film, and then didn't, so we stayed together and went to the Five Spot together. I found his quickness of mind exciting. I was afraid to be attracted, glad of all the obstacles. I do not trust my excitements. But I like to see him at the door. He is articulate. And adroit with words. He is emotional, even though the intelligence is so bright it eclipses the feelings. But they are there. Once he spoke of himself as "dead. I am so dead." But I do not see him as such.

He is difficult to help. He defends himself, cannot take easily. I did all I could, tried to find him an apartment for Gloria. I was touched by his difficulties. His children are young. Gloria pulls him away although she has children of her own. She is still in Europe, was there all summer. He is tall and very thin (my *homme fatal*). His hands attract me. They are extremely thin and sensitive but covered with straight, long black hair. The mixture of sensitiveness and masculinity, of intelligence and feeling wins me each time.

Hugo and Tom made friends, so it helped to make our meetings natural. Once I told Bogner I had managed to dissipate the attraction, understood my compulsion to charm or be charmed, but that this was a friendship I valued and didn't want to spoil. But the week before I left I felt the old, wild desires to embrace. And I called him up from the airport. He responds so quickly to what I say. I became interested in a Chinese junk, which a friend of Walter Trampler got from China for $500.

And immediately Tom said, "But I saw it from the car. I was driving uptown! And I almost drove off the freeway. That would be a perfect way to live!"

Excitement. I couldn't believe that I could ever find such excitement in life. I thought my life was ending, ending in depression and isolation. The excitement of being in the world, of being able to act, to be spontaneous. Of activities. Of a pile of letters in the morning. Of the discoveries of analysis. When I told Tom about realism and surrealism he said, "Those are the things I wish we were discussing. Now it's all acute crises and conflicts."

"Yes, first aid. But these refinements come later."

I recognize how much neurosis interfered with my friendships, publications, etc. and am elated at the freedom from neurosis.

I kept telling Bogner of accomplishments. I could go to a party the same day Grove Press turned down all my work.

The moment of the greatest pain was hearing about Gonzalo's illness. He has cancer of the brain. It affected his throat. He was treated for days with long radioactive needles through the throat. Hearing this, I felt a pain in my own body. Beautiful Gonzalo, who used to say, "I will be unable to bear old age and physical decadence." His neck was one of the most beautiful I have ever seen, smooth and strong. He has lost his hair, which was so abundant, thick, curly and so alive. I wrote him a letter full of love.

The torments that tore us apart are forgotten. I only remember the passion and the tenderness. But because it was so physical, the idea of his body ill and in pain is more intolerable than it would have been had I loved him less sensually. I had days of pain and then a quiet acceptance that comes from the knowledge of our doom, illnesses and death. The intensely personal image is finally dissolved by time and thrown back into some universal ocean where Gonzalo's pain, or Hugo's, or Rupert's, or mine, are all one. We do not die individually, but in fragments with the deaths of those we love.

There are days when I count the dead, like a ritual of black magic, calling up names and being not too certain mine is not among them.

Retrogrades—the news of Gonzalo's illness came when I was preoccupied with completing my Diary portrait of Henry because I had heard he had been very ill.

I thought aging meant the loss of sensibilities, or vibrations. I could not believe that while parting from the dead I would feel more intensely alive than ever. Music pours freely through me; that is how I observe the uncluttered passages, the receptive cords, the purity of receptivity. I thought the feeling flowed less sharply, but I was blessed with continuous aliveness even at the thought of losing Gonzalo and knowing that a part of me will die with him.

Will he find my letter addressed to Café le Dôme?

It is so wonderful to lose the angers, the wounds. My real scar is actually vanishing like the other invisible scars. I thank Dr. Bogner. When Tom was betrayed by his analyst, I felt no qualms about Bogner, who never betrayed the exactitudes of truth even by a word misplaced or misused or carelessly defined! She has a genius for nuances.

But Tom's experience of betrayal awakened my stomach pains for days. Jim had said: "He is probably younger than he looks because he is sapped by some sort of anguish."

The endless sources of love—to love Hugo for his nobilities, his courage: he has overcome depression. He desires me but cannot complete the sexual act. I like his big hand over my face. It covers it. I still feel small and at rest in his arms. He struggles with his own liberation from guilt in the disguise of his abusive Aunt Annie. Bogner is Aunt Annie too. He must tell her, as he told Aunt Annie: "You can't change me." So he has a passport photograph in which he is scowling, his lips thin and compressed (as I often saw him).

How changed he is! He is friendly. He accepts my friends and makes his own friendships with them. He is in business with René de Chochor. He took Tom out for dinner while I was away.

When Jim and Dick met Tom they were jealous—"You are in love with each other," they said. Jim became irrational and attacked Tom's need of secrecy—then recognized his own irrationality. "I was jealous, that's all; he was younger and more attractive than I had expected."

I sought to retrieve the intensity of my communication with Jim—I had felt a change. It was not my feeling about the plays.

I left in a good mood. On the plane I finished the "Letter from New York" for *Eve* magazine.

Hugo entitles his new film *Melodic Inversion.*

I have lost the sense of pain that had closed these portions of my life (opened only by the Diary) and can relive them purely. A distillation has taken place that has dissolved the past, left the experience free of dregs.

I can write freely to Henry and for *Eve.* I can work with Lawrence Lipton as I could not have worked before, out of aesthetic, aristocratic retractions. The first time I went to his house in Venice, California, and I saw a little man whose glasses magnify his eyes and give him a fixed stare, who has black teeth and a lisp, a common accent. His house is like a motel without an object I could love, but it is filled with books, records, tapes. A prosaic, homely evening, at which he played records of readings instead of letting the poets who were there read. When he invited Rupert and me to meet Corso and Ginsberg at a Dadaist evening, the one during which Ginsberg took off all his clothes, we both recognized a primitive force. But I did not go again because of my passion for high-quality beauty and taste. Yet he called me up when *Eve* was born and I responded fully, gave all my time and experience to crystallizing it and carved out a job for myself.

Now *Eve* will publish 8,000 words of *Solar Barque,* my "Letter from New York," and give me a salary. When I arrived from New York, that very evening after wild lovemaking, Rupert and I went to the Poetry and Jazz concert. Lawrence Lipton was backstage. I realized he had had a large role in the new grouping and fusion of arts. I liked him for this, for his association with jazz musicians. The poetry was bad. Rexroth, as I knew long ago, is not a poet, and his prose is lifeless. But in this there is more life, more freedom, and more experimental excitement than in all the rest of American literature. The dead writing is left behind. Jazz has influenced the new writers. They are at least alive and have rhythm. Sunday Rupert and I drove to Venice. My high standards had alienated me from error, trials, experiments. But here, it was an effort, an attempt. I would help them. I could help them associate this with films, which I know. And perhaps they will, in the end, understand what poetry is.

Lawrence Lipton treats me gently. He excerpted *Solar Barque* himself but then said I could change it as I pleased. The excerpts were good. Intelligence and vulgarity were obstacles to me before, but perhaps America could no longer use the old art forms. It had to find its own: jazz. The only writers I singled out of interest lately were the jazz writers—the author of *Solo*, of *Wild Party*, of *On the Road*, the lyricism of Kerouac, the Dionysian rhythms that people were too quick to condemn, as the bourgeoisie in France condemned the bohemian antics of the poets and later of the surrealists. So there it is. American art in writing is being born of jazz.

Los Angeles, December 1957

My connection with the world broke twice: the first time when my father left me. The second time when America slammed the door on my writing. What I have been busy reconstructing was my bridge to the world. I had to find an objective role for a comeback. I couldn't come back just as a writer—that would have been too difficult. But *Eve* helped me.

When creativity is fulfilled there is less fatigue than in frustration. I have accomplished amazing work. I go from writing letters to editing volume 32 of the Diary, to Xmas cards, to the article for *Eve*, to notes, to housework, to telephone calls…but because all of it is living and creating, I do not feel tiredness. And it is affecting Rupert, and even Lloyd. No time for negativities. I sweep them up in my forward motion. Lloyd wants to publish a book. Rupert enjoys the jazz concerts—and the idea of New York begins to charm him. He is forgetting his own defeat there.

Los Angeles, December 24, 1957

Editing volume 33. Writing 15 letters while Rupert sleeps. Then the usual waste of one's life driving in California—driving to have the car repaired, driving endlessly for an hour of sun at the beach, driving to the post office for more letters to answer, more books to wrap up and mail, driving to parties, driving to a market, driving nowhere, to nowhere. But the Bridge to the World is strengthening. I came too soon. I was too far ahead of America. It is like abandoning your children, deserting younger brothers. And the price is solitude. Now I retrace my steps to understand. They were locked and bound. They knew no other way to get unlocked and unbound except for alcoholism, drugs. They knew no other way to trust the flying carpet except that it seemed to have been fabricated by the scientists. So they take the flying carpet of science fiction or drugs. Who knows if the very old, very mystical race resorted to them too? It was jazz that led me to those who were never going to acknowledge their debt to surrealism, never acknowledge what they owe to Joyce, to Proust, to surrealism, to Giraudoux—but pretend to have been born of some spontaneous chemical volition. *Et voilà*. They bow to jazz, but not one of the poets can write its equivalent. It has revealed them as non-poets, non-rhythmics, non-transposers, decomposers. Yes, yes, everyone can see it. The *other* writing, the one I practiced and nurtured, protected and fed, Miller's, Durrell's, etc., etc., etc. is waiting backstage for the fiasco. The public knows there is something wrong. I wish the jazzmen had the courage to shake them off. In any case... retrograde. *Je me met au diapason de l'Amérique* [I am in tune with America]. What separated me was my disbelief in drugs, in alcohol, in the absence of art. Now I enter because only then can one influence, not by standing outside passing judgment. When Gil Henderson comes offering mescaline, the Anaïs B.A. (before analysis) would have refused. I wrote *House of Incest* without mescaline and it is better than Huxley's or Michaux's experiments. But didn't I accept analysis? Bring the mescaline.

Los Angeles, February 1958
LSD experiment:

Dr. Oscar Janiger took Gil Henderson and me into his private office where he gave me a number of blue pills with a glass of water. Then he conducted us to the waiting room.

At first I knew I was sitting on a chair in the doctor's office, looking at the young scientist sitting across from me with his notebook. Then the doorknob began to melt. The walls and carpet began to waver, palpitate and move as if they were seen through water. The motion was slow and rhythmic, like that of algae in the water, or like jellyfish at the bottom of the sea. Designs like wavelets formed on the walls. I could see each hair of the rug moving in ripples, and I felt gay and at ease recognizing the water life. I said: "This is what I was seeking when I lived on my houseboat. Everything breathes and flows. People should not live in houses." I could, alas, hear the singing of the birds outside more clearly and sharply as other sounds began to disappear. Part of my body was dissolving and not felt at all. I could not feel myself walking, but floating. The transformation was gentle, and yet I was becoming aware that some parts of my body were unfeeling and others acutely sensitive, that I was being unglued from my earth gravity and that this was a sea-heaving motion to which I would have to become accustomed. The image of myself standing and trying to get my sea legs amused me.

I could no longer see the scientist or Gil Henderson. The doctor's office disappeared. I saw space. I was in space, and no longer under water. I saw a slender, black arched line that disappeared into infinity, over the horizon. I saw numbers on it, millions of numbers. I laughed and said: "I'm not a mathematician. How can I measure the infinite?" But I do understand it. The numbers disappeared. My eyes followed this endless design in space. I felt then that I was standing on the rim of a planet, alone. I was a child. I could hear the fast rushing of other planets. Then I saw Gil, and I was glad not to be alone. Gil was smiling, with his face the face of a normal man. But his body looked as if seen though a distorting mirror, small and chubby. But then I knew I was small too.

Gil was sitting on the foot of the bed. I explained to him that I felt like a little prince, all alone in space, yet I knew that he was there and that he knew. He had been there. I was weeping, weeping, weeping. I could feel the tears, and I saw the handkerchief in my hand. Weeping to the point of total dissolution. Why should I be weeping? I could see Gil clearly, and the absurdity of weeping when traveling through space struck me. I was aware of Gil handing me Kleenex. Then the Comic Spirit appeared. It was not the Anaïs who was lying down and weeping, but a small, light, gay Anaïs, very lively, wearing a cape, very cold, but who always got up and moved about. The Comic Spirit was aware of Gil's predicament. "Poor Gil, you are out with another weepy female! What a ridiculous thing to weep and spoil a voyage through space. But before we go on I want to explain to you why women weep. It is the quickest way to liquefy, to become fluid and re-enter the ocean, where the colors are much more wonderful."

The Comic Spirit shook itself jauntily and said: "Let's chase away this weeping. Everything is more wonderful under water. It is alive and it breathes."

Having decided to shrug off the weeping I must have asked the way out of the hospital room. Gil opened a green door to a back yard. I saw the sunlight; it seemed terribly crude and stark, and I shrank from it. Particularly because on the door there appeared designs in colors. There were two columns of rippling and undulating Persian designs in green, violet and blue. The designs were formal, symmetrical, and exquisitely perfect, but drawn in jeweled, illumined colors like melted precious stones. They formed patterns that dissolved swiftly to be replaced by other patterns in scintillating transparencies, like filaments of amethyst and emeralds in settings of silver filigrees. They changed without ever ceasing to form designs, and the luminosity was so bright that I was overwhelmed by the beauty, also by the sense of it passing too quickly. I cried out: "It is beautiful, so beautiful; it is passing too quickly." The two long columns were replaced by diamond-shaped designs, not like a kaleidoscope in which the pieces of colored glass break and fall like pieces of glass, but like undulations of light in a rhythm like the strings of an instrument. I clung to the spectacle on the door, but began to feel the intrusion of the daylight and to wish for darkness to see better. I shrank into the little room, and on the wall began small patterns that widened like the design on the surface of water, but I could hear the lawnmower outside, and it annoyed me; it grew louder and louder and I shrank away from it, and just then as the musical patterns evolved on the wall of the room, I was overwhelmed with sounds, swept into a violent wave of sounds and colors, drowned in them. The designs had ceased to be exquisite, detailed, intricate and modulated Persian or oriental designs. They became, to the accompaniment of bells, gongs and Balinese instruments, luxuriant and magnificent towering roofs and pinnacles, arches of red and gold, as if all the towers of Bangkok, the minarets of Arabia, the spires, the domes of India, the gold roofs of Venice, the inside of Buddhist temples, of Japanese temples had all been put together. There were no longer small designs on the doors or walls, but an Arabian Nights city, wildly beautiful, the gold alive, and as all the other colors, mobile, fluid, incandescent. It was the aliveness of the gold and the red that brought out cries of pleasure. They all towered above me, and the sounds matched them, not like an orchestral accompaniment, but as if the sounds were directly emitted by the colors themselves, matching and fusing with them perfectly. The intensity of the music grew, like vast waves of sounds washing over me, but the bells and gongs predominated. I had to look up at the vaults of gold ornaments and red brocades, at the arches, grilles, murals and domes. Long, sustained notes were fused with the long sweeps of gold spirals, every line, every design, every cell *breathing and alive*, but constantly mutating, and so swiftly that I began to feel I could not seize the beauty, could not tell of it, and I was concerned with loving it, enjoying it and telling it. I lamented how quickly they passed (actually, they took two hours).

While inside of the Arabian Nights city, I had a feeling that I was a Japanese doll, or a Balinese dancer. I felt my cape on my shoulder like a heavy, brocaded costume, and I held my hands together in the form of a prayer, and, overwhelmed by the beauty, the music, the splendor, I cried: "My world is so beautiful, so beautiful, but so fragile, so fragile, so fragile." I had a feeling of danger. I was pleading for protection of this evanescent beauty.

The Comic Spirit appeared again. I thought I was the quickest, the quickest, the quickest mind alive and the quickest with words, but words cannot catch up with these changes; these changes are beyond words, beyond words, beyond words. While I repeated these words I felt waves of pleasure like those of the most acute pleasure of lovemaking. The Arabian Nights city vanished, and the infinite appeared again, but now it came between two columns of bejeweled gauzes, filigrees set with rubies, and I understood I must surrender the infinite to enjoy the beauty that lay along the way, on the sides, around it.

The beauty grew in intensity. The two delicate columns vanished, and I was once more within a Buddhist temple.

The Comic Spirit of Anaïs made fun of these Russian Opera extravaganzas. But the other Anaïs became a Balinese dancer. I put my two hands together and I saw the long fingers, the red nails in a gesture of a prayer and pleading.

I awakened and saw the hospital bed. "What am I doing here?" I asked Gil.

He said: "We will go wherever you want."

The Comic Spirit of Anaïs stood in her black cape like an imperious child and said: "I want a pagoda," and I immediately became aware of the unreasonableness of my request, and wept again. Keeping my hands folded, I seem to feel that I could return to my Arabian city and hear the music again, but the music was lost. I felt my cape heavy, and I felt very cold. I was not comfortable there. I looked for darkness. I lay down in a small room again.

In between the loss of the Arabian Nights city, two things happened. First of all, the physical sensation of suffocating became stronger than that of pleasure. I had difficulty in breathing, such as I had under ether. I not only felt a swelling of the nasal passages, a pain in the middle of the forehead (pineal gland?), but the pain of asphyxiation. I could see I was in a hospital room. I could see some mechanical contraption I took for an oxygen tank. I asked for the doctor. I could not see bodies, just faces. I saw the face of the nurse. I heard her ask for the doctor as one hears under ether. I saw Gil's face. Then the doctor came. I could only see his face and shoulders. His face was evenly divided into two sections. The left side of his face was normal, smiling. The right side was slightly lower, and was all one large eye—the whole side of his face was just one eye. I was lying down in a cloud and seeing only faces. I heard myself say: "I am having trouble with my breathing." I saw them both standing there. I must have stood up and tried to walk, for the doctor put his arm around my shoulder and said: "There is nothing wrong, nothing wrong, it will pass. Just lie down quietly and it will pass." I said: "If you say there is nothing wrong, I believe you."

I lay down and relaxed. Gil was sitting in an armchair and smoking. I could only see the smoke. I looked at the small curtain on the window and it was made of gold. I looked at the lamp in the middle of the room and it was made of gold. There was a gold light in the room. The smoke was gold. And as I lay there, I felt the undulations of this intense gold were those of myself becoming gold. I was gold. I was gold. The sensation was like the dissolution of the orgasm without the pulsation. It was more iridescent than sunlight, more penetrating, outside and all around me, within me, and the feeling of being gold was the most marvelous sensation I had ever known. It seemed to be the secret of life.

This state was broken into by the doctor opening the door and turning on the light. The Comic Spirit of Anaïs got up, pushed off the coat and the blanket under which I lay, and said, laughing: "This is the wrong place in which to dream." And so I awakened. I asked for a comb to brush my hair. Gil gave me his, which I used and then threw away; I asked him: "Why am I lying here?" The door was open and I could see the garden outside. I walked out gaily.

Now I was in four worlds simultaneously. I saw the back yard bathed in sun. Leaning against the fence was the doctor and the scientist. The doctor was smiling and talking professionally about introverts and extroverts. The scientist I knew was in a fleeting state but not swept up and down with music or drowned in colors as I had been. I had a clear feeling that I had gone deeper into dissolutions and further up into space. Gil was on my left, a friendly, unobtrusive, smiling presence. I felt friendly towards the scientist too; I removed my magenta coat because he could not bear the color (I could not bear the sun, the crude green of the grass, the crude blue of a car, the crude white of the garage, after the reds and golds and greens I had seen). It seems to me we had a clear discussion. An older doctor came to look at us. I was aware of four levels. Behind me lay a treasure world of magic, and here, outside, a world I did not like but that I understood. Several times during the visions I remember asking playfully: "And how is the scientist doing?" It seemed to me that he was still in a world of daylight and less violent and intense things were happening to him.

Just before becoming gold, I had been concerned with words. It was while watching a shore line in which wavelets of light unfurled, and in the moment of unfurling became wavelets of smoke, wavelets of gold hair, wavelets of radium, of mercury, that I felt the impossibility to tell the secret of life because the secret of life was metamorphosis, transmutation, and it happened too quickly, too subtly.

The Comic Spirit of Anaïs mocks words, and herself. "Ah, so I thought myself the Queen of the symbolists." I thought myself the quickest, the quickest of minds, and there are no words for these metamorphoses.

I was looking at Gil's painting. It was breathing. The red brush strokes were swelling with breathing. The blue palpitated more gently, and the yellow heaved almost imperceptibly. There were gradations in the breathing. "Poor Gil," I said, "you must suffer so much as a painter. This is the way you see your painting, breathing, alive, and others do not. They see it as a still life."

Then sorrow. And this is what I wanted words to do, to breathe, and make others breathe with them, and feel them inside their bodies.

Within my cape, words and gestures became one. I bowed my shoulders at the weight and passage of words, as if they were washing over me and causing me to bow. The words became gestures as graceful and gradual as algae. Let them liquefy and dissolve and become color. That is the secret; watch blue become a sound, the sound become green and green become a cold word. A cold word; now comes the Ice Age again. I am shuddering, shuddering. And now comes the Golden Age again. So the secret is not breathing, flowing, but *being*. I am red, I am blue, I am gold. There come all the precious stones again.

The Comic Spirit of Anaïs gets up, shakes herself in her cape, feels small and fragile, but lively and jaunty and bright. *Now I know why fairytales are always full of jewels.* This is a world of precious stones.

Infinity has disappeared. So has space. So has the planet. While in another cave of diamonds I become aware that I had written how it felt to be inside of a sea diamond. Now I know. I was also aware of walking through some parts of *House of Incest*.

Another awakening. The door of the room is open. I see the door opening on to the sky, the linoleum on the floor, and a certain listing that makes me say: "Oh, I know this is just an ordinary voyage in an ordinary ship, and it's rocking, and Gil is the captain."

The Comic Spirit of Anaïs steadies herself and is glad to know where she is.

But I have lost the beautiful colors and music! Great sorrow.

Now we are walking through the streets. Gil is eating a sandwich. Neither the scientist nor I can eat. We are talking quietly about the experience. There is no alteration of the outside. It is just as crass, as plain, as crude as ever. I cannot bear it. Everything marvelous happened within. I shrink from it. The scientist wants to be alone. He sits in his car. I ask Gil if I can't return home. Gil says it is three o'clock. All this lasted from nine to three o'clock. Later, when I closed my eyes, some of the dreams returned in a gentler form. I was aware that at some time during the day I had felt that this was the world the artist was trying to take people into and that I understood why they were afraid. I felt compassion for them, and also for the artist so desperately trying to tell what he sees. It seems to me that the love for the beauty, the acute awareness of its passing, and the desire to share and tell it were just as strong during the dream as they are outside it.

Later I recalled The Comic Spirit: this is a strange figure. It was very apparent in my childhood. I was said to be very gay, lively and gregarious. When my father left, this changed to melancholy. It appeared strongly in my Diary when I wrote it in French. I felt it had disappeared when I learned English, but I see now it disappeared with my father (he had the same peculiar, whimsical humor) and only reappeared at times in intimate relationships. A merry, humorous, whimsical spirit. Its appearance in this dream has left a permanent effect on me, like a resuscitation of an inhibited personage.

Letter from Anaïs Nin to Lawrence Durrell:
Los Angeles, February 18, 1958

Dear Larry:

On this end of the trapeze, I have been going through a fabulous experiment similar to Aldous Huxley's *New Door to Perception*. Did you read the book? LSD is a refinement of mescaline, the Mexican mushroom, and possibly the Hindu *soma*. It gives visions, hallucinations, and makes you dream in such a concentrated, heightened fashion, telescoped and timeless. But for me, it was merely a proof that the world of the artist, the world of the unconscious, are one, and some can only reach it by chemicals, but the artist already has access to it, as do the analysts... That was all I wanted to know. I will send you a copy of the voyage I took soon. Huxley has an extended knowledge of this lore, and we had endless discussions because he says it is new; I say it is familiar and recognizable, as dreaming is.

Yes, of course, we will take a detour to visit you in France [during Hugo's trip to Brussels], any detour. And we will not give away your address.

Hugo is working feverishly on perfecting his film.

Here is a photo of Rupert Pole, so you can become acquainted with him. He is of Welsh origin, sings and plays the guitar, plays the viola; his father was a famous Shakespearean actor (Cambridge) and his stepfather is the son of Frank Lloyd Wright, the architect. Rupert's obsession is to build a house. He will this summer, by the sea. But Los Angeles is in the middle of nowhere. Have you read Nathaniel West's *Day of the Locust* or *Miss Lonelyhearts*? Los Angeles *est le néant*. But Rupert is non-uprootable.

I look out to a small patio filled with semi-tropical plants. The dog is chewing a bone. Rupert is about to come home from the school where he teaches, and the children are giving him a birthday party today. Then we will have a gin and tonic while I cook dinner. And we will see Romain Gary, author of *Les Racines du Ciel* (did you read that?) and his wife Lesley Blanch (*Wilder Shores of Love*)—do you know her? Romain is a super-neurotic, which is an achievement in the diplomatic service, and Lesley doesn't care whether she buttons up her picnic basket with an old pencil. Hollywood is baffled at such a French consul!

Devotedly,
Anaïs

Los Angeles, March 29, 1958

At 7:00 AM the alarm rings. Beautiful Rupert, with his black hair tousled, and his English skin quite sunburnt and reddish, is deeply asleep in the darkened room. His eyes, closed, with the deep-set shadows over the lids, look innocent and good. There is no trace on his face of the anger, flaring temper, of the stubbornness, the setness of his ways or the concern with petty details. He looks spiritual and sensual, but never quarrelsome. This will only be revealed later when he talks. For the moment he looks like all the statues of beautiful young men, the Donatellos, the elongated Giacometti. There is a cast of innocence. The mouth, so full, promises generosity. One cannot imagine it saying: "You cannot have a maid for an hour. We must save for the house." The perfect ears, so delicately molded, small, glossy, with the blond faun hair on the earlobe which he does not allow the barber to shave "because my wife loves it." The lean and bony shoulders of an adolescent still. The short-fingered, rough, wrinkled hands; because of the shortness, the fingers look childlike too. It all promises warmth and beauty. But if the phone should ring he will say: "You answer." Or if Tavi scratches at the door he will let me open it. He could, during the day, perform an act of the greatest altruism (how well he took care of the men he led to fight fires). It is agreed that he has trouble getting up and awakening. Once or twice I have been too tired to get up first, and then he goes off without breakfast. So I always get up, and quietly go to the bathroom and turn on the electric heater. I slip into my white kimono—and I make the coffee and prepare his lunch for school. At 7:15 he is up. He looks somnambulistic. He is naked. The beauty is there, but he is not alive yet. His eyes are open but he does not see. He puts on the radio, which I hate (think of beginning the day with automobile accidents, fires, skirmishes in some country or other, the death of a cinema mogul, or an advertisement for Bufferin). Rupert says: "It helps me to know the time." I have set a clock on the breakfast table, but it isn't that. He cannot bear silence. This came out when he was taking LSD. I had to keep playing Beethoven records—no others. When silence came he said: "I feel the silence like something concrete, not the absence of sound. It makes me uneasy." He has all the American sicknesses, especially the fear of silence, because then you are confronted with yourself. He has, when he listens to the radio or when he reads *Time*, the illusion that he is connected with the world, but the obverse of this is when he said: "Neither in the Forest Service nor in the school do I feel connected with anyone. Drinks help me feel connected. I didn't like LSD because it made me feel separated from all—I did not feel connected even with you, my darling."

He kisses me on the cheek, grabs his thermos and sandwich and rushes off. He looks very serious and intent. He is gone for the day.

At 9:30 Rose comes to clean. Only a few weeks ago I decided to disregard Rupert's phobia (no money for a maid, but we spend $100 a month on vodka and on movies), and I got Rose so that I could sit at my desk at 7:30 and type ten pages of volume 62. At nine, sometimes Gil's wife Olympia comes. We either work on her novel, or she helps me with typing in exchange. Or I work alone and intensely until 3:00, interrupted only by the need of a massage or to get my hair washed.

By the time Rupert returns, I am full of thoughts, excitements, memories, rediscoveries, a rich world in my head that stirs up Olympia and acts on her like a drug, making her want to live and write. But I can't share this with Rupert. He is only perfunctorily interested, not truly responsive. I have tried so many times to share this with him. I wanted to. No matter what we are talking about, at 5:00 he turns on the commentators, and, more or less, listens to them all through dinner. The excitement generated during the day over an idea or a character is dissolved, not in the *grandes lignes* of our history, but in its petty details. Of course, I would respond to the essential events, but not to the petty squabbles of notions or the competition in science that proves not a love of science, but of the self. Slowly, the world in my head (my paradise and my inferno) has to be quieted. So I take a drink and attend to the dinner, but these thousands and thousands of little deaths of luminous cells have to be equated to thousands of nights of love. Whatever we destroy in others of elations, flights and scintillations causes a strange phenomenon. It is a stratification. *Et encore, tue ceci*, kill it, or silence it, or turn the radio on.

Is it that he wants to possess only what he needs or wants, but not what is of me that does not mingle with him? Yes... He, alas, wants not to be disturbed. That was his first comment on my writing. A smaller world with many doors closed. This was revealed in his experience with LSD. I persuaded the doctor to let me have the pills to take at home. One Saturday at 11:00 he took six pills. He lay down on the yellow couch after starting Beethoven records (later he could not operate the record player). I was correcting *Solar Barque* after Tom's revisions—to

170

leave Rupert alone. He listened to the music. He became highly sensitive to sounds. He heard the doves outside. They were a disturbance. He also heard the neighbors' footsteps above our head—and Tavi. He found Tavi too loud and too smelly.

Because so little happened after an hour and a half, I gave him one more pill. Then, after a while, he began to laugh—he laughed intermittently for two hours.

I read his own version of the experience. He does these things with such a touching earnestness—while hating to write, he sits and reports his experience for Dr. Janiger as if he were doing homework.

There are times when he returns from school with his beautiful face pale with fatigue, and even though I know now the experience has been mostly trivial, prosaic, unimportant, his expression is the one Rimbaud should have had returning from his debauches. His hair, his eyes with purple shadows, make it seem as if he had been washed and beaten by the waves of great mystical illuminations or a night of sensuality. It is the languor, the feeling of abandon, of a feminine defeat, of something that is not man's expression after an encounter and combat with life.

If he only did not, at that moment, turn on the radio and listen religiously to Edward R. Murrow. This is the moment when the absurdity and childishness of America's reactions become apparent: Russia's scientific leadership would not take the place of the vast treasure house I could lay at his feet. The inner labyrinth full of precious stones that nourished Olympia must be locked in their casket, and what takes its place is the shoddy details of an inglorious history of our corruption: vanity, competition, airplane accidents, marriages of movie stars, shootings in Jerusalem, all the ugliness of human beings and none of their accomplishments. No sooner do we hear about the vaccine for polio than we hear about squabbles between those who are to provide it, or even deaths due to neglect and greediness. We only hear about the degradation of France's politicians, but not about the 3,000 modern churches built by French artists. We have headlines of the death of Mike Todd (America's cult of aggression), but so little on the death of Einstein.

Then there is the choice of how we fill our evenings. A batch of paperbound books just arrived by mail will not seduce Rupert for an evening at home. *Any* movie will be preferred. So this man, who should have been the Prince of Wales or Rimbaud reading in a smoky café, drives a battered, damp car to a battered, damp movie of no account, has no more than a newspaper to read and soon to be forgotten, and now it is 11:00 and the day is over. He takes all his clothes off, and, naked, brushes his teeth and gets into bed. This perfect body is an ever-new delight to the eyes. He has a gin and tonic beside him; he is reading *Time* magazine.

He feels "at home" with me. His charm is at its fullest when he feels relaxed, and he blooms, expands in warmth. Then his smile unfolds, not a full smile, a sly smile, but it is dazzling, the teeth so perfect and even, the mouth so full, the outer design of the mouth a work of art; it is not symmetric, but one side of the upper lip is slightly fuller, which gives it an expression of goodness. It does not have, in spite of its fullness, a greedy expression, or a mean one. Even in anger (and he has a flaring temper) it does not tighten into a thin line. His eyes, when he is happy, loved or loving, take on a golden light, the light of sunlight through leaves. His skin is flushed, roseate. His greatest charm appears then; he is full of tenderness, and he is articulate about the relationship, even eloquent. "Nobody else has what we have. We must make a life worthy of it." This wish is always in the future. "*After* we build the house, then we will travel, we will go to New York." He forgets that time is passing and that my time is running short.

If we have an evening with people, he drinks too much. He takes little pleasure in conversation because he has not learned the *pleasure* of talking. In his family life talk is merely used functionally, to impart facts or to have arguments. If I want to share with him a visit I had from a Latin woman who is the head of the International Press reporting about Hollywood for South America on the radio, and I tell him the story she told me of being deprived of her radio station when South America was Hollywood's biggest client, Rupert says, cuttingly and positively: "That is not so." He always knows and makes the assertions on any subject, whatever it may be.

He is full of *idées fixes*. If I happen to lose one shirt (in ten years!), he will ask me about this shirt every evening for a week. He says it was the *only* shirt he could or would wear (out of his collection of beautiful shirts I get for him each time I go to New York, this one was the least valuable, the least beautiful).

The same cemetery of uncreated things surround him as with Gonzalo: we never cut the films we took in Mexico; we never classified our color slides; we never make films together; I have to struggle to get rid of a dirty and torn rug. "In our new house, we will have a beautiful rug."

I have to shake all this off to get to work again. *La vie décendente.* He does not understand that he makes it this way. It does not need to be so.

Another day he set out to guide Lesley Blanch and a diplomat's wife to the desert. Then he became Rupert the traveler of our first beautiful trip. He sang for them under the pines. He was radiant and unforgettable. The people who see him at such moments think I live with a magical being. I will never again believe in faces, because I do not think Rupert contains any magic but that of beauty, and that within himself his landscape is betrayed by the way the house looks when I am not there: unkempt, desolate, chaotic, stagnant. He himself observes the paradox: he *seems* like an extrovert, because he lives in nature and loves the outdoors. But nature is only one of his escapes from a rather somber and restricted introversion. He is not gregarious, and he often resorts to non-action. Peggy said of Walter Trampler: "He chose the viola because the viola never has a solo." Was this why Rupert chose it? His character affects his folk-singing. He starts out beautifully. His voice is expressive. But if anyone suggests a song he does not know, he is apologetic. He encourages others to sing, and they sing fumblingly and amateurishly. He leads them on. He abdicates his own performance, which is excellent and full of character. If someone else wants to take over the guitar, even if less gifted than Rupert, he surrenders. If once I speak of how we could go to Italy and he could have worked in Italian films (I am absolutely sure they would have appreciated his type of beauty) he says, "Oh, I wouldn't stand a chance. I know the film world. I don't believe it would happen." The same about New York. "Darling, I *know* all the people who could get you in... I have very many contacts. It would be an adventure. Even if it did not work out we could have had a year in Italy" (with our savings of $7,000, accumulated over several years). "But then I would be nowhere."

He never thinks that the future might contain a rich, young wife, an inheritance, a new and better job, etc. The spectre of failure bars the entrance to all gambles, adventures, experiments.

The self-frustration accumulates. Then it turns into anger. Montgomery Clift, who started out with him as an actor, "got all the breaks." Leonard Bernstein, who was his roommate at Harvard, was merely "lucky" to have so much talent.

All the time his words, his attitudes are belied by his face, the face of a poet, of a lyrical lover. An actress said: "I look at him and I am baffled by his talk, which does not match his face."

I may be planting the seeds for the future.

I have had the enjoyment of his beauty and of the lyrical lover, but not that of the miracle of his own wish made before a mirror one day: "I wish I were inside what I am outside."

"It is there," I answered. "I will help you get it out."

Then, when I manage to fly (living in the Diary, copying) after a difficult take-off, comes Reginald's lugubrious voice over the telephone at 2:00 AM: "I have swallowed my false teeth. I can feel them in my stomach. You must take me to the hospital for an X-ray."

Rupert answered: "It's impossible to swallow a set of false teeth. You would strangle first, but not swallow them. Have you looked in the car? Look in the car. Then go to sleep, and tomorrow I will help you find them."

He called up someone else who drove him to the hospital. He called up all his friends: "I'm going to the hospital. They may have to operate." Of course, there were no false teeth in the X-ray.

The next day he went to the dentist and ordered 150 dollars' worth of new teeth. At 4:00 that afternoon, as soon as he could leave work, Rupert found the false teeth on top of a carton on the back seat of Reginald's car.

Then we had to move him. He had called his doctor, saying he needed to be hospitalized, was too ill to live on his own, and the doctor wearily said: "I'll get you an ambulance and get you to the hospital." (Like a load of garbage.) That same evening, the hospital rejected him as not a hospital case. We had to find him a room, and move him in again, in another hotel. His old one would not take him back. They were relieved to see him go.

I met Olympia Henderson five years ago. First I met Gil, her husband, at an art gallery. They are young and handsome. Gil is tall, blue-eyed, with delicate features, has a jazz conversation, beat generation habits, having to go, drink, move, stay up. His hand is always on the handle of the door.

Olympia had read my writing and was silent, shy, but interested.

She had a child, two years old. She had the pale, perfect pale skin of Persian harem women in prints. The black hair, heavy and glossy, a narrow face, full lips, coal eyes, and a long, very long, but finely-arched nose. She is Greek. The smoothness engrained in her white skin is her outstanding trait. A slender, full-breasted body, long-legged. She seemed submissive, patient, self-effacing.

She talked very vaguely about her writing. I encouraged her: "Let me see it." Gil was in the foreground, active, but puzzling to me. The necessity of mobility makes contact difficult. He seemed to me like the mass of wires and plugs he dressed himself in for Renate's party. Communication was never established successfully. We exchanged gifts and gentle visits. Gil was extraordinarily generous and gave us paintings and a beautiful rug he designed. I gave them my books. With time, they both went to analysis.

When I returned from one of my trips, I found them both more distinct figures, as if they had been properly photographed and in focus. Even though Gil rarely completed a long phrase, talked fast and punctuated it with the gestures of a jazz musician who is not holding an instrument, he cannot make words an instrument of virtuosity (as Jim Herlihy does). He became very eager, very excited to have me try LSD and took me to the doctor himself.

Then Olympia and I began to work together. She would come in a taxi (we both consider the taxi as a necessity in the same way Gil and Rupert consider alcohol), wearing black tights and a loose black sweater, her black hair floating over her shoulders, glossy and alive, a manuscript under her arm. We were proceeding slowly, organically, cell by cell, to liberate her true flow from taboos, embarrassments, shame and guilt. She began to read the Diary. She was being analyzed. She began to talk, as Gil did not (being too eager for the joke, the quip, the shrug, the gestures that prevent all pyramids of words and meaning). But all the writing she was doing never reached the level she reached with LSD. Suddenly, she was a poet moving comfortably in multiple dimensions. It may, as she says, have happened from a conjugation of analysis, reading the Diary, allowing me to open up her writing, but the dramatic acceleration, the hot-house bloom, the speed camera happened during the LSD experience. How difficult it is to analyze a sole liberating component. It would seem that LSD was the precipitator. I had to admit that her writing *before* and her writing *after* were distinct. Perhaps I did prepare her, and analysis prepared her to enter *de plein-pied* [fully] into the unconscious world.

Her personal experience was interesting, but even more exciting was the relationship drama when she took LSD with Gil and Dr. Jim Macy (Gil's close friend for whom she experienced a desire that frightened him and to which he responded as a homosexual or a voyeur, accepting and giving all caresses except the final possession, wanting to watch her and Gil making love).

Olympia read, and then offered to help me copy the Diary. Every day she reported its effect on her, on Gil, on Jim Macy. I began to copy with more pleasure and conviction of its value and usefulness. Jim Herlihy's response all these years had nourished me.

She said her greatest aids were "analysis, the Diary, and LSD."

The opposite effect to that of the atom bomb—yes—the opposite effect. Radioactive fallout that brings everyone to life. Why does this generation live destructively...because we may be blown to pieces at any moment? What a poor excuse. Men have lived magnificently, have created and discovered *in spite of the certitude of death*.

And even today while the beat generation lives destructively, men are creating and discovering, exploring and giving life.

One of the most fascinating new files in this exploration of man's unconscious is "Exploring Inner Space," in Dr. Janiger's words.

After the LSD, my dreaming was activated, but I only retained hazy images.

Rupert and I are so perverse that the best weeks of our relationship are those following my return from New York or the one preceding my departure. I awakened this morning in his arms, my head on his shoulder. Looking up, I could see his mouth. The clearness of the design, a fine, clear outline, of a different texture than that of the ruddy, transparent cheeks. And when he awakened, he made love to me. I lay perfectly happy for a moment, realizing I was leaving in a week and we were entering a period of heightened feeling on which I thrive and which annihilates doubts and dissolutions.

I had fallen asleep the night before while remembering a "character" in the Diary and adding to the portrait. Today, while Rupert plays a Brahms sextet, I tried to recapture this and couldn't, but I did realize that it was the first time I had looked upon the personages of the Diary as characters and that it revealed I was achieving a work of art and transcending the personal Diary, for I began to see it as "peopled," in fact crowded, as any so-called "social" novel might be. Oh yes, the minor characters were lovingly depicted, but not the ordinary ones, the ones so beloved in America. No, it is true I have not included them—*because they have not included themselves.*

Those who seek to conceal themselves, to remain anonymous...those who are comfortable in this world cannot enter the Diary as characters. There must be some reward for those who made a greater effort at *being* and *becoming.*

The character—I cannot remember him now. It concerns me. Was it the faceless one? The one without a voice? The unborn? Have I not listened enough?

Letter from Anaïs Nin to Hugh Guiler:
Los Angeles, March 1958

Darling:

You must not be surprised at my genuine wish to spend all we have on making a perfect film rather than going to Europe. This feeling has grown entirely from my understanding of what all you have done for my writing has meant to me. I have never been more aware of what it would have done to me to have been buried alive as far as artistic creation and contact with the world go. Even now, the pleasure I have had from the living circulation of *Under a Glass Bell* has been tremendous. Three months later I have sold all but 200 copies. Even at a minimum and most sober addition of an average of fifty cents each, say (counting gifts and some sales at one dollar), I met my expenses. But I know I made more, as it activated sales of other books, and the last 200 copies are extras...

Now, this pleasure of feeling in touch with the present as an artist is one you have always given me, over and over again, and very often at great personal sacrifice. I think your fulfilment as an artist is not only a personal pleasure I want give back to you, but I think it is a contribution to the art of the film for the whole world, and perhaps for the whole development of bringing the unconscious life into consciousness. I have done this in writing, but I am not sure that it will finally have to be done in film because film is simply closer to the way our unconscious functions. In this, I feel you are a pioneer. In fact, any money not spent on this seems rather foolish to me right now. I take all my pleasure in your filmmaking, and in publishing.

I am truly excited about the publication of my LSD journey in the future. I think it may even sell well. Dr. Janiger has a wonderful title: "Exploration of Inner Space." It resembles the statement I made at the YHMA lecture at the time of your film: "Why read science fiction instead of exploring unconscious marvels?" I want to help you, collaborate with you. I even intend to finally take a course on mechanics. My problem will be my impatience with details, which has even ruined some of my writing.

Love,
Anaïs

Rupert Pole, Anaïs Nin, Annette Nancarrow and Stanley Smith, Acapulco, 1955

Renate Druks and Paul Mathieson, 1954

Rupert Pole, Los Angeles, 1956

Anaïs Nin, Eric Wright, Lloyd Wright, 1950s

Joaquín Nin-Culmell, 1950s

Eric Wright and companion; Anaïs Nin and Tavi, Malibu, 1950s

Anaïs Nin, New York, 1959. Photo: Stanley Haggart

Jean Fanchette, Paris, 1959

Lawrence Durrell, Anaïs Nin, Claude Durrell, and children, Sommières, 1958

Ronnie Knox and Renate Druks, Malibu, ca. 1960

Anaïs Nin, Venice, 1959

Antolina Cárdenas (with glasses) and Cuban rebels, 1959

Rupert Pole planting his first tree at Silver Lake, 1960

Hugh Guiler and Piccolo (Bouboule), 1960s

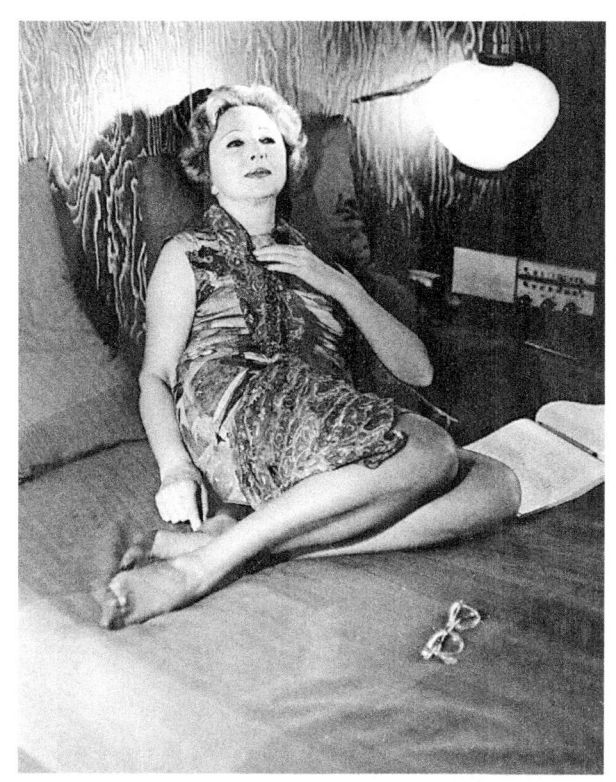

Anaïs Nin in her Silver Lake house, 1963

Anais Nin, Piccolo, Rupert Pole, Silver Lake, 1960s

Dr. Inge Bogner, 1963

James Leo Herlihy, 1964. Photo: Stanley Haggart

Gotham Book Mart owner Frances Steloff and Anaïs Nin, 1966

Anaïs Nin and Rupert Pole with the *Diary*, 1966

BOOK TWO:

OTHERS

1958-1966

New York, April 1958

When Hugo said we could definitely go to the Brussels World Fair with his new film *Melodic Inversion*, at first I felt anguish: anguish of being separated from Rupert, anguish at the possible pain of the return to Paris (I would regret Henry, Gonzalo, my father, Rank), and I would frequent the cemetery and be haunted by the dead.

This anguish took the form of finding the trip so long—too long. At first there was talk of 14 hours. Then came endless discussions with Bogner. Rupert had said: "What difference does it make how *far* you have to go? If you are not here, it is all the same." When Hugo told me they had added an hour and a half to our time by stopping at Montreal, I began to visualize *Kon Tiki* and the 40-day journey on a raft. Fear was added to fear. I would lose Rupert. I would lose everything.

We laughed at the exaggerations, the absurdities, until Bogner said: "Your first journey from Spain, on a slow cargo boat, must have seemed very long to a child." Must have seemed very long to a child. Long, long, losing all, father, country, grandmother, friends, home! The *Monserrat* was on its final voyage. It took a month; it stopped everywhere. *This* journey would be equally long, and I would lose Rupert and Bogner.

I would lose it all, and I was not certain of rediscovering a home, but a place no longer mine and covered with tombstones. If I returned to France and felt I did not belong, especially after my rebellion and hostility towards America and Rupert's American traits, I would discover I had been loving an illusion.

This became clear. I had bronchitis. I felt tightness in my chest. I was tired.

On the last day with Rupert I found on the sidewalk a little aluminum Catholic medal such as I used to wear as a child. I had to pick it up. A symbol? A blessing from the past? I could have left it there. I couldn't...

At the last moment I begged Rupert to write me often and he promised to.

Letter from Anaïs Nin to Rupert Pole:
New York, April 6, 1958

Darling:
Will call you this morning. The worst is over. The cold is breaking up. But what a way to begin a trip!

One hundred films to see and write about in one week in Brussels! So just picture me in a movie house afternoons and evenings with my little pad. Kenneth Anger entered that horrible film *Inauguration of the Pleasure Dome!*

Jim came and cooked me dinner and he talked as I couldn't. He is not spoiled at all by his success—looks at it for what it is worth, and will get $20,000 out of the sale of the film *Blue Denim* (agent takes 40%! His co-writer the other half!), and to avoid taxes, etc., he is in the hands of lawyers and agents. He has no control over his money and longs for the simple days of having $10 in his pocket and no accountants!

He is buying property in Key West, for his health. He looks wonderful. He and Dick will build a small house.

On Sunday the 25th I will leave for Paris and meet with Joaquín. I hear Josephine Premice is there. I leave on the airplane *Sabina*, straight for Brussels. 16 hours.

As soon as you get the geologist report for your property please let me hear, darling.

I hope you enjoy the Kerouac as I did. You felt his freedom was fake in *On the Road*. Jim feels Kerouac's freedom of writing is fake too—but I don't.

Did I tell you to tell Tavi it isn't true I don't miss him? I do.

Sold another 50 copies of *Under a Glass Bell* to the 8th St. bookshop. They have it on the stand next to Kerouac and I see people picking it up—another $25!

Te quiero,

A

Letter from Anaïs Nin to Rupert Pole:
Brussels, April 20, 1958

Darling:

It doesn't seem quite real! I've arrived at Brussels, was whisked off first from the airplane by a respectful chauffeur, and the Baroness Hausi Lambert is in the car with a big dog (she is an Austrian married to one of the Rothchilds—nobility). The guest room is in yellow velvet, and on the spotless white blotter with a *crown* on it, the monogram "R" like a bunch of roses in a vase! So wonderful! Took a bath. Slept. Two maids to unpack my bag, two white-gloved butlers at lunch, a siesta in a downy bed. Now I'm at the desk awaiting dinner and the first evening at the Fair.

There is a crown on my sheets, like in *Harper's Bazaar*, but beautiful and simple at the same time. No ostentation. Hausi is very genuine, a patroness of the arts, music in particular.

There are cigarettes at the bedside, pine oil in the bath, *stamps* on the desk, and a book of poems to read.

Her son, who is not here, at 31 *owns* the Belgian Congo (politically I don't approve but it will be fun to visit him someday).

Anyway, I will heed your warnings to go easy.

A

Letter from Anaïs Nin to Rupert Pole:
Brussels, April 23, 1958

My darling:

I got your letter yesterday. I was so grateful knowing the effort you made for me. You helped me overcome the anguish of going so far. Now you can relax, my love—having heard from you when I first arrived relaxed my sense of distance.

The gods have been so kind. It is as if they had seen my homesickness and decided to give me all of Europe on a silver platter at once. Exhausted by the fascinating life here. Every night ten or fifteen people for dinner (and what dinners!). Owner of the *Times*, Zurich journalists, writers, a specialist on one of my favorite writers, Pierre Jean Jouve, so I will meet Jouve, now old in Paris. All the filmmakers are here. Kenneth Anger too, but can only wave at him from afar. Met the German and Swedish cultural attachés. I'm writing on the American Pavilion for *Eve*.

I got up this at seven this morning to write you, though sleepy and unable to shake off bronchitis.

Don't worry that I will want butlers and maids! It is comical. When I return from the exhibit, it takes me an hour to dress for dinner because I have to find every object that has been whisked away...my shoes are being cleaned, my dresses pressed, my dressing table tidied, etc. The bath tub is so big I almost drown in it.

I asked the IBM machine some questions—what happened in 1903, and it answered that the Wright brothers invented the airplane and Picasso painted the "Guitar." Big crowd around it.

I don't write you about the Fair as there is too much and I'm doing it for *Eve*. I would sum it up for you as a development of the aesthetics of science, new forms and designs created entirely by science.

About 90% of the films at the festival are bad, just like at the Coronet. The jury is not severe enough. Half of the films are American, and most of the best.

In spite of all this, *get this*: I miss you, our little bed, house, and I would not stay here even under magical conditions. All the wonders of the world cannot win over a true love.

Your *mujer*,
A

Letter from Anaïs Nin to Rupert Pole:
Paris, April 29, 1958

Darling Chiquito:

Arrived in Paris Sunday at 9:00 AM so tired and so cold and was handed your letter, which warmed me so much. I went to sleep with it under my pillow. Slept two hours. Went for a walk alone, to where the houseboat was moored, to Montparnasse. It was all beautiful to me, small, tender, human, gentle—so small! In one day I achieved what I consider a most valuable side of the trip: I satisfied a long homesickness but realized it was the *past*, that my new life was with you, a different life, that this was not for us, that this would not have the appeal for you that it has for me. Externally Paris is not beautiful, but it is beautiful with *meaning*. America is externally beautiful and empty of meaning, but America with *you* in it is another matter. Here, there is a mystique of meaning—the past, characters we know, a patina, the fact that art pervades and permeates the entire life, not just a few people—but we will make such a life ourselves in your home. I'm glad I came. It cured me of a longing that pulled me away from your home, but never from you. I am immune to the French, my love, even though they make such a fuss *because* they see in me their dream intact—the ideal France. But though I am immune to the French because I love you so much, I am not immune to croissants and rolls! And the results will be the same! You will divorce me!

The prizes for the films at the Fair were absurd. *Nothing* for Abel Gance, who invented the Cinerama, and an honorary mention for the *Pleasure Dome* by Anger! Everybody was disgusted.

I will return rich and cured of my longing for Europe—because of you.
A

Letter from Anaïs Nin to Rupert Pole:
Paris, May 2, 1958

My darling:

I'm so spoiled I looked for a letter every day and it came! Yesterday was Rupert day. Not only did idleness induce Rupert-sickness, but an American guitar player and singer was rehearsing all day for some nightclub. I could not see him, only hear him in the courtyard, and as it was all the songs you sing, I thought maybe you had managed to come; I felt I was hallucinating, like it was a message from you, and I got so blue that going to a tiny theatre to see Ionesco and eating at an Algerian restaurant with two girls from the theatre did not seem so wonderful. But walking back along the Seine, the buildings were all beautifully lit up, our moon was shining, and even though my body hurt from longing and I was furious at the lovers walking along the quays, I felt peaceful and happy. The beauty of Paris is this strange mixture of excitement and nature—so many trees, gardens, flowers, and then the peaceful river, the flower markets. I was blessed with a real but ideal spring—all the blossoms are out.

Darling, wait for me. Four weeks is our limit. I promise you the 15th is the deadline. I will be home that weekend—will leave the 15th, which is Thursday, I believe.

A

Letter from Anaïs Nin to Rupert Pole:
Paris, May 5, 1958

Sweet love:

Your sad, wistful note this morning about the fault line on our property, and your pleasure at how I felt about Paris, about its beauty and that it is not for *us* as a unit of R and A.

Yesterday a champagne lunch at Graciella's. I saw the Breton family I told you about (one has a Proust MS, another has wife who acted in *Les Enfants Terribles*, another has sailboat). They were leaving for Spain on their sailboat and invited me!

Paris is the Magic City. No wonder starvation and war don't matter. The dream is intact—the magic of art. I interviewed Zadkine, who looks like an old lion-monkey with a mane of white hair. He works in the same old studio. His statues are in the garden. Some of his wooden ones he allows nature to wear away, to give them a patina to prove that death is as beautiful as life and that one must not fear it.

The taxi drivers talk about politics while shaking their heads. "Poor France," they say, "she is like a woman without a husband; she has no leader and she is lost."

But at night the lights on the Sainte Chappelle illumine it like a Bangkok temple.

The amusing thing is that my euphoria is contagious so everybody is beginning to see Paris as I do. At bottom everybody has spoiled-brat reactions to Paris for the simple reason that before the war all this was a bargain and today it is exactly like the U.S.A.—expensive. They still want the most perfect city in the world to cost nothing, as it once did. This explains their crossness.

Deadline May 15 for return.

René and his wife have gone back to Geneva by way of the Dordogne cave paintings. Now I have Joaquín to see, and more galleries, more galleries.

Off to work!

How do you sleep? Are you overworking?

A

Letter from Anaïs Nin to Rupert Pole:
Paris, May 1958

Darling:

About the fault line on the property. All I meant was to keep on wishing—I didn't mean you had not wished enough, love…

I have had my horoscope done by the All-Seeing [Jean Carteret] and his girl last night and I wished I had you here with me. He is 55, a French version of Reginald, carries the same basket, takes the same pills, has the same talk of illness (his is psychic), and has the same woman to protect him. His poor girl is so good to him. He is only happy when talking, though he never listens, but he is a marvelous astrologer.

I haven't written to anyone except you.

I have made no new friends for Tavi, but he doesn't need any, does he?

Well, this is our last weekend away from each other—it is so amazing to think that next weekend I'll be home. It seems years and years!

Today Joaquín plays his concert for a radio recording at the Salle Érard.

I visited Pierre Jean Jouve, and it made him so happy. He is old, has had heart attacks, and nobody has come to see him for 15 years. All these poetic writers have been forgotten during the war, and after the war only realists like Sartre were read. My visit did him good. I left loaded with the books he gave me. Everybody who lives in Europe and lives by forms like the Japanese (rules, rituals, courtesies, etc.) envies the informality of America. Here, people don't write to writers or invade their privacy or call them up (as I have been subjected to); they wait for formal introductions.

I think we should build a tent on our lot to spend weekends on the beach, or buy an old houseboat and dump it there, or a Frank Lloyd Wright pleasure bathhouse—a fantasy.

Te quiero, Chiquitito,

A

Letter from Anaïs Nin to Rupert Pole:
Paris, May 13, 1958

Darling Chiquito:

Saturday night, hearing the Durrells could not come to Paris, I boarded a train and went to Nîmes. I'm so glad I did. Not only are Durrell and his wife wonderful, he so deep and she so gay, but to see the Arlesienne countryside, the Nîmes Arena, to find again the beauty I had missed so much, the river, the house, the Roman town, the bridges, the castles. The Durrells have a small peasant house, but a lovely garden. They grow all their own vegetables. No hot water, no bathroom, no W.C.! It is like Mexico.

You cool bottles by lowering them down the well. He is very poor as they have two sets of children whom other parents take half the time. Both were married before. Claude is more international than I am—brought up in Alexandria, in New Zealand, in France—a saucy girl. They took me to an arena where bulls wear tassels on their horns and the men have to remove them for a prize. They try, and they run for their lives and jump the barrier, and some bulls jump too. The whole thing is very gay as there is no death. The men do get hurt now and then, but not as seriously as during bullfights. They drink red wine from morning till night, which keeps everyone glowing but never really drunk. Durrell has known so much poverty that he is obsessed with succeeding. He has already been compared to Proust in France.

We explored Nîmes, sat at the cafés, talked non-stop for two days, and I returned this morning tired out, but with my spiritual batteries recharged for years to come.

I had to see Durrell to complete the *carnet de bal*. No one could be homelier and so humorous. He has an Irish prizefighter face, a thick potato nose, a large head on a small body, shorter than I, and as fat as Joaquín... So there is nothing to threaten any husband! But you and he would hit it off—he hates cities, loves the sea, used to have a boat; they paddle a canoe down the river and swim. As soon as you get out of Paris you can live on nothing.

Pretty soon I'll be on my way home, a nicer wife for this fulfillment of a long, long desire and grateful to you for having allowed it.

Love,
A

Letter from Anaïs Nin to Hugh Guiler:
New York, May 16, 1958

Darling:

As I leave you in Europe, there is a moment when the awareness of what you are becomes sharply *total*, and I see all of you at once, and it is so wonderful, your many sides, many qualities and many creations. But I think what I am most grateful for is your greater *acte de présence*. Before you used to give me things (in Paris) and leave me more or less alone with them. This time you not only gave me Paris (for which I am deeply grateful), but more than ever before you were there too. I did not have that feeling before, and it made Paris far more real, and *our* experience. Even though you were busy and we were not together much, *you were there*. Only Jean Carteret can explain this achievement (or Bogner). Your presence added greatly to the reality of Paris. I do want to thank you, my darling, because I know that this *second* birth was made by your own efforts, and even if for 35 years I played the role of the one who *wanted you to be born*, as against the negative one played by your parents, nevertheless the great effort was made by you. I hope the world you finally enter will satisfy you. I will try to keep you in it!

Jean said: You were in danger of being condemned to the silence of words. The filmmaking delivered you from silence. You were in danger of utter solitude. You are the secret man, the Chinese box. When you were born you were not wanted. You were, in a way, prevented from being born. Traumatized. And it caused your absences. It was very necessary for you to create your presence in the world by worldly activity (business). Socially, you assured your presence. You cried out to be reached and to reach others. Aware of distance. Your great effort to communicate. But you could not be opened up by way of consciousness. *Seulement par le mystère* (analysis—the unconscious?). Your relationship was usually achieved by giving, by sacrifice. You developed a psychic miracle—a psychic tenacity, and psychological lyricism!

I was so lucky on the plane. I had three seats all to myself and was able to stretch out and sleep for eight hours so that now I can enjoy the rest of my trip and relive it all. As you can see, you get the first letter written on this remarkable dual pad. What a perfect instrument for a *poisson double*—and the *two* fish love you.

I hope all your projects materialize, and mine too.

There are six hours' difference between us. You are already—no, I get all confused, I am ahead of you now. It is 5:00 AM in New York. You are still asleep —I'm no Einstein—I give up. Next time I will wear two watches. Breakfast is coming. I will mail this from N.Y. and more from L.A. Don't get too tired.

Anaïs

Letter from Anaïs Nin to Thomas Payne:
Los Angeles, June 4, 1958

Dear Tom,

Hugo is returning to Paris June 15—he has a job to do there—and I will go there June 23 or so, for the summer. So it will be a long time before I see you, and this is really the first lap of an ultimate return to Europe if I can win over Rupert to the beauty of life there—or let's say just *life*. Perhaps I can persuade you to come too—you're not very happy where you are. In America there is only a choice between a square or a Beat, and people like us, who are neither, cannot make a life. The squares are really too rigid and the Beats too self-destructive. The life I rediscovered in Europe was incredibly lovely, human, intimate.

I feel badly that you haven't written me about yourself, which I take as a bad sign.

Comme toujours,
Anaïs

June 29, 1958
London with Hugo.

June 30, 1958
Planning for Rupert to come to Europe.

Letter from Mark Paterson, Anglo-American literary agent to Anaïs Nin:
London, July 8, 1958

Dear Anaïs,

As you are anxious to get *Children of the Albatross* published sooner rather than later, I have worked on Peter Owen, and they have agreed to publish it (subject to written confirmation) early next year at a royalty of 10% to 3,500, 12.5% to 7,500, and 15% thereafter. I would like to have seen them do it this fall, but I am afraid there would not be enough time to give it the proper pre-publication promotion even if a printer could be found quickly. I hope this is reasonably agreeable to you.
Mark

July 29, 1958
Rupert arrives in Paris.

August 6, 1958
Visit to Durrells with Rupert.

Letter from Jim Herlihy to Anaïs Nin:
New York, August 8, 1958

Dearest Anaïs:
I am up to my Adam's apple again. *Crazy October* is not only going into rehearsal on Sept. 15 for a Nov. 3 opening in New York, but I am going to direct it. So far we have signed Tallulah Bankhead, Joan Blondell, and an old acquaintance of yours, Estelle Winwood. Now we are casting the ingénue and remaining male roles. And rewriting bits of the script. And answering dozens of letters of actors who want jobs. And so many pieces of time-consuming details. It is a very stimulating, exciting period. Starcke is behaving like a magnificent producer, Dick is a very good help in casting ideas. (He thought of Tallulah.) My personal life (fringe-friends, etc.) threatens to become just a small concern, something to be dealt with as it occurs. I remember that you always answer your correspondence, and I wonder if I can manage that; there are so *many* outsiders!

Your beautiful, romantic summer! Every time my mind stops on that, I glow for you.

Dick and I saw the Key West house, but only for a few days. We love it. It is a self-contained world, distilled beauty, usefulness. Remember my old dreams of a winter sun, Anaïs? Now I have it!! I have everything. Strange and miraculous. And thank God I am able to enjoy it, experience it, rather than waste it on guilt and burnt offerings, etc. There is a lot of work this year (I think 1959 will be quite a lot simpler) but I enjoy that, and there has been plenty of rest in between so that it is not a strain.

You know that I will write you when I can, and at all times you have my love and devotion, Anaïs, as I know that I have yours. I don't want to say *come back*, but I do miss you so much.
Love,
Jim

August 31-September 12, 1958
Venice.

September 13, 1958
  Rupert returns to L.A.

Cable from Rupert Pole to Anaïs Nin:
Los Angeles, September 13, 1958

  Await forgiveness for my parsimony. Trip high point of my life. All well here.
  Love, Rupert

Letter from Anaïs Nin to Rupert Pole:
Paris, September 1958

Darling Chiquito:
  As soon as I arrived in Venice I telephoned your hotel—they told me you had gone, had not slept in your room. Such a blue day—we both hated to be separated and to stop traveling—although I feel caught in the Sorcerer's Apprentice trick. I wished for travel but got too much. I would have liked to go home with you.
  Felt so tired but every time I close my eyes I see the high moments of our trip—do you? I do wish I were home ruminating with you. I am only seeing it with half of myself.
  My love, I can't return early (you knew it). My contract says that I can only leave at the real end of the season. I don't know where I will be, so write to the Crillon or to Marguerite Rebois. I think of you.
  You are such a wonderful traveler! Such a skillful driver, such a thorough explorer—always leading me on and seeing so much!
  I like to remember the places where you were happy with the beauty. Forgive me for my not being economical. I know I made you unhappy by not haggling—but between us we reach a balance!
  Te quiero and I wish I were home.
  A

September 28, 1958
  Return to Los Angeles.

Los Angeles, September 29, 1958
  Rereading *Balthazar*. I have decided Durrell is a brilliant cheat who does not have a deep knowledge of character. It shows in *Balthazar* that he is a *soi-disant* psychiatrist. He promised relativity of truth, but that lies in acceptance of subjectivity and that means introspection, going inward, and he has not.

October 20, 1958
  Return to New York.

Letter from Rupert Pole to Anaïs Nin:
Los Angeles, October 1958

Love:

Your first letter today. I am so sorry that we had a tiff and a bad night. Just my lousy temper—was mad at the doorman, not you—I hate the idea of you waiting on that sidewalk for long periods, plus my old fear of parking tickets. I'm so sorry to send you off unhappy just when we need each other's strength. Music was very good that night, but I missed having you there writing and occasionally looking up and listening when it's good.

Work, work, work, work, but that's good while you're gone—time passes so fast.

Tavi is fine. He stays out under the castor bean trees where he can keep tabs on everything that happens. He's really watching for you—and so am I. Hurry back to us, to your slower, sunnier, real life.

Siempre mas,
R

Letter from Anaïs Nin to Mark Paterson:
New York, October 1958

Dear Mark:
Peter Owen came to New York, won Gunther over with much better terms and assurances of presenting my books properly (*Child of the Albatross* and *The Four-Chambered Heart*) and won me over by his enthusiasm. I have waited for an English publisher for a year now; these are old books, and I lack the gift of patience! There are new books coming, a large, full novel (besides *Solar Barque*). One reason for the decision, too, is that the two books are out of print here and have been much in demand. Peter Owen publishing them will take care of that.

I *am* susceptible to enthusiasm and immediacy.

Gunther has written you. We both appreciate your efforts. I have lost so many years with difficulties in America that I cannot afford to lose more years in Europe.

My best to you as ever,
Anaïs

Letter from Anaïs Nin to Joaquín Nin-Culmell:
New York, November 4, 1958

Dear Cuchi:
Hugo is leaving for Lausanne again on December 15, and life in New York has been bedlam. Getting the clothes fixed, doing his errands, winding and filing thousands of strips of film that were being damaged from exposure, plus my private launching of *Solar Barque*—it is selling very well, bypassing all reviewers. I sold *Children of the Albatross* and *The Four-Chambered Heart* to England.

We're up at 7:30 AM. At 8:00 Millicent serves breakfast. I answer my mail, fill orders (if you want any copies for Xmas presents let me know—send me inscribed personal cards and I will mail them—all free).

Took care of my anemia. Saw Thurema, who is well and is making stained glass windows, now married to Jimmy (who is a flavorless American Photostat of you, since Thurema couldn't catch the original!). Met Harry Partch, the man who made all his own instruments and invented a scale of 43 tones.

No leisure until I get to L.A. again—then peace and quiet, which I also appreciate. My spirits are high. I think of you.

Love,
A

November 1958
Lawrence Durrell will do the preface for the English edition of *Children of the Albatross.*

Letter from Anaïs Nin to Hugh Guiler:
Los Angeles, December 1958

Darling:

I didn't write you yesterday because I was trying to resolve a conflict. I have had quite a struggle with myself, William Kozlenko, and Mr. Pink, the businessman. The latter, who is to clinch the *Spy* film option, has been traveling through the country (he owns a vast chain of movie theatres and visits them to see how programs go, studies neighborhoods, takes statistics on demands from the public, etc.). Kozlenko keeps giving me his work and looks upset when I seem to doubt it. He put me to work on a scenario, and I couldn't do it. I have been corresponding with Bogner over it. I have to find out if it is I who have interfered with my own success. I am going through something similar to your more titanic struggles with your neurosis versus your genius for business. I have been "taken in" by mirages here. Bogner says I did not handle it well.

I have to be direct and firm with Kozlenko. I need to say I can't write my own scenario (but I'm afraid to lose the opportunity) and that I have to have an option.

Times are changing. *Lolita* is being filmed!

Deepest love,
Anaïs

Letter from Anaïs Nin to Hugh Guiler:
Los Angeles, December 8, 1958

Darling:

Yesterday enormously depressed by Durrell's introduction to the English edition of *Children of the Albatross*...it seems out of proportion. Tell me what you think of it. I cut out the personal references. They were so flat and absurd. Why, why can't I get understanding of what I'm doing by either critics or other writers?

I took it hard. But I don't know why I should have expected Durrell to understand my work. I couldn't sleep. I'm afraid I'm still trying to make up for the fact that neither one of my parents ever said: "You are wonderful." Only you have. And you, poor darling, have said it a million times. Incidentally, *spell* out amounts you raise for your fund as I cannot count zeros beyond 100,000. After that I'm lost. Some banker's wife I am. It is 7:30 AM and I'm going to work on *Spy.*

Love,
A

Letter from Anaïs Nin to Lawrence Durrell:
Los Angeles, December 1958

Dear Larry:

It would have been so much better if you had written to me that you could not do the preface, did not like prefaces, were too busy, etc.!

I was not going to comment on it, but your letter today was rather irritable. Larry, first of all I would not have asked you for an introduction if I had not needed it, as I know you were busy. It was not because of your name or fame that I asked you, but because I had hoped, or imagined, you understood my writing and would be the one to place proper focus on it. I explained to you that all these years in America I had received no evaluation at all, and that this had, in turn, affected Europe who wondered why I did not get any critical stature at all. But to the sadness of the disappointment in your total lack of understanding, came the added reproachfulness of your last letter—you are deluged in demands for blurbs, prefaces, etc. I was made to feel like one of your many nuisances. Also that bit about my ancient venerable reputation which you were teething in writing—I'm only ten years older than you and I wrote *The Winter of Artifice*, my first novel, after you wrote *The Black Book*, a most mature work.

I had the illusion that I occupied a special niche in your affection. For my friends I usually commit such foolish acts of devotion—both fictions were utterly demolished by your preface. Lines like "embalming" to distill essence, like being in a "casket" in grand hotels, soap bubbles applied to my work, conventional clichés about "feminine subjective" work, a certain disparagement and frivolity—were enough. But your letter today made matters worse. The basic shock was the non-caring and the distortion.

If you know that I had such a fantasy about your understanding or about your friendship, you should have refused to write.

I am not using the preface. It was a matter of great humiliation to me that my English publisher should think I needed to be introduced—but you greatly added to this.

I blame myself, however. I had imagined, invented and created something which did not exist.

My subjective feminine work is a long, careful work in which I am progressing from the dream outward as one way into relative truth.

Anaïs

Letter from Anaïs Nin to Hugh Guiler:
Los Angeles, December 15, 1958

Darling:

Was so depressed after making the decision to see the film possibilities *through* that I couldn't write you. When I realized I wasn't getting on a plane the 20th, I felt how long you had been away, and now that our connection is so strong again, I do feel the separation keenly. Then your letter came, philosophical and adaptable, and I tried not to take changes and fluctuation so seriously—then your cable—I hope a letter from you will make all this clearer, what you are going to do—I was not quite sure of the meaning of the cable.

I am giving Kozlenko a deadline, and meanwhile getting Lesley Blanch to stir things up for me. The victory in terms of analysis will be if I can stop giving people the feeling they can exploit me, feed on me, get ideas for their own work and give me nothing in return.

But humanly I miss you. When I go to the beach on weekends I wear the same cape, bathing suit and basket I had with you in Venice, and I feel I am going with you. When I wear my Venetian dresses, look at my watch, use my miniature camera, I feel your presence in all these moments. I have enjoyed my little camera so much! I keep it in my handbag and handle it easily.

Partch will stay on in our apartment unless his music project is on. He seems to be the best tenant we ever had! I love you, darling. I have a gift for you for your return. Analysis remarried us.

A

Letter from Anaïs Nin to Lawrence Durrell:
Los Angeles, December 1958

Dear Larry:

I'm so glad you wrote me as you did. I regretted my emotionalism which came out of a million accumulative distortions in twenty years of life in America, and which made me expect and count too deeply on your word. I realize so well you are overworked, had little time, and why should I have dreamt of the perfect preface? I don't want to go back to what hurt me. I value the alliance of the Three *Mousquetaires* too much. Let's just forget about it. Poor Peter Owen—he clung to the preface so desperately and I'm grateful you let me cut out what I felt to be detrimental. I might add that your lightest words were the heaviest to digest—soap bubbles! I do not understand Peter's qualms anyway—*Spy* sold very well in England.

You don't mention anything about the film version of *Justine*. Has it come through? I'm seeing Gore today and will enquire.

Love to both of you,
Anaïs

January 10, 1959
Return to New York.

Letter from Anaïs Nin to Rupert Pole:
New York, January 17, 1959

Spy is definitely sold to Germany, thanks to Gunther. Awaiting the check from Cotta, the publisher, now.

Being here, I got window displays at the Gotham Book Mart and the 8th St. Bookstore. Val Telberg made enlargements of the cover of *House of Incest*—very striking. I was interviewed by the *Village Voice*.

The days are productive. I'm getting over Kozlenko's failure at a script for *Spy*.

I saw my analyst and discovered that in Spanish families, only the boys count (as in China). Father and Mother were disappointed to have a girl first! When Thorvald was born, he became the favorite. Then, when Joaquín came, *he* was the favorite—the baby. I was just left to be the little mother of both, and I felt left out (this explains my dislike of Xmas)—I was left out of the family and was desperate to be the favorite. So every failure in the world—no film, no commercial success —is always from not being the favorite. Now that this is all clear, it doesn't hurt anymore.

I'm the American representative of a magazine in two languages coming out of France soon (*Two Cities*), edited by Jean Fanchette, who was introduced to me by Durrell. It is literary, which means no money but lots of prestige.

My nights are bad, like yours—I'm in the sleeping pill habit again, as I have to be up at 7:00 AM.

I'm trying to keep my New Year's promise to be less jealous. I remember sweet moments at night—it helps me to finally sleep. Your basket of presents from Haiti was so beautifully chosen—a fairytale.

A

New York, January 1959

Dream: Hugo, with a gesture of kindness and protectiveness, opened the deep freezer and showed me a newly born doe. It stood there naked and without fur, pink with sad eyes, and I was horrified by the realization of how it must feel, the sensation of freezing. Hugo felt it would freeze to death. I said it needed warmth. I took it up and warmed it in my arms. It became a little girl, unusually small but not a baby, more like a diminutive girl of five or six. I was delighted. It seemed as if many days passed during which I enjoyed mothering the little girl, playing games. Then suddenly I found her lying on the ground, absolutely stiff, her feet rigid, her face blue from asphyxiation. It seemed to me she was dying. Hugo placed her in the cat's valise and took it to the hospital. I was so certain she had died that I did not even ask Hugo. A few days passed and she returned lively and well.

Dream: I was lying in bed with Rupert and he told me what Hugo said to me in Venice: "I can't make love to you because I have a severe blister on my penis." I wept. At the same time a red fire engine drove into our bedroom, breaking down one wall.

Letter from Eve Miller to Anaïs Nin:
Big Sur, February 3, 1959

Dear Anaïs:

The great news! Henry has at last agreed to a "trip" to France! He thinks of it as such. For me, I pray it turns out to be far more than that. A "return," if you wish. I've done nothing but dream of this for the past six years. Nor is it entirely a selfish need on my part. Henry *needs* France. This hunk of veritable paradise in which he's put down tap-roots is insidious for him, and he refuses to recognize it. I watch this vital man dissolving. He is another person in Europe. My own personal needs I'm fully aware of. I'll never realize my own potential in this country. I've got to breathe at this point. Start living. The inertia breeds like a fungus here! How do *you* tolerate it, Anaïs??

We will take the two children with us. Their mother has given permission…(this has always been the number one "excuse" for not being able to go back to Europe). We've arranged the passports, the tickets, passage! We leave New York the afternoon of the 16th of April, and are in Paris at 10:00 AM the next day. We want six weeks, I insist, in Paris, after which we'll go to the south of France and spend the summer months. Probably where Durrell is. He'll have a houseful of assorted children through the summer months. Val and Tony will come along—it's essential that they have other children to be with if they're going to have a taste of "living" in France. (Henry is unaware of all these hidden dreams and hopes, of course. I doubt he has ever asked me once during our seven years together what my hopes and dreams might include!)

We aim to rent the Big Sur house out. We're asking $125 per month. Available from April 15-August 15, as things are planned now. An ideal time of year here. Two studios, three bedrooms, large living room. Kitchen. Furnished. This income, combined with the money from New Directions, will take care of Henry's sister's rest home.

Love,
Eve

Letter from Anaïs Nin to Gunther Stuhlmann:
Los Angeles, February 1959

Dear Gunther:

I am quite distressed at the acrimony in the situation with Neville Armstrong. I did not make myself clear to you. He had not acted behind my back. What happened was that four years ago he said casually he would show *Spy* on the Continent but not formally. And I never heard about the activity again. He did write me that he had sold *Spy*, and I wrote back: OK, but I was expecting a contract to follow as a matter of course. When I talked to you, I said this was three or four months ago and I had received no contract. I agreed with all the points in your letter, but I do feel you were a little harsh with him. He is still the publisher of *Spy*, and I would have liked to have done it with more diplomacy. He was casual and unorthodox, but not sneaky.

Now—to prevent further difficulties: In Paris I have become associated with the French poet Jean Fanchette, a friend of Durrell who is starting a magazine I told you about, *Two Cities*. He is mad about *Spy* and wants to translate it. He is writing about it in *Two Cities*. He is trying to persuade his publisher. He wants to be sure I am not trying elsewhere. His chances of getting it in are good. I will let any contract, etc. go through you. But before I write Jean, I must ask you if *Spy* is being shown in France.

From now on I will have to make carbons, date my letters, and be altogether more organized. Writers should never tamper with such matters. Do, please, send Neville a little salve! I still have to work with him on *Spy*.

Anaïs

Letter from Gunther Stuhlmann to Anaïs Nin:
New York, February 11, 1959

Dear Anaïs:

Many thanks for your communiqué re: Armstrong.

I wrote to him from here giving, in substance, pretty much the same facts as you did in your letter to him, but keeping it all on a friendly basis, acknowledging his efforts, etc. but making the strong point that no contract should be made without your approval and that we cannot recognize anything he arranged for unless we have seen and approved in writing any such arrangements.

Naturally, being the person that he is, he will try to wiggle himself out of the situation by turning around and accusing us of being ungrateful, etc.—which has nothing to do with good business practice whatsoever.

I will certainly try to keep the whole affair—as I have until now—on a friendly basis, but my impression of him is that you have to stick to your guns, otherwise he will do what he pleases.

Now to your question about France: I am not showing *Spy* anywhere there, as we had previously discussed, and thus Jean Fanchette can go ahead. Good luck.

I am sorry that we are having such difficulties with Armstrong, but I hope we can clear this up one way or another in the near future. As soon as I have a reply from him, I will try to "salve" him in the interest of future relations.

All my best,
Gunther

New York, March 1, 1959

Double pneumonia, at Mt. Sinai Hospital. Told Rupert on the phone that I have a cold.

I had wanted to expand my Anaïs Nin Press to include other writers, but I'm afraid it is a heavier burden than I had expected and takes several hours a day away from writing. I wanted to reprint the lost books and maintain a quality of writing. I have too many "children," too, symbolic ones. Most of the writers I nursed have been terrible disappointments.

Letter from Rupert Pole to Anaïs Nin:
Los Angeles, March 1959

My love,

I fear I will never make it on your typewriter. The "o" is sticking impossibly—no, I have fixed it now.

Don't know what my horoscope for today is. But do know that I will never believe any astrologer again after saying I'd make money with *land*—fates seem to be against us here. I went to Lloyd's after your call feeling so optimistic only to have a big fight and walk out on him—I can't take the raging anymore. He refused to even look at the places I had lined up for him here, and he got livid when I told him you couldn't take the mountain—this was the wrong thing to say and I knew it, but I can always try to say the right thing. We may get a decent house someday, but right now I feel like it will never happen. After all these years not one break, either in the mechanical or human side of a house.

Must be something basically wrong with my planning. I don't think we want too much, or things too far beyond our means, but others just seem to find a lot and build and be happy and have little of the struggle we've had. The moral, perhaps, is not to come from a family of artists.

Please take care of your cold and take it easy till you get your strength back again—you must have some to instill life and hope again into your blue husband.

R

New York, March 11, 1959

Mt. Sinai Hospital: Strange feeling—as if the neglect or hostility of America had finally silenced me, I could not write last year. I even had doubts of myself, my work. I reached the lowest ebb of faith when I received Durrell's preface. But recently, starting with Jean Fanchette, the letters I receive and things I hear (Val Telberg said at a party: "Anaïs survived years of vilification and now she is being rediscovered"), I feel the warmth and nourishment I need given to me. People praise my "integrity," but my integrity lies only in the consistent nature and quality of the work, not in the absence of doubts, discouragement and fears. Now I am beginning to feel support. Without Hugo, I would not have continued.

And now Elizabeth Moore, Peter Owen's wife, writes me a beautiful letter about *House of Incest*, saying I "have plaited, as it were, music and prose together (which, of course, equates poetry)," and that I, unlike so many other writers, "flow with life."

Letter from Rupert Pole to Anaïs Nin:
Los Angeles, March 1959

Love:

So good to hear your voice from outside the hospital. You sounded much more optimistic. I was so worried about the pneumonia—it's much easier to fight with new antibiotics, but it still can leave permanent scars on the lungs, which means extra care from now on. I know you didn't want to worry me, but I'd still rather know right away. It's true I couldn't help much from here, but I could have gotten off more letters (straight to the hospital) and talked about more important things during our calls. But the important thing is you had the best care and are out of danger now and (I hope) will take it very quietly until the plane leaves.

All goes well here. Lots of work but would rather have that when you're away. Musical evenings, looking for a new lot, and I go to the beach on weekends. Still nothing but disappointment with finding a lot. I found some charming ones, just right for us, but the owners won't sell. Maybe the fates have something better in mind for us!!

But whenever I get really mad at them (the fates) I remember that they did bring us together, and that was so wonderful I guess they figure we were not entitled to anything more—and they're right, we're greedy; we have so much just with each other, we really don't need anything more.

I love you—and always will.

R

Letter from Anaïs Nin to Lawrence Durrell:
En route to Los Angeles, March 26, 1959

Dear Larry:

Such a wonderful letter from you. Just as I was going to write you how elated I was at *Mountolive* being selected [for the] Book of the Month Club.

I am writing you on the plane, flying to Los Angeles. So weak I can't carry a handbag—but the intensity of New York was preventing me from convalescing—and Rupert was getting desperate. My only outing was a visit to Varda because he wanted me so much to see his paintings before he takes them back to Sausalito. He cannot live in New York. He is a marvelous painter—he never left the fairytale—white-haired and so battered by life. His Greek wife is giving him up, and they gave a party to celebrate divorce!

I am working hard at distributing *Two Cities*, collecting subscriptions, etc. Sent 1,400 announcements to University libraries.

[Continued in] Los Angeles

Rupert sends his love.

The pneumonia has made my trip [to France] impossible—by the time I can travel Hugo will be back.

Don't feel badly about the preface anymore. I know exactly how it happened. Owen rushed you. You were in the middle of a book, with personal harassments, moving, children, correspondence, and in no mood for it. You opened a bottle of wine and out of friendship set out to do something you were in no mood to do. No time to reread books, etc. Also you didn't know how important it was, crucial, etc. It was for America. England can read. But America has no inner evaluations, only what other people say.

I don't think you need to be concerned about Henry. It is Eve, I feel, who wants to live, not to be isolated and a cook-hostess to whoever wants to come. But she will have her time in Paris.

Love to you and Claude,
Anaïs

Los Angeles, March 28, 1959

I thought it might be the illness that accelerated the detachment from Rupert—residual filaments—I could no longer enter into life with him, even when we made love. The spark and illumination are gone. He touches me humanly, but that is all. His charm works magic for a little while but is annihilated by the selfishness.

When I see him blindly working on his destiny—his unrelatedness to others except on a superficial plane—it is frightening, as is his illusion of closeness to me.

Now I see the role that contradiction plays in the disharmony with people. Rupert was so curious about the lovely Italian girl at Cornelia's, Tommy Runyon's fiancée, yet I heard him across the room loudly saying "That is not so!" in response to something she'd said. They began to argue, and she turned away from his willfulness. Arguments at parties are in bad taste, if nothing else.

The case of the olive oil. When I first met Rupert he had the dry skin of an old man. He would tan and peel. His back was rough. I told him the story of the French doctor saving my badly burnt eyelids with a week of olive oil, and the skin never broke! So I taught him the use of olive oil and he acquired beautiful tans—his back became satiny and his face stopped peeling.

He spilled hot coffee on his arm, and we had no tannic acid. I offered him oil. He would not use it. His arm is now blistering. And tonight, sitting among the musicians, one of them said the latest scientific attitude towards burns was to do nothing. So Rupert says to me: "Did you hear that?" triumphantly. A sickness of the ego, self-defeating. The need to assert himself in a negative way. This is carried to excess with everyone. One evening an old college friend of his reappeared after 15 years, and Rupert spent the evening contradicting him. I saw the irony on his friend's face—cool, objective, lawyer-like.

We can't talk to each other.

Yet I know he is desperately lonely in his autistic world and that I am the only one he feels close to. But I don't feel close to him. I would have to stuff my ears.

But human life goes on...

I am writing to find out Sylvia Yelton's address and I will write her—she may be the one to make him happy. I must try.

A strange split between the empty outer lives—I dreamed that Gonzalo, vividly there with his powerful stature and intensity, was telling me that he had never known the orgasm with me in all those years, that he was never satisfied with me, only with whores... I wept desperately, and awakened, thoroughly shaken.

I awakened feeling alone, like a mother with a child to care for. 7:00 AM. Went to the sunny front room where the big desk is. Wrote to Hugo. Walked out quietly to mail letters. Made coffee.

At 10:00 Rupert awakened. I gave him coffee. We boiled eggs for the beach, packed our bathing suits and towel, Tavi's crackers, and got into the old, battered car. A long drive. Sometimes Rupert says: "Read me the letters." I read him a letter from Jim, a letter from Joaquín, or Ruth Witt Diamant, but never a fan letter. I realize now that he is jealous of the letters I get, my friendships.

Another night, more nightmares. Hugo is lying on his bed. He is alone. I leave him to go to my brothers. I am in bed with one of my brothers. He makes love to me. Thorvald? Joaquín? Rupert?

I can't start my major work. With Rupert there is an absence of magic, a pedestrian, superficial life—even the movies! I thought they were his opium. But he does not feel them. I am the one who has to leave Jack London's *Call of the Wild* because I can't bear the sadism. Occasionally he is emotionally involved (*Diary of Anne Frank*), but he cannot put himself in others' places—not if it threatens his pleasure.

I'm sinking in his life.

We return from the beach towards 3:00 when the wind grows too cool for me, and my voice grows rusty.

We take a bath. We make love.

The next night another nightmare—this one I cannot remember. The more sun-filled and pleasurable the day life, the darker the nightmares.

I must write my novel, find a way to utilize the Diary, escape into creation. I would prefer to be with Hugo cutting his Venice film in the apartment he allowed me to make beautiful, as Rupert does not allow me.

He says: "When you talk about New York, you talk about your world, but what will I be there, what will I do, what job will I have? How do I know what my life will be?"

"My friends always love you."

This is the tragedy. Rupert cannot take my world. Because he is not sure of his place in it.

My spirit is heavy. I hear the cliché jokes. And I begin to think that Rupert's eyes, his face, his smile, are like the sea, the mountains, the landscape of California without any inner beauty.

Letter from Anaïs Nin to Rebecca West:
Los Angeles, March 1959

Dear Rebecca:

I wanted to write you about your books fully, but I am here in Los Angeles without them, recovering from double pneumonia. That will have to wait until I return home. Alas, I will be unable to go to Paris in April with Hugo, when I had expected to go to London for the publication of *Children of the Albatross* and we could have had a visit.

Yes, I understand when you speak of active opposition, but in America there is not even that, just chaos, lack of values, absence of quality, a blind barbarism. I never realized until lately what a perfect symbol of America was: a total lack of insight.

So much I wanted to ask you! But I'm sure now we will be going to Europe often. I always remember our lunch in New York when you told me America reminded you of those scientific experiments made with rats when after many manipulations the rats were restored to their original state but *with something missing.*

I wonder if I may ask you to contribute to our magazine—*Two Cities*—in French and in English, edited by Jean Fanchette in Paris. It may become a monthly. As soon as the first number is out I will have one sent to you—so you will see. I would be so proud to have you in it. I'm affiliated with it on the American end.

All these years I have worked on a *roman fleuve*, slowly, almost organically, and now I am doing the last volume. The collection will be *Cities of the Interior.*

In the diaries I found a marvelous portrait of you, all in warm tones, your love of life and your keen perceptions.

Anaïs

Letter from Hugh Guiler to Anaïs Nin:
New York, Sunday, April 5, 1959

Darling,

For once I had a real rest today. Read and dozed in the morning and in the afternoon actually slept until about 6:00 PM. So I am feeling fine now, but realize I had to have a day like this and must have them regularly and recover from accumulated fatigue.

Had a dream about going up into a high place looking down at a beautiful valley. At the top I found you. I had walked through a small gate in a wall that was a boundary line between two countries and discovered the one I entered was Canada. I don't know why. Perhaps the association was Canada Lee! Anyhow, you said to me that in that place you had at least found people you could talk to and who could express themselves as you had always wanted to hear. You had found communication with them after a long time and much searching. And I was glad we were together there. The only thing that made me sad was that as you walked ahead and down a long corridor, I noticed that you had hurt your right ankle and limped and I felt so terribly sorry. I think I felt I had hurt you. But, apart from that, the dream was a happy one, for we were together overlooking such a beautiful valley, and I felt we both *breathed* better.

In another part of the dream, I saw you naked and your body was so beautiful.

In the analysis, Bogner has many times, and more recently, brought up the question of how much I trust her, and we are working on this now. I can see more clearly now that the attitude of the analyst is symbolical of an attitude towards ourselves. When we withdrew from her, physically or by withdrawing any part of a thought or forgot our dreams and so avoided telling her about them, we were withdrawing a part of ourselves from contact with an awareness of another part of ourselves. Total communication with ourselves is impossible if it does not start with total trust in a total communication with the analyst. It is probably very significant, for example, that I have, ever since my slipped disk, sat in an upright chair opposite her, with the glass table between me and her. This is, I guess, a picture of what happens inside me, mistrustful of myself, on the defensive against a part of myself. This is all pretty obscure yet, but I can sense we are getting into an important phase. And only a week and a half before I go.

But I have made all possible plans now to cut down my absences from New York to the minimum while Bogner is here. For now I know how vital it is for me to know myself better than I do, and I have the feeling that I am on the boundary of some entirely unexplored region. Perhaps that was the gate I went through in my dream today. I am so glad it was you I wanted to find on the other side!

I miss you a great deal, darling, and I know you will find me close to you when we are together again.

All my love,
H

Letter from Hugh Guiler to Anaïs Nin:
New York, April 8, 1959

Darling,

Just a line before I go to the office to ask you to let me know, as I am leaving next Wednesday, the 15th, whether you will need any funds before I return about May 20-22. I would like to provide anything you need in advance so that you will feel completely secure and comfortable. So let me know.

My new salary at G. D. & Co., which, however, will be subject to adjustment every three months according to results, will be $2,000 a month, from which, of course, the withholding tax will be deducted and income tax. I believe it will be about $1,300 per month. But everything is going well, and the Nassau office has opened with very large orders.

Roger Boulogne is taking over all my accounts and will have power of attorney to pay all my bills and see that my bank balance is OK. So if you have any bills to pay in my absence send them to him.

Otherwise I am seeing Bogner regularly, four times this week, and am feeling a lot more rested after a long sleep last night.

In haste, all my love,
H

Letter from Anaïs Nin to Hugh Guiler:
Los Angeles, April 8, 1959

Darling:

I'm so mad at the pneumonia cheating us of this period in New York. Time has dragged this time. When I return I have to work with Bogner on this matter of concentration. In N.Y. I am unable to concentrate—at all—but here I find that my problem and struggle with writing is similar: organization of vast fragments, and although I have peace and no interruptions, I still find it hard to construct, and it must be an inner problem.

I loved your dreams. Funny about my looking for people who could talk! It's true, except that now *you* talk, and all you say now was worth waiting for! And as for hurting me, darling, you, of all people, are the only one who has not—I always think of that. It has spoiled me for all other relationships. I also think how you wish to fulfill my every wish. "You want that? Get it"—as if to make up for all I did not get from the world. No, the opposite of hurt is what you did—reconstruct, protect, and allowed to grow, with analysis as your gift to me too.

I was thinking, too, that when you overwork, I feel guilty—I feel drowned in guilt, and I connect all that you give me with the overwork; then it turns from pleasure to guilt and I run away from your strain, as in Paris, even though I know overworking is your opium and escape from other problems.

I'm getting sick of my "escape." I'm at my desk at 7:30 AM with nothing to stop me, not even a phone!

But I keep working...

Karl Shapiro, poet and critic, editor of *Prairie Schooner*, writes me: "I find myself reading your novels in secret and crying. *In a way I want to keep you a secret.*" I wonder if this is not true of many people—the fear of seeing neon lights on me.

Peter Owen has been wonderful to work with! Writes every week, sent the book to Rebecca West, to reviewers, etc.

I have been checked once a week at the doctor's, and all is normal. But it is when I think of suddenly going to Paris with you that I realize my lack of stamina.

All my love, darling,
A

Letter from Hugh Guiler to Anaïs Nin:
New York, April 11, 1959

Darling,

I was never so sorry you were away than last night when, with the Ruggles, Millie Johnstone, Varda and Peggy, I saw Harry Partch's "The Bewitched." It was the most beautiful and moving creation I have ever seen. I expected to like the music and was enchanted with it, but the decor, the lighting and the ballet that went with it were equally sensitive and effective. Above all, it was the same kind of rare alchemy of music, image and movement that took place in *Bells of Atlantis*. But this time it arose out of that very American indigenous material that has so repelled us. As in *Jazz of Lights*, where you said that you could never again see New York with the same eyes, Harry has proved himself the best poet of the whole American scene—a really original poet owing nothing to anyone else, as far as I could see.

This is the one work that should obviously represent the U.S.A. abroad. It would be understood in all countries, would reveal so much that has been concealed, inarticulate and waiting for the American poet to express.

We stayed up late into the night telling Harry how we felt and he was obviously touched. He needed this because this morning John Martin lambasted and ridiculed him in the *Times*, giving whatever credit that was due to the man who did the costumes and saying that he wished the musicians had "got lost." It was cruel and criminal—absolutely unforgivable for a performance at which the entire audience went absolutely wild. It was, in fact, a triumph, and you were certainly the one who brought it about, so what a pity you could not have seen this. Harry says that after tonight he will go back to Illinois with the same troupe, but that the stage equipment will be lacking, as that only exists in N.Y.

Harry had the satisfaction of a tremendous personal ovation, and he says there is a hope that he may get an appointment out of it at Julliard, which would enable him to continue his work.

He is really a delightful man—I am very fond of him. Coming back in the taxi after the performance, he even asked me if I had found everything in order in the apartment after he left!

So glad your checkups are OK. So now just use the next month to recover completely and come back to Bogner and me.

This last period with Bogner has brought me to a realization that nothing is as important to me—not business, not art, not my films—as human life itself. That is my theme this year and what a theme it is to discover at this time.

All my love,
your Hugo

Letter from Jim Herlihy to Anaïs Nin:
Key West, April 1959

Dear Anaïs,

I like what *Masterplots* wrote about you. I hope they are influential and widely read. And how wonderful that the Avon *Spy* has sold so well. I don't think you should bother doing a reprint of it, since they are still selling it in the Avon edition. The project that really excites me is the two-volume edition of all the novels together. If you could find a good and reasonable binder, you might have a quantity of them done in hardbound and offer them at a slightly higher cost than the paperback. But I like your idea of keeping the prices low. If there is one suggestion I would offer about your little books, it is this: there is not enough information about you in them; I think the back of the book should have bibliography, blurb, quotes, etc. You don't need that so much for mail order, but I think it helps the bookshops.

I am anxious to know about your health; it is so important because without it the spirits flags, and I want you high-flyin'. I am amazed at the way you handled your hospital period, making plans for what you would do with the press, writing letters, continuing. You didn't even seem depressed!

Bill Noble was here for two weeks. He has just come from another period in the hospital as a result of a bout with alcohol. He is in bad money trouble; all of his *Blue Denim* money sort of slipped through his fingers. Much of it he loaned to people who have disappeared.

Dick has found some wonderful jazz musician friends here. They play at a place called the Regency Room. I kicked up my heels on marijuana one night; stupendous reaction! But I am still suspicious of drugs. Lee Shaw, the drummer, says Anaïs Nin is a real cool cat, and he "turns on" with your books. You have many readers here, but he is the most colorful of them. One night as I was leaving the nightclub, some sailors came in; someone introduced us, we talked, and somehow I said something (don't remember what) that made one of the sailors say: "You sound like Anaïs Nin!" This floored me. Anyway, he is another Nin aficionado. I'm convinced that your new editions are doing a lot to broaden your readership—but the Navy!

Is anyone staying at 35 W 9? Jimmy Spicer has been reckless with my friendship; he asked if he could have Patchen at our apartment (to stay there with him). I don't like Patchen because I remember your experience with him. Anyway, I said no—and Jimmy went ahead and let him stay. I have not scolded him about it, but I am offended and am not going to offer him the apartment anymore.

I am not writing. No guilt either. I sun and read and swim and enjoy. I take it as it comes. I love this warm country.

Your reasons for calling your press the Anaïs Nin Press are very good.

Please be kind to your body; don't overdo it! Demand your rest; steal it if you have to!

Love,
Jim

Letter from Gunther Stuhlmann to Anaïs Nin:
New York, April 1959

Dear Anaïs:

I don't see any reason why you should not authorize Jean Fanchette as your translator for the *Spy*, but I firmly believe that we ought to conduct all business discussion as to terms and contracts, etc., through our office and subject to your and our scrutiny so that we do not get into another situation that would be embarrassing for all of us. It was no mean trick to solve the Spearman entanglement, and I am somewhat wary of getting into a similar situation now in France.

Hope you are well and productive.

All my best,
Gunther

Letter from Anaïs Nin to Hugh Guiler:
Los Angeles, April 16, 1959

Darling:

I felt your going away to Paris yesterday so sharply I wonder if it means the end of my having to go away myself now that I know it is a problem of concentration and the need of peace outside. Anyway, your voice sounded good.

I hope you like *Two Cities*. I was disappointed. Don't tell Jean it has no guts and it is not particularly new, daring or contemporary. It seems like a clique, a class reunion, a banquet of old friends!

I am entering artistically into a more objective state of seeing all I did not see before. It is frightening, this limitation of the vision. The dreamer wears velvet blinders. I am writing what I did not see before.

Still struggling with an overall title to the first five novels—*Cities of the Interior* is not perfect.

I work from eight to five, except for one hour of massage. I read at night, write letters and try to follow you on your voyage! I will get my reservation for May 10th to meet you on the 11th. I'm waiting for your first record and record player.

Love, and go easy on yourself, darling,
A

Letter from Anaïs Nin to Daisy Aldan:
Los Angeles, April 1959

Dear Daisy Aldan:

I would have written you sooner, but I have little energy. Thank you for your subscription to *Two Cities*, for the copy of your *Folder* magazine and your very wonderful translation of Mallarmé.

I'm very interested in your Press. It is what I have done for my own work—rescued it from oblivion—I wish I could do this for other writers, but I can't both write and publish, and have been overworked the last year.

Are you close to Wallace Fowlie? We were good friends once. I admire him. He has become cool and formal towards me, and I don't know why. *Mystère*. I invited him to contribute to *Two Cities*, as I would like to invite you anytime you have something for us.

Amicalement,
Anaïs

Letter from Anaïs Nin to Claude and Lawrence Durrell:
Los Angeles, May 1959

Dear Claude and Larry:

How I wish I could have joined you this spring to talk over *Two Cities*, to celebrate the success of *Montolive*. You must be enjoying Henry's and Eve's visit.

Rupert and I just returned from sitting on the site in Silver Lake he chose to build his home, following true California tradition—overlooking a small lake, with mountains in the back. He is fulfilling a long, old fantasy. He will begin to build this summer.

I'll be in New York May 11. Write me there at 35 W. 9th, New York City 11. Soon you will have all the children again and no time for letters.

Working on 1,000 pages these six weeks—but had to give up the Anaïs Nin Press—no strength.

Hope you'll have a happy summer. Please try and see Hugo's film at the Cinémateque if you go to Paris.

My love,
Anaïs

May 11, 1959
Return to New York.

Letter from Anaïs Nin to Rupert Pole:
New York, June 1, 1959

Chiquitito:

At the time I usually call you I am now at the hospital with Bebe Barron because she insists I see her baby boy as if it were one of the seven wonders of the world. My unconscious had chosen presents for a girl. A gift from you (not to exceed one doll) was included in the shower at Maya Deren's. A tiny, tiny bottle of perfume. A tiny Japanese fan. A Japanese doll. Oh, my intuition.

I have had extra work on account of my great flaw, which you know all about. For the recording of *On Writing* (we had to postpone it till next week), I had to organize my material (where have I heard this word before?) as you could so well do, my love, but your wife is in hell at such moments just as when you have to write a letter. Poor Stuhlmann wanted me to include an introduction and a proper intermission while the record is flipped and told me that I pass too quickly from one idea to the next, that I begin in the middle. *Et voilà.* Whenever one has a weakness it betrays you sooner or later. He does understand and did help me. He thinks I have good ideas, novel ones in fact, but toss them off so lightly! Tossed salad, eh what.

Darling, I got your letter. Please call up the cleaner and tell him not to come. You do not enjoy it. I was wrong to think it would please you. Do whatever you please. You always think the bad exceeds the good. I release you from your promise. It will only mean more cleaning when I return to chase away the horse shit from every corner and the smell. *C'est la vie.*

Te quiero,
A

Letter from Rupert Pole to Anaïs Nin:
Los Angeles, June 1959

My Love,

I know it's been so long and only my first letter. So much to do with our lot—seeing Roberts, the contractor, the pool man, trying to get the lower wall placed right, etc., etc.

Then, of course, there are troubles selling the beach lot at the last minute, but I hope all will clear up and he will sign the escrow next week.

You have sounded so good over our last phone calls. You promised when you were feeling down you'd tell me so I can believe it when you sound so good!

Lloyd and Mother are going to Chicago for a funeral next week—hope to get Eric's full-time attention to the house then. As I plan each detail, I think, "Will my love like this? Will it be beautiful enough for her? Will it be convenient and easy to clean?"

Hurry back to help and to make our house—and life—complete.
R

Letter from Hugh Guiler to Anaïs Nin:
New York, June 22, 1959

Darling,

Am worried about Mitou. Since yesterday she has not only been completely asthmatic, her spirit seems less lively. I am afraid the time the doctor gave her may be shorter rather than longer—I have to prepare myself for that. If I could only have had her massaged and analyzed it might have had been different.

Now you must take extra care of yourself, my darling. You looked prettier than ever looked in your life when you left.

You probably have absolutely no chance of getting the polar flight to Europe as it is only once a week and booked months in advance. Let me know as soon as you can. Meanwhile I will ask the Crillon to reserve a hotel for Venice the 13th or the first night they can after that, so you can avoid so many nights of traveling. Leaving on the 13th will give you the night of the 12th in Paris, on the assumption you will get there the hard way and not by the polar route. But telegraph me as soon as you know.

Deepest love,
Hugo

Letter from Gunther Stuhlmann to Anaïs Nin:
New York, June 23, 1959

Dear Anaïs:

Just a day after you left for L.A., I had word from India (Mysterious East Department) that Rupa and Co. in Calcutta would like to bring out five of your titles in paperback editions of 3,000 copies each.

They offered a royalty of 5%, which, on the basis of the current exchange and their low pricing of the book, should amount to about a little more than 2 cents a copy at 3,000 copies sold, half of which they are willing to pay upon signature of the contract as an advance against royalties, and as a guarantee.

Given the situation in India and all, this is not a lot of money, and will add up to a few hundred dollars altogether, but I think it is good to have you published there and I went ahead and drew up five contracts of four copies each, as they requested (my fingers are still sore from typing all this, but I wanted to get the thing settled fast).

As soon as I get the rest of the German contracts, I will pass them on to you for signature.

More soon, and don't get a cramp in your hand from signing all this.

As ever,
Gunther

Letter from Hugh Guiler to Anaïs Nin:
New York, June 25, 1959

Darling,

On Monday, as I wrote you, Mitou became obviously and progressively worse and finally started to fall over as she walked. Millicent and I took her to the animal hospital yesterday, and they made X-rays, which three of the doctors examined. They then asked me if the cat had a bad accident or a fall recently and when I said no they said then it was congenital ostosis imperfecta, a bone deficiency in her spine from birth that had brought about so much deterioration of the cortex (the outer layer of the bone on the spine) due to calcium deficiency, that it had caused the spine to cave in above the heart. As a result the heart was pressed out of its normal place from the pressure of the bone on top and pressed against the chest bone. This caused a lack of flow of the blood and was the cause of the sporadic coughing and now also a lack of flow of blood to the brain. The cat has been suffering from this, and not from asthma at all, and has been in pain all this time without our knowing it.

I asked the doctor if it would be possible to do an operation and he answered no—nothing. I asked him then if he would advise putting the cat away so that she would not suffer anymore. He said definitely he would so advise without any hesitation in a case like this.

I had to make a terrible decision, but as I could not bear to bring Mitou back to the house knowing this, I said he should go ahead. I turned away without being able to look at Mitou. Of course, I broke down and wept, and I don't need to tell you what my feelings have been.

I saw Bogner afterwards, and she said I had done the only thing that was possible under the circumstances and again assured me that I could have confidence in the animal hospital as they are known to be first class.

So Mitou was put to sleep yesterday afternoon, painlessly, by an overdose of anesthetic injection.

Bogner went over with me all that Mitou had meant to me. One was the fact that I identified her with you, and that she was a symbol of you, as well as a companion when you have been away. And one reaction is that I started to worry because you did not complete your checkup here, so even still we have no final report on your metabolism, etc. You must do this for me when you come back in the fall.

I had gone to work after the decision and worked feverishly to forget it all, but of course I broke down again when I saw Bogner. When I recovered somewhat, I brought out that I do not want another Siamese cat. The doctor told me they are delicate animals and are particularly prone to this bone deterioration, which can only be arrested when they are very young.

It helped me that we can talk about a dog—perhaps a poodle. Bogner told me how wonderful her dog is—that it is so delicate in its way that it is like having an animal that is half cat and half dog.

We also talked about what it meant that I could consider a dog instead of a Siamese, and it became clear that in so far as Mitou was *me*, too, I had been identifying her not with you (beautiful, harmonious, cathartic) but on the other hand with the more withdrawn part of myself, and so the wish for a dog is a wish that I myself should be less withdrawn and more outgoing and demonstrative in my affections.

So there it is, darling, and I know you will weep for our Mitou, but also that you will approve of the terrible decision I had to make.

Deepest love,
Hugo

July 22, 1959
Arrival in Paris with Hugo.

Letter from Anaïs Nin to Rupert Pole:
Paris, July 28, 1959

Darling:

Yesterday I sent you a night letter because I had not been able to write you for three days, being on the road to catch writers who have gone away for the summer. It has been wonderful to work in Paris and to catch a glimpse of Venice. These cities give me the strange feeling of living many lives in one day. It must be the rich past, though I tried to read a history of Venice and it was so gory I could hardly finish it. But even today a refined Italian told me the best thing for America to do would be to have Fidel Castro assassinated—so simple!

It is 7:00 AM and I'm starting my day.

All my love,
A

P. S. I'm sitting in the same café in St. Germaine where you and I sat for a while, waiting for the *Two Cities* group who is always late, and I find that although I love Paris with passion, I keep thinking of it with you in it even though we had such short moments here. It has become your city with you haunting it. I guess, after all, my true home is in your arms...

August 1959
Return to N.Y. alone, ill.

Letter from Hugh Guiler to Anaïs Nin:
Venice, September 2, 1959

Darling,

The news that the pain has stopped made me very happy and that you are feeling recovered. The fact that you now feel the pains were related to an ulcer brings the whole thing close to a psychological problem, which is what Bogner is trying to help you with. But I agree the time was too short for you to return here as I only have one week free from business, and the weather, although sunny, is cooler than what you would have enjoyed.

I have already over 3,000 feet of sound for the new film—some of it I think usable—the difficulty is that the microphone does not *select* sounds the way our ears and brain do, so much is overloaded with background sounds—OK sometimes, but otherwise confusing. As I wrote you, I have made a discovery of Venice *at noon.* Happened by accident because the weather at first did not look good for the beach. It cleared up and we were in canoes in clear, bright sunlight, to see the fish market. The clothes were hanging out all across and if these shots come out they will be wonderful. Am going back today to make sure and am swimming in the late afternoon. Not so good for swimming, but this new Venice is too good to miss.

Deepest love, and so glad you are well again.

H

Letter from Anaïs Nin to Rupert Pole:
New York, October 5, 1959

My sweet darling:

Yesterday I had a surprise. Jim arrived, and Dick and Stanley, Anne Bancroft and a movie director, on the occasion of the publication of Jim's book of stories. We had a gay, light talk. Anne is quite a dynamo, and imitates everyone. They cheered me up in a superficial way. They are all tanned, and have many stories to tell about Tennessee Williams. Everybody sends their love. Stanley said: "Rupert was so, so, so, so handsome, I got stage struck when I tried to photograph him." It was a good thing they came, chattering away, as later Hill Kluver came, in a state of shock, and ready for another suicide try. These Swedes. "I have lost Billy. He really loves that woman in Paris. I don't want to live." Looking down, doll-like, small, turned-up nose, child-like (the woman in Paris is a kind of Sabina). So this morning I had to call Dr. Hammerschlag (what a name), the analyst, to see if I can prevent another suicide. The last time she only lived because Billy came back for something he had forgotten. I tried to tell her it was selfish to take her life and make Billy feel guilty for something he cannot help.

I told you a radio station will do your reading of "The Party." Let me know if there is anyone in New York you want me to notify. I don't know the date yet.

Te quiero, don't work too hard. There are no deadlines worth keeping, only life. No deadlines. Just the preciousness of life.

A

Letter from Anaïs Nin to Rupert Pole:
New York, October 1959

My love:

Yes, your jealousy is blind (as you know) and destructive (as you know) and negative—and it all hurts so much I don't want to go into it until later. I never want to see Reginald again, for he is evil and loveless and destructive. How could you believe what he says about me?

Anyway, I'm still under the shock of your suspicion. I'm trying to wind up the work.

New developments: Peter Owen, my English publisher, is a friend of the new head of British Book Centre. They are well off and willing to repair unethical behavior of the former head. He asked me to lunch. I told him the story of 5,000 copies of *Spy* offset without a contract or any money given me. Even if they settle for a little part of it, it should mean a few hundred dollars. I do feel I must do all I can this time. I know my time in N.Y. is shortening, but we do need the money. I can't keep this up, but I must make all I can *now*.

Several other problems: I'm undergoing sinus treatment, a possible ear abscess, so I thought I may call you. Don't see how I can come before Tuesday, the 10th of November. Friday night I leave for the Harvard lecture, and then I lecture at Dartmouth Sunday evening at their Writers Club. I return Monday to lunch with British Book Centre, and Tuesday, I hope, home to you.

Undivided love,
A

New York, October 14, 1959
Notice in *The Village Voice*:
Eighth Street Bookshop and The Living Theatre present: ANAÏS NIN reading "The Party" from *Ladders to Fire* and IAN HUGO four films including *Melodic Inversions* (premiere) Monday, October 19 at 8:30 PM. Adm. $1

Letter from Anaïs Nin to Rupert Pole:
New York, October 18, 1959

My love:

I have a good excuse for not dating letters! Oh, I remember, it is Oct. 18—as I'm giving a reading tomorrow evening. I'm writing you in case I do not reach you today. Last night the Barrons drove me for one hour out of N.Y. to New Jersey to the Swedish couple's farewell for the Swedish Museum of Modern Art Director.

A real nice Swedish evening. Champagne and much to eat. Good records, good books, and lovely women.

The world is full of good films we don't see. It's the same problem of mass taste. If we had 10 or 20 steady friends, we could see one interesting film a week or month. The Swedes have so many more films that are banned here. They think we are as "censored" as Russia!

We definitely must go to Sweden. They are so charming, really, full of learning, humor.

Fearfully busy—yet time drags. I've given up the idea that we get used to living apart.

There is an actor reading your part in "The Party," a homosexual, but fortunately has a good male voice and does not show it. Has a French boyfriend. He doesn't read as well as you, love, but it's fun having a real stage.

A

Letter from Anaïs Nin to Rupert Pole:
New York, November 1959

My darling:

You sounded as lonely as I feel! Life is cruel sometimes. Here I do have all the excitement, novelty, change, contact with all that is happening in art but no Rupert. So that half of the pleasure is cancelled—and it is also too much of a good thing. The fact that the opening of the Guggenheim is the same night as my reading put my friends in a terrible spot! But they came, faithfully, warmed up the hall—no defections! I was so proud of my friends that night.

All the seats were sold—20 or 30 were turned away. I gave a good reading. Kept remembering what you said: put into your reading what you do when you get mad at me. Some said that I had the power to create magic without acting.

I postponed calling you—to be able to tell you it was good.

Work, work, work. I'm slipping responsibilities of *Two Cities* on two other people. Poetry editors.

Brooks Clift tells me Monty tried to commit suicide. How can a person become that unhappy? I wonder if the actor's life would have driven you to such anxiety. Of course, you don't have the problem of homosexuality—only the problem of a Spanish wife! And that can only be solved by separation, which causes me to return home very docile and penitent.

Lecture Monday at City College. Working on it this weekend. Will call you.

A

Letter from Rupert Pole to Anaïs Nin:
Los Angeles, November 1959

Love:

Such a nice, long letter yesterday; so glad the reading went well. I'll bet lots passed up the Guggenheim to hear it. When we get set in the house let's spend our Christmases (two and a half weeks) in N.Y. You can plan ahead and I'll come out to do readings, parties, etc. with you.

I would love to go to Sweden in the summertime.

The film idea is marvelous—our house will easily hold 20 or fewer for films. I have unlimited use of projectors from school—let's have a film month (by subscription) where we show the best three or four recently produced films. This is one reason I want the house—to do things others cannot or will not do.

Glad for what N.Y. does for you aesthetically and spiritually but hate what it does to you physically—take it easy and come back ready to swim again and to love again…soon.

R

Letter from Anaïs Nin to Rupert Pole:
New York, November 1959

Darling:

You sounded so gay and well yesterday on the phone except for the body-surfing voice! I saw Jim and Dick on their last evening here. It was very funny, for we started out with just Jim, Dick and Gil Henderson, and we had dinner together. Then we ran into Starcke, who joined us and walked the Village streets to show Gil around. Then we ran into Stanley and his Greek boy, and they joined us, and as we walked two more hung their heads out of the windows and wanted us to celebrate one of them getting divorced! It was hilarious. Eight homosexuals and Gil and I. I looked for an exit and finally I got away. Too much, really! Gil has left determined to return to New York. He feels he can make it as a painter here and that in L.A. he has become a businessman. Olympia may change his mind.

Restful weekend, relatively, arranging with the Phoenix to sell *Cities of the Interior*, five novels in one, for $3.50.

With love, the best vitamins, Vitamins A and R

Letter from Jim Herlihy to Anaïs Nin:
Key West, November 20, 1959

Dear Anaïs,

Though I have not yet read all of *Cities of the Interior* straight through, I have studied it carefully, trying to get an idea what effect the new sequence and continuity have on the whole body of work. I feel it is terribly important, and wish they were being presented now as a first, in this form. The pattern or tapestry you were creating seems to define itself by the association of its parts, and in a way that a reader of single portions would have to take for granted. I had not meant to say this so complicatedly. I only mean that I believe each part is stronger in this context than when it stands alone. When I see it on my shelf I can hardly believe that the day has actually come, the long dream fulfilled. Do you remember how often we talked about this book, all the novels in one volume?

I finished the second draft of the novel, changed the title to *All Fall Down*. Now I have a big typing job ahead of me.

I miss seeing you. The few hours we had in New York were deeply important ones for me. I wish I had seen Hugo. I miss him very much, too, but in a different way. I still feel about him that he is my real papa, and when I don't see him for such long periods, I feel, irrationally, that he has disowned me or something. His engravings in your new book cause in me a kind of nostalgia that is like a memory from childhood. He is one of the very few people in the world whom I truly love. Please give him my wishes and regards.

I feel that I am about to embark on some big project, and I am suffering all the excitement and anxiety of wondering what it will be. The first big rush of Golconda lethargy that seemed to threaten me forever, last winter, has definitely subsided. I think that with the writing of my novel I broke it entirely. Now I am a palm, moving only with the wind, but moving. I wonder if you would be happy here.

Love always,
Jim

Los Angeles, November 1959

Dreams: I am walking parallel to a man who is walking with a giant bear on a chain. He is seeking to catch me with a chain with a hook at the end of it. He makes one attempt, but I free myself and I fly into space. I stay in space. I see him down below waiting for me to get tired out and come down to earth.

There is a young woman who keeps away from men. I try to reunite her with them. Then I turn to someone and say: "There is nothing to be done. *Elle a peur bleu...*" [she is scared to death].

Rupert falls into a well. I shout for help. Then I rush to help him out. I pull him out and give him artificial respiration. He moans as he spits water from his lungs.

A man has a coat with a fur capelet.

Letter from Anaïs Nin to Daisy Aldan:
Los Angeles, December 1959

Dear Daisy:

My energy has been so low that I am contemplating withdrawing from *Two Cities*. I have written to Jean. I have to reduce my activities. Would it make much difference to you, would you continue with Serge Gavronsky, to be sole editors and I will give indirect help? Will you think this over? I will not act hastily. I want to know how you and Serge feel. How do you get on with him?
Anaïs

Letter from Daisy Aldan to Anaïs Nin:
New York, December 5, 1959

My Dear Anaïs,

You are absolutely right in your decision concerning *Two Cities*. There is no reason whatsoever that someone like you should devote her time to distributing that magazine, or reading hundreds of mediocre and poor manuscripts, and carrying on the work of returning them with comments. That kind of work is one reason I gave up publishing *Folder* as a magazine. No, I also do not intend to take over that chore for *Two Cities*. I will be delighted to send Jean any manuscripts I receive that I feel to be publishable, and even to solicit some from friends, but I do not wish to be the recipient of all those that come from the same old people whose work may be seen in any inferior little magazine in America! There are hundreds. All you should be doing, Anaïs, is writing and experiencing and resting, particularly at this time. The other is a complete waste for you, and I'm glad you wrote to Fanchette and told him. Perhaps Serge can take over that other job, and you and I can do some editing of the choices (semi-final ones) and send some things when we receive them. We'll talk further about this.

Will Hugo want to go abroad to rest? Will you too? You must try now not to work very much... Simply renew yourself. If there is any strength that can come from my affection for you, please use it.
Daisy

Letter from Anaïs Nin to Jean Fanchette:
Los Angeles, December 8, 1959

Dear Jean:

    I am afraid your last letter may alienate me if we cannot clear the misunderstandings with good will and patience. First of all, it was not because of differences of opinions that I asked you to let me resign, but because of my health. You are a doctor, and you must know my handicaps and what they mean: I have chronic anemia, incurable, and a demanding, intense life, full of duties and responsibilities. I minded very much your mention of "selfishness" in my withdrawal, after the proof I gave you of the opposite, even incurring an extra expense to help you, which I should not have done when the debts of my own Press are still pending. I had no idea it would mean so much labor, and so much correspondence.

    Also, dear Jean, threatening me with the loss of your friendship—but what kind of friendship is it that has no human consideration for the friend, and only for the magazine? What will I lose? Someone who does not care about me, only that the magazine should go on! The only selfishness I have been guilty of is to burden Hugo with a luxury at the wrong time, and when I had debts incurred by my own Press. I know you were thinking of *Two Cities*, and not of me, but I hope you did not mean anything you wrote me, for then I would be forced to resign.

    I did not think you would be irritated to receive opinions to be objectively and quietly studied, and then equally quietly disagreed with. It is the life of the magazine in America we are working upon, all of us, with good will and objectivity. I had sympathy for you this summer when you were breaking down with fatigue.

    I do wish you would write me a different letter so I could tear up the last one and forget it. We are all under stress, and I want to believe that it is because you are too that you have been irritable when there was no cause to be.

    Have I answered all your points, or is there any other reason for your sharpness?
Anaïs

Letter from Jim Herlihy to Anaïs Nin:
Key West, December 21, 1959

Dear Anaïs,

    I tried to telephone you the other day, for no particular reason except that I wanted to talk with you, but you were out each time I tried.

    I was very much disturbed to hear about the close call of the midnight telephone call, and the increase of tensions because of it. I have thought about it a lot and have even dreamed about it at night. I do wish you could give up the trapeze, but I know that it is necessary to be emotionally ready to do so. When the time does come, I know you will do it well. I wish I could help, but I know that there is nothing I can do except to assure you that if at any time you need a buffer state, a rest, or any other help within my power to give, it will be yours for the asking. I love you and don't want you hurt.

    A mortgage that costs $150 a month for 20 years for your house seems such a frightening burden, a terrible price for security, which does not even exist in the first place. It is the kind of madness that is impossible for me to truly understand. It is exactly the security of a prison term. Incredible that Rupert has learned so little from you, when there was every opportunity to learn freedom.

All my love,
Jim

New York, December 31, 1959
A few hours before 1960.

I was weeping. I considered myself an incurable melancholic—a mental case.

Hugo sat me on his knees, and consoled me, reassured me, assured me of his love. We went out to dinner and to a Japanese film. He was too tired to go to a party. We came home and drank a bottle of champagne, talked gaily, tenderly, and fell asleep. I did not remember Rupert. Was it because in his letter he said he would drink to us and the house? Or because this time he asked me to go to Paris or New York on my fictional job because we needed money (for the house)?

I feel that having failed at my intimate, personal life, I should try to achieve a good work of art.

In 1960:
Work at completing all the characters in the journals
At rounding out portraits
At expanding dimensions

Letter from Rupert Pole to Anaïs Nin:
Los Angeles, January 1, 1960

Darling:

Getting very good ideas for the house, and poor Eric is trying to incorporate them. One is to have a planting box come right inside the living room, so we'll have a living decoration—nothing dead. Getting very excited about the house.

Very quiet New Year's Eve. Called Gil and Olympia but they were having his mother over, so it was dinner with Eric (Mother and Lloyd went out to a party, Reginald to another party) and to *400 Blows*, a wonderfully sensitive movie.

Counting the days till you return—so many things to tell you and ask you about the house. Horribly cold here—left Tavi at Mother's this evening as it is much too cold to leave him out here and so cold that my car doesn't warm up. Come soon and bring warmth and love—my love is big, but it needs you here to really glow—and set our house on fire…

R

Letter from Jim Herlihy to Anaïs Nin:
Key West, January 22, 1960

Dear Anaïs:

Poor Eduardo—what will he do? He seems so utterly unqualified for poverty. I feel that Castro is a madman, a dangerous megalomaniac. I pray for his downfall. Batista was a far lesser evil, I think. Here, only 90 miles from Cuba, there are many refugees with dreadful stories of their treatment at the hands of a government of beatniks. It's sad, because the Cuban people don't deserve it.

How I wish your Nassau-Key West plan had worked. We have had many weeks of constant sun, beauty; you would have loved it. I hope it will happen one day soon. I miss you so much.

I have in my locked cabinet here a set of keys to the filing cabinets with the black children; if you want me to send them to you, let me know. Otherwise I will keep them until they are needed. I just wanted to remind you that I have them.

The news of your new apartment sounds really wonderful, but it is hard to imagine that 35 W 9th is no longer yours. A new shell now and then is an excellent idea, I think.

Love,
Jim

Letter from Anaïs Nin to Jim Herlihy:
Los Angeles, January 1960

Dear Jim,

So happy to hear from you on the phone. Letters, even though we are writers, do not make up for the talks!

Yes, it was difficult to take the decision of leaving 35 W 9th, but the owners wanted us to buy it at $20,000 and they are untrustworthy people and nothing worked—electricity, plumbing, heat. We were not allowed colored lights or air conditioning. Our new apartment is a million times more comfortable. It is in a new building, modern, doormen with capes, air conditioning, proper heat, two bathrooms, a balcony with a view, as much space as in 35 with more comfort. It is south of Washington Square, a new development near New York University. View is of West downtown and some of Washington Square. We're on the 14th floor, where there is air and sun.

I'm getting letters from a man in Joliet, Illinois, Roger Bloom, a writer and actor serving a sentence for violence.

An important year in decisions: to accept the conventional life of both Hugo and Rupert because of their affection, goodness, sincerity. A woman cannot create her own life unless she lives like George Sand, and I'm not the type.

To discard the novels and work only on the Diary, I'm free of rebellions. I know you'll be glad.

You don't miss New York? Will you ever return? Now that you find you can write down there I'm afraid you won't come back. Do you still rent your place to Bill Noble? The Hendersons will be looking for a place.

Rupert is so happy building his house! It is on a hill, overlooking Silver Lake and the mountains—beautiful, open view, the lot is flat. The pool is already dug. It is strange to see a house built from the beginning.

Hugo will go to Venice before coming home for a few more shots for his film.

Love,
A

Letter from Henry Miller to Anaïs Nin:
Big Sur, March 18, 1960

Dear Anaïs,

I hope to get down your way the middle or end of next week.

No, Grove Press is not bringing out the *Tropics*. They wanted to, and offered a staggering advance (guaranteed), a very liberal arrangement and all, but my conscience wouldn't let me. Too much trouble involved, bad publicity, etc.

Henry

P. S. Forgot perhaps to say I am leaving for Europe April 4th. Have been invited to act as one of the judges at Film Festival in Cannes (in May). Have accepted. Simenon will also be "*un membre du jury.*" We'll meet finally. Wonder who else?

Letter from Artur Lundkvist to Anaïs Nin:
Stockholm, April 8, 1960

Dear Anaïs Nin,

Excuse me for answering your letter so late. I have been abroad for several months and all communications have been difficult.

Now I just want to say that I am extremely glad you and your husband are coming to Stockholm. I will be here at that time to meet you, and I hope Stockholm will be at its best at the end of May.

Your book *Cities of the Interior* I have received and I thank you for it. Only the very last part of it was new to me, but it is nice to have all the books in one volume.

I wish you a very warm welcome to Stockholm and look forward to your visit.

Sincerely yours,
Artur Lundkvist

Los Angeles, April 12, 1960

Reading at a small theatre, American Playwright Theatre, with Rupert Pole, reading "The Party."

Letter from Anaïs Nin to Roger Bloom:
New York, April 1960

Dear Roger Bloom:

I was very moved by the story of your life, how you were so desperate for money that you held up a bank with a toy gun. The most natural impulse in the world when there is so much injustice in the distribution of money. When will they come to believe that the man of last year is not the same man today? How far we are from understanding man's changes, evolutions.

I can't have the Miller books mailed to you, as it is against the law. I will send you an autographed set of my books, and you can give your other set to the library or lend them out, as you wish. I like to wait until I feel I know the person before I autograph books. And now I do.

I particularly want you to have a good typewriter now if it is a matter of writing a Writ, which may be important to you.

Home again and still typing. More soon!

Anaïs

Letter from Anaïs Nin to Roger Bloom:
Los Angeles, May 1960

    Henry is in France now, for the Cannes Festival, as you probably know. I am going over in the middle of the month, to give a reading from my work in Brussels, Stockholm and Rome, and to see my German publisher who is bringing out *A Spy in the House of Love.* In Paris I will meet with a painter and a writer who bought a sailboat in Amsterdam for only $1,300, 30 ft., and are going around the world. He is Ronnie Knox, the famous football player, and she could be one of the characters in my novels, an Austrian girl named Renate Druks. They named their boat after my last book, *Solar Barque*, and asked me to go along, but I can't. Too much work and two homes to keep up.
    Anaïs

Letter from Gunther Stuhlmann to Anaïs Nin:
New York, May 2, 1960

Dear Anaïs:
    Here, at last, is the check for the various monies that came in recently. The monies amount to the following:
    Royalties from Peter Owen, up to December 31, 1959, after the deduction of the advances for both novels showed a balance in your favor, which amounted to $7.48 in exchange, after commission: $5.98.
    Royalties from Spearman, according to his statement, up to December 31, 1959, amounted to $46.49, after commission this comes to: $39.49.
    Advance payments from Rupa & Co, for the first four paperbacks came to $30 per book, or a total of $120.00. Of this, two times 25% go to Peter Owen, based on our negotiations when he was here, and after the commission is deducted this amounts to a total of: $84.00
    Grand total: $129.47
    I have to rush off. All my best, as ever,
    Gunther

Letter from Anaïs Nin to Rupert Pole:
Paris, May 15, 1960

Darling:
    The flight was terrible. Weather was bad over the North Pole, so we went by way of New York. An hour-and-a-half wait there, two hours late, seven babies crying and people talking all night. Every woman in Paris still looks like Bardot. I took a special insurance as I am flying so much, so often. It insures me for the whole month on plane or land.
    I'm still dazed by the trip. Not writing very brightly. Paris is full of police and tension (Algeria). How good it is to be able to escape the oppressive, heavy, ugly political world into other worlds of creation. A French taxi driver only earns 60,000 francs a month and pays 18,000 for rent. No old age pension. Even the priests are turning communist. A mess.

I hope to hear from you before I leave Saturday.

The weather is grey, but for some reason Paris gives me euphoria. It has so much character and flavor.

And now to work!

Love, deeper and deeper and deeper into the night,

A

Letter from Anaïs Nin to Rupert Pole:
Paris, May 16, 1960

Darling,

The walk between Place Clichy and Place Blanche is a walk we should have taken. It is the rough Paris, cafés full of pimps, pushers, etc. The side streets are dark, lit up only by a few hotel signs and prostitutes standing by the door—tough, interesting, like those we saw in Mexico, like those you see in paintings, so vivid. There are crowds walking, jazz musicians, nightclub barkers, dirty postcard sellers, penny movies (no longer sexual scenes, just stripteases), an animation like the streets of Spain, so lively. The bookstores are open, there are pinball games like on Broadway, a Japanese Review at the Moulin Rouge, so alive and sensuous, and such good food and good, mellow wines that one becomes high in a gentle way, mellow, everything mellow and gentle and loving life. Paris affects your wife like LSD! Only in a good way. I was showing all this to my Swedish friends. Their eyes were popping.

In the evening, a fancy dinner with Graciella Archibald and her husband, a mature champagne, no preservatives. And afterwards, we went to see a Greek painter's exhibit. The galleries would not have him, so he set up shop under a bridge. It was a huge arcade with plenty of room for his big paintings under floodlights. It was under Pont Neuf. The black river, the heavy bridge—a lovely summer night. In the afternoon I was at the Mistral bookshop. Everybody was browsing. I signed some books.

Last night I could not sleep. I was overexcited by the city, its beauty.

Graciella's dog reminded me of Tavi. I worry about Tavi. Will he be there when I return?

A

Letter from Anaïs Nin to Rupert Pole:
Paris, May 17, 1960

Darling:

Tonight I have an autograph party at the English Book Shop, and then dinner with the Fanchettes. He has a pale, blue-eyed child although he is so dark and his wife is a dark French girl with black hair.

I hope the house is going well, darling. I hope Tavi won't fall into the pool.

I'm glad they didn't send me to Cannes. It's a real Hollywood affair. I feel sad that the Europeans only get the vulgarization of America, never *the other*. I keep talking about the America they don't know or hear of. You would be proud of all I say and would forgive me some of my sputterings.

Te quiero, Chiquito—I think of you before going to sleep. Keep well. Don't work too hard. Pretty soon you'll have a rest and the beach.

A

Letter from Rupert Pole to Anaïs Nin:
Los Angeles, May 17, 1960
Sunday at the beach

My Darling:

Tavi is *recovering* from his stroke—natch. Like Reginald, he has the stubborn, tough quality of life itself—just refuses to give up. The vet saw him Monday, and by Wednesday he seemed to recognize me, and Thursday his interest in food revived with a bang. Right now he's determined to go down to the stream but can't make it, can only walk sideways (his balance is still impaired). Of course, I'm really glad he's pulled through. I want him to see how radiant you look when you get off the plane again—and to live in the new house for at least a few months!

Beautiful day here—windy but warm in *our* corner and *huge* waves just waiting till I finish this. Tavi has to be *tied up* to keep him from wandering all over the beach—sideways.

House is going to be very spectacular—raised ceiling in the living room with glass all around at top will make a very *dramatic* room. I am trying for *poetic* and *practical* lighting—each on *separate* switches.

No more room on this paper, my love—except for you in my heart and in our house, where there are no limitations. Don't try to keep too fast a pace—want you back beautiful and well. Will try to write every other day.

Love,
R

Letter from Anaïs Nin to Rupert Pole:
Paris, May 21, 1960

Darling Chiquito:

Your letter about Tavi upset me so much I was sad all day. Just before I left I whispered in his ear that he should wait for me and keep well. I had an intuition, and I wrote you about it. I was at Graciella's, and, seeing her dog, I worried about Tavi. I know what he means to us; yet, darling, old age is so cruel it is better not to be alive, and the Tavi we have known lately is not the *real* Tavi. He has had much love and care, more than any dog I know. You know, he often wobbled to one side—he must have had a slight stroke before. I hate to think of Tavi being ill when I am not there to console you, to greet you when you come home. I hope perhaps it was a false alarm and he may be all well now. I thought of you all day. Got your letter in the morning.

At five o'clock the English Book Shop started its autograph party. All sorts of people came—old friends, new ones, writers, poets, Sylvia Beach, an art critic who gave me an introduction to the biggest Swedish newspaper, singers, painters. We stayed until nine o'clock. I was dead tired and hungry. Then eight of us went to dinner at a small place. Fanchette got drunk and talked a lot of nonsense. There were two girls from Vienna who couldn't talk at all. Then on to Deux Magots, where I dumped them at midnight. I returned wishing to be in my little home with you, realizing more than ever I am made for intimate life, not public life. I'm tense and not happy with most people. I need the tropical warmth of my Acapulco marriage, our life *à deux*.

I can perhaps get LSD from Jean Fanchette, who is working at a psychiatric hospital.

Te quiero, Chiquito. Love to Tavi...tell him to wait for me.

A

Letter from Anaïs Nin to Rupert Pole:
Stockholm, May 1960

Darling:

First scene from the airplane: Swedish lakes, hills with pines, small red houses like candy houses. Too many lakes, islands and all dark green. Stockholm itself would be dull except for rivers, canals, boats. Billy Kluver is all ears and teeth; Hill is all freckles, a pug nose, like a puppy. The museum man is red-faced. The professor who has a boat has a long, long nose and small blue eyes. They all look like peasants. Little cars, brown buildings. Staying at a small hotel in the center of town, facing the bookshop that has all my books. It looks like one of Reginald's hotels, only it is one of the best! All the luxury is in the linen. No bathroom. It is outside. The bathtub is big enough for *four* Anaïses—I almost drowned. We could have had such a fine bath together. I rested, took two aspirins. The airplane gives me a headache. At 6:30 they will all take me to the museum man's home. What a difference from Paris. No, I do not feel at home. It is foreign to me, to my temperament. The palace is earth-color, the trolley cars bright blue and yellow. Manners are stiffly polite. The maid is not your type! I think of you and give Tavi my love.

Yesterday was a holiday, so we packed into a small car and drove to the country. First they showed me suburban building projects, just as monstrous and dull as ours, all alike, but then Hugo Nils, the driver, took us to his family's property: 25 acres on a lake, so much like Bergman's settings for *Illicit Interlude*, a cold lake, gulls, but spring vegetation, wildflowers of all kinds, birches, red-leaved trees, big old trees, deer and snakes. The house is like a big Southern home, all in wood, ruined by vandals—being unoccupied—and finally burnt by teenagers who prowl about. While we were there a man came with his fishing rod and Nils argued with him. They almost had a fight. Billy went to get the police. They pay no attention to private property. Socialism has taken care of all problems except the cussedness of bums and nature. It is a country full of restrictions on drinking, etc. All the wives do social work, which is paid like any other job. It was all truly sad, with the strange feeling that summer is only three months—that is all they have to enjoy their boats, lakes, nature. Imagine a city in which it takes all of 15 minutes to be out in the wildest country! So many lakes instead of pools. Everybody has a boat and a tiny cottage.

Every newspaper has an article on me—what I say, wear, etc.

Will rest Saturday and Sunday at Brussels.

Te quiero, Chiquito, and long to be at home, at peace, with you. I'm not made for public life even when it spoils me.

A

Letter from Anaïs Nin to Rupert Pole:
Paris, May 1960

Darling:
The last evening in Sweden was the most interesting of all. In the old quarter, the medieval chartreuse-colored houses have peaked roofs. We all stood in the narrow street shouting, "Here we are!" The painter we went to see finally leaned out of his attic window and threw down the key (they lock the doors at six). We climbed the old stairs to the fifth floor. Jazz records, but *bread* made by the painter —a real big round loaf like a cratered moon—and wine. So simple. Everybody was there. I felt I had made lifelong friends, really loved them all. At eleven I gave out.

We almost wept at parting, and they made me promise to return. The big taxi could hardly get through the narrow streets. My room was full of flowers, not from florists, but wildflowers they all pick from the countryside. Lilies of the valley from the waiters, wild bluebells, violets, wild lilac, something very naïf and touching. They are passionate people frozen in conventions and old forms and a kind of puritanism that creates neurosis. They all criticized a girl who had lived in Chile for a year and danced rather jazzily! The artists can run away to Paris or Italy. Anyway, they won my heart, red ears and stiffness and slowness and all!

I could not get to Brussels directly, so a brief stopover in Paris. Saddened by the news of the death of Gonzalo from throat cancer—and Helba, the sick monster, is still alive! There is no justice in death. It kills the useful ones and keeps the useless ones alive!

Te quiero in all languages. *Tu mujer,*
A

Letter from Rupert Pole to Anaïs Nin:
Los Angeles, May 1960

Love:
So many good letters from you. I so, so enjoy hearing your adventures and being with you through the letters, and how wonderful to have one in the box each day. I'm surprised at your reaction to Stockholm, but forgot that the midsummer light was still a cold light, and that the old part of the city was still so primitive. So glad you're seeing the world and can compare all kinds of life with our sun life here. And wait till you see the new sun house—a very ornate and poetic balustrade all around. It's going to be a very warm, open, light-filled house, just as you wanted.

Very pleased at your indigestion of people in Paris and your realization that café life until wee hours *every* night is just not for us.

Tavi has recovered *completely*—in fact, he has saved up *so much* energy just to plague me with. He goes sideways and falls down occasionally, but then as you say he's been doing that for some time. He probably had his first stroke long ago. I have to put Tavi out at five each morning—he just can't hold it any longer than that.

If you see Renate tell her that her car was a most unwelcome gift (no, don't tell her that). I hope she and Ronnie are as happy in their Solar Barque as we will be in our Solar Castle. Tell them our Castle is built to last forever (no, don't tell them that either, because their Barque isn't).

Reading my Harvard 20-year class reunion report; such horribly dull lives most have led. I'm so proud of the last three words in my three-line life story: "married Anaïs Nin."

Too sleepy for more. I do love to write you from the beach; I feel closer to you (even though it's the wrong ocean) and always feel our love life is tied to the sea and the sun, and I am as big and warm as both put together.

R

Letter from Rupert Pole to Anaïs Nin:
Los Angeles, June 1960

My darling:

Started the wood panels on the house today. The wood is really beautiful. They are fine panels of a satin tone and grey finish, the one you liked best at the Builder's Exhibit. It will be just stunning. I may not even have to stain it—looks like old driftwood now.

So busy with final exams, projects, end-of-year work, but will try to get good black and white photos to send before you leave. So glad you love wood and that you've seen really fine use of it in Sweden, but wait till you see *our* new use of it, and we'll have our wild forest country view right in the heart of the city. Well, OK, so L.A. isn't much of a city, but it does show all the Bergman films, and our beach life here is twelve months a year, my love, not three, and we can read without having to be snowed in. You'll have left Sweden by the time you receive this, but tell all your friends we'll see them next summer. I'm so glad you were really fêted, but also glad you see now you wouldn't have lasted long if you were fêted everywhere, all the time.

Tavi has not been swallowed by the lion, but is his old impossible self—only more impossible—he now distains canned food, so I cook pork liver for him, and every day is a holiday for senior dogs.

Tavi sends his love (he's sleeping on the purple couch right now)
But I send the most love
Because I have the most
So much—that we must live more and more intensely
To live it all out
In the next thirty years.
Rupert

Letter from Rupert Pole to Anaïs Nin:
Los Angeles, June 1960

Love:

A little blue today, with no reason really, but whenever I brag about the house I regret it—it is poetic, but the design fascia going around under the roof is really too thin and too fussy—and Eric knows it—he was first to point it out. He thinks it can be remedied later—but I don't. But all the troubles are so minor compared to the overall house. It will be beautiful and *golden*. I'm going to stain all the wood inside and out with gold highlights.

Tavi fell into pool again yesterday but seems none the worse for it. I felt sorry for him whining in the car and let him out (as you warned me not to do). I got talking to the men and then when it was time to go, I found Tavi in the pool, wet and quite happy with himself. I hope he fell down the steps at least!!

Torn between wanting you back and wanting the house to be well along by time you arrive. We will leave it up to fate—as long as you come back well, and with love. Tavi will wait and so will *su amor.*

Siempre,
Rupert

Letter from Anaïs Nin to Rupert Pole:
Paris, June 9, 1960

Darling:

Your letter of yesterday sounded blue, about the duration of the house. I understand how you feel, but judging from my own experience now (my feeling of heaviness of the roof) sometimes these defects get less pronounced as the rest of the house is built. A detail one may not like is less emphatic as another is added. I hope the total effect will make you happy. And please don't think of my return as a deadline for anything or plan any surprise. I shall be so happy to be home with *you*, just you, even if there were no house, only a spot in the desert. It is *you* I miss, want. Great as my passion is for Paris, for Europe, for their way of life, what would it be without you? I think of this when I see lovers walking along the Seine, and my heart tightens. Your letters have helped me so much. I need outward signs of connection. Writing is very real to me, and I know you are doing it for me. I like all the details—Tavi in the pool! Why don't you tie him to a long rope, too short to reach the pool? Poor Tavi!

Last night George Whitman of the Mistral Book Shop gave a farewell to his friends. After ten years at the bookshop he is going to Tokyo. He is a pie-baking bohemian. He made *three* pies like any Midwest housewife, feeding his Beats! We sat in a little room overlooking the Seine, lit by candles in bottles.

Big batch of mail today, a big load of work. Everywhere at once. Weather cool and rainy. I did want to do all I could for the house.

A

Letter from Rupert Pole to Anaïs Nin:
Los Angeles, June 1960

Love:

So terribly much work here. This year the house and Tavi have really kept me running about, and now I'm fighting with Eric about the lights—he's sold on lumiline, which is a cold light and too soft for any kind of work. But again this is minor—the house will be beautiful—if the lights are no good, I'll change them later.

Tavi is brimming with health. He'll outlive all of us. There's no problem in his waiting, but he does miss you.

Never have I felt our relationship so strong, my darling. Please forgive me for not writing every day, but that is too much for me. Next year we'll be in Europe together and hope to see all your friends and to have a little café life, but now all I want is you, my love, before our huge fire, which we will shame into an anemic, lukewarm glow compared to our own fire...

Soon,
R

Letter from Rupert Pole to Anaïs Nin:
Los Angeles, June 11, 1960
Saturday at the beach

My love:

Your letters are so wonderful. I got up late today after the most marvelous *sleep*. Took your letter from the box, then went to the post office to buy *more* air letters, then to the house for a big hassle with Eric. Eric is a rock with all the stubbornness of the Wrights plus the feeling that he is an artist and everything must be perfect (according to him) on his first house. But in spite of disagreements (the study is much too small, the carport too big, etc., etc.) it will be a lovely house, taking full advantage of the view, which is more poetic every time I see it—details, details, but finally got away at 2:00 to get to the beach at 3:00 with water, food, Tavi, took him for a swim, had a beer and a sandwich, and now your letter.

So glad you're meeting artists you like this trip. We can have a wonderful trip through Europe in the summer visiting all you like best.

We move in *July*, to *our* home, with our lake, our pool, our mountains, our sun, and our own moon surpassed only by *our love*.

R

P. S. You say nothing at all about coming back in any letter—ever. My school year ends next week, June 17. Can't have the house ready, but want you back anyway to help make decisions—and to make love.

Letter from Anaïs Nin to Rupert Pole:
Paris, June 13, 1960

My love:

A month ago I left L.A. and it seems like years! The only balm is the beauty of Paris. It is clear the war broke the true spirit of France—the values and civilization—and on top of that breakdown, the influence of violence from America found a fertile ground here. Today they receive Ginsberg and Kerouac as they might a Giraudoux or a Proust. I feel for the first time the full extent of the damage and the end of a civilization. It will be hundreds of years before the sons of A & P become civilized and fund artists like the Wrights. We will never see it. I can't bear the world when I look away from the artist.

Still no word from Renate!

Hope for a letter from you before I leave. I leave Thursday for N.Y. Will phone you from there as soon as I arrive, and leave N.Y. within a day or two. I want to bring back as much money as I can. When is school over, I wonder. I have to swim away all the brioches and croissants! It is 8:00 AM and I am getting ready for a full day. Home is closer. I'm happy. I would not stay away even if I could. You are the core of my life, darling.

A

Letter from Anaïs Nin to Rupert Pole:
Paris, Tuesday, June 14, 1960

My love:

Your little card yesterday. You sound dead tired. And I am not to be able to fly directly home. Too many complications and difficulties with *Cue* magazine, many diplomatic obstacles, rivalries. They want a verbal discussion. I could do it all Friday and arrive for the weekend, but I must see Jacobson. I'm very low. Saturday I will call you up as soon as I arrive, to hear your voice.

Because of the Barrons I went last night to a whole evening of Musique Concrète in the same Salle Gaveau where my father gave 1,000 concerts. Science fiction music, not to be taken seriously, done by Japanese, Italians, French, Americans (the Barrons were too neurotic to send a tape). Distortion of voices, sounds like satellites, planets, wind in the Grand Canyon, much of it like the noise of a jet plane taking off, electric mixers, our ice maker, Tavi's feet scratching on glass, Tavi's medal hitting his dinner dish, you shuffling your school papers. The conductor stands by a board of colored push buttons. Sounds came from all over the hall, from giant plastic forms like Mexican pottery with a top open like an oyster shell. People went to sleep it was so monotonous—whistles, factory grinds, stellar bumps, choked voices. A human voice cut off, and as a Frenchman said aloud: "*Elle a la vie dure!*" The musicians (!?) came on stage for a bow.

I saw the first American drugstore on the Champs Elysées—Snack bars, vegetable juice bars.

I do hope you did not get my letters all at once.

I imagine Reginald is probably preparing a way to move into our house—selfish people outlive the unselfish ones.

I'm getting closer to home.

A

Letter from Anaïs Nin to Rupert Pole:
Paris, June 1960

My darling Chiquito:

Rain, rain, rain, so I live off your Sun. Bouboule the poodle does not object to getting wet, but you can imagine how much time I spend toweling him. Caring for him prevents me from thinking of myself as only a half human being or perhaps a quarter, with all my happiness on Hidalgo Avenue. I do hope the heat continues. My love, don't work too hard. You know I get enthusiastic about work on the house, but I do want you to enjoy your vacation and rest, please, for both of us or

rather the three of us.
Yours,
A

Letter from Anaïs Nin to Hugh Guiler:
Los Angeles, June 1960

Wish I could give you some of this summer weather! Bouboule is out all day. He is interested in archeology. He brings me bones of all shapes and colors. Very disappointed that I do not keep them. We miss you, darling.

I did my ten pages of copying already, and my cold is almost gone. In a way I'm hoping we don't have to go to Europe so you will have time to work on your film.

Wrote a letter to the warden of a man in jail, saying that I believed he had changed from the man he was years ago—then I wondered. I know how much you and I have changed, but we had help. We had a difficult month, you with your health and I psychological. Eventually I tried to reach an enjoyment of little things, home, all I *do* have, but Bogner stirred up the "abdications" and I had difficulties talking. Of course, this state of serenity I achieve here simply not doing anything is not right either. But today I really felt as we did in Acapulco—and it was genuine enough. Why write?

The day was beautiful, calm, windless. Bouboule lay in the sun—hair so white—he never gets black here—just garden dust.

Cuba seems so bad. It upset me to read the paper.

All my love,
A

Letter from Anaïs Nin to Stanley Haggart:
Los Angeles, June 1960

Dear Stanley:

On which planet are you staying now? Neptune, or Plutonic New York? Are you still thinking of traveling?

Wish you could see Rupert's house. I will soon send you a photo. It *is* beautiful (third generation Wright). Desert stone, wood, big glass windows overlooking a pool, Silver Lake Reservoir disguised as a lake, and San Bernardino mountains on the right. It will be ready to live in in two months. I have painted a thousand nail heads with anti-rust silver as expertly as I do my own nails, and I am the gardener of fifteen baby trees. Otherwise I'm inside the new novel.

I don't know my own plans. I may be back in New York by the end of July. Hugo wants to go to Venice.

Affectionately,
Anaïs

P. S. Our N.Y. apartment has become a motel for Cuban family refugees, otherwise I would have offered you the use of it while we were away.

Letter from Anaïs Nin to Hugh Guiler:
Los Angeles, July 6, 1960

Darling:

Mario Grut from Sweden wrote a crazy review, absolutely as silly as *Time* magazine—not hostile, but stupid. He writes me: "I do not think it is possible for a professional artist—be it his or her influence upon the world of limited scope—to strike an attitude of such graciousness and take such humble interest in those who have yet to be recognized, unless it is sincere and based upon the knowledge and practicing of the finest values of civilization. Your visit was short, but the lesson you and Hugo gave us had its immediate result and will long be remembered."

A strange thing has happened, my darling: I was once clear-minded, clearly oriented; I used the image of a searchlight to describe myself in relation to you, you being the nebulous planet. Now I feel I am the nebulous one and you the searchlight. I look to you for clarity. It is as if I had gone down too deep into the unconscious, too deep and where there is no light. I am writing blindly. But I shall let you and Bogner lead me out of this disorganization. The peace helps, the tranquility of the life.

I feel also that I have had too many angry reactions to the actions of others. I do feel it is because of our over-ideal behavior (or at least our attempts), so I get angry that people allow themselves such latitudes. It's the anger of the self-made man for the hobo! We were in danger of becoming reformers!

I received a letter from Renate. Ronnie couldn't sail the boat. Renate couldn't take the boat life. They are selling it. They didn't like the Riviera.

All my love,
A

Letter from Anaïs Nin to Rupert Pole:
New York, August 1960

Bless the telephone company! It is so much better than a letter.

Jim is getting rave reviews for *All Fall Down*, which I could barely get though. He is a celebrity. Marlon Brando is reading his novel; he has interviews by *Esquire*. He will clean up again. God, all it takes to make money is to pander to the lowest form of life—and now he takes himself seriously.

Quietly writing today. New York is so quiet on weekends. Temptation of the Big City for me is: there are telephone booths on almost every corner of the street, which make me think of you! I wish you could have the feeling you could get me at the end of the wire, darling, but first of all I have no permanent home here, then most of the time I manage to call you free from the office and I know the expense would deter you.

I will be able to work on my articles and on my own work. I am copying diary 82 because it has a passage I need for the novel, on the death of my mother, which is very simple and good.

Love, *comme toujours—cariños* of passion,
A

Letter from Jim Herlihy to Anaïs Nin:
Key West, Summer 1960

Dear Anaïs,

I received your letter, in which you clarified our discussion of the novel, character selection, etc. Your point of view is much clearer now; and there is so much more to be said about it that I don't know if it is possible even to begin. I do understand and accept your point of view. I even like it. But it is no longer mine. Does that seem to be contradictory? Perhaps it is, on the surface; but on a deeper level I'm certain it's not. My work has become a part of the total of my life in a way that it had not been previously: my subjects and characters select me as much as I select them. They are like friendships or love affairs to me. If I find myself fascinated, delighted, preoccupied more and more with a group of people, or a character, or a situation, or a combination of them, I come to the typewriter and let them have their lives. (It is a far less objective process than you know; and the novel, for instance, was deeply personal, in that the dilemma and the characters are my own family's.) Since I found myself working in this way, my life has found a new integration and form; it is at once more natural to me and happier. And I feel it has made me freer in profound ways, particularly in the freedom to love. By contrast with these powers, writing, in itself, is of no importance to me—only in that it contributes and forms an essential part of the whole, which is my life. I am not really tempted to concern myself with whether or not this makes me a more or less significant artist, though I confess I am tempted to believe that, in my case, my work is better for it.

I agree with you that the artist must accept every challenge to his vision, so that it can expand. Any kind of freedom in which there is stasis, a lack of growth or expansion, is false. You must trust me to know that my own expansion has been tremendous; if, in your own view of my work, this does not seem to be true, it is purely a question of vantage point, the difference between yours and mine. Yours is of great value to me when I am in shadows or darkness; your insights have cast much light on those moods and conditions in me, and you have contributed to my freedom. Now that my work has taken a face that is strange or unexpected, from the point of view of your own tastes and preferences, I can understand why you would be tempted to place upon it this interpretation: namely, that I am not using my full powers. I can only say, again, that I deeply appreciate your devotion, which is what made you speak out at all; and most important, I hope you will trust me that I have not turned away from the challenging in favor of the easy. Oddly enough, I demand more of myself than ever before...

Love,
Jim

August 17, 1960
Account of The Anaïs Nin Press: January 1, 1960 to August 15, 1960
Books Sold: (Items marked * represent recordings.)
1,116 copies @ 20¢: $223.20
234 @ $1.50: $351.00
10 @ $2.00: $20.00
2 @ $1.25: $2.50
*26 @ $2.45: $63.70
Total: $660.40
Purchases from Press: $28.00
Total: $688.40

Postage, etc. (on behalf of Press) $51.33
Purchases by Press $21.35
Paid to Printer (2-15-60) $456.72
Total Expenses: $529.40

Net Profit: $159.00
Outstanding accounts at this time, about $500.00

Letter from Anaïs Nin to Hugo Nils:
New York, August 1960

Dear Hugo Nils:

I look out of a huge window upon the skyscrapers. New York in the summer is slow-paced, everyone is away. Hugo is cutting his film on Venice in the next room. The view is not as beautiful as your view of Stockholm. The air is clear, sharp, and it looks like a city of giant children's wooden blocks. No graciousness or grace or sensuosities. Violence and toughness. The Village is tough too. Hoboes, clochards, thugs. The Italians and the negroes are at war over the girls. The Beats and the hoboes are rivals. Our new development looks like a sanatorium.

I want to thank you for translating Mario Grut's article. He had promised to send it. Frankly, I find him very confused, and he did misquote and misinterpret. He has mixed up *House of Incest* and the novels. And the stories. And I had asked him not to use the photo he took. I said it would break my heart. It was so bad. But he is the only one who broke my heart in Stockholm, and American journalism is far more inaccurate. In fact, it is usually a burlesque. So, I am still appreciative.

Last Saturday we spent the day with Hill. She was alone and we took her to the beach in a rented car, forty minutes away. It is almost 90 percent negro, and they are very handsome, and look as if they belonged on the beach. We swam and talked. We talked about you. When we came home Hugo showed her the bits of film of Stockholm, you and your daughter and your family home, and the old house where we stopped, and a beautiful shot of the bay with the sailboats looking like brides or a first communion of swans. I told Hill you were my favorite of everyone we met, and she agreed and said you had always been her favorite.

Twilight, not as subtle as yours, lights going on, and you know they are not reading, but watching TV. Your life in Stockholm had more depth than the American life, all surface, all gloss. And boring.

Affectionately,
Anaïs Nin

Letter from Joaquín Nin-Culmell to Anaïs Nin:
Oakland, September 29, 1960

Dear Anaïs,

Your letter received yesterday along with a letter from Hugh asking me to look after some Italian friends of his from Rome. Was most pleased with the former and will take care of the latter…

239

Too bad about things in Cuba. Don't believe I want to send my clippings to Thorvald. He has enough worries as it is with so many refugees on his hands. Kay, as usual, is doing her part too.

Thank you for Eduardo's address. Augusto (Tia Anaïs's eldest son) is now in Chicago with his family. Sorne (Tia Anaïs's youngest) and her husband and family are stuck in Havana and can't seem to leave. What a mess!

Am well although too damned busy at the university. My classes are far too big and I don't know what to do with them. Too bad I take my teaching so seriously! Should learn to give myself with an eye dropper! Too late to learn, though. Hope to do some work of my own soon.

Am having a friend sharing the house until further notice. Met him last year during the opera season. He is trying to settle down in this area and so I offered him the possibility of sharing expenses, etc. Hope it works out. Might be a good way to keep the house occupied while I am away and also cut down on expenses and make my yearly trips to Europe less painful. What do you think? He is an architectural draftsman and very fond of music. Has also read your books and admires you very much. We shall see.

Love,
Joaquín

Letter from Anaïs Nin to Henry Miller:
New York, September 1960

Dear Henry:

I have been working at sorting and arranging our correspondence for the future. Somehow in the medley of the belongings during the war I ended with up a box containing all my letters to you, and yours to me up to a certain date. Some of yours, however, are carbon copies. If this letter reaches you before you go to Japan, would you mind telling me whether you have the originals of these letters, whether you would lend them to me, if they are not in Larry Powell's hands at UCLA? I would like to make a complete series, in order, and I can give the originals to Powell later, since that is your wish, and keep only an offset copy. They are very wonderful and worth preserving. With all our travels they might have been lost many times. The carbons will not offset very clearly. Also, you may have more. Do please let me know, if you can.

Anaïs

Letter from Anaïs Nin to Hugo Raes:
New York, October 10, 1960

Dear Hugo Raes,

What caused my long silence was Hugo's illness, a long one. He caught hepatitis, was four weeks in the hospital, came out, went back again and is now at home but with very little energy. And yet he has to go to Europe on a business trip Oct. 28 but, alas, only to Paris and Rome, not Brussels.

I turned in my novel to Peter Owen in England. It begins with *Solar Barque* (which was only done in a limited edition, expands and completes the other novels.

I have no good title yet. I no longer like *Seduction of the Minotaur*. *Spy* is coming out in Germany. I am busy now taking some light, humorous sketches of characters out of the diary for magazines. I gave a reading at the Maison Française; I read the original French version of *Un Coup de Dés* by Mallarmé, and Daisy Aldan read her English translation. It was very much liked, even by those who do not know French.

I am going to travel with Hugo—I rarely go on quick business trips because going to Europe in a hurry makes me rebellious, but this time, as he is not well, I feel I must go. If we should happen to be in Paris during a weekend, perhaps we could invite you to spend a day with us.

The feverish pace of New York. At 8:30 AM I was at the veterinary for our dog Bouboule. At 9:00 getting manuscripts offset...at 11:00 meeting a Swedish journalist on his way to Cuba...lunch for Maude Hutchins, who came from the country. Tonight the electronic musicians. Last night it was a party for *The Village Voice*. Friends passing through...

Anaïs

New York, October 1960

I arranged the Miller letters in chronological order for three hours. Such a beautiful image I carried away with me, of Rupert in the pool, as Greece must have appeared to the cave dwellers (cave dwellers being New Yorkers). So much light, sun, warmth. Bought presents for everyone at a Japanese shop.

Letter from Anaïs Nin to Rupert Pole:
New York, October 1960

My love:

I have been worried about your constant complaint that I don't tell you everything, and I am trying as hard as I can to be clear. The Miller letters are being appraised. I had to rework them, placing them in chronological order and taking out the personal ones following your suggestion. Peter Owen went away with my novel manuscript without paying because he needs a permit to export money from England, and also because I had no title for the contract; I'm stumped for a title. Never have been before.

I will call you up to see if you agree about the extra week in Europe, which would mean finishing the pool for Christmas. It is something to work for.

I am working so hard I have not done anything for myself, not seen Bouboule, all day out and about and evenings for writing articles. There are four flights for me to walk up, so I don't go out as often as you might think. If I am not invited to dinner I eat in small Italian restaurants, really cheap, on MacDougal St. Tonight I will go to Millie Johnstone to see her son's slides of Guatemala, and this will make me think of you, and our trips, and your slides, and I will be off in a reverie again ...and suddenly I will remember: Rupert said I was so vague, never very specific, or clear, or tell him how it is...

Anaïs

Letter from Anaïs Nin to Rupert Pole:
Paris, November 1960

My love:
I felt I should accept this trip to Paris because of the delay in the Miller letters (they are valuable, but it is a slow business to get estimates from colleges) and our wanting the pool and not to be broke for Xmas.

Spy is on again. André Bay of Stock is tired of Stock's purchase of best sellers from New York magazines; has found a backer, will have his own collection of foreign novels, wants it translated by someone other than Fanchette because he knows Fanchette will never get it done. No advance, just royalties because he is sure it is non-commercial. Whatever has not been a success in America is non-commercial and won't sell. Americans know what sells! But he loves the book, thinks it is original, bold, poetic, and told him things he didn't know about women. Was invited to his apartment to meet his wife, see his books, his own paintings, which are watery, delicate, Debussian, and he said: "Now you see why I like your book." Again, my coming here clinches publication—isn't it strange? Stuhlmann was here a month ago!

Paris is tense. They expect a real fascist coup. De Gaulle has been too severe on protests for Algerian independence. He has police in the bookshops so they won't sell books on Algeria or torture, etc.

Peter Owen is doing only the Lillian section of the new novel—the fool—leaving out two wonderful sections (Mother's death among them).

Leaving tomorrow, finally flying to Milan, taking a train to Florence.

Te quiero siempre. Tu mujer,
A

Paris, November 4, 1960
At 5:30 I awakened with the following thought: I should abandon my life with Hugo and my life with Rupert, stay in Paris among the artists, publish my Diary and begin new *vrai vie.*

I saw the life of Paris as opening my compassions, natural, impulsive, instructive, giving free reign to my eroticism, imagination, creation. I even saw the evil, the sensuality, the honesty of it—a series of images—two plays—*Biedermann et les Incendiaires* and *The Balcony*—the whore, Miller's world, of myself as I am truly, and not as the loving wife of Hugo, the helpmate of Rupert, the mother or sister or friend. It was such a strong impulse that I went to the window, opened the curtain, as if to escape from all the Crillon symbolized, the soft bed, the valet, the *femme de chambre*, even the dog with his red coat and red leash (like other fashionable women—*un chien de spectacle*, a show dog), and Hugo in a conference, on the phone, talking of business, Hugo at dinner always while I have a martini and want to enjoy the evening talking. I have a project by which I can get his firm to pay my traveling expenses and wonder why we couldn't eat at a bistro for 700 francs and be carefree. I wanted to escape out the window. I saw the rue Boissy d'Anglas—a stormy night. I went quietly into Hugo's room as if he could help me. He was asleep (with sleeping pills). I saw in the mirror a woman still desirable, but not young, kept alive by doctors. I knew I was a prisoner of my fears. I could not endure poverty, solitude.

I would return to my role—a smartly dressed woman, perfumed by Guerlain, carrying a slim lavender and gold umbrella, in a black suit, a fur cape, detached from the people I see, their interests (politics and economics).

I would return to bed, read a Simenon book in which he describes a hundred times a man awakening to the disconnection from his life.

I fell asleep. I dreamed I was going to church, but it was on an incline, and the chairs were kept from slipping downwards only by being fastened together. I sat on the last one feeling precariousness—then the sea rose and began to engulf me. I walked uphill just fast enough to keep from drowning, but my legs felt wet and cold and stiff. Everything was being covered by the sea.

I slept.

I awakened again at eight. The noises in the street seemed like those of a revolution.

I write to Rupert. I cannot feel him. I do not feel Hugo. I see and hear things that charm or fascinate me, but it is all deadened by an incurable illness.

Moments of sweetness. The taxi driver quoting Socrates and Balzac, the small intimate restaurants, the gentleness and politeness, the personal, intimate feeling between people, a waiter is not a waiter, a client is not a client, a relationship is established, he knows me, knows what I eat. I know him, what distinguishes him among other waiters.

I see George Whitman, a ghost; I see André Bay, a tall, handsome man, editor at Stock, who loves *Spy*, paints lyrically and is like Debussy in the world of Ondine.

On rue de Lappe, Bal Musette is covered with colored posters. The musicians are up in a balcony. A woman is playing piano like a pianola-accordion. A gigolo. A whore. Servants. Montique, St. Geneviève. Harry's Bar. Election night. Bouboule is a link with humanity. Silence is broken. Waitresses, shopkeepers, even bookkeepers. Henri Michaux is a misanthrope. I belong nowhere. Allegra—a pixie in a beaded evening dress—an incongruous, thoughtful *maitresse de la maison*, playing. Serenity and order of countryside. Allegra knocks at midnight to talk, a role, hard brilliance. Pinocchio is at the head of the table—red tablecloth embroidered with white flowers and black dishes. One candle, one rose. Roses in fingerbowls. A film show. Want to weep at the beauty.

Letter from Anaïs Nin to Hugo Raes:
Los Angeles, November 1960

Dear Hugo:

We passed through Paris like a comet, or a satellite. I can hardly believe it. As it was for Hugo's work, we spent all our time with his clients.

Here I live on top of a hill, in a house with eight big glass windows opening over a pool and a lake, but chose a small room without a view to work in. As a friend said, your thoughts bounce back at you in a small room; they do not dissipate into space.

They say Henry Miller will settle in Europe so you may meet. I think he wants a change of cycle, following his divorce from Eve, the best wife he ever had, and an escape from the lack of respect America gives him, official, I mean. It hurts him to

see Durrell get so much official recognition.
Anaïs

December 21, 1960
Arrival in Paris with Hugo.

Letter from Anaïs Nin to Rupert Pole:
Paris, December 21, 1960

My love:
The trip was rather rough and we were slowed down by bad weather. Bouboule and I slept through most of it. He is a great traveler.
I have so much to do: a book show (for Xmas), Festival of Toys for children in the Science Fiction vein, new plays, concerts, a surrealist exhibit... Every day I say to myself: "This means another tree in our garden," and that sends me cheerfully out in the rain! I miss our life. You have truly made me love home more than travel! I wish Bouboule and I could chew on your ears—they tasted so good!
A

Paris, December 24, 1960
Hotel de Crillon
All those who signed the plea for Algeria are out of work and in trouble—actors suffered the worst as they cannot act—writers always manage. People are so tired of the war.
Exhibitions of Pop Art. A large plywood board as large as a wall. Fake sponges. Real ones. They cover plywood boards with them, place them on, spray with cobalt blue powder. It looks like the craters of the moon. Or they make ink-blots with colors, casually folded paper, open, exhibited, only when the colors have blotched real well. There was an enormously intricate cage at the entrance, with labyrinths, spirals, complex meanderings, and it was filled with bewildered lovebirds. When Zadkine came in he noticed them and exclaimed in a loud voice: "What grotesque sadism! To enclose birds in such a torture prison! They will die of boredom, sorrow and pneumonia. Anyone who thought that up should be locked in such a cage too!"
Paris is full of refugees from Algeria.

Paris, December 1960
Graciella Archibald talks about the plight of Cuban refugees, thousands of them. Her nephew is being trained by the American Army to fight Castro—all of them are 17 to 20 years old. Cubans were promised training and arms. Charlie Cárdenas escaped to Miami and from there to Mexico.
People comment on my sound knowledge of politics. It comes from Hugo and Rupert, who have the same attitudes and opinions.
I have no compassion for the wealthy refugees and my relatives who had more than the poor, the workers, the negros, and us when we were poor. They have lived spoiled and selfishly like aristocrats.

Letter from Anaïs Nin to Roger Bloom:
Los Angeles, December 1960

Dear Roger:

I went to Paris to help Hugo with his work, to watch over his health, not for myself. But Paris won me over just the same, with its unequalled charm. Went to the quiet bookshop by the Seine, the Mistral. Heard Henry had passed by there a week before. Visited Henri Michaux, whom I consider the greatest of all poets, who is untranslated. He is old and sick, and so I am glad I saw him, to console him for the fact that he was not published in America in spite of all my efforts, in spite of the fact that he has used drugs for inspiration and that drugs are so fashionable now. So I explained to him the reason for this was that most Americans like to remain outside of experience, to be objective and scientific about it. They prefer Huxley's scientific, cool descriptions, not the kind of oceanic, unconscious wildness of Michaux's experience, which sweeps you into visions and dreams so intense you think you will never return to earth.

I am so glad you enjoyed your typewriter. And that it makes writing pleasurable.

About Djuna Barnes: I was a beginner in writing, a young woman, when she was in full bloom, a handsome, red-haired, full-bodied woman I used to admire from afar on the terrace of a café, in a tailored suit, seeming like an Amazon. Later, when I wrote *The Winter of Artifice*, I wrote her a long, admiring letter that she did not answer. Later I heard there was so much resemblance between our lives that she said I had stolen her life story. I answered that I could not have stolen her life because I was writing about my own. (Particularly, the father characterization must have been similar). The great difference between us was that she was truly a lesbian and I am not. During the war I used to see her in the Village, and she looked different; she looked like a masculine maiden aunt and had a tongue everyone feared. She will not see anyone who wants to see her as a writer, but will talk to strangers in bars. I finally met her at the house of her lawyer. She was bitter and caustic. I still love *Nightwood* as one of the most poetic novels ever written. She felt she had a copyright on the name Djuna. She also told me, by way of a friend, that her father had invented the name for her. I had found the name in a dictionary of Welsh names, and used it for my character, probably out of my respect for Djuna Barnes, as I remember.

I think Henry went to Paris to make a break from the loss of Eve. He felt that, I hear. And at his age I doubt if he will marry again. I think he also felt badly about the easy way in which Durrell got acclaim, what took Miller thirty years to get, and even then, the real, open, official respect comes to him from Europe. America has never said anything about him openly, or is, I believe, proud of him. I know one critic who thinks well of him but does not dare to admit it. But I am sure he will come back for the sake of his children, as he can only see them in the summer, and I doubt if he will be able to pay their way to Europe every summer.

Grove Press wanted to publish *Tropic of Cancer*, but it is Henry who refused. I think he recoiled from the kind of three-ring circus that was accorded *Lady Chatterley* in New York at the time of the obscenity trial. In England it was more or less dignified, but in N.Y. it was a spectacle that was most humiliating to writers and critics.

Anaïs

January 1961
Dreams:
1. I am visiting Larry and Ruby Wallrich. They are in the bookshop, *en famille*, with their two children, as they were when we were friendly. I trusted him. They were making coffee for me in the back room. There was an atmosphere of books, family, and Ruby's gentleness and friendship. I woke up to the realization that this concealed his dishonesty in his handling of my books.
2. Rupert is preparing an injection of blood. I'm very disturbed because I want him to make love instead.
3. Gonzalo is there, at his best, groomed. But he has just driven Helba away. He is telephoning someone. He tells me he will marry and make a new life. I weep and ask why I wasn't able to save him from destruction.

Letter from Anaïs Nin to Hugh Guiler:
Los Angeles, February 9, 1961

You poor Cat, it's a good thing you don't hate the snow and cold as much as I do. And I feel badly about your film difficulties. I should really look into technicians here in Hollywood, for I believe they are superior to the N.Y. people who only work for TV. I don't know where to start. But superimposition should not be as hard as all that. Perhaps you should take the job to England. Americans don't use their intelligence on technique; they think the machine can do it all.

Daisy sent me a tape of the Mallarmé reading we did. It is exceptionally good, so good that I would like to make a record of it. I read French better than I read English, or perhaps the language is more poetic.

Gilbert Neiman will publish a fragment of the *Minotaur* in *In Between Worlds*.

Bouboule, now called Piccolo because it seems to suit his nature well, is well and happy and frisky. But he cannot get used to being left in the car.

You don't mention your own notes on analysis and your father that I sent you, which inspired the moon section in *Minotaur*. About your Venice film. I had some thoughts yesterday. I saw it this way, the sea lapping, corroding, eating away, caressing disintegrating everything slowly and finally its submergence. Coming gradually, water on the rocks, on the steps, in the cellars, eating the wood, wearing away, and then the flood, the superimpositions, the sinking, the unconscious, the double image. The sea wins. In spite of exorcisms, cleaning, repairs, rituals of the "wedding" of the two.

A

Letter from Anaïs Nin to Roger Bloom:
Los Angeles, February 1961

Dear Roger:
The reason I want to publish our correspondence someday, in the far-off future, if possible, is to impress upon the world the need to help man recreate himself. Did you know America has the greatest number of mental cases? And the greatest number of crimes?

You see, I feel stealing is symbolic; it is done not for its own sake (money) but for some other deeper reason (anger, sense of injustice, of having been wronged, deprived). There are some genuine criminals, but they are closer to the insane. I can give you a most interesting example of what I mean. My father was a spoiled pianist, adored by women, always on tour, who should never have married and had three children (a Don Juan). He was not interested in us (he had wanted us not to be born). My mother was too worried by him and his egocentric demands to pay us much attention. So, because I did not have what is called a "close" family, I took a dislike to "family" life of all kinds, wanted to be an adventurer, a nomad, a traveler. But it was out of anger for having been deprived, really. And by dint of exploration and finally of understanding, a little late (but better late than never), I am beginning to love home, and children, and others' close family life rather than turn away from it. From this early "anger" derives a great many hostile acts we are all capable of, an anger that is really envy and jealousy, and a kind of revengefulness for what was not given to us.

Don't worry about my occasional complaints about my work! I am unable to find a publisher. I was never a bestseller, and they have all given me up. Well, I decided that instead of feeling frustrated I would publish the books myself. But now I find that the distributors are dishonest and never pay, and neither do the bookshops. So I am, in a way, stymied. That is why sometimes I exclaim. And also for ten years I supported and helped Henry, and yet he has not once extended any help with publishers. I even paid for the publication of *Tropic of Cancer* when he started out. He can get anything published that he wants to by praising it. Yet I know my work means a great deal to many people. It has insight. My readers always talk about understanding themselves better. Incidentally, I cannot send you Miller's books, or my diary under the conditions of censorship. You will have to read them when you are pardoned, as I am sure you will be someday.

More soon,
Anaïs

Letter from Anaïs Nin to Alan Swallow, publisher:
Los Angeles, February 1961

Dear Alan Swallow:

It is many years since we visited you in Denver, when I was on my first visit West. I was reminded of it when I saw your name in Glenn Clairmonte's books and talked about you with Maude Hutchins, whose *Victorine* you published.

As you probably know, for years I continued with my own Press, doing my own books, but I am having difficulties with distributors who do not pay, and so I am two books behind and seeking a new solution. I have one new unpublished manuscript, and one that has long been out of print and for which I get orders: *Winter of Artifice* (which I meant to put together with *The Voice* and *Stella*, as three novelettes). I wonder if there is anything we can work out together. Would you care to do the new manuscript *Seduction of the Minotaur*, or the reprint? I could guarantee that I myself would sell 1,000 copies. Do you have any organization such that you might consider distributing my books? They have sold well and continuously without advertisement, without reviews, without any outside help, at the rate of 2,000 or 3,000 a year. The Avon paper edition of *A Spy in the*

House of Love sold 120,000 copies (but the editor who worked with Avon is no longer with them, and now, with Hearst ownership, the titles and quality of the books have changed). Have you any suggestions? I know you only print hardcover books. Would you like to do an omnibus of *Cities of the Interior*, which I did in a limited edition and put a hard cover on it with your imprint? Do think this over and write me. There is one added factor, that I have always said whichever publisher puts out my novels I will give an option on the Diaries (for the future).

For the distribution of the books I would give sixty per cent on condition that they are paid for in cash. Do you have copies of my books? Shall I send you some?

Sincerely yours,
Anaïs Nin

Letter from Alan Swallow to Anaïs Nin:
Denver, February 13, 1961

Dear Anaïs Nin,

It was a real pleasure to hear from you. You mention having read Glenn Clairmonte's book on Calamity Jane. This is in my Sage Books imprint—an imprint devoted solely to books about the American West. Of course, under the Alan Swallow imprint I do the work in my literary materials—original poetry, fiction, criticism, etc.

The enclosed overall catalog will indicate this to some extent.

Furthermore, you do not seem aware that about a year and a half ago I did enter the field of "quality paperbooks" with the Swallow Paperbooks series. The enclosed list will indicate something of this, too, which is now up well more than 20 volumes.

I should be interested in your work a great deal. My rates are the very standard royalties on sliding scale for cloth editions (I do a great many now offering cloth and paper simultaneously, and it seems to work pretty well; or sometimes offer the cloth for a time and then also offer a paper edition later), and the regular royalty for paperbacks.

First, about your new manuscript, unpublished. Indeed, I should like very much to see it.

Second, *Cities of the Interior*. I would be glad to see a copy of this as you have done it. Perhaps, by some device we could go ahead with this as a Swallow Paperbook, too—or I could take over some distribution, etc. I do a bit of distribution for others but do not like to do so, concentrating primarily on my own books, of course.

Third, the reprint material you mention. I am sorry to say that the only two books of yours I actually own are *Under a Glass Bell* (which I see contains *Winter of Artifice*, which you mention); and *Ladders to Fire* (which I see contains something called *Stella*). It is possible I could be interested in reprinting *Winter of Artifice* or perhaps the new arrangement you suggest of that title plus *The Voice* (which I have never seen) and *Stella*. I would need to know why you wish that arrangement, the length of *The Voice*, and if the versions of *Winter of Artifice* and *Stella* that I have in those two books would be the versions you would wish to use in the reprint. At least I shall be glad to consider these various alternatives.

Cordially,
Alan Swallow

Postcard from Anaïs Nin to Gunther Stuhlmann:
Los Angeles, February 1961

Dear Gunther:
What made me write to Swallow was not hearing from Atlantic Press, to whom you sent my books. I hear indirectly Swallow is interested. I'll be back March 14 and will be able to talk. I'll give you the Miller letters then, and stories, etc.

As Atlantic Press wrote me a personal letter once, do you think you might get a definite answer by suggesting we all meet? I would have liked an answer from them before hearing Swallow's offer. Originally I had thought of him only as distributor, but he now publishes quality paperbacks and at least I'd be free of the book business, which we agree is not good for a writer.

Hope you've avoided bad colds after such a rough winter.

À *bientôt*, your friend,
Anaïs

Letter to from Anaïs Nin to Alan Swallow:
Los Angeles, February 1961

Dear Alan Swallow:
On Friday I will have sent to you by way of my agent Gunther Stuhlmann the new manuscript of *Seduction of the Minotaur*. Today I sent you a copy of *Cities of the Interior*. This is a hardbound copy, but I also printed a limited edition of paperbound. You can study the various possibilities. If you have the Dutton edition of *Under a Glass Bell* you will find the *Winter of Artifice* and *The Voice* are in it, and in my own edition they are both there. They are two novelettes long out of print and for which I get requests all the time. *Stella* (at the beginning of *Ladders to Fire*), turned out to be a novelette all by itself, unrelated to the long novel I wrote subsequently, so I left it out of *Cities of the Interior*, which includes all the novels except the last one. I found through the years that the plan of writing a continuous novel and publishing the volumes as they were written was not good. People did not get a sense of the total design, and the early volumes went out of print. I think to have a real impact they should all be published together in one omnibus volume, a reprint. If you should want to do this then I will simply send the existing edition (incomplete) to England to be distributed there, so as to give you a clear field for the complete work. My best seller has been *Under a Glass Bell*, used in schools as text, and constantly reordered every six months. Whatever you decide to do I will get rid of my own leftover copies so as to make the way clear for your edition. I have had offers from England, but the shipping cost made it so it would barely cover the cost of the books; but in this case, if the books are available under your imprint, then I don't mind. I can send you my good mailing list. And I will naturally forward all the orders that come to me.

So as I see it there are several possibilities:

Taking over *Cities of the Interior* and putting your imprint on it—2,000 or 3,000 copies. I don't know the cost of that. Does it mean redoing the binding? Binding these in hardbound, and making a paper edition? And then publishing *Seduction of the Minotaur* as an "End" separately?

Reprinting *Under a Glass Bell* or changing the imprint of it. (I don't know how many I have left but I can let you know).

Reprinting *House of Incest*, which also sells continuously (or changing the imprint, or taking them all *at cost* and distributing them, and when they are finished then reprint them in paperback). As you can see, we have to study various combinations.

Gunther will write you. He is my agent and a friend and very pleasant to work with.

In any case, whatever book you do, you will be my sole publisher in the U.S.A.

Do write me soon as in March I will be on the road again!

Anaïs Nin

Letter from Alan Swallow to Anaïs Nin:
Denver, March 6, 1961

Dear Anaïs,

I have now read the materials you sent me, including the manuscript of the new novel, which came from Gunther Stuhlmann.

I think it makes just about perfect sense that I become your U.S. publisher. The sales of your works have apparently demonstrated that they are not suitable or of interest to the large commercial publishers. Yet, there is a kind of victimization involved for an author to be handled by too many smallish "avant garde" publishers who seem to be fly-by-night much of the time, who appeal to a certain clientele (an avid one, but a limited and changeable one); or for you to be attempting self-publication of the works. I fall in between. I don't manage the very large, large sales; but I am a determined and persistent devil, and I manage a very respectable sale for the materials in which I am interested. (Indeed, for many books I feel that my methods will get more sales over a period of time than can be achieved by others—for I have seemed to develop them for the kind of work in which I am interested, which I find will not support themselves well upon a publishing situation of high overhead, etc., but are quite satisfying to me and, in the end, to the author.) As I say, for the kind of sales that seems to be your destiny in this country, I feel that I am in a better situation than anyone else. I am loyal to my titles; I keep them in print if humanly possible.

Furthermore, I publish only what I admire, and everybody knows this; and I admire your work. So it should be a fairly good "wedding" of work and publisher, I think. I shall hope so, anyway!

I would be willing to embark upon a long-range program with your work. One cannot do it just overnight. So far as taking over any of your present stock, there is no problem about imprint; I would fashion a label or I would tip in a new title page to indicate this. Physically it could be done.

All right, in summary: I am indicating my willingness, even my eagerness to do this. I would sign any contracts, of course, after seeing your willingness in the overall

plan and the particular contracts, etc., that is, that they be such that I can approve. I don't think we would have any problems there. The big problem now is the ultimate intent and then the development of the plans.
   Cordially,
   Alan Swallow

Letter from Rupert Pole to Anaïs Nin:
Los Angeles, April 1961

LOVE:
   Yesterday (Sunday) first day of spring and 94 degrees in the shade—so I put on a bikini (bought one here) and worked and swam and worked more and swam more, and, of course, without you to tell me not to overdo it, ended up with royal sunburn—could hardly move today and had very rough day teaching. The garden is going to look really wonderful, but hard to work alone day after day without anyone to admire what you are doing—hint.
   Love, you misunderstood me on the phone. I didn't suggest you ask for a raise. You had just told me you would have to work more days to fill out the week (you never said anything about the flu then) and I blew up because I miss you and thought it petty of them to haggle over a day or two when they pay you $100 a week. Have missed you more this trip than ever before, perhaps because of spring vacation, or because I'm doing so many things I want to show you.
   I put the top down on the car and it's wonderful, but it's so heavy I can't get it back up again!
   Must go now; I'm snowed under with school work after Easter. Heard all the dogs were in the Easter parade in N.Y.—wonder if you were there with Piccolo.
   Hurry back. I'm keeping the pool, and the bed, WARM...
   R

Letter from Anaïs Nin to Rupert Pole:
New York, April 1961

Darling:
   So much to write you that I couldn't get going.
   It's too windy to go out. Both Piccolo and I get blown away, almost in the Hudson! He misses you. He runs after tall, slender, young men, but when he sees their faces he is just as disappointed as I am!
   Thorvald's daughter was in a coma for 56 hours, cause unknown.
   Joaquín was here for a visit. The Cuban youth are about to fight Castro, which will be tragic, bloody, terrible.
   Swallow and Stuhlmann are working things out very nicely—same type of men, sincere and not greedy. He will pay the *cost* of books' printing and give me regular royalties on their sale.
   Time is dragging. I'm just as busy but I do less in the evenings. I'm beginning to like this quarter—the Village was getting rowdy. Piccolo likes 57th Street, because it's full of poodles! What a healthy dog, and he is 20 times lovelier than his relatives!

I think you ought to work up a guitar program for FM radio, to keep your singing going.

Te quiero, mucho,

A

Letter from Alan Swallow to Anaïs Nin:
Denver, April 1961

Dear Anaïs,

Things are shaping up more clearly now since *Under a Glass Bell* and *House of Incest* will be out of print shortly. The one imponderable left is the quantity of *Cities of the Interior*. At the same time, I completed my royalty payments and found out I was a bit better off than I had expected.

So I think we can get down to cases.

1. Sign immediately a contract for *Seduction of the Minotaur*. Price should go up to $3.75 cloth and $1.65 paper on *Seduction*, I think. I propose the same terms regarding rights, percentages of royalty. Publication either Sept. or Oct. Advance $500.00.

2. Sign immediately a contract for the novelettes. (What *is* the title to be?) Same proposal of $3.50 and $1.45 paper. Advance of $250.00. Publication Sept. or Oct.

3. Sign immediately contracts for reprinting *Under a Glass Bell* and *House of Incest*, $1.00 each, paper edition only, with assignment of your negatives to me. Advance $100.00 each.

These advances total $950.00. I am willing to make it $200.00 a month on these starting May 1 until I've paid $950.00. Also publication Sept. or Oct., or even Aug.

I must know the titles, prices, etc. no later than May 15 so I can get them into my new annual catalog (hence, into *Trade List Annual* and the very important *Books in Print*. If we miss those, it would be a pity).

Cordially,
Alan

Letter from Anaïs Nin to Hugh Guiler:
Los Angeles, April 21, 1961

I am so sorry you had difficulties with Harry Partch. That was a beautiful, a generous and a very subtle and tasteful letter you wrote him. And I am glad you kept your temper, and handled him so well. It is a terrible thing to see those misdirected angers destroy the valuable things, your appreciation of him, and I am afraid that all of us are guilty of such misplacements. He is angry at the way he has been treated as an artist (because the only artist who succeeds is the one who plays the game), at the failure of his last production, and he lashes out at the very ones who are faithful and devoted to him.

I was about to write you on a similar theme. I feel that Bogner very often stressed how we judge in others the very trait we do not like in ourselves. I think, just as Harry hurled his anger at you (an innocent victim of it), we attack anxiety in the other, knowing it is our own we would like to be rid of.

It is reasonable, I think, to wish for a life that would put less strain on our already strained temperaments. We would like to be like Piccolo. I am learning from him! The only occasion in which he is definitely nervous and difficult is in the car. He has a hysterical need to get out of it, not to be left in it, to leap out the window. Should I go on training him or let him stay home, since that is what he likes, just like Mitou, remember, when you wanted to take her to the beach?

A

Letter from Anaïs Nin to Roger Bloom:
Los Angeles, April 22, 1961

Dear Roger:

It takes me days to recover from the intensity of N.Y. to catch up with my correspondence, to catch up with the neighbors' demands and invitations. A friend, Leslie Blanch, came with real trouble: Romain Gary is divorcing her after eighteen years of marriage, not because he wants to, but because Jean Seberg, the young actress, wants him to (the French believe in mistresses, not divorces, usually), and the film she was working on, *Madame L*, collapsed as many Hollywood films do from internal conflicts, bad scenarios, squabbles between producers, actors and directors, etc., etc.

Yes, I understand what you mean about knowledge of the arts; I do feel that because the arts were disparaged and looked down upon in America, they are paying the price in crime. It is when you are given things to believe in, to enjoy, to love, that you do not get angry and rebellious and destructive. Art teaches creativity, and America has been very anti-art. Every child, as even we were in public school in New York, was exposed to all kinds of influences, yet what protected me was not external laws, police, or fear of consequences, it was my love of other things, music, painting, books, which made up a world of beauty as against whatever world of ugliness I came upon. Recently I found much ugliness in the commercial aspect of literature and it almost stopped me from writing. There is an ugly world and a beautiful world that one can choose if one knows about it. With the Kennedys, I think America is entering into its golden era of education, of art, of knowledge of how to create and believe in one's self-made world. The knowledge of art has always made human beings better. The knowledge of science does not affect human beings one way or the other, but art does.

It's funny, I can't see the connection, or any connection between your past and the person you are now. No sign of natural love of violence or money in any of your thoughts and feelings today. Is that true?

Anaïs

Letter from Alan Swallow to Anaïs Nin:
Denver, April 25, 1961

Dear Anaïs,

Four of the contracts now signed. I sent back those for *House of Incest* and *Under a Glass Bell* yesterday.

All that remains for settlement is about the stock of *Cities* and the agent has promised a list and price indication soon.

I had heard that Grove might try *Tropic of Cancer*. Glad your original preface will be in it. Can you tell me the date they will release? Would like to use the timing for some publicity about your books, you see.

Cordially,
Alan

Letter from Anaïs Nin to Hugh Guiler:
Los Angeles, April 27, 1961

Darling:

Yesterday I was invited to a dinner for Varda at Holiday House. I did a little writing, had a massage, did gardening, much resting, and drove halfway, the rest of the way with Renate and Ronnie. Their house is right on the beach.

I was relaxed. There were about 20 people. Piccolo was his usual success and Jeannie Murphy had a dog named Tequila exactly the same size and age, but tan, and they played together all evening, made everybody laugh. I left early, about 11 o'clock, and I was utterly exhausted. I can't understand it. Today I was "recovering" as if I had really stayed out all night.

Today Piccolo and I walked up the hill at noon, and I took a swim in my private pool, no one around, but it was too windy for a sunbath. I wonder what your plans are. I'm sorry I called at such a bad time Saturday. I know we had agreed not to call, but I felt something in the air, a need to hear your voice.

Tomorrow writing, massage, and a visit to Renate and Ronnie. I will call you Sunday for news.

Do you have news of our friend? Was he on that ill-fated invasion, the Bay of Pigs? The American idea that if everybody concentrates on politics the world would run better is so false. Never was there a Darker Age politically. I yearn for the romantic years before the war when no one knew what was happening.

The place is full of wild yellow poppies. They fold up and go to sleep late in the afternoon until it gets warm in the morning.

Piccolo does *not* understand about the bees and the red ants. He chases them both. Nor does he know the difference between male and female.

Love,
A

Letter from Anaïs Nin to Roger Bloom:
Los Angeles, May 1961

Dear Roger:

I hope you received your copy of *Tropic of Cancer*. I wish Grove Press had made it less expensive—so many of my friends can't get it—but now I hope it will be in paperback. Isn't it amazing that it did not have any trouble? America has finally become mature on the freedom of expression—it is in full bloom with flowers that smell like honey.

Los Angeles State College offered me a job teaching Creative Writing, but I've been away from Hugo for such a long time.

Your friend,
Anaïs

Letter from Anaïs Nin to Hugh Guiler:
Los Angeles, October 6, 1961

Darling:

It was rather sad to know you were in N.Y. for only two days, to talk with you, and then to feel you gone again. Never expected such a long separation. There was no mention of Paris, so I am sending you only one letter to Lausanne.

Swallow sent four hundred review copies. He has done the job well. I hope when you get to Lausanne you get the two books I sent you, *Winter of Artifice* with your engravings, and *Seduction* with the Varda collage. I did not dedicate them as I thought you might want to give them away. It cost one dollar to airmail, so I can send you two more for important people only. Otherwise they take a month.

You missed Gunther in Paris. He will be back Oct. 20. I will miss Peter Owen but I am glad of that.

Tracey Roberts, the ideal actress for Sabina in *Spy*, now has the flu. She sounds more and more like my characters. Weeps over the telephone, acts so dynamically but really helpless, and fights helplessness... Mirages. Mirages.

This confirms my desire to be Piccolo has the power to break my somber moods. I don't know how such a small body can convey so much intensity of feeling. He still loves Alyssum flowers, white, and it is quite a sight to see him walking among them, eating them, or else sitting on top of a rock so he can survey the landscape. He will write you soon. At the moment he is sleepy, and something tells him he had better continue to sleep as there is a bath in the offing, for weekend visitors. The druggist told me he had a poodle, and he stopped the tearing with cod liver oil every day, so I am giving it to him faithfully. Would much rather be taking care of you, darling, but you move so fast, I would have been unable to keep up with you, though once I wanted to try. After this trip we owe each other a good quiet time together.

All my love, and Piccolo's,

A

Letter from Anaïs Nin to Rupert Pole:
New York, November 1961

My love:

A girl from Chicago University is writing her thesis on me (it will be published); Gotham has decided to give an autograph party the first week in December; and Marguerite Young, the writer I most admire, is reading from *Winter of Artifice* to her New School class as a classic example of stream of consciousness. How I wish we could have celebrated this with martinis! But the phone has been a blessing, picked my spirits up, gave me courage.

Poor darling, what a torment Reginald has become. I must come back and help you. It's so depressing. I hope the nurse's reaction won't be to take care of you instead! That would be mine!

Letter from Piccolo:

Dear Rupert: There is a serious shortage of dog psychologists. Nobody understands that I only pee at the United Nations just to be polite and international, I pee on 57th at the corner of Tiffany's just to be fashionable, but I reserve my fullest pee for my temporary home, to assert my temporary ownership, and each time the old German elevator man comes out and grumbles. It's true I'm not paying any rent. It's a cold, rainy day. Anaïs tells me you had the same. She hangs on that phone. I don't feel I own her whole heart! But she brought me leftovers from her dinner with rich couscous.

I want you to know I was made a permanent member of the United Nations. It's about time. I'm the most peaceful member they will ever have. I have not been such a good letter writer this time because, frankly, I spend all of my energy following Anaïs about. Up and down stairs, elevators, conference rooms. I hear so many languages that I'm all mixed up. What adds to the confusion is that the girl from Nepal in the sari has an English accent. Why? And the minister from Liberia has a French accent, and his French representative has a Harvard accent, and the Haitians speak like Marius, the Italians sound like Russians. Finally, all I recognize is my name. In the evenings I'm so tired that all I can do is pick up the bathroom rug and lie on the cool floor—the steam heat is terrible. As soon as Daisy goes out Anaïs turns it off. As soon as Daisy comes home she turns it on.

I'm worried about my weight. I can't stand up in the wind here—I get swept off my feet. Now I don't mind being swept off my feet by a pretty girl like you do, but not by any old wind!

Love,
Piccolo

Letter from Anaïs Nin to Tracey Roberts:
New York, November 1961

Dearest Tracey:

I understand your dilemma with the *Spy* film. You must never be concerned about what Gunther Stuhlmann writes: he is a friend. What happens is this. He told me that he did not know what to ask, that he had been told that the writer would receive five per cent of the total budget for the picture, and the screenwriter the same.

I am with you in this, not for money. This is important for you as an actress, and for me as a writer. Gunther will always do what I say. The only problem has been the order, which comes first, and, according to Gavin Lambert, the usual procedure is for the producer to assign the screenplay, with an advance.

The Gotham Book Mart is giving a big autograph party December 7, so I am terribly busy, but glad to be busy. Hoping all is well with you...

Anaïs

Letter from Alan Swallow to Anaïs Nin:
Denver, November 19, 1961

Anaïs, dear:

Don't be too anxious about reviews. I think that they misunderstood. But I think we get nowhere by pressure, enquiry, etc., about reviews. The only thing to do is for you to go ahead and contact more and more people to whom we have not sent material earlier, if you wish. But lay off the standard review media. We can't cure their stupidity; and too much personal contact does harm, builds resentments. So I have a hands-off policy; if they choose to review, all right; if they don't, no sense counting on anything except their stupidity. And in the end they start to come around, like *The New York Times*, who wrote to me for information, and that is a much better situation for all! I do hope they will review, for it is the most important place other than perhaps *Library Journal* (if we can hope for good library sales at all). I think a few of the slower places will come through.

I think some of the academic people (if one doesn't consider this a curse word) will come through gradually. I know a couple who have already proposed that they would like to deal with you in articles.

What is surprising is that some of your friends have sufficiently misunderstood or been "low" enough that they have not gone ahead to secure some places for you to review. That business about *Solar Barque* and *Seduction* has puzzled them, I guess. I upbraided Felix Pollak at Northwestern, who said you had asked him to review, and he apparently had made the mistake of considering *Seduction* to be *Solar Barque* over again. He hasn't replied to that upbraiding yet. He is probably angry with me. I begin to think he is a pipsqueak.

I wish Geismar could help more. I think he could. He overstates the situation at *The New York Times*. They *do* review a number of my books every year. And if they miss yours, I shall be very disappointed and puzzled.

Please show my letter to Daisy Aldan. I am sorry that I can't go for her book. It was good of you to think of me; and I appreciate what you try to do for your friends. Too bad, as you noted, that they don't return the favors more!

Well, we'll keep at 'em! And win, by golly.

Take care of your lovely self.

Love,
Alan

Letter to Anaïs Nin from Alan Swallow:
Denver, November 19, 1961

Dear Anaïs,

So good to hear your sweet voice. Glad to talk with you.

The one who wrote me from *The New York Times Book Review* was Nona Balakian. Now, whether or not you should approach her directly, I don't know. I tend, as I said, to lay off. She has been good to me and my books, on the whole, and I think she is interested and will try for something. If you already know her and thus have a contact, then I would say phone her or get in touch with her on a friendly basis, not particularly asking for a review; just assuming that she is going to arrange it. But if you don't know her or have a very informal, non-pressure way of getting in touch with her, leave her alone. My policy has been by far the best so far, for good, serious books.

Alan

Letter from Joaquín Nin-Culmell to Anaïs Nin:
Oakland, November 20, 1961

Dear Anaïs,

Thank you for the postcard and for the news about the family. I had no idea that Antolina's plight was so dramatic. Is there nothing we can do? I can't honestly say that I worry too much about Tia Anaïs or Thorvald Sánchez. Poor Graciella! She must have had quite a shock! I keep correspondence with Sorne (in Miami) and Augusto (in Chicago). Like typical second generation Sánchezes, they are not on speaking terms... Maybe Castro was needed after all...

Would love to have some of your books for Christmas and for giving later. Have met a few young English instructors and I am sure that they would enjoy reading you. Most of them have heard of you and a good number have even read you. Bravo for them!

What do you want for Christmas? And Hugh?

Love,
Joaquín

Letter from Henry Miller to Anaïs Nin:
Pacific Palisades, November 25, 1961

Dear Anaïs:

I had a letter from Dr. Hoffman (Paris) a couple of weeks ago, saying you wished to publish some of our correspondence. I asked him to have your agent send me details and your address, but have heard nothing further. Now I have your address—or are you in New York at the moment? You're such a traveler!

I'm here in Pacific Palisades since two months and may be leaving after Xmas to return to Europe. I have a furnished room near my children. The address on the envelope is theirs. I get all my mail there—as I have to keep my whereabouts secret or be plagued to death. I am there every day, usually, between six and eight in the evening. (Phone is Gladstone 4-4080.)

If you're here in L.A., perhaps we can meet. It's about time.

All the best to you!
Henry

Letter from Hiram Hayden of Atheneum Publishing to Anaïs Nin:
New York, December 13, 1961

Dear Miss Nin:

Thanks for your letter. I have called Gunther Stuhlmann and he's agreed that when the time comes if Alan Swallow doesn't feel up to doing the diaries, I shall be next in line for them. I can answer your question about the past and the failure to take your novels very simply. I was an editor working for another publisher in those days. Hence I had little final authority in the acceptance or rejection. Moreover, what may be eminently suited to one publishing list is not necessarily to others. I am sure you have no doubt.

Sincerely,
Hiram Haydn

New York, December 1961
Dream: A French girl is at the consulate, dying of cancer. Beautiful, 20 years old. Dressed seductively. Making love as often as she could. She did not lack for lovers. Not only because she was beautiful, but because of the attraction of a night of love that might never be repeated, which is very strong in man. It allows them to revel in an absolute, a total gift of themselves that is certain not to become a contract. Assurance of discontinuity is an inspiration to man just as continuity is an inspiration to woman.

Letter from Alan Swallow to Anaïs Nin:
Denver, December 18, 1961

Dear Anaïs,
I was glad for the report on the Gotham book party and glad it went so well, that Karl Shapiro was there (hope you liked him), Marguerite Young and Maude Hutchins. Sounds fun. And also Nona Balakian. I hope this last augers well for what she is hoping for at *The New York Times*. You probably impressed her well as not being too "far out"!
Cordially,
Alan

Los Angeles, December 26, 1961
Reginald had to be institutionalized. He imagines a hostile world of poisoning, being beaten and robbed. We visit him every day. He recognizes Rupert but starts telling mad stories immediately. The place is like a jail—locked doors, etc.—really, madness is worse than death.

Los Angeles, January 1962
Alan Swallow suffers a coronary occlusion.

Los Angeles, January 1962
My French publisher invited me to go to Paris and I have an appointment to meet the director Jean Gabriel Albicocco in March. He had expressed interest in *A Spy in the House of Love*. He can do a shooting script in May. That means it will be a film to be proud of, a new wave film. It is his wife, Marie La Forêt, who reads English and has the book. She had to translate it for him.

Letter from Gunther Stuhlmann to Anaïs Nin:
New York, January 8, 1962

Dear Anaïs:
I had hoped to see you around these parts this week but from your most recent note I see that you may go off to Europe. So, in haste, first of all a check for the Stock advance and Alan Swallow's monthly payment.
Thanks for the word on Miller, though your note did not give his address. Did you talk to him? Did he tell you anything about what conditions he wanted on the letters? I do need that information, and Hoffman in Paris stays mum. Could you

possibly contact Miller about this, or have him drop me a note as to what his conditions are for the letter edition: advance, etc. Arthur Wang is most anxious and keeps calling me about this. They would like to do the volume, but we have to get Miller's specific okay and draw the contract with him.

Pollack's review is fine, but I don't really care for the postscript and in general it probably sounds better over the air than it reads, to me at least. How do you feel? I am not totally happy about the thing as it stands. It's a bit too precious and does not do you full justice, to my mind. But I may be too critical.

As ever,
Gunther

Letter from Hugh Guiler to Anaïs Nin:
New York, January 15, 1962

Darling:

Have just spent an hour and a half reading your 37 pages of the *Spy* scenario. It seems to me that this is perhaps the form you have always been looking for. It suits you so well because it gives you the two freedoms—to let the character act and monologue—and so to express as much as she can and also to let you explain what she must express beyond her own consciousness (which is pretty penetrating too). It will be a great challenge to a director, but I would have liked to have a try at it as I think I could at least suggest what you mean. Whether the spectator would be able to translate it back into your works will, of course, be important to him, but if he is as interested as I am he will probably want to buy a copy of the scenario.

As a director I would say the only problem is how to leave enough space between the various love affairs of Sabina so that she does not give the impression of being a nymphomaniac, which is, of course, far from what you intend.

I can see a great movie come out of this and can't imagine that you will not be able to find someone to see the great possibilities you open up. But I have a hunch that the ideal would be for you to direct it yourself, and I hope someday you have a chance to do this.

This would be a fulfillment of your old desire to be an orchestra conductor!

And so, to sleep.

I do miss you and certainly it seems difficult to coordinate things at present, but I also feel this is an opportunity you must not miss, and your scenario confirms this completely. Just believe. I love you.

Your
H

Letter from Anaïs Nin to Hugh Guiler:
Los Angeles, January 18, 1962

Darling:

Today I finished the new version of *Spy*. You will see many changes. Your letter gave me confidence. The danger of having Sabina considered a nymphomaniac is a flaw that worked against me in the novel. Tracey once called it the "Lost Weekend of Sex." I have not solved yet how to make one aware of time passing, because of the *La Ronde* structure I chose, the wheel turning. I have to find a solution for that. But you will see how much more visual work I have done. It is very amusing that there has been an exchange of dependencies. I see now my interest in film was directly influenced by you, so that I cannot see, work, or imagine anything except in terms of how you would do it. You have formed me as a filmmaker! How do you like that? If I once formed you as an artist, you certainly are getting back at me. Now I'm dependent on you as a scenario writer. I mailed you the batch this morning, special delivery. I am pinning Tracey down tonight. Making her come down, sit there and read the damn thing. But she is so volatile, it's like trying to catch a minnow.

I feel very happy today. I have not had pleasure in my work for a long time. Frankly, I thought I was "through." This may be good discipline for the writing. Less abstract. Have to learn to describe concretely.

I have a clearer idea of my feeling about movies. I feel it is the art of our time. I feel writing is an anachronism. People don't know how to read anymore. America precipitated the death of writing. What Americans read is the equivalent of *Reader's Digest*, prefabricated, preheated, prefrozen, predigested, prepared functional writing. Not the art of writing. Not even the French write as Jouve, Giraudoux, Proust did. They only want writing to be functional. The scenario will be the only writing left. Even the profession of teaching has taken up films. Not books. America the inarticulate has achieved the death of the art of writing...

Piccolo has no more fever. I will let him speak for himself.

Dear Papa: I was certainly glad to get a letter from you. Now I know what you have gone through with your throat. But with a Scotch father and two Scotch veterinarians, nothing can happen to me. He poked his finger down my throat and said my tonsils were swollen. Anaïs takes a squirter and squirts a white powder down my throat every day. No fun. On top of that, since the day I tangled my leash around her arm and made her drive her car against a wall, she takes taxis when I'm with her. This, plus the fact that she has no talent except for losing or spending money, makes me sorry to be sick. So today I have no fever. I hope your throat is better. Why are vets all Scotch? Last night I certainly wished you were around. Tracey the actress kicked off her shoes, removed her necklace, and sat down to read, and nobody paid attention to me. Anaïs was pasting corrections. They didn't even talk. Tracey is pretty nice, and she lavishes us with words like darling, honey, lover, is a sweetheart to everyone. She's always pushing her hair around. She should get a haircut and get rid of the nuisance. She pushes it off, and then around her face, away from her neck, and against her ear. Women are funny. I would get her a poodle cut, myself.

I would have written you oftener but sometimes I believe I react against so much writing. I hear that damn typewriter tap tap tap tap all day, and decide to go out and bird watch. My own growling is not as reasonable and just as yours. Often a sheet on a chair, socks hanging on a laundry line, a rug flapping from a window will make me growl, and then Anaïs and other people think I'm seeing ghosts.

The old Belgian lady is very nice to me. Anaïs takes me to her apartment for a massage every day because it is she who has the massage table. It's too high for me to jump.

Anaïs must be homesick because every day she runs to the mailbox, often ahead of time, and she was quite blue when she heard you were going to Europe. Anyway, she tells me now we are joining you, and that's fine with me. I'm eager to play with you. I read the article on obedience. As a matter of fact, I have become a very obedient dog, without any formal education. I guess Anaïs, not having had a formal education, thought I shouldn't either.

Your devoted,
Piccolo

Los Angeles, January 1962

Norbert Auerbach, producer of *Girl With the Golden Eyes*, left saying to Tracey: "Show me a budget," and to me, "Show me a treatment." So all I could do was to sit and do it myself, quickly. What I did was a basic layout upon which others with more craft can embroider, elaborate in filmic terms. Evidently Albicocco came to him with a complete treatment, budget, package, and he accepted it. He does not want to coordinate these elements. So the treatment is ready and the budget, too, and then Mr. Auerbach neither came back nor answered letters.

Tracey: in my efforts to discover the "search" of the failures, like a doctor's diagnosis intended to fight the disease, I feared to lose compassion. Yet I felt the compassion for Tracey because the knowledge of the self-destructive impulse is just as tragic as the blows that come from the outside, the accidents, the fatalities by other causes, for these are as inevitable and cause as much suffering.

Tracey *should* be recognized as an actress, and, naturally, as I could never resist a battle with the dragon of self-destruction, I was for a long time determined I would succeed. Once again I courted a potential Tracey I could *see* as Sabina, or Lillian, or Djuna.

I was not aware of it at first, but when Tracey began to introduce me to scriptwriters, I observed a curious attitude towards Sabina. They were all *judging* her; they were all fundamentally unsympathetic to her behavior, even hostile. They denigrated her according to the old morality rules! There was either an open contempt in the characterization, or a vulgarization, or a de-poetization. It was so obvious in their interpretation that I began to wish for a European production, and when I saw *The Girl With the Golden Eyes* I knew this was the right tone, the poetization of passion free of judgment.

I seem to be the only one among my friends who sees the genuine actress in Tracey and intuitive intelligence behind the Hollywood trappings. Everyone is misled by the makeup, the dress. Renate said she always wanted to put Tracey in a bath and wash away all the Hollywood tinsel. Perhaps I got to know the emotional Tracey over the telephone. We have long conversations, intimate—and honest. I feel her life has been tragic.

The most important thing is to obey the flow of life if you have it in you. Our growth is like that of plants; if they are not permitted to grow, they become stunted and twisted. It is not easy for the woman. Man usually fulfills all his desires, but woman has a need to protect and to preserve at the same time. I have known all the torments of guilt for expansion which seemed a threat to those I loved, yet I know that if those life impulses had been crippled, they would have turned into destructions. I needed constant absolution.

If you don't grow, you die inside. A dead woman can make no one happy.

I live quietly, avoiding publicity around *Tropic of Cancer*. The obscenity trial has been so vulgar. Everyone displaying ignorance and prejudice.

Letter from Daisy Aldan to Anaïs Nin:
New York, January 1962

Dear Anaïs,
 I think the proof of our friendship is that under the circumstances, neither one of us has completely dropped the other. Generally, I think this would have occurred. Since it has not, it shows we both respect and care enough about each other, and what has sometimes seemed like utter impatience on both sides, is really great patience.
 As for "understanding," you know very well that one can realize intellectually what a situation is, and if one cares deeply enough, emotionally respond with utter loss of judgment at a particular moment. So do not feel so utterly "misunderstood." Perhaps I understand you more than most.
 It seems to me that within the past year, you have been afraid to show any particular affection openly for fear I might misinterpret it, and deepen the intensity. You have been wrong, if this is so.
 I enjoyed our visit, finally, and I hope you realize through it how easy our relationship can be if we don't anticipate all kinds of strains and deeds. I like Rupert very much. I think Piccolo was utterly friendly and unrestrained.
 How it hurts me to read that your life is a strain to the breaking point. The compensation must be great for you to be willing to endure it so.
 I hope your cold is all better and you are feeling well again, and Rupert is feeling better about his father. He should feel better now that he is being really helped.
 Love,
 Daisy

Letter from Joaquín Nin-Culmell to Anaïs Nin:
Berkeley, February 5, 1962

Dear Anaïs,
 I tried to reach you by telephone this morning but you had just left for the hospital. Will try again tonight. Hope Hugh is better.
 No news about the Madrid business and so I doubt very much if I will make the trip at this time. The recording is going through, however. I suspect that they would prefer that the composer stay home. According to some performers, the only *good* composers are dead ones. They can't talk back!
 Glad to hear that Miller has done something nice for a change by giving you the rights to his letters to you. I didn't realize that one's letters could be sold by somebody else. Always thought that they belonged to the writer. Music manuscripts are something else again. Someday I will give them away but *not* to the University of California. I hate this place.
 Best wishes to Hugh for his prompt recovery and my love to you both.
 As ever,
 Joaquín

Letter from Alan Swallow to Anaïs Nin:
Denver, February 19, 1962

Anaïs darling:

I realize that the review in *Minnesota Review* was upsetting. It was to me too. When I read this guy's comments, I thought long and seriously all evening. He was so unscholarly, and then his critical assumptions were patently so damned silly, that I thought I might write something. But it is so useless to protest; it seems one is partial to one's own books. So, although I have not resolved the conflict entirely, I have not written him. Most of the time, my experience is that these things bury themselves, they are so bad, and it is just as well to let them die their own deaths. But it is annoying, and it is annoying that the very first of the quarterlies to review you did this. But, as I wrote, I think perhaps the best attitude is to feel that the space itself is a gain and what they say is of little significance (I am quite sure that this is true, but it still does not quell the disturbance that it was so bad). Experience says let it go to prove its own stupidity; the emotion says lash out in return with a direct pointing out of the stupidity!

Love,
Alan

March 1, 1962
Arrival in Paris with Hugo.

Letter from Oliver Evans to Anaïs Nin:
Urbana, Illinois, March 4, 1962

Dear Anaïs:

I am glad that you wrote me, for I was on the point of writing you to inquire if you had an extra copy (or knew where I could obtain one) of a brochure of yours published more than ten years ago and entitled—I think—*Realism and Reality*.

I found that pamphlet enormously helpful, and (since it is true that I am going to do a long piece on you for Karl Shapiro), I am quite upset that I cannot find it anywhere in my files. For many years I kept it, but it seems to have disappeared for good. It had a violet-colored cover, as I recall, and a photograph of you, quite a good photograph, as a matter of fact, on the cover.

I realize that as you are now in Paris you may not have access to this little leaflet, but I am wondering if you could perhaps have your husband send it to me: I swear faithfully that I will return it when I have taken a few notes.

Do you ever see Gore or Tennessee anymore? I hear from Gore quite often; he has recommended me for a Guggenheim next year, and so has Tennessee. Tennessee was in Chicago a couple of months ago trying out the new play, and I had dinner one evening with him, Audrey Wood and Bill Inge, who happened to be passing through town just then. The Middle West is a dreadful place: one has to depend on fortuitous accidents like these to see one's old friends, and these accidents occur so seldomly it is increasingly difficult to re-establish the old intimacy.

Next year I will be in California, unless the Guggenheim materializes. In Northridge, a suburb of Los Angeles. I don't know a soul there. Do you know anyone in that area whom you think I'd enjoy meeting?

I've enjoyed my friendship here with Harry Partch, who I think is also a friend of yours.

Let me hear from you!
Cordially,
Oliver Evans

Letter from Anaïs Nin to Rupert Pole:
Paris, March 4, 1962

Darling:
A week since I talked with you. It seems like a long time.
Paris is full of policemen and soldiers. Last night I was invited to Anne Metzger's by an old sculptor and his wife, the painter Anita Caro, on the Left Bank. Lovely place. He is wealthy, comes straight from his studio to work. Next door to them a journalist's home had been bombed, and a fire followed. During dinner there was a noise and the maid was shaking. She was sure it was another bomb. She had worked in the resistance during the war. The bombs have stirred the people against the Organisation Armée Secrète because usually it kills innocent people, children, passersby. This contrast between art-loving, pleasure-loving people and political unrest and tragedy is strange. The French here think the behavior of the Algerian French is shameful.
Tomorrow I see Norbert Auerbach and Gabriel Albicocco. I have to find out if they are on good terms after the film, since Albicocco gave me the impression his backers had both cut and restricted him. Meanwhile I had to be here to force Fanchette to finish a rough translation of *Spy*, which Albicocco needs. He had done half and I'm reviewing it with Marguerite Rebois.
The fashion is black leather coats and suits in every window, puffed-up dresses.
Your photos didn't come, nor a letter. If you have not written me, darling, won't you send me a night letter just once? It is hard to be without news. I should have had at least one letter last week. It's such a small thing to ask—even a penny post card—I will never understand how you can read my letters, which are so full, and not *respond*.
Love,
A

Letter from Rupert Pole to Anaïs Nin:
Los Angeles, March 1962

LOVE:
Dark, cold, rainy night, like all the nights alone here, but beautiful *now* that I have made a huge fire and brought the typewriter into the living room. The clouds are just beginning to lift, the rain is still falling in the pool, making magic circles within circles within circles, but the magic circles are lighted now by shafts of brilliant moonlight piercing the clouds through the rain-washed air. It is so lovely and dramatic I had to think of anything but how much I love you and miss you and want you here by my side to share this—and how little it really means without you, except that I can sit here and plan ways to make it even more beautiful for your return.
Well, to work, writing this letter, that is, and it is work to even write to you, my love—I have never pretended otherwise. I write only because I know how much it

means to you and because your letters mean so much to me. It would help if I could know you receive my letters (let alone get your reaction to them), but usually you are on your way back by the time my first letters arrive. This is my fifth letter, and I write it only on the horrible possibility that you'll still be in Paris when it arrives. If all goes according to the mail's sense of time, we'll both read this together with our feet in the pool this summer!

Tracey just phoned (from Jerry Gessner's, natch) that she's trying to arrange a showing of *Golden Eyes*. She's still all aflutter, very moved by Albicocco. She wants terribly to work with him but still says (and I believe her, because they're cheap Hollywood people) her backers want a screenplay before they will put up any money. I said that usually by the time a screenplay is finished all the money is raised. That shook her up a little. She still asks Jerry for advice on each step, which I can't take because I can't take him! But we'll see; I imagine it's something of a record for Tracey to have stuck to anything this long!

Tell Piccolo there are many new smells here, and none of them are proletarian. There are so many white flowers since the rains that he won't need baths anymore—he can just eat the white flowers. Tell Piccolo he can have anything he wants if he'll just bring you back soon.

LIKE NOW
Rupert

Letter from Rupert Pole to Anaïs Nin:
Los Angeles, March 1962

My Darling with the Green Eyes!!

The Girl with the Golden Eyes is the most beautiful, sad, poetic, marvelously directed, wonderfully acted film I have *ever* seen anywhere. I'm still so much under its spell that it's hard for me to collect my thoughts for you. Everyone at the showing was very moved, very impressed, all, that is, but (guess who) Jerry, of course—but such a beautiful film. It would seem something like a sacrilege if he had liked it. I have to hand it to Tracey; she persevered till she got this film.

Albicocco is a great artist, my love. If we can get him to do *Spy* it will be the finest work of art in motion pictures. He is exactly right for your work. He is a poet—his father is a poet—he chooses wonderful actors and then lets them act. He understands relationships, he digs sex in the deepest way—that scene toward the beginning where he's passed out on her bed and she puts her hand inside his shirt—sexiest I have ever seen. Tracey was very moved—in the right way—she's all stirred up now to work with Albicocco, but money is still a problem. There were about ten people at the showing, but I don't know if any of them were backers. Tracey went out to dinner with Jerry afterward so I bowed out and came *home* like a good little boy—which I always do so I can think of you and Piccolo so far away—don't worry about the separation—if Albicocco will do the film I'll take a leave and come along to help!

Horribly cold here, very cold nights and cold, windy days. In fact, it's been cold ever since I turned the pool heater on (I might have known). But saving warm weather up just for your return. Easter vacation isn't till April 16 this year so no danger we'll miss it.

Stay as long as you need to, but come back soon to bring back my sun, my life, my love.
Rupert

March 29, 1962
Return to Los Angeles.

Letter from Oliver Evans to Anaïs Nin:
Urbana, Illinois, April 1962

Dear Anaïs:
Am reading your work. I have decided that you are the best. Better than Ann Porter, better than Carson McCullers. Will it be known during your lifetime? I hope so and I want to help. *Seduction of the Minotaur* is a masterpiece.

From time to time I have heard rumors that you were working on a diary and that there is the possibility of publishing it. What I would like to know is the relationship, if any, that it bears to your prose fiction...which is another way of asking to what extent are your novels (and the characters Djuna and Sabina) autobiographical. I hope you will not think these questions impertinent; the truth is that I have not been in with you for long and that I must rely on the grapevine for much of my information. And we all know how twisted grapevines can be!

As ever, cordially,
Oliver Evans

Letter from Anaïs Nin to Gunther Stuhlmann:
Los Angeles, April 1962

Dear Gunther:
We are waiting for the Albicocco script. Tracey will supply $2,000. Would you talk to the group you once mentioned who sponsors films made in Italy? Financiers are beginning to think backing foreign films is a good investment. They are setting up companies to make European-type films! (As if anything could be imitated.)

As you know I'm very fond of you and you're the most patient, helpful, clever literary agent in the world, *but* you never write me! And *please* send the 30 pages of *Spy* in French done by Fanchette—I need them!

Affectionately,
Anaïs

Letter from Alan Swallow to Anaïs Nin:
Denver, April 6, 1962

Dear Anaïs,
Relieved to hear from you, but surprised to hear from Los Angeles. You had said two weeks in Paris, and when I wanted to respond to your letter from Paris I saw that the time was up and sent it to New York. I take it that you returned straight to L.A. and did not stop in N.Y. This creates a problem, since you did not

handle the Gotham Book Mart event when you were there in February, and it dangles.

Now in this letter you say you are going back to N.Y. on April 1 or so, but since you postmarked the letter April 4, I guess you mean May 1. At any rate, I guess the Gotham thing will have to be postponed until you get back.

No new reviews that I have seen. I think we are finally going to get into *Books Abroad.*

Sales continue, nothing setting a house on fire, but a steady going out. That is pleasant.

Love,
Alan

P. S. Glad to hear Oliver Evans is reviewing you; probably for *Prairie Schooner.* I hope the contacts in Paris are going to mean that film for you!

Letter from Anaïs Nin to Alan Swallow:
Los Angeles, April 9, 1962

Dear Alan:

Hugo's job (foreign department of a stockbroker) is highly unpredictable. He stays in Europe until his business is done. That is why I never know quite what our plans are and have learned to accept this. When he started to travel quickly again (one day in each city) I came back to Los Angeles to report to the actress and the backers on what I had achieved in Paris. (But my mail is always forwarded from N.Y.) I guess it is hard to follow my motions, but I do try to keep you informed as far as I know myself.

I am glad the books are selling in spite of practically no reviews. But an article by Oliver Evans should be good for us. And Karl Shapiro wrote me: "I will see that *Seduction of the Minotaur* is reviewed. *Prairie Schooner* is not being edited by me this year, but I will be back in the fall. May I say stupidly that I love the way you write?"

All I got out of Paris is assurance and guarantee that *Spy* will be an art film, not a Hollywood production, but having captured the interest of a young genius as a director helps in securing backing. Though they are all waiting to see the script!

My best to you, as always,
Anaïs

P. S. What I can't understand is *The New York Times* and *Tribune* ignoring the books. I hope Oliver Evans' article will be good. They always write about personal and biographical details—want to know if it is my life, is it me, etc. Why? It is unethical, isn't it? If I wanted to publish my life, I'd publish the Diary. I answer patiently—but it annoys me. Why should my life be necessary for a review? Don't you agree?

Letter from Anaïs Nin to Hugh Guiler:
Los Angeles, April 9, 1962

Darling:

Yesterday I took the day off, went with Renate and Ronnie to the beach; it was 90 degrees, a desert wind and sun, took a dip in the icy sea, and then we drove up to the mountain top where Lloyd Wright will someday build a spectacular home (he is seventy now) for a last picnic with them before they leave for Japan. It was five o'clock when we got there. Sunset time. Sea and mountains as far as one can see... Eric's wife (who has been in Japan) served a Japanese dinner on two hibachis. I put the chicken and vegetables on wooden skewers, and we had sake and tea. Then, as evening came, we built a pioneer fire (just branches piled high, unbroken, as the Indians taught pioneers instead of chopping up wood)—it makes a wide, round fire to warm everyone, and each one keeps pushing a branch in as it burns... Eric played the flute, and it seemed like a peaceful, serene moment that I have come to enjoy more and more. It did seem to me that neurosis destroys nature and that as one emerges from it, the link with nature is resumed. I had it when I was a girl in Richmond Hill.

Piccolo was very happy, liked the Japanese food, chased quail out of their nesting places as he did in Fontainebleau but did not run around so much.

Jerry Gessner is a strange man. He bulldozed his way into Tracey's life; he is rough, too authoritarian, too anxious to succeed. He may be intelligent, but he is not sensitive. I could not work with him. He did say he thought Tracey was *in love with failure*. And sometimes I do get discouraged with her. She has not yet sent the photographs, so perhaps the cleverest thing you ever did was to get part ownership of the script.

I do hope you had better luck with your business and will feel you accomplished something. I felt so badly you had disappointments while I was there. Piccolo and I talk about you, and remember all our games. I guess we are fundamentally fonder of playing than of working...wish you were too...

Anaïs

Letter from Anaïs Nin to Hugh Guiler:
Los Angeles, April 1962

Darling:

So relieved after talking with you yesterday that you should be given time at least to turn around. The suddenness and shock were really inhuman. I hope now you will never, never, never again work with people whose unconscious hostilities to you and others were so apparent all along. It is hard for people like you to realize the evil in others. I know it is easy to say as I did: St. Phalles is destructive and will always harm you. In every relationship there is a potential danger. Anyway, now, we can work this out, and you sounded good yesterday, and optimistic. I am going to see if I can arrange intermittent teaching jobs. I find people are very eager to work with me.

Please bear in mind my suggestion not to mention the facts of your split with G. D. and Co. unless absolutely necessary, and I don't see that it is except in the most intimate case (such as John Chase), which I interpret as goodness and your incapacity to see destructiveness in others that businessmen might interpret otherwise. Most men are born with a canny self-defensive system, shrewdness; but you, because of past relationships, were born vulnerable and idealistic, and always

drowning in harmony (as Renate always imagines your relationship with animals to be serene and loving). I discovered that part of my failure as a writer was that I was honest about my failures, and I created in others an image of failure; I never bluffed, you know. Since I have taken to building an image of success, others follow suit, especially Americans who have a cult of what others admire and follow like sheep. I am now playing the game, and it works. We have been too sincere. Too open. Too trusting. I, for one, do love you for this because I know it comes out of your incapacity to do this to others.
Anaïs

Letter from Anaïs Nin to Hugh Guiler:
Los Angeles, April 1962

Darling:
I am not depressed by problems, but saddened by what hurts you. I think you should not economize on Bogner at this moment, for she will help you in your decision. I fear that the hurt may make you do emotional things. And I hope you won't *tell anyone* what happened (except close friends who can help you), as I think your choice of partners must have always puzzled people who were aware of your quality. For the sake of your prestige, avoid discussing St. Phalles openly. Your letter, which I reread carefully, sounds calm and wise. But don't save on Bogner. It is I who can cut down expenses drastically. I don't have Bogner. I don't need massages when I can swim (there's $100 right there). I don't dress up. I don't go anywhere. I gave up a second-hand car. People who want to see me come and get me. I don't need a cent. I want to unburden you. To relieve your mind, I will bring Tracey's check. I'm waiting eagerly for the results of your interview on Monday. I wish you would tell me clearly what your income will be. If you could rent out your apartment for the summer we could sublet Daisy's at less than half the price (big living room, big bedroom and you could move your film stuff to a loft nearby). Thinking of you lovingly and constructively.

Dear Papa: I hear you're going to change jobs. Why don't you just play the guitar? Anaïs and I like having you around. I will try and help you, too, by eating the food I am given and not being so capricious. We love you.
Anaïs & Piccolo

Letter from Jim Herlihy to Anaïs Nin:
Key West, April 1962

Dear Anaïs:
I was surprised to get your card from Paris! And to hear that you've broken through in France. It always seemed curious that you hadn't been published in French all these years. Also, pleased to hear that mine sold well. I hadn't known that it had come out yet, as they didn't send me copies. Do you think if I wrote to Bay, he would have a couple of them sent to me?

Last night in bed I was reading biographical notes on the Swedish writer, Stig Dagerman, who killed himself at thirty-one because he couldn't write anymore; and experienced a moment of terrible identification with him. Then, inexplicably, I woke up this morning rather elated! I've been having a difficult time understanding the fluctuations of my spirits, and am still uncertain whether to attribute it to the flu I had for a month, or vice-versa.

Anaïs, about photos of the *All Fall Down* film for Bay: I don't have any, but have written to MGM suggesting they send him some. I'm not sure to what extent I want to be identified with the film—not having seen it yet. But I still have the gnawing suspicion that it is going to be just violence for the hell of it, and that I won't like it at all. It's playing in Miami now. They wanted me to take a bow at the local premiere; but I ran like the wind from such a situation. It'd be quite different if I'd written the script, or felt that it accurately represented the book in tone and meaning.

This has been a difficult period, Anaïs. If I had to make a guess about what the hell is going on here lately, I would say that this is probably what I am trying to do: trying to grow up and away and beyond the fairy tale, the medieval legends of one-true-love, etc. You and I have talked about this many times over the years, and I understand it oh so well, except that understanding has very little to do with actually rooting it out; the legend is seated in the soul itself. And then, too, there's this: the danger of becoming free of that legend by adapting its even more deadly antithesis: that love does not exist, etc.... And so, dear Anaïs, to bring you up to date on my doings, I suppose it is fairly accurate to say I'm trying to maintain some balance between these poles; and I wouldn't be a bit surprised to discover that there has been some headway. But it is a long process for me, and God knows where it is leading to... I hope it won't seem strange to you that I go from not writing any letters at all to speak of—and then suddenly plunging to these matters of the soul: I have to assume that I can always speak to you on these levels without initial waltzes, prefaces, attitudes, shenanigans, etc. And that my silences will be accepted and understood; or forgiven. There is never a time when I don't think of you a great deal, and always with so much love.

Jim

Los Angeles, May 1962

I sit here waiting for the script by Albicocco, writing the story of Renate's friend Raven. Watching nightingales, swimming in a pool that smells of honey, with Elysian flowers all around, reading Michaux's *Miserable Miracle* over the FM station, pursuing elusive and stereotyped backers with Tracey, mere computers. One of them showed me a scrapbook with photographs of actresses. Under each name there was a box office evaluation calculated by the banks. At the present moment, after the success of foreign films, Japanese, Italian, French, they want to make films *like* foreign films, but certainly not with authentic products like Jean Gabriel Albicocco.

Letter from Alan Swallow to Anaïs Nin:
Denver, May 16, 1962

Dear Anaïs:
I was pleased to have the *Village Voice* review, thanks much for having one sent to me.

I keep getting enquiries concerning the diary. You have mentioned it several times that I am to have the first chance at it, but do you have any notions yet about when you may want to be publishing this? I am just in the dark, is all.

Love,
Alan

Letter from Anaïs Nin to Hugh Guiler:
Los Angeles, June 6, 1962

Darling:

It is 9:00 AM. Piccolo is still lying on his back. He watches me with one eye. He is never sure whether I am just writing or writing to you.

The papers write up the Wall Street market slide again, and I can't tell how you feel. I was tempted to call you last night, but I realized it would be midnight for you and did not want to wake you up. I keep thinking of you so much. It seems so ironic that in my eagerness to accept and embrace what you love (visits to lawyers, examining trusts, talking about business to Bogner, wanting to "regulate" my expenses, putting a limit on myself, etc.), only the negative aspect should have come out. I hope I can overcome this. I have written to Bogner.

It is still cold. I am typing a copy of the Oliver Evans article for *Prairie Schooner* because it will please you. It is sound and solid. I hope it means a change of winds.

I also have to pack the diaries I copied so patiently during all these years of solitary life, to send to New York.

People in Europe will certainly need your reassurance, your equilibrium. I do admire deeply how you have come through. It was probably the biggest crisis in your life, and what a contrast to your emotional feeling about the first Crash. My darling, my vulnerable love, don't you think it is this knowledge of the vulnerability that we had about each other and that we tried to protect? Some of my desperation is that I cannot protect you from the hurts of the business world. I feel I can protect everyone except you. Perhaps it is not protection you want, but a listening ear...

I love you, as you well know, and think of you more than ever.

Anaïs

Letter from Anaïs Nin to Oliver Evans:
Los Angeles, June 1962

Dear Oliver:

This may reach you before you leave. I am delighted about your article. Also delighted at your plans to move to Los Angeles. I have many interesting friends here, and in the last years, many people have some from the East and stirred up what was once a lethargic place. It is good for work, the peace in between, the sun, and enough going on to stimulate.

What I like so much about your article is the balance and solidity of it—the integration of so many elements. I will send a copy to my French publisher, André

Bay, of Stock, who reads English and is a writer. I would love it as a preface. I don't know what his plans are. You may achieve what you offered to do in your telegram, to reverse the negative verdict during my lifetime.

I'm always amazed to be an enigma to anyone. It seems to me I avoid publicity and live for my loves and friends more than publicity. It's painful for me to appear in public. As you so greatly avoided personal references in your article, I feel you are a friend and will tell you whatever you want to know.

How I liked what you said about "illimitable space" when you first read the stories.

Your study of Carson McCullers was very illuminating. You answered many questions I had in my mind about her. There is much to say about allegory and the "human"...a good point. How you sum things up. You're a fine critic. Gore's idea that you do a book is fine; we need good critics. Are you going to do it?

If you see Tennessee Williams in Florida, you will probably also see a good friend of mine, James Leo Herlihy.

Do you see much of Partch? Tell him his music for Hugo's Venice film was much admired, and commented on in Paris at both UNESCO and Musée des Arts Décoratifs. It was noticed, separate from the film, by composers.

Anaïs

Letter from Anaïs Nin to Hugh Guiler:
Los Angeles, June 1962

Darling,

My poor darling, what a difficult time you have had. I am glad you are withdrawing your feelings from these situations, which are in essence factual and not feeling. Wish I had been there to help you. What can I say? I will do everything that helps you. I do see the necessity of saving, and if you are going to be traveling so much, then we must move anyway. And save for such emergencies. I want to save money. Not invest it. I want savings. Each one has to arrive at his own idea of security. I have several things I am working on.

I was just about to write you about my lecture yesterday. Yesterday I gambled. Having seen the peasant faces, heard the moronic questions, experienced the hostile sulking, I had given the simplest part of my talk. Called upon to replace someone suddenly, I had to give them the heights. All that I had left out. It's funny, the first speaker was the most prosaic, the most A-B-C, the most beginning, middle and end. And I came and gave them the most difficult, abstract, poetic lecture...and I had them all with me, tired as they were... They refused to allow questions, but the audience wanted more. They gathered around me and the gist of what they said was, "You are the first who talked to us as if we were intelligent human beings, did not talk down to us..." Nobody moved or coughed. Bebe and Louis were flabbergasted. And some of it was inspired by you, on science and poetry, etc. It was all taped, so I hope I can get a tape... Gambled for the heights and won this time. In this way I hope to help you.

Anaïs

Letter from Anaïs Nin to Hugh Guiler:
Los Angeles, June 8, 1962

Darling:
This is what Albicocco writes me:

> I wonder if you are a little helpless without news from us, so I apologize, but this trip to South America has dragged on until today with problems and difficulties that we have occupied our minds in search of quick solutions. We have not forgotten our commitments, but we still want to do quality work, and I must admit that we have not yet sufficiently expanded the first work that we have just completed. I ask you kindly to grant us another two good months so I could, despite the preparation of my film in South America, finish our cinematographic construction of your book. That's it; trust that we have not given up on you. Believe me when I tell you that dear Anaïs has our friendship.

I can understand how you and John Chase feel, and the injustice of being scapegoats. I even think this stock market drop was planned by Big Business to discredit Kennedy. It is directly said in *Time* magazine that Kennedy had undermined confidence in Big Business.

I am teaching for a good reason, to be able to help out in case of need. I want to add to your fund now rather than deplete you.

As soon as I heard from you and that you sounded all right, and were seeing Bogner often, my spirits recovered. Your happiness is the most essential thing in my life. Everything rotates around you.

Piccolo sends his love and says we must have a conference before you get another dog. He is fonder of you than you think, and he knows that it is when I am not there that you need him. What a problem! But he thinks what you really want is him, not any old dog. He thinks there is a bond there. He wants you to discuss it with Bogner.

A

Letter from Alan Swallow to Anaïs Nin:
Denver, June 15, 1962

Anaïs dear:
To catch up a bit. The Oliver Evans article is long and appreciative; it is so good that *Prairie Schooner* will publish it.

Now to the diary: Let me make one thing clear: so far as I am concerned, you need not wait "till it is time to get ahead with the books." We are getting ahead, slowly, but surely; and I would be prepared at any time to go ahead with the diary, in any reasonable way (publishing 70 volumes all at once might be impossible; but even if that were what you wanted, perhaps I could go into the market for money and do it, but I am sure that is not what you had in mind, for probably the work should be set upon a good, swift schedule to get the work all out within a reasonable time for it to be digested, etc.). So the pertinent matters *rest with you and your commitments on time.* I see that 70 volumes (which I assume is most of it; you do not say) cannot be published until after your husband's death. Okay, I will be ready, if I am still alive by then. But at any time any volumes are ready (and I am never too overburdened to do the necessary things, so don't worry about that), I am ready. It does seem clear from what you say, there are some volumes

that you are now reediting, condensing, etc., which could precede your husband's death. I can only repeat that there is no reason here why I should not be able to go ahead on some reasonable publishing plan.
   Love,
   Alan

Letter from Anaïs Nin to Gilbert Chase:
New York, July 1962

   I missed Henry in New York. He was not well in Mallorca. The obscenity trials have been insane, haven't they? One was *won* because a woman spoke up and read whole passages. It was said that because a woman accepted it, they won! *Tout le même.* And a woman caused it to be printed—myself. And a woman prefaced it—myself! It is all senseless. And the ignorance displayed, and above all, the lack of humor. Why should not women accept the same writing men do?
   Anaïs

Los Angeles, August 1, 1962
   Poor Marilyn Monroe. No one helped her—a defeat for psychiatry.

Los Angeles, August 8, 1962
   Over the years I accumulated many griefs against Henry. He had allowed Fred Perlès, staying in his house, to write a shabby description of our relationship; he had given my letters to him to the UCLA library; he had refused to preface my books in England. I stopped writing to him. When in need of money I sold some of his letters. More than the thoughtless acts he had committed, I hated my own anger. I wanted to be free of it. So when he wrote offering me the royalties on the publication of his letters to me, I answered it was not money I wanted, but his help in obtaining my letters back from UCLA. His answer was pure Henry—no empathy or sympathy for my motivation—but offering help. So I let him help me, in the way he wanted to—financially. He sent me $2,500 at a most critical moment and relieved me of economic anxiety.
   To thank him, I visited him at Pacific Palisades. Unconsciously, there were other reasons. I had heard he was not well, had had a heart examination, and I wanted to recover the genuine goodness of the relationship. I couldn't bear hostility. I let Rupert drive me to a typical, ordinary little California house, cream-colored, with neat lawns—his ex-wife's home, his children's home. When Henry opened the door, there was the negroid warmth of his voice and the shock of his aging. It was no longer the pink-skinned, clean, clear face. He was not fat, but there was the slight tremor and the slackness of seventy. The eyelid falling over the right eye slightly—giving to his left eye more fixity by contrast. This eye gave me a strange uneasiness. It was an indication of my own aging—because this time, even while softened by the voice, and the acute mentality, and the past, I saw the slyness, the deep lack of feeling I had not observed before. This dual vision was that of the dead romantic Anaïs.
   But I felt grieved about his aging. He talked about his children. He had not slept the night before because his 16-year-old daughter had not come home; at 4:00 AM, when he was about to call the police, he came to the telephone and found her

asleep on the living room couch—she had not wanted to wake him. His son had broken his ankle surfboarding. They came in. They looked like a million other California teenagers. I could not have distinguished them or said: these are Henry's children.

"Success—oh success, Anaïs, doesn't mean anything. The only thing that means anything are the few letters one gets a year—personal responses." He was unchanged, modest, unaffected, naïve at this moment. No ego showing. The Henry who wants to be thought of as a saint. I asked him about his health. He said: "I had the flu in Mallorca, and while treating me for the flu the doctor said my heart was in a bad state. He gave me digitalis. When I returned to the States all they found was an irregular beat. I believe in reincarnation. I believe I will have a great deal of time somewhere else."

He continued, "I fell in love with this woman in Germany. She is a publisher. I would have stayed in Europe, but I missed my children. They make me feel young. When I hear them talk, play games, live, I feel their age. Jesus, I get all stimulated. What about you? Are you or are you not married to Rupert? Are you a bigamist?"

"No, I'm not. I just say we are because of his family, his students."

He told me an opera was being written out of *Smile at the Foot of the Ladder*. And how in Germany he had written a play. "This German woman, she had to go and visit her children during Christmas, and too late I found I could not buy food. So I ate what I found and got in a good mood—and wrote a play. And what do you think, the French found it too sentimental. They thought Henry is getting old: "He, the ruthless one, is becoming soft..."

Soft...he was always soft, gentle, and so one believed he was compassionate. But he does not believe in protection. He tells me the story told by the Indians—a child wanted to watch a butterfly break through the chrysalis—he was told not to help it, and instead bruised its wings forever. I told him how Hugo had suddenly lost his commissions and job in the Wall Street turbulence and how his gift of the letters relieved me as I was starting teaching to supplement his shrunken salary. No more trips to Europe for me. We also talked about Roger Bloom in jail. On him he lavishes compassion. He can identify with Roger's humble beginnings, handicaps, sentimentality. Not with Hugo, or my desire to protect Hugo from the truth. The light made his eyes twitch (the weak eyes of the Clichy days). He was no longer fresh and sensual. It hurt me to see Henry old because he was a symbol of life, of pleasure. I felt tenderness, forgiveness. He suggested I steal my letters from the UCLA library.

He said he was not done with writing, but that the world did not give him time now. He was on his way to a writer's conference in Edinburgh, then to Paris, Germany, etc. Would be back in November. He pulled the curtain. On the fireplace there was a mountain of empty cigarette boxes. His children collected them to win a competition on the amount of cigarettes smoked. His son came in to ask him to pay for some shorts, which would be delivered. Made to order. "He dresses better than I do," said Henry admiringly. "And my daughter came home the other day with a poem by Rimbaud to translate. I never thought my children would be reading and translating Rimbaud." I can see why Eve complained that he loved his children more than he loved her. Because Henry has remained one of them—has more affinity with them than with adults. He told me Eve had remarried.

Success has not spoiled him. But it has given him a load to carry, letters to answer, obligations. Young writers ask for help.

He can't understand my shunning publicity. He has always lived his life openly.

I do not think he is a lonely man. His relationship with the world is more important than his personal, intimate relationships. He can easily transfer his love here and there. I have never worried about Henry being lonely. To be lonely, you have to love the other person as a part of yourself you cannot live without. That has never been Henry's feeling about anyone except his children. Women were necessary to him, but he would never die of a broken heart!

When Hugo told me over the telephone that he lost his partnership and had three days to "turn around"—then that he was taken in by Hayden Stone at $1,300 a month—and that salary is not certain (commissions), no more expense account for trips—and having to pay taxes twice—once for last year and again for this year—every month taken out of his pay…it was a shock. I rushed to sustain his battered and injured pride. His relationship with St. Phalles, a constant battle, had climaxed in treachery and his loss. I helped him surrender luxuries and take a small apartment in the same building, which gives him the same comforts but less space. Bogner said he had handled the crisis well, had not been self-destructive. But I could see that what he had done at the age of 64 was to sacrifice the present to an "illusion" of the future, to selling a fund that "might" bring him a large reward, but which actually brought in less than the others and thereby antagonized his partners and made them feel they were sharing in high expenses and not being compensated by his "mad" schemes. He still lives in the future, and so the present is sacrificed. I had to conceal my anger at this, the fact that I am not in accord with him. So many concerns. Like all men working with expense accounts, Hugo is spoiled—he abuses phone calls, cables, telegrams, is used to luxury restaurants and hotels, secretaries, typists, etc. All this he has to face. Poor Hugo. It is easier for me to economize than it is for him. Rupert has trained me well. My only luxuries are my trips. So now I have to earn this money. I tell Hugo and Rupert I earn money when I am away from home. Henry's money saved me for a few weeks. I started to teach at $10 a lesson. I helped Hugo. We went to the beach, Riis Park. He was less depressed than he would have been years ago.

Saw the lawyers to arrange the problem of the Diary. Had to ship the originals to New York because under California law, the husband would have a right to them. They were misplaced for several days at Railway Express. I had to search for them, relive the trauma of their loss during the war. By persistent detective work I traced them—and deposited them in a bank vault in Brooklyn. I made a trust, with Dr. Bogner and Gunther Stuhlmann as trustees. Money is to go to Hugo and Rupert, Joaquín, or Hugo's brother Johnnie.

A summer day in New York. The garden of the apartment house. Hugo and I are throwing a tennis ball to Piccolo. Piccolo arrived around two years ago, when Hugo was ill with hepatitis and said he wanted a dog. He sent me to look them over. Piccolo, a white poodle, two or three months old, looked me over and chose me. Because I had to take care of him, he became my dog. It was I who was enslaved. Hugo enjoys his playfulness, speed, liveliness.

Hugo talks obsessively about business. At breakfast, at lunch, at dinner. And when not talking to me, he talks to Roger Boulogne over the telephone.

Los Angeles. We drive in a second-hand black Thunderbird on the driveway downhill to our home. The house looks like a Japanese house. The silver paint has oxidized into a mellow grey-red. The sun is setting behind the hills across the lake, which is a disguised reservoir. One can see several rows of hills—the first dark and violet, the second grey and olive green, the third misty, ghostly outlined, infinitely far—the sea coast. The pool glitters. It smells of lepin and alyssum. Piccolo rushes out to chase away a wandering cat, to assert his ownership of the garden. I throw off my dress, shoes, and swim in the pool that Renate calls the child of the lake for we made it dark-bottomed so it would match the lake. Rupert looks so happy in the pool, his eyes doubly green, the green of the water added to his natural green. He smiles. His dark hair is curled by the water. He is heavier but evenly distributed, and it gives him a voluptuous quality. Happy moments, never purely happy because they are tainted by guilt over Hugo. The happiness I cannot *give* him. The happiness he is not capable of experiencing. Could we have reached this happiness without each other? I could, without him. But Hugo clings. When disaster befalls him, he writes me: "What would my life be without your love?"

His paternal role masked his need of my maternity. This is clear now. And the image of his dependency on others, on Millicent, on his secretary, on Boulogne, on Bogner, on his doctor, on advisors, lawyers, confidants—is utterly painful to me. I am fully aware of it. It is an abnormal dependence. He depends but he does not *share*. He creates his own solitude. He is my cross to bear.

Rupert is my happiness in the physical world. His home gives me peace. His gardening is miraculous. A Japanese gardener, I call him. The sprinklers are playing like fountains. The sun is setting. Acapulco sunsets. Soon the moon will spill its twin into the pool. The musicians will come. Their playing will be reflected in the pool too. Piccolo lies outstretched on rose-colored cement steps. I suffer the loneliness of Hugo interwoven with my fulfillment here. I grieve over the illusions that sustained me and that I no longer have. Hugo considered me a cripple because I could not earn a living, yet he wanted me to be dependent. When I met him, I was supporting my mother and brothers. I cannot forgive him for always living for a future that I do not believe in. His goodness, his goodness was the Hugo I loved. Now at times this goodness wears the mask of masochism, and I rebel against its exposure to the world. Who is to blame that I could not give to Hugo what I gave to others?

I stopped writing in the Diary because everywhere I turned lay pain. But I have come back to complete the impersonal Diary, not to what I left out. This is the most violent experience I suffered this year—the discovery of the missing dimension. Jack Hirschman, poet, teacher of English at UCLA, was planning a program on Artaud for Pacifica. I was to contribute memories of him. But when I arrived, each member of the group had already planned to set forth his particular contribution and were only concerned with that. One had translated a one-act play. Another had written a thesis. Jack had translated poems. They had ransacked libraries and bookshops. They had more formal, academic and objective knowledge of Artaud than I had. We never came to my portrait of Artaud. And in a way I was glad, because I was struck by the awareness that the Artaud I knew was Artaud the human being, intimate and confessional. And I could not give them that. They did not want it. I came back silent from this evening. I felt my knowledge of Artaud was not valuable. I condemned myself, my Diary, my need of intimacy. I felt the failure of all I had done: to attain this deep, personal knowledge of human beings, I had sacrificed the other knowledge this group had (bibliography, theories, etc.). Objective knowledge. I could have attained both. I touched only the personal Artaud.

So I return to Henry, the vision of Henry, of Hugo, of Rupert. I wanted to atone for the failures. To see all around them, to relinquish the personal intuition. I began to look at Henry in this way the other day, Sunday at three o'clock, outside of my personal range. The man who went to a party and was outraged by the sullenness, indifference, absence of expansive talk, and who insulted them: "I'm 70 and more alive than you are!"

There was a narrowness in my vision. I have time to expand it. And to conquer my anger. This inexplicable anger Henry had when I first met him. Does this anger disappear with reciprocated love—between artist and world? Mystery.

I am beginning to copy Hugo's diary of our most crucial moments. To let him speak.

Letter from Anaïs Nin to Hugh Guiler:
Los Angeles, December 4, 1962

Darling:

I skipped writing because Sunday night was a late night. It started late because Tim Leary, head of research on LSD at Harvard was giving a seminar first. He is a quiet, scholarly man, and talked with Huxley and everybody listened. But the one who really impressed me was his associate, Richard Alpert. Under ordinary circumstances he would be a brilliant scientist, but, caught up in LSD, he adds an inspired, an absolutely uninhibited poet's imagery. He is the one who started the Zihuatanejo Project, a utopia based on LSD (controlled). And then someone brought *Seduction* for them to read, and they read it with amazement. It was a description of how they felt, and of the place, etc. (swimming, unity with the sea, nature). He said I was a "natural" who, without drugs, had access to the unconscious. Of course, they invited me there next summer. I want them to see your films. Invitations there are rare and special. Richard said something I found hard to remember: he said that wounds come from the ego, that under the effect of the drug, they are forgotten. He was high when he went to visit his family, with whom he always quarrels. He regressed to an ideal state of love and sympathy and they all felt it; no quarrels. He forgot whatever they had said or done that had made him defensive.

Monday I was so tired, and I received a deluge of letters from Chicago University I had to answer: a letter from the dean's wife: "How very kind of you to send us an autographed copy of *Under a Glass Bell*. It is the nicest reminder of your visit to us. I don't need to tell you what a success the My Life and Yours program proved to be. You gave so much of yourself in thoughtfulness and understanding and patience, and in real illumination. I have heard nothing but enthusiasm for your talk. And, for myself, I think you have been our most gracious and amazing guest. I am only sorry that I couldn't have talked with you more. Perhaps when you're in Chicago again you might have time to call us and we can have a quiet lunch or dinner."

Best of all, the students want to enter your Venice film in the April Film Festival. I would like you to let them.
Received my French copy of *Ladders to Fire*.
Waiting for news of you, darling.
Love,
Anaïs

New York, December 1962
Saw parts of the NYU student film of *Under a Glass Bell*. Good and bad. Good: genuine antiques and a real glass bell. The girl is a theatre actress but overacts. The young man is bad. Piccolo barked at him. One lovely shot of the girl asleep seen through a glass bell like Sleeping Beauty. It was made in a small, overcrowded museum-like apartment. Jeanne was free and sophisticated in the story. When a young admirer comes to see her, she keeps pulling her dress over her knees.

Letter from Anaïs Nin to Hugh Guiler:
Los Angeles, December 16, 1962

Darling:
I seem to be surrounded by new plans and prospects. New producers, young directors, new backers... There is a ferment in L.A. caused by French films, a rebellion against the way they have been made. You never know how much creativity is inhibited by commercial setups. Can't understand Albicocco not writing back to me.
So glad you are sleeping well without the pills. They leave a depressing hangover, I feel. I never need them here because the life is unstimulating, but when I hit New York and take them, I notice irritability and depression. However, the Christmas complex has come back strong, and I am grateful to you for letting me keep busy at something.
Did you notice the big controversy over LSD? The dean of Harvard is conducting a campaign against it. Alpert, the man I met, answered that it is not "deforming" or distorting, but is, rather, a conscious-expanding drug.
Anaïs

Letter from Anaïs Nin to Hugh Guiler:
Los Angeles, December 19, 1962

Darling:
I was just about to write you that things were becoming clearer when you wrote me about your possible trip. In a way, I hope it may not materialize, as it will be too long an absence. But this is the way it looks here now. You are right to imagine that having the movie script, I will want to go on pushing. But to avoid this I am doubling up on activities, seeing all the contacts I can.
Did you receive my story about Djuna Barnes and Dr. Norman? Did you like it? I have polished it considerably.
In any case, whatever happens, I will be in N.Y. on January 15. Before, if you don't leave.

It seems like a long time. I will let Piccolo finish this letter.

Dear Papa: I guess I'm not turning out to be a professional writer as Anaïs had hoped. What about filmmaking? Letters probably don't interest me anymore because I see Anaïs writing all day, and it's a bore. She has no time for anything else. My lack of success with the little white poodle around the corner continues. She barks at me furiously when I go for a walk. Do you think women really mean yes when they bark no, and I should not take it seriously? Aside from that, my best playmate is the Kesslers' huge black poodle. At first he frightened me. But he is very gentle, in spite of his size, and he obeys much better than I do. I certainly miss you. Nobody knows how to play as well as you. I love my walks with you in the evening. Will you teach me to make films when you come back? Writing is anachronistic. Pretty soon we'll be able to talk with you all day and all night carrying a little tape recording machine in the pocket. Who wants writing then?

Love,
Piccolo

Letter from Henry Miller to Anaïs Nin:
Northridge, California, January 19, 1963

Dear Anaïs:

Here for a few days to paint watercolors (for tax deductions!). Back Tuesday evening. Sorry about all the "financial" talk—that's all I have thought of for the past two months. Just coming out of the woods now. Go to Big Sur next weekend for 10 days or so, to start writing again.

Just got a *box* full of letters from fans—sent to Big Sur. Knocks me over.

We move Feb. 1 to 444 Ocampo Drive, Pacific Palisades. Same phone number.

I started reading your letters—very moving. (I always think of them as yours instead of mine—strange.)

Yes, I do want to see the rest, please.

June is always in bad shape. I send her a little something monthly. I don't see how she can possibly live much longer. Eve writes her fairly regularly. She is quite a wreck—physically—but full of spirit—and lots of complexes too. We are on good terms. But I got a terrible shock when I visited her a year ago in N.Y.

I certainly do want to see your place. One day I'll manage it.

I notice from the letters how my handwriting has changed. Not yours!

This in haste, my best,
Henry

Letter from Anaïs Nin to Hugh Guiler:
Los Angeles, February 13, 1963

Darling:

Such lovely and rich letters you sent me. I am so sorry you were ill, for you were in such a good, active period.

Yesterday I was all taken up with Varda. First a dinner for him Monday night. Varda is in full production, effervescent, healthy; he looks like fifty and is seventy. Then yesterday he came to see me because I told him I had been writing a story about him. He wanted to tell me more stories, and I wondered why I could not remember them—the atmosphere of them, yes, but not the actual stories. Then yesterday I realized it was because there is no link between them; he wanders about and starts a new one without connection. This does not bother him, the *enchaînement* or association. To the average person he sounds mad. So I have to extricate from this some artistic coherence as you do when you cut your film. He took LSD once with Alan Watts and confirmed his theory about color, that it is all dependent on relativity. My story is charming, really, about Varda and his daughter. But listening to him for four hours was tiring.

I wish you could stop smoking. Your throat seems to be sensitive.

Secretly I feel in sympathy with De Gaulle. I share his fear of the influence of America...don't tell anyone.

Anaïs

Letter from Anaïs Nin to Hugh Guiler:
Los Angeles, February 1963

Darling:

How happy I am that the London business is going well.

Yesterday the Barrons gave a party, Gavin, Renate, Curtis, the Hirschmans, the Kesslers, Alan Watts, his girl, Virginia the yoga teacher, Ronnie, Daisy Aldan.

The day before I read at Pacifica with Daisy, the Mallarmé again, Breton poems, Eluoard, Baudelaire, Rimbaud. And then the orchestra section from "Winter of Artifice." I am reading better.

I went through a deep depression over two French reviews of *Spy* that are no better than the Americans ones: "Lillian should be good to her children and husband"; "a lack of objectivity"; "there are dedicated and loyal women in the world, but this is not one of them"; a bourgeois moralism, quoting the preface and turning it against me, picking out the small flaws, and though I had prepared for my idealization of French criticism, I am not prepared for hostility. All we can both say is that we are not immune to the blows, but we can recover. I went down, had one bad day and one bad night, doubted my work, myself, felt like a leper, and then slowly came back again.

Today I see Miller and his ex-wife Lepska and their children, as the French say, for the "relation" advantages. I am far from my romantic concepts of friendship.

Anaïs

Letter from Henry Miller to Anaïs Nin:
Pacific Palisades, February 23, 1963

Dear Anaïs,

Went straight to bed a few days ago with a bad cold after returning from Big Sur. Now up and fine. Lovely place, this new house. I have a good pool too. Feel I can work here—at last. Won't have to go to Paris till May or even later—just leaves me time to finish *Nexus*. And then I'm through. Don't need to write another line—unless I'm crazy enough to do so. Would rather paint now. Did quite a few recently—*forty*.

I haven't looked at the letters since I'm back, but will tonight on retiring. Somebody tells me the Durrell-Miller letters are wonderful. So, maybe after things cool off, we can get these out too. I'm sure they're good—from what I have read so far.

Yours is the last letter I have to answer—and then to work. What a relief! I go crazy sometimes with all there is to do single-handedly.

Now the Brooklyn authorities are after me again—trying to extradite me. Another mess. I count on my horoscope—which says prison is not for me. I'm charged with a *felony* this time—imagine it!

Henry

Letter from Anaïs Nin to Marguerite Young:
Los Angeles, February 1963

Dear Marguerite:

My renewed friendship with Miller was a Proustian experience. It was as if when I loved him I saw only one side of him, and now in friendship, the other side, the negative. I have yet to see him as the world sees him. In both him and Durrell I see this frightening lack of empathy, a lack of insight into others. They live in a completely fabricated world. Perhaps analysis has made me feel that such fabrications add to the blindness of the world, and I expect something clairvoyant from writers. And then I wonder—perhaps clairvoyance is not what people seek from a writer, but only fiction to add to the fictions they live with and in. Never before have I observed the fiction that love creates, the illusion (as, for example, of his honesty and simplicity) as when I see Miller today unhappy and alone with the world loving him, but he is somehow unable to accept it, feeling guilt, as he says.

How true what you say that the mature one does not feel guilt, but responsibility.

Hugo has finally achieved a great change with analysis. I hope the most recent downfall, to almost no income at all, will be the last. But his aim has not changed, and he continues his quest for "fortune" at 65; I had hoped he would surrender this living for projects that develop "later" to enjoy the present. He is happy when he travels.

I am writing stories around Renate, a woman painter I know here, and others. The theme (one you will appreciate from analysis) is how we often perform for the other a role that will mask our own needs or desires, as, for example, Miller's obsession about how the lies of his second wife, June, masked his own lies. In focusing his attention on her, he turned away from the knowledge that his life was filled with insincerities. He is one of those who take care of the weak to mask their own weaknesses.

It is 8:00 AM. Rupert has already gone to his school. The phone is quiet here, not like New York, where it rings every five minutes. Nature is quiet. The desk is covered with work to be done, letters to be answered. Do not see the Italian film *Mondo Cane*, about a man who went around the world dwelling on bloodshed, sadism, cruelties of all kinds. It will make you ill.

Anaïs

Letter from Joaquín Nin-Culmell to Anaïs Nin:
Oakland, April 20, 1963

Dear Anaïs:

Here are the "facts" with regard to Father for the diary: Born in Havana in 1879. Studied in Barcelona with Vidiella and Pedrell and in Paris with Moszkowsky and Vincent d'Indy. Was the first to perform and publish modern editions of Padre Antonio Soler and other Spanish classics of the XVIIIth century. His excellent settings of folk songs from all regions of Spain (primarily *Vingt Chansons Populaires Espagnoles* and *Ten Christmas Carols*) are classics of their type of music. He also wrote music for the piano, many articles on musicological subjects and two books: *Pour l'Art* and *Idées et Commentaires*. The books deal with the aesthetics of music and denote an uncommon thoughtfulness of attitude. His career as a first-rate pianist was overshadowed, particularly in his later years, by his reputation as a composer. He lived most of his life in Paris, but returned to Havana in 1939. He died there ten years later.

Quite agree with you about Cuba. It was a mess and still is. Too bad we never seem to learn... Much better to write books and music and bring a little gaiety to the grim mess we have made of the world.

Love,
Joaquín

Los Angeles, May 1963

Before retiring as the major character of this journal, I made one more sortie to take a look at Henry Miller 20 years later—when America began to pamper him, enrich him, praise him. It was not a very beautiful spectacle. Or was my vision clearer? He was utterly self-centered, and his enthusiasms were always projections or extensions of himself. He could only love what was like himself, the Beats, Kerouac (who was embarrassed by the exaggeration of his praise). He talked a great deal about money. He had sold my letters but would not tell me where. He was concerned only over his play being presented in Germany, and *Cancer* being filmed in France. He criticized my novels because they were not the Diary—when he, at one time, wanted me to abandon the Diary for the novels.

He refused to keep me in France, completely—I left hating him for his egoism. His falsely naïve questions. How could anyone believe his naïveté? It was like Fred's. It was an "act" intended to disarm. A comedy. The caricatural aspect, which was the first one I saw as a young girl; how could anyone fail to see it? What coldness too. Was I blind? Or was he different? Two more failed marriages, Lepska and Eve. It is strange that when passion has blinded one, one has a compulsion to become super-lucid, but I can't get this lucidity by looking at him through the eyes of others—it has to be through my own. But lucidity is dangerous. It exposes a Henry I did not know.

"People kissed my hand in Germany."

I prefer to think of Marguerite Young, who calls me up and tells me what she is writing about.

Once when I went to Smith College to read, there was a professor there [Newton Arvin], and Truman Capote was visiting him. They both came to my reading. I visited them for a little while. Later, this professor wrote an article for *Harper's Bazaar* on Romantic Realists in Writing. He did not mention me. I feel he should have, so I sent him *House of Incest* and *Under a Glass Bell* with a letter. He replied curtly and returned the books (one of a million incidents). Marguerite Young now tells me somehow or other his papers fell into the hands of the FBI, his intimate diaries and correspondence. It contained what the law calls moral turpitude and implicated Truman Capote. The professor was committed to a mental institution. Truman stayed abroad, she says, for this and for his open allegiance to Castro. Has he matured? He is one person I must complete, seek out.

Sylvia and Ted Ruggles: so late, so late, the illusions collapse, the façades, the mirages, and suddenly Sylvia has an expression I never saw before: soberness. There was always, until now, a triumph of humor in her eyes in spite of fatigue or illness, an expression of gayety. After 30 or 40 years a wife can say: he was perhaps not the right man, and I not the right woman.

When Swann marries Odette, one does not know why, but he discovers that he has suffered jealousy, has been a slave to a passion, has married a woman who was not really his "type" and whom he did not really love...

In love affairs, the end of illusion is not fatal. In marriage it is a sterile discovery—after 20 or 30 years—at age of 50 or 60. Too late to begin anew.

Sylvia has lost her physical charm. Ted is overweight and withdrawn. They depend on each other. Sylvia is Ted's connection with life. It is Sylvia's friends who fill the house with excitement. Ted hardly talks. He keeps a journal. He travels. When he travels he calls up Sylvia every night. "He is *so* dependent." He drank heavily. She was first divorced from a wealthy Southerner. She has experienced a frivolous, candied Southern life. She has intelligence, wit and shrewdness. She tried many professions (she writes poetry, draws, is well-read, and has all the social graces and amenities). She drifted into fundraising (Ted was a fundraiser) for the UN, for the handicapped, for colleges, for orchestras. It was the first time I had known a professional fundraiser, discovered the vast organization behind foundations—an organization woman.

We talked at first in the elevator of 35 W 9th St. She resembled Elsa Lanchester, but prettier—in miniature—but the same English roses-and-cream complexion, slight drawl on the lips. It was just after the war—she was traveling to Washington —he elsewhere. I met him early in the morning walking a homely, old dog (whose cleverness, *chantages*, mischievous inventions, mutinies and caprices Sylvia still tells of), shy—and evasive. Then there was tea in her apartment—old paintings, old furniture, many books. Impersonal talks. When Hugh had his film shown they both helped with advice, but we shied away from the organized wooing of the press, mimeographed announcements. (Hugo later took on a professional public relations person who was a fraud, a friend of Stanley.) Friendship developed. They came to our parties. At first it was an impression (although they were younger) of visiting uncomfortable parents—because of their plumpness, the atmosphere of the home seemed physically and mentally streamlined by comparison. But later this impression of niceties, old-fashioned virtues, a Southern lady, a Harvard graduate, faded. It was only a décor.

Sylvia's life appeared gradually as a parody of the lady at tea time. She led a hectic, dynamic life, full of agitation, contrasts, one moment doing publicity for the children of UNESCO, one moment for a circus, one moment for musicians. Her friends changed from dancers to the handicapped, committees in Washington, friends in trouble for whom I did personal favors (nursing, a little money, lending the apartment, etc.). I slowly gave her Peggy Glanville-Hicks, Harry Partch, Julian and Judith Beck, Jimmy Spicer, for more professional help. She enjoyed their talent, was tolerant of their neuroses, and explained she could not bear her commercial work if she could not associate with real artists to bring charm into her life. And so we shared this adoption bureau until it came to Marguerite Young. By this time, 15 years later, Sylvia's profession was no longer a skillful game that she covered with glamor (a telephone under a tea cozy was the image I had at first). It had become as all professions are in America—grim and sordid. At a party at our home she met Tennessee Williams. The next day she was on the telephone with him to get money for Peggy. People began to fear introducing her to their rich or powerful friends. Everyone knows rich people suffer a complex at being asked for help. To them it means: "I do not love you. I need you." You are either a friend or a beggar. I never had this complex, although people have always made inordinate demands on all I had, energy, time, etc., until recently when Americans who don't even bother to read my work or know me ask me for help only because of my name!

Anyway—Sylvia's professional experience failed to move foundations. I suppose foundations are cynical about professional fundraisers.

A merchant of illusion.

As Ted withdrew (he hated his business, wanted to be in education, is a scholar planning a book on philosophy), Sylvia became more and more assertive. She dominated conversations. Her business invaded the household. She was always on the telephone. When she moved to 47 W 9th, the salon looked like an office. She had a secretary. What parts were delusion, illusion, pragmatism? "Of all Sylvia's schemes," I asked Jimmy Spicer, now her assistant (I saved him from being exploited by Living Theatre), "how many come through?" "About 50%," Jimmy answered. But in the adventure now there was a note of hysteria, fatigue...and signs of faltering. She fell down some steps and broke her ankle. Ted was near a breakdown and went to an analyst.

In the upper classes (Caresse Crosby, Millie Johnstone, Sylvia Ruggles) there is a freedom, a reserve about the personal life that makes intimacy rare. *Il y a une coquetterie*—a certain form.

Sylvia had her "confidantes"—but for some strange reason our friendship never penetrated into the lower depths of our life. I veiled mine too. I don't know why. When drinking, she confided in Jimmy Spicer, who resented her confidences, felt them like a weight he could not carry. He wanted to leave. We had a false pride—perhaps because we first entered a partnership as parents do with hysterical, desperate children, and their troubles seemed more urgent. We were like two dutiful nurses who did not want to betray any weakness, inadequacy, or ill health.

Perhaps, too, I could not judge her *desire* to help—the need also to conceal one's own needs and wishes, being ashamed of them, and therefore disguising them by giving. To disguise one's desire to be given to—how well Bogner exposed my fantasy. Sylvia has not built up a fortune or an income such that she and Ted may stop working one day and become artists. They lived out their artist selves though others. But worse than this, Sylvia suffers the greatest killer in America: her profession makes her dislike herself.

Letter from Anaïs Nin to Alan Swallow:
Los Angeles, May 1963

Dear Alan:

I received the books in time for the lecture Monday. I must confess it was a huge success. Only Ray Bradbury can fill a hall here in California. About 100 students belong to the conference, but 200 came. I really roused them. I have become more concrete, more down to earth, more specific about writing, and they loved it. Also, in the last lap of my life, I have become more humorous. They all asked for a copy of the lecture and set about mimeographing it out of love. I was very happy and proud. This will be added to my new book on writing.

I was trying to get a fellowship so as to concentrate on writing. My lectures take a lot of time and energy. But they are good for the books. I have one in Boulder, and several in San Francisco. Boulder will bring me to Denver. I worked on a one-hour lecture all month. No wonder the students felt it was the only one that gave them something to study and write about. All meat and no fluff, they said.

Take good care of yourself.
Anaïs

Letter from Anaïs Nin to Alan Swallow:
Los Angeles, July 1963

Dear Alan:

Gunther will take good care of you. You deserve to be well-treated and included in every way, as you took me on when nobody else would. I will never forget these acts of personal devotion, and I am, so far, a writer who has brought you much, and I want whatever good comes to be for you too.

In a week or so you will get a draft of the new book of stories. I want to prepare you, it is not bulky, but it has humor (a new element) and a new form.

As soon as I am through with this book, I have to get the book on writing together. We will see who is nicest to you, Doubleday or Putnam. Ferlinghetti too. I have never respected those who "follow" the trends, but those who have the courage to start them out of their own convictions. Like Mr. Swallow.

Anaïs

Letter from Anaïs Nin to Oliver Evans:
New York, July 26, 1963

Dear Oliver:

I am so glad you and Hugo met. Now I am sure you understand my life better. I am interested in all you tell me about Carson, about separating the writer from the woman. I don't feel that way. Perhaps because the writing and I are the same, so I feel loved when someone cares for the writing. I can see the book presents problems, having to write it from her eyes. If Peter Owen should not turn out as scrupulous as you are, do not worry, for your book on my work will easily find a publisher. I can now talk about it to a representative of Doubleday who came to L.A. to meet me and hear my lecture. I have three publishers interested in me now.

In fact, now I worry because if they take the new book, somehow, I feel that poetic justice demands that you should be, as you are, my "discoverer," and I would like your book to point the way.

After you left, I had a beautiful month, writing early in the morning and going to the beach in the afternoon. I wanted to tear myself away.

How much more I gave in that one-hour lecture than at the panel, which bothered my scrupulous nature. How I wish you had lots of time and could write the book on writing with me. Publishers are waiting. I have fulsome material. But it requires a skill in coordination I do not have. We could make a textbook of it. The time is so right.

I am lengthening the new book of stories. I have no title for it. Several new sections. Was afraid at first to spoil the light mood, to unbalance it.

Anaïs

Letter from Alan Swallow to Anaïs Nin:
Denver, September 20, 1963

Anaïs dear,

On the new novel—yes, I like it. A great deal. Hasn't the conclusive power of *Minotaur* (that is, bringing the story to a close of altitudes achieved) but the making it a sort of "minor chord" is exquisite and tremendously funny. I'd go ahead with it at any time if these N.Y. boys won't come through with something decent for you and me.

Getting along okay, getting out lots of books, etc.

My leg is giving me a very bad time, just finished 30 days of an antibiotic treatment that hasn't worked, so I don't know just what will come of it. We are trying a few other things. Chiefly, I hope to avoid surgery on it. But, otherwise, okay. Still have problems getting time at the typewriter for more enjoyable correspondence, etc.

Love,
Alan

Letter from Henry Miller to Anaïs Nin:
Pacific Palisades, October 4, 1963

Dear Anaïs,

You will be receiving from me shortly—either in N.Y. or here—a formal letter gifting you the rights to my letters to you that are to be published. It will come to you from my lawyers who insisted that such a letter be written—for the usual legal reasons.

Hope to hear from you when you get back from N.Y.

All the best now,
Henry

Letter from Daisy Aldan to Anaïs Nin:
New York, October 1963

My dear Anaïs,

It looks as if the Henry Miller painting will have a hard time being sold. To give you my honest opinion, it's awful. He's really terribly untalented as a painter. Doesn't he realize it? Or does he just do it to earn money in that way? He'll have to answer for such conduct on the day of judgment.

Oh, yes—about the "humiliation" in New York—the humiliation must never be yours. It's the stupidity, cupidity, commercialism of the publishers that is wicked. *They* should be humiliated. You, never.

It is your destiny not to be commercialized…alas! In one way it is a shame, since you need the money, but then what great work was ever appreciated in its day? We'll just have to become big thermo-fax publishers ourselves—but I'm afraid we are both so unbusinesslike, we'll probably be doing copies for all our "friends" for free. So let's not tell anybody we have the machine. But we must really do a couple of limited edition little books.

Love,
Daisy

Letter from Anaïs Nin to Daisy Aldan:
Los Angeles, October 1963

Dear Daisy,

I was told not to ask for a grant to edit the Diary, and yet this is my major work, and it is what I want to do now. To be in control of my craft. I could never edit so tightly before, so surely, so objectively. I have done, edited and typed and re-written 175 pages since I came here. I seem to be typing all day and often in the evening while Rupert receives his quartets.

Nona Balakian. I wonder if she knows what pain she caused me. She came to my Gotham party. Gunther and Swallow wanted her to do a piece on me, for all the books just reprinted, and the new one just out. Not a word. And I thought, because of her sister's book on surrealism, she would have some feeling. I hope she will be kinder to you. You can tell her. They all let me sink in silence.

Just like Rimbaud, I am abdicating as a poet. I am writing no more poetic prose. I am starting now as a diary writer and realist. For the rest of my life I will be at work on this. The poetry and the fairytales (Oliver calls the last book Arabian Nights; he loves it) have alienated me and isolated me too much.

Love,
Anaïs

Los Angeles, October 1963

Contemporary stories begin generally with a telephone call. Virginia Dinesen has a light, fragile, girlish voice. She is crying. She has no one to talk to but me because her relationships are so complex and unconventional. I say: "Meet me at the beach—we can talk there." She arrives wearing a straw hat woven so loosely that the sun shines through the interstices and makes a checkered pattern over her face and shoulders. Her figure is slim and youthful, trimmed to perfection by yoga exercises and teaching yoga to others. Her face is older than her body, with large, green, dreaming eyes, her dark hair cut short and looped over the cheek. But sometimes the color of her skin turns pasty, as if she had not slept and the tired blood is stagnant behind the static makeup. This morning it shows traces of weeping. She spreads out her Japanese straw mat, lays her basket beside her, and Saki, her tiny, long-haired dog begins to grunt—like a small pig. After an attack of bronchitis its bark turns to a grunt. The sun shines on her bikini, on her half-exposed breasts. She has fine spider-web lines on the corners of her eyes.

Oliver arrives with his new dog, a slate-grey puppy with opal eyes. Virginia and I take a walk.

Virginia has a dual nature. If the Centaur were a woman (mythology favored men) the animal half of her body belongs to André, a young dark-haired singer in nightclubs, and the upper part (yoga, LSD, occultism, search for serenity, wisdom) to Tim Leary—when Leary was here and it seemed as if the plans to open a Freedom Center in Zihuatanejo were crystallizing, he was a guest of Virginia who was then occupying the beautiful house of her ex-husband Henry Dinesen (they had met in a Buddhist monastery). Virginia admired Leary's ideas, his pioneering in LSD, and either with or without the influence of LSD, they were lovers. He was an unsatisfactory lover. The chemical fluids, electrolades of sex concentrate in the brain. There is a diversion of energy. He removed his hearing aid to sleep. And André arrived at dawn, knocked Virginia down, broke some furniture, threw a bottle through a window, kissed her and proposed to her, slapped her and left while Leary remained blissfully asleep.

She said, "It is true André is brutal, but there are two sides to his nature. He can be utterly charming and so sensual and alive, and we can remain in bed for days without need of anyone. But when he loses his balance, becomes angry or jealous, he is like a madman. Everyone says to leave him, that he is bad for me, but, Anaïs, I look at all the relationships around me and they are so dead, so dead! At least with André it is wild. Look at the Barrons! Look at others around us. It is like Antonioni's *La Notte*. I prefer the violence, the beatings. I did wrong to laugh in his face when he proposed, but in the middle of the violence, it seemed absurd. I made up for it by trying to live entirely for him after Leary left. I acted like a wife. I did not go anywhere, but he becomes cruel as soon as I'm in his power. One night he called me up at midnight and said he was coming over, and I fell asleep and he never came. I called up his apartment at dawn and a woman answered. I asked her what she was doing there; she said she was playing with the dogs and handed André the phone." (André wants to make his way as a singer on TV, and the woman can be of great help to him.) "An hour later they were at my place to 'explain.' I refused to see her. André knocked me down and said, 'You want to destroy my career!'"

I usually combine a mixture of affection, sympathy, analysis, consolation and awareness, and Virginia stopped crying—André demolished her studies. But this has lasted five years, and she has to live it out, the extremes of a savage and an explorer of the unconscious with a hearing aid.

In the sun, on the beach, this image of hell is difficult to retain and dwell upon. I see Virginia on the terrace of Dinesen's beautiful house, in the morning, in a fitted jersey and ballet tights, on an orange mattress, doing yoga exercises and teaching Rupert and me how to breathe deeply, slowly, completely.

Letter from Hugh Guiler to Anaïs Nin:
Paris, October 22, 1963

Darling,

Georges Borchardt just called me to say he has heard from Marguerite Duras, who says she has read *Spy* and likes it. She is busy now and would not be able to do the screen treatment until next year, probably in the summer. Meanwhile, she thinks the choice of a director is of first importance and would like to know whom the producers have in mind. Borchardt suggests you send him a list, including Albicocco, Antonioni and others with whom Jerry Bick may be in touch and who would consent if Marguerite Duras does the screen treatment. Borchardt mentioned an American director in Europe called Joseph Losey as a possibility if the U.S. producers want an American, but of course Bick would have to approach him and get his consent in principle, at least.

Will be back in New York, according to the present plan, in a few days, so it will be a quick trip.

All my love,
H

Letter from Gunther Stuhlmann to Anaïs Nin:
New York, October 24, 1963

Dear Anaïs:

Here are three copies of the contract with Swallow for *D. H. Lawrence: An Unprofessional Study*. Would you please sign all three and return them to me?

I will have a check for you covering the advance tomorrow, when my new checkbooks come in.

Swallow liked the idea of Harry T. Moore introducing the book and he asked whether you or I wanted to write to Moore about this. Let me know.

Also, Swallow will reset the book and he asked whether there were any changes, corrections of typographical errors, etc. you wanted to make before he sets type.

As ever,
Gunther

Los Angeles, October 1963

Ronnie has asked Renate to let him live apart from her. He repudiates the mother in her and wants to rescue the lover relationship. At first Renate weeps, and her green eyes are so large she looks as if her whole body were weeping. But later she accepts the situation, and now she believes the relationship is balanced.

In August I finished a story about her, one about Varda, one on Lesley Blanch, one on Lila and her magazine, Henri the chef, Holiday House, Annette Nancarrow, Colonel Isham and Caresse, Djuna Barnes and Dr. Norman, and, untitled, it went to Peter Owen in London, André Bay in Paris, Peter Israel at Putnam, Alan Swallow in Denver. Various people read it, Gore Vidal, Gavin Lambert, Pierre Brodin, Daisy Aldan, Sylvia Ruggles, Varda, Marguerite Young, and love it. It was my first light, humorous book.

On September 20 I went to New York. Hugo was working on a marvelous long section of the Venice II film, the realistic one. He was learning theories of sound from Varèse. He was alive and enthusiastic—I helped him. I observed what he had done first (the myth and essence of Venice) was really the climax, the finale. It made a beautiful unit, beginning in the mud, and ending in a symphonic complex illusion and reflections.

I filed his cans of film in a big cabinet, built shelves in his dressing room, swam with him, ate in a newly-discovered French restaurant, saw Daniel Petrie and his wife (who wanted to option *Spy*), Pierre Brodin and his wife (Brodin said, in answer to my "What am I doing in the American literary stream?": "You are working for the future of American letters"), Varèse and his wife (Louise and I celebrated Lawrence Ferlinghetti publishing her translation of Michaux's *Miserable Miracle*, which I peddled indefatigably for years).

Letter from Anaïs Nin to Henry Miller:
Los Angeles, November 1, 1963

Dear Henry:

I wanted to free you from accountants, but I guess I don't understand the rules and regulations of economics! I do understand how you feel about going back and writing about the past, but I had an idea today while I was working (I was not able to do this job, which you did years ago, until now) that might help you. When themes begin to become weary, it is because they lose their life, and what restores them to life and our interest is a new vision into them. I see everything differently because I have changed. I was wondering (and I was going to talk to you about it) whether you had thought of reversing your vision of that past, not *finishing* a story, but telling about how differently it looks today. Everything looks differently. It took me twenty years to understand your interest in June's lies, and so everything takes on a new aspect. A new aspect! That's the thing that restores one's appetite. I jumped into the present this summer, wrote a book about the characters around me now, but there was not so much to say about them, so I went back to the major work of fullness.

You'll be glad to hear that I have walked out, like Rimbaud, of poetry forever. I could tell you what aspect of you you have left out of the last books, but that's too long and I will keep it for a talk, an aspect which might be its denouement!

Anaïs

Los Angeles, November 1963

Renate was at home. She had her sewing machine on the table with her paint brushes. On the couch lay a piece of black textile. On the back of a chair a black jersey jumper dress. On the dining table yards of black lace wrapped around yards of tissue paper. Her face was red from effects of typhoid fever shots. "I'm making a black wardrobe for the divorce. We are going to Mexico in two weeks. Ronnie has been very good to me. He has given me several thousand dollars. He loves me. He is already tired of his rich, young girl."

For two months, Rupert and I arrived and found her weeping; Ronnie had not made love to her. He, for years, was writing the same story. It was always a story about a prostitute. The last one was a one-act play in which the prostitute was preferred to the girl who loved the young man and wanted to marry him. Marriage was described as having the smell of diapers. It was such an infantile, hackneyed theme, that Renate should have been suspicious of it. And to the prostitute he did not give the lusty approval Miller did. Renate was too strong for him—that was obvious—too motherly, too dominant. She overwhelmed him. He had become more and more passive. He had returned to college. His writing was thin and without quality. Corny, tasteless, flavorless words!

The afternoon Rupert and I arrived, Renate wore her pale blue bikini and looked worn and deflated, more maternally fat than voluptuous.

She played the role of prostitute and they made love a few more times. She made him *pay* and she framed the first dollar he gave her. These games revived the relationship. Ronnie's first reason for leaving Renate was that he wanted to separate the mother and the mistress. Now, she was a "kept woman." But this was not enough. He had to be a man kept by a rich girl. The rich girl entered the scene. And she is paying for the divorce. I can see Renate all in black lace, traveling with Ronnie through the same towns they had visited as honeymooners four years earlier.

Letter from Anaïs Nin to Hugh Guiler:
Los Angeles, November 9, 1963

Darling:

Working at a rate of 20 pages a day on the edited Diary for the library. Worked on getting a title for the new novel. What do you think of *Twelve Pearls and Thirteen Oysters, Riding a Comet, Inscription on a Meteorite, Luni-Solar Fiestas, Ivory Boat, Statues Walk at Night, Statue on a Bus*?

Oliver came. He is a masochist. Tied himself up with Peter Owen so he cannot get an advance from an American publisher. Gunther writes me but always leaves something out and answers only a part of my questions. He does not look at the letter he is answering.

I'm writing like Niagara Falls. Must tell Bogner.

Wish I could see your film. You will have to have a print made for me for the University of Southern Illinois by December 10. What are your plans? If I go to Illinois I will go to Denver, too, and pick up $100 there. UCLA gives $2,500 for three lectures to Carson, Alberto Moravia, Tennessee, and here I am at $100 a shot. *C'est la vie…* How are you, darling?

Your A

Letter from Gunther Stuhlmann to Anaïs Nin:
New York, November 14, 1963

Dear Anaïs:

This Monday Peter Owen came into town and I had a long session with him. He asks me to tell you that he is enthusiastic about you, and that you should never have gotten the impression that he has "cooled off." I am seeing him again to get a contract for the new book signed. We are still discussing a title. I like *Count Laundromat*, and Hugo and I discussed other possibilities with his suggestion: *Count Laundromat and the 13 Oysters*. For British consumption Peter had put in the catalogue *Count Launderette* since this is the British term.

Miller letters. Peter has made a big pitch for these, offering you an advance of 500 Pounds if he could get them. I have stalled him, pending your feeling about this. Arthur Wang is also interested, and he wants to know how much money we want. Have you any thoughts? We can go shopping.

DIARY. I have had no further word on the committee meeting, but the question of publication rights has come up, and this will give us a chance to up the price from $50,000, which I had quoted for the diary copy per se. It gives us the feeling that they can do better, but it may also have depleted their coffers.

As ever,
Gunther

Letter from Anaïs Nin to Hugh Guiler:
Los Angeles, November 18, 1963

First of all, my darling, do not worry about Marguerite Young's impression of my "loneliness." As you know, she has such an imagination. I may have been blue. No, I am used to this rhythm of our life together, and then alone; Marguerite wants us together all the time. She projects her own loneliness, to which she has confessed, adding at the same time that she could not live with anyone around all the time. She is devoted to you, and feels all "separations" as we did. What she referred to may also have been the ostracism I have felt while writing poetic prose, the isolation as a writer. I have no closeness to any writer, although I have been generous and friendly (except to Marguerite, and that is good, for she is not destructtive nor jealous nor envious, but very maternal and helpful).

I have respected your wishes to leave you out of all this. It started with the index for universities, but ended by writing myself out fully...

Thank you for talking to Gunther. He has finally written. No, I won't have the title *Count Lauderette.* That's silly. Writing to Peter Owen.

I am glad you will be in Paris, love, and don't worry about me.
Anaïs

Letter from Gunther Stuhlmann to Anaïs Nin:
New York, November 22, 1963

Dear Anaïs:

Just a brief note—I am still under the shock of the Kennedy assassination, which just was announced—to acknowledge contracts. I have passed a copy on to Peter and we should have the advance soon.

His offer for the Miller letters only covers the British rights and it leaves us free in the States. We should also get a decent advance here, and I have invited bids from a number of people.

As ever,
Gunther

Letter from Anaïs Nin to Hugh Guiler:
Los Angeles, November 1963

Darling:

I will call you today but this is just a note for your trip. Have been very upset by the death of Kennedy, as everyone was. Like a death in the family. He represented quality and intelligence and many other things. The ugliness of it all is overwhelming. I believe it had a deep unconscious effect on America, perhaps first of all rousing their almost dead capacity to feel, then to become aware of their hostilities. And the dangers of it. All they can think of is to outlaw guns. But deeper thinkers are exposing underlying hostility. And the worst of it is that many (I don't know what you think) feel it may not even be political, or psychotic, but purely money and oil well interests. That would be the final humiliation. Exposure of the ruthless element. I would have liked to know what you felt and thought.

I am so sorry you had so many difficulties with the film. It seems to be in the nature of filmmaking and I do hope from now on we will not accept any deadlines. They are not good for you when you have your other job to attend to.

Don't waste your energy on Albicocco. Or on Duras. Or Bay. These things take time and energy. Your time is too short. Albicocco proved himself an irresponsible person. *Spy*, according to Anne Metzger, is being revised by Bay; he made changes she does not like, changes that she considers taking liberty with my text (don't tell him she wrote me), so my destiny is to continue to work as usual—bitchy. I am writing to Bogner, so I can handle all this with coolness. I don't want you using your energy on all this. Not worth it.

Take care of yourself,
A

Letter from Luthor Nichols of Doubleday to Anaïs Nin:
San Francisco, November 27, 1963

Dear Miss Nin:

I'm terribly sorry to have to report that, after much top-level consideration in New York, Doubleday has regretfully decided it cannot make an offer for the untitled manuscript you so kindly let us see.

Just between us, I'm afraid that in the final analysis your work was too unconventional for our house. The more conservative element had its way.

This will come as no great shock to either of us, I'm sure. Longstanding preferences in publishing are not easily broken in any firm, but I had hoped your work would be an instrument for piercing our barriers here and getting us into more experimental literary fields. Alas, that will now have to await another day.

Will return the MS under separate cover.

This may seem completely at variance with the sad note of this letter, but here's wishing you a very happy Thanksgiving.

Cordially yours,
Luthor Nichols

Letter from Harry T. Moore to Anaïs Nin:
Carterville, Illinois, November 28, 1963

Dear Anaïs:

Here is a copy of the preface for *D. H. Lawrence: An Unprofessional Study* I have sent to Alan Swallow. I hope you will like it—I was honored to be asked to write it. Rereading your book, I am struck again with its fineness—and I am indeed delighted it is being reprinted. Indeed, hooray!

Caresse was here with us during the horrible days after the Kennedy murder; we all sustained each other. On Saturday night we didn't call off a social event to introduce Caresse to some of our friends; we have since had many phone calls and notes from people saying how glad they were that we went ahead with the affair. It was a time for friends to get together, and everyone loved Caresse. But the assassination has left a scar on us all. The crushing of such wisdom and youthful eagerness; in time he would have been one of the few really great presidents; he almost is now, potentially.

All best to Hugo,
À la bonne heure,
Harry

Letter from Daisy Aldan to Anaïs Nin:
New York, November 1963

Dearest Anaïs:

About your decision to avoid poetic writing...

I'm glad you are working on the diaries. No doubt this is what you are supposed to be doing now. And if you're being "realistic," because your inner impulse at this time in your life is to be so, then, great. But if it's compromise...well, you know my feelings about this. Yes, great fame in your lifetime would be pleasant (perhaps)—but what great writers, artists of all kinds, thinkers, ever achieved it?

Darling, you haven't "sunk in silence" yet. If you look at all the "crap" (forgive me) that is published by big publishers, you must realize it's business—commercial. All this work will be wafted away like useless dust in a short time. Your work, bred in truth, art and love, *will live*. It isn't important (believe this!) for it to get a hundred million readers right now. It isn't wasted. It is important for the development of the world—the earth needs it if the earth is to live. It is being noted...not lost, believe me...not only by some people, but by the gods. They will do with it what is important for the earth, in the time that it will have the most significance. I know this. I believe this. If you are to fulfill what you are supposed to fulfill as a special and conscious Being, which you are, gifted with the *word*, the most important aspect of humanity, you must believe this and never despair. It is *absolutely true*. The important thing is to go on working—in truth, in newness, never compromising, never stopping a style or an insight because it isn't popular or accepted. (You said it yourself...you were right then.) They (those Beings who direct our lives) are wiser than us. Perhaps it is necessary for you not to be a popular success now.

Love,
Daisy

Letter from Anaïs Nin to Hugh Guiler:
Los Angeles, December 3, 1963

Darling:

Received your letter. It's funny I wrote you about similar assassinations in Paris and similar reactions (right blaming left, left blaming right). All the more striking as I went to see *Lord of the Flies*. The reversion of children to barbarism was very unconvincing in that story, based on finding themselves alone and having to hunt for food. Weak. As you say, not facing the real issue, which is hostility within.

I am glad you gave up cigarettes because your throat is so sensitive anyway. I am glad you feel Marguerite is a great writer. I wish now I had helped her instead of Miller. But sometimes dealing with one's opposite is better than seeking harmony. I am very glad about your salary raise. And our next year looks good, I am sure with the Diary, etc.

Did the French hostess say to you: You are the most handsome, the most modest, the most charming man that I ever had the honor to meet? Well, I do now.

Piccolo just had a much-needed bath.

I have given up the idea of the film.

Proofreading my book on Lawrence for Swallow.

Much work.

Carter Harman did the sound recording on *Lord of the Flies*, but did not compose the music.

Love,
A

Letter from Gunther Stuhlmann to Anaïs Nin:
New York, December 12, 1963

Dear Anaïs:

I will deposit Peter Owen's check in your account. He told me it was on the way. He also mentioned that apparently you had agreed to call the new book *Collages*?

He has also been after me regarding the Miller letters and mentioned that you had agreed to his proposal of an advance of 500 Pounds. I have been stalling him a bit since we have to have Henry's approval first before we can sign anything. I could always explore the possibility of Henry's English publisher, blaming this on Henry as far as Peter is concerned, and we could take the best offer. Here, I am still talking with Hill & Wang. I told them we needed a substantial advance.

As ever,
Gunther

Letter from Henry Miller to Anaïs Nin:
Pacific Palisades, December 12, 1963

Dear Anaïs,

Once again I'm getting dubious about my getting through the letters. I'm going to bed now—with a cold. Would love to read them in bed but my eyes are watering so I probably couldn't get far.

In addition I've been saddled with more work—things I can't escape doing. Drives me crazy sometimes—never seem to get free to do my own work—*writing*, I mean. Am always putting the writing off.

Well, I'll see what's what over the weekend—then, if I see it's impossible, I'll have to ask you to select for me—and then read. Am very sorry about this. But I am sure it will all work out all right.

More soon,
Henry

Letter from Alan Swallow to Anaïs Nin:
Denver, December 13, 1963

Anaïs, dear:

How very wonderful to have 200 pages of the diary! I appreciate it very much. Sending, as you suggested, 100 pages at a time is fine indeed. I will return each 100 in turn. Now I know you are getting this "ready," in part so that you can let go of the original. Right? What does this work on it mean now? Is it getting ready for publication? I am eager, of course, about that; but I understand that you will let me know when it is ready in the sense that you *can* go ahead with publication. As for publishing it, I don't know what I will need in terms of capital; depends upon just how fast it comes, in a sense; if it is to be done in one big swoop, yes, the printing costs would require extra capital, and if Henry Miller would be interested, fine. If it goes more slowly, a volume at a time, I could handle it, undoubtedly, as money would be coming in continuously on each volume.

I feel dull and the fingers are not operating well. Have still had a time of it. The reason I feel vague right at the moment is that the leg woke me up two hours early this morning (only three hours of sleep, then) with pain, and I took a painkiller—I can't use aspirin, and this ones I do take makes me feel that way. Have continued with such troubles, but I still have some hope that we will get the answers and that, although I will have *some* trouble with it the rest of my life, it will be a minor annoyance.

Alan

Letter from Gunther Stuhlmann to Anaïs Nin:
New York, December 17, 1963

Dear Anaïs:

Though I have heard from you no further about the Miller letters, I am airmailing you a very rough assembly, which goes from the time of Dijon to that of Corfu. There is enough for a book, a big book in there, and it is developing as a fascinating discourse. There is much pruning, dating, ordering, etc. to be done, but I felt it was better to show Henry the maximum from which we can subtract, rather than the smaller selection. Once he has approved all of this, we can use less. There are some points of remarks about people, etc., which will have to be checked. Work, yes, but fascinating. I am really getting into this and am excited. It will be a big thing. There is still quite a batch of the U.S. letters, which may almost make another volume.

Tom Payne asked me for some letters for *Playboy*, and he wanted to make us an offer for Putnam's. I told him he had to make this offer on my say-so, sight unseen, since I am tired of their hemming and hawing.

Let me know when you get this. The other section will follow in a day or so. Once Henry has given the okay, I can settle down to the fine work.

Happy holidays,
Gunther

Letter from Henry Miller to Anaïs Nin:
Pacific Palisades, December 24, 1963

Dear Anaïs:

I found the new batch of letters and will start going through them just as soon as possible. I'm in a terrible mood—really depressed, discouraged, no desire to do anything—but suppose it will burn off, like the fog, before too long. Feel bad not having gone through all the other letters. Each day new chores come up, new problems—on *all* levels. It's driving me nuts.

Yes, I want to return the big batch of letters to you. But I don't want to mail them. Is there someone who could pick them up here? Would need to know in advance *when* the person would call so that I will be here. Maybe just send me a card and I'll answer by phone if OK or not. I don't answer the phone at all anymore.

Sorry to give you such a dismal picture of things. It's always this way at Xmas for me. Maybe a little worse this year, that's all. But I won't die! I didn't send out any cards or give any gifts—not even to the children. That's a step in the right direction, I feel.

Henry

1964
Mon Journal
Journal des Autres

Letter from Alan Swallow to Anaïs Nin:
Denver, January 3, 1964

Dear Anaïs:

Your note from N.Y. dated yesterday arrived just a moment ago. I shall try to be patient and get off this reply immediately. I say "patient" because I have been a bit beside myself to know what to do. I received, you recall, a letter from you a week ago saying you had postponed your trip to N.Y. because of the flu, and I just didn't know where to write you. Finally, two days ago or so, I did write you at L.A., but, of course, now you are gone. I do wish you had sent me an airmail card the moment the decision was made, all you had to do was to say "off to N.Y." and I would know.

I get a better sense now of the diary. In this preparation you have done, selection, rewriting, etc., are you getting close to publication? When can we proceed? Are you at liberty to go ahead with this section (involving Henry) ahead of some others that you must hold back? If so, fine. Are you at liberty to publish any of that which precedes this part dealing with Henry, etc.? I certainly would like to get a clear picture. But I am ready at the drop of the hat, so to speak.

Best always, even if I do get a bit impatient!
Alan

Los Angeles, January 1964
University of Southern Illinois—a retrospective of Caresse Crosby's life: Letters of Kay Boyle to Caresse. Letters of D. H. Lawrence, Joyce, Crevel, Aldington, Nin (mine are under glass for my visit, exhibit Nin, *Under a Glass Bell*, dead already, living in the future for biographers and students; it gives me a ghostly feeling).

I see Hugo's engravings given to Caresse, Miller's letters and watercolors, Cartier-Bresson photos, snapshots, portraits of Caresse and Harry Crosby, Harry's diaries, red leather bindings, letters of Glenway Wescott, etc.

A strange world. Collections. Bibliophiles. First editions. It is frightening to see one's self or friends becoming history—what was personal and intimate made public. In the old days, people waited for this to happen until after their death, their own and the death of friends and lovers. But today there is amorality, an absence of ethics, a great impatience; the acceleration of life precipitates the young, the not-yet-famous to donate or sell things—the new libraries are eager to get *filled*.

Under a glass is the story of the days when Gonzalo and I worked for Caresse, printing a book—the exacting, capricious taskmaster she was to us was recorded in the Diary.

It was a visit to tombs, mausoleums, pyramids, to the past, which is also the future, but not the present.

That night at the museum, Max Jacobson was there, injected with so much of his B12 that he smelled of it, in the snow and in the cold, and he took care of Maya Deren, of McGregor of New Directions, etc.

The web: Hugo shivers with fever and chills and I would gladly become ill to make him well. He does not deserve to suffer. I do. I fabulate to keep Rupert waiting a few days. I call Dr. Bogner, and René de Chochor is having dinner there! René met her at a summer beach colony one summer, and he knew Dr. Manrique, who was a friend of Gonzalo's and whose wife seduced Tana's third husband and married him. At Dr. Bogner's office Brooks Clift read my books while waiting, showed them to Kim Stanley. Gonzalo died of the disease he most feared, cancer. Helba survived him, but he was spared old age, which he feared even more. Hepatitis undermined Hugo's vitality, but even more, his obsession with business, which his neurosis, prevented him from being truly successful so that he gambled, invested, wasted almost as much as he made. Wasn't Rupert wiser to retreat from challenges that his neurosis would have doomed to failure? To retract and contract from conflict?

How many people I sent to Bogner who did not go—refused to go—Jim Herlihy (he failed), Hill Kluver, who committed suicide, Daisy when she is haunted by her succubus.

Daisy first appeared to me dressed in rough, lesbiany tweeds, a bag hung from her shoulder, low-heeled shoes, plump and small, not beautiful but with a charm of voice and animation. We went to dinner in the Village and talked like shocked idealists outraged by the callous behavior of people—Daisy drew up her list of outlandish hostilities, I mine, and it made a bond, a devoted friendship, faithfulness, a love that had to be prevented from becoming desire. I experienced for the first time not the cruelty of the one desired, but the strange resentment toward the one who desires me when I cannot respond. Why anger? It should be anything but anger. When you do not desire, the desire of the other seems like an illness, a wound, a reproach. Never fathomed this. When Walter Starcke is cruel, openly jeering at homosexuals, I'm outraged at him. He is the first I did not romanticize. His is a cold mind, arrogant with far too high an opinion of himself. Oh, the American brat. The first film he makes, the first poem he writes, the first painting he paints, is exhibited, advertised, pushed, for sale, and then he is busy propagandizing.

There is also the Astrologic Web. Daisy continues the sign of Virgo, my father's sign, only with her I was able to break the barrier, and his persona was so much more impregnable, insulated. But when Eduardo's cold fire reappears in Walter, I can see what I dislike and repudiate—a coarser form of it—in Eduardo the retractions of tenderness and sensitivity, in Walter a vulnerable self not sensitive to others.

Much of this extraordinarily rich material I did not fully encompass, delve into. I was living a lover's life too feverishly, and all that I sensed and perceived intuitively (like the understanding of Artaud) I did not take time to expand. I did not have the care, the patience, the craftsmanship, the thoroughness I have now. It is no accident that I find Artaud's letters in the vault, that I read them with new eyes—rediscover them and will be able to complete the picture. As I wrote to Henry, I am enjoying this journey and these relationships now because I am free of my hypersensitivity, which made them painful at the time.

Years ago, Maya Deren came to my group of friends to seek her actors, appropriated Gore Vidal, a beautiful girl who lived with a negro musician, a South American painter and his girl, a dancer. She called us up, and we reported for work at Riverside, at Central Park, in her studio.

"Take a taxi, I'll pay for it!" was the classic order, and at first we believed it, but later recognized the myth and took subways. We went to New Jersey, to a park filled with statues, a hot house, a formal garden. We danced. There were sadistic scenes. In Central Park the dancer (a ballet dancer whose life depended on his legs) did not want to leap across jagged, uneven rocks. Maya taunted him as if her film were a major work of art worth any human sacrifice. She used her Mable Dodge Luhan will, threats. "You are a coward!" We asked him not to leap. I placed my coat over the rocks when I saw Maya was going to win. She made the dancer feel if he did not jump, he was a weakling. He leaped. He did not break his leg. But our faith in Maya as a human being was shattered. It was our first glimpse of the monster, the one who later learned the hexing of voodoo rituals with facility and practiced them on Stan Van der Beck.

But the Maya among the community of women at the pink baby shower for Bebe Barron was impossible to superimpose over the Maya in gypsy *oripeaux* [tinsel], dancing primitive dances, or setting her camera before a cat who was expecting kittens, or Maya sending Sasha Hammid out for a walk while she tried to seduce Charles Duits, then seventeen years old, who telephoned me: "Anaïs, please come over, Maya has started her war dance, and I'm the next victim..."

How could someone who calls herself Maya produce a genuine life or work—I see her on a horse, a Cossack woman with a leather belt six inches wide, boots, blouses, furs, knives...

When her Japanese husband's father died and they had hoped for an end to poverty, he was deprived of the inheritance by a family plot; after the stormy meeting, on the way home, Maya had a stroke.

She died of anger.

Daisy helped me to decipher Antonin Artaud's handwriting when I missed some words. Daisy, whose first appearance as a dowdy schoolteacher, changed with time. She dressed better, took a new apartment, decorated it, modernized herself, had an affair with Karon Kehoe and found her rough and violent (her lovemaking was like her words and attitudes, sadistic, primitive); Daisy confided her love for a Spanish-French woman in Algeria and later in Nice (in the watering holes of Fellini's *8½*), which may have unleashed her desire for me (echoes and resemblances of type). This desire was what unbalanced our friendship, as I was forced into elusiveness and escapes even after I told her directly that I was not attracted to women sexually (if I had been, I would have desired Tana), so slowly Daisy emerged on the New York scene reading poetry at the FM station and The Living Theatre. At the Maison Française we read together. We collaborated on *Two Cities*—she took over the editorship because she wanted the "credit" for her PhD, but found Fanchette impossible to work with.

The lurking desire for physical warmth warped the friendship, but she was loyal, devoted, and finally we overcame the obstacle.

She now reads Artaud because Jack Hirschman does, because Mary Caroline Richards translates him. Was it my fault that I did not proselytize these writers I loved? I always felt my talk fell on deaf ears—Jouve's novels, Giraudoux, Dumas.

Today, recreating and rediscovering them, I feel a deep, wild, painful nostalgia for my life in France. What a violent contrast to America! How can I compare the poets I knew here—Patchen, Duncan, Daisy—to Artaud? Marguerite, yes, she has stature, but it is limited to America; it is not international.

Bogner opens a pocket of guilt at the same time as she opens a well of guilt in Hugo for his "business" of helping the rich avoid taxes (trusts, foreign investments, etc.). It was his profession to help the rich remain rich. And it bothered his scrupulous soul.

Doctor's Hospital, New York, January 1964

Hugo is ill with bacterial pneumonia. I should be in Los Angeles. I have to tell Rupert I need Jacobson's care for a week for a low blood count. Hugo sleeps. I am merely a nurse. My Proustian work on the Diary is my only joy, tracing webs and correlations.

The web: Gonzalo met Lila—both left-wingers; Lila sang and played her guitar; Gonzalo gave her *House of Incest* to proofread while I was away. (He told me he had met a girl who loved my writing. He tried to sleep with her, but she hated men sexually.) Lila is now friendly with Woody Parrish Martin, who has changed from an utter snob to a quieter, sincerer man. She is cured of drinking, is writing stories, having an affair with a negro painter (who makes Woody the scapegoat for his "humiliations," and who, during fights for integration, could not sleep with Woody because he felt "guilt" at loving a white man).

Years ago, when I had to go to the hospital for my tumor operation, everyone said, "Well, that is one event Anaïs will not be able to alter, color, enhance, heighten or romanticize." A brutal fact. A prosaic common occurrence. Anaïs and her "genius for living." *Rien à faire.* Hard, stony realism, the hospital.

Well, Anaïs took care of that too. She went the same day as the King of the gypsies. According to gypsy tradition, when the king falls ill, his subjects must all gather around him and stay near him. 600 gypsies camped outside the hospital in an empty lot. All day they came in and out. Tired of the invasion, the hospital barred them from filling the elevator. They climbed up and down the stairs. I saw them—met them in hallways. Black hair and swarthy or olive skin, moon-faces, necklaces, sandals—even in winter they were not heavily covered.

When I had pneumonia at Mount Sinai, I wore my red wool Moroccan burnouse in the chair on the way down for X-rays. An ideal, warm wrapping—like a blanket. The color cheered everybody, was a note of joy. I spread it over my bed.

Letter from Anaïs Nin to Alan Swallow:
Los Angeles, January 1964

Dear Alan:

Here is Henry Miller's comment on *Collages*:

"The book abounds in magical descriptions of a highly original and sensuous nature, often spliced with a sly and wanton humor which is never vulgar, never cloying. The miracle is that, despite the miniature aspect of these delineations, they demand no padding, no psychological insight to be relished and digested. The best of collages fall apart with time; these will not. Like the Persian rugs the author mentions in one of the stories, these tales even when worn out will be readable."

Affectionately,
A

Letter from Henry Miller to Anaïs Nin:
January 12, 1964

Dear Anaïs:

I finished reading the letters today. Should I turn them over to Dr. Macy now—to ship to Gunther or to deliver to you? Let me know.

It will make a fat book, if all of these letters are published. They were in pretty good order, I think. Where they were out of order, I indicated it. I also marked places in margin where I thought passages should be cut for one reason or another. Sometimes real names should be changed—or else sentences cut. Too compromising or else derogatory—I think of Hugo, Wambly Bald, June, Caresse, etc.

Also, if you remember, there's a lot of talk about money—you giving me money constantly. I am not sure that *you* want all that mentioned. I checked quite a few spots—maybe *you* should now check, or else wait until galley proofs are made, then go over everything with a fine comb, all three of us.

There was one letter on the Royal Opera letterhead, Monday afternoon, mentioning Kahane, Gallimard, June in an incriminating way. Don't know now if I checked that.

By the way, I have photos of two wall charts mentioned in the letters—one on my Lawrence book and another on the Brochure. Also a cover of a big notebook mentioning Walter Lowenfels. These might be good to reproduce in the book.

I notice quite a difference between the letters from Europe and those from America. Makes two neat divisions. You mentioned recently a tentative title, but forget what it was now.

So, I'll wait to hear further what to do with all three batches of letters. Sending this c/o Gunther, to forward to you, as I'm not clear where to write you at this point. Will drop Gunther a line too. Good luck!

Going back to bed—with a fresh cold.
Henry

Letter from Gunther Stuhlmann to Anaïs Nin:
New York, March 5, 1964

Dear Anaïs:

The contracts for the Miller letters arrived safely and went out to Putnam's right away. They also have a copy of the latest letter signed by Miller, which was drawn by George Shively and supersedes the previous ones. So all is in order on that front. To speed up things I gave Putnam's Hugo's social security number for the tax return since his accountant said this was all right, and I think Putnam's will go along.

So, the check should be there any moment and we can finally drink the champagne.

Hugo seems to be better.
All my best,
Gunther

Letter from Hugh Guiler to Anaïs Nin:
New York, March 1964

Darling:

No letter from you this morning, so I have to hope for one on Wednesday. Saw *The Servant* last night directed by Losey and did not like it at all. The scenario, by Harold Pinter, was for the most part crude and sometimes quite vulgar, when it was not childish, apart from one frankly homosexual scene that contained the only real emotion in the whole film. I would particularly think you would do well to steer away from Losey as a director for your subtleties.

Nobuko, with whom I saw this film, was equally disappointed with it; I had the impression that she is gradually maturing, at least as far as her critical sense is concerned. She was on a TV show, but I did not see it; she is still dieting and taking off more weight, but she remains pleasant to look at.

Tana is back from Cuba and talked to me over the phone for about three quarters of an hour about how wonderful things are there and how misinformed we all are. She will invite me to a meeting at her apartment when she will have many of her friends who are interested in Cuba, to show her photos, etc.

Love,
H

Letter from Anaïs Nin to Hugh Guiler:
Los Angeles, March 10, 1964

Darling:
Your letters gave me a permanent pleasure. You feel a return to life, and one is so grateful for all one did not notice before. You feel now as I did when I came out of the hospital after the tumor operation, when I had really thought I was going to die…and nearly did under the anesthetic…and then found myself in the Yucatan, on the pyramids, starting anew…and again after the pneumonia.

Worked well today. Am at page 619 of the Diary. Was just asked to be on the tribute symposium on Huxley at UCLA on May 10. Dates are always difficult for me to accept... I hem and haw...not knowing… You plan to go to Europe in April. Will you be strong enough?

Did I tell you about the "happening" Renate invented for her unveiling of her Pisces painting? She used me, as Ondine. Fishes, sea, an arch, and a collage of all my book covers. I am bound like a mummy—Ondine in strips of ticker tape paper with writing on them. She and John Houseman were the two fishes. But the symbolism got rather mixed up, as they were dressed in white. Tom (Renate's new lover) shot at them and blood came on to the dress (when the artist is shot through the heart he gives birth to flowers) and red roses popped out of the dresses, while I turned and unwound some kooky phrases on the meaning of Pisces. But people laughed, and now Curtis Harrington wants to film it. They said we made the painting come to life. The truth is that a happening is merely action. For better or for worse, we are all trying to make images flow (as only you do)...the poor painting looked pretty dead! The fish were frozen...but if Renate has anything, it is spirit and ebullience.

Love,
Anaïs

Letter from Gunther Stuhlmann to Anaïs Nin:
New York, April 15, 1964

Dear Anaïs:
Just got your card and thus hope this still reaches you in L.A. I received the two charts from Henry that you sent along and I have not yet had time to decipher them.

A few days ago I put about $70 into your account here, Swallow royalties, up to the end of December. He keeps selling in small batches, but it goes on. I wish he would keep me posted re: reviewers so that we might stir up some life here at this end since I don't think he has the manpower to do so.

As for Bay, I just got a letter from him making me the same offer for the Miller letters he had already made to you, and he mentioned that *Spy* would be coming out. At the same time, he writes: "As for *Collages*, I have the manuscript, but if I have to make a decision now, it will be negative." So, this would give us an out with him if we wanted to break. If you do go to Paris, tell him the Miller letters are in my hands and you don't know what's going on, and the same goes for Peter Owen. I have already had some correspondence and I explained to him simply that we have to have Miller's okay and that there are "complications"—so don't write or talk to him about this. The same with Bay—I wonder why he doesn't want to commit himself to *Collages*—so why should we give him the Miller letters? I want to keep things friendly, i.e. dangling at the moment, so he does not louse us up on the *Spy* any more than he has already.

I will have a contract with Swallow for *Collages* drawn up—he offered a $350 advance, which is the best he can do. How does that strike you?

As ever,
Gunther

Letter from Anaïs Nin to Alan Swallow:
En route to New York, April 20, 1964

Dear Alan:

We corresponded with Marguerite Duras in Paris (my agent and I) and she accepted the terms of Robert Wise, the director. Now we are all meeting in Paris and going to Salzburg where Wise is making a film. If Duras and Wise get along (unknown chemical reaction) and he likes her ideas, then all is set for an art film—not a big production. If this succeeds, it will be great for all of us.

Anaïs

Letter from Renate Druks to Anaïs Nin:
Los Angeles, April 27, 1964

Dearest Anaïs:

I received *Collages* and it is heaven. No one will ever be able to compliment me again. Thank you so much for seeing me so beautifully.

Putting *my* ego aside for a moment, *the rest of the book is heaven too*. And what genius to have it begin again at the end.

Love,
Renate

May 1964
Trip to Paris with Hugo.

Letter from Anaïs Nin to Rupert Pole:
Paris, May 2, 1964

My love:

What a rush of things! This morning I had an interview with *Art* (the paper I used to read for news of France) at 10:30. Can't remember if I told you that Duras was in Paris and didn't ask me over, but I will see her Sunday evening. I had a lot to do for Bay. Dinner with Marguerite Rebois last night. City so soft and beautiful with new lighting on more and more buildings. So alive. On St. Germaine the light comes through the trees and the whole church is dappled with moving shadows.

Bay is really impossible, dreamy, vague, *distrait*. It turns out he was tubercular at one time. I hope to get away from him. My press agent is called Sabina! I'll be photographed Monday walking along the Seine (looking for my houseboat?). Sun is shining today. I expect Jerry Bick Tuesday but don't know what time, damn it.

Full of blue marks: when I come out of the bathtub I hit my elbows on the wall, my knees on the tub edge, my head on a lamp! I miss our castle! Our sumptuous home! The Lord and Sire! The only thing I find human about Paris, however, as against massive proportions of N.Y., are those tiny, tiny houses, tiny windows. People sitting at a table with small red lamp look like puppets in a puppet house. After the U.S.A. Paris looks toy-like. The *little* policeman photographing the tourist last night as we walked. Imagine a big Irish cop doing that!

With my love. It will be a useful trip, I feel.

More soon, all yours,

A

Letter from Anaïs Nin to Rupert Pole:
Paris, May 4, 1964

Darling:

Bay's vagueness and stupidity. He never sent the MS to Duras. He sent *Ladders to Fire* (*Miroir* in French—she loves it, loves the Party—thought of what a film *it* would make). She is *now* reading *Spy*.

If I hadn't come! Comedy of errors.

Duras likes the poetry. I will hold this till later when I know how she feels about *Spy*.

I'm n-e-r-v-o-u-s.

Later: OK, she *loves* it.

All the interviews have been successful—the French really want to understand me.

Darling—I know this is hard on you, my trip—but this one will enrich our lives, I know—I'm at a good moment. The *toughest* TV interviewer became sweet with me.

But I long for you, my home. I feel so nervous all the time—like you onstage—or before stage. I couldn't *live* onstage. My love for Duras and her reciprocity has been a blessing.

Spring is here at last.

Love, love,

A

Letter from Anaïs Nin to Rupert Pole:
Paris, May 7, 1964

Darling:

Leaving for Salzburg tomorrow morning. We really kidnapped Duras, who was not ready, because Jerry's time here is short. Her English is very limited. But she is cooperative, conscientious, scrupulous. No ego. Her last book is number 7 on the best sellers list. We are in the same paper today. My book *Spy* is in every window. What fun. But oh, my love, I don't *thrive* on publicity as some people do. I'm tired. Duras calls TV interviews the electric chair.

No news of you—because of holiday, I guess.

All my love,

A

Letter from Anaïs Nin to Rupert Pole:
Paris, May 10, 1964, Sunday morning

Darling:

Wondering how you are and Piccolo.

Wise's older brother is a business manager. He will draw up contracts with Jerry, who returns to L.A. Tuesday or Wednesday. Mine will be only a $500 option till shooting begins in February.

Poor Gunther—his mother is dying in Hamburg. We talked on the phone.

Of course, there was talk about actresses. Duras said Jeanne Moreau. Jerry said Ava Gardner. Wise said nothing. Is Marie La Forêt too young, too girlish?

Your wife was "cool." Publicity will be good for me.

Burroughs, Mary McCarthy and my English *Collages* in the windows together!

Love,

A

Postcard from Anaïs Nin to Alan Swallow:
Paris, May 1964

I talked about you over Radio-Canada—your story. One-hour interview. Really made it in Paris! Met all the critics and journalists, made new friends. Could you possibly get in touch with *Newsweek*, give them news of the film to be made: ROBERT WISE, DIRECTOR; JERRY BICK, PRODUCER; MARGUERITE DURAS, SCENARIO. *It is news.* They should synchronize with *Collages*, too, which has *good* reviews in England. I feel this is the time. The reception of Paris healed me. Such a soft, gentle city. But I am exhausted. Must have seen 100 people—can only fly to L.A. to regain strength. Visits till the last minute.

A

Letter from Anaïs Nin to Hugh Guiler:
Los Angeles, May 28, 1964

Darling:

8:00 AM and I am writing you before the day catches up with me. I may call you up this morning when I go down to mail this letter as the most important thing of all is that Gunther must sell *Spy* to a paperback publisher. There are already demands for the book. It is ridiculous, pathetic, and a little repulsive to see the people all around me who never bothered with the books, but as soon as news of the film is in the papers they are rushing about…sad. And all those lamenting that they did not take an option, and some saying: but I wanted to do that book. I don't know how anyone can ever be taken in by "publicity" like that. But they are. So this is what Gunther must make use of now to force Random House to come through.

Joaquín will be coming to stay with you. He will phone or write you. I am terribly sorry to miss him, and not to be there also to help you. But remember, let people take care of you. It is all in your attitude. Joaquín is no trouble. I will only call you if there is no letter from you today. We have to be careful. How are your finances?

Jack Hirschman's review of the Lawrence book has done me a lot of good.

But I don't like "business," and as soon as our economics are stable, I quit. It makes you aware that 99 per cent of the world is an inert, unthinking mass, led by the nose, empty, blind, deaf and dumb, whom a few people manipulate. It's a rather sad picture.

No summer yet, but Piccolo is in fine form. Sends his love.

A

Letter from Gunther Stuhlmann to Anaïs Nin:
New York, May 30, 1964

Dear Anaïs,

I was pleased to see the announcement of the film, and I do think it would be good to have something in writing worked out beyond the option letter you mentioned to me, since I am by nature suspicious of all Hollywood people, and I would like to work something out with Jerry for your protection, particularly since the announcement made mention of the fact that Jerry is part of the production team and thus not really in a position to represent you 100%, wearing two hats. Can you send me a copy of the option letter?

Did you see the stupid notice of the Lawrence in the current *New Yorker*, which is really superficial, arrogant and quite idiotic?

Now to my activities in Paris: Miller letters: It looks as though we are in solid with Gallimard on this—I spent two days with Madame Karvelis and we hit it off quite well. They are also interested in *Collages* and I have sent her a copy of the English edition for final word from Claude Gallimard.

All in all, I was very glad I had a chance to follow up on the spot and I am quite optimistic about the French scene now. I think your being there had a miraculous effect on all of this. More details will follow.

I am so glad, also, about the effect Paris had on you—we should go there more often.

As ever,
Gunther

Letter from Daisy Aldan to Anaïs Nin:
New York, June 1, 1964

Dearest Anaïs,

I am delirious with your success. All I can say is, "I told you it would come when it was ready..." Be careful with your favors to all and sundry late admirers.

Nona Balakian just called me and said that she was going to Paris, and that she is looking for a French publisher for her book; so I told her to write to you, and you'd make some suggestions. This is a good way to be in touch with her again directly. She said she remembered you as being very lovely...so you see, all those thoughts about her neglect were really unfounded. Also, I've told her so many things about your work by now; she's very sympathetic.

As you know now, Nobuko will have my apartment while I'm traveling, so we're keeping it in the family, as it were. I feel very happy about this.

If you need money before February, let me know. You'll return it when you can.
Love,
Daisy

Letter from Anaïs Nin to Gunther Stuhlmann:
Los Angeles, June 1964

Dear Gunther:

Jerry Bick will send you the contracts as soon as they are ready. I understand your disappointment, but you know I have no choice and no bargaining powers, with my "reviews" as non-existent as they are. Jerry made a mistake in rushing to say he was a producer, because there is an unwritten law about being agent and producer, as you say, he now regrets this youthful eagerness—it is affecting his agent business, and your reaction to this conflict of interest is natural. But what can I do? We are in no position to "bargain."

Los Angeles State College is inviting Swallow to speak, which will please him, and we will try to make it a tribute to independent publishing. Leon Surmelian knows him and admires him.

Miller is crazy about *Collages*. Tells everybody it's marvelous. He wants to meet the different women. He thinks it is a harem.

How is your father? And are you healing from the loss of your mother? It took me so long to accept the death of my mother. Your being so busy must help. But she was younger than my mother, and that is harder to resign one's self to, as one counts on a longer life.
Anaïs

Letter from Anaïs Nin to Hugh Guiler:
Los Angeles, June 2, 1964

Darling:

Trouble now with the British Book Centre having printed *Spy* as if they owned the copyright, even though they have no contract to show it. This has held up everything until Gunther clears it up with a document. The fine point of logic is that they believe the British Book Centre, but not me, even when I printed "copyright by the author." René de Chochor's carelessness here is still plaguing me.

I have lost my confidence, gaiety and faith. I need the love and approval of France and can't face the prejudice here. I do not want to read what came out in the *New Yorker*. It angered Gunther. I am seriously thinking of studying French, and writing in French from now on. I can't go on spending money on analysis to get rid of my deep-seated hatred of America. It's getting to be a new sort of sickness. Nausea. Nausea at everything I hear, see.

Anaïs

Letter from Hugh Guiler to Anaïs Nin:
New York, June 5, 1964

Darling,

Your letter of the 2nd reached me this morning, and alarmed me, for it seemed you went into an emotional tailspin over the frustrating question of the rights for *Spy*. And, according to what Gunther has told me this afternoon over the telephone, it has been settled legally since you wrote. So I imagine you are now feeling relief. But what of the deeper roots to which this surface storm must have been connected? In my case, I am only now beginning to find out something about these roots, and you must also, as soon as you can.

The only thing that now worries Gunther, as I believe he told you, is the agreement you signed last year with Bick, and which he would have advised you against if you had consulted him. He does not want to take any strong measures about this until the negotiations with Wise's lawyers are further along. But when I asked him if he is seriously concerned about the paper Bick has in his hands, he replied, "Yes, I am, because Bick has a conflict of interests." And Gunther says he has too often seen writers losing out in similar cases in Hollywood. He has also, I understand, told Bick that the financial considerations for the option are not what they should be, so already it would appear that Jerry has had other interests than yours to look out for. So I think what you should do from now on is to put yourself completely in Gunther's hands, since he is the one who has only your interests at heart.

Tonight I see *The Silence* with Gunther and Tamara, and I must now close this and get a bite, so I can get there in time.

Deepest love,
Hugo

Letter from Anaïs Nin to Hugh Guiler:
Los Angeles, June 15, 1964

Darling:

A dragging month. I heard from Duras again. She is sending the script untranslated. Partly because she wants my opinion, I guess. I hope as soon as it arrives Millicent will send it airmail special delivery. The danger is that this is playing into the hands of Jerry who will want to alter it, and I will have to do it fast so I can send Duras the original to show Wise. He has been delayed in Salzburg due to the weather, so he will not come through Paris till the end of June. If I do the translation, I insist on being paid for it. That means a lot of rushed work.

I hear that Nobuko is happy about Daisy's apartment (if you want to call her after July 1 Daisy's number is in our phone book). The story of Nobuko is people's favorite in *Collages*.

A

Letter from Gunther Stuhlmann to Anaïs Nin:
New York, June 18, 1964

Dear Anaïs:

I just got some documents from Wise's lawyer, and I believe they sent you the same for your signature. Please hold off signing these till we have worked out the papers with Jerry Bick, from whom I have had no further word yet, since I don't want to sign up stuff with Wise that puts Jerry in the driver's seat without our having worked out details with Jerry. Once things have been signed, we are completely in Jerry's hands.

I heard that the screenplay is in and Hugo promised me a copy; I won't mention it to anybody till you have had a chance to look it over.

Best,
Gunther

Letter from Anaïs Nin to Hugh Guiler:
Los Angeles, June 1964

Darling:

A warm day at the beach. Up to see Renate, who was sick from her shots for Mexico—she is preparing to go with Ronnie for their divorce. She had her sewing machine out, and the room was full of black lace, a black corset, a black sheath, etc. She *lives* symbolically—so she wears black for the divorce, but I noticed mostly negligées, more negligées, breakfast coats, and I wondered if this widow's mourning was not a devious way of seducing Ronnie again!

Now I'm going to write to Nobuko. I have neglected my correspondence. 10 or 15 pages a day of writing is really enough.

Love,
A

Letter from Hugh Guiler to Anaïs Nin:
New York, June 27, 1964

Darling:

I can see you have a difficult problem with the Duras script, and that you are feeling frustrated, but I don't see what more you can do than you are doing, which is to let things take their course and put in a tactful word when you can. You can rely on me not to say anything about all this.

I can also see you need to wait until Wise arrives and get his reaction, since everything depends on that, so don't worry about the delay. I would rather you come home when your problems are cleared up and your mind is at rest.

Jean Clarence has very little good to say about Japan. He came to the same conclusion we did from our meeting with some of those who came here—that they are a most inhibited people living in the nineteenth century.

Love, and do take care of yourself, darling.

H

Letter from Anaïs Nin to Hugh Guiler:
Los Angeles, June 28, 1964

Darling:

Today I am working on my lecture for next Monday. Meanwhile, Jerry is expecting Wise to arrive tonight. Max Lamb, his right-hand man, read the Duras script as it was, and agrees with the need for changes, so at least we are all in accord. I am sending you a review of her book, which is related to the problem of the script. Frankly, I never believed an intelligent and good artist could be as unfaithful to the meaning of the book, unless she is psychoanalytically blind...

A

Letter from Anaïs Nin to Rupert Pole:
New York, July 21, 1964

Darling:

I don't know what to do—we can't discuss the script over the phone. And your annoyance depresses me so much I can't sleep, and I can't work the next day. Your obsession with people being *vague*—me, and others—is only because you want things black and white and they just aren't. Life is not that simple. People are complex. So are you. You are insecure, and you want *certainties*—and life is never so. Don't work on the proofing if you feel so uneasy. I'm used to the artist life and people's unstable behavior, like yours tonight—very confused, vague, and rather unfair. I have a heavy load of work.

It is muggy, stormy and over 90. I spend my evenings either trying to write a realistic Sabina, or dating the Miller letters. Yet calling you brings me no comfort, only irritation added to strain. Perhaps I should not call you. You hate to write. And all you do is complain. You should really give it up. I am ready to—why don't you? It is best not to do a thing in such a state of rebellion and exasperation. You make me feel guilty for accepting your help, guilty for having written a poem, not a standard story. To hell with Wise! I never chose him.

But please don't go on making me pay too high a price for your help. Many times I have told you to not do things unless you are *with it*, love it, want to do it.

I can't face the phone anymore. I will call you once more, and if you pile up exasperated comments—I will give up calling.

I have to cut 1,200 pages of the Diary to 500 for Random House, retype pages and hand it in before I leave it to Gunther.

I love you—just the same.

A

Letter from Anaïs Nin to Rupert Pole:
New York, July 24, 1964

Darling:
Your page has wonderful, clear and well organized. It sounds to me as if you were really doing it. You had a right to be temperamental. I guess I felt guilty because I know writing is a pain for you, and I felt I was responsible. Yet I never know why we quarrel because five minutes later we both think the other was right after all. I struggled vainly on my side to make a contribution. I am hard pressed at Random House (deadline Sept. 15). I spent several evenings dating Miller's letters, but it is a work which will pay off in the long run. Always later. I cut into the 1,200 pages, and retyped to see if Gunther agrees with this kind of cutting before I refine it.

Then two evenings with Varèse, who is like Lloyd and demands all my attention, plays the score [for *House of Incest*] over and over again. Last night his singer did not come, so I had to pretend I was singing the lines. Loud music, all through the house.

Love,
A

Letter from Anaïs Nin to Rupert Pole:
New York, July 1964

Darling:
I was being a "business woman"—but oh, with an added charm. Nobuko invited the son of biggest Japanese publisher. He came with a big shopping bag full of tiny presents, real doll-like objects, tiny fan earrings, tiny fans, tiny scarves, tiny bells, buttons, a jade bird! You know how I love small things. He could not speak English, but he was so sweet and responsive. Nobuko had to translate—and she told stories of Noh plays. I have been going to her rehearsals. One lovely story was the insistence that the door for people entering with props should be very, very low to *teach* them *modesty* as they enter the stage. The stage has to be clean enough to *lick*. Students have to *scrub it* before stepping on it. Discipline, order, form.

Well, anyway—the Japanese publisher, Mr. Kawade, will do *Spy* in Japanese, and the Miller letters. He is right now talking with Gunther via an interpreter.

Gunther is really sold on the Diary—found only a few minor repetitions and one gap—said wonderful things: Solid, strong, better than Proust, rich, etc. What he admired most, he said, was that most writers were content with reflecting their time, the society they lived in—none were concerned with *making* their own world! Not sure of the ending—as you said and wondered, too, where it should end.

Time magazine asked for photos. It may not mean anything—I had to give the one you took of me with the Varda collage—as the best of candid photos!

But so much to do. Have to solve with the publisher if they will take *whole* project on, book after book (with income), stand behind me, and make a big investment.

Grey day. I miss you terribly.

Nobuko will help to make our Japanese trip lovely!

Love,
A

Los Angeles, July 1964
Symptoms: Ringing in the ears sometimes, face swollen, feeling of pressure in the head, difficulty in concentration, confusion. Feel very badly in the morning. Bad taste, poor elimination, the worst feeling towards five, just before dinner. Entire body aches. Any part I touch is painful, chest, neck, especially nape of neck. Stiff neck. Wandering arthritic pain, now feet, now shoulders. Heaviness in chest. Heavy, contracted feeling when carrying weight. At times legs feel heavy. Dry, burning mouth. Small hemorrhages on the temple, over the eye—a small bruise will spread far—black veins inside of the mouth. Loss of hair. Gaining weight. History: Chronic anemia. Typhoid fever. Appendicitis. Loss of ovary. Watery discharges. Pneumonia. Bronchitis. Feel worse with: alcohol, sleeping pills, humidity. Worst symptoms: tension, depression.

Letter from Anaïs Nin to Hugh Guiler:
Los Angeles, August 19, 1964

Darling:
Situation with Wise is so unsatisfactory. I was hoping he would give up, and perhaps let Losey do it, as Jerry said he might finance this; he likes Losey, but then Jerry continues to hold on with his teeth, writing memos, and yesterday they had a big talk. It is all so contradictory that all I can gather is that Jerry holds his interest. And that Duras' new pages (about fifteen) came closer to Wise's idea. Almost a caricature of how films are made. Impossible to get a synthesis from all these random notes, but my hands are tied. What I did do was to send the script to Losey confidentially, and start activities there. Meanwhile, to endure it, I type all day. Cutting, retyping, cutting, editing, etc. to have the Diary done for Random House, at least.
I will do all I can to return as soon as possible, darling. Take good care of yourself. I think of you.
A

Letter from Hugh Guiler to Anaïs Nin:
New York, August 22, 1964

Darling:
Sorry to hear how unsatisfactory the Bick-Wise business is. If Losey replies that he could work something out with Duras, I think you may have to step in and assert your own rights. But then you would need to consult with someone, and Gunther's advice might be valuable before you do anything. I am surprised you did send the Duras script to Losey, as it might kill the project with him too. I suppose you were counting on his friendship with Duras to work something out.
I am glad you have the job for Random House to occupy you in this trying period.

Chico has learned to bite me *gently* you will be glad to hear, and his purring is becoming deafening. The lady and her husband along the corridor who have the little Yorkshire terrier we like so much now has also a real toy poodle about ten weeks old, slightly off-white and very wooly. She and her husband called me over especially to see it, and the little thing reminded me of Piccolo.

All my love,
H

Letter from Alan Swallow to Anaïs Nin:
Denver, October 22, 1964

Dear Anaïs,

I can't figure out what happened to *Time*. They were so hot on the thing, had the local man rounding stuff up fast, said they'd contact you for photos, etc. Very, very strange: this is the second time a large weekly of that sort (*Newsweek* with Lawrence, you remember) went to all this trouble, and then didn't publish. Can't figure it all out.

Leon Surmelian was supposed to review *Collages* for the *L.A. Herald*; hope he has. But as far as I can see, he's a most difficult person to deal with.

Excuse me if I don't reread this for errors; it is after 4:00, I am bone weary and my leg has been giving me a very bad time the last week (again on antibiotics and painkillers), and I just will have to send it off.

Alan

Letter from Eduardo Sánchez to Anaïs Nin:
Florence, Italy, October 25, 1964

Dear Anaïs:

It would be impossible to explain in a letter the negative mood I am in, and have been in for the past year, ever since I came face-to-face with old age and death, and the shock has been so terrible that I have not been able to react except negatively. I have become a stark existentialist. Life is absurd.

So, being in a negative state of mind, and not wanting even "immortality" or notoriety, and therefore, wishing to be forgotten, the thought of your publishing part of your diary (1931 to 1935 no less!) depresses me considerably. And I don't see how a discussion over it would be of any help. But don't mind me. You just go ahead. Don't tell me about it, and don't send me a copy. Just remember that the less you say about me the better—that is, while I am still alive. OK?

Love,
Eduardo

Letter from Anaïs Nin to Gunther Stuhlmann:
Los Angeles, October 30, 1964

Dear Gunther:

I know better than anyone how hard you worked on the Miller letters, and how you are trying to do the very best for both of us. But you have also more patience than I have, and more *time*. The time wasted on negotiations is appalling. I asked Hugo to talk with you as I know you have much to do and a million letters to write as well as contracts.

Also, I feel I cannot let Swallow wait indefinitely just to read more of the Diary when he will know others are reading it. Just as a matter of relationship (and it will take him much time to read 800 pages), I feel we should send him a copy.

Are you unable to show the Diary to anyone else while negotiating with Random House (I mean, Japan, France, etc.)?

Tell me what you think of this. I get desperate for news.

My best to you, as always,

Anaïs

Letter from Anaïs Nin to Hugh Guiler:
Los Angeles, October 30, 1964

Darling:

Yesterday I sent you the new section of the Diary. Airmailed one to Gunther. Now we have a letter from André Bay offering $1,000 for the Miller letters, and only if we give him the letters he will do *Four-Chambered Heart* and *Children of the Albatross* (in one book, which he wants to call *Le Livre de Djuna*). Now, Bay is the last one I want to deal with, but I would rather go ahead, at any price, with any conditions. Gunther is young and not aware of time. The time is now. Today. Please talk with him. We wasted at least six months with other publishers. I have another lecture on Monday. Will rest on the weekend.

Daisy Aldan is having a marvelous time in Kashmir on a houseboat. Flowers, music, etc. 6,000 feet up. She is reclining on pillows, and being transported by a small boat (attached to the houseboat) through lakes and gardens. The lakes are so filled with lotus and water lilies, that it seems as if the boat is actually moving across a field of flowers instead of water.

I will phone you over the weekend for news.

All my love,

A

P. S. Have you thought of dictating your autobiography?

Letter from Anaïs Nin to Hugh Guiler:
Los Angeles, November 1, 1964

Darling:

Joseph Losey writes me: "My feelings about the screenplay are very mixed and complicated and I would hope that we can meet to discuss them personally rather than doing it by letter. I have talked to Duras a little bit about it. I don't like the screenplay as it stands, although I like many ideas very much and as you know I like the material. I feel that Duras and I could arrive at a very exciting screenplay and I should be happy if Bob Wise wants to set it up and produce, allowing me reasonable artistic control." So Jerry will work on this when Wise returns.

I am waiting for a Random House memo to work on revisions, but, as I told Gunther, I don't think I should work on revisions without them being committed and knowing for whom I am revising, because another publisher might take it as is. I hate being not able to work with France only because America pays better. Critics would be so much better in France.

A few weeks, Gunther says. The other publishers took six months.

I do have confidence in Gunther. But I have heard rumors about the Miller-Durrell letters not selling well in France.

Today I gave a lecture and am real tired, but the fulsome mail gave me energy.

Love, love,
Anaïs

Letter from Jimmy Spicer to Anaïs Nin:
November 1, 1964

Dear Anaïs:

Thank you for sending me to Carson McCullers. It was quite an afternoon, an exciting and loving experience. We became friends quickly, I feel. She is in bed, partially paralyzed, not an alcoholic, but with a drink constantly by her side. Both the maid and the nurse refer to her as "sister," an amusing Southernism. I was supposed to have had dinner with her the following Saturday, but when I phoned to confirm it she cancelled. Seems that she might have to go to the hospital for another hip operation. Although I wrote her a note and phoned her that second time, I feel that I must phone again. Nothing was really decided—at least by me. But I just might go up there for several months... A "retreat" is tempting. And she would be a good person to be near.

I'm sure I've said it before, but let me say it again: you are almost the only person I've ever met whom I can truly *trust*... All the people I've met through you have been important in my life. Again, I thank you for your friendship.

Love,
Jimmy

Letter from Gunther Stuhlmann to Anaïs Nin:
New York, November 2, 1964

Dear Anaïs:

Thank you for your letter of the 30th.

I wired Tom Maschler in England to make us an offer for the Miller letters and this morning I got back a cagey note saying that he might offer half of $2,500 or something in that order, which means that I have already gotten a better offer from Peter Owen (after much wrangling), amounting to an advance of roughly $1,800. So if you feel you don't want to waste any more time, let's go with Peter Owen. And rather than going with a house that has not done you, there may be an advantage in staying with Peter, though Miller perhaps will not like it because he doesn't trust him. What do you say on that? Miller has no legal point, but I'd hate to offend him. If Peter plunks down what for him is a lot of money, he will probably do a good job, at least that is the purpose of my holding out for more.

The diary pages are only with RH at the moment, and, as I told you, I expect to get Jim Silberman's letter this week. I have a hunch that we may not quite see eye-to-eye on their idea of the books, after various talks with him on minor points. But we will know shortly. I certainly would have no objection to Swallow reading the diary—it's just that I feel he just is not equipped to handle such a project to your best interest, but if you want us to, I can send him a copy. Meanwhile, Henry and Eduardo could read the present version—and if you want, I can send you a copy. I have held off on other countries for the simple reason that I feel we have to get the U.S. situation in hand, otherwise we will have problems of different variations—no?

As for the André Bay proposition—if you like the idea of the *Livre de Djuna* as a proposition, we can go ahead on that—I already had written to him about the situation with Gallimard. Again, I feel that if André gives a decent advance he will push the book to get his money back. I will be diplomatic about this, though, with Bay and Gallimard, and I would like you to keep mum for the moment because I have told André I have to discuss this with you first—to get a little leeway in negotiations. It worked with Peter Owen, so I hope it works there too. I will always be the dragon—am used to it by now.

Please don't worry too much about all this—things are getting better, and we will even lick the time problem, I'm sure. I know it is frustrating for you sit in California and wait—but I feel strongly that all will turn out.

As ever,
Gunther

Letter from Hugh Guiler to Anaïs Nin:
New York, November 3, 1964

Darling:
I have read the new section of your diary and want to tell you right away that it deepens and reinforces all that went before, as I am sure the rest will, too, when it comes out. Also, it is good to have it end just before the departure for New York, as it will whet everyone's appetite.

The part about your suffering in the stillbirth, I had to force myself to read again as I have not been able to read it ever since the first time *I* suffered with you, when you included it in *Under a Glass Bell.* It is just as devastating as ever. I sweated when I read it. If I could be objective, though, I think I might say that this section is the keystone of the whole diary, hitting, as it does, the bottom of the ocean floor in a way that no novel could ever do. This is what I meant when I referred to its unique lapidary style, composed of sound waves that reflect from your own body and blood, in a way that no other narration could possibly do. Apart from that, there is the growing sense of utter integrity, arising out of this very kind of direct contact with your own deepest foundations—an integrity that caused you to see clearly the limitations, as far as you were concerned, of so many others—Miller and Rank among them—something all the more dramatic because all the separations caused you more pain than it did them. I don't think that anywhere, except in nature itself, has there been an example of such persistent, individual growth in a seemingly frail nature.

Gunther may have made a mistake about Maschler in England, and overplayed his hand, but this is the only way he can feel out the market, and I think he now has that feel and is acting in your best interests; to bring pressure on him now and make him feel that you are willing to sell at any price would, I think, only hurt you.

All my love. I also love you enduringly, and think of you.

H

Letter from Oliver Evans to Anaïs Nin:
Northridge, November 3, 1964

Dear Anaïs:

I don't in the least blame you for being impatient about your book: I am quite as anxious to get started on it as you are. No one could have foreseen that the McCullers project would prove so very time-consuming: had I written for her what I am planning to do for you (a straight critique), it would have been finished long ago, since it was the biographical material that gave me so much difficulty. That problem does not exist where your book is concerned, and once I get started on it I expect to sail right through with no delays.

Love,
Oliver

Letter from Anaïs Nin to Hugh Guiler:
Los Angeles, November 4, 1964

Darling:

I was helping at the polls yesterday and so could not write you. I am a real community type now! But today I received your beautiful letter about the Diary. What struck me is not so much what you said at first, but the wonderful way you said it. By gosh, you're turning out to be the writer of the family after all. After observing your artistry, I settled down to enjoy what you said. It must be hard for you to read a story from which the principal character is absent—yourself. But someday the truth will be out, when you are rich enough to thumb your nose at the whole world.

Bebe Barron is busy destroying herself at forty, sick, passive, neurotic, in a far worse state physically than you or I. I can't get her out of her paralysis.

I feel that Gunther, to spare me, and because of his European upbringing, does not tell me all that Random House said. In his last letter I gather they have reservations. I was right to feel that when people quibble about little things, it is because they do not accept the big ones.

Love,
A

Letter from Anaïs Nin to Gunther Stuhlmann:
Los Angeles, November 1964

Dear Gunther:

Well, now that we are free of concern over the voting (I worked here this time to get votes for Lyndon Johnson), we can think about Random House. My intuition may be wrong, but I feel that in order to spare me, you are perhaps holding back some of the doubts on Jim Silberman. I did not feel he was sure, or had faith, to carry it off. Let us see what happens after they read the last part. I try to put myself in their place, but I can't, for they would not have written the Diary. Please tell me what you know. Are they afraid? Do they miss the scandal, want the whole truth and nothing but the truth; is it too strong, too personal, unsalable? If they make too much fuss, I feel, Peter Israel won't. He is not as clever as Silberman. He will either do it or not do it. Yes, I agree with everything. I know the delays bother you as much as they bother me. Yes, let us go ahead with Peter and with Bay. I am writing only friendly letters to Bay, and telling him everything is in your hands. I learned my lesson and I realize I make it harder for you when I correspond with them. But it seems as if I have to accept that they only publish me to be able to publish Miller.
Anaïs

Note from Henry Miller to Anaïs Nin:
Pacific Palisades, November 5, 1964

Dear Anaïs:
I'm almost sunk with work. OK on the release for the diary. Suppose I ought to see proofs of the *Letters*—don't trust that publisher Owen! Soon as pressure lets up I'll call you to meet Oliver Evans.
Glad to hear you're so active. Wonder how the film is going—with Duras.
Henry

Letter from Gunther Stuhlmann to Anaïs Nin:
New York, November 6, 1964

Dear Anaïs:
I just had a long talk with Nona Balakian at the *Times* and it now looks as though a lengthy essay review of *Collages* will be in the week after next. She also wants to do a brief interview with you. She wants to finish her piece by Friday morning, and I think this would be a good promotion.
Jim Silberman is still formulating his editorial suggestions on the first hundred or so pages, and I have not shown him any more since he asked to see first whether we agree with his suggestions. I begin to feel, as I already indicated, that we may not get together with them. Jim is still waging strong condemnation of the material, of covering a larger span of time, etc., all the things that came up in our talk, and he seems to feel that some of the slower, low-key sketches in the current manuscript are excessive for the "blockbuster" launching. But I should have his memo any day now. I don't feel you should follow any of his suggestions for editorial work until we have worked out the situation with RH and just go on with your editing as you have done. This will not be wasted work and time—it has to be done regardless of who publishes. I also have a feeling that Silberman may—perhaps subconsciously—be missing what you call the "schedule," although he has never said anything to that effect. I don't think he feels it is too strong, too

personal. I think his concern is still mostly about the impact the book will make when it comes out, to compete with the confessions of Simone de Beauvoir et al., and one of his recurring themes is the thought that we "have to justify the expectations" that have been built up for so long. This seems to be the main point he is riding, and this is why, I feel, he is against some of the reflective material in the mss., which is why he wants to have more people, more sharp, close stretches like the ones he mentioned (Miller, June, Rank, West) and less of the "personal" material, of the slow emerging of feeling and evaluation. In other words, he is looking for more "portraits," more "action," and he seems to feel that "condensation" will "speed up," make the book more "solid"—all this is, I gather, from the publishing point, from the competition, from the feeling of having to offer more. All this is interpretation on my part—I am trying to see it from his point of view.

As ever,
Gunther

Los Angeles, November 1964

Today I read in the paper: "Ronnie Knox, UCLA football star of 10 years ago, now a writer and actor, today was divorced by his artist-wife, Renate. 'He never contributed to my support, and he stayed away from home too much,' she testified in Superior Judge Harold W. Schweitzer's court. Sometimes her husband would stay away all night without explanation, she also told the judge. Her witness, actress Raven Harwood, corroborated the allegation of frequent absences from home. Attorney Ridgeway Sutton, for Mrs. Knox, informed the court she was asking for no alimony. Her paintings, including portraits, have been shown widely in the West, he added. Born in Vienna, she came to this country after World War II and won acclaim for her works under her maiden name Renate Druks. She and Knox were married in Taxco, Mexico, on June 4, 1959 and separated on Nov. 22, 1963. They have no children."

Letter from Eduardo Sánchez to Anaïs Nin:
Florence, Italy, November 8, 1964

Anaïs, for goodness' sake, don't spend eighty dollars for a copy of your diary for me. All I ask is that is if it is humanly and artistically possible for you to leave out my personal life, and to tone down as much as possible my homosexual relationships. Is that too much to ask? While I am still alive I do mind very much this display of my miseries.

My plans are to stay in Italy for another year at least—the archives and my research are the necessary drugs that I need acutely at this stage of my life. Of course, if I can afford it, I shall visit the States next year.

Hope Hugo enjoyed his trip to France, and I hope you are doing well, and if you see Joaquín give him my *cariños*.

Love,
Eduardo

Letter from Anaïs Nin to Gunther Stuhlmann:
Los Angeles, November 9, 1964

Dear Gunther:

I never worry about what I say to you because I know you understand, and that basically we are in accord. I remember the first time you called me I felt that there was something wrong, but I hate to be prima-donnaish. I can see now from your last letter that what Random House wants would destroy the integrity of the Diary. A diary is not an action film. What people. What greed, too, and *entre nous*, there is more in my Diary than in the diary of Simone du Beauvoir. There is no action in hers, and no life at all. It is deadly dull. And all this talk about expectations. It shows lack of faith. No, I feel, they are wrong. But I will wait for the memo.

I have not been able to edit because I did not know what was going on and was troubled by the cloudiness. I just went on doing more of the same. I do want to preserve the integrity of the document. What do you think of Hiram Haydn at Harcourt instead of Peter Israel? I may be wrong, but I do not feel that what RH asks would improve the Diary. It is a false concept. They are trying to turn it into a novel and take the authenticity out of it.

Don't you agree it is silly to want to take out the *growth* of the personality, to have it all external? Tell me your real feelings. Don't spare me. In work I am quite toughened by now, thanks to America.

Anaïs

Letter from Anaïs Nin to Hugh Guiler:
Los Angeles, November 10, 1964

Darling:

I did not want to spend a lot of money to talk about our plans, as it is better to discuss these things without pressure. I do hate the way people always operate with urgency. Why the urgency in the matter of preparing an article, getting photos and material, tension and pressure? Why did Nona bother you with all that when on Thursday she was talking to Gunther who has photos, lectures, etc.? Poor organization. Pressure. Gunther has everything there. You have enough to do and enough pressures, enough worries. I was very annoyed at all that. Ran down in pouring rain to mail off the photos. Are these people incapable of planning? I have done this twice for *Newsweek* and for *Time* magazine, telephones, expenses, special deliveries. It is all absolutely unnecessary.

Anyway, my plans depend greatly on your doctor's opinions. I would like to stay here until I receive the memo from Silberman. If he asks too much—and it looks that way (this is what Gunther writes me)—then I'll return. But if you are well and have no surgery in the future, I would like to stay a little longer and work, and then prepare for a vacation at Xmas. Gunther writes me: "Silberman wants less of the personal material, of the slow, emerging of feeling and evaluation. In other words, he is looking for more portraits, more action, and he seems to feel that condensation will make the book more solid…" MORONS MORONS MORONS.

All my love,
A

Letter from Anaïs Nin to Hugh Guiler:
Los Angeles, November 12, 1964

Darling:
I am so sorry I wrote irritably the other day. I seem unable to take the slightest "stress," and I live to avoid it. Pressure. Anyway, I calmed down and called up Nona, talked well, and she has all the material she needs for the review. I am afraid she was trying to pump you for personal touches, which I resent very much. What place do they have in a review? They have persecuted me for being subjective, but all they ask are personal questions. It is a real invasion of privacy and I think out of place. Anyway, I hope it comes out well.

Wise said NO. No to everything. He does not like the script and will not finance the film. Nor will he spend another $4,000 on another script. I can't blame him. It would not have got off the ground without a "name," and the "name" betrayed him. Jerry is not giving up, but he is depressed. He cannot get an answer from Malraux about writing a script; he would have made much money that way and it would have been good for me ultimately. I don't suppose you have any contact with Malraux.

A sad day yesterday, with the Wise news. Was taken to *Cleopatra*, which is worse than I thought it would be, it is a real Folies Bergères, Radio City Music Hall, but not even as good as they were at times. The feathers close up, and green eyelids from near cannot create illusion. An impotent film. Even the teenagers laughed and talked all through it.

Love. And forgive my depression.
A

Letter from Anaïs Nin to Hugh Guiler:
Los Angeles, November 14, 1964

Darling:
I am terribly sorry; I did not mean to cut our conversation short. I am simply very aware of the terrible expenses and I try to discuss only factual problems, and then you ask me what my plans are in the middle of an uncertain situation. Plans have been very uncertain, because the attitude of RH has upset me deeply. I admit that. I cannot understand it, and I do not want to discuss it with anyone, nor for anyone to know, as I have had too much of that and most people have no faith.

Jim Silberman said: "I know, of course, the importance to Anaïs of these diaries and the importance to her of the day-by-day development of character. I simply do not feel how this unfolding will be interesting to enough to make it possible for us to do the diaries on the scale Anaïs proposes. The very least that should be encompassed in a single volume is the entire thirties, and my guess is that these volumes would contain no more manuscript pages than this present section and perhaps less. What I am saying is that my second reading makes me feel that Anaïs and I are so far apart in our conception of what this book should be that we had probably best end our discussion now."
A

Letter from Anaïs Nin to Gunther Stuhlmann:
Los Angeles, November 15, 1964

Dear Gunther:
With the best will in the world, the RH letter made no sense to me. What they ask, if I read it well, would destroy the authenticity of the Diary (organic development), would destroy the sole unity that brings all the fragments, sketches, impressions and minor portraits into a whole, which is the relation of all the characters to the self that catalyzes, and what they really want is a "cream," or excerpts that would destroy the full development of the Diary and its momentum. I realize from your letter that you feel the same way. It all is really double talk, contradictory and conventional, stuffy and standardized, which all translates as *No Sales*. Well, I feel absolutely sure they are making a business error, but I had not thought Mr. Silberman was so lacking in individual insight. They flounder, they have no convictions, they are unable to think for themselves or to act; they are like robots, probably because Silberman does not have the power he wishes us to believe he has, and when he let the committee read it (girls of seventeen out of college) they said: it has no beginning, no middle and no end. I am sorry because I know how much time and care you have given to this situation. It is the kind of blindness that makes me wish to be published first in Europe.
Let me know what is next.
Anaïs

Letter from Gunther Stuhlmann to Anaïs Nin:
New York, November 17, 1964

Dear Anaïs:
Thank you for your note on *l'affair* Random House, which I think we can now chalk up to another experience, but which has shown once more, as you say, what publishing is like here.
I will get the material back from Silberman and we will assume another tack.
I had a hard time persuading Nona at the last minute not to include any marriage material in the *Times* piece, and I resorted to the fact that this would present legal complications, that the previous statement in the *Current Biography*, etc. is erroneous—just so you know should this question come up again. You had mentioned I should use this as a last resort, which I had to do since this indicates that this was a matter of record, etc.—so I told her the record was wrong.
As ever,
Gunther

Letter from Anaïs Nin to Hugh Guiler:
New York, November 23, 1964

Darling:
Feel relieved about Chico in that you know there was nothing you could have done to save him. It is difficult with animals when no symptoms appear but a loss

of appetite. I watch Piccolo constantly and even then cannot prevent certain troubles.

The sun is out. I took Piccolo to the beach from where I wrote you a card. Waiting for my glasses, for the photos, to terminate a few interviews with new people for *Spy*, to sustain Jerry through a black moment, and then I will come, darling, which will be Tuesday, the first of December if that is convenient for you. Monday might be difficult to get off. I am in a quandary about Piccolo. Whether to bring him back to the ugly winter of N.Y., no exercise, and for the companionship he will give you, but a real slavery to taking him out, which I dread, on winter mornings at seven and at night in the snow. I have the feeling he is an apartment dog.

A

Letter from Alan Swallow to Anaïs Nin:
Denver, December 13, 1964

Dear Anaïs,

This week Hugo's surgery comes up, and I hope it will go well—and that, for your part, it won't be a poor experience. I suppose you have a lot of extra duties while Hugo is in the hospital.

The diary material arrived safely.

Now, let's see what you have in mind. I'd like answers to these:

1. Is the diary material you have now prepared going to be released for publication soon—next year or so? Or must it still await clearance for all?

2. If this much is being released, what are plans for the rest? Just waiting, or do you have parts you will continue to get ready and release?

3. If this is intended for publication, is it complete as I have it? Or how much, for this segment, is yet to come?

4. Is there serious concern that we may be able to manage a joint imprint with Putnam or someone else? Or is it an either/or choice? Either they or I, that is?

I did not know the full financial situation about the Miller letters until you told me, of course. I do need to know the picture a bit better, if it is clearer to you, at all.

Cordially,
Alan

Letter from Alan Swallow to Anaïs Nin:
Denver, December 27, 1964

Dear Anaïs,

In my last letter, about the diary, I did not mean to suggest doubts. I just sought some clarification. It still is not too clear. But I think I get the gist, all right. You see, last I had heard, as I explained, was that the diary was not to be published, any of it, until after Hugo's death. The assumption in my mind was that as you got this ready into copies was that, this being a drawn-out process, you wished to get at it so that ultimately the diaries could be sold and the typescript would be ready for the time it could be released for publication. Then it dawned on me that you were actually getting this Paris part ready for publication—that perhaps the objections Hugo might have (or whatever those sensitivities about the whole) would not be to this part. So the first thing I had to get clear in my mind was this: was this part actually to be published as soon as it was ready, rather than later? In my letter of being nettled, a month ago, after this had dawned on me, I had supposed that this was to be like the Miller letters and go to Putnam. But this has been clarified to me, just recently; I just wanted to be sure if the thought was still in mind (after all, after the letters went to Putnam without any suggestions of joint imprint, I had heard absolutely nothing from you or from Gunther about this matter and felt in the dark about it) that we might proceed thus. This seems clear now: my assumptions are that the diary, in this part you are working on now, can be published ahead of other parts; and that you and Gunther wish to work in an overall cooperation, etc. You know, if this is true, I could have some ideas, too, about where we could get the right cooperation, for I know several people in N.Y. publishing quite well and could readily, I think, help in finding a joint imprint. And I think we could possibly get this moving quite soon after I complete reading—since this part is a "cycle"—and get some advance money. If Gunther will not object too much to my feeling out one or two of my connections in New York, I might help on the hurdle of cooperation, which apparently Putnam may object to (I say "apparently" because I have only the experience (a) that they refused to do *Collages* on such a basis, and (b) because the letters went ahead without such joint effort, my final judgment to replace the word "apparently" is reserved).

I never suspected secrecy; I have never doubted that. I just felt that the pressures were such that decisions had been made there without my being informed, and it did appear so for a time.

Cordially,
Alan

Letter from Anaïs Nin to Alan Swallow:
New York, January 3, 1965

Dear Alan:

It is important that you tell Gunther if there is a publisher who would cooperate with you. I thought all of them were monsters. Peter Israel is like the others, but if there is such a thing you'd better tell Gunther. Of course, Gunther would have no objection in discussing plans with publishers who would behave decently towards you. This has been the major problem. Peter Israel is reading the Diary now. As you say, I realize all this takes years, years of time wasted, indecisions, discussions, etc., and I wanted to get it started before I die. I am editing the second volume. I did write you quite clearly about the time that I was so happy to discover a way of editing that made it possible to publish now.

The fact you bring up the Miller letters being done without discussing it with you is not quite fair, Alan; the Miller letters are not my writing. They are his, it was his say, his rights, his choice of publisher. It does not enter at all in any of the joint plans. And *Collages* was not turned down on the basis of refusing collaboration; Peter just did not think it was a big enough book to enter into such a big plan. He was proved wrong and was generous enough to admit it. It was not big, but it certainly has been popular. There was no reason to spend hours writing you about the adventures of the Miller letters. Both Gunther and I spend our days at the typewriter. We have more letters to write than we can ever get written. Neither one of us had any reason to tell you all the details of a publishing problem that had no relation at all to my work, aside from the fact that Miller gave me the money from it. You are usually a very fair-minded man, and this quite surprised me. In fact, I never mentioned it out of tactfulness. Miller wanted me to get a lot of money because he is paying off what he considers a big debt to me.

Now there are revisions to be made on the Diary. I cannot show it to Miller until the letters are all cleared, because he is beyond anything you might believe, swamped in letters, in visitors, in reading from all over the world. It took his having the flu to get through reading the first proofs because he has to OK the final proofs. This cannot be rushed.

I would suggest you write Gunther immediately on the publisher who might cooperate graciously with you. We never knew of them. As soon as Miller has agreed (he loves to be written about, but lately has had twinges of conscience about its effect on other people), I will change a few names, that is all. I did not want to be held up by names. This cannot be rushed. But I repeat, we cannot work together if you do not have confidence and trust in us and if you still believe we were concealing things we had no reason to discuss with you at all.

Anaïs

Letter from Anaïs Nin to Eduardo Sánchez:
Los Angeles, January 1965

Cher cousin:

I am amazed that you could think I would publish anything to hurt you. I cannot make myself plainer than I did: I would send you the 850 pages of the Diary to take out not only whatever you wanted out, but all or any reference to you at all. Nothing will be published without your full consent. There are two solutions offered: one is to leave you out altogether; the other is to change the names. I gave Joaquín the Diary to read during Xmas under the same condition; he could make notes of whatever he did not want in it. His comment was: "You forget that I have grown up too." He took it with him to Berkeley to annotate errors or facts, dates, etc. You will do the same. What more can I say? I think you are feeling undue anxiety about this. I am not Miller. My main concern has been not to hurt. What I have left concerns people who are dead. What refers to you is all harmless and certainly not on homosexuality. Will you please stop worrying? I am no male ego, more intent on fame than on my human relationships. I have sacrificed everything to my human relationships. Have I not? Don't confuse me with Miller and other males, please, whose ego is more important than human beings. At 73 Miller is having twinges about how others feel. Too late. He is entering his Gagaist period after Dadaist. He is babbled by Hollywood, flattery and money. You are absent from his letters (where he only referred to your scholarship, your book, and astrology, on which he is now very seriously hooked); please do not have neurotic anxieties. I had them about Miller because I know he does not give a damn, but you have never known me not to care.

Hugo is well again. In a good mood. Joaquín spent Xmas with us. I am in Los Angeles, doing twenty pages a day on the next batch. I feel like Proust, that I must get this done before I die, and even though I have no grave organic crisis, I know that each time I have been to hospital—the last with double pneumonia—anemia makes it near-fatal, so I don't expect to survive the next crisis. I even mastered anemia, as you know. But I have known the joy of being recognized in France, which is the only thing that mattered to me. *House of Incest*, good reviews, correspondence with everyone I met there, critics, the world of intelligence I lost forever by exile to moronic America. It will take centuries, and I am not sure it is intelligence in which America will ever excel. Science. That is another kind of intelligence. Not the one I prize. But see Cousteau's film at the bottom of the sea. Prodigious. And trust me.

Anaïs

Letter from Hugh Guiler to Anaïs Nin:
New York, January 4, 1965
Darling:

Got your letter today and am glad you have got Miller softened up. I don't understand what his approval of the letters for the magazines means for the publication of the letters in book form, but I will ask Gunther whether this means you are OK for that also.

This was an important day for me. Following up on my determination to get business for myself from the Banco de Bilbao, I invited my Cuban friend Parajon to lunch. Parajon is the son of a Cuban banker and is also an engineer. He now is an official of both Altos Hornos, the Spanish Steel Co. controlled by the bank, and also of the bank itself. He told me confidentially about some of the important plans the bank has, and when I told him about my trust experience, he became very much interested and said they would want me to be their consultant.

All this should come to a head in February and March, and I now feel great confidence that I stand solidly in with the bank. If this materializes, and I think it should, this one account could well be enough for us to live on comfortably. This is no magic wand, but the result of my whole experience in banking and on Wall Street. I simply today seized the opportunity to bring up all my guns, and I did not miss a shot.

And your year, darling, seems to be starting out well too. Just have confidence, for I believe you also are going to have a wonderful year.

I am particularly pleased that for the first time in a long while my own experience, apart from Chase, is appreciated. Anyhow, I feel very good tonight, and wanted you to know that at once.

All my love,
H

Letter from Anaïs Nin to Hugh Guiler:
Los Angeles, January 5, 1965

Darling:

Yesterday Renate came. She is no longer in shock. She has courage. But I have never seen such tragic eyes. Peter did not have the courage to tell her he was deeply drug-addicted and died because of it. He did not confide in his psychiatrist, paid for by UCLA. He feared the analyst would report him to the University. The university is full of addicts. It could be a scandal, so they are being very quiet, erasing his debts, trying to get the film done he made of drawings for a memoriam, etc. (I wrote the text). Ronnie behaved beautifully, never left Renate's side.

A

Letter from Anaïs Nin to Hugh Guiler:
Los Angeles, January 1965

Darling:

Here is what Peter Israel writes me about the Diary: "The main thing I want to tell you is how fascinated I am with the diaries. I had no idea what was in them except by reputation and no idea that I would become so utterly engrossed in the pages. Surely they stand as one single example of the confessional genre. Perhaps I expected depth of self-revelation and it is certainly there, but I never anticipated that people about whom I knew little and didn't particularly care, Allendy, your father, etc. would come so vibrantly alive, like characters in some great Proustian novel. I have not quite finished these 800 pages, but I am most of the way through them, and I find myself hoping that they never end. In sum, I don't know whether these pages are commercial or not, or what the answers are to the commercial questions. (By which I mean that I don't know how a reader who knows nothing about Anaïs Nin will react.) Personally and unprofessionally I think they are terrific—a great personal expression—and somehow I wanted you to know that first off."

Then he goes on about having given them to his new wife to read (they are on a honeymoon trip until January 20). As you can see, with the praise there are still the commercial reservations. He will now try it on his wife, on the salesmen, on the doorman, the elevator man, the night watchman, the cleaning woman, the delivery boys, the telephone girl, and then he will ask me to make it sound like *Candy*, like Mary McCarthy, and yet keep it clean for the *Ladies' Home Journal*, and perhaps rewrite it in the third person, make Allendy a negro physician, my father a taxi driver, for human interest, and instead of a dead child, write about nine children, and my life in Harlem and in Indo-China as a missionary (for the social angle) and throw in a few more famous names, but be sure to do no name-dropping as Charlie Chaplin did. Also I might perhaps have one of the characters have an alcohol problem, make Joaquín a dope addict (he could not stand the strain of concert playing), and aside from that it's a great work.

All my love, darling. And don't worry about my crossness, any more than I will about yours. I had Intercostal Neuralgia, allergies, headaches, pains in the jaw, arthritis of the left toe, etc., etc.!

A

Letter from Eduardo Sánchez to Anaïs Nin:
Florence, Italy, January 11, 1965

My dear Anaïs:

You finally answered that you were not going to expose my homosexuality, but I don't see how you are going to do it. I have reasons for mistrusting you since you once told my sister and Mama, and then later you and Hugo told Archibald! But honestly, now that my blood has chilled completely, I cannot for the life of me comprehend how I could have been homosexual. What an *idiot* I've been for the best part of my life! What's worse, this is only an acute stubbornness against publicity. My most profound mulishness is dead-set against any publicity whatsoever. My poor Anaïs, who would have thought that your loving cousin would, in the end, let you down! Somehow even writing under a pseudonym seems to be a poor subterfuge. I used to amuse myself by calling this singular complex the "Greta Garbo Complex," in other words, an unmeasurable desire for fame accompanied by a horror of being *known personally* (this is while I was an actor).

At this moment, because I am a scholar and consequently impersonal, I am doing my damnedest to break through this complex by forcing myself to publish a document I've just discovered—I am trying to be very clever, cornering myself in such a way that I should have to go through with it—for instance, I've already written to an editor. If he says yes, I must perforce finish the introduction I've already half-finished!

Rereading your letter, I find that it is only fair that I read your diary before I make up my mind to ask you to cut me out altogether (the solution of changing names I do not accept).

Love,
Eduardo

Letter from Gunther Stuhlmann to Anaïs Nin:
New York, January 1965

Dear Anaïs:

Good news. Saturday I received a card from Henry that the galleys for the Miller letters were on their way back here, and on the card he mentioned that he assumed that I was taking care of the intro. This should mean more or less that we have settled the whole thing and that I won't have to go through this with him again. I have made some changes he requested in the intro where they affect facts or things he does not want to say, but the rest remains as is.

This noon the galleys arrived and after a glance, there are apparently very few changes and corrections, and it seems that we are over the worst hurdles—thanks no doubt to your good work on the other end.

I spent last weekend finishing off an index, and now we are all through on this and I hope off to bigger things. People's advance reactions to the book seem very good.

I have no objection to Alan's "feelers" and I'll stand by to hear what comes of it. Sooner or later we will have to face that problem anyway, particularly since I expect to see Peter Israel any day now, and I will keep you posted on that.

As ever,
Gunther

Letter from Hugh Guiler to Anaïs Nin:
New York, January 27, 1965

Darling:
 Following your call I had a talk with Gunther over the telephone about André Bay. Gunther says he wrote Bay about three weeks ago a very clear letter and that Bay is just trying to do what he has done before, i.e., to work on you to get what he wants, just as Peter Owen did. Bay offered $500 for the novel, or two of them if he could get the Miller letters for $600. You remember Peter Owen finally paid $2,000 for the Miller letters and Gunther feels you should have at least $1,500 from Bay. Also, he does not want him to be taking you only as a package with Miller, but feels he should be interested in doing your novels for their own sake.
 In general, Gunther wants to stop anyone from taking you only as a package with Miller, which he thinks is not good for you. Also, he has had a terribly frustrating time with everyone in France, first Gallimard, who don't answer letters or even cables sent to their own N.Y. office, and de Roux also just keeps silent, after raising the package question.
 As I can see, Gunther is doing what he should with the bastards who are trying every trick of the trade to take advantage of you, and at the present juncture I feel it is important that you leave things in his hands, and simply send Bay's letter to him for a reply. Gunther has, in fact, written Bay today asking him for a reply to his letter of three weeks ago, suggesting that he deal with him directly and not go about things by a circuitous route. He believes this will bring the best results for you, and that he may even change his mind about *Collages*. Gunther has also again cabled Gallimard in a last effort to get a reply from them, as they promised him several times. This is obviously an irritating process both for Gunther and you, but I do believe, darling, your agent is doing the best possible job, that he has been quite clear with Bay, and while it is, of course, right for you to keep in touch with him, he deserves your confidence and that it is best to leave things in this case in his hands. I see nothing unreasonable about his stand with Bay, and you yourself know how niggardly he is.
 Love,
 H

Letter from Anaïs Nin to Eduardo Sánchez:
Los Angeles, February 1, 1965

Cher cousin:
 Since you have my promise that not a word will be published concerning you, let us study this problem with detachment and calm. I am sending you the pages as they are now (subject to revisions). Joaquín made his helpful revisions, comments, etc. in a charming, very mature letter, concerned only with mis-facts.
 Now, I can take you out altogether, which would be a shame, because you contributed to the mental climate, books, knowledge and ideas of the group. (Also, occasionally I slipped you in instead of Hugo where an objective scene took place.) In any case, remember that the name will be changed. I can remove all clues to your identity so that if any of the family will read it (which I doubt, as none of them read anything at all, and Graciella could not get through the novels) I

can leave you as a friend, influence, and mentor, which you were, leave you wherever you wish, as a part of talks, games, charades, etc. Now, I beg of you, read quietly, gently and without anxiety. Whatever troubles you, displeases you, make note of it. Page so-and-so. Comment.

For example, Joaquín had a totally different version of what happened at his concert, and I rectified that. Do not feel exposed. You won't be. I was going to precede each section with a physical description of character: you as an even handsomer Louis Jouvet. There are beautiful things that are a shame to lose, in the Proustian sense. For example, my bearing the name of your mother and sister, and therefore symbolically explaining the taboo, are hard for a poet to sacrifice. I could stress one element, and efface another. The romantic brother-and-sister attachment and our influence on each other, and you taking me to Allendy. Weigh these things. Try to think of them as Proust would. You were important. If I respect the homosexuality completely, do you object to the other things? (Always under another name, of course. The only real names I left are those who wish to be named, such as Miller, and others I will consult over time, such as Rank's wife and daughter, etc.) Above all, as the new generation says, *keep cool.* Keep your mind alert. Make your comments. If you wish to draw a red line through all of your existence, do so (not on the script because each copy costs me so much). By the time you return it, Joaquín will have another batch coming. I am up to page 1,400... A life's work. Trust me. Weigh things that should not be buried as an artist, as a thinker, as a personality. I have long ago understood that some of us cannot bear to expose one's self, and also to respect the image one has. Others' images of us are never matched to our own. I suffered hell when Fred wrote his obtuse book and distorted every fact. I do not think I distort. I will send you a copy of Joaquín's letter. Send it back to Los Angeles, where I do the major part of my work. N.Y. is just hell for work. Here I am at my desk at 8:00 AM till I drop with fatigue.

Anaïs

Letter from Anaïs Nin to Hugh Guiler:
Los Angeles, February 1965

Darling:
Something very important has happened that may delay my return a few days. It took a long time, but I finally made a good reconciliation with Miller via my French professor, whom I share with Henry's son. What happened first was that I understood the change in Henry, partly due to three years of pains from an arthritic breakdown of the hip bone. The doctor is going to attempt replacing the bone so he will not limp. This prospect, three weeks in a cast and three months on crutches, affected him. Then the French professor has a student near where Henry lives and offered to bring him to lunch. I cooked a lunch, we talked French, and this finally broke the ice, as he said himself. I was then able to talk to him honestly and simply about the problem of the Diary, and he took the edited pages with him to read while in the hospital. This is a turning point for the fate of the Diary, as you know. And as it is the best part, and I told him I would take out whatever bothered him, I feel I want to stand by, visit him, etc. For the first time, there is sincerity in our dealings. We talked about his children, his problems, his friends, etc. Until now

there was strain, and on my side a resentment for his not helping me and talking badly about the novels. This will lead to other things. I am calling Gunther up today.

For example, Henry tells me *Vogue* asked him for an assignment in Hong Kong, which Henry does not want to do. Why shouldn't *Vogue* take some of his letters from Greece? I don't feel Gunther has been active here. I can't understand. To get Henry's good will in all this is very important. He has enormous, almost unbelievable power, because as you know, in America, once a name is made, then everything happens. For example, I told him that I told Bay that his offer for the letters was derisory, and Henry laughed and agreed. On the other hand, he was impressed with the Putnam advance of $6,000, though he thinks they are the lowest on the rung of publishers, the cheapest. He would prefer Simon and Schuster for the Diary. And so on.

I hate to stay away so long, darling; it always seems as if everything comes to a climax just as I decide to leave. But I know you understand diplomacy better than anyone. When I first came, you remember, I had a job to do about the letters, and it was my praise of the letters that finally did it. Varda's visit, and now the French professor, who is round, bald, jolly and a wine drinker who amuses Henry, the atmosphere has finally become unstrained.

This, plus work with Oliver Evans and work on the new Diary, will really mean a *gigantic* accomplishment. But I notice that the same jitteriness I feel in New York affects me here when things get social and hectic. Perhaps because of my over-responsiveness (the source of my work) I feel like a machine that gets a *survoltage*. The peaceful life here usually removes that overcharged feeling. But when I am active socially (Varda, Partch, Miller and Oliver) I feel the same way. The only remedy is the pool! I am now helping Partch to get a good crowd for his concert at Pasadena Museum.

Miller is going to the hospital Monday. He may read all week while in a cast. I will visit him, and I will definitely, even if he has not finished, be home by Sunday. I hope he will have finished. To return with an OK will be very wonderful for the publishers.

A

Letter from Joaquín Nin-Culmell to Anaïs Nin:
Oakland, February 4, 1965

Dear Anaïs:

Delighted with your delight and so glad that my comments were helpful. I felt a little bit like Tom Thumb following some giant footsteps, but even so I could make an attempt at jumping from one imprint to the other... The fact remains that your writing is extraordinarily fluid and bell-like at the same time. It rings true (regardless of the bookkeeping details, which are my specialty), but the sound is never harsh. How you can manage to *see* people as you do and still *love* them is beyond my capacity to understand. You must have a monumental capacity for love. No small wonder that human beings fall short of your expectations. It is God you seek.

About Father's need for bolstering the surface things. It was his most disarming quality (if you caught on to it) and the most destructive (if your life depended on it). I still feel he was a child in many ways. An adolescent husband and a competitor with his children. He had genuine accomplishments but never quite fulfilled the promise of his talent. Perhaps I should say *talents*. He applied his iron-clad discipline to the wrong things. Having escaped from his father, he proceeded to "punish" himself in lieu of his father. And so he never quite escaped from his "guilt" but rather added to it like a little boy who can't keep out of the cookie jar. He was ready to make peace with himself and with religion, but it had to be done on his deathbed (!!!) like some bad novel he had read and wanted to act out. I could not prevail upon him to see Padre Rey in Havana. I might add that Padre Rey was ready and willing to see him and was quite a different cup of tea from the usual. He wanted his deathbed scene and he got it! St. Peter must have a special place for children who never grow up.

All my love,
J

Letter from Eduardo Sánchez to Anaïs Nin:
February 7, 1965

Dear Anaïs:

From your last letter I am convinced that you do need me—and want me in your book. All right. Send me a copy, and let's see.

Let me repeat again: now that I am an old man with chilled blood, I look at my homosexual interludes as a series of aberrations ending in miserable failures. I have been a complete and utter idiot! So, the less said about it, the better. Of course, if I am going to remain in your diary, my homosexual tendency must or should be implied. But I will not allow any discussion of my relationship with Feri (was that his name?), and his relation to me and to you, and his confessions, and my confessions, etc., etc. *ad nauseum*. See?

If only my life could have been on the same level of objectivity, coolness, steady purpose and deep satisfaction I am in now. What satisfaction!

Love,
Eduardo

Letter from Anaïs Nin to Hugh Guiler:
Los Angeles, February 1965

Darling:

Your last letters are full of activity and interesting events. No, I am not discouraged, but that is not true. I am. I am terribly disappointed that magazines have not taken the Miller letters, that Gunther does not keep me informed, that Putnam does not decide on the Diary, that Bay won't do my next novel unless he gets the Miller letters. No, of course, I do mind all that. But I am working. Next big hurdle is Henry's opinion of the Diary. Also, in his mellower frame of mind, I hope to get his help with publishers and magazines. He is going to the hospital today.

I am terribly sorry to miss your birthday because I know that it means something to you, my darling, but I do feel I can't run away from this job that may make it easier with publishers (Putnam was already uneasy when they saw Henry fuss over the letters).
Love,
A

Letter from Hugh Guiler to Anaïs Nin:
New York, February 8, 1965

Darling:
Your letter came this morning, and I was surprised at your decision to show the diary to Miller, as I thought you were sure that his reaction would not be good, and that this might make everything more difficult. But, as Gunther said to me over the telephone, we must trust your intuition and believe you have good reasons. However, now that you have taken the step, I think you would do wrong to leave, as you suggest, before he finishes reading the diary and before he has given his approval in writing, as there would always be the danger of his changing his mind after you left. Do think this over carefully, and this time it is I who urge you to see this thing through, as the consequences of your succeeding or failing in this could be very important either way, and I can imagine your hanging on the telephone here if you return before you have seen this through, and living in a state of distraction.

If Miller prefers Simon and Schuster for the diary and has influence with them, you may do well to consider them if, as Gunther thinks, it may be possible in the next two weeks that certain changes will take place at Putnam's. But this is something he asks not be mentioned until the situation becomes clear, which he says will happen very soon. I don't know whether he even thought he could mention it to you over the telephone, and it would probably be well not to say I mentioned it. I have only done so so that you can keep the Simon and Schuster idea warm in the meanwhile, without mentioning anything else to Miller. Gunther is right on top of this situation, and will let you know as soon as he knows himself, but here again is another reason for you to follow through with Miller and settle everything with him before you return. Perhaps you should stay at least until Gunther receives definite news about Putnam's. And I will be in close touch with him myself so I can let you know.

I do miss you, darling, but I feel that you have to act in your best interests at this critical juncture. Let me know what you feel about this.
Love,
Hugo

Letter from Henry Miller to Anaïs Nin:
Pacific Palisades, February 11, 1965

Dear Anaïs:
Writing (and reading) from bed. Have now read about 200 pages. The stuff about June is dynamite. Aren't you worried she may sue for "libel and slander"?

I've checked (lightly in pencil) places that need revision, for clarity or what. Will go over it all with you when I'm up again. Am enjoying it immensely. Feel that you need to cut here and there because of repetitiveness.

You say I am half German, half *French*? (A mistake, or did you mean influenced by the French?) You also report a visit together to the rue Blondel brothel. Didn't you make that up? I don't recall such a visit.

The part about Allendy I enjoyed very much.

I think if publishers knew now what you have to offer they would descend on you in a swarm. Much of it is truly sensational. You'll have to hide away once the book is out.

More later. Should be up and about by Saturday or Sunday.

Henry

P. S. I wonder what June will make of it if she ever reads it. It's a Goya portrait. Would make *me* turn over in the grave. Funny, eh?

Letter from Henry Miller to Anaïs Nin:
February 17, 1965
Dear Anaïs:

I'm now at page 470! Lucky I'm still in bed and can read. Have very bad bronchial cough and a minor heart condition. Won't be able to undergo any operation for some weeks yet.

First thing I wonder about is—do you expect a publisher to bring out all these 900 pages at once—in a single volume, or two or three volumes? It would be very expensive if in several volumes, I imagine. Also I think it better, for the readers' sake, to allow an interval of time between volumes. No one can take the whole biz at one blow. Too intense, too compact.

It does seem to need more editing—mostly elimination of repetitious phrases. I don't feel I want to touch your work—that you are the one to decide what stays or comes out. But I've checked a number of places, and when we can go over it together, I'll explain what I mean.

I take it that Mme. Allendy, as well as Dr. A., is dead now? That's a slanderous bit you include—with his ex-patient, the whip biz and all that.

By the way, I don't think *I* attended any Artaud conference with you. I remember my first and only encounter with him—at the Dôme—when he struck me from behind with his cane—thought I was making fun of him, which I wasn't.

Louise de Vilmorin and her family seem horrible. I would have taken them all to the guillotine myself, if necessary.

(Incidentally, you always seem to go places alone—the question will arise—were you married, a widow or what?)

Some material about me—my notes, charts, etc.—has been covered in the "Letters" to you.

There are many little things to point out—must wait. I haven't much energy yet.

All in all, what impression I imagine readers will get—*of you*—is of a most complicated individual—and perhaps of a "solipsist"—one about whom the world revolves. No matter how clearly you analyze people and situations, one is left mystified.

(One little thought—several times you quote me as saying "Life is foul!" I doubt this extremely. I may have said the *world* is rotten, and people too—but not life itself! Quite a difference.)

However, more in the next. It's an overpowering dose. There's an occasional risk that your uttered seriousness verges on the ridiculous. Watch for this—in editing. Repetitious phrases augment this danger. Enough now!

Henry

Letter from Henry Miller to Anaïs Nin:
Pacific Palisades, February 24, 1965

Dear Anaïs:

Still in and out of bed and will be till next week, at least. No energy at all. But feel OK despite all this—just tired, listless. Now in this 900 pages of the diary. It's a Niagara. Five pages on Rank and his ideas.

Yes, June *had* been in an asylum for two or three years, has been out for some time now, and holds a civil service job for city. Had an accident recently. I hear from her off and on—and help her, of course. I don't know whether she's read *my* books (*Rosy Crucifixion*) or not. I have a chance now to get five books published by Grove Press—but am in a quandary because of the libel and slander issue both from June and from my first wife. I've got to decide soon, because they can be printed legally. Changing names is no use if the character can be identified. Why don't you ask Gunther his opinion—and then some reputable lawyer? June ought to be flattered—but with a woman, who can tell?

Do you have copies of Peter Owen's edition of the *Letters*? Hope I can get six, at least, and a similar amount from Putnam's—yes?

You've done your father well too. Just in these 900 pages you've shown yourself to be a most complicated individual. You're not just a contradiction, but a thousand ones.

By the way, regarding Simon and Schuster—I would say see only Max Schuster. The others I don't trust. But be sure to tell him that the pages are "selected" and possibly pruned and modified. He may think he's getting the authentic diary. Tell him that I said it's the chance of a lifetime—for him. Unless I'm mistaken, he has a great respect for me.

I wonder if you realize today how much judging, condemning, annihilating you have done in the diary. You're not a bad "caricaturist" yourself!

More later. In bed again—2:30 AM. (Answered 20 letters myself and gave the girl 25 more to answer.)

Stay well in that cold N.Y.!

Henry

Letter from Henry Miller to Anaïs Nin:
Pacific Palisades, March 2, 1965

Dear Anaïs:

Still confined to the house, but improving slowly now. Don't mind the illness—a vacation. The other night I finished the diary. It's a tremendous dose to take in one lump. All the material on Rank and *your* acting as analyst is very exciting. (Although I think you end on a weak note—the end occurs before, I'd say.) All you touch on with regard to your early life in N.Y. is also very moving—wish there were more of it. I come away with the impression that no experience, no relationship ever offers you complete satisfaction. You seem insatiable.

It will be quite a job to go over all this together. I take it you will go over it alone first. I have only checked certain passages in question—made no notes—too much for me. (Suddenly I remember one little item—your mention of my "affair" with my first wife's mother. Better cut this out. I am in a spot now as to what to do about certain passages in my books, which are of a libelous, slanderous nature. That is, if the books are published *here*.)

Don't know yet when I can get out and move about. Need full recuperation for the hip operation.

By the way, *The New York Times* wrote Larry Powell of UCLA to do an interview on our long relationship and use the *Letters to Anaïs Nin* as point of departure. I assume he can get a copy of the book—the *Times* already had one. This may be very good for the book. Powell writes well, you know. Especially on literature.

By the way, you mention a number of people (in the diary) by real names. Be wary of certain ones!

Hope everything goes well for you in N.Y. Don't worry about rejections. I feel in my bones that you are soon, and suddenly, going to become a figure of great prominence in the literary world. (Like you sneaked in by the back door.) Good luck!

Beautiful, warm, sunny days here.
More soon.
Henry

Letter from Daisy Aldan to Anaïs Nin:
New York, March 9, 1965

Bien chère Anaïs:
About the journals: These are no longer "diaries" with deletions, but journals. This, to me, has a nuance of difference. Diaries imply spontaneous intimacies; journals—clarified experience. A personal reaction. I prefer journals for publication. Thus, you have superbly succeeded. Only a special type of reader who is not interested in literature, but in gossip and scandal, would prefer the first. What you have done justifies revelation to the world, for the living has become art, and so your experience becomes the reader's.

Your analysis of Miller—*incomparable*—complete, unequalled. Even if this Miller had never existed (which he did), this character you depict has so many nuances, is seen from so many angles, with such sweeps, shadings, highlights, perspectives, that it becomes one of the great character studies in world literature.

And your father! Creating that remarkable tension in contrast to Miller! With what skill you relate his nature to your own—such objectivity, and yet warmth, not the scalpel! How difficult this is for a writer!

And then the impression one receives of *you*, Anaïs Nin! Vast: intelligent, subtle, intuitive, delicate, vain, modest, strong, weak, searching, aware, pretentious, unpretentious, mature, child-like, compassionate, giving, reserved—in short, a *real* being with the contradictions of humanity. Every creative woman will find a part of herself here, and each a different part, because the Anaïs Nin that is formed from the reader's experience is unusual (as I always knew her to be), special, and *many*-faceted.

I think this journal is a superb work of writing. Never think of it otherwise, no matter what money-hungry, ridiculous publishers may say at *any* time. What is written here is already beyond the criticism of the mediocre. It will find its way into the future, *I absolutely know*.

What you have succeeded in doing by deletion and editing, is to have made an outstanding work of art.

When you wrote me about the terrible experience in Florida with Thorvald and that you had cried and trembled all the way home, I felt like crying myself. No one should be permitted to act in such a way. You, for whom all life should be made beautiful—it is your destiny to suffer—but out of this, you have become wise and have created exquisite works.

Daisy

Letter from Joaquín Nin-Culmell to Anaïs Nin:
Oakland, March 11, 1965

Dear Anaïs,

Terribly upset by your note from New York and the result of your visit to Miami. I did warn you about Thorvald (one has to see it to believe it) and I did warn you about assuming that he is behind Charlie's [Cárdenas] in-born anxiety about his investments [with Hugo]. I was against bringing up the subject to Thorvald at all by anybody at any time... *Ceci dit*, I understand and sympathize with your reactions from A to Z. Patience is the only answer and, as you say, if it were not for Kay, Thorvald would be a real problem for himself as well as for others. As it now stands, he must not be crossed. Sweet reasoning has no place in his mind... And yet he needs those around him...

I had no idea he was hostile and sadistic as a child. I remember being sat upon by him as a child, but then you must admit I was an awful brat. He was always so neat, so studious, so surrounded with friends. Mother always used to say: "Why can't you have friends like Thorvald?" I lost track of his development by the time we lived in Paris. In New York, when Mother and I returned, he was sullen and difficult, but then he was having difficulties, marital and otherwise. He tried to sit on me then, but without too much success. I find that it takes two to be sat upon. One does the sitting and the other does the sitting upon. Since then I have felt that he respects and loves me *in his own way*. I must admit that I often fail to see the humor of his ways but then I have *tried* to understand what makes him relive the matrimonial battles of his parents. For me that is the clue of his behavior. There has never been a picture of his father or of his mother in any of the houses I have visited. Not even the large picture of Papa, which he requested from Mother in Williamstown. Forgive me if I seem to be finding excuses, but you know better than I do, my sweet one, that love is the only cure.

If I had been there I would have covered you up with my Spanish cape as I did after that famous concert in Paris. My love will always cover you, you know that.

Kay is taking it on the chin and so is Ken. I feel I must do my share in some way. And forgive us our trespasses as we forgive those who trespass against us...

All my love,
Joaquín

Letter from Joaquín Nin-Culmell to Anaïs Nin:
Oakland, March 20, 1965

Dear Anaïs,

I quite agree with all you have to say about your visit to Miami, but I don't quite see how one can oblige anybody to seek psychiatric help. As for endurance rather than active help, I don't see what else I can do. I still feel that by just being there, I can and do help. In fact, I encouraged Kay to send Ken away to school as soon as possible, and although I have never confided in her, she has confided in me. As for Thorvald himself, all that I can do at the moment is not rise to the bait. The day he will want to confide in somebody, I may be there and I may be able to supply what you call "active help." Meanwhile, I consider it fruitless to go over the past and to pin down blame. In the large sense, we are all to blame. We are all responsible for each other's actions. Who is guilty or who is innocent? God only knows. Besides, nobody is ever completely innocent or completely guilty. To say nothing of the trickiness of words and the way they take on symbolic meanings under certain circumstances.

In any case, don't worry about me and don't worry about what Thorvald might attempt to say about you or Hugh. Silence is a devastating criticism, particularly as Thorvald is a past master of this technique himself.

Kay is under great stress, but I would never talk openly with her. She loves Thorvald and will always, in the final analysis, be on his side. I find that natural enough. That is why I dislike "taking sides." My "serenity" and "balance" is trying not to judge, but to understand. Perhaps it is the only way I can really help, and hence I must help in this way. *Au fond,* you do, too, and that is why I am a little surprised at the violence of your judgment. Don't let him upset you and don't let him turn you away. And always know and feel assured that my love for you is complete, unconditional and ever-present, to say nothing of my respect for you on an intellectual basis. As for Hugh, he has been and always will be more of a brother than my own brother. I can afford to be generous with Thorvald. Life has been good to me.

Love,
Joaquín

Letter from Eduardo Sánchez to Anaïs Nin:
Florence, Italy, March 23, 1965

Dear Anaïs:

Yesterday I mailed "registered" your diary ms. in two packages. It may take five weeks to reach Los Angeles. I do hope they will arrive safely and well.

You succeeded so well in eliminating Hugo that I am encouraged to believe that with just a little effort you can erase me completely. Do try again. Please. Besides,

I believe you are not exercising your instinct for selectivity. You are bringing forth out of your diary people who should remain there, and not clutter your ms. I am a neurotic, negative being, so why bring me in? Why not stick to the famous, the important, the interesting, the creative? (You have certainly brought out vividly Allendy, Rank and Miller.) I met Artaud? Possibly once, but I can't remember.

I know you don't want criticism, but just the same I will criticize people who are colorblind. Anaïs, you are vulgarity-blind, and when you try to be vulgar, or try to imitate Miller, the result is so out of color, so preposterous, so utterly vulgar, that instead of shocking, it *dismays*. That description of your and Henry's visit to the whorehouse is *awful!*

At one moment, I thought you had found a brilliant way of showing Henry's vulgarity: by publishing *his own notes,* so that when on page 99 he uses the word "shit," that four-letter word, that strident note was perfect, just the right and necessary note to climax Henry's sense of vulgarity. But when you try to describe his vulgarity literally, and on page 103 you give a string of four-lettered words, the result is a vulgarization of vulgarity that is preposterous and pitiful (and while we are on this subject, let me advise that if you use "cunt-writer" once, it should be enough).

Now, on a more personal level, I do question your intuitions or your taste at times. You had worried that I wouldn't accept the three Anaïses—conceit. I didn't bat an eyelash. But did you think that your having me, in front of your future public, masturbate at the age of six would make me chuckle with glee? Anaïs, this is an intimate, psychoanalytical, clinical, professional secret. (Besides, it is only a psychoanalytical Freudian supposition. I only remember the punishment and the guilt, etc. Why wouldn't my crime have been that I tried to rape my mother?!)

You seemed to have felt a sense of delicacy in not exposing your father. It's his own type of masturbation (the ripped trouser pockets—and his manipulating girl-pupils while at the piano). He is dead now, and wouldn't mind. I am alive, and wouldn't mind? As though you had me already dead! I was doing so well in your ms., quiet, silent, in the background, mysterious, coming forward now and again, to take Hugo's place, or someone else's, saying just a phrase, or just a sentence, not important, just to keep myself alive until—bango!—I masturbate at the age of six, or, what is silly and even the epitome of banality, until you have me say (page 131): "I have a feeling I am coming to my mother…"

No, my dear Anaïs. I shall be 61 next month. Please try the impossible: be realistic. I cannot change my negative pattern. I did not change when I was young, and I cannot change now.

I am so sorry, so terribly sorry.

Eduardo

Letter from Anaïs Nin to Hugh Guiler:
Los Angeles, March 24, 1965

Darling:

Tell Gunther that this morning I remembered that when I told Bay in May that Gallimard was interested in the Miller letters he made this significant remark, the bastard: "Oh, young Gallimard and I were in a tuberculosis sanatorium together, and I can speak to him." Now I know he meant to tell Gallimard to keep his hands off.

Again, it is a matter of no money. But, my love, it will never be a matter of money with the films or my work. I am giving the Diary a one-year tryout. If no money comes from it, I will take a teaching job and give up writing.

I'm sick of being a parasite.

But with you it is different. You are working hard and working to allow yourself freedom and integrity in your films, and showing them is a luxury, as is going to Miami or buying clothes or pearls and minks or horse race gambling for other people. We should concentrate our efforts on a well-run, efficient showing at home, with help, to important artists and people who matter. As a luxury. Instead of parties.

How is your shoulder, darling? What does Bogner say? Is she back? Does she find you well? Is your relationship with the Open Theater unspoiled by their childishness? I hope so.

A

Letter from Anaïs Nin to Hugh Guiler:
Los Angeles, March 26, 1965

Darling:

Eduardo's reaction to the diary is absolutely irrational, personal and highly distorted. But I promised to leave him out altogether.

André Bay wants to publish only half of the diary, 450 pages. Wonder what you and Gunther think of that, whether that is endangering my reputation in France, to do a truncated work. If only I could get away from Bay.

Starting to revise the first batch, having had time to cool off.

Have you had any repercussions from Charlie Cárdenas? I still regret my flare-up in Miami. But I guess, as you say, I was a time bomb, held back for a lifetime and which was set up with Thor's teasing and denigrating and sapping my self-confidence as a child.

Sometimes I wish I had not been analyzed. I would still be a (fake) Japanese woman (my ideal). Alas...

A

Letter from Anaïs Nin to Daisy Aldan:
Los Angeles, March 26, 1965

Dear Daisy:

The Selma to Montgomery march had a deep effect on me. I wish I could do something. It seems too little just to do things for Millicent or her family. Not enough. I was so moved by their singing and endurance. Wish I could talk to you about the negro marches. I felt I wanted to be there. I felt that all I do personally is not enough. Or is it? Helping Millicent's daughter here, when she had a touch of meningitis, her husband out of work, going to hospital, giving her money, a radio, etc. Is that as good as collective action? All my life I have weighed the personal help against collective action. I have doubts now. The woman who leaves her five children and husband (forever) to help thousands. God, what a problem that is. Rupert says his duty is with his students.

A

Letter from Anaïs Nin to Henry Miller:
Los Angeles, March 26, 1965

Dear Henry:

This is what André Bay, of Stock, writes me: "The Miller letters are indeed of an exceptional, natural, living, effervescent quality. They are very natural (that was not the case with Durrell, and even less with Fraenkel)."

Bay has been publishing all my books and so it was natural that he should bring them out. I would like to know who your favorite translator in France is in order to suggest him.

What I meant yesterday, and I repeat, was that I did not want you spending your energy on general comments on the Diary, merely on what concerns you. You have too much to do, to read, write, etc.

I will try and come one evening while Rupert is playing music, or could your secretary bring you one evening while Rupert is playing nearby?

I am unable to get a publication date from Putnam's. This may be because the young editor who took them has decided to take a year off to write his own novel.

I am editing the first batch of the Diary right now for repetitions, etc. So your mentioning what concerns you would be useful now.

No luck with the magazines. They felt they had to do a big batch of the letters for a cycle, and had no room.

Anaïs

Letter from Anaïs Nin to Gunther Stuhlmann:
Los Angeles, March 26, 1965

Dear Gunther:

Please do all you can to get me out of Bay's hands. His last attitude was really the last straw. To publish only 450 pages of the Diary, his doubts ("I am fascinated with the diary, but what will it mean to people who do not know Allendy or Rank?") is even worse than Peter's, who was at least responsive to the "characters" as such (even if he wanted them to be like the heroine of *Candy*). And then Bay dropping the novel when he has the Diary. What can I say? Or do? How do you feel? Can you make him at least pay an advance on the novel when he has the contract for the Diary? They have to be together, according to his blackmail letter. I am keeping my reactions for you and myself. Next week I will send him the beautiful chapter Oliver Evans wrote on the Diary as an organic part of the total works.

Alas, I cannot get at the photos until I return to N.Y. Will that be too late? If it is absolutely necessary before May 1 let me know. There is a way. But you would have to "burglarize" my apartment with the key I gave you. Get into my closet, find the box with the other keys, lying there, visible, open the files, and there are photos. Can you wait?

I have not seen Miller yet, but there seems to be no trouble in that direction. Eduardo has been the only neurotic who wants every mention out. He wants to remain the invisible man. But he is not an important element. His obsession is secrecy.

I am now starting revisions of first volume, having had enough time to become objective. The only thing everyone agrees upon is the matter of repetitions. I will have that all done by the time I come back. Other reactions, as you know, have not been useful. Yours and two or three others are the only ones by which I can respect and guide myself.

Anaïs

Letter from Gunther Stuhlmann to Anaïs Nin:
New York, March 29, 1965

Dear Anaïs:

Just got your letter of March 26. I think there is a misunderstanding somewhere: judging and interpreting André Bay's letter, it was my understanding that he wants to start out doing the diary with the first 400 pages of the mss. on hand as volume 1 of a series, since he felt that for France it would be better to do a series of volumes rather than a very big book. Am I wrong? He spoke of *Tome 1* and did not say anything about not doing all that comes his way.

Maybe I am interpreting him wrong, but that is how I translate his long letter to me. Well, I'll check this out right away. My feeling was that he was enthusiastic, rather than reluctant.

More soon. I just got back into town and hope to pound the last nail with all this.

As ever,
Gunther

Letter from Henry Miller to Anaïs Nin:
Pacific Palisades, March 31, 1965

Dear Anaïs,

The jacket for the letters book looks very good, I think. Excellent photo of *you*. I seem to recognize the photo of me as one by Carl Van Vechten in 1940 on returning from Greece. You? The drawing of me is quite good, too, I thought.

Am only now about to go through the diary for the places I had checked. Hope to type out my remarks for you, to save time and effort.

I told Gunther I hoped Putnam would not send a review copy to *Time*, but to try *Life*, which, though short, is usually far better. I asked for a dozen copies of the book, either to be mailed by the publisher to names I give or to me—and to send me a bill for same, if they don't want to make it gratis.

I had two good letters from the German publisher recently, and though she is still in straits, she is getting out more publications. She had some good write-ups in important German reviews. She explained how busy she had been—and I can well believe her—and that she would be writing you soon. I know she's very keen to do the diary. If Rowohlt takes the Miller letters, it would help a lot toward a good reception for the diary over there. I urged Gunther to see that Putnam gets copies off immediately to all the foreign publishers. That is where I think the letters will sell well.

Noted what André Bay said—very flattering. Hope he knows English well.

As for a translator, the best is the one who translated Durrell's *Quartet*. He's really excellent. He did one of my books only, and I forget which it was now, also forget his name! He's married to a beautiful Martiniquaise. My good friend Georges Belmont is also very good, but I think he is trying to avoid taking on such assignments now. He gave up all work to do his own writing recently. In a pinch, however, one might try him. He's a marvelous fellow, even though he was on the wrong side (Vichy) during the war. At his trial after the war, the judge got down from the dais, embraced him (accolade) and said he wished there were more Frenchmen like him. Quite a victory—and he deserved it, believe me.

More soon. Carry on!
Henry

Letter from Eduardo Sánchez to Anaïs Nin:
Florence, Italy, April 2, 1965

Dear Anaïs,

I am so grateful that I am being left out—a million thanks (just a most inadequate expression for expressing the inexpressible).

Good luck, my dear, as ever, your cousin,
Eduardo

Letter from Anaïs Nin to Hugh Guiler:
Los Angeles, April 9, 1965

Darling:

Eduardo's request to be completely out of the Diary is what Joaquín aptly describes as a strange way to commit suicide. All he had, after reading 815 pages, was a violent reaction to a ten-line episode on masturbation, which was going to come out, as per our agreement, and had nothing to say about the entire Diary except an outraged criticism of the visit to the whorehouse. My most negative statements about him have been confirmed by time. Negative, neurotic and petty. Above all, he is absolutely without a sense of history, for I cannot help but regard the past as history, no longer personal. Don't you? The real artist has to transpose; he can't live with all that alive-and-kicking in the womb all the time.

A

Letter from Anaïs Nin to Alan Swallow:
Los Angeles, April 16, 1965

Dear Alan:

You may have received a letter from Morrow of Putnam's as Gunther did. Here is what they said to Gunther: "To be perfectly frank, we found this first section of the diary disappointing from a purely editorial point of view and style. We did not find in this section the forthrightness and the sense of contact with real people (!)

that one expects from a journal. It was all as if it were half fictionalized even as it was first set down and the form into which it was edited strengthens this impression. It read almost like a loosely constructed novel. In short, we could not see that this would appeal to more than Anaïs Nin's present, devoted, but we think small audience, and that accordingly the project represents a disproportionate investment even with Swallow's help."

No comment. I prefer Gunther's crude remark: "The bastards can't read."

So another wasted month or more. And now we have to try Miller's friend Max Schuster. How I wish you were rich enough to do it alone. But you know, it is not the money, as I will get money from every country in Europe, it is the fact that we will get no reviews, as with the other books. I am depressed and disgusted. I won't write more today. I am doing such a fine revision job. Then I will have it typed clean, all ready for publication. Miller is writing me his unimportant and small excisions. Nothing serious. But I have taken out repetitions, changed a few names.

Tomorrow I may be able to see the ironic humor, that the fact that the Diary reads like fiction is exactly what pleased my severest critics (those I trust), such as Oliver, so that they were interested in characters they did not know.

How these publishers mask their commercial calculations with phony judgments. I would rather they said: "We don't think it will sell." They are nothing but machines.

I did want, for both of us, Alan, some economic retribution. Some status.

Miller tells me Sydney Omarr will review the Miller letters for the *Los Angeles Times*. An astrologer, a man of no literary quality at all. And an article for the *New York Times* about the UCLA Miller collection will not mention the letters book because the letters are not in the collection!

How is your leg? How is everything with your new projects?

I am up to page 1,500 now—my encounter with Durrell, the summer before the war, always dramatic and *fiction!*

As soon as Oliver has typed his study of the Diary I will send it to you.

Anaïs

Letter from Alan Swallow to Anaïs Nin:
Denver, April 19, 1965

Dear Anaïs,

Yes, I had got the letter from Morrow. Sorry they didn't "go." I don't think there is any sense in vilifying them. These are good people, but they are in publishing for other reasons than you want or than I am. They do their job conscientiously as they see it; the only trouble is that they don't see it very well, in our terms. Because they are at least decent, I am sorry that it didn't work, for I could have been confident of what they would do merchandising-wise. I'm not so confident of some of the others.

You indicate "now we have to try Miller's friend Max Shuster." I don't understand the "have" in this sentence. There are plenty of others. Do you recall that I said earlier that I could contact some others I know to see if they might be interested in a joint imprint? Morrow was only the *first* one I was going to contact. But now it appears the work is being already submitted independent of this situation.

Still one more thing I don't understand: your assumption that I can't do this alone. As for reviews, we didn't do too badly with *Collages*, and there is a continuing upswing, so that after that one, we'd be getting more. It doesn't appear we are going to vault in one jump into a big, "bestselling" kind of attention; we will have to go at it gradually, as we have. (For example, I don't think the *Herald-Tribune* would again pass it up, after their apology for goofing on *Collages*.) I still don't have an answer to the question I asked: When are the *Letters* appearing? Or do you know? Did Putnam go slowly on this, or what happened with regard to the publication date?

Don't be discouraged: you have a most enviable reputation, one better and sounder than that of 90% of the writers today. I wouldn't trade it for Henry's, for example, because it is solid, believed in, and growing quite rapidly now.

Cordially,
Alan

Letter from Anaïs Nin to Hugh Guiler:
Los Angeles, April 1965

Darling:

Yesterday I had Miller to lunch, limping, very old, frail, full of nervous tics, cold, thin, and we talked out his notes, as it is always easier then. I have always given in to the foolish little things to keep his good will for the important ones. Not too much. His Lolita secretary, who looks like his daughter, was hardly able to carry the box of the Diary. But all in all in good temper, and he gave me, verbally, the compliments he did not give in his letters. He does insist and finally explained that though I feared to hurt more than he ever did, my lucidity in the end was more terrible than his cruelties!

Catalonia will publish two of my books.

No reviews from Putnam or Gunther on *Letters*.

But the pool is my reward.

I will have to spend a dollar after nine o'clock to call Gunther. Was always afraid to call him because he talks so long.

My love to you, darling,
A

Letter from Anaïs Nin to Joaquín Nin-Culmell:
Los Angeles, April 30, 1965

Dear Cuchi:

You have proved to be the most understanding of all my readers. I am glad we had this opportunity for me to discover your insight, and more of you than I knew from our rare encounters. Your comments deserved careful consideration.

You are wonderful at catching repetitions. I will ask you to be my number one editor.

Enormous job of revising. Now I must consider Miller's comments. Complying with small things so he won't get mad at the big ones. Such as that Fred has brains, that *Tropic of Cancer* never had 1,000 pages, that he never suffered from not being a handsome man, that June was Romanian and not Hungarian, that he never hated America, etc. *C'est très drôle*, but it is a fact that portrait painters are well acquainted with.

How do you feel about being more present in the Diary? You were, of course, in the early ones, in the early Paris period, rue Schoelcher, in Louveciennes. It was after that really that you were farther away, traveling, etc. I cut out a lot because it was intimate, always doting on you, and maybe I felt you did not want to be featured too much. Think about it. I would like to put things in that do you good as a composer. Help me. You deserve star billing. Only the closer a person is, the more one keeps a portrait in a niche marked "not literary."

I thanked Thor for the ring he sent me, warmly, and gave him advice for his arthritis and said let's be easy on each other, none of us are feeling so well and we need kindness.

Anaïs

Letter from Gunther Stuhlmann to Anaïs Nin:
New York, May 7, 1965

Dear Anaïs:

The check from Peter Owen for the Miller letters advance finally cleared the books and I have deposited a check for $1,120.59 in the First National City Bank here to your account.

After deducting for books you had ordered from him, the check we received was for $1675.24, from which we deducted 10% commission, based on the total amount due, and I have taken off 20% under our agreement for the editing of the book. I did not deduct the extra 10% on the Putman payment that you wanted me to have, since we can work this out on some future money that comes in. I figured your account needed some replenishing.

The French edition of *Collages* should be settled soon, too, once we cleared the last hurdles of the bickering.

Don't worry, I'll work with you on the diary as much as you want me to. You know this is the most promising thing, and I'm glad the editing is progressing.

I was not too keen about Swallow's further thoughts (you got copy of his letter) and I have started again on my own to see what we can do here. Maybe Hiram Haydn will turn out (awaiting word from him).

Maybe I will have to retire and devote myself wholly to the project. Glad that Henry is working out. As I told you, I had two good letters from him in which he suddenly liked all I did, including the preface.

Soon more, as ever,
Gunther

Letter from Nobuko Uenishi to Anaïs Nin:
New York, May 18-19, 1965

Dearest Anaïs:

You have I am sure no idea how relieved and terribly delighted I was upon opening the mail box and finding a letter from *you!*

I thought I must have offended or hurt you, or maybe you were already flying back for your lecture of May 28th (as I had been told by Mr. Hugo).

Tomorrow morning, first thing I'll do is to go down to Grand Central Post Office to have the Miller letters sent to Japan, and I shall write an airmail letter to Mr. Kawade.

Otherwise, what has happened is so dramatic that you can see its like only in Hollywood pictures... The other day, I rushed out to Gaiety East as usual for a salad, where I was spoken to by an elderly gentleman, who turned out to be the president of 20th Century Fox, Mr. Darryl Zanuck. He asked me to try out for the film, *Sand Pebbles*, which Mr. Robert Wise is to direct... Shooting has been arranged by 20th Century Fox.

The final decision, I don't know yet. The part is a Chinese girl's part. Which I happen to not be...

Anaïs...I simply wait for your return to New York.

Nobuko

Letter from Gunther Stuhlmann to Anaïs Nin:
New York, May 20, 1965

Dear Anaïs:

Thanks for the marvelous review of the letters in the *Los Angeles Times*—and the diary chapter by Oliver Evans, which is very important and helpful.

And congratulations on the editing of the diary, which seems to be going well—you probably won't even need my hand on this.

Enclosed are three copies of the contract for *Collages* with du Rocher in Monaco. Would you please sign and return to me all three, and I'll eventually get you a copy signed by the publisher for your files. We had a good deal of haggling back and forth and finally agreed on the terms spelled out.

I will also send you copies of the contract with Stock for the Miller letters. I am still haggling with Bay on the novel and diary commitments and awaiting his reply to my various memos. But we can get the Miller letters contract ready, anyway. I still feel he has a strong obligation to commit himself on the novels.

Doubleday wants to see the diary. Haydn has not answered yet.

Also sent Peter Israel at Putnam's a note complaining about the lack of promotion and publicity of the letters, just to go on record. I already discussed this on the phone. More soon.

All my best,
Gunther
P. S. Still waiting for *The New York Times* review!

Letter from Alan Swallow to Anaïs Nin:
Denver, May 31, 1965

Dear Anaïs:

I wrote to Hiram Haydn, and he was most interested and said that he had talked with the president of Harcourt as well, and that neither of them felt there would be any difficulties in the joint imprint idea. So I sent that on to Gunther too. I had

written Hiram that I'd have it sent over to him as soon as possible. Either of these would be good; I hope we get some interest there.
Cordially,
Alan

Letter from Alan Swallow to Anaïs Nin:
Denver, June 16, 1965

Dear Anaïs:
A letter this morning from Hiram, which was most encouraging.
Mae will be going with me to the L.A. State conference on July 7. We found out yesterday that she can get off work. So we will fly in on Tuesday, arriving about 1:30. Since we will be there that long, we will arrange to have a car ready for rent and use it, delivering it back to the airport as we leave. We will go immediately to the hotel. Then, after settling a bit, we will be out to your house at 2335 Hidalgo Ave. We can make it an exact hour, or we can come on out, and if ahead of the other guests, then that would just mean a little more chance to chat beforehand.
I'm sending this in care of Daisy Aldan. I understand that officially you are there, but I wasn't sure if I should write thus.
Of course I remember Rupert when you came through visiting his father.
Cordially,
Alan

Letter from Alan Swallow to Anaïs Nin:
Denver, June 21, 1965

Dear Anaïs:
Mail has just come and a letter from you.
1. I am sorry that you felt the royalties check was so discouraging. It is a false indication, however. If you examine the report, you'll see that we maintained sales and improved. Then you took a good, *big* credit, and the *advance* to be paid off—because we managed all that, we did very well.
2. I am going to speak about the diary once more. I felt hurt by your sentences: "I know you have been prevented from enjoying the Diary or responding to it by your anxiety about my loyalty." This is a *false* assumption. I indicated to you that I have lived with the diary on practically a daily basis. I backed you to the hilt on it. You *knew* it would be published. So how can you speak of my not responding? The only thing I did not do was to wade into it as an editor. So I was content to read and enjoy; to back it up with everything, being prepared to go all the way in publishing it; and until the publishing situation was settled, I could do little except a disservice to interfere, as I would think of it. There will be a joint imprint; this is a necessity, if we find someone willing, as Haydn is. I won't stand for anything else unless none of my friends in publishing wants it. I think it will be Harcourt Brace from what Hiram wrote and from your report on your conversation with him.
Cordially,
Alan

Letter from Oliver Evans to Anaïs Nin:
Northridge, California, June 1965

Dear Anaïs,
My reason for treating *Winter of Artifice* as personal history is that from certain extracts from the diary which I reproduced in Chapter 1, it would be immediately obvious to anyone who read the chapter on *Winter* that it was, in part at least, autobiographical. To pretend it was not would be to raise the suspicion on the part of a careful reader that I was simply not very bright. It needn't be *stressed*, of course; and perhaps I did over-emphasize it, but I did so by way of accounting for what I think is the basic weakness of the book: you did not have the necessary distance from your material. Obviously it is the job of an honest critic to account for weaknesses where they exist, or where he thinks they do.

Again, when you deny that you and Miller are romantic writers, you are using the term in its popular sense as the opposite of realism rather than in the traditional literary sense in which I am using it (as the opposite of classicism). I enclose excerpts from two handbooks of literature so that you can see the sense in which I use the word. In this sense, of course, Miller is a romantic. And so are you.

I hope I can continue with the book, and I shall certainly show you the finished product. But it is too exhausting to have to cope with individual and random objections that involve rewriting the chapters as soon as I have finished with them. My mistake for inviting them!
Love,
Oliver
P. S. The term romantic does not, as you seem to assume, have a pejorative meaning to scholars and students of literary history.

Letter from Gunther Stuhlmann to Anaïs Nin:
New York, July 1, 1965

Dear Anaïs:
Swallow is delighted with the Harcourt situation and told me I could go ahead with a contract while he is working out the joint imprint with Haydn.

Had a four-hour visit with Abe Rattner and his wife—very pleasant and was shown a great deal of material, including his oil portraits of Henry. Quite stunning.

Bay sent back contracts unsigned and will return all material. He keeps assuring me that he is still your friend. So we can pursue other avenues in France.
All my best,
Gunther

Letter from Gunther Stuhlmann to Anaïs Nin:
New York, July 7, 1965

Dear Anaïs:
I think you have done very well in bringing the text of the diary down by another 100 pages or so, and I think this is all it needs, for this would bring us to 150,000 words, as we discussed, and I don't think you should cut any more. I am not sure whether it would be good to cut out the little scene with the prostitutes—

this is the sort of "worldly color" that I would hate to lose. Also, I would not cut out much more about Allendy than you have. The Miller cuts seem good, and maybe if we can't name Vilmorin, your suggestion to cut her out is a good one. In the disguise it won't mean much to the American reader. Hiram is away, but they are working on the contracts and the October deadline is simply for contract purposes; if the book is ready earlier, we can turn it in earlier. But we would not be able to publish it before Christmas, anyway, and it seems to me to be best for early next year. More soon.

As ever,
Gunther

Letter from Anaïs Nin to Alan Swallow:
Los Angeles, July 9, 1965

Dear Alan:

It was such a real pleasure to see you in person after so many years. If Leon Surmelian had not been so possessive we might have had more time to talk. But I was grateful for what we had, and I must tell you that you made a wonderful impression on *everyone*. What a contrast between you and the other panelists. My own respect for your attitude and affection for your human qualities, integrity and genuineness were reinforced. I hope you enjoyed your trip, and I wonder what you felt about Los Angeles. It would be wonderful if you moved out here! They need men like you, and it might be good for your health. More relaxed.

Everybody liked you. I was very proud of you. I hope Mae had a good time. That panel was not worthy of you. But you talked vigorously and made important points. I hope we can do this again.

Your friend,
Anaïs

Letter from Daisy Aldan to Anaïs Nin:
New York, July 12, 1965

Beloved Anaïs:

I am neglecting Rudolf Steiner to read Miller's letters to you. I am about up to May 1934. By now, I like him a little more. I read his ideas with interest, but also critically—ideas about Spengler, Nietzsche, etc. What an ego! He rarely mentions your work with any detail—or his concern for you, but uses you as a great Ear and a "fairy Godmother." You must have been too wonderful to him. It is fantastic to me how he wrote everything with the idea that he was writing for posterity—and I guess he was right, because, look—*I'm* reading those letters, and a lot of other people are and will be.

I'll bet, after reading this book, a lot of your admirers, fans, "friends," correspondents, will write you long letters about themselves. It must inspire them to do this. I feel I'm beginning to do it myself. As you know, it was always very painful to me to consider myself as being one of those people. I always wanted to be special to you; I suppose they all do. I feel now I am. If I didn't, I'd stop seeing you.

My love to you.
Daisy

Letter from Anaïs Nin to Hugh Guiler:
Los Angeles, July 14, 1965

Darling:

Cannot get over Daisy's pettiness, but I analyze it as a basic jealousy and envy, which will appear now as I get known, as she is the kind of friend who is kind while you are a failure and then resents it when you become successful. Deep down, she is very egocentric.

But her friend [Marlis Schweiger] made marvelous reproductions of the old photos for the Diary, even a spoiled newspaper photo of Allendy. And I won't have to pay—that is, the publisher will pay if he uses them.

Still working on the Diary. Gunther gave October as the deadline, but I would like to turn it in before that and get it out of the way. I hope the next volume won't take as much preparation.

A

Letter from Anaïs Nin to Gunther Stuhlmann:
Los Angeles, July 15, 1965

Dear Gunther:

I sent you the final index, and a page of references to Henry that enabled me to check every repetition. To my surprise, there were few. The way we have made the cuts enables you and Haydn to accept or refuse them.

André Bay told Pierre Brodin over the telephone that the Diary was not "*commerciale, un gros risque,*" etc. But as I told Brodin, it was not the decision we minded, it was his taking *two years to make it.*

What do you think of the *Los Angeles Times*, who would not review *Collages*, but enables me to achieve great distinction as a clue in their crossword puzzle? I thought this would make you laugh. It is worth framing, or pasting on your bathroom walls!

Hugo writes me he thinks you have a better understanding of the Diary than anyone. He is glad you are writing the preface.

A

Letter from Alan Swallow to Anaïs Nin:
Denver, July 1965

Dear Anaïs,

It was so wonderful to be with you and Rupert. You were awfully good to us; and I am sorry that we shortened our Wednesday evening by getting so lost. But it was really enjoyable; and it was sweet of you two to drive to the motel Thursday evening for a bit more togetherness. I hope it was not too tiring for you, Anaïs.

We enjoyed very much getting to know Rupert more too; we thoroughly enjoyed him.

Again, much love to you both.
Alan

Letter from Anaïs Nin to Joaquín Nin-Culmell:
New York, August 1965

Dear Cuchi:
Came to N.Y. because Hugo was not recovering from a month-old bronchitis, and he is better now. Will return to L.A. August 20 because of a possibility of a new script writer for *Spy*. I am sorry I have been lazy about letters. I must tell you that Ayme is coming through with contracts for *Ladders to Fire* and *Spy in the House of Love* in both Spanish and Catalan. I am signing contracts this week. I am sure you had a hand in this.
New York is muggy, hot, occasionally rainy. Almost everybody is away. I hope you had a rest.
My publisher Hiram Haydn is a darling man, an older, scholarly Jew, a writer himself who treats me perfectly, so I permitted many cuts (not vital) to tighten the text.
Write me in L.A. Give my love to Mary.
Un abrazo de Anaïs

Letter from Henry Miller to Anaïs Nin:
Pacific Palisades, August 13, 1965

Dear Anaïs,
Just got your card from N.Y. Glad to know it's fixed for the diary with Harcourt Brace.
About June—so very hard to say. Unpredictable. So far she hasn't said anything to me about the mention of her real name (June Edith Smith—dance hall girl) mentioned by tactless reviewers of *Sexus* and other books. Would you really have the courage to see her? I got a terrible shock when I saw her two or three years back. She has two very good friends whom I introduced to her—Dr. James E. Baxter (a young psychiatrist) and his wife Annette K. Baxter, who wrote a book about me. They are truly lovely, wonderful people. Maybe you should sound them out first. (They know of you, of course.)
They have really helped June materially, morally, spiritually. I just heard from Annette the other day. She said June has improved greatly of late. (Annette is Armenian—a person you would like, I am sure. And to be trusted.)
June's address is: Mrs. June E. Corbett, 63-65 100th St. (Apt. 4-D), Forest Hills (75) N.Y. Tel: Br 5-5659 or/and 275-7861 (area code 212). Think the latter is her home telephone.
Gunther could tell you whether a mere change of a (real) name of a character in a book is legitimate or safe enough. I doubt it! Especially where there is any possibility of libel, slander or defamation of character.
June shouldn't need any material assistance. I send her something every month. And she gets a salary for her work in one of the city's departments. (I think as a typist—imagine!)

Someone sent me Gore Vidal's review of *Sexus* in the *Sunday Times* (or else the *San Francisco Examiner*). What a stinky, niggardly spirit! He must be a fag, isn't he? Imagine giving *that* book to a homo! It's like putting a stiletto in one's back.

We have had and still have a real heat wave here—around 95-100 degrees for days. I'm dripping with perspiration—and am only in pajamas.

Enough now. Can't go in the pool yet as I just had three growths carved out of my back. Nothing serious.

Take good care of yourself *repeatedly*, as the Japanese say.

Henry

Letter from Anaïs Nin to Annette Baxter:
Los Angeles, August 1965

Dear Annette:

Some thoughts about June, and what I would have said to her if I had had a chance. What she calls my treachery was my effort to prevent Henry from breaking up the relationship between them, my desire to have it continue, my feeling that hers would outlive his need of peace and a writer who would help him to write. I didn't want them to break. June would never have been displaced if she herself had not made a scene, and Henry, always being passive, let things happen. He has never struggled to hold anyone. When I made a scene about his selfishness, he let Lepska take over when he did not really want to marry her. Perhaps you can convey this to her. I was not deceiving her. As you could see, I really admired her. If she wants me to change her name or delete her portrait, I can't do that. The facts are true.

Thank you for your letter. I had a good talk with Henry. You are right about his not writing to her, and I am sure he won't. He is eager for peace. We all want that. I would like June to have it too.

My love to you both,
Anaïs

Letter from Alan Swallow to Anaïs Nin:
Denver, August 23, 1965

Dear Anaïs,

No word from you for a long, long time. Concerned and worried a bit. Did something happen to offend you? Or are you ill? I hope not the latter—or the former, either!

As I understood it, Hiram is primarily responsible for the editorial job, but in the background I can help at any moment if there might be differences of opinion, etc., in a protective capacity. I believe that is the way we wished it, from our conversation, oh, six weeks and more ago. If you have expected and wished more from me, please let me know. But it seems to me to be going beautifully, and it is just a matter that if Hiram doesn't agree, then I can help. I haven't noted anything I'd object to, anyway.

May I keep the old version of the diary? Or do you wish it back? A good thing to have in my effects for the depository, ultimately, if this is of no use to you; but if it is, I'll send it right off.

Good news from Harcourt. I had a phone call from the VP in charge of the trade dept. He was calling after they had all had a conference after the return of the president Jovanovich. What they propose for the joint imprint is all right with me. It doesn't involve any investment on my part; they will invest and figure a reasonable amount for sales overhead (but not for any other overhead, so they are being fair), and then out of the gross profit I would get a little. He made the point that this would simplify the bookkeeping. Well, we are in a culture of bookkeepers and accountants and lawyers, so I guess we have to bow to them. I had figured on making an investment and thus sharing more largely the risks and the profits. But since there is no investment, this is all right with me. At least I am in as I should be (that is, I believe I should be, as we all seemed to agree, in view of my support for your work), and the joint sponsorship is assured—that should be the main thing.

Cordially,
Alan

Letter from Anaïs Nin to Alan Swallow:
Los Angeles, August 28, 1965

Dear Alan:

I saw Hiram Haydn a few hours about cuts. There were few disagreements, and he is not inflexible. He wanted the visit to the prostitute out, and I, too, but Gunther defended it as typical of Miller's world. He wanted Artaud having dinner at his publisher's home taken out, and I felt everything that concerned Artaud was important in literary portraiture. You are kind to offer to mediate. I will call on you if necessary.

I don't understand why Harcourt did not let you share everything—both burden and profits. But in a way, I am glad you did not have the burden of an advance, printing, etc. They are cutting to keep the book within an easy price, which, I hope, means they hope to sell enough. Be sure your name is on the front page of the Diary. Is that in the contract? I hope your sort of "royalty" arrangement will be fair. What I will see to is that you get the *credit* (in interviews or reviews) you deserve. Already preparing a KPFK interview on the Diary with Frances Roberts in which I will talk about you.

Your guess was intuitive. While in N.Y. I had a checkup and found two things wrong that will require surgery—gallstones and a fibrous growth in the uterus. Not very happy about it. But you have had a much worse time, and I think you show remarkable patience and endurance. The old version (uncut) of the Diary I find useful to lend to friends who can't wait till May 1966—lend it to me. Oliver used it to work with, now Frances Roberts, etc. I return to N.Y. September 9.

Love,
A

Letter from Alan Swallow to Anaïs Nin:
Denver, August 31, 1965

Dear Anaïs,

So good to get your letter and its spirit! Glad that the cuts seem pretty much in agreement with Haydn. Henry Miller and the prostitutes would probably help popularity; but everyone knows this, in a way, through his work, and I agree it can be dispensed with without any great harm.

I haven't had the promised letter concerning details with Harcourt Brace, but they are always slow about such things. I am sure that we understood together, as per the original offering, that there will be a joint imprint on the book; I shall see to that, all right.

As for the financial thing, of course they do a lot of "bookkeeping" and the dominance of such in publishing; but I don't mind. It will be all right. I wanted a little more, but in their terms, I can see their reasoning. I'll mail on the uncut version. Fine, if you can use it.

Sorry you have to face the surgery. Both are relatively light, I understand from friends who have had them. I don't mean to belittle them, and any time in a hospital is to be regretted (although I confess that is the way I manage to rest up; I once figured that I'd spent a year of my life in the things); but I trust you'll have the hysterectomy (seems to be extremely worthwhile) and get at the gallstones too. Should make you pert again!

Cordially,
Alan

Letter from Anaïs Nin to Rupert Pole:
New York, September 12, 1965

Darling:

The Lincoln Center Festival takes all my time and is overwhelming—films afternoon, morning and evenings.

Marguerite Young's success is a pleasure to me as she is the first breaking down of the Four-Letter-Word school. Today I attend the gathering of the press at her agent's place from five to seven and then it's over, but it is good for me, and Marguerite goes around praising me and will introduce me to everyone. What will amuse you is that she is also receiving mean and bitchy remarks. I thought I got them because I was a foreigner. They hold against her the *size* of her book, her age and her being a spinster! I advised her to say she is 40, married four times. There is so much envy and jealousy in the world.

So you are working hard again, but our trip to Japan is assured: $300 from Spain, $200 from Japan, $1,500 from Harcourt Brace (next year), 200 pounds from England (Miller letters in paperback), etc., etc. All is well. Energy good; feeling the benefit of a good vacation. Still using your *fine* corrections. Eagle eye! Your perfectionism a great help. Photos of the Diary came out very well.

Love love love,
A

Letter from Anaïs Nin to Alan Swallow:
New York, September 28, 1965

Dear Alan:

New York catches me like a maelstrom. There were three days of celebration for Marguerite's book (sold over 40,000 copies), errands for Harcourt, photos reproduced, a chart of names, a woodblock lithograph by a young girl artist that they may use for a cover, etc. I *saw* Hiram write your imprint for the designer with Hilda Lindley of the publicity department. They are *all* people you would like and who would like you. I work well with them.

Then time wasted at the doctor's to get built up for surgery. I return to Los Angeles in a few days to rest up or at least not strain—correct proofs Oct. 15—return Oct. 29 to N.Y. Enter hospital for surgery Nov. 2—Doctor's Hospital 170 East End Ave. will be my glamorous address for two weeks.

No disagreements on cuts—Gunther, as the preface writer and editor (we agreed to name him editor so he could protect me from malicious questions), makes final selections. I do hope the Diary will bring you prestige as an independent publisher.

Affectionately,
Anaïs

P. S. How do you feel? How is your leg behaving? Give my regards to your sweet wife.

Letter from James E. Baxter to Henry Miller:
New York, October 3, 1965

Dear Henry,

As you may know, we recently spent a splendid evening with Anaïs, talked with June last weekend about her appearance in the diary, and found her unexpectedly obstinate. Since then we've twice spoken with her by telephone about another matter (she heard me on a silly radio program), and she brought the diary up in a considerably more cooperative tone. We've been in touch with Hiram Hayden at Harcourt Brace and feel pretty sure that it will work out all right.

I'm writing to you now to suggest that if you haven't mentioned this in writing to June, it might be just as well not to, not right now, anyway. We don't want her to feel that she's being pressured, or that there's some conspiracy, etc.

The diary, of course, is a monumental document, and we'd hate to see a word of it changed.

I'm sending a copy of this to Anaïs to keep her posted.

Have a good month!
Jim

Letter from Anaïs Nin to George Shively, lawyer:
Los Angeles, October 1965

Dear Mr. Shively:

On November 3 I am going to have surgery, and I wanted to ask you to make a change in my trust. I hope it will not be too difficult. I would like to make Rupert Pole heir to my literary estate. You have his name and address on the trust. Can this be done? Will it be a great deal of trouble? I am returning to New York October 31. I could be at your office November 1 for a signature. I will telephone you that morning, but I thought if I gave you time to prepare the change it would be better.

Sincerely yours,
Anaïs Nin

October 29, 1965
Return to New York.

Letter from Joaquín Nin-Culmell to Anaïs Nin:
Barcelona, November 9, 1965

Dear Anaïs,

So glad to receive your note of November 5th from the hospital and to know that "*tout va très bien*" even though the stay in the hospital must be far from amusing... I still feel badly about not waiting for you, but given the circumstances, I *was* upset and still am. Must be going through (I hope!) a bad period but don't you worry, I'll pull through. Partly work, partly future, partly personal life, partly religious crisis. I must sound more like 20 than 57! In any case, don't worry and get well soon.

Hugh was as nice as he could be. I'm afraid that I wasn't a very appreciative guest. Do thank him for me again.

The weather here is cold and snappy, but I manage to heat my little study with a well-directed electric heater.

Mary is well, but we seem to have grown apart. I have the impression that my planetary influences must be raising hell!

Of one thing I am sure. I do love you, my sweet, and hope that you are being patient and "sage" and taking all of your pills on time.

Thank you for writing so soon!
Love,
Joaquín

Letter from Rupert Pole to Anaïs Nin:
Los Angeles, November 1965

My darling,

So glad you went ahead—and did it—"out, damned spot," out now—you sounded tired today (Sunday)—but that must be normal for the 4th day when the pain killers wear off.

Gave a test Friday, so working late tonight correcting papers. The maid just called to say she had the flu and can't come tomorrow—OK as not much to do anyway—Piccolo and I have a new system—we *never* get anything dirty! Tired after a hard day's work in the garden. It was nice of Robert Haas to mention you—you are no longer just "The Writer's Writer"—now the reader's writer—and my writer—whom I will love always,
R

Letter from Henry Miller to Anaïs Nin:
Pacific Palisades, November 10, 1965

Dear Anaïs,

Delighted to hear that all's well. Bravo! You are lying very near to where I was born—85th and York Avenue—top floor (over a saloon).

Wondering how much time they give you before the second operation. Hope the first one was the toughest.

Heard all about the "blackout" in N.Y. on TV yesterday. Must have been spectacular.

Get well fast now and come back soon. We miss you. Do you have a TV in your room, I wonder. If you need anything, let me know.

Good luck!
Henry

Letter from Hugh Guiler to Anaïs Nin:
En route to Paris, November 18, 1965

Darling,

So sorry it was so hectic we had little time for each other. Will be in Paris in a half hour or so, and I have slept and rested and read and feel ready for work.

I am happy about the way things turned out for you. You have a wonderful spirit. And it all made me realize once again how precious you are to me.

Rest well in the sun, darling—I promise not to strain on this trip.

All my love, your
H

Letter from Anaïs Nin to Gunther Stuhlmann:
Los Angeles, November 30, 1965

Dear Gunther:

I called you up when I got the proofs to ask if you were going to proofread, then decided I had to do it anyway to see the cuts, etc.

Also to tell you I had not noticed that in the preface you speak of me "as a fledgling writer in the 1920s"; I am not trying to play ostrich, but I was not yet a fledgling writer in the '20s. Everything began in the '30s, and I think it makes it sound as if it was in another period. My first book was in the '30s. So if you don't mind I am changing that, as it corresponds to the idea of the Diary of everything beginning in the '30s. The same with the fact that I agreed with Hiram that we had to say the Diary was from such-and-such a date to such-and-such a date so people would not expect to get the whole thing, but I feel that Harcourt exaggerated the emphasis by putting the years in such bold type on the back, and as one friendly bookseller observed, it will scare away the young who pick it up. Enough will be said about the dates.

I like the preface very much, as I read and reread it. It should orient the critics.

I am appearing on Channel 28 about the Miller letters.

I am glad you put the Miller letters in the bibliography with my books.

Affectionately,
Anaïs

Letter from Annette Baxter to Anaïs Nin:
Scarsdale, N.Y., December 1, 1965

Dear Anaïs:
   Thank you so much for your letter written in flight. We are happy to know that you will be resting quietly, away from the inescapable distractions of New York.
   You say there is still time to change a word or two. After going through the entire manuscript, I recently reread the material on June. Knowing her in this later phase is not very different from knowing her as a young woman. It astonishes me to discover how little the passage of time affects our essential natures. At any rate, I am convinced that tampering with your manuscript would be a tragic error. There are just a few phrases, however, that might conceivably antagonize her, although again my judgment of this is sheer guesswork. June seems to resent having her imaginative narratives crudely labeled as lies. So while the tone of everything you write makes clear to the sensitive reader that the "truth" or "falsity" of her stories is the least relevant question, I think you might soften or eliminate the following passages for the sake of avoiding June's possible misinterpretation.
   1. page 20 "June could never tell the truth."
   2. page 45 "It was mostly lies."
   3. page 52 "But I am also aware that June is lying to me."
   Please don't be concerned if you feel you cannot, with integrity, change any or all of these passages. It is so difficult to predict what would strike her wrongly, and it may be futile to try at all. Remember that we have told her that in our view you have written a loving portrait of her. And as I reread your words, I marvel at the way in which you have been true to the many contradictory facets not only of her personality but of the interactions between the three of you. I would have despaired at trying to walk along that maze of mirrors. You have done it, and what is more, emerged in triumph.
   June was with us for Thanksgiving and seemed in the best of spirits. Her single reference to you was a good-humored one. It is almost as if, of the diary, she would be guilty of a lapse of judgment, not so much a lapse of loyalty, were she to take a position different from ours. It's a little like being outside the circle of enlightenment.
   Love from us both,
   Annette

Letter from Anaïs Nin to Gunther Stuhlmann:
Los Angeles, December 7, 1965

Dear Gunther:
   Henry had a cold, so until yesterday I was not able to talk over with him the harsh statements he might have made on June that might antagonize her and which he asked me to watch for. Annette asked me to watch out for appellation of "lies,"

and as you may notice, I tried at the beginning and then gave up because all of us referred to each other's lies, so it was a shared affliction.

However, Henry wanted this taken out:

Page 28:"Extreme vulgarity and lack of pride" (June).

Page 90: I describe battles with June, I may have cut it out, but Henry said it was all right. Genius for botching, tangling, aborting in a blind, instinctive way. OK.

Page 93: Line about June's body seeming heavy and big could be taken out.

Page 109: Ugliness and brutality. If Henry says it directly, it should be cut, but Henry said over the phone I could leave it if it was stated indirectly. I can't remember if statement came from me. It may be fine.

Don't feel badly about the cuts. It is something we had to experience, which will serve in the next volume. Either people have to be complete, or not at all, for the Diary is impressionistic enough and the various appearances have to make a whole portrait. I may have to work on this for the French edition where Bradley and Vilmorin are better known.

Anaïs

Letter from Henry Miller to Anaïs Nin:
Pacific Palisades, December 17, 1965

Dear Anaïs:

Sorry to hear you're not feeling well. Hope it's not serious. I'll probably talk to you on the phone before you get this.

So Buchet didn't take the letters or the diary. Just as well. He's not very successful as a rule. (Wasn't Denoël to bring these out?) There's Gallimard, of course, and Julliard and Plon, and Albin Michel and others. Can't Gunther advise which are best to try first? I'm trying to think of someone who knows us both—our work—and who can advise wisely. By the way, didn't the American publisher of the *Letters* suggest a French publisher?

And what about Rowohlt (Germany), Hans Reitzel (Denmark) and one of my three Italian publishers—Einaudi (Turin), Feltrinelle, Longanesi (latter two in Milan)?

Is Gunther sending out your texts, or the American publisher (for the *Letters*)? You shouldn't have to do all this yourself!

More later.

Henry

Postcard from Anaïs Nin to Alan Swallow:
Los Angeles, December 1965

Every day I can do a little more work. Corrected proofs of the Diary, which Gunther is doing too, so that's one job spared you. How are you feeling?

I am leaving for New York on Saturday. I am almost well, except that the operation I went through did not solve the problem, and I will have to go through it again. They ran into complications, so they did not remove the cyst—they needed the presence of a second surgeon as well as a psychologist—so I was naturally depressed that nothing was accomplished and two months have been wasted—plus the money.

Will write you again when I see Hiram. Gunther is on the alert for every detail—for what will be written in the jacket, etc. They make mistakes—like praising the Diary and disparaging the novels, which would have harmed the novels. Every detail. But they will use a big chart I designed of all the characters in the Diary as an announcement. It will intrigue and reveal scope.

W. Colston Leigh lecture bureau is taking me on—if I have the energy to do all that!

Keep well.
Affectionately,
Anaïs

New York, January 1966
1965 sales figures:
Peter Owen $1,128.59
Swallow $1,404.85
Kawade Shobo $144.50
Spearman $40.32
Peter Owen $458.00
Harcourt $800.00
Kawade Shobo $246.00
Total $4,222.26
Expenses $3,500.00
Net $722.26

Letter from Tomohisa Kawade (publisher) to Anaïs Nin:
Tokyo, January 12, 1966

Dear Miss Nin:

We are very glad to hear that you have wished to come to Japan for a long time. Please come if you possibly can, and we will welcome you. Your book will be published this April. We wish we could find the way that might reduce your fare. Please tell us what we can do for you. We intend to bear the expense of your stay in Japan. Please let us know the date and time of your arrival.

With best wishes for you, yours sincerely,
Tomohisa Kawade

Los Angeles, February 1966
I am up to page 300 editing volume 2.

On January 27th I went to the hospital for surgery. The usual nightmare—fear of death, fear of anesthesia. Saying goodbye to the world from the window of Doctor's Hospital, early dawn, before the familiar cart comes, the familiar injection causing drowsiness. Pain. Stays in the hospital should be erased, forgotten. The only event I remember with pleasure was the devotion of my Scotch nurse who was about 70. Because her husband died, the doctor advised her to return to work. When I saw her devotion I felt I had won the devotion of Hugo's mother, a fantasy, the opposite of reality.

Before that I had written a review of D. H. Lawrence's plays, which had been rewritten by *The New York Times*. I refused to let them publish the rewritten review. The original was "too feminine," they said.

(These are notes, for my energy has not returned yet. As soon as I was well enough, I returned to Los Angeles.)

It was during my stay at the hospital that I received an invitation from my Japanese publisher to visit Japan. This became my talisman. I wanted to live and go to Japan with Rupert.

Japan was woven into the life of Frank Lloyd Wright. Lloyd Wright had worked at the construction of the Imperial Hotel when he was 18. Frank Lloyd Wright collected Japanese prints. Lloyd had a beautiful Japanese screen in the living room.

And my childhood was influenced by a travel book on Japan. The illustrations had remained in my memory. Also, naturally, Pierre Loti and *Madame Butterfly*.

This became the vision into the future by which I heal myself of the weight of the present.

Los Angeles, February 1966
Slow recovery from surgery. Work on volume 2.

Letter from Anaïs Nin to Alan Swallow:
Los Angeles, February 13, 1966

Dear Alan:

We are a pair! I was rushed to the hospital January 27 and operated on again, but this time successfully. When I was nine, a ruptured appendix caused so many adhesions that on November 4 they could not remove the fibrous tumor. This time a stomach surgeon cleared things up and I'm mending rapidly because of a better morale, knowing it's over. Before, in November, I felt this hanging over my head. So let us both keep well this year!

Spent most of my convalescence proofing the Diary.

And *Publishers Weekly* has already written about the Diary.

My friends were wonderful, spoiled me, and even those I had quarreled with wrote to me, Edmund Wilson and Maxwell Geismar! Hiram Haydn is kind and active. But I will give all the thanks to Alan Swallow due him, on television and radio. Will write more when my energy returns. Love to you and your wife,

Anaïs

Letter from Anaïs Nin to Hugh Guiler:
Los Angeles, March 1, 1966

Darling:

I didn't write you yesterday because I was hard at work.

I stopped the sleeping pills. I am feeling much better than I did at the same time after the last operation.

365

I am also working on the Diary. Made all the corrections suggested by Hiram Haydn. It will lighten your burden.

I agree with Mrs. Lindley that showing your film in a chaotic setting of the Gotham Book Mart would not be good. That is not where publicity is needed, but in small, out-of-the-way places.

All my love,

A

Los Angeles, March 1966

Activities prior to publication of the Diary. Susan Stanton made a woodcut out of the upper half of my face, mostly eyes, which was accepted for the cover. She visited me.

I had lunch with the publicist, Hilda Lindley. We disagree on the way she spends my budget for publicity (a certain percentage of royalties). She advertises in magazines that never supported my work—the *New Yorker, Partisan Review, The New Republic*. She will not advertise in the inexpensive *Village Voice*, which has supported me. She says: "I am trying to remove you from the underground into a more general readership."

"But I *am* part of the underground, and I want to remain with them. They are the ones who supported me. The others tried to destroy my work. *Life, Time, Saturday Review* ignored me."

She cannot see my point of view. Even if my readers are now more general, I belong to the underground.

I saw Bogner several times. Daisy. Went to Gunther's engagement party. He is marrying Barbara Ward, a beautiful and charming young woman.

Letter from Anaïs Nin to Hugh Guiler:
Los Angeles, March 22, 1966

Darling:

The talk to the Beats who started their own college in a nightclub went wonderfully. I devoted most of it to *Miss MacIntosh, My Darling* and Marguerite to make my point about prose and poetry, etc., and not to repeat myself. It was taped and Marguerite will be able to hear it. Walls were bright red, stage set for jazz, nightclub lights, not rowdy.

They were so pleased they wanted me to teach there.

I am beginning to understand the need to save ahead, for I like the idea of my doing my own savings account.

Oliver Evans' book on Carson is a success in England, which is good for us.

Now I await copies of the Diary to fulfill my commitments here.

All my love and hope you feel better. Don't rush into activity too fast.

A

Letter from Gunther Stuhlmann to Anaïs Nin:
New York, March 23, 1966

Dear Anaïs:

Here are two copies of the signed contract with Rowohlt for the Miller letters. Would you please sign both copies and return them to start the tax exemption proceedings with Germany?

Also, I just had word that Mondadori wants to buy the diary for Italy and take an option on the second volume, so we have started negotiations for a contract.

Fischer Verlag in Germany just said no on the diary, but I have a long line of people waiting.

Hope all is summery with you.

As ever,
Gunther

Letter from Hilda Lindley to Anaïs Nin:
New York, March 23, 1966

Dear Miss Nin:

I'm back from my holiday and looking forward very much to working with you on the diary, which is due in from the printer tomorrow. There's been a great deal of advance interest created in the book and I have been deluged with requests for advance copies from reviewers as well as people in publishing. So it looks as though you will have an exciting time ahead.

I wondered if you could tell me now when you will be in New York? As you know, we have scheduled the party for April 13 at the Gotham Book Mart, but I would also like to begin working on radio, television and newspaper interviews on or about the publication date of April 20, and it would help us plan these things if we knew what your schedule would be like in New York.

I hope that you are feeling well and looking forward to adding another book to your string. Warm regards from all of us here.

Cordially,
Hilda Lindley

Press release:
THE DIARY OF ANAÏS NIN—1931-1934; Harcourt Brace.
News Note
ANAÏS NIN, Manhattan Easter, one of the foremost novelists of our times, will have her Diaries published in April by Harcourt Brace. These Diaries, which Anaïs Nin has kept since childhood, have been called by those who had previews of them, notably Henry Miller, a work of writing stature on a par with Proust and Joyce. The literary community is awaiting them with impatience as one of the outstanding literary and biographical documents of the times. The first Diaries cover Miss Nin's life in Paris during the early 1930s. Included are full-length portraits of such notables as Henry Miller, the extraordinary Surrealist writer Antonin Artaud, and the great psychiatrist Otto Rank.

The intensity, clarity and vision of these Diaries will be appreciated by readers. They contain 16 illustrations, and the price of the first series will be $6.95.

Those familiar with Miss Nin's previous work (now translated into eight languages and world renowned), will find here the struggling artist and profound, creative woman.

Letter from Hilda Lindley to Anaïs Nin:
New York, April 8, 1966

Dear Miss Nin:

It will be good to see you on Monday. I would be grateful if you could come to the office, not only to talk over plans for promotion of the diary, but also to sign some copies of your book for a Houston bookseller who has asked us, as a great favor, if we would get him 75 autographed copies. Could you plan to have lunch with us too? I hope so.

I will be glad to send a copy of *The Diary of Anaïs Nin* to James Spicer, but I need his address.

I agree with you that the *Los Angeles Times* is an important paper and we have scheduled an ad for your book there.

We will certainly explore the possibilities of a Los Angeles autographing party for you. When do you plan to return to California?

The responses to the party invitations are pouring in and it should be a very festive occasion. I'm looking forward very much to seeing you next week.

Cordially,
Hilda Lindley

Telegram from Kathleen and Gilbert Chase to Anaïs Nin:
April 13, 1966

Received your great book. Thank you. Bravo. Bravo. Best wishes for a splendid party. Feel miserable not being there.

Love,
Kathleen and Gilbert

Letter from Alan Swallow to Anaïs Nin:
Denver, April 1966

Dear Anaïs:

It was such a pleasure to have your card of joy, and also the very nice letter that Hiram sent so enthusiastically. It seems to be launched well. I am sick that I didn't make it back for the event!

I'll be anxious to see *The New York Times* review. I'll appreciate the copy you send. I am not sure my clipping service will be alerted to catch the Swallow Press name in association with Harcourt, but probably will. They are quite diligent and observant.

Love,
Alan

Postcard from Henry Miller to Anaïs Nin:
Pacific Palisades, April 18, 1966

Dear Anaïs:

Good review you sent me. Let's hope *Time* will do as well by you. How about the *Saturday Review of Literature*? Don't let the interviewers wear you out. Cheers!

Henry

Letter from Annette Baxter to Anaïs Nin:
Scarsdale, N.Y., April 19, 1966

Dear Anaïs,

The *Diary* came, with your generous inscription. You must know how it will be cherished!

And again, many thanks for speaking to us at Barnard—the students were deeply moved by the viewpoint of your talk. It is rare that anyone communicates with them—and never with much grace—about the profoundly personal realms; I can still sense their gratitude for this, after the event.

The *Diary* couldn't have had a happier sendoff than the Gotham party. Thanks for including us, and for coming to dinner the next night when you both must surely have been exhausted, although miraculously showing no signs of it.

Love,
Annette

P. S. We were thrilled to hear the first edition is sold out already—I predict the statistics will become more, not less, spectacular as the weeks go by.

Postcard from Henry Miller to Anaïs Nin:
Pacific Palisades, April 23, 1966

Dear Anaïs:

Martindale's—Beverly Hills—sold out the *Diary* the first day—100 copies! Ordered 100 more. Now I can see you will soon be a best seller. Cheers!

Henry

New York, May 1966

A month of good reviews, love letters, appearances on television. Has the sniping really stopped?

Diary is selling well. Hiram Haydn thought its sale would be limited. He only printed 3,000. They were sold in a week.

A month which made up for every disappointment, every poison pen, for all the past obstacles. The sound of opening doors is deafening! Suddenly love, praise, flowers, invitations to lecture.

BIOGRAPHICAL NOTES

Daisy Aldan (1918-2001) was a poet, translator, teacher and editor of *Folder Magazine of Literature and Art* in New York City. She interviewed Anaïs Nin in 1959 and became her friend and supporter. Her translations of the French Symbolist poet Stéphane Mallarmé won respect amongst her fellow translators.

Louis and Bebe Barron (1920-1989 and 1925-2008 respectively) are best known for their innovations in electronic music. Early on, in order to make a living, they began "Sound Portraits," recordings of authors reading their work, among them Anaïs Nin, whom they met in 1949. Their music was used in soundtracks for movies, including Ian Hugo's *Bells of Atlantis* (1952) and *Jazz of Lights* (1954), and the Hollywood film *Forbidden Planet* (1956).

Inge Bogner (1910-1987) was a New York psychiatrist whom Hugh Guiler began seeing in the 1940s, and Nin in the early 1950s. Both continued analysis with her for the rest of their lives.

Caresse Crosby (*née* Mary Phelps Jacob, 1891-1970), born to a prominent American family, was a close friend and confidante of Anaïs Nin beginning in 1940. With her husband Harry Crosby, she founded the Black Sun Press to publish their own poetry and the writings of several up-and-coming writers, including D. H. Lawrence, Eugene Jolas and James Joyce.

Rosa Culmell (1871-1954), a classically trained singer born in Cuba and of Danish and French descent, married pianist/composer Joaquín Nin in 1902 and gave birth to three children: Anaïs (1903), Thorvald (1905), and Joaquín (1908). After her husband abandoned the family in France in 1913, Rosa and her children went to Barcelona, and the following year they came to New York where she took in boarders and did mail-orders for her wealthy Cuban relatives in order to make a living. She lived with Anaïs, her husband Hugh Guiler, and her brother Joaquín in France, and in 1938 she returned to America and lived with Joaquín Jr. in Williamsburg, Massachusetts, and then in Oakland, California.

Renate Druks (1921-2007), one of Anaïs Nin's closest friends, was born in Vienna and studied at the Vienna Art Academy for Women. She came to New York, moved to Mexico and later to Malibu, where she had a house and studio overlooking the ocean. She lived there with her son Peter (from a previous marriage) and was a prolific painter, all the while supporting herself with day jobs. Her home became a salon of sorts, attracting the likes of Colleen Dewhurst, John Houseman, and Christopher Isherwood.

Marguerite Duras (1914-1996), born to French parents in what is now Vietnam, was a novelist and screenwriter who was perhaps most known for her film script of *Hiroshima mon amour* (1959), for which she earned an Oscar nomination.

Lawrence Durrell (1912-1990), an English writer born in India, was one of the "three musketeers," a literary collaboration with Henry Miller and Anaïs Nin that produced three books, all published in Paris by the Obelisk Press: *The Black Book* (Durrell, 1937); *Max and the White Phagocytes* (Miller, 1938); and *The Winter of Artifice* (Nin, 1939). Durrell went on to achieve literary fame when the first installment of *The Alexandria Quartet* was published in 1957.

Oliver Evans (1915-1981) was the first American scholar to write critically about the work of Anaïs Nin, both in article and book form.

Jean Fanchette (1932-1992), born in Mauritius, was a poet, doctor, and friend of Lawrence Durrell who founded and edited the bilingual literary periodical *Two Cities*.

Millicent Fredericks, Anaïs Nin's faithful maid beginning in 1940, was born in Antigua to African and Portuguese parents. When she came to America she became a housekeeper after she failed to get a job teaching. She played a key role in keeping Nin's two husbands—Hugh Guiler and Rupert Pole—unaware of each other.

Maxwell Geismar (1909-1979) was an American critic, author, and editor who wrote the introduction to Eldridge Cleaver's *Soul on Ice*. He and his wife Anne befriended Anaïs Nin and her husband Hugh Guiler in 1951, and he was one of Nin's few ardent literary supporters during the 1950s.

Hugh (Hugo) Guiler (1898-1985) married Anaïs Nin in 1923. His prominent Protestant family initially disowned him for marrying a Catholic "foreign" woman. Guiler's difficult relationship with his father, a successful businessman, haunted him throughout his life as a banker who never reached his potential. In the 1940s, Guiler began to express himself artistically by engraving copper plates (he used a pseudonym—Ian Hugo—to keep his straight-laced colleagues from discovering that he was dabbling in the arts) for prints that were often used in Nin's books produced by her Gemor Press. In the 1950s, again as Ian Hugo, he began making experimental and critically praised films, most notably *Bells of Atlantis* (1952), which included Nin reading from *House of Incest* and a soundtrack by electronic music pioneers Louis and Bebe Barron.

James Leo Herlihy (1927-1993), born in Detroit to a working class family, was a novelist, playwright, and actor, best known for his novels *All Fall Down* (1960) and *Midnight Cowboy* (1965), the latter of which was adapted into an Oscar-winning movie of the same title in 1969. Herlihy met Anaïs Nin in 1947 when she visited Black Mountain College, and they formed a close friendship, each supporting the other's work.

Helba Huara (1900-1986) was a Peruvian dancer whose second husband was Gonzalo More. At the height of her career she became too ill to continue dancing. She was entirely dependent on More by the time he became Anaïs Nin's lover in 1936, and her jealous rages helped end the affair ten years later.

Max Jacobson (1900-1979) was a German-born physician who was aided in fleeing Europe at the beginning of World War II by Hugh Guiler and Anaïs Nin. As a way of thanking them, Jacobson treated Nin gratuitously, and they had a brief sexual affair in the early 1940s. Nin recorded in her diary that she often turned to Jacobsen's "vitamin shots" when her energy was low. Jacobsen gained a reputation as "Dr. Feelgood" or "Miracle Max" and was visited by celebrities, athletes, and politicians, including John F. Kennedy.

Paul Mathieson was a painter and a lover of Renate Druks, whom he introduced to Anaïs Nin.

Henry Miller (1891-1980) was the author of *Tropic of Cancer* (1934), *Black Spring* (1936) and *Tropic of Capricorn* (1939), all written in Paris during his love affair with Anaïs Nin, which lasted for a decade beginning in 1932. After their breakup in 1942-43, a long estrangement ensued.

June Miller (1902-1977) was the second wife of Henry Miller and a muse for Miller and his lover Anaïs Nin, inspiring his character "Mona" and Nin's "Sabina" in their respective fiction.

Gonzalo More (1897-1959) was born in Punto, Peru, of Incan, Scottish, and Spanish blood. He met Anaïs Nin in Paris in 1936 and they carried on a torrid, emotional love affair for a decade. During the 1940s, Nin and More worked together in New York to print her books as well as those of others on an old handpress and called their enterprise "Gemor Press," after his name. More's jealous wife and his irresponsible behavior helped end the affair with Nin in 1946.

Joaquín Nin (1879-1949), a pianist and composer, born in Cuba and of Spanish descent, married Rosa Culmell in Cuba in 1902 and fathered three children: Anaïs (1903), Thorvald (1905), and Joaquín (1908). He fell in love with one of his teenage students (whom he later married) and left the family in 1913. After a twenty-year estrangement, he and his then thirty-year-old daughter embarked on an incestuous affair that lasted for several months. After his second wife divorced him and left him destitute, Joaquín left Paris for Cuba at his cousins' invitation in 1939. He died there ten years later.

Joaquín Nin-Culmell (1908-2004) was the younger of Anaïs Nin's two brothers. Born in Berlin, Nin-Culmell studied piano at the Schola Cantorum and the Paris Conservatory with prominent instructors, most notably Manuel de Falla. He gave his first recital in New York in 1936 and later became the head of the music departments at Williams College in Williamsburg, Massachusetts and later at the University of California at Berkeley. During the 1950s he took sabbaticals to Spain and composed some of his most important works there, including *Tonadas*.

Thorvald Nin (1905-1991) was the elder of Anaïs Nin's two brothers. Unlike his parents and siblings, all of whom were artists, his passion was for the sciences and business. After being forced to eschew higher education and to financially help his brother's musical studies, in the 1920s he bitterly estranged himself from the family to pursue a business career in Latin America. In 1936 he had a brief incestuous relationship with Anaïs.

Alfred Perlès (1897-1990), born in Vienna, was Henry Miller's friend and companion during his Paris years in the 1930s. Perlès was the author of *Sentiments limitrophes* (1936), in which he based a character on Anaïs Nin.

Reginald Pole (d. 1971), born in England and a student at Cambridge, was heralded as a Shakespearian actor, director, writer, and playwright. He married Helen Taggart and was the father of Rupert Pole. His declining health and bouts of hypochondria later in life turned him into an unwanted presence among his family members and friends.

Rupert Pole (1919-2006), Anaïs Nin's "west coast husband," was born in Los Angeles to Reginald Pole and Helen Taggart. His mother divorced Reginald and married architect Lloyd Wright when Rupert was a boy. In the early 1940s, Rupert began a short and unsuccessful acting career, appearing in a few plays and on the radio. He was drafted into the army in 1943, refused to bear arms, got very ill in boot camp, and was medically discharged. He was briefly married to Janie Lloyd Jones, a cousin of his stepfather. Pole met Anaïs Nin at a party in February 1947 and became her lover. He invited her to drive from New York to California with him, and she accepted. Nin bigamously married Pole in 1955.

Tracey Roberts (*née* Blanche Goldstone, 1914-2002) was an American stage, television, and movie actress who later became a well-respected acting coach.

Eduardo Sánchez (1904-1990) was Anaïs Nin's cousin for whom she had a romantic attraction as a teenager, and with whom she had a brief sexual relationship in Paris as an adult. He was an early and ardent supporter and confidant of Nin's during the 1930s.

Nobuko Uenishi (b. 1940), a Japanese-born writer and student of the Noh theater, inspired one of the more popular characters in Anaïs Nin's last work of fiction, *Collages* (1964).

Jean (Yanko) Varda (1893-1971) was a Greek/French collage artist, painter, and friend of Henry Miller and Anaïs Nin.

Gore Vidal (1925-2012), novelist, essayist and playwright, was twenty years old when he met Anaïs Nin. Although homosexual, he developed a close relationship with Nin and proposed that they get married and have outside lovers, a notion Nin considered but ultimately rejected. He was instrumental in getting some of Nin's fiction published by E. P. Dutton. Vidal dedicated his second novel, *A Yellow Wood*, to Nin. After Nin became Rupert Pole's lover, she and Vidal drifted apart.

Helen Taggart Wright (1892-1977) was married to actor Reginald Pole when their son, Rupert, was born. She divorced Pole in 1923 and married architect Lloyd

Wright a short time later. With Wright, she bore a son, Eric, who became an architect as well.

Lloyd Wright (1890-1978) was an architect and the son of Frank Lloyd Wright. After divorcing his first wife, he married Helen Taggart, thereby becoming Rupert Pole's stepfather. Anaïs Nin was an admirer of his work, highlighting it in her heavily edited *Diary of Anaïs Nin* and later in the documentary *Anaïs Nin Observed*.

INDEX

400 Blows (film) 224
8½ (film) 302
Albicocco, Jean Gabriel 259, 262, 265, 266, 267, 271, 280, 291, 295
   letter from (excerpt) 274
Albin Michel (publisher) 363
Aldan, Daisy 241, 246, 256, 257, 270, 282, 291, 300-301, 302, 312, 317, 351, 354, 366
   letters to 213, 222, 289, 343-44
   letters from 222, 263, 288-89, 296, 309-10, 339-40, 353-54
Aldington, Richard 300
Aleksander, Irina 7
The Alexandria Quartet (Durrell) 346
Algren, Nelson 132
All Fall Down (Herlihy) 221, 237, 271
Allendy, René 330, 333, 336, 337, 342, 344, 353, 354
Alpert, Richard 279, 280
Anaïs Nin Press viii, x, 204, 212, 214, 223, 238, 247
Anger, Kenneth 115, 136, 189, 190, 191
Annie, Aunt 162
Archibald, Graciella Sánchez 86, 115, 117, 192, 228, 229, 244, 258, 332
Archibald, Roy 115
Armstrong, Neville 12-13, 17, 18, 25, 203, 204
   letter to 19
   letter from 31
Art (periodical) 306
Art and Artist (Rank) 140
Artaud, Antonin 90, 278-79, 301, 302, 337, 342, 357, 367
Astor, Mrs. 117

Atlantic Press (publisher) 249
Auerbach, Norbert 262, 265
Avon (publisher) 86, 87, 110, 158, 211, 247-48

Balakian, Nona 257, 259, 289, 310, 321, 323, 324, 325
The Balcony (Genet) 242
Baldwin, James 101
Baldwin, Lanny 76
Ballet Mécanique (film) 57
Balthazar (Durrell) 197
Bancroft, Anne 218
Bankhead, Tallulah 196
Barker, Bill 147, 156
Barnes, Djuna 245, 280, 291
Barron, Bebe 52, 54, 72, 117, 129, 134, 159, 214, 219, 235, 282, 290, 301, 320
Barron, Louis 52, 54, 72, 117, 129, 134, 159, 219, 235, 282, 290
Bates, Sydney 72
Batista, Fulgencio 224
Baudelaire, Charles 282
Baxter, Anne 55, 95, 106
Baxter, Annette K. 355, 362
   letter to 356
   letter from 369
Baxter, James E. 355
   letter to Miller 359
Bay, André 242, 243, 270, 273, 291, 295, 306, 307, 317, 319, 321, 332, 334, 335, 342, 343, 344-46, 350, 352, 354
Beach, Sylvia 229
Beauvoir, Simone de 99, 321, 322, 323
Bells of Atlantis (film) 57, 211
Belmont, Georges 346
Bergman, Ingmar 230, 232

375

Bick, Jerry 291, 307, 308, 309, 310, 311, 312, 313, 315, 317, 322, 326
Biedermann et les Incendiaires (Frisch) 242
The Black Book (Durrell) 148, 158, 160, 200
Black Spring (Miller) 148
Blanch, Leslie 150, 152, 253
Blondell, Joan 196
Bloom, Claire 117, 152
Bloom, Roger 225, 276
   letters to 226, 227, 245, 246-47, 253, 254
Blue Denim (film) 189, 212
Bogart, Humphrey 74
Bogner, Inge 1, 2, 3, 6, 7-8, 9, 11, 13-14, 15, 30, 33, 40, 41, 44-45, 49, 52-54, 59, 61, 63, 64, 66, 67, 71, 74, 78, 79, 81, 83-84, 93, 94-95, 96, 99, 100, 101, 102, 105, 107, 110-11, 113, 114, 118, 119, 120, 124-25, 127, 128, 131, 139, 140, 141, 142, 144, 145, 146, 150, 157, 160, 161-62, 189, 194, 199, 209, 210, 211, 216-18, 236, 237, 252, 270, 272, 274, 277, 278, 286, 293, 295, 300, 302, 343, 366
Bonjour Tristesse (Sagan) 28, 38, 39
Borchardt, Georges 16, 17, 25, 159, 291
   letter from 19-20
Bouboule (*see* Piccolo)
Bowles, Jane 72, 100
Bowles, Paul 5, 69, 72, 100, 138
Boyle, Kay 300
Bradbury, Ray 287
Brando, Marlon 137, 237
Breton, André 282
Brier, Samson de 115
British Book Centre (publisher) vii, 3, 4, 10, 83, 219, 310
Brodin, Pierre 291, 292, 354

The Brothers Karamazov (film) 152
Brown, James (agent) 9, 10, 19, 20, 25, 30
   letters from 16, 24-25, 85
Brown, Teddy 45
Brynner, Yul 97
Buchet (publisher) 363
Burford, William 148
Burroughs, William S. 308

Cairns, Huntington 5
Call of the Wild (film) 207
Camino Real (Williams) 78
Campion children 37, 49, 83, 108
Campion, Pam 35, 39, 45, 59
Campion, Paul 39, 45
Capote, Truman 284-85
Cárdenas, Antolina 86, 258
Cárdenas, Charlie 244, 340, 343
Caro, Anita 265
Castle, Katarina 96
Castro, Fidel 217, 224, 244, 251, 258, 285
Cat on a Hot Tin Roof (Williams) 44
Carteret, Jean 193, 194
Chaplin, Charles 330
Charm Magazine 90
Chase, Deirdre 12
Chase, Gilbert 12
   letter to 275
   letter from 368
Chase, John 269, 274, 329
Chase, Kathleen
   letter from 368
Chase, Paul 11, 12
Children of the Albatross (Nin) 113, 138, 143, 196, 198, 199, 208, 317
Chochor, René de 25, 141, 142, 162, 193, 300, 310
Cities of the Interior (Nin) viii, 208, 213, 221, 226, 248, 249-50, 253

376

Clairmonte, Glenn 247, 248
Clarence, Jean 313
Cleopatra (film) 324
Clift, Brooks 1, 220, 300
Clift, Montgomery 1, 173, 220
Colette 50
Collages (Nin) 297, 303, 306, 308, 309, 310, 312, 316, 321, 327, 332, 348, 349, 350, 354
Confidential (periodical) 122, 123, 137
Corey, Irving 142
Crazy October (Herlihy) 105, 117, 118, 196
Crevel, René 300
Crosby, Caresse 3, 5, 6, 8, 21, 112, 121, 147, 286, 291, 296, 300, 303
Crosby, Harry 5, 300
Cue (periodical) 6, 10, 235
Culmell, Rosa (mother) x, 2, 3, 5, 8, 30, 35, 39-41, 44, 61-62, 71, 76, 78-79, 86, 102, 106-108, 114, 127, 129, 144, 145, 154, 156, 202, 237, 247, 278, 310, 340
   death of x, 2, 35, 39-40, 61, 71, 79, 237, 242, 310
Current Biography 325

D. H. Lawrence: An Unprofessional Study (Nin) 291, 295, 297, 304, 309, 316
Dalí, Salvador 6
Day of the Locust (West) 169
De Gaulle, Charles 242, 282
Debussy, Claude 70, 243
Denoël (publisher) 363
Deren, Maya 214, 300, 301-302
Diamant, Ruth Witt 43, 49, 89, 207
Diana (friend of Barker) 147
The Diary of Anne Frank (film) 207
Dietrich, Marlene 108
Dinesen, Henry 290

Dinesen, Virginia 289, 290
Djuna (Nin character) 91, 262, 267, 317, 319
Don Quixote (de Cervantes) 152
Dostoevsky, Fyodor 152
Doubleday (publisher) 287, 295, 350
Downes, Olin 101
Druks, Renate 33-34, 36, 37, 49, 50, 53, 55-57, 59, 63, 93-94, 106-107, 109, 136-40, 147, 151, 158, 159, 174, 227, 231, 234, 237, 254, 262, 268, 269, 270, 271, 278, 282, 283, 291-93, 305, 306, 312, 322, 330
   letters from 159, 306
Duane, Dick 4, 8, 11, 20, 28, 43, 57, 78, 87-88, 91, 97, 98, 99, 100-101, 111, 123, 125-26, 127, 128, 130, 139, 141, 154, 162, 189, 196, 212, 218, 221
Duits, Charles 302
Dumas, André 302
Duncan, Erika ix, x
Duncan, Robert x, 302
Duras, Marguerite 291, 295, 306, 307, 308, 311, 312, 313, 315, 317, 321
Durrell, Claude 194
Durrell, Lawrence 148, 158, 163, 196, 197, 199, 202, 203, 205, 244, 245, 283, 344, 346, 347
   letters to 157, 168-69, 200, 201, 205-206, 213
   visit to 193-94
Dutton, E. P. (publisher) 140, 249

Edith (Hugo's sister) 41
Éditions Stock (publisher) 242, 243, 259, 273, 344, 350
Einaudi (publisher) 363
Eluoard, Paul 282
Emperor Jones (O'Neill) 57
Erskine, John 65, 145

Esquire (periodical) 237
Evans, Oliver, ix, 268, 272, 274, 289, 290, 293, 321, 334, 344, 346, 347, 350, 357, 366
  letters from 264-65, 267, 320, 352
  letters to 272-73, 287-88
Eve (periodical) 158, 159, 162, 163

A Face in the Crowd (film) 141
Fanchette, Jean 202, 203, 204, 205, 208, 212, 222, 228, 229, 230, 242, 265, 267, 302
  letter to 223
Feinstein, Harold 132
Feltrinelle (publisher) 363
Ferlinghetti, Lawrence 287, 292
Field, Frances (Brown) 62, 63, 76-77
Fischer Verlag (publisher) 367
Fisher, Vardis viii
Folder (periodical) 213, 222
Forbidden Planet (film) 117
Forêt, Marie La 259, 308
Fortune (periodical) 15
The Four-Chambered Heart (Nin) 20, 85, 86, 198, 317
Fowlie, Wallace 160, 213
Fredericks, Millicent 1, 5, 52, 54, 71, 99, 102, 119, 128, 198, 216, 278, 311, 343
Fromm, Erich 159

Gallimard (publisher) 16, 309, 318, 331, 332, 342-43, 363
Gallimard, Claude 304, 309, 342
Gamez, Tana de 91, 300, 302, 305
Gance, Abel 191
Gardner, Ava 308
Garrigue, Jean viii, x
Gary, Romain 74, 138, 143, 150, 169, 253
Gavronsky, Serge 222

Gedin, Lena I. 85
Geismar, Anne 29
Geismar, Maxwell 13, 20, 29, 95, 132-33, 140, 143, 257, 365
  letter to 46-47
  letter from 27
Genet, Jean 20, 28, 35, 50, 147
Gessner, Jerry 266, 269
Ginsberg, Allen 90, 162, 234
Giraudoux, Jean 39, 163, 234, 261, 302
The Girl with the Golden Eyes (film) 262, 266
Glanville-Hicks, Peggy 41, 69, 72-73, 96, 100, 101, 138, 159, 172, 211, 286
Goodwin, John 5
Gotham Book Mart 201, 255, 256, 259, 268, 289, 366, 367, 369
Goyen, William 44
Graeffe, Edward 40
Grath, Dr. 71
Grove Press (publisher) 142, 161, 226, 245, 254, 338
Grut, Mario 237, 239
Guiler, Hugh (Hugo) vi, vii, x, 1-4, 5, 6-7, 8-9, 11, 12, 13-14, 15, 16, 17, 18, 20, 25, 27, 28-29, 30, 33, 35, 36, 37, 38, 39, 40-41, 44-45, 50, 53-54, 57, 60-62, 64-67, 68, 72-73, 74, 76, 79, 80-83, 85, 86, 90-92, 93-94, 95-97, 98, 99-100, 101, 102-104, 106, 107-108, 109, 110-13, 114, 115, 116, 117, 119-20, 122, 123, 124, 127, 131, 133, 134, 139-40, 141-45, 147, 148, 154, 155, 157, 160, 161, 162, 189, 195, 198, 202, 205, 206, 207, 208, 214, 217, 221, 222, 223, 224, 225, 236, 237, 240, 241, 242, 243, 244, 245, 254, 264, 277, 278-79, 283, 285, 287, 293, 300, 302, 303, 304,

312, 317, 322, 326-27, 329, 331,
332, 340, 341, 342, 350, 354, 355,
365
  letters to 83-84, 89-90, 105-106,
175-76, 194-95, 199, 200-201,
210, 213, 236-37, 246, 252-53,
254, 255, 260-61, 268-70, 272,
273-74, 279, 280-82, 293, 294-95,
296-97, 305, 308-309, 310-11,
311-12, 313, 315, 317-18, 320,
323-24, 325-26, 329-30, 333-34,
335-36, 342-43, 346, 348, 354,
365-66
  letters from 80, 208-10, 210-11,
215, 216-17, 217-18, 260, 290-91,
304, 311, 312, 315-16, 319, 329,
332, 336, 361
  AN's dissatisfaction with 2, 4, 52,
64-67, 68, 128, 129, 278
  banking career of 1, 20, 62, 63,
268, 276, 277, 302, 340
  as filmmaker 26, 125, 162, 169,
189, 207, 239, 273, 291

Hadyn, Hiram viii, ix, 323, 349,
350, 351, 353, 355, 356, 357, 359,
361, 364, 365, 366, 368, 369
  letter from 258
Haggart, Stanley 68-69, 115-16,
129, 159, 218, 221, 285
  letter to 236
Hammerschlag, Dr. 218
Hammid, Sasha 301
Hampton Manor (house) 6
Hans Reitzel (publisher) 363
Harcourt (publisher) viii, ix, xi, 323,
350, 351, 352, 355, 357, 358, 359,
361, 364, 367, 368
Hartford, Huntington 31, 34
Harman, Carter 40, 297
Harrington, Curtis 32, 134, 282, 305
Hawkins, Eric 159

Heaven and Hell (Huxley) 63
Heifetz, Sasha 48
Hemingway, Ernest 14, 46, 123, 149
Henderson, Gil 116, 164-68, 170,
173-74, 221, 224
Henderson, Olympia 170, 171, 173,
174, 221, 224
Herlihy, James Leo 4, 9, 11, 20-21,
28, 32, 39, 42, 43, 44, 52, 61, 67,
68, 76, 78, 80, 91, 97, 98, 99, 100-
101, 102, 110, 111, 112-13, 117,
118, 119, 123, 125-26, 127-28,
129, 130, 139, 140, 141, 143, 147-
48, 149, 150, 162, 174, 189, 190,
207, 218, 221, 237, 300
  letters to 38, 57, 75-76, 85-86, 225
  letters from 38-39, 75, 87-88,
104-105, 152-54, 196, 211-12,
221, 223-24, 224-25, 237-38,
270-71
  diary excerpt of 63-64
Herskovitz, Harry 76
Hilda (friend of Reginald Pole) 109
Hill & Wang (publisher) 297
Hirschman, Jack 278, 282, 301, 309
Hodiak, John 55
Hoffman, Georges 258, 259
Holmes, Burton 147
House of Incest (Nin) 8, 10, 19, 132,
164, 168, 201, 205, 239, 250, 252,
253, 285, 302, 329
Huara, Helba 33, 35, 45, 59, 60, 72,
107, 108, 111-12, 113, 121, 151,
231, 246, 300
Hugo, Ian (*see* Hugh Guiler)
Huston, John 84
Hutchins, Maude 241, 247, 259
Huxley, Aldous 164, 168-69

Idées et Commentaires (J. Nin) 284
Illicit Interlude (film) 230
In Between Worlds (periodical) 246

379

Inauguration of the Pleasure Dome (film) 189, 191
Inge, William 264
Isham, Colonel (Nin character) 291
Isherwood, Christopher 135
Israel, Peter 291, 321, 323, 327, 330, 331, 350

Jack (Cuca Sánchez's husband) 115
Jacobson, Maxwell 6, 23, 27, 28, 63, 70, 97, 101, 117, 124, 131, 139, 157, 235, 300, 302
Jaeger, Martha 77
Janiger, Oscar 164, 171, 174, 176
Jason, Philip K. x
Jazz of Lights (film) 4, 26, 211
Jeanne (Nin character) 280
Johnson, Lyndon 321
Johnstone, Millie 211, 241, 286
Jones, Janie Lloyd 152
Jouve, Pierre Jean 190, 193, 261, 302
Joyce, James 78, 163, 300, 367
Justine (Durrell) 148, 156, 157, 201

Karvelis, Mme. 309
Kawade Shobo (publisher) 364
Kawade, Tomohisa 314, 350
  letter from 364
Keating, Mrs. 6
Kehoe, Karon 90-92, 93, 95-97, 99, 100, 101, 105, 108, 116, 142, 159, 302
Kelly, Grace 62
Kennedy, John F. 253, 274, 294, 295, 296
Kerouac, Jack 163, 190, 234, 284
The King and I (Hammerstein) 97
Kirkland, Alex 70
Kirsch, Robert R. viii, x
Kitt, Eartha 152
Kluver, Billy 218, 230

Kluver, Hill 218, 230, 239, 300
Knox, Ronnie 227, 231, 237, 254, 269, 282, 291, 292, 293, 312, 322, 330
Kon Tiki (raft) 189
Kozlenko, William 199, 201

l'Invitée (de Beauvoir) 107
Ladders to Fire (Nin) 10, 50, 219, 248, 249, 280, 307, 355
Lady Chatterley's Lover (Lawrence) 27, 245
Lam, Wilfredo 159
Lamb, Max 313
Lambert, Gavin 291
Lambert, Hausi 190
Latouche, John 117
Lawrence, D. H. 27, 152, 300, 364
Leach, Bob 77
Leary, Timothy 279, 290
Leigh, W. Colson 364
Lepska, Janina 282, 284, 356
Les Enfants Terribles (film) 192
Les Racines du Ciel (Gary) 137, 169
Letters to Anaïs Nin (Miller) 293-94, 297, 298, 304, 306, 309, 313, 314, 317, 318, 326, 327, 328, 331, 332, 335, 342, 344, 345, 347, 349, 350, 358, 361, 367
Lewis, Janet viii
Library Journal (periodical) 257
Life (periodical) 366
Lillian (Nin character) 2, 91, 242, 262, 282
Lindley, Hilda 359, 366
  letters from 367, 368
Lindsley, Mrs. ix, 6
Lipton, Lawrence 162, 163
  letter from 158-59
Lolita (Nabokov) 199
Longanesi (publisher) 363
Loomer, Peter 158, 159, 330

Lord of the Flies (film) 296, 297
Los Angeles Free Press viii, x
Los Angeles Herald 316
Los Angeles Times viii, x, 347, 350, 354, 368
Loti, Pierre 365
Lowenfels, Walter 304
Lundkvist, Artur
  letter from 226

Macy, Jim 174, 303
Madame Butterfly (Puccini) 365
Maggini, Donald 115
Mangones, Albert 92, 121
Mallarmé, Stéphane 213, 241, 246, 282
The Mandarins (de Beauvoir) 95, 101, 103
Martin, John 211
Mason, James 122, 137
Masterplots 211
Mathieson, Paul 33-34, 36, 37, 45, 49, 50, 53, 55-56, 59, 63, 93, 94, 107, 109, 135, 135-37, 138, 140, 151
McCarthy, Mary 308, 330
McCullers, Carson 134, 149, 267, 273, 287, 293, 318, 366
McKinley, Hazel ix, 59, 69-70
Melodic Inversion (film) 162, 189, 219
Merrill, James 140, 148
Messiah (Vidal) 122
Metzger, Anne 265, 295
  letters to 15-16, 50-51
Metzger, Deena viii, x
Michaux, Henri 164, 243, 245, 271, 292
Miller, Eve 276, 281
  letters from 88, 202-203

Miller, June 35, 91, 107, 147, 281, 283, 292, 303, 304, 322, 336, 337, 338, 349, 355-56, 359, 362
Miller, Henry vii, x, xi, 3, 8, 13, 14, 16, 25, 31, 32, 33, 35, 36, 40, 60, 66, 74, 83, 88-89, 99, 102, 107, 111-12, 113, 114, 128, 148, 161, 162, 163, 189, 202-203, 206, 213, 227, 243, 245, 247, 279, 284, 289, 297, 298, 299, 301, 305, 319, 331, 333-34, 335-36, 342, 348, 349, 352, 354, 356, 358, 362-63, 367
  letters from 17-19, 225-26, 258, 281, 282-83, 288, 297, 298-99, 303-304, 321, 335, 336-39, 345-46, 355, 361, 363, 368-69, 369
  letters to 240, 292, 344, 359
  AN's reunion with 275-77
  blurb for *Collages* 303
Millett, Kate ix, x
Minnesota Review (periodical) 264
Miserable Miracle (Michaux) 271, 292
Miss Lonelyhearts (West) 169
Miss MacIntosh, My Darling (Young) 366
Mitou (cat) 76, 91, 103, 215, 216-17, 253
Moby Dick (film) 83, 84
Molaine, Pierre 79
Mondadori (publisher) 367
Monserrat (ship) 189
Montolive (Durrell) 213
Moore, Elizabeth 205
Moore, Harry T. 291
  letter from 295-96
Moravia, Alberto 292
More, Gonzalo 3, 6, 8, 14, 32, 33, 35, 36, 45, 60, 66, 72, 74, 76, 77, 97, 99, 102, 107, 108, 112, 113, 114, 121, 128, 138, 151, 172, 189, 207, 246, 302

illness of 161
death of 231, 300
Moreau, Jeanne 308
Moricand, Conrad 32, 33, 88
Morrison, Jane 158
Morrow (Putnam employee) 346, 347
Morrow, Felix 10
Moulin de Soleil (house) 6
Murphy, Dudley 57
Murphy, Jeannie 254
Murrow, Edward R. 109, 171
My Friend Henry Miller (Perlès) vii, 13, 16, 17-18, 18-19, 25, 31, 83, 275, 333

The Nation (periodical) 74
Neiman, Gilbert 246
Ness, Kenneth 12
Neuman, Dr. 129
Neurath, Otto 121
Neville Spearman (publisher) 12, 212, 227, 364
New Directions (publisher) 203, 300
New Door to Perception (Huxley) 168
The New Republic (periodical) 366
New York Herald-Tribune 348
New Writing (periodical) 63
The New York Times 43, 211, 257, 259, 268, 321, 325, 339, 347, 350, 365, 368
The New York Times Book Review viii, x, 257
The New Yorker 309, 310, 365
Newman, Paul 135, 152
Nexus (Miller) 282
Nichols, Nick 22, 43, 49, 56-57
Nichols, Luthor
letter from 295
Nietzsche, Friedrich 353
Nightwood (Barnes) 245

Nils, Hugo 230
letter to 239
Nin, Anaïs
on America 2, 4, 5-6, 13, 19, 20, 26, 28, 29, 30, 31, 33, 34, 38, 40, 44, 45-46, 50-51, 68, 69, 72, 74, 98, 118, 122, 125, 132-33, 140, 155, 163, 164, 170, 171, 175, 189, 191, 193, 195, 198, 200, 201, 205, 206, 208, 228, 234, 239, 242, 245, 246, 253, 254, 261, 270, 282, 286, 295, 302, 311, 323, 329
on the diary 3, 16, 19, 20-21, 28, 29, 30, 31, 46, 57, 59, 66, 76, 77, 79-80, 111, 112, 114, 119, 121-22, 125, 133, 144, 145, 161, 163, 168, 174, 175, 225, 242, 268, 277, 278-79, 284, 289, 293, 302, 305, 313, 314, 315, 317, 320, 323, 325, 327, 328, 330, 333-34, 335, 343, 344, 346, 347, 348, 349, 351, 354, 357, 358, 359, 361, 362, 363, 364, 365, publication of 366-69
on the double life 2, 61, 79, 80-82, 85, 92, 94, 96, 108, 128, 139, 157, 168, 223, 276
on Los Angeles 116, 155, 169, 278
on New York 48, 82, 107, 108, 109, 110, 115, 117, 120-21, 151-52, 155, 198, 206, 208, 237, 239
on Paris 65, 189, 191-92, 194, 203, 217, 227-28, 233, 234, 242, 244-45, 265, 307, 308
on publishing problems 10, 295, 305-306, 310, 316, 323, 330, 332, 335, 344-45
on fiction writing 2, 37-38, 77, 79, 89, 133, 207, 237, 241, 249, 282, 283, 291
illness of 27, 30, 36, 57, 71, 204, 205, 302-303, 359, 363-64, 365

382

dreams of 1-2, 8-9, 29-30, 44, 45, 52, 73, 76, 79, 81, 83, 86, 87, 92, 98, 103-104, 106, 108, 112, 117, 118, 127, 131, 133, 139, 142, 145-46, 168, 202, 207, 222, 243, 246, 259
Nin, Joaquín (father) 5, 8, 9, 28, 39, 79, 99, 102, 103, 107, 119, 133, 135, 138, 143-44, 145, 163, 168, 189, 202, 235, 247, 283-84, 301, 330, 334, 338, 339, 342
Nin, Kay 154, 240, 340-41
Nin, Thorvald (brother) 114, 145, 154, 202, 207, 240, 251, 340, 341, 343, 349
Nin-Culmell, Joaquín (brother) 15, 22, 23, 29, 30, 35, 41, 42, 43, 44, 70, 71, 73, 123, 127, 144, 145, 154, 189, 193, 194, 202, 207, 251, 277, 309, 322, 329, 330, 332, 333, 346
  letters to 198-99, 348-49, 355
  letters from 86, 239-40, 258, 263, 283-84, 334, 340-41, 360
Noble, Bill 212, 225
Norman, Dr. (Nin character) 280, 291

Omarr, Sydney 77, 347
On the Road (Kerouac) 163, 190
On Writing (Nin) 214
Owen, Peter (publisher) 196, 198, 201, 205, 206, 210, 219, 227, 240, 241, 242, 255, 287, 291, 293, 294, 297, 306, 318, 319, 321, 332, 338, 344, 349, 364

Pansies (Lawrence) 27
Parrish, Woody 68-69, 115-16, 302
Partch, Harry 199, 201, 211, 252, 264, 273, 286, 334
Partisan Review (periodical) 366
"The Party" (Nin) 218, 219, 226

The Passionate Years (Crosby) 5
Patchen, Kenneth 212, 302
Paterson, Mark
  letter from 195-96
  letter to 198
Payne, Thomas 110, 113-14, 115, 130-31, 141, 146, 148, 158, 160-61, 298
  letters from 86, 87
  letter to 195
Peck, Gregory 140
Peiquot, Marie-André 86
Perlès, Alfred vii, 17-19, 25, 31, 80, 83, 111, 275, 284, 333, 348
  letter from 12-13, 16
Petrie, Daniel 292
Piccolo (dog) 235, 236, 241, 244, 246, 251, 253, 254, 255, 261, 263, 266, 269, 270, 272, 274, 277, 278, 280, 297, 308, 309, 316, 326, 360
Pinckard, William 40, 96, 133-34, 143, 144
Pink, Mr. 199
Playboy 298
Plon (publisher) 10, 16, 17, 20, 30, 50, 363
Pole, Reginald 17, 33, 36, 37, 41, 45, 57-59, 60, 61, 82, 91, 95, 98, 106, 108, 109, 113, 115, 116, 119, 129, 133, 135, 138, 151, 173, 193, 219, 224, 229, 230, 235, 255, 259
Pole, Rupert vi, vii, x, 2, 4, 6-7, 11, 15, 17, 21, 25, 27, 28, 29, 30, 31, 32, 33, 34-37, 38, 40, 44-45, 47-50, 52, 55, 56-61, 62, 63, 66, 67, 73, 74, 75, 76, 77, 79, 80, 82, 84-85, 91-92, 93-95, 96-97, 98-99, 101, 102, 103-104, 106-107, 108-109, 110-15, 116, 119-22, 123, 125-29, 131, 133, 134-35, 136, 137, 138, 139, 140, 143-44, 145, 150-51, 155-57, 161, 162-63, 169,

172-75, 189, 195, 196, 202, 204, 206-208, 214, 222, 224, 225, 226, 236, 241, 242-43, 244, 246, 259, 263, 275, 276, 277, 279, 283, 289, 290, 292-93, 300, 302, 344, 351, 354, 359, 365
letters to 8, 9-10, 21, 22-23, 23-24, 42-43, 70-71, 92-95, 97, 109-10, 123-24, 129, 154, 158, 190-94, 197, 201-202, 214, 217, 218-21, 220-21, 227-29, 229-31, 233, 234-36, 237, 241-42, 244, 251-52, 255-56, 265, 306-308, 313-14, 358
letters from 10-11, 21-22, 24, 42, 51-52, 73-74, 74-75, 89, 106, 197-98, 205, 214-15, 224, 229, 231-33, 234, 251, 265-67, 360-61
AN's description of 36-37, 54, 63, 169-70
AN's passion for 30, 40, 53, 54, 74, 82, 108, 120, 126, 128, 278
AN's frustration with 15, 28, 32-33, 53, 95, 116, 141, 142, 143, 147, 151-52, 170-72
Pollak, Felix 26, 257
Pollak, Sara 26
Porter, Anne 267
Pour l'Art (J. Nin) 114, 284
Powell, Larry 240, 339
Prairie Schooner (periodical) 210, 268, 272, 274
Premice, Josephine 189
Proust, Marcel 20, 32, 61, 73, 101, 133, 148, 152, 163, 192, 194, 234, 261, 314, 329, 333, 367
Publishers Weekly (periodical) 365
Putnam (publisher) viii, x, 287, 291, 298, 304, 326, 327, 334, 335, 336, 338, 344, 345, 346, 348, 350

Raes, Hugo
letters to 240-41, 243-44

Random House (publisher) viii, 309, 313, 314, 315, 316, 317, 318, 320, 321, 323, 324, 325
Rank, Otto 153, 189, 319, 322, 333, 338, 339, 342, 344, 367
Rattner, Abe 352
Realism and Reality (Nin) 264
Rebois, Marguerite 197, 265, 307
Reid, John 155
Rexroth, Kenneth 162
Richards, Mary Caroline 302
Rimbaud, Arthur 171, 276, 282, 289, 292
Roberts, Frances 357
Roberts, Tracey 255, 260, 261, 262, 266, 267, 269, 270, 271
letter to 256
Robinson, Edward G. 137
Rodríguez, Altagracia 101-102
Roots (film) 155
Rosenblum, Lila 11, 67, 291, 302
Rosés, Mary 355, 360
The Rosy Crucifixion (Miller) 338
Roth, Samuel 11
Rowohlt Verlag (publisher) 345, 363, 367
Rudyar, Dane 73
Ruggles, Sylvia 14-15, 23, 90, 211, 285-86, 291
Ruggles, Ted 14-15, 23, 90, 211, 285-86
Runyon, Cornelia 106, 206
Runyon, Tommy 206
Rupa and Company (publisher) 215, 227

Sabina (Nin character) 91, 137, 147, 218, 255, 260, 262, 267, 313
Sánchez, Anaïs 72, 240, 258
Sánchez, Augusto 240, 258
Sánchez, Cuca 115, 117

Sánchez, Eduardo 80, 110, 115, 117, 122, 135, 142, 224, 240, 301, 319, 343, 345, 346
  letters from 316, 322, 330-31, 335, 341-42, 346
  letters to 328-29, 332-33
Sánchez, Sorne 240, 258
Sánchez, Thorvald 257
Sand, George 225
The Sand Pebbles (film) 350
Satie, Erik 70, 74
Saturday Review (periodical) 366
Schneider, Duane x
Schuster, Max 338, 347
Seberg, Jean 253
Secret of the Reef (film) 103
Seduction of the Minotaur (Nin) viii, 240-41, 246, 247, 249, 250, 252, 255, 257, 267, 268, 280
The Servant (film) 304
Shakespeare, William 152
Shapiro, Karl 210, 259, 264, 268
Shively, George 306
  letter to 359-60
Sierra Madre vi, 7, 21, 53, 56, 57, 59, 60-61, 65, 68, 71, 79, 103
Silberman, James 319, 321, 321, 323, 324-25
The Silence (film) 311
Simenon, Georges 32, 42, 54, 99, 101, 103, 226, 243
Simon and Schuster (publisher) 334, 336, 338
Smile at the Foot of the Ladder (Miller) 276
Sokol, Thurema 49, 76, 91, 99, 108, 142, 144, 198-99
Solar Barque (Nin) viii, x, 2, 37, 57, 61, 64, 78, 79-80, 85, 87, 89, 136, 141, 142, 158, 159, 162, 163, 170, 198, 227, 240, 257
Solo (Whitmore) 118, 163

Spewack, Bella 23, 28, 39, 73, 127, 140
Spewack, Sam 23, 28, 127, 140
A Spy in the House of Love (Nin) vii, x, 2, 3, 10, 12, 13, 19, 20, 25, 83, 86, 87, 100, 110, 141, 199, 201, 203, 204, 211, 212, 219, 227, 241, 242, 243, 247, 255, 256, 259, 260, 265, 266, 267, 268, 282, 290, 292, 295, 305, 306, 307, 308, 310, 311, 314, 326, 355
  attempts to film 199, 201, 255, 255, 259, 260, 265, 266, 268, 291, 295, 306, 307, 308, 311, 312, 313, 315, 317, 323-24, 349, 355
St. Phalles, Claude de 20, 41, 62, 269, 270, 277
Staff, Clement 77
Stanley, Kim 300
Stanton, Susan 366
Starcke, Walter 111, 115, 123, 125, 127-29, 130, 131, 196, 221, 301
Steiner, Rudolph 353
Stella (Nin) 247, 248, 249
Stern, Daniel x
Stuhlmann, Gunther viii, xi, 159, 160, 198, 201, 213, 249-50, 251, 255, 256, 258, 277, 287, 289, 293, 294, 303-304, 308, 309, 310-11, 313, 314, 315, 318, 320, 323, 327-28, 329, 332, 333, 334, 335-36, 338, 342, 343, 345, 346, 347, 348, 350, 354, 355, 357, 359, 362, 363, 364, 366
  letters to 203, 249, 267, 310, 316-17, 320-21, 323, 324-25, 344, 354, 361-62, 362-63
  letters from 157-58, 203-204, 212-13, 215-16, 227, 259-60, 291, 293-94, 294, 297, 298-99, 305-306, 309, 312, 318-19, 321-22,

325, 331, 344-45, 348-49, 349, 350, 352-53, 366-67
Surmelian, Leon 310, 316, 353
Swallow, Alan viii, x, xi, 249, 251, 255, 258, 259, 289, 291, 295, 297, 305, 306, 310, 316, 317, 319, 349, 352, 364
   letters to 248, 249-50, 257-58, 268, 287, 303, 306, 308, 327-28, 346-47, 353, 357, 358-59, 363-64, 365
   letters from 248-49, 250-51, 252, 253-54, 256-57, 259, 263-64, 267-68, 271-72, 274-75, 288, 298, 299-300, 316, 325-26, 326-27, 347-48, 350, 350-51, 351, 354-55, 356-57, 357-58, 368-69
Swallow, Mae 351, 353
Swanson, Gloria 34

Take a Giant Step (Peterson) 112
Tate, Allen viii
Tavi (dog) 30, 42, 77, 116, 120, 122, 129, 143, 156, 169, 171, 190, 193, 198, 207, 224, 228, 229, 230, 231, 232, 233, 234, 235
Telberg, Val 15, 201, 205
Ten Christmas Carols (J. Nin) 284
Time (periodical) 32, 33, 37, 123, 143, 156, 170, 171, 237, 274, 314, 316, 323, 345, 366, 369
Tookey, Helen xi
Trampler, Walter 160, 172
Trapeze (Nin) vii
Tropic of Cancer (Miller) 245, 247, 254, 262, 348
Two Cities (periodical) 202, 203, 206, 208, 213, 217, 220, 222, 223, 302
Uenishi, Nobuko 304, 310, 312, 314
   letter from 349-50
Un Coup de Dés (Mallarmé) 241

Under a Glass Bell (Nin) 28, 158, 160, 175, 190, 248, 249-50, 252, 253, 279, 280, 285, 300, 319

Van der Beck, Stanley 301
Van Druten, John 111, 125, 126, 132, 154
Varda, Jean 49, 206, 211, 254, 255, 281, 282, 291, 314, 334
Varèse, Edgar 291, 292, 314
Varèse, Louise 292
Victorine (Clairmonte) 247
Vidal, Gore vii, 2, 91, 96, 117, 122-23, 133, 134, 135, 136, 138, 140, 144, 148, 149-50, 151, 152, 154, 201, 264, 273, 291, 301, 356
Viking Press (publisher) 141
The Village Voice (periodical) 201, 219, 241, 271, 366
Vingt Chansons Populaires Espagnoles (J. Nin) 284
Viqué, Jean 86
Visit to a Smaller Planet (Vidal) 122, 134
Vogue (periodical) 334
The Voice (Nin) 248, 249

Wages of Fear (film) 74
Wahlström & Widstrand Forlag (publisher) 85
Waiting for Godot (Beckett) 78, 86, 98
Wakoski, Diane ix, x
Wallrich, Larry and Ruby 246
Wang, Arthur 259, 294
Ward, Barbara 366
Waters, Frank viii
Watts, Alan 282
Weigel, Henrietta 159
Wescott, Glenway 300
Whitman, George 233, 243
Wild Party (March) 163

The Wilder Shores of Love (Blanch) 150, 169
Williams, Tennessee 6, 44, 78, 117, 134, 135, 149, 152, 218, 264, 273, 286, 293
Williwaw (Vidal) 149
Wilson, Edmund 143, 365
Winter of Artifice (Nin) viii, 148, 200, 245, 247, 248, 249, 255, 282, 352
Winters, Yvor viii
Winwood, Estelle 196
Wise, Robert viii, 306, 308, 311-13, 315, 317, 323, 324, 350
Wood, Audrey 264
Woodward, Joanne 135, 152
Woolf, Virginia 20
Wreden, Nicolas 117
Wright, Eric 35, 36, 47, 55, 89, 106, 116, 119, 121, 269
   building RP's house 215, 224, 232, 233, 234
Wright, Frank Lloyd 30, 116, 157, 169, 365
Wright, Helen Taggart 24, 34, 36, 42, 47, 48, 53, 55, 95, 98, 106, 107, 110, 114, 116, 119, 121, 146, 151, 215, 224
Wright, Lloyd 28, 30, 31, 34, 36, 43, 45, 47-49, 55, 59, 60, 89, 95, 98, 106-107, 109, 110, 116, 119, 121, 122, 151, 154, 163, 169, 204, 215, 224, 269, 314, 365

A Yellow Wood (Vidal) 149
Yelton, Sylvia 207
Young, Marguerite 62-63, 255, 259, 284, 285, 286, 291, 294, 297, 302, 359, 366
   letter to 283

Zadkine, Ossip 192, 244
Zanuck, Darryl 350
Zina (friend of Barker) 147, 148

ALSO AVAILABLE FROM SKY BLUE PRESS

Mirages: The Unexpurgated Diary of Anaïs Nin, 1939-1947 by Anaïs Nin (print, ebook)

Trapeze: The Unexpurgated Diary of Anaïs Nin, 1947-1955 by Anaïs Nin (print, ebook)

Reunited: The Correspondence of Anaïs and Joaquín Nin 1933-1940 by Anaïs Nin and Joaquín Nin (print, ebook)

Auletris: Erotica by Anaïs Nin (print, ebook, audiobook)

Letters to Lawrence Durrell 1937-1977 by Anaïs Nin (print, ebook)

The Quotable Anaïs Nin by Anaïs Nin (two volumes; print, ebook)

The Portable Anaïs Nin by Anaïs Nin, ed. Benjamin Franklin V (print, ebook)

D. H. Lawrence: An Unprofessional Study by Anaïs Nin (ebook)

House of Incest by Anaïs Nin (ebook)

The Winter of Artifice: 1939 Paris Edition by Anaïs Nin (print, ebook)

Under a Glass Bell by Anaïs Nin (ebook)

Stella by Anaïs Nin (ebook)

Ladders to Fire by Anaïs Nin (ebook)

Children of the Albatross by Anaïs Nin (ebook)

The Four-Chambered Heart by Anaïs Nin (ebook)

A Spy in the House of Love by Anaïs Nin (ebook)

Seduction of the Minotaur by Anaïs Nin (ebook)

Cities of the Interior by Anaïs Nin (ebook)

Collages by Anaïs Nin (ebook)

The Novel of the Future by Anaïs Nin (ebook)

Anaïs Nin: The Last Days, a Memoir by Barbara Kraft (ebook)

Anaïs Nin's Lost World: Paris in Words and Pictures 1924-1939 by Britt Arenander (print, ebook)

Anaïs Nin Character Dictionary and Index to Diary Excerpts by Benjamin Franklin V (print, ebook)

A Café in Space: The Anaïs Nin Literary Journal, Vol. 1 by Anaïs Nin, Janet Fitch, Lynette Felber… (print, ebook)

A Café in Space: The Anaïs Nin Literary Journal, Vol. 2 by Anaïs Nin, Benjamin Franklin V, Masako Meio… (print, ebook)

A Café in Space: The Anaïs Nin Literary Journal, Vol. 3 by Anaïs Nin, Gunther Stuhlmann, Richard Pine, James Clawson… (print, ebook)

A Café in Space: The Anaïs Nin Literary Journal, Vol. 4 by Anaïs Nin, Alan Swallow, John Ferrone, Yuko Yaguchi… (print, ebook)

A Café in Space: The Anaïs Nin Literary Journal, Vol. 5 by Anaïs Nin, Duane Schneider, Sarah Burghauser… (print, ebook)

A Café in Space: The Anaïs Nin Literary Journal, Vol. 6 by Anaïs Nin, Joaquín Nin y Castellanos, Tristine Rainer, Christie Logan… (print, ebook)

A Café in Space: The Anaïs Nin Literary Journal, Vol. 7 by Anaïs Nin, John Ferrone, Kim Krizan, Tristine Rainer…

A Café in Space: The Anaïs Nin Literary Journal, Vol. 8 by Anaïs Nin, Benjamin Franklin V, Anita Jarczok, Kim Krizan… (print, ebook)

A Café in Space: The Anaïs Nin Literary Journal, Vol. 9 by Anaïs Nin, Anita Jarczok, Joel Enos… (print, ebook)

A Café in Space: The Anaïs Nin Literary Journal, Vol. 10 by Anaïs Nin, Benjamin Franklin V, Kim Krizan, William Claire, Erin Dunbar… (print, ebook)

A Café in Space: The Anaïs Nin Literary Journal, Vol. 11 by Anaïs Nin, Henry Miller, Alfred Perlès, John Tytell… (print, ebook)

A Café in Space: The Anaïs Nin Literary Journal, Vol. 12 by Anaïs Nin, Kim Krizan, Benjamin Franklin V… (print, ebook)

A Café in Space: The Anaïs Nin Literary Journal, Vol. 13 by Anaïs Nin, Barbara Kraft, Danica Davidson… (print, ebook)

A Café in Space: The Anaïs Nin Literary Journal, Vol. 14 by Anaïs Nin, Jessica Gilbey, Joaquín Nin-Culmell… (print, ebook)

A Café in Space: The Anaïs Nin Literary Journal, Vol. 15 by Anaïs Nin, Rupert Pole, Steven Reigns… (print, ebook)

A Café in Space: The Anaïs Nin Literary Journal, Anthology 2003-2018 (print, ebook)

ANAIS: An International Journal, Anthology 1983-2001 (print, ebook)

Forthcoming:

A Joyous Transformation: The Unexpurgated Diary of Anaïs Nin, 1966-1977

Printed in Dunstable, United Kingdom